존경하는
장 종철 회장님 혜존

저자 김 희국 드림
Rockville, MD
March 27, 2021

A SUMMARY OF READINGS
THE TRANSFORMATION OF
POLITICS, ECOMNOMY, AND SCIENCE
The Twenty-First Century

History of Politics and Economy
Book VII

Photo 0-0-1. The U.S. Shale Revolution influences global energy markets,
Accessed 1 April 2019,
http://culvercitycrossroads.com/wp-content/uploads/2017/04/Chevron.jpeg.

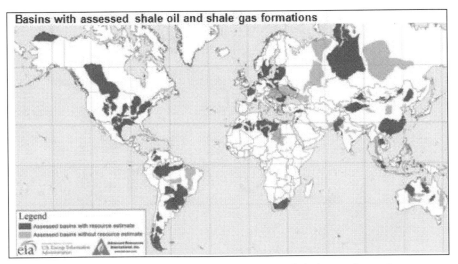

Map 0-0-1. Basins with assessed shale oil and shale gas formations
Accessed 2 April 2019,
https://www.eia.gov/todayinenergy/images/2013.06.10/shalemap.png.

A SUMMARY OF READINGS
THE TRANSFORMATION OF
POLITICS, ECONOMY, AND SCIENCE
The Twenty-Frist Century

History of Politics and Economy
Book VII

Hugo W. Kim

CreateSpace
North Charleston, SC

The Transformation of Politics, Economy, and Science:
The Twenty-First Century
History of Politics and Economy, Book 7
Copyright © 2020 by Hugo W. Kim

First published in the United States of America in 2020
by CreateSpace, an Amazon company,
4900 LaCross Road, North Charleston, SC 29406.
www.createspace.com

Library of Congress Cataloging-in-Publication Data

Name: Kim, Hugo W. (1941 -), author.
Title: The Transformation of Politics, Economy, and Science:
The Twenty-First Century / Hugo W. Kim
Description: North Charleston, SC: CreateSpace, 2020.
Includes bibliographical references.
Identifier: ISBN: 9781656263926 (print, 392 pages)
Subjects: 1. World politics. 2. International Relations. 3. A new world order.
4. Capitalist economy. 5. The future of capitalism. 6. Digital transformation.
7. Technology for national security.   I. Title.

Printed in the United States of America

Photo 0-0-2 on the previous page
21st Century Manufacturing: A World of Difference by Jeremy Leonard
https://www.uschamberfoundation.org/sites/default/files/styles/detail_image800w/public/article/fo
undation/21st_century.jpg?itok=QOS2N33w, accessed 5 January 2020

A SUMMARY OF READINGS
HISTORY OF POLITICS AND ECONOMY
HUGO W. KIM, AUTHOR

Book	The Title of Each Volume	Chronology
I	From the Beginning to the Rise of Islam: The Greco-Roman Civilization	- 750 A.D.
II	The Middle Ages From 750 To 1400 Feudalism and the Commercial Revolution	750 - 1400
III	From the Renaissance to the Scientific Revolution: Humanism and Mercantilism	1400 - 1715
IV	The French Revolution and the Industrial Revolution: Liberalism and Capitalism	1715 -1815
V	The Consolidation of Nation States and Industrialization: Nationalism and Socialism	1815 - 1914
VI	The World Wars, the Cold War, and Terrorism: Globalization and Interdependence	1914 - 2015
VII	**The Transformation of Politics, Economy, and Science: The Twenty-First Century**	**2015 - 2100**

Hugo W. Kim (1941 -), Author

Hugo Wheegook Kim was born to a family cultivating a small land in a town of southern part of South Korea in 1941. He received basic education during the Korean War, graduated from a teacher's high school in Suncheon city in 1959, and taught at a primary school in his hometown until he was admitted to the Korea Military Academy in 1962. Receiving a BS from KMA in 1966, he was commissioned to the second lieutenant of the Korean Army and assigned to an infantry division. After thirteen years of his service with tactical and strategic trainings, Hugo had an opportunity to receive overseas graduate education: three years for a Master's program, and another three years for a Doctorate program. Receiving a MPBA from the Southeastern University, Hugo earned MA and Ph.D. in economics from the Catholic University of America in Washington, D.C. Teaching at the National Defense University in Seoul, he retired from the Korean Army in 1987, when he moved to Virginia. Teaching at the Southeastern University during 1989-91, Hugo participated in research activities linking with CSIS during 1994-99. Meanwhile, he has taken part in Asian studies by joining the International Council on Korean Studies as a founding member, organizing its annual conferences, and publishing its academic journal IJKS as Editor-in-Chief. Hugo has taught graduate courses at the Washington University of Virginia since 2008. Hugo published articles in academic journals, and books including the *Korean Americans and Inter-Korean Relations* in 2003. Since then, owing to his devoted wife, Hugo had worked for an ambitious book project - a series of seven volumes of the *History of Politics and Economy: A Summary of Readings*, all of which were published in 2020. Hugo and his wife EJ have two daughters: the first Hejune married Sanghe, living in Fairfax, Virginia with their two children Ashley and Jaden; and the second Heji married Christopher, living in Berkeley, California.

TO THE READERS

This is the last volume of my book project: *History of Politics and Economy: A Summary of Readings*, Volume VII, *The Transformation of Politics, Economy, and Science: The Twenty-First Century*. I started this book project, first, to widen my intellectual scope, frankly speaking, to escape from my ignorance; and second, to keep records of my efforts towards burning desire for knowledge in my life. I have spent my time and resources to study and write this series of seven volumes until now for over sixteen years. In the beginning of studies, I was energetic and matured at the age of 62, but now passed 78 of my age with less physical ability. Fortunately, I have been able to finish my book project before I reach the point losing my memories, though I am still healthy. I have nostalgic memories during the period. In closing, I want to say some retrospective points to the readers as follows.

In politics, the concept of democratic peace lies in that democratic states are hesitant to engage in armed conflict with other identified democracies since they can resolve tensions through diplomacy to avoid high costs of war. Nevertheless, if the gains from war are much larger than the losses from peace, a nation-state may choose war for gains. In fact, the United States helped China join the World Trade Organization for trade and investment, but China's unfair trade practices and stealing of intellectual property rights brought China's huge trade surplus with America continuously. Moreover, China has caused territorial disputes in the South China Sea by occupying some of Spratly Islands. President Xi Jinping strengthened his authoritarian rule by removing the term limit and challenged the U.S. supremacy with the Belt and Road Initiative and Made-in-China 2025. "President Donald Trump in 2018 began setting tariffs and other trade barriers on China with the goal of forcing it to make changes to what the U.S. says are unfair trade practices." Democratic peace with India seems to be successful, but not with China. If Washington takes containment strategies against Beijing, the impact would be deep, wide, and long in various aspects of international relations.

In economy, efficient growth versus equal distribution must be essential goals of any nation state. Democratic politics is based on equality – a vote per person; while capitalist economy is based on efficiency – more profits per unit cost. Therefore, democratic capitalist countries pursue not only efficiency in growth but also equality in income distribution. However, efficiency and equality are in trade-off relations, so that more efficiency loses some equality, while more equality loses some efficiency by certain degrees. In the United States, the Republican Party has been in favor of policies for more growth, while the Democratic Party in favor of policies for better distribution. Hence, the policies of the Democratic Party collect more taxes for better distribution of income or welfare of the poor by transferring wealth from the rich to the poor. Meanwhile, the policies of the Republican

Party reduce taxes to encourage consumption and investment for more growth. Thus, government policies move towards growth or distribution just like a pendulum of the clock, according to the change of the Administration. Because of limited resources in a certain period of time, the political system cannot sufficiently reduce the income gap between the rich and the poor. The last resort to overcome the gap between individuals coming from initial conditions must be the will power of individual, who is eager to escape from one's own fate given from the birth, either material or genetic.

In science, artificial intelligence (AI) has experienced "a resurgence following concurrent advances in computer power, large amount of data, and theoretical understanding; and AI techniques have become an essential part of the technology industry, helping to solve many challenging problems in computer science, software engineering and operations research." There are various challenging areas such as AI as reasoning and problem solving, knowledge representation, planning, learning, natural language processing, perception, motion and manipulation, social intelligence, and general intelligence. Any individual, company, or state can develop a leading edge of AI technology to be a great beneficiary. The nation state may wisely manage the progress of technology, effectively and efficiently, which will change the coming centuries of human civilization. More importantly, this author hopes that the coming century is able to be led by good people and good nation states making the civilized world more peaceful and prosperous.

Finally, I cordially remind you of that I am not a historian, but a forever student who loves to read about history, politics, economy, and some others. Hence, this book is *a summary of readings* with many quotes from various sources, but not my creation of theories or new findings, although opinions and comments were expressed here and there in the book. Please note that *The Transformation of Politics, Economy, and Science* was an independent version previously published, but the same contents as this Book VII that is merged under the series of the History of Politics and Economy. I would very much appreciate for any feedbacks to me at <hugo33kim@gmail.com>. Thank you very much and God bless you, my respectful readers!

With truth and humbleness,

Hugo W. Kim, Author
Fairfax, Virginia, U.S.A.
5 January 2020

THE TRANSFORMATION OF POLITICS, ECONOMY, AND SCIENCE
The Twenty-Frist Century

CONTENTS

PART II. The Future of Capitalism: Efficiency in Growth vs. Equality in Distribution

LIST OF TABLES, FIGURES, AND PHOTOS

LIST OF MAPS

Map 0-0-2. Territorial Disputes in the South China Sea
Accessed 6 November 2019,
https://tse4.mm.bing.net/th?id=OIP.4wNFhcplw-
oHX40OyWRcAQHaID&pid=Api&P=0&w=300&h=300

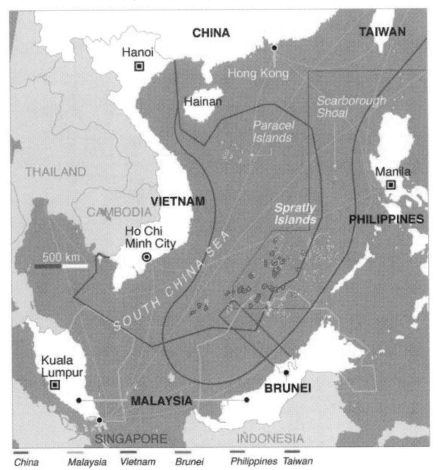

"The ***Spratly Islands dispute*** is an ongoing territorial dispute between China, Taiwan, Malaysia, the Philippines and Vietnam, concerning ownership of the Spratly Islands, a group of islands and associated maritime features (reefs, banks, cays, etc.) located in the South China Sea. The dispute is characterized by diplomatic stalemate and the employment of military pressure techniques (such as military occupation of disputed territory) in the advancement of national territorial claims. All except Brunei occupy some of the maritime features." The Spratly Islands are important for economic and strategic reasons like oil and natural gas, fishing, maritime trade route, and military base.
Accessed 6 November 2019, https://en.wikipedia.org/wiki/Spratly_Islands_dispute.

INTRODUCTION

In his essay "7 Best Case Scenarios for the Future of Humanity" of 2012 George P. Dvorsky, a Canadian futurist, predicted as follows. 1. Status quo: "Our ongoing survival…Many have suggested that we've already reached our pinnacle as a species." 2. A bright green earth: We can use technologies to clean up the Earth and to live in harmony with environment. 3. Watched over by machines of loving grace: It is possible "that a machine intelligence could create a veritable utopia for humanity" with friendly artificial intelligence – "Machines of Loving Grace." 4. To boldly go where no one has gone before: Improved science and technology allow human civilization to colonize other solar systems with the expansion of digital intelligence. 5. Inner space, not outer space: "Alternatively (or in conjunction with space travel), we could attain an ideal existential mode by uploading ourselves into massive supercomputers…a single multi-layer Matrioshka Brain could perform about 10^{42} operations per second." 6. Eternal bliss: "Given our modern materialist proclivities, many of us no longer believe in heaven or anything else awaiting us in some supposed afterlife. But that doesn't mean we can't create a virtual heaven on Earth using our technologies." 7. Cosmological transcension: Human civilization is increasingly migrating into smaller and smaller increments of matter, energy, space, and time, eventually, "we'll take our collective intelligence into a cosmological realm …as a black hole – where we'll essentially escape the universe."[1]

In BBC Future of 2014, Rachel Nuwer views that Western civilization would collapse by agreeing with a research that there are two factors that mater: ecological strain and economic stratification. "The ecological category is the more widely understood and recognized path to potential doom, especially in terms of depletion of natural resources such as groundwater, soil, fisheries and forests – all of which could be worsened by climate change." Under this scenario, "Disaster comes when elites push society toward instability and eventual collapse by hoarding huge quantities of wealth and resources." Another sign entering into a danger zone is "the increasing occurrence of nonlinearities' or sudden, unexpected changes in the world's order such as the 2008 economic crisis, the rise of ISIS, Brexit, or Donald Trump's election." Moreover, "Western societies' collapse will be preceded by a retraction of people and resources back to their core homelands. As poorer nations continue to disintegrate amid conflicts and natural disasters, enormous waves of migrants will stream out of failing regions, seeking refuge in more stable states." "Meanwhile, a widening gap between rich and poor within those already vulnerable Western nations will push society toward further instability from the inside." If democratic and liberal society fail, then stronger governments, like China and Russia under authoritarian rule ignoring humanity, will be the winner.[2]

As discussed in Introduction to my *History of Politics and Economy* in Volume I, the rise and fall of a nation state or a civilization depend largely on interactions between politics and economy. The economic strength allows a state to build up military power to expand its political domain, while excessive military expansion causes economic decline and collapse of its regime at the end. Democratic politics pursues equality of rights, while capitalist economy pursues efficiency of dollars. Political equality and economic efficiency stand generally in trade off relations in nature. The fall of communism in 1991 proved that a serious loss of economic efficiency cannot support the ideal of political equality. As long as poverty remains significant in a state, socialist measures will continuously threaten economic efficiency although the solution lies in a cyclical way by cooperation or competition rather than a dialectic way of confrontation between opposite values. Generally speaking, political power affects economic decisions, while limited resources restrict political and military maneuvers.

The economic growth without democratization creates the political-economic complex due to lack of checks and balances in the system, which disturbs fair competition and encourages monopoly in the market with increasing corruption of society. As a result, resource allocation is distorted, which creates bottlenecks here and overcapacities there, so that economic efficiency declines, which reduces the national wealth in the long run. Therefore, interactions between politics, economy, and society evidently appear in the process of economic development. Developing countries choose one of three possible routes of political and economic transition or development: (i) the simultaneous growth, (ii) the autocratic path favoring economic growth first, and (iii) the democratic path favoring democratization first. In the autocratic path like current China, its economic growth without democratization interrupts continuous growth since economic power purchases political power or vice versa, which makes it possible to create conglomerates or huge state-owned companies, monopolizing both politics and economy, and even jeopardizing social justice.

Moreover, we have to consider two sets of boundaries: one is politics vs. economy, and the other is domestic vs. international. First, politics and economy are two main subsystems pushing and pulling human history. The interactions between politics and economy are so influential that political scientists always consider economic elements in politics, and economists consider political elements in economic policies. Because of the rapid progress of science and technology such as the fifth generation of data networks and artificial intelligence, science and technology become the third influential sub-system of civilization. Therefore, this book consists of three parts: politics, economy, and science. Second, since a nation state is an actor integrating its politics, economy, and science; domestic and international boundaries should be separately considered in our discussions. For example, a nation state has three actors: individual, corporation, and government. Their activities are integrated into maximized national power competing with other countries. In other words, the maximization of national strength is constrained by foreign states opposing to this nation.

This book consists of three parts. **Part I** evaluates a new world order in the twenty-first century: which power will run the world? It consists of five sections: 1 A historical overview of international relations; 2 Theoretical background of international relations; 3 Liberal hegemony and globalization; 4 The decay of liberal order and the resurgence of nationalism; and 5 Which power will run the world in the twenty-first century. After two World Wars, the Allies created the United Nations to avoid a third world war. The Cold War increased geopolitical tension between capitalism and socialism, that caused the Vietnam War, the Korean War, and the Arab-Israeli War of 1973. While Realism dominated the world with the balance of power, the two Oil Crises made Liberalism with complex interdependence more influential in foreign affairs than Realism based on military power.

After the fall of communism, liberal hegemony and globalization help expand trade and investment throughout the world. But the liberal order began to decay because of the rise of China, the returning of Russia, and the development of nuclear weapons in Iran and North Korea. Therefore, Realism with Nationalism became the dominant theory of international relations in the United States to maintain its supremacy to lead the world. China may decline because of inefficient allocation of resources, political involvement in business management; huge debt finance by provincial and central governments; income inequality between the rich and the poor; the decline of active population; manipulations of foreign exchanges; and huge corruption throughout society. To maintain the U.S. supremacy, Washington should take the containment strategies against China and Russia based on Realism with Nationalism. Military superiority should be held with wise diplomacy. Defense spending should not hurt economic growth. Harmony of society is essential for a healthy nation. Finally, the United Nations should be the center of conflict resolution among nation states.

In **Part II** the future of capitalism consists of five sections: 1 History of economic transformation; 2 Theoretical background of capitalism; 3 A historical overview of socialism; 4 Capitalism and democracy: efficiency versus equality; and 5 The future of capitalism. The fundamental issue in the future of capitalism lies in the conflict between efficiency in growth and equality in distribution. The main cause of income inequality is in different initial conditions between individuals. A person who was born to the rich family will get better education and receive some inheritance, which generate higher labor income with additional rent income than a person who was born to the poor. Moreover, A person, who inherited better gene with wiser brain, warmer heart, and better physical abilities, achieves better output than a person who inherited not better gene. Hence, the former performs better and gets paid more in working place. Therefore, the initial condition makes individual person achieve differently. The world should maintain not only capitalist economy for efficiency in growth by promoting competition and minimizing monopoly, but democratic politics for equality in distribution by enforcing such policies as progressive taxation, public education, minimum wage regulation, nationalization of essential goods and services, and so on. However, resources are so limited in a state during a certain period of time that unfortunately there is no sufficient way to change the initial conditions of human society. The only way to overcome differences lies in personal motivation to be successful in his or her life.

Finally, **Part III** science, technology, and national security deals with 1 Digital transformation and information age; 2 Cyberwarfare and national security; 3 Space warfare and national security; 4 Weapons of mass destruction and national security: nuclear, chemical, and biological weapons. Bernard Marr of Enterprise Tech introduced "The 7 Biggest Technology Trends in 2020 Everyone Must Get Ready for Now," which includes Artificial intelligence (AI) in a service, 5G data networks, Autonomous driving, Personalized and predictive medicine, Computer vision, Extended reality, and Blockchain technology.[3] They are all sensitive for national security. For example, "China is building the world's most powerful facial recognition system with the power to identify any one of its 1.3 billion citizens within three seconds. The goal is for the system to able to match someone's face to their ID photo with about 90 per cent accuracy. The project…is under development in conjunction with a security company based in Shanghai."[4] Scanning people's faces as they lawfully go about their daily lives, to identify them, is "a potential threat to privacy that should concern us all." Thus, a bad government can use AI technology for bad purposes to maintain an authoritarian regime.

Endnotes

[1] 7 Best-Case Scenarios for the Future of Humanity, accessed 26 October 2019, https://io9.gizmodo.com/7-best-case-scenarios-for-the-future-of-humanity-5958479.
[2] BBC Future, How Western civilization cold collapse, accessed 26 October 2019, https://www.bbc.com/future/article/20170418-how-western-civilisation-could-collapse.
[3] Bernard Marr, The 7 Biggest Technology Trends (8 October 2019), accessed 31 October 2019, https://www.linkedin.com/pulse/7-biggest-technology-trends-2020-everyone-must-get-ready-bernard-marr/.
[4] Stephen Chen, "China to build giant facial recognition database to identify any citizen within seconds," *South China Morning Post* (12 October 2017), accessed 30 October 2019, https://www.scmp.com/news/china/society/article/2115094/china-build-giant-facial-recognition-database-identify-any.

Part I. World Order in the Twenty-First Century
Which Power Will Run the World?

The Peace of Westphalia in 1648 inaugurated a modern system of sovereign independent nation-states in Europe, which did not bring peace because it was a compromise settlement that regulated relations between Catholics, Lutherans, and Calvinists. After the fall of Napoleon, the world order was reestablished by the *Congress of Vienna* in 1815 based on the balance of power between member states. Metternich adopted the principle of intervention "that the great powers had the right to intervene militarily in other countries to crush revolutionary movements against legitimate rulers." But the system became powerless because of the rise of nationalism, the liberal wave of revolutions across Europe in 1848, and the Crimean War in 1853. As Bismarck led the German unification in 1871, the Concert of Europe lost its flexibility. Over the second half of the nineteenth century, a unified Germany and a modern Japan rose, the Ottoman Empire and Russia declined, and France and United Kingdom grew stronger. Experiencing World Wars, the United States arranged the Marshall Plan and NATO to lead world peace. With the collapse of the Soviet Union in 1991, the United States became the unipolar superpower, but the rise of China and the resurgence of Russia have challenged the U.S. supremacy in world politics.

Civilization has made the continuous progress in politics, economy, society, and culture; in which Part I deals with international politics - the world order which power will run the world in the twenty-first century. To answer to this question, five steps are considered as set in the box above. Section 1 overviews the history of world politics from ancient time to present days. Section 2 investigates the theoretical background of international relations, and Section 3 analyzes why and how the trend of realism moved to liberal hegemony and globalization after the oil shocks and the fall of the Soviet Union. Section 4 discusses about the decay of liberal order and the resurgence of nationalism because of the rise of China, the returning of Russia, and the development of nuclear weapons in Iran and North Korea. Section 5 provides answers to the raised question above. Following three books gave me a significant guidance for discussions in Part I: *World Order* of 2014 by Henry Kissinger, *The Accidental Superpower* of 2014 by Peter Zeihan, and *The Next 100 Years* of 2009 by George Friedman,

1. A Historical Overview of World Politics

In this section, history is divided into three periods before the death of Louis XIV in 1715, and another three periods after the same. The former includes the Greco-Roman civilization (-750 AD), the Middle Ages (750-1400), and the Ages of the Renaissance, the Reformation, and geographical discovery (1400-1715). The latter includes the French Revolution and the Industrial Revolution (1715-1815); the consolidation of nation states, industrialization, and commercialization (1815-1914); and the World Wars, the Cold War, and liberal order and globalization (1914-2015). Since then, we have been facing the resurgence of realism with nationalism in theory until now.

The Greco-Roman Civilization (- AD 750): One of the human species lived 2.5 million years ago and began to use fire as a source of light and heat around 500,000 years ago. The first modern humans appeared in Europe in around 250,000 BC and Africa around 200,000 BC who migrated to the Middle East in around 100,000 BC. The latter moved to Europe, Australia, Asia, and America in tens of millennium ago. In the prehistoric period, Paleolithic people (-10,000 BC) used tools made of stone for hunting, fishing, and gathering food; Mesolithic people began to cultivate land by attaching a stone blade to wooden hand; Neolithic people (7000-3000 BC) ended the hunting way of life and developed agriculture with metal tools; and Bronze people (3000-1200 BC) heated metal-bearing rocks and molded them to produce tools and weapons. Since then, the use of iron became common in daily life. The early civilization independently developed in Mesopotamia, Egypt, India, and China in the fourth millennium BC owing to favorable environments of nature: river valley, rich soil, fine weather, and the dense population. The other factor was in "the capacity of the peoples on the spot to take advantage of an environment or rise to a challenge" as well as external contacts for exchanges of goods with new knowledge. The basic economic and social organization was an agricultural village as a tribal community. Since natural endowment and technological progress were different, there appeared exchanges of surplus for deficiency between tribes. As farming, manufacturing, and trade were gradually expanded, the villages were transformed into urbanized towns and cities; which became the center for political, military, economic, social, cultural, and religious development. Economic power formed a new social structure: kings, high priests, political leaders, and warriors were on the top; farmers, artisans, and craftsmen in the middle; and slaves at the bottom. The development of writing made it possible for the people to keep their records, and artistic and intellectual activities were performed with material progress. Since India and China did not closely affect the western hemisphere in this ancient period, our survey here begins from two civilizations, Mesopotamia and Egypt.

Mesopotamian civilization was created by the Sumerians who established independent city-states in the valleys of Tigris and Euphrates Rivers by around 3000 BC. Semitic peoples migrated into the river valleys of Mesopotamia and developed later civilizations among which the Babylonian Empire was most significant under the rule of Hammurabi. By around 2000 BC, the Hittites, Indo-European people, migrated into Asia Minor, destroyed Babylon and established their kingdom, which power reached at Syria and northern Palestine. Meanwhile, the Egyptians created another civilization on the bank of the Nile: the early dynasties lasted four centuries until 2700 BC, and the middle kingdom remained five centuries until 2200 BC. The rise and fall of dynasties created the new kingdom (1550-1070 BC) expanding its territory to the south and the east. By around 1200 BC, the destruction of the Hittites and weakening of Egypt caused power vacuum in the Near East, which invited small kingdoms or city-states to emerge. The Sea Peoples - Philistines, Sicilians, Sardinians, and Etruscans - swept over Asia Minor and Syria; the Phoenicians became "the traders, shipbuilders, navigators, and colonizers" in the Mediterranean; and Hebrew established a new kingdom. All of them had enjoyed political freedom until the Assyrians dominated the Near East in the eighth century BC. The Assyrian Empire was defeated by the coalition of the Chaldeans and Medes in 605 BC which were also conquered by rising Persia in 539 BC. The actors of ancient Mesopotamia and Egypt were Caucasians, who are classified into three linguistic groups: Hamites, Semitics, and Indo-Europeans. The Hamites evolved in north and northeast Africa; the Semitics in the Arabian Peninsula; and the Indo-Europeans came from southern Russia by 4000 BC and entered Asia Minor by 2000 BC. The latter group includes the Indo-Iranian, Balto-Slavic, Hellenic, Italic, Celtic, and Germanic speaking peoples. During 2000-1500 BC, the Semitic people mingled with the Indo-European speaking people in Mesopotamia, while the Hamites with the Semitics in Egypt.

Passing the Dark Age, the ancient Greeks experienced two developments during 750-500 BC: evolution of city-state and colonization of Greek cities. Each city-state needed the unity of citizens relying on local patriotism, which created a new military system of hoplite forming a phalanx in the battle. The rising population and lack of arable land forced the Greeks to migrate toward the Mediterranean and the Black Seas; that increased their trade with colonies. Among Greek city-states, the Spartans created a military state, while the Athenians developed a democratic system. In the classical period, the Greeks fought two major wars: the Persian Wars and the Peloponnesian War. As Darius expanded the power of the Persian Empire, the rising Greeks supported the Ionian Greek cities against Persia. The Persian Wars (499-449 BC) came from a conflict between Greek freedom and oriental despotism, but more from Persian expansion and revenge for Greek intervention. Darius invaded Greek cities in 490 BC and Xerxes did in 480 BC, but both were defeated. After the wars, the Athenians formed the Delian League against Persia in 478 BC, which became an instrument of Greek imperialism. The Peloponnesian War (431-404 BC) was caused by the arising fear of the Spartans to the growth of Athenian power. Athens finally fell into Sparta, but the Greek cities were so exhausted that rising Macedonia dominated them in 338 BC, when Philip II forced the Greek cities to join the Corinthian League, controlling their foreign affairs but giving autonomy of their domestic affairs. His son Alexander the Great suppressed the revolts of the Greek cities; invaded and conquered Asia Minor, Syria, Palestine, Egypt, Persia; and subdued modern Pakistan and entered the Indus valley. Alexander destroyed the Persian monarchy and extended Greco-Macedonian rule to the region, but after his death in 323 BC his empire was divided into four Hellenistic kingdoms – Macedonia, Syria, Pergamum, and Egypt – ruled by his powerful generals. Hellenistic ideals pursued imperial cosmopolitanism through cultural exchanges with the east, but their rule lost efficiency in controlling of resources in the overextended territory, so that the rising power of Rome took over and inherited them.

The Roman monarchy began in 753 BC as an oligarchy of seven tribal leaders and moved to the Roman Republic (509-30 BC) by expelling the Etruscans. Until 133 BC, the Romans developed a more democratic institution by extending political and social equality to the plebian lower class and expanded its political and military control in Italy and later the Mediterranean region. The Romans destroyed Carthage by three Punic Wars and subdued Macedonia by four Macedonian Wars. During 133-30 BC, the territorial expansion faced serious problems with the decline of small land-owners and corruption in the government. Roman reformers were assassinated, and the republic moved into the empire through three civil wars: Marius vs. Sulla, Pompey vs. Caesar, and Octavian vs. Anthony. Augustus (27 BC - AD 14) transformed Rome from a city-state to the Roman Empire by pursuing a defensive imperialism limiting the boundaries to the Rhine and Danube, the Euphrates, and Arabia and Africa. He restructured the army into legions, Praetorian Guard, and auxiliary forces; and used the army as an agent of Romanization. As the civil wars stopped, the Romans achieved peace and prosperity. Military expansion and continuous campaigns induced economic downfall; the urbanization of provincial towns made its economic center shift to provinces, which expedited the depopulation of Italy. As the empire rapidly declined since Commodus, Diocletian (284-305) pursued aggressive reforms by dividing the empire into the east and the west, which demanded more supply, payroll, and recruitment. Constantine (272-337) recognized Christianity as a lawful religion in his proclamation of the Edict of Milan in 313 and moved his capital to Constantinople in 330. Since 400, the imperial army had heavily depended upon Germanic recruits, and both military and civil positions in the government were filled by Germans.

Romanization by the army meant militarization, and recruitment of Germans in military and civil services caused barbarization of the empire. Finally, the Western Roman Empire fell into the hands of Germans in 476 with the rise of the Christianity internally and the Germanic pressure externally.

After the fall of Rome, we can observe three developments: Germanic kingdoms, the Byzantine Empire, and the rise of Islam. First of all, the Huns moved into the Black Sea region in the late fourth century, and pushed Germans - Visigoths, Vandals, Ostrogoths, Lombards, Burgundians, Franks, and Angels and Saxons. Moving westward, the Visigoths finally settled in Spain and established a kingdom, which was conquered by the Muslims in 713. The Vandals moved westward to Spain, crossed the Strait of Gibraltar, and settled in northern Africa, but were defeated by Justinian in 534. Being ruled by the Huns, the Ostrogoths regained independence and established a kingdom in Rome in 491 but were conquered by Justinian in 535. The Lombards invaded northern and central Italy and established a kingdom in 568 but were conquered by Charlemagne in 774. The Burgundians settled in Savoy and spread toward Lyon, and moved into the Roman land, but were overthrown by the Franks in 532. As the Franks rose from the northern corner of Gaul, Clovis (482-511) inherited the Merovingian throne, conquered both Gaul and Germany, and moved his capital to Paris; which dynasty had remained until Pepin III opened the Carolingian dynasty in 751. The Angels and Saxons conquered the Britons after the withdrawal of Roman legions in 409. Meanwhile, the east was largely divided into two powers: the eastern Roman Empire and the Persian Empire. In the eastern Roman Empire later called the Byzantine Empire, Justinian (527-65), making peace with Persia, restored the Mediterranean world by destroying the Vandals in northern Africa, the Ostrogoths in Italy, and the southern shore of the Visigoths in Spain; though the empire could not maintain the expanded frontiers. Justinian codified the Roman law as the basis of the empire, which was a great contribution to western civilization. On the other hand, the Persians invaded and captured Syria, Palestine, and Egypt from the Byzantine during 616-19. Byzantine emperor Heraclius (610-41), after ten years of preparation, counter-attacked Persia from the rear through the Black Sea to revenge the past. Since then, the Persians became extremely weakened, and its Sasanian dynasty, the last kingdom of the Persian Empire (224-651) finally fell to the Arabs with the rise of Islam.

In religion, the peoples of ancient Mesopotamia and Egypt worshipped many gods of nature: the former prayed for earthly goods, not for heavenly rewards; but the latter believed immortality, revival of life after the death. The Persians worshipped Zoroaster (630?-550? BC), who preached an ethical dualism: the followers of truth will be led to paradise and the adherents of lie will fall into hell. Judaism has been the religion of the Israelites entering into the covenant agreement with the God: Yahweh protects the Israelites while the Israelites worship Yahweh as written in the Hebrew Scriptures. The Greek cities worshipped the Olympians with intense cults of local deities: the Olympians were the twelve major gods and goddesses having their home at the mount of Olympus. The Romans had three main gods – Jupiter as a sky god, Mars as a warrior god, and Quirinus as god of war – and they accepted the Greek gods and adopted Greek mythology. Jesus of Nazareth (6 BC - AD 29) and his twelve apostles established Christianity by preaching on love of God, love of neighbor, the existence of heavenly kingdom for salvation, and the continuity of the Hebrew Scriptures. The Christian church developed a centralized administration in accordance with the Roman imperial system. After the fall of Rome, the Catholic Church played an important role to civilize wild barbarians in the west. Muhammad (570-632) established Islam at Medina with the Holy Scriptures, the *Koran*, largely adopted from Judaic doctrines. After his death, Abu Beker succeeded him, followed by the Caliph Omar (634-44), which clan became the Shiites. When the Byzantine and Persians exhausted themselves by wars, the Arabs conquered Syria in 640 and Persia and Egypt in 651; and a half million Arabs migrated into the conquered lands. After the death of Omar, the Quraysh aristocracy in Mecca gained power. Muawiyah established the Umayyad Caliphate (661-750), which became the clan of the Sunnites, and moved his capital from Medina to Damascus. Conquering North Africa, the Muslims invaded Spain and subdued them, and expanded its territory to the Central Asia beyond the Oxus River during 711-13.

The Middle Ages: *(a) The Early Middle Ages* (750-1000): After the fall of the Western Roman Empire, Europe experienced three centuries of transition until the rise of the Pepins. The Pepin III founded the Carolingian dynasty in 751, and his son Charlemagne was coronated by Leo III in 800, which recognized him as the first Roman emperor ever since the fall of the empire: it was a beginning of the Holy Roman Empire. The Treaty of Verdun made in 843 opened the modern states of France, Germany, and Italy; but the political partition with the middle kingdom located between France and Germany expedited the disintegration of the new empire due to their socio-cultural differences. The empire was divided by the ecclesiastical provinces and individual bishoprics, which made their lands in far-off regions, are under foreign political control.[1] Meantime, a wave of invasions hit Europe. The Vikings were Germanic invaders from Norway, Denmark, and Sweden; their motives lay in political instability from dynastic struggles and economic difficulties from the rising population with bad harvest; and their shipbuilding skill and navigation knowledge helped them to follow the existing trade route for raids. The Magyars invaded Hungary, Venice, the Bulgarians; raided provinces of France and Germany; penetrated the Flanders but were defeated by Otto I; eventually established the Christian

Kingdom of Hungary in 1000-1001.[2] The Muslims invaded and ruled Egypt, Tunisia, and Morocco in northern Africa; and the west collided with them in two fronts - southern Italy and Spain. They colonized the islands of Corsica, Sardinia, Crete, Malta, and Sicily; and the caliphate of Cordoba in Spain maintained its independence from Baghdad even under the Abbasids, and Arab vessels from Spain invaded coasts and rivers to the Mediterranean and raided villages and towns. The Umayyad (Sunnites) previously were Arabs who had no contact with Christian states in the west, but traded with Pakistan, east Africa, and China through the Indian Ocean. But the Abbasids (Shiites), initially supported by the Persians, pursued to be a more Muslim state than a pure Arab or Persian state.

The Muslims created a new civilization from Gibraltar to the Indus in the three centuries of ascendancy. Unlike Christianity, the Muslim state had no conflict between church and state, and they were advantageous in their armies to be the strongest in the east.[3] The major caliphates succeeded as follows: "the Rashidun Caliphate (632–661), the Umayyad Caliphate (661–750) and the Abbasid Caliphate (750–1258).[4] In the fourth major caliphate, the Ottoman Caliphate, the rulers of the Ottoman Empire claimed caliphal authority from 1517."[5] Harun al-Rashid (Reign 786-809) centralized his power and rooted out abuses in tax collection. Baghdad needed the revenues from the provinces to pay salaries and pensions to soldiers largely recruited from Khurasan, which nobles wanted to spend their tax revenues locally, that was not acceptable to Baghdad. To resolve the revolt, Harun visited Khorasan but he died of ill there.[6] Al-Mutasim hired 4,000 Turkish soldiers for his bodyguards; but later on, they took the palace and murdered caliph al-Mutasir in 862; which caused war and anarchy for decades, and finally the fall of the dynasty and the rise of local powers: the Buwayhids, the Curds, and the Hamdanids. The Seljuk Turks conquered most of Iran and Iraq in the eleventh century. The Byzantine lost lands to Muslims, Slavs, and Bulgars in the seventh and eighth centuries; and held only Asian Minor, some lands in the Balkans, and southern coast of Italy. The empire handled many difficulties but reached its peak in the tenth century; however, the old aristocratic families of Byzantium were gradually replaced by others drawn from Anatolians and Armenians. The Slavs migrated and formed political units in Poland, Bohemia, and Russia in the ninth and the tenth centuries. The Polish tribes established a kingdom between Oder and Vistula under Mieszko in 962 and converted to Christianity through Bohemia. The Bohemians migrated to the region during the fifth to eighth centuries and founded a state in Czech and Slovakia in the tenth century. The Swedish Vikings invaded the Slavonic tribes in Novgorod, and occupied Kiev in 882. Trading with Constantinople, Kiev became a commercial center, where the Vikings and the Slavs fused into one, the Russians. The other Slavs migrated to the south into the Balkans: They are the main population of the Eastern and South-eastern Europe of "Bosnia and Herzegovina, Bulgaria, Croatia, Montenegro, North Macedonia, Serbia and Slovenia."[7]

(b) The High Middle Ages (1000-1300) experienced three major affairs: political centralization, religious reforms, and the Crusades. The clergy was troubled in spiritual quality, religious discipline, and educational function; the feudalism made church officials hold fiefs from nobles with military obligations forcing their spiritual duties to be secondary; while clerical marriage and simony corrupted the church. The reform movement of the Catholic began from the abbey of Cluny in eastern France in 910, which was followed by the Cistercian monasticism joined by Bernard in 1113. In the thirteenth century, other religious orders became active for Catholic reforms: the Franciscans and the Dominicans. Meanwhile, the European kingdoms were centralized as the economy revived with the end of anarchy from external invasions. In England, William the Conqueror invaded England and took the throne in 1066. John fought against Philip of France, and the heavy burden of taxes caused rebellions of barons; which made the king seal the *Magna Carta* for equal access to court and due process of law. In France, Philip IV needed money for military campaigns, and summoned the Estate-General consisting of the noble, clergy, and commons in 1302, which was the first parliament of Paris. In Spain, the Christians fought against the Muslims in the twelfth century and conquered all of southern Spain ruled by the Muslims in the thirteenth century. Spain was finally consolidated into Castile and Leon, Aragon, and Portugal except Granada of a Muslim state until 1492. In Germany, Frederick II gave up the hegemony in Europe, and focused on the control of northern Italy based on Sicily by leaving Germany to feudalism; which resulted in a loose confederacy in Germany and independent city states in Italy. The Seljuk Turks expanded into the former Persian territories; the Mongols invaded Russia and central Asia and established the Golden Horde in the thirteenth century. The Crusades fought two centuries against the Muslims, but Jerusalem fell into the rule of infidel and the Christians finally failed. The original purpose of the Crusades was in religion, but their impact became wide and deep.

(c) The Late Middle Ages (1300-1400) encountered economic turmoil, war and political instability, and religious downturn. First of all, famine and plague killed more than a half of the people in Europe though the death rate differs by region; and the change of factor intensity with rising wages and falling rents as well as the intensive use of money in exchanges expedited the collapse of the manorial system. In fact, the destruction of law and order by the plague and subsequent economic dislocation exacerbated social tensions, which stimulated the peasant and urban revolts; which was helped by the ravage of the war between England and France. Second, the Hundred Years' War (1337-1453) formed the two axes: England was supported by Germany, Scandinavia, and the papal state; and France by Spain, Scotland,

and southern Italy. The French won the war, so that the English lost all lands gained in France during the war except the town of Calais. In the war, the English infantry was more successful than the French cavalry, which reduced the necessity of knights and loosened the lord-vassal relations. In Germany, Charles IV approved the Golden Bull in 1356, allowing the seven electors to choose the German king and the Holy Roman Emperor, which became significant in history. Third and finally, the papal system began to decline because of economic and social changes, political centralization, and lack of self-adjustment. By about 1200, the church owned a third of lands in France, and the papal state received more income than the total revenues of all secular sovereigns in Europe. Since the French king wanted to impose taxes on clerical revenues and to judge some clerical crimes at the royal court, the conflict between Philip VI and Boniface VIII caused the Great Schism after his intervention in the election of the pope: two legitimate popes had existed at Rome and Avignon from 1378, and one more at Pisa from 1409 until Emperor Sigismund intervened by initiating the Council of Constance, which ended the Schism in 1417. Considering that the Black Death failed in providing spiritual comfort by the church, the Great Schism largely damaged the prestige and respect of the papacy. Since then, the church became part of the political authority as Masilius of Padua wrote.[8]

The Renaissance, the Reformation, and Geographical Discoveries (1400-1715): Passing the Dark Ages, the Black Death, and the Hundred Years' War, the population began to rise from 1450 that expanded the economy until 1600. In *the Renaissance period*, Italy was divided into five major powers: the Dutch of Milan, Venice, Florence, the Papal State, and the Kingdom of Naples. They used foreign forces to maintain the balance of power on the peninsula. The French army invaded the Kingdom of Naples by an invitation of Milan, but the Spanish expelled them and ruled both for two centuries. The Hundred Years' War caused depopulation, desolate farmlands, ruined industry and commerce, and independent nobles. Obtaining the right to levy direct taxes on properties, Charles VII strengthened the authority of the king and secured the control over the church in France from the pope. Charles VIII and Louis XII were engaged in the Italian wars, and Francis I also invaded Italy but was captured and detained in Spain for months. He negotiated with the pope to obtain the right to nominate the prelates in France. In England, the War of the Roses gave the throne to the Yorkists, but Henry VII challenged and founded a new Tudor dynasty in 1485 and strengthened the royal power during his reign until 1509. In Spain, Isabella of Castile married Ferdinand of Aragon in 1469, ruled two kingdoms as equal partners, and finally unified Spain. They conquered Granada and expelled the Muslims and Jews from Spain in 1492, when Isabella allowed the expedition of Columbus. Being engaged in the Italian wars, Spain gained and ruled Milan and the Kingdom of Naples until 1713. The Holy Roman Empire includes princely states, ecclesiastical states, some fifty of imperial free-states, and some thousands of imperial knights. The emperors were elected by seven electors set by the Golden Bull of 1356 (including archbishops of Mainz, Cologne, and Trier; King of Bohemia, Count Palatine of the Rhine, Duke of Saxony-Wittenberg, and Margrave of Brandenburg).[9] The emperors such as Albert II, Frederick III, and Maximilian I were rooted to the Habsburgs, which had gained territories through marriages, so Charles V of Spain became the emperor in 1519. Meanwhile, the Ottoman Turks founded the empire of vassal states in the Balkans and Anatolia - Mehmed II conquered Constantinople in 1453. Moreover, the Turks threatened Hungary and Austria in the 1520s.

The demand for reformation of the papal system was accumulated, exploded, and advanced by the combined forces of the state and society. In the early Renaissance, rejecting papal claims on temporal authority and property, both Wycliffe and Hus attacked corrupt church. The Reformation rooted in mysticism of Groote and Kempis and humanism of Erasmus and More, emphasizing "a true inner piety into Christian faith" by following the life of Christ in the Bible, which was more important than the external forms of religion. Martin Luther issued the Ninety-Five Thesis in 1517 against the abuses of selling indulgence by the pope. He views that works cannot glorify God, and faith alone brings complete salvation without works; there is no difference between clergy and laity so that the temporal estate should exercise its power over the spiritual estate; and every Christian is a priest to interpret the Bible that is final authority for doctrine and practice. Martin Luther suggested no annual tribute to Rome, marriage of priests, and reformation of sacraments; but he faced problems with internal radicalism, external opposition, and social revolution. But he was against revolts and supported complete obedience to the state enforcing law and order. Charles V failed in containing the spread of Lutheranism because of the French, the Turks, the pope, and the Lutherans in Germany. Other movements appeared in Zwinglians, Anabaptists, Calvinists, and Anglicans. In the mid-sixteenth century, Lutheranism gained roots in parts of Germany and Scandinavia; Calvinism rose in parts of Switzerland, France, the Netherlands, and Eastern Europe; and England created a protestant church of Anglicanism by splitting with Rome. Finally, the Peace of Augsburg in 1555 was a turning point of reformation in history allowing that Lutheranism is legally equal to Catholicism in Germany. The papal system had been challenged by internal and external demand for reformation: the Society of Jesus was successful in reform by establishing highly disciplined schools around the world. The Council of Trent, held between 1545 and 1563 in Trent as the embodiment of the Counter-Reformation, reestablished the Catholic doctrine and unified the Catholic Church under the papal supremacy.

In the sixteenth century, ***geographical discoveries*** gave opportunities for Portugal and Spain to expand political power to and to exploit economic gains in Asia and America, followed by the Dutch, English, and French. Meanwhile, the Reformation caused the wars of religion in Europe until 1648. In France, the conflict between Calvinism and Catholicism ignited a civil war: the duke of Guise killed thousands of Huguenots in 1572. Henry of Navarre became Henry IV in 1589 by converting into Catholic and issued the Edict of Nantes in 1598 allowing religious co-existence in France. In Spain, Philip II ended Italian wars with France and England in 1559 that secured the Spanish control over Italy; and expelled 5,000 of Moriscos from Castile in 1568. Forming a Holy League with Venice and Rome, Philip won the war against the Turks at Lepanto in 1571. He invaded and occupied Portugal during 1580-1640, when the Dutch and English attacked the Portuguese who dominated the Atlantic slave trade and the spice trade with Asia. In the Low Countries, the Calvinist movement ignited anti-Spanish revolts in 1566, and Philip sent Alva with 10,000 troops to the Spanish Netherlands to secure the law and order. In 1579, the southern provinces formed a Catholic union accepting Spanish rule, while the northern formed a Protestant union opposing it, which was supported by 6,000 of English troops. Philip sent the Spanish Armada of 130 ships to invade England but was defeated by the English navy at near Calais in 1588. Spain finally recognized the United Provinces at a truce of 1609. In England, Elizabeth settled religious problems with a moderate Protestantism, but Catholics and Puritans were dangerous to the Anglican Church, while the Puritans became the majority of the House of Commons in the 1570s. Elizabeth aided French Huguenots and Dutch Calvinists to weaken France and Spain. In Germany, the conflict between Lutherans and Catholics caused the Thirty Years' War (1618-48), which was developed to war between Bourbon and Habsburg for hegemony rather than religious conflict between Catholics and Protestants.

The Thirty Years' War was "the last major religious war in mainland Europe, ending the large-scale religious bloodshed accompanying reformation, which had begun over a century before. Other religious conflicts occurred in the years to come, but no great wars." By the Treaty of Westphalia of 1648, Protestants and Catholics were redefined as equal before the law, and Calvinism was given legal recognition. Louis XIV consolidated a Catholic dynasty by revoking the Edict of Nantes, suppressing Huguenots to escape to foreign countries, intervening in church affairs and trying to keep the Catholic throne in England. But religious differences no longer justified disputes between nations. Political affairs were settled without reference to opinions of the church, and the popes could not effectively participate in political affairs of Western Europe. Since the Enlightenment emancipated the medievalism submitting individual will to the heaven, the scriptures were less sympathetic. In fact, the Deists insisted that reason and observation determine that God created the universe and rejected super-natural events like prophecy and miracles. In England, the Anglican Church was established, and Evangelicalism arose "as a reaction against the lack of spiritual fever and enthusiasm in the Church" and John Wesley's Methodists broke away from the Church of England. In France, the Jansenists opposed to the Jesuits in high places, and "Quietism was a mystical protest against excessively intellectual ways of apprehending the divine." Monasteries and convents declined in the absence of spiritual vitality, and skeptic deism expedited secularization of society. But the clergy had their own courts, and controlled marriage; the church still possessed huge wealth and property exempted from taxes, and monopolized education and the care of the sick. In Germany, the pietistic spirits reacted against the Lutheran rigidities.

Religious wars, rebellions, and crises weakened the creditability of Christianity, secularized society, and centralized politics. In the seventeenth century, there appeared absolute monarchy in France, Spain, Germany, and eastern and northern Europe; limited monarchy in England and Poland; and the republic in the United Provinces. In France, Louis XIV consolidated his power and entered wars to conquer new lands in the Netherlands, to secure natural borders along the Rhine, and to make peace in the War of Spanish Succession. He revoked the Edict of Nantes in 1685 to suppress Huguenots. In Spain, Philip III expelled all remaining Moriscos of 250,000 to North Africa in 1609, which caused an economic crisis. In the War of Spanish Succession, Spain lost all possessions in Italy and the Netherlands. When Germany became free from the Holy Roman Empire by the peace of Westphalia, Frederick William of Brandenburg built the standing army of 40,000 by 1678 by requiring *Junkers* to serve him as army officers or civil leaders; that became the foundation of Prussia. Leopold I of Austria extended the Habsburg's possessions, created an imperial standing army, and consolidated the Austrian administration. In Russia, Peter the Great westernized its old system, and built a new standing army of 210,000 and the navy of 28,000 by 1705. Peter won the war with Charles XII of Sweden at Poltava of Ukraine in 1709 but lost the war with the Turks and withdrew by giving up Azov in the Black Sea in 1711. Peter invaded Sweden and gained some lands in 1721 which secured the control of the Baltic. The Ottoman Empire advanced to Vienna in 1697, but the Austrian army defeated them at Senta of Serbia; and Austria and Russia continuously forced the Turks to leave the Balkan. England experienced the Civil War between Charles I and Parliament during 1642-46. The Navigation Act of 1651 caused the Anglo-Dutch Wars during 1652-74 that restricted the Dutch expansion. The Glorious Revolution of 1688 offered the throne to William and Mary, who accepted the Bill of Rights confirming England to be constitutional monarchy based on social contract, which ideas reflected those of the political thinker John Locke.

The French Revolution and the Industrial Revolution (1715-1815):
Passing the age of Louis XIV, the Treaties of Utrecht, Rastatt, and Baden of
1713 made Europe being able to keep the peace with a new balance of power
between emerging five powers – France, Britain, Prussia, Austria, and
Russia. Philip, Duke of Anjou, received the throne as Philip V of Spain by
renouncing any claim to the throne of France; Spain ceded the Netherlands,
Milan, Naples, and Sicily to Austria; Britain, being strengthened by the
union of England and Scotland, obtained Gibraltar, Minorca, and the
commercial privilege of the *asiento* from Spain, and Newfoundland and
Nova Scotia from France. "Utrecht strengthened the sense of useful international law and inaugurated an era of relative stability in the European state
system, based on balance-of-power politics that no one country would
become dominant." In France, the nobility was too powerful to give up their
privileges, and resisted reforms demanded by the people. Louis XV (1715-
74) failed in controlling state affairs and Louis XVI knew little about his
jobs. The public debt was accumulated by foreign wars; that caused the
financial crisis and threatened the supply of necessities for the people, which
finally led to a violent revolution. In Great Britain, the Glorious Revolution
prevented absolutism by sharing political power between king and parliament with the passage of the Bill of Rights. The new Hanoverian dynasty -
George I and George II (1727-60) - was established. In Germany, Frederick
William I of Prussia established militarism, and his son Frederick the Great
(1740-86) further developed army and bureaucracy and challenged the
Austrian Habsburgs. In Austria, Maria Theresa (1740-80) succeeded her
father's throne, when Prussia invaded Silesia, which ignited the two great
wars between European states. In Russia, Elizabeth Petrovna (1741-62) led
the country into the two European conflicts, and Catherine the Great (1762-
96) continued the war against Prussia in the Seven Years' War. Poland was
partitioned by Russia, Prussia, and Austria in 1772, and disappeared on the
map in the 1790s. Russia contained Sweden and pushed the Ottoman Turks
out of the Black Sea, to be discussed later.

In around 1700, Sweden had many enemies: Russia wanted to access to
the Baltic that had been blocked by Swedish-held costal lands; Denmark-
Norway resented the loss of their lands such as Skane to Sweden in the past;
Brandenburg coveted Swedish Pomerania; and Poland wanted to recover
Swedish Livonia. *The Great Northern War* (1700-21) resolved those
conflicts: Prussia gained Swedish Pomerania, and Sweden ceded Ingria,
Estonia, Livonia, and a strip of Finish Karelia to Russia. In *the War of the
Polish Succession* (1723-38), the Bourbon powers, Spain and France,
attempted to check the power of the Austrian Habsburgs in the Western
Europe; which resulted mainly in "a redistribution of Italian territory and an
increase in Russian influence over Polish affairs." *The War of the Austrian
Succession* (1740-48) involved most of the powers of Europe, questioning

Maria Theresa's succession to the House of Habsburg. France and Prussia challenged Hapsburg power, while Prussia invaded Silesia, which was supported by Great Britain and the Dutch Republic. Spain had been at war with Britain over colonies and entered the war in northern Italy later. At the peace, Theresa's succession was confirmed, but Prussia gained Silesia.

In *the Seven Years' War* (1756-63), France, Austria, Saxony, Sweden, and Russia were aligned on one side against Prussia, Hanover, and Great Britain on the other. It was the first true world war having taken place before World War I of 1914. The war arose out of the attempt of the Austrian Habsburgs to win back the rich province of Silesia, which had been wrested from them by Frederick the Great of Prussia. "The Seven Years' War also involved overseas colonial struggles between Great Britain and France, the main points of contention between those two traditional rivals being the struggle for control of North America and India." Moreover, it was also the war between France and Great Britain that allied with Prussia partly to protect Hanover from the threat of a French takeover. At the peace, France ceded its possessions east of the Mississippi River, Canada, Granada, and the Northern Circars in India to Britain, west of that to Spain; Spain ceded Florida to Britain; and Caribbean islands were divided between Britain and France. "Britain aligned itself with Prussia, in a series of political maneuvers known as the Diplomatic Revolution. However, French efforts ended in failure when the Anglo-Prussian coalition prevailed, and Britain's rise as among the world's predominant powers destroyed France's supremacy in Europe, thus altering the European balance of power."[10]

The Russo-Turkish War (1768-74): This was a by-product for the first partition of Poland. The Polish-Lithuanian state became a protectorate of Russia that caused guerrilla warfare in Poland, which threatened livelihood of many a poor noble. A band of Orthodox Cossack crossed into the Turkish territory, in pursuit of Polish confederates. Russian operations against the confederates concentrated in areas closer to the Turkish border, which threatened Turkish security. The Turks allied with the Polish opposition forces declared the war against Russia supported by Britain for its naval operations. Catherine the Great wanted to separate Crimea and the Balkans from the Turks as independent states. At peace, Russia returned Wallachia and Moldavia to Turkey subject to the protection of Christians; the Crimea declared its independence; and Russia gained the north of the Crimea and Kerch, and part of the Odesa region at the mouth of the Dnieper; which allowed Russia to access two outlets to the Black Sea. Through the second Russo-Turkish War (1787-92), Turkey recognized annexation of the Crimea and ceded Ochakov to Russia that could control the western Ukraine coast of the Black Sea from Kerch to Dniester.

The American Revolutionary War (1775-83): After the Seven Years' War, Britain faced financial constraint, which required more taxes from the

American colonies in order to pay expenses of the British army defending her colonies. The British parliament issued a series of acts to collect more taxes from America. American intellectuals like Thomas Paine and Patrick Henry with leading planters, merchants, and clergymen set fire on a common sense: the spirit of independency, which generated a momentum for mass movements. The Americans fought against British regular troops, won the war with the support of France, and founded a new independent state. The constitution of the United States was a social contract of American people, ratified by all states in 1789, and the Bill of Rights was added. American intellectuals learned liberal ideas – liberty and equality – from the Enlightenment, and their experiences re-entered Europe and shook their societies.

The French Revolutionary War (1792-1802) was a liberal movement to extend political rights and power to the bourgeoisie class, which was the major turning point in European history. It destroyed the old regime and created a new order based on individual rights, representative institutions, and loyalty to the nation not to the monarch. The main cause of the French Revolution was in the near collapse of the government finance. When the government was forced to call a meeting of the Estate-General to raise additional taxes, the activists of the Third Estate with reform-minded individuals among the First and Second Estates drafted "statements of grievances" advocating a constitutional government that would abolish the fiscal privileges of the church and nobility. The Third Estate considered itself as a National Assembly and swore "that they would continue to meet until they had produced a French constitution." This was the first step of the revolution, and the urban rising like the fall of Bastille and the marching to Versailles pushed it forward to be successful. In August 1789, the National Assembly adopted the "Declaration of the Rights of Man and Citizen" affirming natural rights - men are born and remain free and equal in rights - which should be protected by the government. In September 1792, the assembly passed its power to the National Convention dominated by the Jacobins that created the Council of Public Safety, and Robespierre used the "Reign of Terror." In October 1795 when the radicals failed in policies, the moderates created the Constitutional Republic consisting of the Directory as the executive and two Councils as the legislative. However, the Directory faced political enemies from the right or royalists, and from the left or the proletariat. The failure of the Directory in managing the state resulted in anarchy in France that required an able man breaking the deadlock. The Directory appointed Napoleon Bonaparte to the commander of the Parisian garrison in September 1799. Thus, the French Revolution destroyed the old regime and created a republican state, which was terminated by inefficiency and anarchy and finally invited military dictatorship.

The Napoleonic Wars (1803-15): Napoleon established a military dictatorship in November 1799. As external threats, Britain had sought a commercial empire based on her maritime supremacy; Russia had pushed upon Poland and Turkey with expansionary strategies; Prussia had sought the leadership in northern Germany by consolidating its territories; and Austria was less aggressive due to rising Prussia and Russia but dreamed of its ascendancy competing with Prussia. Since France had been at war against major European states, Napoleon faced a choice of either war or peace in foreign relations. He chose peace with them in the first stage in his reign but chose war in the following stages. As internal threats, Napoleon faced many serious problems in all aspect of French society. The Treasury was empty, religion was in constant opposition, public education was in ruin in the absence of church commitment, the family was shaken in the freedom of divorce, and public spirit of patriotism was dying in the skeptical future of the revolution. He could be challenged either from the left or the right; any faction was able to be against the coming regime if new policies were harmful for their interests; and friends and foes could be changed according to the political environment. At the time he took power, he wished the revolution to end by healing its internal strife and neutralizing factions for peace and prosperity. He favored compromises rather than his iron fist in dealing with impending issues. Napoleon introduced many reforms in law, administration, education, and others. His victory against the Austrians at the Battle of Marengo in 1800 encouraged him to embark on the Napoleonic Wars. After the loss of the Battle of Trafalgar with the Royal Navy in 1805, Napoleon established the Continental System to block all ports against Great Britain. When Napoleon invaded Iberia to extend the Continental System in 1808, the Spanish and the Portuguese revolted with British support, and the Peninsula War lasted six years, featured extensive guerrilla warfare.

As the Russians routinely violated the Continental System (while France realized that extensive trade was going through Spain and Russia), the French launched a major invasion of Russia in the summer 1812 with the Grand Army of 685,000 soldiers from Germany, Poland, Italy and France. As Napoleon marched on Russia, Moscow had been burned to the ground by the Russians: the whole city was on fire for three days. As Napoleon retreated from Moscow, "fewer than 70,000 had returned, leaving 400,000 dead and more than 100,000 prisoners of the Russians, with an unknown number of stragglers and deserters making their way back unrecorded." [11] Further battles, in which Napoleon was driven back relentlessly westwards by a coalition of European armies led by the British, the Prussians, the Austrians and the Russians, had caused further carnage. Finally, in 1814, the Allies had occupied Paris, forcing Napoleon into exile on Elba. In March 1815 Napoleon returned from exile to Paris, but he was finally defeated at Waterloo in June, and sent in exile to St. Helena. Napoleon ended the French Revolution and replaced entrenched custom and privilege with rationality and uniformity based on the rights of property, liberty and equality. He conquered European states: its occupation and rule caused resentment and resistance against France and stimulated patriotism and nationalism of the oppressed people. His Russian campaign was the worst mistake by strategic misjudgment, as the peninsular war forced France to divide resources into two fronts. He developed efficient models of political organization and authoritarian rule, but the failure of the Continental System made Britain a dominant industrial and commercial power, which ended two centuries of Anglo-French competition.

The Consolidation of States, Industrialization, Commercialization (1815-1914): As a reaction to the radicalism of the French Revolution, Allies as victorious powers of the Napoleonic Wars resolved to suppress liberalism and nationalism and revert largely to the status quo of Europe prior to 1789. *The Concert of Europe* was "a system of dispute resolution adopted by the major conservative powers of Europe to maintain their power, oppose revolutionary movement, weaken the forces of nationalism, and uphold the balance of power." The Kingdom of Prussia and the Austrian and Russian Empires formed the Holy Alliance with the expressed intent of preserving Christian social values and traditional monarchism. "Every member of the coalition promptly joined the Alliance, except for the United Kingdom, a constitutional monarchy with a more liberal political philosophy. Britain did however ratify the Alliance, signed on the same day as the Second Peace Treaty of Paris (20 November 1815), which became the known Quintuple Alliance when France joined in 1818. It was also signed by the same three powers that had signed the Holy Alliance on 26 September 1815." So France became the fifth member of the Concert. The leading personalities of the system were British foreign secretary Lord Castlereagh, Austrian Chancellor Klemens von Metternich, and Tsar Alexander I of Russia. The Concert of Europe had no written rules or permanent institutions, but at times of crisis any of the member countries could propose a conference. "The Congress of Aix-la-Chapelle (1818) resolved the issues of Allied occupation of France and restored that country to equal status with Britain, Prussia, Austria and Russia. In 1822, the Congress of Verona met to decide the issue if France could intervene on the side of the Spanish royalists in the Trienio Liberal. After receiving permission, Louis XVIII dispatched five army corps to restore Ferdinand VII of Spain." "In 1818, the British decided not to become involved in continental issues that did not directly affect them. They rejected the plan of Alexander I to suppress future revolutions. The Concert system fell apart as the common goals of the Great Powers were replaced by growing political and economic rivalries."[12]

(a) *The Conservative Order*: The Concert had tried to maintain the prerevolutionary conservative order, but the rising liberalism and nationalism pushed the oppressed people towards revolutionary movements in the 1820s and beyond. In France, Louis XVIII (1814-24) was restored to the throne of the constitutional monarchy, succeeded by Charles X (1824-30). In fact, during 1827-30, the French peasants suffered from worsening grain harvest, rising food prices from high tariffs on grain imports, and industrial downturn, which contributed to the rising poverty levels among Parisian artisans, while they were suffered from the economic policies of Charles X. In March 1830, when liberal members of the Chamber objected to the ministry, Charles dissolved the Chamber, and called for an election, which returned a majority unfavorable to the King himself. He issued four ordinances for his power, but the liberal bourgeoisie-controlled Chamber of Deputies elevated Louis-Philip (1830-48), Duke of Orleans, to power. Meanwhile, the Belgian Revolution broke out in 1830, after the performance of a nationalistic opera in Brussels that led to a minor insurrection among the capital's bourgeoisie, protesting against Dutch rule imposed in 1815. Heavy fighting took place between Dutch forces and Brussels revolutionaries. Dutch garrisons were pushed out of the area, the provisional government of Belgium was formed, and Belgian independence was proclaimed. Leopold I became the King of - the Belgians under the new constitution.[13]

After its Partitions, Poland was ruled by Russian secret police. By 1829, Nicholas I (1825-55) of Russia crowned himself as the King of Poland in Warsaw. The uprising began when the young Polish officers of its military academy revolted. They were soon joined by large segments of society, but was eventually crushed by an Imperial Russian Army; henceforth, Poland was an integrated part of Russia, with little more than a military garrison in Warsaw.[14] In Italy, by 1830, "revolutionary sentiment in favor of a unified Italy began to experience a resurgence, and a series of insurrections laid the groundwork for the creation of one nation along the Italian peninsula. The Duke of Modena, Francis IV, was an ambitious noble, and he hoped to become king of Northern Italy by increasing his territory. In 1826, Francis made it clear that he would not act against those who subverted opposition toward the unification of Italy. Encouraged by the declaration, revolutionaries in the region began to organize. New French king Louis-Philippe had promised revolutionaries such as Ciro Menotti that he would intervene if Austria tried to interfere in Italy with troops. Fearing he would lose his throne, Louis-Philippe did not, however, intervene in Menotti's planned uprising. The Duke of Modena abandoned his Carbonari supporters, arrested Menotti and other conspirators in 1831, and once again conquered his duchy with help from the Austrian troops. Menotti was executed, and the idea of a revolution centered in Modena faded."[15] The Austrian army marched across the Italian peninsula, crushing resistance in revolting provinces.

In Latin America, when Bourbon monarchy of Spain was toppled by Bonaparte, Spanish authority in its colonial empire was weakened. "By 1810, the disintegration of royal power in Argentina had led to that nation's independence. In Venezuela a bitter struggle for independence was led by Simon Bolivar, hailed as the Liberator. His forces freed Colombia in 1819 and Venezuela in 1821. A second liberator was Jose de San Martin who liberated Chile in 1817 and then, in 1821, moved on to Lima, Peru, the center of Spanish authority. He was soon joined by Bolivar who assumed the task of crushing the last significant Spanish army in 1821. Mexico and the Central American provinces also achieved their freedom, and by 1825, after Portugal had recognized the independence of Brazil, almost all of Latin America had been freed of colonial domination." Moreover, "After the royal court returned to Lisbon, the prince regent, Pedro, remained in Brazil and in 1822 successfully declared himself emperor of a newly independent Brazil."[16] Louis XVIII of France sent his armies to suppress the liberal uprisings against Ferdinand VII in Spain in 1822. On the other hand, the Greek Revolution was a successful war of independence waged by the Greek revolutionaries during 1821-32 against the Ottoman Empire. The Greeks were later assisted by the Russian Empire, Great Britain, the Kingdom of France, and several other European powers.[17]

   (b) *The Revolution and Reforms*: The revolutions of 1848 were a series of political upheavals throughout Europe, which remains the most widespread revolutionary wave in European history. "The revolutions were essentially democratic in nature, with the aim of removing the old feudal structures and creating independent national states. The revolutionary wave began in France in February, and immediately spread to most of Europe and parts of Latin America. Over 50 countries were affected, but with no coordination or cooperation between their respective revolutionaries...some of the major contributing factors were widespread dissatisfaction with political leadership, demands for more participation in government and democracy, demands for freedom of press, other demands made by the working class, the upsurge of nationalism, and the regrouping of established governmental forces. The uprisings were led by shaky ad hoc coalitions of reformers, the middle classes and workers, which did not hold together for long. Tens of thousands of people were killed, and many more forced into exile. Significant lasting reforms included the abolition of serfdom in Austria and Hungary, the end of absolute monarchy in Denmark, and the introduction of parliamentary democracy in the Netherlands. The revolutions were most important in France, the Netherlands, the nations that would make up the German Empire in the late 19th century and early 20th, Italy, and the Austro-Hungarian Empire."[18] As legacy, "Democrats looked to 1848 as a democratic revolution, which in the long run ensured liberty, equality, and fraternity. Marxists denounced 1848 as a betrayal of working-class ideals by a bourgeoisie indifferent to the legitimate demands of the proletariat. For nationalists, 1848 was the springtime of hope, when newly emerging nationalities rejected the old multinational empires. They were all bitterly disappointed in the short run. In the post-revolutionary decade after 1848, little had visibly changed, and most historians considered the revolutions a failure, given the seeming lack of permanent structural changes." Austria and Prussia eliminated feudalism by 1850; France gained universal male suffrage; Russia freed the serfs by 1861; with political economic gains of the middle classes.[19]

   (c) ***Nationalism and Unification***: Napoleon III (1848-70) was a strong supporter of popular sovereignty and of nationalism. "In Europe, he allied with Britain and defeated Russia in the Crimean War (1853–56). His regime assisted Italian unification and, in doing so, annexed Savoy and the County of Nice to France; at the same time, his forces defended the Papal States against annexation by Italy. Napoleon doubled the area of the French overseas empire in Asia, the Pacific, and Africa. On the other hand, his army's intervention in Mexico which aimed to create a Second Mexican Empire under French protection ended in failure." In the German Confederation, the Austro-Prussian War (1866) was fought between the allies of the Austrian Empire and those of Prussian Empire, resulting in Prussian dominance over the German states. This conflict also paralleled the Third Independence War of Italian unification. As a result, power among German states shifted away from Austrian towards Prussian hegemony; which abolished the German Confederation and partially replaced by a North German Confederation. The Italian unification became crucial after the Franco-Austrian War of 1859 that transferred most of Lombardy to Italy from Austria. In 1860 Giuseppe Garibaldi with a thousand Red Shirts landed on the west coast of Sicily, crossed the strait and marched northward, entered into Naples. He handed over his dictatorial power to Victor Emmanuel II (1861-78) of the House of Savoy with the title of King of Italy. His alliance with Prussia in the Austro-Prussian War allowed Italy to annex Austrian-controlled Venetia, which brought the Italian unification in 1866. The Pope lost Rome to Italy in 1870. The Franco-Prussian War (1970-71) was a conflict between France and the North German Confederation led by the Kingdom of Prussia. The Treaty of Frankfurt of 1871 gave Germany most of Alsace and some parts of Lorraine. The Prussians conquered France and proclaimed the German Empire in 1871, which upset the European balance of power. The Prime Minister, Otto von Bismarck, led European international affairs for two coming decades.

   After the Austro-Prussian War, the Austro-Hungarian Compromise of 1867 established the dual monarchy of Austria-Hungary, governed by separate parliaments and prime ministers. "The old historic constitution of Hungary was restored…The common diplomatic and military affairs were managed by delegations from the Imperial Council and the Hungarian parliament…All common decisions had to be ratified by the Austrian and Hungarian parliaments to be valid…A common finance ministry was founded, only for the expenditures of the Common Army, the navy and the diplomatic service and for the issue of banknotes. It was headed by the Common Finance Minister."[20] The Compromise was formally terminated by 31 October 1918. Alexander II of Russia (1855-81) ruled Russia, Poland, and Finland. His reforms were emancipation of serfdom and other reforms, reorganizing the judicial system, setting up elected local judges, abolishing corporal punishment, promoting local self-government through the *zemstvo* system, imposing universal military service, ending some privileges of the nobility, and promoting university education. In foreign policy, "Alexander sold Alaska to the United States in 1867, fearing the remote colony would fall into British hands if there were another war. He sought peace, moved away from bellicose France when Napoleon III fell in 1871, and in 1872 joined with Germany and Austria in the League of the Three Emperors that stabilized the European situation. Despite his otherwise pacifist foreign policy, he fought a brief war with Turkey in 1877–78, pursued further expansion into Siberia and the Caucasus, and conquered Turkestan… Among his greatest domestic challenges was an uprising in Poland in 1863 …incorporating it directly into Russia. Alexander was proposing additional parliamentary reforms to counter the rise of nascent revolutionary and anarchistic movements when he was assassinated in 1881."[21]

Great Britain was in the period of relative peace in Europe (1815-1914) during which the British Empire became the global hegemonic power and adopted the role of a global police force. Historians have characterized the mid-Victorian era (1850-70) as Britain's Golden Years. Much of prosperity was due to the increasing industrialization, especially textiles and machinery, as well as to worldwide network of trade and engineering that produced profits for British merchants, and exports from across the globe. The American Civil War (1861-65) was an internal conflict fought in the United States. "The Union faced secessionists in eleven Southern states grouped together as the Confederate States of America. The Union won the war, which remains the bloodiest in U.S. history…Four years of intense combat left 620,000 to 750,000 soldiers dead, a higher number than the number of American military deaths in World War I and World War II combined, and much of the South's infrastructure was destroyed. The Confederacy collapsed and 4 million slaves were freed. The Reconstruction Era (1863–1877) overlapped and followed the war, with the process of restoring national unity, strengthening the national government, and granting civil rights to free slaves throughout the country."[22] In Canada, British four provinces – Ontario, Quebec, Nova Scotia, and New Brunswick – agreed on Constitution Act that proclaimed Canadian Confederation on July 1, 1867. On the other hand, "The Japanese knew that they were behind the European world when American Commodore Matthew C. Perry came to Japan in large warships with armament and technology that far outclassed those of Japan, to try to conclude a treaty that would open up Japanese ports to trade. In Japan however, unlike China, foreign ideas were not associated with opium addiction. Figures like Shimazu Nariakira concluded that if we take the initiative, we can dominate; if we do not, we will be dominated, leading Japan to throw open its doors to foreign technology."[23] The Meiji emperor realized that the best way to counter Western influence was to modernize. He sent diplomats to Europe and North America to study Western ways. The emperor energetically supported following the Western pass of industrialization. The Japanese economy had become as modern as any in the world, including shipbuilding and railroad construction.

(d) *The Growth of States*: "In Britain, the working classes that had given the country the greatest successes in the industrial revolution clamored to be heard by the ruling elite. Eventually, workers threw their support behind the Labor Party, a political party based on trade unions that advocated the creation of the government welfare state. A similar development took place in Germany, where the Social Democratic party emerged as a political force despite the numerous attempts by the ruling elite to destroy its power. In France, the modernized and centralized state that emerged in the Third Republic united the nation and allowed a mass media culture to emerge. The entire population, receiving the same information and the same interpretation of the news, was galvanized by various events, such as the Dreyfus Affair, which cut right to the heart of French society. In Austria-Hungary, the power of the bourgeoisie, who had identified their interests with those of the aristocracy, began to weaken as the entire outsider population - ethnic minorities, students, and radical right-wing groups - began to emerge in Austrian politics in an atmosphere of demagoguery and fantastic politics."[24] The Russo-Turkish War (1877–78) was a conflict between the Ottoman Empire and the Eastern Orthodox coalition led by the Russian Empire and composed of Bulgaria, Romania, Serbia, and Montenegro. "Fought in the Balkans and in the Caucasus, it originated in emerging 19th-century Balkan nationalism. Additional factors included Russian hopes of recovering territorial losses suffered during the Crimean War, reestablishing itself in the Black Sea and supporting the political movement attempting to free Balkan nations from the Ottoman Empire. The Russian-led coalition won the war. As a result, Russia succeeded in claiming several provinces in the Caucasus, namely Kars and Batumi, and also annexed the Budjak region. The principalities of Romania, Serbia, and Montenegro, each of whom had had de facto sovereignty for some time, formally proclaimed independence from the Ottoman Empire."[25]

(e) *Imperialist Exploitation*: "Foreign policy throughout this era was generally dominated by the imperial game. By 1914, nearly the entire continent of Africa was dominated by Europeans. The ancient states of Asia also generally succumbed to European invasion. Only the Japanese, after years of modernization and westernization, were able to become imperialists themselves and exert their own interests on the Chinese mainland." The Berlin Conference of 1884 regulated European colonization and trade in Africa during the New Imperialism period and coincided with the sudden emergence of Germany as an imperial power. The Conference can be seen as the formalization of the Scramble for Africa. "The conference ushered in a period of heightened colonial activity by European powers, which eliminated or overrode most existing forms of African autonomy and self-governance."[26] The Boer War (1899-1902) was a conflict between the British and the Afrikaner population of South Africa caused by British interests in mining gold. "The war progressed rather poorly for the better-equipped, better-trained, and larger British army. Under inept leadership and harassed by effective Afrikaner guerrilla tactics, the British were forced fight the Boer War for three years. In 1902, the British accepted the conditional surrender of the Afrikaners in which the entire colony was united under British rule; however, the British promised the Afrikaners that no decision to include the black majority in government would be made before rule was returned to the Afrikaners." The Opium Wars (1839-42) were conflicts between China and Britain over Britain's illegal trading of opium in the Chinese market. "The British blockaded Chinese ports, besieged Canton, and occupied Shanghai before the Chinese sought peace in the Treaty of Nanking." The Boxer Rebellion of 1900 was that "with secret encouragement from the Chinese empress, the Boxers, dedicated to ending foreign exploitation in north China, killed scores of European and seized the large foreign legation in Beijing. Reacting immediately, an international expeditionary force of Japanese, Russian, British, American, German, French, Austrian and Italian troops sacked Beijing to protect the interests of their respective countries. Afterward, the European powers propped up a weak central government for their own economic benefit."[27]

(f) *Military Affairs*: The military discipline is largely related to the change of the armed forces, the art and science, and technology. Europe experienced such major wars as the Crimean War (1853-56), the Austro-Prussian War (1866), the Franco-Prussian War (1870-71), and the Russo-Turkish War (1877-78), while America fought the Civil War (1861-65). As nationalism encouraged imperialism, European states expanded colonial territories in Africa, Asia, and the Americas with many wars. Karl von Clausewitz (1780-31) was a Prussian general and military theorist who stressed the moral and political aspects of war as written in his *On War* published posthumously (1832-35) by his wife. It is one of the most important treatises on political-military analysis and strategy ever written and remains influential on strategic thinking. Antoine Henri de Jomini (1779-1869) was a Swiss officer who served as a general in the French Army and later in the Russian service, and one of the most celebrated writers on the Napoleonic art of war. He published the *Treatise on Major Military Operations* (1803) and *The Art of War* (1838). Helmuth von Moltke (1800-91), a German Field Marshal, published *The Russo-Turkish Campaign in Europe, 1828-29*. Moltke regarded strategy "as a practical art of adapting means to ends." Alfred Thayer Mahan (1840-1914) was a U.S. naval officer and historian, who published *The Influence of Sea Power upon History, 1660-1783* (1890) and *The Influence of Sea Power upon the French Revolution and Empire, 1793-1812* (1892). He viewed that "if the United States were to build an isthmian canal, it would become a Pacific power, and therefore it should take possession of Hawaii to protect the West Coast." He supports for American imperialism - its annexation of the Philippines.

(g) ***Religion and Politics***: In the 19th century, Christianity showed as evangelical revivals in some Protestant countries and the effects of modern Biblical scholarship on the churches. Liberal theology was one consequence of this. "In Europe, the Roman Catholic Church strongly opposed liberalism and Georgia culture was launched in Germany, Italy, Belgium and France. It strongly emphasized personal piety. In Europe there was a general move away from religious observance and belief in Christian teachings and a move towards secularism. In Protestantism, pietistic revivals were common." Antisemitism may be manifested in many ways, "ranging from expressions of hatred of or discrimination against individual Jews to organized pogroms by mobs, state police, or even military attacks on entire Jewish communities. Although the term did not come into common usage until the 19th century, it is now also applied to historic anti-Jewish incidents. Notable instances of persecution include the Rhineland massacres preceding the First Crusade in 1096, the Edict of Expulsion from England in 1290, the massacres of Spanish Jews in 1391, the persecutions of the Spanish Inquisition, the expulsion from Spain in 1492, the Cossack massacres in Ukraine from 1648 to 1657, various anti-Jewish pogroms in the Russian Empire between 1821 and 1906, the 1894–1906 Dreyfus affair in France, the Holocaust in German occupied Europe, official Soviet anti-Jewish policies, and Arab and Muslim involvement in the Jewish exodus from Arab and Muslim countries." The development of nationalism allowed Jews to be patriotic about the country in which they lived. However, many of their non-Jewish fellow citizens still considered Jews to be outsiders. Islamic modernist ideas promoted a re-interpretation of Islam which would fit in with the modern world, attempting to reconcile Islamic faith with modernity. "They were formulated during the last decades of the nineteenth century and implied an acknowledgement that the Muslim world had lost its position in the world. For many modernists the reason for this loss rested in the lack, in Muslim countries, of a modern and dynamic understanding of science. Ironically…Islamic medieval knowledge with its transmission of classical science to the West was instrumental in the development of modern European science and technology."[28]

The World Wars, the Cold War, and Globalization (1914-2015): As a result of industrialization and unification of nation states, European states became more powerful, while the United States and Japan emerged as a major power by around 1900; which led to imperialist competitions through-out the world, so that a series of conflicts was unavoidable between world powers. (i) Scramble for Africa: Great Britain, France as well as Germany, Italy and Portugal, expanded their colonies in Africa, and Belgium controlled Congo. The Suez Canal was initiated by France, becoming a joint British-France project, but the Anglo-Egyptian War (1882) resulted in the British occupation of Egypt for seven decades. (ii) With rapid modernization starting in 1860s, Japan provided a base for imperial expansion: the Sino-Japanese War (1894-95) and the Russo-Japanese War (1904-05) made Japan annex Taiwan (1895) and Korea (1910), which became its basis to invade Manchuria. (iii) In China, European powers and Japan took effective control of certain port cities and their surrounding areas from the mid-nineteenth century until the 1920s, by forcing a series of unequal treaties with China. (iv) In the Balkans, Bulgaria, Greece, Montenegro and Serbia had achieved independence from the Ottoman Empire, but large elements of their ethnic populations remained under Ottoman rule. The Ottoman Empire was unable to deal with the rising ethnic nationalism of its diverse people; the great powers quarreled among themselves and failed to ensure that the Ottomans would carry out the needed reforms; and the Balkan League (1912-13) was confident in that it could defeat the Turks. As a result of two Balkan Wars, the Ottoman Empire lost all its European territories. (v) The Russian foreign policy shifted from Germany toward France though Russia fought France in the Napoleonic Wars and the Crimean War. Germany stopped lending to Russia, which became to depend on Paris banks. In the Balkan Wars, Russia supported the Serbian, against which Germany took the side of Austria-Hungary that was extended to World War I.

(a) *World War I* (1914-19) began in the Balkans because of following reasons. (i) Mutual defense alliance: The Triple Alliance was a secret agreement between Germany, Austria-Hungary, and Italy formed in 1882; and the Triple Entente was signed by Russia, France, and Great Britain in 1907, supplemented by agreements with Japan and Portugal; which, though was not allied, could be a powerful counter-weight to the Triple Alliance. (ii) Imperialism: In Africa, France and Germany competed for new colonial possessions; the Ottoman attracted the attention of European powers. During 1898-1913, German exports grew more rapidly than British exports, and in 1913 German exports to Russia and the United States largely exceeded British exports to the same. (iii) Militarism was intrinsically connected with nationalism and imperialism. Military leaders were influential to formulate defense policies, demanding more armed forces with corresponding defense spending, so the world entered an arms race. The expansion of militarism helped push the countries involved into war. (iv) Nationalism is an extreme form of patriotism and loyalty to one's country. The Germans placed great faith in Prussian military efficiency, and its army had supreme confidence in the Schlieffen Plan, a preemptive military strategy designed to win a war against its neighbors. The pan-Slavic nationalism inspired the assassination of Archduke Franz Ferdinand in Sarajevo in June 1914, which led directly to the outbreak of war. (v) Immediate causes of war: Serbian officials were involved in the plot to murder the Archduke visiting Bosnia; Austria-Hungary delivered to Serbia on 23th July the unacceptable July ultimatum. Russia ordered general mobilization for the related military districts, and fleets of the Baltic and the Black Sea. Servia decreed general mobilization on the 25th. Following this, Austria-Hungary broke of diplomatic relations with Serbia; and declared war on it. Germany mobilized and declared war on Russia on August 1st, then France and Great Britain were engaged in war. Thus, World War I became unavoidable.

The Germans were watching the change of politics in Russia, in March 1917, demonstrations in Petrograd (Saint Petersburg) culminated in the abdication of Tsar Nicholas II and the appointment of a Provisional Government, sharing power with the Petrograd Soviet socialists; which arrangement led to confusion and chaos at the war front and home. "Following the Tsar's abdication, Vladimir Lenin was ushered by train from Switzerland into Russia 16 April 1917. He was financed by Jacob Schiff. Discontent and the weaknesses of the Provisional Government led to a rise in the popularity of the Bolshevik Party, led by Lenin, which demanded an immediate end to the war. The Revolution of November was followed in December by an armistice and negotiations with Germany."[29] On the other hand, the United States declared war on Germany on April 6, 1917. During the war, the U.S. mobilized over 4 million military personnel and suffered 110,000 deaths, including 43,000 of the influenza pandemics. At the Peace of Paris during 1919, the Big Four (France, Britain, Italy, the U.S) leaders dominated the Conference. "The major decisions were the establishment of the League of Nations; the five peace treaties with defeated enemies (including the Treaty of Versailles with Germany); the awarding of German and Ottoman overseas possessions as 'mandates', chiefly to members of the British Empire and to France; reparations imposed on Germany, and the drawing of new national boundaries to better reflect the forces of nationalism. The main result was the Treaty of Versailles, with Germany…This provision proved humiliating for Germany and set the stage for very high reparations Germany was supposed to pay. As the conference's decisions were enacted unilaterally, and largely on the whims of the Big Four…the Treaty of Versailles itself weakened Germany's military and placed full blame for the war and costly reparations on Germany's shoulders."[30] The post-war reality began to diverge from Wilson's vision.

(b) *The World Between Wars, 1919-1939*: Following the Armistice of 11 November 1918 that ended World War I, in the next five years of 1919-19, Europe struggled to recover from the devastation of World War I and the destabilizing effects of the loss of four empires: the German, Austro-Hungarian, Russian, and Ottoman Empires. "There were numerous new nations in Eastern Europe, most of them small in size. The United States gained dominance in world finance. Thus, when Germany could no longer afford war reparations to Britain, France and other Allies, the Americans came up with the Dawes Plan and Wall Street invested heavily in Germany, which repaid its reparations to nations that, in turn, used the dollars to pay off their war debts to Washington. By the middle of the decade, prosperity was widespread, with the second half of the decade known, especially in Germany, as the Golden Twenties." The major issues of interwar diplomacy and international relations included resolution of wartime issues such as "reparations owed by Germany and boundaries; American involvement in European finances and disarmament projects; the expectations and failures of the League of Nations; the relationships of the new countries to the old; the distrustful relations of the Soviet Union to the capitalist world; peace and disarmament efforts; responses to the Great Depression starting in 1929; the collapse of world trade; the collapse of democratic regimes one by one; the growth of economic autarky; Japanese aggressiveness toward China; Fascist diplomacy, including the aggressive moves by Mussolini's Italy and Hitler's Germany; the Spanish Civil War; the appeasement of Germany's expansionist moves toward the Rhineland, Austria, and Czechoslovakia, and the last, desperate stages of rearmament as the second world war increasingly loomed."[31] The Great Depression, that was originated in the United States in 1929 and lasted until the late 1930s, led to the collapse of democracy in most European countries and the rise of expansionary dictatorships in Russia, Italy, Japan, Germany, and elsewhere.

(c) *World War II* (1939-1945) involved the vast majority of the world's countries eventually forming two opposing military alliances: the Allies and the Axis. It was the deadliest conflict in human history, "marked by 70 to 85 million fatalities, most of whom were civilians in the Soviet Union and China" including massacres, the genocide, strategic bombing, premeditated death from starvation and disease, and the use of nuclear weapons in war.

Japan aimed to dominate Asia and the Pacific, and its war with China began by 1937, though neither side had declared war on the other. "World War II is generally said to have begun on 1 September 1939, with the invasion of Poland by Germany and subsequent declarations of war on Germany by France and the United Kingdom. From late 1939 to early 1941, in a series of campaigns and treaties, Germany conquered or controlled much of continental Europe, and formed the Axis alliance with Italy and Japan. Under the Molotov–Ribbentrop Pact of August 1939, Germany and the Soviet Union partitioned and annexed territories of their European neighbors, Poland, Finland, Romania and the Baltic states. Following the onset of campaigns in North Africa and East Africa, and the Fall of France in mid-1940, the war continued primarily between the European Axis powers and the British Empire. War in the Balkans, the aerial Battle of Britain, the Blitz, and the long Battle of the Atlantic followed. On 22 June 1941, the European Axis powers launched an invasion of the Soviet Union, opening the largest land theatre of war in history." In December 1941, Japan launched a surprise attack on the United States and European colonies in the Pacific, such as Hawaii at first. "Following an immediate U.S. declaration of war against Japan, supported by one from Great Britain, the European Axis powers quickly declared war on the U.S. in solidarity with their Japanese ally. Rapid Japanese conquests over much of the Western Pacific ensued, perceived by many in Asia as liberation from Western dominance and resulting in the support of several armies from defeated territories." [32]

"The Axis advance in the Pacific halted in 1942 when Japan lost the critical Battle of Midway; later, Germany and Italy were defeated in North Africa and then, decisively, at Stalingrad in the Soviet Union. Key setbacks in 1943, which included a series of German defeats on the Eastern Front, the Allied invasions of Sicily and Italy, and Allied victories in the Pacific, cost the Axis its initiative and forced it into strategic retreat on all fronts. In 1944, the Western Allies invaded German-occupied France, while the Soviet Union regained its territorial losses and turned toward Germany and its allies. During 1944 and 1945 the Japanese suffered major reverses in mainland Asia, in Central China, South China and Burma, while the Allies crippled the Japanese Navy and captured key Western Pacific islands. The war in Europe concluded with an invasion of Germany by the Western Allies and the Soviet Union, culminating in the capture of Berlin by Soviet troops, the suicide of Adolf Hitler and the German unconditional surrender on 8 May 1945. Following the Potsdam Declaration by the Allies on 26 July 1945." Japan surrendered on 15 August 1945 after the U.S. dropped atomic bombs, which brought total victory in Asia for the Allies.[33]

World War II changed international relations. "The United Nations was established to foster international cooperation and prevent future conflicts; the victorious great powers—China, France, the Soviet Union, the United Kingdom, and the United States—became the permanent members of its Security Council. The Soviet Union and United States emerged as rival superpowers, setting the stage for the nearly half-century long Cold War. In the wake of European devastation, the influence of its great powers waned, triggering the decolonization of Africa and Asia. Most countries whose industries had been damaged moved towards economic recovery and expansion. Political integration in Europe emerged as an effort to end pre-war enmities and create a common identity."[34]

(d) ***The Cold War Between Superpowers*** (1945-1990): The USSR was a Marxist–Leninist state led by its Communist Party of the Soviet Union. The Communist Party controlled the press, the military, the economy and many organizations. "It also controlled the other states in the Eastern Bloc, and funded Communist parties around the world, sometimes in competition with Communist China, particularly following the Sino-Soviet split of the 1960s. In opposition stood the West...democratic and capitalist with a free press and independent organizations...The two superpowers never engaged directly in full-scale armed combat, but they were heavily armed in preparation for a possible all-out nuclear world war. Each side had a nuclear strategy that discouraged an attack by the other side, on the basis that such an attack would lead to the total destruction of the attacker: the doctrine of mutually assured destruction."[35]

The first phase of the Cold War began in the first two years after the end of the Second World War in 1945. "The USSR consolidated its control over the states of the Eastern Bloc, while the United States began a strategy of global containment to challenge Soviet power, extending military and financial aid to the countries of Western Europe and creating the NATO alliance. The Berlin Blockade (1948–49) was the first major crisis of the Cold War. With the victory of the communist side in the Chinese Civil War and the outbreak of the Korean War (1950–53), the conflict expanded. The USSR and USA competed for influence in Latin America, and the decolonizing states of Africa and Asia. Meanwhile, the Hungarian Revolution of 1956 was stopped by the Soviets. The expansion and escalation sparked more crises, such as the Suez Crisis (1956), the Berlin Crisis of 1961, and the Cuban Missile Crisis of 1962. Following the Cuban Missile Crisis, a new phase began that saw the Sino-Soviet split complicate relations within the communist sphere, while US allies, particularly France, demonstrated greater independence of action. The USSR crushed the 1968 Prague Spring liberalization program in Czechoslovakia, and the Vietnam War (1955–75) ended with the defeat of the US-backed Republic of Vietnam, prompting further adjustments."[36] Israel won the Six-Day War of 1967 and the Arab-Israeli War of 1973 against Egypt or other Arab countries.

By the 1970s, both the U.S. and the USSR had become interested in making accommodations "in order to create a more stable and predictable international system, inaugurating a period of détente that saw Strategic Arms Limitation Talks and the US opening relations with the People's Republic of China as a strategic counterweight to the Soviet Union. Détente collapsed at the end of the decade with the beginning of the Soviet–Afghan War in 1979. The early 1980s were another period of elevated tension, with the Soviet downing of Korean Air Lines Flight 007 (1983), and the Able Archer NATO military exercises (1983). The United States increased diplomatic, military, and economic pressures on the Soviet Union, at a time when the communist state was already suffering from economic stagnation. In the mid-1980s, the new Soviet leader Mikhail Gorbachev introduced the liberalizing reforms of perestroika (reorganization, 1987) and glasnost (openness, c. 1985) and ended Soviet involvement in Afghanistan. Pressures for national independence grew stronger in Eastern Europe, especially Poland. Gorbachev meanwhile refused to use Soviet troops to bolster the faltering Warsaw Pact regimes as had occurred in the past. The result in 1989 was a wave of revolutions that peacefully overthrew all of the communist regimes of Central and Eastern Europe. The Communist Party of the Soviet Union itself lost control and was banned following an abortive coup attempt in August 1991. This in turn led to the formal dissolution of the USSR in December 1991 and the collapse of communist regimes in other countries such as Mongolia, Cambodia and South Yemen. The United States remained as the world's only superpower."[37]

(e) *The Post-Cold War Era (1990-2015)*: During most of the latter half of the 20th century, "the two most powerful states in the world were the Soviet Union and the United States. These two federations were called the world's superpowers. Faced with the threat of growing Japanese, German and Italian fascism and a world war, the western Allies and the Soviet Union made an alliance of necessity during World War II. The alliance between the USA and USSR was simply against a greater common enemy and the two countries never really trusted each other. After the Axis was defeated, these two powers became highly suspicious of each other because of their vastly different ideologies. This struggle, known as the Cold War, lasted from about 1946 to 1991, beginning with the second Red Scare and ending with the August Coup, a coup d'état attempt that destabilized the Soviet Union and later contributed to its dissolution."[38] The collapse of the Soviet Union caused profound changes in nearly every society in the world.

The fall of communism formed an existential threat for many institutions. "The US military was forced to cut much of its expenditure, though the level rose again to comparable heights after the September 11 attacks and the initiation of the War on Terror in 2001. Socialist parties around the world saw drops in membership after the Berlin Wall fell and the public felt that free market ideology had won. The end of the Cold War also coincided with the end of apartheid in South Africa. Declining Cold War tensions in the later years of the 1980s meant that the apartheid regime was no longer supported by the West as a bulwark against communism and they were condemned with an embargo. In 1990, Nelson Mandela was freed from prison and the regime made steps to end apartheid, which were on an official basis completed by 1994 with the new election. Libertarian, neoliberal, nationalist and Islamist parties on the other hand benefited from the fall of the Soviet Union. As capitalism had won, as people saw it, socialism in general declined in popularity. Socialist Scandinavian countries privatized many of their commons in the 1990s and a political debate on modern institutions re-opened. Scandinavian nations are now more seen as social democrat. The People's Republic of China, already having moved towards capitalism starting in the late 1970s and facing public anger after the 1989 killings in Beijing moved even more quickly towards free market economics in the 1990s...Stock markets were established in Shenzhen and Shanghai late in 1990 as well. The restrictions on car ownership were loosened in the early 1990s, causing the bicycle to decline as a form of transport by 2000. The move to capitalism has increased the economic prosperity of China, but many people still live in poor conditions, working for companies."[39]

(i) Liberalism and Globalization was based on the commercialization of the internet and the growth of the mobile phone system. "The ideology of most-modernism and cultural relativism has according to some scholars replaced modernism and notions of absolute progress and ideology. It has seen the United States become by far the most powerful country in the world and the rise of China from a relatively weak developing country to a fledgling potential superpower. Reacting on the rise of China, the United States strategically rebalanced to the Asia-Pacific region. It has also seen the merging of most of Europe into one economy and one military bloc. Accompanying the NATO expansion, Ballistic Missile Defenses (BMD) were installed in East Europe. These marked important steps in the military globalization. Environmentalism has also become a mainstream concern in the post-Cold War era. Recycling has become commonplace in many countries over the past 30 years."[40]

(ii) The Global War on Terrorism was ignited against Sunni Islamist fundamental-ist armed groups located throughout the Muslim world, "with most prominent groups being Al-Qaeda, the Islamic State, the Taliban, Tehriki-Taliban Pakistan, and the various franchise groups." After the September 11 attack in 2001, the Bush Administration strengthened security measures against possible attack by terrorists. In May 2013, two years after the assassination of Osama bin Laden, President Barack Obama announced that the Global War on Terror was over. On 28 December 2014, U.S. officially ended the combat role of the U.S.-led mission in Afghanistan.[41]

(iii) The New Nationalism rose in the mid-2010s in Europe and North America and to some degree in other regions. "It is associated with several positions, such as right-wing populism, anti-globalization, nativism, protect-ionism, opposition to immigration, opposition to Islam and Muslims, Sinophobia, and Euroscepticism where applicable. According to one scholar, nationalist resistance to global liberalism turned out to be the most influen-tial force in Western politics in 2016." More specifically, it includes the rise of China, the resurgence of Russia, Iran and North Korea developing nuclear weapons, Britain's exit votes in 2016 from the European Union, and the 2016 election of Donald Trump as U.S. President.[42]

2. Theoretical Background of International Relations

International relations theory attempts to provide a conceptual framework upon which international relations can be analyzed. The most prominent theories are realism focusing on the balance of power among states, and liberalism considering interdependence between international institutions in economic and cultural exchanges.[43] Realists were dominant to explain international relations until the oil crisis of 1980, when the world recognized that economic interdependence is more influential than the power of military forces, so that liberals became influential when the Cold War ended in 1991. The liberal hegemony prevailed with globalism but began to decay because of challenges of the rising China, Russia, Iran and North Korea, resulting in the resurgence of realism with the new nationalism.

REALISM

Realism is a belief "that world politics ultimately is always and necessarily a field of conflict among actors pursuing power," which idea is contrasted to cooperative ideals of liberalism. Realists can be divided into three classes: "Classical realists believe it follows from human nature; neorealists attribute it to the dynamics of the anarchic state system; neoclassical realists believe it results from both, in combination with domestic politics." The theories of realism revolve around four central propositions: "1. states are the central actors in international politics, rather than leaders or international organizations; 2. the international political system is anarchic, as there is no supranational authority to enforce rules; 3. states act in their rational self-interest within the international system; and 4. states desire power to ensure self-preservation."[44] Realism is associated with real politics, and priorities of realists have been described "as Machiavellian, single-mindedly seeking the power of one's nation over others." Hans J. Morgenthau introduces the six principles of political realism, in which he writes that the difference between political realism and other schools of thought is real and profound, by taking three examples: (i) "In 1930 the Soviet Union attacked Finland. The action confronted France and Great Britain with two issues, one legal, and the other political." (ii) The rise of the Communist government in China confronted the Western world with two issues, one is moral, the other political. (iii) "Great Britain, as one of the guarantors of the neutrality of Belgium, went to war with Germany in August 1914 because Germany had violated the neutrality of Belgium." This could be justified in legalistic-moralistic terms, but one could argue realistically.[45] Generally, realists assume that national security is the primary issue for the state so that political-military issues dominate the agenda of the state involved.

Some intellectuals have written the realist tradition or discipline in their works. Thucydides (471-400 B.C.), in his *History of the Peloponnesian War*, views that the real or underlying cause of the war was fear associated with a shift in the balance of power. Machiavelli (1469-1527), in his *The Prince* (1523), suggests that the security of the state is so important that it may justify certain acts by the prince that would be forbidden to other individuals not burdened by the princely responsibility of assuring that security. Thomas Hobbes (1588-1679), in his *Leviathan* (1651), writes that as anarchy prevails in the state of nature, so too is anarchy a dominant characteristic of international politics. Without a hegemonic power or world state, suspicion-distrust-conflict-war are seemingly inevitable. In the absence of any social contract among them, there are no moral obligations to govern the relations of states. In his *On the Law of War and Peace* (1625), Hugo Grotius (1583-1645) insists on that changing circumstances might lead to the alteration of rules, but the important point is that order in international relations and matters of war and peace involve both power and values or norms. Carl von Clausewitz (1780-1831), a Prussian army officer who served the Napoleonic Wars, views that the military element of a state's power is extremely important but subordinate always to the political; and that the military is a political means, so that war is a continuation of political activity by other means. Edward Hallett Carr (1892-1982), in his *The Twenty Years' Crisis, 1919-1939* (1939), argues that "any sound political thought must be based on elements of both utopia (i.e. values) and reality (i.e. power)."[46]

(a) ***Power in International Politics***: Politics involve conflict of power; once the conflict is resolved, the political issue becomes an administrative matter.[47] "Some realists understand power to be the sum of military, economic, technological, diplomatic, and other capabilities at the disposal of the state. Others see power not as some absolute value determined for each state as if it were in a vacuum but, rather, as capabilities relative to the capabilities of other states." The power is often evaluated as its capabilities relative to those of other states. A state influence is not only determined by its capabilities but also by its willingness to use these capabilities.[48] Political scientists or practitioners of international relations consider the concept of political power as a goal of states or leaders, a measure of influence or control over outcomes, victory in conflict and the attainment of security, control over resources and capabilities, and or status which some states or actors possess and others do not.[49]

Some theorists distinguish between two types of power: Hard and Soft. "Hard power refers to coercive tactics: the threat or use of armed forces, economic pressure or sanctions, assassination and subterfuge, or other forms of intimidation. Hard power is generally associated to the stronger of nations, as the ability to change the domestic affairs of other nations through military threats. Realists and neorealists, such as John Mearsheimer, are advocates of the use of such power for the balancing of the international system. Joseph Nye is the leading proponent and theorist of soft power. Instruments of soft power include debates on cultural values, dialogues on ideology, the attempt to influence through good example, and the appeal to commonly accepted human values. Means of exercising soft power include diplomacy, dissemination of information, analysis, propaganda, and cultural programming to achieve political ends. Others have synthesized soft and hard power, including through the field of smart power...ranging from soft to hard."[50]

(b) *System and its Stability*: The system maintains equilibrium or balance but moves toward elsewhere according to the change of internal and external forces. We have to examine the system dynamically as patterns of interactions, and anarchy and the distribution of capabilities or the balance of power. The anarchy brings forth images of violence, destruction, and chaos in the absence of any hierarchy of authority. The realists try to maintain the equilibrium with the balance of power among states to avoid the triumph of a dominant power. Henry Kissinger views that a balance of power is a foreign policy creation, constructed by statesmen; it does not just occur automatically – voluntarism. Kenneth Waltz sees the balance of power as an attribute of the system of states that will occur whether it is willed or not – determinism. However, Hans Morgenthau attempts to combine two perspectives: acknowledging the balance of power "as a tendency within international politics while, at the same time, prescribing what statesmen should do to maintain the balance."[51]

As an international system moves from being bipolar to being multipolar, the amount of overall uncertainty in the system increases, because the number of international actors increases. Kenneth Waltz argues "that greater uncertainty makes it more likely that a decision-makers will misjudge the intentions and actions of a potential foe. Hence, a multipolar system, given its association with high levels of uncertainty, is less desirable than a bipolar system because multipolarity makes uncertainty and thus the probability of war greater." But David Sinter and Karl Deutsch make opposite arguments. "They believe that a multipolar system is more conductive to stability because uncertainty breeds caution on the part of decision-makers...the increase in number of independent actors diminishes the share that any nation can allocate to any other single actor." On the other hand, Bruce Bueno de Mesquita argues that "if the system's structure – be it bipolar or multipolar - does not change, there will be little uncertainty because learned patterns from prior behavior will aid decision makers to anticipate the likely consequences of similar behaviors under similar circumstance. Hence, the level of systemic uncertainty, by itself, neither increases nor decreases the likelihood of war."[52] Both theories are opposite but persuasive.

(c) *Interdependence among States*: Three concepts are considered here. (i) The balance of power is a kind of interdependence that is not necessarily a good thing for any one particular state since it does not affect all states equally so is vulnerable. (ii) "If a state wants to be more powerful, it avoids or minimizes economic dependency on other states just as it avoids political or military dependency on other states." Increasing interdependence may produce conflict as opposed to peace. (iii) "The hegemonic state or states benefit, but so too do other, less powerful states. By contrast, the decline of hegemony and the consequent fragmentation of power in international politics is said to produce disorder – a breakdown or unraveling of previously constructed international agreements." The absence of hegemony may result in chaos and instability, so that the theory of hegemon stability has been applied to a wide range of issue areas. There are certain virtues in having a hegemonic power capable of enforcing stability.[53]

(d) *Change of Political System*: Balance of power involved in states has existed at least since the fifteenth and sixteenth centuries. Lewis Richardson, in his *Statistics of Deadly Quarrels* (1950), found that "world population increases seem not to have been accompanied by a proportionate increase in the frequency or severity of war"; and that "such factors as similarity of language and common religion had little bearing on the incidence of war or the maintenance of peace." Using statistical methods in the *Correlates of War Project* of 1963, J. David Singer and his associates found "that big powers have participated in more wars, that major powers undergoing rapid growth in capabilities are more likely to fight with other major powers, and that international disputes between larger countries tend to escalate to war if there has been an arms race between them." In his *War and Change in World Politics* (1981), Robert Gilpin views "that international political change is the result of efforts of political actors to change the international system in order to advance their own interests." Gilpin lists five assumption concerning the behavior of states: in his second assumption, "A state will attempt to change the international system if the expected benefits exceed the expected costs." Power transition theorists see the international system as hierarchically ordered, with the most powerful state dominating the rest, which are classified as satisfied or dissatisfied with the ordering of the system." George Modelski argues "that the global political system goes through distinct and identifiable historical cycles or recurrent patterns of behavior... The dominant power is inevitably faced with the growth of rival power centers and attempts to maintain territorial control around the globe prove to be a costly task that drains the vitality and energy of the home country. Each cycle, therefore, exhibits a particular nation-state in an ascending and then a descending phase" in line with the rhythm of global politics.[54]

(e) *Changing Character of Realism*: Stanford Encyclopedia writes on it as follows: Realism is "a practical and evolving theory that depends on the actual historical and political conditions and is ultimately judged by its ethical standards and by its relevance in making prudent political decisions.

Realism also performs a useful cautionary role. It warns us against progress ivism, moralism, legalism, and other orientations that lose touch with the reality of self-interest and power...Nevertheless, when it becomes a dogmatic enterprise, realism fails to perform its proper function. By remaining stuck in a state-centric and excessively simplified paradigm such as neorealism and by denying the possibility of any progress in interstate relations, it turns into an ideology. Its emphasis on power politics and national interest can be misused to justify aggression. It has therefore to be supplanted by theories that take better account of the dramatically changing picture of global politics. To its merely negative, cautionary function, positive norms must be added. These norms extend from the rationality and prudence stressed by classical realists; through the vision of multilateralism, international law, and an international society emphasized by liberals and members of the English School; to the cosmopolitanism and global solidarity advocated by many of today's writers."[55]

LIBERALISM

Liberals believe "that international institutions play a key role in cooperation among states. With the correct international institutions and increasing interdependence, states have the opportunity to reduce conflict. Interdependence has three main components: that states interact in various ways, through economic, financial, and cultural means; that security tends not to be the primary goal in state-to-state interactions; and that military forces are not typically used. Liberals also argue that international diplomacy can be a very effective way to get states to interact with each other honestly and support nonviolent solutions to problems. With the proper institutions and diplomacy, liberals believe that states can work together to maximize prosperity and minimize conflict."[56] Four assumptions for liberalism are as follows: (i) Nonstate actors are important entities in world politics. (ii) The state is not a unitary actor. "It is composed of competing individuals, interest groups, and bureaucracies." (iii) Liberalists challenge the realist assumption of the state as rational actor, by viewing that "the clash of interests, bargaining, and need for compromise do not always make for a rational decision-making process." (iv) Though national security concerns are important, "the liberals are also concerned with a number of economic, social, and ecological issues arising from the growth of interdependence among states and societies."[57]

Liberal ideas resulted from the fall of feudalism in Europe and the growth of a market and capitalist society. The rising middle class conflicted with the established power of absolute monarchs and landed aristocracy. The English Revolution of the seventeenth century and the American and the French Revolutions of the late eighteenth century were distinctively liberal.

Liberals challenged the absolute monarchy and supported the movements for religious freedom. In the nineteenth century, liberals advocated indust-rialization and capitalist economy. In fact, Frederick Hayek argued that economic freedom is essential for political liberty. In the economic front, liberal ideas for individual were reinforced by Adam Smith and David Ricardo, who emphasized the important role of individual entrepreneur. Jeremy Bentham and James Mill developed utilitarianism that promotes actions maximizing individual happiness and well-being within available resources. Economic liberalism is the ideological belief in organizing the economy on individual line. "The spirit of liberalism and its emphasis on the individual prevailed all spheres of life and thought – scientific, political, economic, social, and religious. The industrial revolution, however, event-ually resulted in modifications of liberal doctrine, which, although retaining an emphasis on the individual, now allowed the state to be given a somewhat active role in order to mitigate the most harmful effects of unrestrained economic competition." Since the state was not some unitary actor pursuing its own course independently of the public, decisions were supposed to be made by the public opinion and political consensus among conflicts of interests...liberals assume that "There could be a harmony of interests among individuals within a given state, so too did liberal theorists argue that a harmony of interest among states was possible."[58]

Liberals believe that liberalism can reduce the possibility of war. "First, advocates of *commercial liberalism* argue that the expansion of the inter-national economy makes it costly more for states to go to war. As economic interdependence increased, there would be a disinclination to cut profitable economic ties. Second, advocates of *domestic liberalism* claim that the spread of democratic political systems means that questions of war and peace are no longer confined to a small group of political and military elites, as in the past. Instead, leaders would have to be concerned with domestic public opinion that could act as a brake on any moves toward international confrontation and the outbreak of hostilities. Third, *regulatory liberalism* claims that the benefits of international law accepted rules of the game, and international organizations would contribute to the peaceful settlement of disputes among states and enhance global cooperation. Finally...western civilization had suffered enough from war, and...leaders and citizens had learned how costly it was to wage it."[59]

In his *To Perpetual Peace*, Immanuel Kant (1724-1804) set the way by forming guidelines "to create a peace program to be applied by nations. This program would require cooperation between states as well as the mutual pursuit of secure freedom and shared benefits. One such idea was the Democratic Peace Theory...Kant put forth the idea that democracies do not fight wars because leaders were too worried about re-election. Because war was naturally unpopular, Kant thought that leaders would avoid burdening voters with its costs. After seeing success in intertwining states through economic coalition, liberal supporters began to believe that warfare was not always an inevitable part of international relations."[60] Kant's democratic peace theory has been revised by **Neoliberals** like Robert O. Keohane and Joseph S. Nye: democracies do fight wars, but they do not fight wars with other democracies because of capitalist ties. "Democracies are economically dependent and...more likely to resolve issues diplomatically...citizens in democracies are less likely to think of citizens in other democracies as enemies because of shared morals."[61]

(a) **Decision Making and Interdependence**: In the decision-making system, comparative studies became useful since 1970. "Although different levels of analysis and different variables were used, what these studies have in common was a commitment to discovering common patterns or progresses in the foreign (and defense) policies of states."[62] (i) If decisions are made by the individuals or small groups for a state, cognitive distortions commonly appears due to the lack of professional knowledge and experiences. (ii) Liberals consider the decision-making process of organizational management in order to make the best choice among available alternatives by applying proper models for various cases. (iii) Military was often interested in integration, which emphasizes how economic unification would contribute to the development of political integration. (iv) The interdependence between states involves reciprocal effects among countries or among actors in different countries, which means that benefits may outweigh costs, or vice versa. If complex problem exists, military force tends to have less utility than other measures in order to resolve it.

(b) *System of Liberalism*: The concept of system for Pluralism (with Liberalism) is considered with four different ways. "First, for some pluralists, the international system is merely the sum of the foreign policies of all states. Governmental actions are the principal focus...pluralists also tend to emphasize the role of specific bureaucracies and pressure groups in the formulation of foreign policy. Second, other pluralists view the system as the sum of foreign policies plus the activities of nonstate actors. Nonstate actors include multinational corporations, terrorist groups, international banks, and transnational interest groups such as Amnesty International, the Red Cross, and Greenpeace. Third, certain pluralists include all the foregoing elements in their definition of a system but add all other types of transactions such as ideas, values, communications, trade patterns, and financial flows. Fourth, despite the fact that many pluralists reject the concept of anarchy, a number of prominent pluralists accept the concept and the assumption that anarchy makes international cooperation difficult." Perhaps not surprisingly, "the most fruitful issues for the pluralist approach have been the non-security ones – those dealing with social, cultural, economic, technological, and related subjects."[63]

(c) ***Change of System***: Compared to realists, pluralists (liberalists) place much greater emphasis on the possibilities of change, particularly peaceful change. Similarly, much of the work on decision-making emphasizes feed-back processes – actors monitoring responses to actions they have taken so that future policies can be adjusted if necessary. In observing changes, Ernest Haas focuses on cognitive variables,[64] while James Rosenau looks into the micro level, noting, for example, the effect on global processes of an expansion of analytical skills among individuals everywhere.[65]

(d) ***Neorealism vs. Neoliberalism***: Neorealists such as John Mearsheimer propose that structural constraints will determine behavior in international relations, departing from classical realism led by Hans Morgenthau. Robert O. Keohane and Joseph S. Nye, in response to neorealism, develop an opposing theory – *Complex interdependence* which sometimes comes closer to reality than does realism. First, "transgovernmental relations occur when one relaxes the realist assumption that states act coherently as units. It is through these channels that political exchange occurs, not through the limited interstate channel as championed by realists." Second, they argue "that there is not, in fact, a hierarchy among issues, meaning that not only is the martial arm of foreign policy not the supreme tool by which to carry out a state's agenda, but that there are a multitude of different agendas that come to the forefront. The line between domestic and foreign policy becomes blurred in this case, as realistically there is no clear agenda in interstate relations. Finally, the use of military force is not exercised when complex interdependence prevails. The idea is developed that between countries in which a complex interdependence exists, the role of the military in resolving disputes is negated. However, Keohane and Nye go on to state that the role of the military is in fact important in that alliance's political and military relations with a rival bloc."[66]

NATIONALISM

A state is a political entity consisting of people, territory, government, and sovereignty, while a nation is a cultural and ethnic one. The nation-state implies "that a state has chosen to adopt and endorse a specific cultural group as associated with it." The origin of the state is based on the evolution theory, the force theory, the divine right theory, or the social contract theory. "Nationalism is a political, social, and economic ideology and movement characterized by the promotion of the interests of a particular nation, especially with the aim of gaining and maintaining the nation's sovereignty (self-governance) over its homeland. Nationalism holds that each nation should govern itself, free from outside interference (self-determination), that a nation is a natural and ideal basis for a polity, and that the nation is the only rightful source of political power. It further aims to build and maintain a single national identity—based on shared social characteristics such as culture, language, religion, politics, and belief in a shared singular history—and to promote national unity or solidarity. Nationalism, therefore, seeks to preserve and foster a nation's traditional culture, and cultural revivals have been associated with nationalist movements. It also encourages pride in national achievements and is closely linked to patriotism."[67]

Nationalism has been an important driver in independence of movements such as "the Greek Revolution, the Irish Revolution, and the Zionist Movement that created modern Israel, and the dissolution of the Soviet Union." (i) English *Puritanism and nationalism*: "In the English Revolution an optimistic humanism merged with Calvinist ethics; the influence of the Old Testament gave form to the new nationalism by identifying the English people with ancient Israel…The rise of English nationalism coincided with the rise of the English trading middle class."[68] (ii) *The French Revolution*: Nationalism was a revolutionary and democratic creed – the subject became the citizen as an owner of France.[69] (iii) *German nationalism*: "The earliest origins of German nationalism began with the birth of romantic nationalism during the Napoleonic Wars when Pan-Germanism started to rise. Advocacy of a German nation-state began to become an important political force in response to the invasion of German territories by France under Napoleon… Aggressive German nationalism and territorial expansion was a key factor leading to both World Wars."[70] (iv) *During the Russian Revolution*, some nationalists proposed a westernized Russia, while others stressed the distinctive character of Russia and Russianism. World War I was the triumph of nationalism in central and Eastern Europe. During World War II Stalin appealed to nationalism and patriotism against foreign invaders. After World War I, the Paris Peace Conference established the principle of national self-determination that is a nationalist principle. It also recognizes the basic equality of all nations and transcends a narrow nationalism. "At the same time, Asian and African colonial territories, seeking to cast off imperial bonds, were developing nationalist movements."[71]

(a) *Central Themes of Nationalism*: (i) *The Nation*: "While all nationalists agree that nations are a blend of cultural and psycho-political factors, they disagree strong about where the balance between the two lies. On the one hand, exclusive concepts of the nation stress the importance of ethnic unity and a shared history, but nations are held together by a primordial bond, so nation tends to blur the distinction between the nation and the race. On the other hand, inclusive concepts of nation highlight the importance of civic consciousness and patriotic loyalty, suggesting that nations may be multiracial, multiethnic, multireligious…This tends to blur the distinction between the nation and the state, and between nationality and citizenship."[72]

(ii) *Organic Community*: It has been observed that humankind is naturally divided into a collection of nations, each possessing a distinctive character and separate identity. Nationalists argue why a higher loyalty and deeper political significance attaches to the nation than to any other social group. "Whereas, for instance, class, gender, religion and language may be important in particular societies, or may come to prominence in particular circumstances, the bonds of nationhood are more fundamental. National ties and loyalties are found in all societies, they endure over time, and they operate at an instinctual, even primordial level."[73]

(iii) *Self-Determination*: Traditionally, the goal of nationalism is the founding of a nation-state. "To date, this has been achieved in one of two ways. First, it may involve a process of unification. German history, for instance, has repeatedly witnessed unification. In medieval times, the German states were united under Charlemagne in the Holy Roman Empire, referred to by later German nationalists as the First Reich. Germany was not reunited until Bismarck founded his Second Reich in 1871. Hitler's Third Reich completed the process of unification by incorporating Austria into Greater Germany...The two Germanys were finally reunited in 1990. Second, nation-state can be created through the achievement of independence, in which a nation is liberated from foreign rule and gains control over its own destiny."[74] The nation state is the only variable political unit.

(iv) *Identity Politics*: "All forms of nationalism address the issue of identity. Whatever political causes nationalism may be associated with, it advances these on the basis of a sense of collective identity, usually understood as patriotism. For the political nationalist, objective considerations such as territory, religion and language are no more important than subjective ones such as will, memory and patriotic loyalty. Nationalism, therefore, not only advances political causes but also tells people who they are: it gives people a history, forges social bonds and a collective spirit, and creates a sense of destiny larger than individual existence. Indeed, it may be precisely the strength of nationalism's affective elements and the relative weakness of its doctrinal ones that accounts for the unusual success of nationalism as a political creed. Certain forms of nationalism, however, are less closely related to overtly political demands than others. This particularly applies in the case of cultural nationalism and ethnic nationalism." [75] As political nationalism is rational, cultural nationalism is mystical, and ethnic nationalism is united by race or ethnic groups.

(b) *Nationalism and Politics*: (i) *Liberal or civic nationalism* adheres with traditional liberal values of freedom, equality, and individual rights. Liberal nationalists "defend the value of national identity by saying that individuals need a national identity in order to lead meaningful, autonomous lives and that democratic polities need national identity in order to function properly. (ii) *Conservative nationalism* tends to develop in established nation-states, rather than ones that are in the process of nation building. "Conservatives care less for the principled nationalism of universal self-determination and more about the promise of social cohesion and public order embodied in the sentiment of national patriotism...The conservative character of nationalism is maintained by an appeal to tradition and history." (iii) *Expansionist nationalism*: The dominant image of nationalism is "one of aggression and militarism, quite the opposite of a principled belief in national self-determination. The aggressive face of nationalism became apparent in the late nineteenth century as European powers indulged in a scramble for Africa in the name of national glory and their place in the sun." That was imperialism of the century. Chauvinism is a form of extreme patriotism and nationalism and a belief in a national superiority and glory. (Male chauvinism is the belief that men are superior to women.) (iv) *Anticolonial and postcolonial nationalism*: "Anti-colonialism came to express the desire for national liberation in both political and economic terms, and this has left its mark upon the form of nationalism practiced in the developing world. Most of the leaders of Asian and African anticolonial movements were attracted to some form of socialism, ranging from the moderate and peaceful ideas represented by Gandhi and Nehru in India, to the revolutionary Marxism espoused by Mao Zedong in China, Ho Chi Minh in Vietnam and Fidel Castor in Cuba."[76]

(c) *Internationalism* is characterized by "the more radical belief that political nationalism should be transcended because the ties that bind the peoples of the world are stronger than those that separate them. By this standard, the goal of internationalism is to construct super-national structures that can command the political allegiance of all the people of the world, regardless of religious, racial, social and national differences." (i) *Liberal internationalism*: "Liberals have rarely rejected nationalism in principle. They have usually been prepared to accept both that nations are natural entities, in that cultural similarities tend to build a sense of identity and common belonging, and that nations provide the most appropriate units of political rule – hence the existence of liberal nationalism." There are two bases of liberal internationalism: democratic constitutionalism (reducing the tendency towards militarism and war) and the principles of individualism. (ii) *Socialist internationalism*: Socialist thinkers like Karl Marx, Friedrich Engels, and Vladimir Lenin argue that economic class, rather than nationality, race, or culture, is the main force dividing people in society, and that nationalist ideology is a propaganda tool of a society's dominant economic class. Communist Internationals were socialist political groupings which sought to advance worker's revolution across the globe and achieve international socialism. The effective collapse of the Second International in 1916 dramatically demonstrated the failure of socialist international movements or socialist internationalism.[77]

DISAGREEMENTS: LIBERALS VS. REALISTS

Robert O. Keohane and Joseph S. Nye published *Power and Interdependence* in 1989, based on their previous work on the same topic. This book contrasts the realistic perspective on international relations with the complex interdependence perspective on the same associated with liberalism. On the other hand, John J. Mearsheimer published *The Great Delusion: Liberal Dreams and International Realities* in 2018, arguing that liberal hegemony, the U.S. foreign policy has pursued since the Cold War ended, is doomed to fail. Both books are reviewed with my interpretations in order to introduce readers their argument points against the opposite theory, either liberalism or realism in international relations.

Background: After World War II, the world had experienced such real wars as the Korean War (1950-53) and the Vietnam War (1955-75) in Asia and the Arab-Israeli Wars (1948-73) in the Middle East, though they were counted in the period of the Cold War (1945-1990). "Traditionally, classical theories of world politics have portrayed a potential state of war in which states' behavior was dominated by the constant danger of military conflict." This concept of political realism was accepted by theorists and practitioners of international relations. After President Richard Nixon's visit to China in 1972, the Soviet Union was interests in "gaining implicit recognition of its postwar hegemony in eastern Europe through guarantees of the inviolability of frontier and noninterference in the internal affairs of states." The 35 states, including the United States, Canada, and most European states signed the Helsinki Accords in July 1975 in an attempt to improve relations between the Communists and the West, that was a starting sign of changing relations from confrontation to cooperation with coexistence.[78]

The Arab-Israeli War of 1973 caused the first oil crisis due to the OPEC oil embargo, which raised the crude oil price from $3 to nearly $12 per barrel in the global market; and the second oil crisis occurred in 1979 due to decreased oil output in the wake of the Iranian Revolution, which caused the crude oil price more than doubled to $39.50 per barrel over the next 12 months. "After 1980, oil prices began a 20-year decline, except for a brief rebound during the Gulf War, eventually reaching a 60 percent fall-off during the 1990s. As with the 1973 crisis, global politics and power balance were impacted. Oil exporters such as Mexico, Nigeria, and Venezuela expanded production; the Soviet Union became the top world producer; North Sea and Alaskan oil flooded the market. It seemed that the United States of America and Norway had much more oil reserves than forecasted in the 1970s. OPEC lost influence."[79] Through the two oil crises, the world recognized that the power of military forces was obsolete and economic interdependence became important in international relations.

"Interdependence in world politics refers to situations characterized by reciprocal effects among countries or among actors in different countries. These effects often result from international transactions – flows of money, goods, people, and messages across international boundaries." Moreover, we can see that "Interdependence affects world politics and the behavior of states, but government actions also influence patterns of interdependence." Considering costs and benefits arising from transactions, we must be cautious about the prospect "that rising interdependence is creating a brave new world of cooperation to replace the bad old world of international conflict." [80] We must not define interdependence entirely in terms of situations of evenly balanced mutual dependence. "It is *asymmetries* in dependence that are most likely to provide sources of influence for actors in their dealing with one another. Less dependent actors can often use the interdependence relationship as a source of power in bargaining over an issue and perhaps to affect other issues."[81]

Power can be defined "as the ability of an actor to get others to do something they otherwise would not do. Power can also be conceived in terms of control over outcomes...When we say that asymmetrical interdependence can be a source of power, we are thinking of power as control over resources, or the potential to affect outcomes." It is observed that "A less dependent actor in a relationship often has a significant political resource, because changes in the relationship will be less costly to that actor than to its partners." We can consider two dimensions to measure the cost of dependence: sensitivity and vulnerability. *Sensitivity* interdependence rests on the relative availability and costliness of the alternatives, but *Vulnerability* interdependence is measured by the cost of effective adjustments to the environmental changes over a period of time. Asymmetrical interdependence by itself cannot explain bargaining outcome, even in traditional relations among states. In the Canadian-American relationship, the use or threat of force is virtually excluded from consideration by either side. Although Canada is weaker in military strength than the United States, the Canadians can take advantage of their superior position on such economic issues as oil and natural gas exports without fearing military threat by the United States.[82]

Power and Interdependence (Robert Keohane and Joseph Nye, 1989): The realist assumptions about world politics are that states are dominant actors in world politics, that force is a usable and effective instrument of policy, and that "the high politics of military security dominates the low politics of economic and social affairs." The liberals introduce *complex interdependence* of world politics by assuming that non-state actors are important in world politics, that the state is not a unitary actor, that foreign policy-making and transnational processes involve conflict, bargaining, coalition, and compromise, and that international politics is extensive.

(a) ***Complex Interdependence: Characteristics***: (i) "Multiple channels connect society, including informal ties between government elites as well as formal foreign offices arrangements; informal ties among non-governmental elites; and transnational organizations. These channels can be summarized as interstate, trans-governmental, and trans-national relations. *Interstate* relations are the normal channels assumed by realists. *Trans governmental* applies when we relax the realist assumption that states act coherently as units"; *transnational* applies if we relax the assumption that states are the only units. (ii) "The agenda of interstate relationships consists of multiple issues that are not arranged in a clear or consistent hierarchy. This absence of hierarchy among issues means, among other things, that military security does not consistently dominate the agenda. Many issues arise from what used to be considered domestic policy, and the distinction between domestic and foreign issues becomes blurred. These issues are considered in several government departments, and at several costs. Different issues generate different coalitions, both within governments and across them, and involve different degrees of conflict. Politics does not stop at the waters' edge." (iii) "Military force is not used by government toward other governments within the region, or on the issues, when complex interdependence prevails. It may, however, be important in these governments' relations with governments outside that region, or on other issues. Military force could, for instance, be irrelevant to resolving disagreement on economic issues among members of an alliance, yet at the same time be very important for that alliance's political and military relations with a rival bloc. For the former relationships this condition of complex interdependence would be met; for the latter, it would not."[83] Among industrialized liberal countries, the perceived margin of safety has widened: fears of attack in general have declined and virtually nonexistent.

(b) ***The Political Processes of Complex Interdependence***: There are five factors: (i) Goals of actors: Military security will be the dominant goal in realism; but in complex interdependence, "Goals of state will vary by issue area; trans-governmental politics will make goals difficult to define, while transnational actors will pursue their own goals." (ii) Instrument of state policy: Military force will be most effective in realism; but in complex interdependence, power resources specific to issue areas will be most relevant, and major instruments will be manipulation of interdependence, international organizations, and transnational actors. (iii) Formulation of agenda: Political shift in the balance of power and security threat will set the agenda in high politics and will strongly influence other agendas in realism. But in complex interdependence, "Agenda will be affected by changes in the distribution of power resources within issue areas; the status of international regimes; changes in the importance of transnational actors; linkages form other issues and politicization as a result of rising sensitivity interdependence." (iv) Linkages of issues: Linkages will reduce differences in outcomes among issue areas and reinforce international hierarchy in realism. But in complex interdependence, "Linkages by strong states will be more difficult to make since force will be ineffective. Linkages by weak states through international organizations will erode rather than reinforce hierarchy." (v) Role of international organizations: Roles are minor, limited by state power and the importance of military force in realism. Nevertheless, in complex interdependence, "Organizations will set agendas, induce coalition-formation, and act as arenas for political action by weak states. Ability to choose the organizational forum for an issue and to mobilize votes will be an important political resource."[84]

(c) *Concluding Remarks*: Complex interdependence is characterized by three characteristics, "involving (i) the use of multiple channels of action between societies in interstate, trans-governmental, and transnational relations, (ii) the absence of a hierarchy of issues with changing agendas and linkages between issues prioritized and the objective of (iii) bringing about a decline in the use of military force and coercive power in international relations." Nye and Keohane thus argue "that the decline of military force as a policy tool and the increase in economic and other forms of interdependence should increase the probability of cooperation among states. The work of the theorists surfaced in the 1970s to become a significant challenge to political realist theory in international politics and became foundational to current theories that have been categorized as liberalism (international relations), neoliberalism and liberal institutionalism. Traditional critiques of liberalism are often defined alongside critiques of political realism, mainly that they both ignore the social nature of relations between states and the social fabric of international society. With the rise of neoliberal economics, debates, and the need to clarify international relations theory, Keohane (2002) has most recently described himself as simply an institutionalist, nothing purpose for developing sociological perspectives in contemporary International relations theory. Liberal, neoliberal and neoliberal institutional theories continue to influence international politics and have become closely intertwined with political realism."[85]

The Great Delusion (John Mearsheimer 2018): Mearsheimer argues in his book that "realism and nationalism will overcome liberalism because liberalism does not take into consideration how the world actually operates thus it lends itself to foreign policy failures which the US has experienced since the end of the Cold War." Here is my review on his book.

(a) *The Impossible Dream*: Mearsheimer argues what happens when a powerful state pursues a strategy of Liberal Hegemony at the expense of balance of power politics. "The key to understanding liberalism's limits is to recognize its relationship with nationalism and realism." (i) Nationalism:

We live in a world of nation-states, which means that liberalism must coexist with nationalism. "Liberal states are also nation-states. The influence of nationalism often undercuts a liberal foreign policy…nationalism places great emphasis on self-determination, which means that most countries will resist a liberal great power's efforts to interfere in their domestic politics… These two isms also clash over individual rights. Liberals believe everyone has the same rights…Nationalism is a particular ideology from top to bottom, which means it does not treat rights as inalienable…Liberalism oversells the importance of individual rights." (ii) Realism: "A state is needed to keep the peace. At its core, liberalism assumes that the individuals who make up any society sometimes have profound differences about what constitutes the good life, and these differences might lead them to try to kill each other. Thus, a state is needed to keep peace. But the structure of the international system is anarchic, not hierarchic, which means that liberalism applied to international politics cannot work. Countries thus have little choice but to act according to balance-of-power logic if they hope to survive." "Our world has been shaped in good part by those two powerful isms [meaning nationalism and realism], but not by liberalism."[86]

(b) *Human Nature and Politics*: There are two assumptions of human nature. One is the survival that is the most important goal of human being, although "there is often intractable disagreement about the answers to the important ethical, moral, and political questions that all societies confront, and which have profound implications for daily life." The other is "that humans are profoundly social beings. They do not operate as lone wolves but are born into social groups or societies that shape their identities well before they can assert their individualism. Moreover, individuals usually develop strong attachments to their group and are sometimes willing to make great sacrifices for their fellow members. Humans are often said to be tribal at their core. The main reason for our social nature is that the best way for a person to survive is to be embedded in a society and to cooperate with fellow members rather than act alone…On balance, however, cooperation [society] trumps selfish behavior [individual]. Social groups are survival vehicles." "Social groups have a propensity to expand, because greater size usually augments their power relative to rival groups and thus enhances their prospects for survival…There are limits as to how far any group can expand because the potential victims almost always have powerful incentives to resist and ensure their own survival."[87]

Mearsheimer discusses various issues on human nature, among which I want to review *Our Social Essence*. "Humans are psychologically disposed to want to be part of a society." (i) The Survival Imperative: Survival is the foremost reason that humans naturally operate in groups larger than the family. Groups are more efficient than individuals or single family at providing food and life's other necessities. A social group is a survival vehicle. (ii) The Importance of culture: Culture is enormously important in shaping how individuals think and behave. The social group that a person is born into is forever a part of his identity. Nevertheless, culture alone is not enough to hold a society together. The most important way societies prevent disintegration is by building formidable political institutions, for which there is no substitute.[88]

(c) *Political Liberalism*: Political liberals have a three-pronged strategy to deal with the possibility of deadly conflict. (i) They emphasize that everyone's set of inalienable rights includes the right to life, which means not only the right to survive but also the freedom to live the good life as one sees fit. (ii) The second prong in the strategy is to purvey the norm of toleration. If individuals have the right to pursue their own way of life, others have an affirmative duty to recognize the right. (iii) But tolerance has its limits. The state writes the rules that define acceptable and unacceptable conduct while going to great lengths not to trample on individual rights. These rules allow individuals or groups to interact in civil ways as each pursues its own version of the good life. The state acts as an arbiter when serious disputes arise, to ensure that conflicts do not lead to violence. The state functions as rule maker, umpire, and night watchman. In any liberal society, political liberalism has a universalist strand that emphasizes the power of reason, inalienable rights, and nonviolence as well as a particularist strand that stresses the limits of reason, and disagreements with principles.[89]

(d) *Cracks in the Liberal Edifice*: Two most salient features of political liberalism are individualism and inalienable rights, but nationalism places serious limits on its influence. We live in a world of nation-state; liberalism must always coexist with nationalism; liberalism operates within the confines of nation-states, so it loses when it clashes with nationalism. (i) The problems of nationalism: First, *the essential function of a nation*: Nations are primarily survival vehicles but fulfill important emotional needs under special culture. In this sense, nationalism is much like religion. Second, *why nations want states*? A state is a political institution that controls a large territory with well-defined borders and has the ability to employ force to break or discipline the individuals and groups living within those borders. Nations covet a state for two reasons: self-determination, and the best way to maximize their survival prospects. Third, *why states want nations*: "Nationalism is essential for economic as well as military success, both of which matter greatly for a state's survival." The logics of nationalism work "to meld nations and states together into nation-states and have made them the dominant political form in the world."[90]

(ii) Living with the Dominator: First of all, liberalism focuses on the individual and pay little attention to social groups, but nationalism does the opposite. Second, natural rights and toleration are central components of liberal theory, but nationalism pay them little attention. Third, liberalism has a particularistic strand coming from no final truths about the good life and its emphasis on inalienable rights. Fourth, with liberalism, the state's main functions are to act as a night watcher, arbitrate disputes, and do significant social engineering to promote individual rights. Fifth, liberalism and nationalism view territory differently. Nationalists tend to think of the land they live on as their fatherland, but liberalism has no room for hallowed territory. It is important to emphasize that liberalism always operates within the context of a nation-state. Liberalism without nationalism is impossible. Nationalism is a more powerful force than liberalism. Liberalism always has to operate in the context of a nationalist state.[91]

(e) ***Liberalism Goes Abroad***: What happens when a powerful state adopts a liberal foreign policy? A state pursuing liberal hegemony aims to spread liberal democracy, toppling authoritarian regimes in the process, with the ultimate goal of creating a world populated solely by liberal democracy to remake international system. (i) Causing Peace: Liberals want to spread liberal democracy not just to protect the rights of individuals but also because they believe it is an excellent strategy for causing peace. (ii) Protecting Liberalism at Home: Non-liberal countries can join forces with those domestic anti-liberals and threat the liberal order. Liberal states have three reasons for a policy of regime change: protecting the rights of foreigners, facilitating peace, and safeguarding liberalism at home. (iii) Ethics, the Public, and Liberal Hegemony: Liberal hegemony is largely an elite-driven policy: A liberal foreign policy is mainly concerned with maximizing the number of liberal democracies in the world. Particularly, nationalism is all about self-determination, and people who live in a nation-state will want to shape their own politics.[92]

(f) ***Liberalism as a Source of Trouble***: "The costs of liberal hegemony begin with the endless wars a liberal state ends up fighting to protect human rights and spread liberal democracy around the world. Once unleashed on the world stage, a liberal unipole soon becomes addicted to war."[93] (i) Liberal Militarism: "One of liberalism's core missions is to protect people whose rights are being seriously violated. The urge to intervene in other countries is especially powerful when large numbers of those foreigners are being killed."[94] (ii) Making Diplomacy Harder: Liberal hegemony makes diplomacy with authoritarian states more difficult, further increasing the likelihood of war. "Diplomacy is a bargaining process between two or more states that have conflicting views on an issue that matters to all of them." "War and diplomacy are distinct instruments of statecraft – each is an alternative to the other. One relies on dialogue and negotiations to settle dispute, while the other employs military force." (iii) Liberalism and Sovereignty: Liberalism undermines sovereignty, meaning that states have the ultimate authority over what happen inside their borders, and that foreign powers have no right to interfere in their politics. Liberalism and sovereignty are fundamentally at odds with each other. (iv) Instability and Costly Failures: A liberal unipole is unlikely to use military power to protect individual rights or foster regime change in a major power, mainly because the costs are too high. Nevertheless, it is likely to interfere in that country's politics in other ways. The pattern of behavior appears in recent U.S. actions toward both China and Russia.[95]

(g) *Liberal Theories in Peace*: "Liberal Hegemony is built around three missions: increasing the number of liberal democracies in the world, facilitating an open economic order, and building international institutions." Liberals compete with realists to lead more peaceful world.

(i) The Primacy of Survival: States worry about "their survival above all else, and this motivates them to pursue power at each other's expense." To supersede realism, a liberal theory may offer more than simple survival.

(ii) Democratic peace theory maintains that liberal democracies do not go to war with each other, because of following reasons: "Democratic leaders are forced to accept culpability for war losses to a voting public; Publicly accountable states-people are inclined to establish diplomatic institutions for resolving international tensions; Democracies are not inclined to view countries with adjacent policy and governing doctrine as hostile; and Democracies tend to possess greater public wealth than other states, and therefore eschew war to preserve infrastructure and resources."[96] Liberal democracies provide "no persuasive explanation for why they would never fight against each other. There is neither a compelling institutional story nor a normative story underpinning democracy peace theory."[97]

(iii) Economic interdependence theory: Countries having economic relations rarely fight with each other, because the costs of war are too expensive to fight each other. But the costs of going to war for economically interdependent countries are not always high, and wars sometimes lead to economic gains. The primacy of politics over economics is really possible.

(iv) Liberal institutionalism: States that join international institutions are more likely to cooperative with each other, because they will be constrained by the organization's rules, which is almost always in their long-term interest to obey.[98] The central problem is the absence of a higher authority that can credibly threaten to punish state if they disobey the rules.

(h) *Concluding Remarks*: According to John Mearsheimer, (i) The U.S. should abandon its grand ambition of liberal hegemony. (ii) "Washington should adopt a more restrained foreign policy based on realism and a clear understanding of how nationalism limits a great power's room to maneuver." (iii) "A powerful state can pursue liberal hegemony only in a unipolar system in which it need not worry about threats from other great powers. When the world is bipolar or multipolar, on the other hand, great powers have little choice but to act according to realist dictates, because of the presence of rival great powers."[99]

3. Liberal Hegemony and Globalization

A stable world order is rare in history because stability is dynamic. "When one does arise, it tends to come after a great convulsion that creates both the conditions and the desire for something new. It requires a stable distribution of power and broad acceptance of the rules that govern the conduct of international relations. It also needs skillful statecraft, since an order is made, not born. And no matter how ripe the starting conditions or strong the initial desire, maintaining it demands creative diplomacy, functioning institutions, and effective action to adjust it when circumstances change and buttress it when challenges come. Eventually, inevitably, even the best-managed order comes to an end. The balance of power underpinning it becomes imbalanced. The institutions supporting it fail to adapt to new conditions. Some countries fall, and others rise, the result of changing capacities, faltering wills, and growing ambitions. Those responsible for upholding the order make mistakes both in what they choose to do and in what they choose not to do. But if the end of every order is inevitable, the timing and the manner of its ending are not. Nor is what comes in its wake."[100]

After the Napoleonic Wars, the world order was reestablished in 1815 by the *Concert of Europe* led by four European powers – Austria, Great Britain, Russia, and Prussia; while other states - Spain, Portugal, Sweden, Denmark, the Papal States, and others - sent their representatives to the Congress of Vienna for their own interests. In 1818 France became the fifth member of the alliance of the Congress of Vienna, which was based on the balance of power between five member states in Europe. In order to maintain the new conservative order, Metternich adopted the principle of intervention, meaning "that the great powers had the right to intervene militarily in other countries in order to crush revolutionary movements against legitimate rulers." During 1815-53, "Europe's political borders changed very little, especially when compared with similar eras in the 18th and 20th centuries, as well as later 19th century."[101]

However, the liberal wave of revolutions across Europe in 1848 was swift and severe. "Uprising in Vienna forced Metternich's resignation and flight from Austria, an event that galvanized additional liberal successes in Prussia, Italy, Hungary, and elsewhere." When the Concert was no longer shielded from domestic politics in this way, "it became much more difficult for elites to justify to their people their continued cooperation with odious foreign regimes at the expense of seemingly more-immediate national interests." With the rise of Napoleon III with the 1848 revolution, the Crimean War (1853-56) broke up the unity of conservative states – Austria, Prussia, and Russia. The Franco-British force landed in the Crimea to seize the city of Sevastopol. While Prussia stayed neutral, "Austria foolishly decided to take advantage of Russia's isolation to improve its position in the

Balkans, mobilizing Austrian troops there." Russia lost the Crimean War to Turkey, Prussia won the Austro-Prussian War in 1866 that was followed by Italian unification; and then Prussia won the Franco-Prussian War in 1871, which created the German Empire.

Metternich was a traditional conservative to maintain the balance of power particularly by resisting Russian territorial ambitions. He wanted open and more prosperous Europe but disliked liberalism and strove to prevent the breakup of the Austrian Empire, which resulted in lack of reforms of the system. Bismarck as a German nationalist wanted German domination and encouraged German isolationism to increase the nationalist ideal. The German unification of 1871 was a greater political event than the French Revolution of 1789. The former totally destroyed the balance of power in Europe, and caused France to remain its fixed adversary, so that the Concert of Europe lost its flexibility. After the forced departure of Bismarck in 1890, France and Russia began exploring an alliance, and Great Britain joined the Entente Cordiale of France and Russia in 1904. "Over the second half of the nineteenth century and the start of the twentieth, a powerful, unified Germany and a modern Japan rose, the Ottoman Empire and tsarist Russia declined, and France and the United Kingdom grew stronger but not strong enough. Those changes upended the balance of power that had been the concert's foundation; Germany, in particular, came to view the status quo as inconsistent with its interests." [102]

World War I caused by such reasons as mutual defense alliances, economic rivalries of imperialism, militarism, nationalism, and the immediate cause of assassination. As changes in technology like submarine and railroad affected the system of armed forces, military mobilization became speedy. The Germans developed the Schlieffen plan to overcome the two fronts of enemies – France and Russia. Russia left the front because of the Russian Revolution in 1917, when the United States declared war on Germany. The Paris Peace Conference, under the leadership of President Woodrow Wilson, ended the war in 1919, but failed to enforce peace with the League of Nations and eventually allowed a despotic Germany to rise again. Suffering from the Great Depression, the leaders of the United States believed that "the best way to protect American interests was to use American power to transform international politics." [103]

After World War II, "Europe was in ruins, revolutionary nationalism was rising, the Soviets were playing hard-ball, and the American public was quickly turning inward again." In 1947 Washington launched a bold movement. "The Bretton Woods system was thus supplemented by the Truman Doctrine, the Marshall Plan, and NATO, a new set of arrangements designed to revive and protect an American sphere of influence run along liberal lines." [104] While the Soviet Union was influential to the Korean War in the 1950s and the Vietnam War in the 1960s, Washington applied a containment strategy to win the conflict with Moscow. The fall of the Berlin Wall in 1989 was followed by the collapse of the Soviet Union two years later, which was the end of the Cold War and of the bipolar system. In the 1990s, the Bush and Clinton administrations skillfully managed the unipolar world, and by the turn of the millennium the United States became strong and rich enough to secure the world order. But liberal hegemony with globalization began to decay with the rise of China. It is now questionable how to manage the Hegemony with the growing rivalry between America and China.

Hegemonic Stability Theory (HST) indicates "that the international system is more likely to remain stable when a single nation-state is the dominant world power, or hegemon. Thus, the fall of an existing hegemon or the state of no hegemon diminishes the stability of the international system. When a hegemon exercises leadership, either through diplomacy, coercion, or persuasion, it is actually deploying its preponderance of power. This is called hegemony, which refers to a state's ability to single-handedly dominate the rules and arrangements...[of] international political and economic relations. HST can help analyze the rise of great powers to the role of world leader or hegemon. Also, it can be used to understand and to calculate the future of international politics through the discussion of the symbiotic relation between the declining hegemon and its rising successor... the economic chaos between World War I and World War II that led to the Great Depression was partly attributable to the lack of a world leader with a dominant economy."[105] In order for a nation-state to rise to the level of hegemon, there are some more advantageous attributes. First, it must have "political strength, military force, and superior national power that is necessary for its ability to forge new international laws and organizations." Second, a hegemon must have a large and growing economy with unrivaled supremacy. Third, hegemon must have the will to lead and the will to establish a hegemonic regime, with the capability to lead and enforce the rules of the system. Finally, "a hegemon must commit to the system, which needs to be perceived as mutually beneficial for other great powers and important state-actors."[106]

According to Robert O. Keohane, "Hegemony is related in complex ways to cooperation and to institutions such as international regimes. Successful hegemonic leadership itself depends on a certain form of asymmetrical cooperation. The hegemon plays a distinctive role, providing its partners with leadership in return for deference; but, unlike an imperial power, it cannot make and enforce rules without a certain degree of consent from other sovereign states. As the interwar experience illustrates, material predominance alone does not guarantee either stability or effective leadership. Indeed, the hegemon may have to invest resources in institutions in order to ensure that its preferred rules will guide the behavior of other countries. Cooperation may be fostered by hegemony, and hegemons require cooperation to make and enforce rules. Hegemony and cooperation are not alternatives; on the contrary, they are often found in symbiotic relationships with one another. To analyze the relationships between hegemony and cooperation, we need a conception of cooperation that is somewhat tart rather than syrupy-sweet. It must take into account the facts that coercion is always possible in world politics and that conflicts of interest never vanish even when there are important shared interests…cooperation should be defined not as the absence of conflict – which is always at least a potentially important element of international relations – but as a process that involves the use of discord to stimulate mutual adjustment." [107] Hegemony is an important aspect of international relations with various schools of thought and theories.

(a) ***Long cycle theory***: In his *Long Cycles in World Politics* (1987), George Modelski defines that "long cycle describes the connection between war cycles, economic supremacy, and the political aspects of world leadership. Long cycles, or long waves, offer interesting perspectives on global politics by permitting "the careful exploration of the ways in which world wars have recurred, and lead states such as Britain and the United States have succeeded each other in an orderly manner." Many traditional theories of international relations are based on anarchy, but Modelski's long cycle theory states "that war and other destabilizing events are a natural product of the long cycle and larger global system cycle."[108]

(b) ***The neorealist interpretation***: In his *The Tragedy of Great Power Politics* (2001), John Mearsheimer outlines "how the anarchic system that neorealists subscribe to create power hungry states who will each attempt to install themselves as regional and global hegemons. His theory is not widely embraced by fellow realists who argue that the hegemon supports the system so long as it is in their interests. The system is created, shaped and maintained by coercion. The hegemon would begin to undermine the institution when it is not in their interests. With the decline of a hegemon, the system descends into instability. Other realists argue that the anarchic system does not actually give causal motivation to aid the creation of hegemons."[109]

(c) ***The neoliberal interpretation***: "Neoliberals argue that the hegemon wishes to maintain its dominant position without paying enforcement costs, so it creates a system in which it can credibly limit the returns to power and credibly commit to neither dominate nor abandon them. This is done through institutions, which are sticky. These institutions favor the hegemon but provide protection and a stable world order for the rest of the world. The more open this world-order, the less likely that there will be a challenger. With the decline of the hegemon, institutions don't automatically die, because they were constructed in a way that benefited all stakeholders; instead, they take on a life of their own."[110]

(d) ***Hegemonic Cooperation***: In the short to intermediate term, the U.S. hegemonic cooperation aided the economic and political recovery of Europe and Japan and maintained alliance solidarity during the Cold War, although the strategy failed in institutionalizing an international regime and maintaining a strong resource base to exercise of American power. "The Cold War legitimated U.S. leadership, but the ability of the United States to carry out its strategy of redistribution depended on its own previous measures to control and exploit oil supplies abroad as well as to ensure the central position of the United States in multilateral trade and monetary regimes."[111] To be successful, any hegemonic strategy must recreate the conditions for its own existence, while any hegemony coexists easily with extensive cooperation with policy adjustment.

(e) ***Robert G. Gilpin's Argument***: In *War and Change in World Politics* (1981), Gilpin observes that "Hegemonic war historically has been the basic mechanism of systemic change in world politics. Hegemonic conflict, arising from an increasing disequilibrium between the burden of maintaining an empire or hegemonic position and the resources available to the dominant power to carry out this task, leads to the creation of a new international system…The conclusion of one hegemonic war is the beginning of another cycle of growth, expansion, and eventual decline. The law of uneven growth continues to redistribute power, thus undermining the status quo established by the last hegemonic struggle. Disequilibrium replaces equilibrium, and the world moves toward a new round of hegemonic conflict. It…always will be, until men either destroy themselves or learn to develop an effective mechanism of peaceful change."[112]

Helen V. Milner wrote on *Foreign Affairs* in the memory of Robert Gilpin as a leading realist of international political economy as follows: "Gilpin's realism posited that the primary mover of politics was competition between states trying to maximize their national interests, often by using or threatening to use force."[113] Unlike other researches in political economy, "Gilpin argued that economic interdependence, or globalization, did not matter much. Most governments were not that constrained by it and could indeed use it as a resource to manipulate other countries that depended more heavily on the global system. It had changed politics little, he suggested; states were still far more concerned with competing for power and wealth than they were with pursuing economic efficiency or maximizing welfare. Nor did Gilpin believe that technology had transformed international politics. Even nuclear weapons were not, in his view, radical enough to end the prospect of war. Gilpin viewed military power as the greatest cause of political change, and war between existing hegemons and aspiring ones as the motor of the global system. And because states control territory and military power, they were the main actors in world politics. Rivalry between them, especially the great powers, determined the world order."[114]

The End of the Cold War: U.S. President Richard Nixon established diplomatic relations with Beijing in 1972, but Ronald Reagan had taken a hard line against the Soviet Union. His administration began to provide military support to anti-communist armed movements in Afghanistan, Angola, Nicaragua and elsewhere. In 1987 the Intermediate-Range Nuclear Missile Treaty was signed by both Reagan and Gorbachev. As Saudi raised oil production, its falling prices reduced Soviet export revenues. Rising defense spending and falling production in the primary and secondary sectors caused a heavy burden of the Soviet economy.

Mikhail Gorbachev assumed the reins of power in the Soviet Union in 1985 and introduced the policies of glasnost and perestroika to the Soviet Union. "Gorbachev hoped these changes would be enough to spark the sluggish Soviet economy. Freedom, however, is addictive. The unraveling of the Soviet Bloc began in Poland in June 1989. Despite previous Soviet military interventions in Hungary, Czecho-slovakia, and Poland itself, Polish voters elected a noncommunist opposition government to their legislature. The world watched with anxious eyes, expecting Soviet tanks to roll into Poland preventing the new government from taking power. Gorbachev, however, refused to act. Like dominoes, Eastern European communist dictatorships fell one by one. By the fall of 1989, East and West Germans were tearing down the Berlin Wall with pickaxes. Communist regimes were ousted in Hungary and Czechoslovakia. On Christmas Day, the brutal Romanian dictator Nicolae Ceausescu and his wife were summarily executed on live television. Yugoslavia threw off the yoke of communism only to dissolve quickly into a violent civil war."[115]

"Demands for freedom soon spread to the Soviet Union. The Baltic States of Estonia, Latvia, and Lithuania declared independence. Talks of similar sentiments were heard in Ukraine, the Caucasus, and the Central Asian states. Here Gorbachev wished to draw the line. Self-determination for Eastern Europe was one thing, but he intended to maintain the territorial integrity of the Soviet Union...Gorbachev was placed under house arrest. Meanwhile, Boris Yeltsin, the leader of the Russian Soviet Republic, demanded the arrest of the hardliners. The army and the public sided with Yeltsin, and the coup failed. Though Gorbachev was freed, he was left with little legitimacy...In December 1991, Ukraine, Byelorussia, and Russia itself declared independence and the Soviet Union was dissolved. Gorbachev was a president without a country. Most Americans found it difficult to get used to the idea of no Cold War...the Soviet invasion of Afghanistan, and the Star Wars defense proposal. Now the enemy was beaten, but the world remained unsafe. In many ways, facing one super-power was simpler than challenging dozens of rogue states and renegade groups sponsoring global terrorism."[116] The publications explain political ideas in response to the collapse of the Soviet Union and beyond.

(a) *The Rise and Fall of the Great Power* (Paul Kennedy, 1987): Paul Kennedy views that the strength of a Great Power can be measured relatively to other powers. "Great Power ascendancy correlates strongly to available resources and economic durability; military overstretch, and a concomitant relative decline are the consistent threats facing powers whose ambitions and security requirements are greater than their resource base can provide for." He sees that "declining countries can experience greater difficulties in balancing their preferences for guns, butter and investments."[117]

"The triumph of any one Great Power in this period, or the collapse of another, has usually been the consequence of lengthy fighting by its armed forces; but it has also been the consequences of the more or less efficient utilization of the state's productive economic resources in wartime, and, further in the background, of the way in which that state's economy had been rising or falling, relative to the other leading nations, in the decades preceding the actual conflict. For that reason, how a Great Power's position steadily alters in peacetime, is as important to this study as how it fights in wartime... The relative strengths of the leading nations in world affairs never remain constant, principally because of the uneven rate of growth among different societies and of the technological and organizational breakthroughs which bring a greater advantage to one society than to another."

The strength of a state is measured by "population size, urbanization rates, Bairoch's per capita levels of industrialization, iron and steel production, energy consumption, and total industrial output of the powers, to gauge the strength of the various great powers." Kennedy emphasizes productivity increase, based on systematic interventions, "which led to economic growth and prosperity for great powers in the 20th century. He compares the great powers at the close of the 20th century and predicts the decline of the Soviet Union, the rise of China and Japan...He predicts that continued deficit spending, especially in military build-up will be the single most important reason for decline of any great power."

"The United States has the typical problems of a great power, which include balancing guns and butter and investments for economic growth. The U.S.' growing military commitment to every continent and the growing cost of military hardware severely limit available options...As military expenses grow, this reduces investments in economic growth, which eventually leads to the downward spiral of slower growth, heavier taxes, deepening domestic splits over spending priorities, and weakening capacity to bear the burdens of defense...The task facing American statesmen over the next decades, therefore, is to recognize that broad trends are under way, and that there is a need to manage affairs so that the relative erosion of the United States' position takes place slowly and smoothly and is not accelerated by policies which bring merely short-term advantage but longer-term disadvantage." But the Shale Oil and Gas became a windfall.

(b) *The End of History and the Last Man* (Francis Fukuyama, 1992): "Fukuyama argues that the advent of Western liberal democracy may signal the endpoint of humanity's sociocultural evolution and the final form of human government. What we may be witnessing is not just the end of the Cold War, or the passing of a particular period of post-war history, but the end of history as such: that is, the end point of mankind's ideological evolution and the universalization of Western liberal democracy as the final form of human government. Fukuyama's position contradicts that of Karl Marx, who predicted that communism would displace capitalism. Fukuyama himself identifies on some level with Marx, but more strongly with the German philosopher Georg Wilhelm Friedrich Hegel."[118]

"According to Fukuyama, since the French Revolution, democracy has repeatedly proven to be a fundamentally better system than any of the alternatives. The most basic (and prevalent) error in discussing Fukuyama's work is to confuse history with events. Fukuyama claims not that events will stop occurring in the future, but rather that all that will happen in the future is that democracy will become more and more prevalent in the long term, although it may suffer temporary setbacks...Fukuyama has stated: The End of History was never linked to a specifically American model of social or political organization...I believe that the European Union more accurately reflects what the world will look like at the end of history than the contemporary United States. The EU's attempt to transcend sovereignty and traditional power politics by establishing a transnational rule of law is much more in line with a post-historical world than the Americans' continuing belief in God, national sovereignty, and their military."[119]

Criticisms: Despite favorable arguments, there were some critics below. (i) Critics of liberal democracy: Jacques Derrida criticized that "For it must be cried out, at a time when some have the audacity to neo-evangelize in the name of the ideal of a liberal democracy that has finally realized itself as the ideal of human history." However, let us never neglect the fact making of innumerable singular sites of suffering.

(ii) Radical Islam, tribalism, and the Clash of Civilization: "Huntington argued that the temporary conflict between ideologies is being replaced by the ancient conflict between civilizations. The dominant civilization decides the form of human government, and these will not be constant."

(iii) The resurgence of Russia and China: China is governed by the Communist Party, while Russia has a democracy form though *de facto* authoritarian, but liberal democracy remains strong.

(iv) Failure of civil society and political decay: "Twenty-five years later, the most serious threat to the end-of-history hypothesis isn't that there is a higher, better model out there that will someday supersede liberal democracy...some version of democracy. Fukuyama also warned of political decay which...could also affect established democracies."[120]

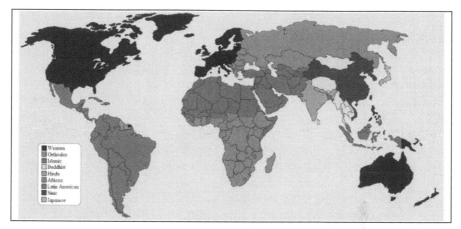

Map I-3-1. The clash of civilizations according to Huntington (1996)
https://upload.wikimedia.org/wikipedia/commons/thumb/3/34/Clash_of_Civilizations_mapn2.png/
750px-Clash_of_Civilizations_mapn2.png, accessed 11 January 2019

(c) *The Clash of Civilizations* (Samuel P. Huntington, 1997): Samuel Huntington argues "that the trends of global conflict after the end of the Cold War are increasingly appearing at these civilizational divisions. Wars such as those following the breakup of Yugoslavia, in Chechnya, and between India and Pakistan were cited as evidence of inter-civilizational conflict. He also argues that the widespread Western belief in the universality of the West's values and political systems is naïve and that continued insistence on democratization and such universal norms will only further antagonize other civilizations. Huntington sees the West as reluctant to accept this because it built the international system, wrote its laws, and gave it substance in the form of the United Nations. Huntington identifies a major shift of economic, military, and political power from the West to the other civilizations of the world, most significantly to what he identifies as the two challenger civilizations, Sinic and Islam."[121]

"East Asian Sinic civilization is culturally asserting itself and its values relative to the West due to its rapid economic growth. Specifically, he believes that China's goals are to reassert itself as the regional hegemon, and that other countries in the region will 'bandwagon' with China due to the history of hierarchical command structures implicit in the Confucian Sinic civilization, as opposed to the individualism and pluralism valued in the West. Regional powers such as the two Koreas and Vietnam will acquiesce to Chinese demands and become more supportive of China rather than attempting to oppose it. Huntington therefore believes that the rise of China poses one of the most significant problems and the most powerful long-term threat to the West, as Chinese cultural assertion clashes with the American desire for the lack of a regional hegemony in East Asia."[122]

Huntington argues "that the Islamic civilization has experienced a massive population explosion which is fueling instability both on the borders of Islam and in its interior, where fundamentalist movements are becoming increasingly popular. Manifestations of what he terms the *Islamic Resurgence* include the 1979 Iranian revolution and the first Gulf War. Perhaps the most controversial statement Huntington made in the *Foreign Affairs* article was that 'Islam has bloody borders'. Huntington believes this to be a real consequence of several factors, including the previously mentioned Muslim youth bulge and population growth and Islamic proximity to many civilizations. Huntington sees Islamic civilization as a potential ally to China, both having more revisionist goals and sharing common conflicts with other civilizations, especially the West."[123]

"Russia, Japan, and India are what Huntington terms swing civilizations and may favor either side. Russia, for example, clashes with the many Muslim ethnic groups on its southern border (such as Chechnya) but... cooperates with Iran to avoid further Muslim-Orthodox violence in Southern Russia, and to help continue the flow of oil. Huntington argues that a "Sino-Islamic connection" is emerging in which China will cooperate more closely with Iran, Pakistan, and other states to augment its international position. Huntington also argues that civilizational conflicts are particularly prevalent between Muslims and non-Muslims, identifying the bloody borders between Islamic and non-Islamic civilizations."[124]

Huntington views that in the future, the central axis of world politics tends to be the conflict between Western and non-Western civilizations. "(i) Non-Western countries can attempt to achieve isolation in order to preserve their own values and protect themselves from Western invasion...(ii) According to the theory of band-wagoning non-Western countries can join and accept Western values. (iii) Non-Western countries can try to balance Western power through modernization. They can develop economic, military power and cooperate with other non-Western countries against the West while still preserving their own values and institutions."[125]

"Amartya Sen (1999) argues diversity is a feature of most cultures in the world. Western civilization is no exception. The practice of democracy that has won out in the modern West is largely a result of a consensus that has emerged since the Enlightenment and the Industrial Revolution, and particularly in the last century or so. To read in this a historical commitment of the West - over the millennia - to democracy, and then to contrast it with non-Western traditions (treating each as monolithic) would be a great mistake. In his 2003 book *Terror and Liberalism*, Paul Berman argues that distinct cultural boundaries do not exist in the present day. He argues there is no Islamic civilization nor a Western civilization, and that the evidence for a civilization clash is not convincing, especially when considering relationships such as that between the United States and Saudi Arabia."[126]

(d) *Culture Matters*: Lawrence E. Harrison and Samuel P. Huntington co-edited *Culture Matters: How Values Shape Human Progress* in 2000 with the articles presented to a 1999 Harvard University symposium.

Under Why Culture Matters, Harrison writes that: "(i) The collapse of communism and socialism have removed the Marxist explanations concerning economic development. (ii) The passage of decades has removed the colonial past as an ongoing excuse for the developmental failures of third world nations. A logical 'statute of limitations' increasingly makes such arguments untenable...(iii) The 'racism/discrimination' explanation for black underachievement has lost its viability as blacks in the U.S. move increasingly into the middle class, although some racism and discrimination undoubtedly continue. (iv) Explanations based on tropical geography and climate are undermined by an increasing number of exceptions that have succeeded with economic development like in Hong Kong, Barbados and Singapore. (v) Economic policy explanations are undermined by those multicultural nations where certain minorities clearly outperform other groups... (vi) The complaint of dependency fails for similar reasons."[127]

Major issues discussed in this symposium are: (i) The link between values and progress: "Skepticism about the link between cultural values and human progress is found particularly in two disciplines: economics and anthropology." (ii) The universality of values and Western cultural imperialism: "The idea of progress I suspect for those who are committed to cultural relativism, for whom each culture defines its own goals and ethics, which cannot be evaluated against the goals and ethics of another culture." (iii) Geography and culture: "It is clear that geography, including resource endowment, and climate are major factors in explaining the wealth and poverty of nations. Almost all the advanced democracies are in the temperate zones, and the large majority of the poor countries are in the tropical zone. But the exceptions are noteworthy." (iv) The relationship between culture and institutions: "Culture is the mother; institutions are the children,' this is particularly true in the long run. In the short run, institutional modifications, often impelled by politics, can influence culture." (v) Cultural Change: "Approximately half of the Hispanic high school students in Colorado and most of the other states in the west are dropping out...the heavy immigrant flow from Latin America impedes the working of the melting pot...one of the reasons for the aversion to confronting culture is that it touches the highly sensitive nerves of national, ethnic, and personal self-esteem by communicating the idea that some cultures are better than others, at least in the sense that they do more to promote human well-being." In general, "The role of cultural values and attitudes as obstacles to or facilitators of progress has been largely ignored by governments and agencies." On the other hand, however, at least in Latin America, a number of homegrown cultural change initiatives are already under way.[128]

Globalization: The fall of the Soviet Union and its satellite countries ended the Cold War, which made the world free from the ideological conflict between the East and the West, which removed various restrictions in economic transactions between countries. The relaxed and less controlled borders have expedited trade with and investment to foreign countries like Brazil, Russia, India, and China (BRIC) –the emerging market economies.

"Globalization is a process of interaction and integration among people, companies, and governments worldwide." Some consider that globalization "as a form of capitalist expansion which entails the integration of local and national economies into a global, unregulated market economy. Globalization has grown due to advances in transportation and communication technology. With the increased global interactions comes the growth of international trade, ideas, and culture. Globalization is primarily an economic process of interaction and integration that's associated with social and cultural aspects. However, conflicts and diplomacy are also large parts of the history of globalization, and modern globalization." In 2000, the International Monetary Fund identified four basic aspects of globalization: "trade and transactions, capital and investment movements, migration and movement of people, and the dissemination of knowledge."[129]

"Economic globalization is the increasing economic interdependence of national economies across the world through a rapid increase in cross-border movement of goods, services, technology, and capital." "Cultural globalization refers to the transmission of ideas, meanings, and values around the world in such a way as to extend and intensify social relations. This process is marked by the common consumption of cultures that have been diffused by the Internet, popular culture media, and international travel." Political globalization refers to the growth of the worldwide political system including "national governments, their governmental and intergovernmental organizations as well as government-independent elements of global civil society such as international non-govern-mental organizations and social movement organizations." This makes the nation-state decline.[130]

An essential aspect of globalization is the movement of people, and state-boundary limits on that movement have changed across history. "The movement of tourists and businesspeople opened up over the last century. As transportation technology improved, travel time and costs decreased dramatically between the 18th and early 20th century."[131] In addition to tourism, immigration, international education, and transnational marriage help people move widely. (ii) Before electronic communications, speed of global communications was limited by the maximum speed of courier services until the mid-19th century. The electric telegraph was the first method of instant long-distance communication." The Internet has been instrumental in connecting people across geographical boundaries.[132]

(a) The Earth Is Flat (Thomas L. Friedman, 2005): "Friedman recounts a journey to Bangalore, India, when he realized globalization has changed core economic concepts. In *The Earth Is Flat*, Friedman views that flattening is a product of the convergence of the personal computer with fiber optic micro-cable with the rise of work-flow software; and that multinational companies led the way in driving global integration." Friedman defines ten flatteners leveling the global playing field: (i) Collapse of the Berlin Wall 11/9/1989; (ii) Netscape 8/9/1995; (iii) Work-flow software; (iv) Uploading - open source software, blogs, and Wikipedia; (v) Outsourcing; (vi) Off-shoring; (vii) Supply-chaining; (viii) Insourcing; (ix) Informing – Google and other search engines and Wikipedia; (x) The Steroids – wireless, voice over IP, file sharing, all analog content and processes.[133]

Proposed Remedies: "Sawyer Stock believes that to fight the quiet crisis of a flattening world, the US workforce should keep updating its work skills. Making the workforce more adaptable…will keep it more employable. He also suggests that the government makes it easier for people to switch jobs by making retirement benefits and health insurance less dependent on one's employer and by providing insurance that would partly cover a possible drop in income when changing jobs…there should be more inspiration for youth to become scientists, engineers, and mathematicians because of a decrease in the percentage of those professionals who are Americans."[134]

Conflict Prevention known as the Dell Theory: According to Friedman, "No two countries that are both parts of a major global supply chain, like Dell's, will ever fight a war against each other as long as they are both parts of the same global supply chain. That is, as long as corporations have major supply chain operations in countries other than that corporation's home country, those countries will never engage in armed conflicts. This is because of the economic interdependence between nations that arises when a large corporation (such as Dell) has supply chain operations in multiple global locations and when developing nations are reluctant to give up their newfound wealth." Developing nations do not want to risk the trust of the multinational companies that include them in the global supply chain."

"Thomas Friedman also warns that the Dell theory should not be interpreted as a guarantee that nations that are deeply involved in global supply chains will not go to war with each other. It means, rather, that the governments of those nations and their citizens will have very heavy economic costs to consider as they contemplate the possibility of war. Such costs include long-term loss of the country's profitable participation in the global supply chain. This theory relates with how conflict prevention occurred between India and Pakistan in their 2001–2002 nuclear standoff, wherein India was at risk of losing its global partners. The relationship between…China and Taiwan…have strong supply relations with each other, and a war between the two seems very unlikely today."[135]

(b) *The Paradox of American Power* (Joseph S. Nye 2002) introduces an astutely argued case for American multilateral engagement. "America's paradox, according to Nye, is that it is too powerful to be challenged by others but not powerful enough to achieve its goals by going it alone. Indeed, popular notions of American unipolarity and hegemony are misleading and potentially dangerous, for the world's power structure is complex and multi-layered. The United States has unprecedented military power, but economic power is widely shared with Europe and East Asia. Meanwhile, a booming world of transnational relations lies outside Washington's control. If the United States pursues a heavy-handed, unilateral foreign policy, it will hasten the demise of its preponderance and destroy its ability to shape the global playing field. By binding itself to the outside world through multi-lateral treaties and agreements, Nye points out, the United States may lose some freedom of action - but it gains far more by turning other countries into predictable and cooperative partners. Other states are more likely to accept rather than resist American power when that power is exercised within at least a loose framework of multilateral rules. This kind of soft power - the ability to influence other states through nonmilitary means -- is critical to America's success...Hence military might alone will not buy the United States much leverage in the coming decades, as economic inter-dependence and information flows make stable rules, credible commitments, and soft power the coins of the new global realm." [136]

"The U.S. is too strong to be effectively challenged but lacks the power to alone achieve such desirable goals as nuclear nonproliferation and the minimization of global terrorism. In pursuing its foreign policy objectives, it needs cooperation and coalitions that require a complex array of compro-mises and accommodations. Vanity and one sidedness can undermine the effectiveness of the US power, especially the adorableness and effects of its soft power policies and leadership style, Nye says...US strategic restricts is comfortingly the open and pluralistic attitude where its external policy is improved decreases uncertainty and surprise.

On the other hand, military globalization consists of networks of interdependence in which force is employed. During the Cold War, the global strategic interdependence between the United States and the Soviet Union was acute and well recognized. Not only did it produce world-straddling alliances, but either side could have used intercontinental missiles to destroy the other within the space of thirty minutes. Such interdependence was distinctive not because it was totally new, but because the scale and speed of the potential conflict were so enormous. Today, terrorist networks constitute a new form of military globalization. Social globalization is the spread of peoples, cultures, images, and ideas. Migration is a concrete example. In the nineteenth century, some eighty million people crossed oceans...more than in the twentieth century." [137]

(c) *Why Globalization Works* (Martin Wolf, 2004): According to Wolf, the anti-globalism movement is anti-liberty like communism and national socialism. They oppose globalized international business because it "• Destroys the ability of countries to control and regulate their own economies. • Undermines democracy. • Destroys the livelihood of farmers. • Prevents the poor from obtaining needed medicines. • Lowers real wages and causes rampant economic insecurity. • Destroys the environment. • Incites nations to reduce regulatory standards and lower taxes and wages. • Allows global markets to generate a series of economic crises, the costs of which are disproportionately paid by disadvantaged countries. • Pushes greed to the status of the primary motivator of all human behavior. • Devours humanity's legacy of diverse cultures." In fact, "The September 11 attacks were aimed at the U.S., the leader of globalization, and their immediate effect was a severe restriction of the normal flow of passenger traffic worldwide...those who backed the attacks want the world to return to an existence more akin to the eighth century than the twenty-first."[138]

"John Locke argued that the individual's right to own and use property freely...was essential to liberty. In this sense, a liberal society automatically becomes a commercial one. Because markets are continually in flux, liberal societies require embracing perpetual disruption and change, as individuals take advantage of economic opportunities...A strong, benevolent state is essential to liberal democracy. Freedom requires that the state protect the individual, and that the individual be protected from the state. Ignoring this fact has tragic historic consequences, as exemplified by the state excesses seen in the late Soviet Union."[139]

The 10 commandments of Martin Wolf's globalization are as follows: "1. Recognize the market economy as the only system capable of giving individuals material well-being. 2. States remain the centers of political debate and authority, but corporations gain legitimacy from the states that foster their operations. 3. In their own best interests, countries and their citizens should participate in international treaties that remove barriers to trade and permit the free flow of capital. 4. These treaties need to be specific, clear and enforceable. 5. Although the World Trade Organization has been enormously successful, its role should be reevaluated because it has allowed a few countries with minimal world trade impact to wield disproportionate power. 6. Create new systems and agreements on investment and global competition. 7. Countries should integrate fully into the global financial markets, but they should do so while being completely aware of the risks. 8. Countries should accept the possibility that their sovereign debt occasionally can be renegotiated. 9. Increase development assistance to countries with reasonably sound political and economic policies. 10. Countries must learn from their mistakes, and the global community needs to improve its capacity for intervention when states fail."[140]

(d) ***Globalization and Its Discontents*** (Joseph E. Stiglitz, 2002): The book draws on author's personal experience as chairman of the Council of Economic Advisers under Bill Clinton from 1993 and chief economist at the World Bank from 1997. "Stiglitz argues that IMF policies contributed to bringing about the East Asian financial crisis, as well as the Argentine economic crisis. Also noted was the failure of Russia's conversion to a market economy and low levels of development in Sub-Saharan Africa. Specific policies criticized by Stiglitz include fiscal austerity, high interest rates, trade liberalization, and the liberalization of capital markets and insistence on the privatization of state assets."[141]

"The theories which guide the IMF's policies are empirically flawed. Free market, neoclassical, and neoliberal are all essentially euphemisms for the disastrous *laissez-faire* economics...This approach seeks to minimize the role of government - arguing that lower wages solve problems of unemployment and relying upon trickle-down economics to address poverty. Stiglitz finds no evidence to support this belief and considers the 'Washington Consensus' policy of free markets to be a blend of ideology and bad science...Without equal access to information between employer and employee, company and consumer, or lender and debtor, there is no chance of free markets operating efficiently. Stiglitz explains that globalization could be either success or failure, depending on its management...Globalization is beneficial under the condition that the economic management operated by national government and the example is East Asian countries. Those countries were based on exports through which they were able to close technological, capital and knowledge gaps...if the national economy regulated by international institutions there could be an adverse effect."[142]

"Stiglitz believes the IMF and World Bank should be reformed, not dismantled - with a growing population, malaria and AIDS pandemics, and global environmental challenges...He advocates a gradual, sequential, and selective approach to institutional development, land reform and privatization, capital market liberalization, competition policies, worker safety nets, health infra-structure, and education...Lastly, democratic disciplines are needed to ensure that financial institutions serve general interests. Debt forgiveness should be extended, building on the success of the Jubilee Movement. Since the IMF loans primarily benefited foreigners and government officials, he argues it is unjust and onerous that citizens of developing nations be heavily taxed to pay them off...Stiglitz believes that promoting local and international democracy is fundamental to reforming global economic policy. Democracy aids social stability, empowers the free flow of information, and promotes a decentralized economy upon which efficient and equitable economies rely." Extending IMF and WTO voting rights to developing countries would be a good start promoting democracy comes before promoting business.[143]

The Global War on Terrorism is an international military campaign that was launched by the United States government after the September 11, 2001 attacks against the United States. "U.S. President Barack Obama announced on 23 May 2013 that the Global War on Terror was over, saying the military and intelligence agencies will not wage war against a tactic but will instead focus on a specific group of networks determined to destroy the U.S. On 28 December 2014, the Obama administration announced the end of the combat role of the U.S.-led mission in Afghanistan. However, the unexpected rise of the Islamic State of Iraq and the Levant (ISIL) terror group—also known as the Islamic State of Iraq and Syria (ISIS)—led to a new operation against terror in the Middle East and South Asia."[144]

"The war on terrorism was a multidimensional campaign of almost limitless scope. Its military dimension involved major wars in Afghanistan and Iraq, covert operations in Yemen and elsewhere, large-scale military-assistance programs for cooperative regimes, and major increases in military spending. Its intelligence dimension comprised institutional reorganization and considerable increases in the funding of America's intelligence-gathering capabilities, a global program of capturing terrorist suspects and interning them at Guantá-namo Bay, expanded cooperation with foreign intelligence agencies, and the tracking and interception of terrorist financing." Continuing efforts were made to maintain a global coalition.[145]

Criticism of the War on Terror were on "the issues, morality, efficiency, economics, and other questions surrounding the War on Terror and made against the phrase itself, calling it a misnomer. The notion of a war against terrorism has proven highly contentious, with critics charging that it has been exploited by participating governments to pursue long-standing policy/military objectives, reduce civil liberties, and infringe upon human rights. It is argued that the term war is not appropriate in this context (as in War on Drugs) since there is no identifiable enemy and that it is unlikely international terrorism can be ended by military means."[146]

As other wars on terror, "In the 2010s, China has also been engaged in its own War on Terror, predominantly a domestic campaign in response to violent actions by Uighur separatist movements in the Xinjiang conflict. This campaign was widely criticized in international media due to the perception that it unfairly targets and persecutes Chinese Muslims, potentially resulting in a negative backlash from China's predominantly Muslim Uighur population. Xi Jinping's government has imprisoned up to 2 million Uyghurs and other Muslim ethnic minorities in Xinjiang re-education camps, where they are reportedly subject to abuse and torture." On the other hand, "Russia has also been engaged on its own, also largely internally focused, counter-terrorism campaign often termed a war on terror, during the Second Chechen War, the Insurgency in the North Caucasus, and the Russian military intervention in the Syrian Civil War."[147]

4. The Decay of Liberal Order and the Resurgence of Nationalism

Since the collapse of the Soviet Union in 1991, the United States created a stable and benign global environment by "providing international public goods such as global and regional security, freedom of the commons, and a liberal trading system. From 1989 to 2016, global product more than tripled. Standards of living skyrocketed. More than a billion people were lifted out of poverty. Infant mortality plummeted. New technologies continuously improved daily life and connected people in extraordinary new ways."[148] Nevertheless, macro-stability coexisted with regional disorder, and the spread of capitalism and the current phase of globalization were far beyond expectations. More money created more problems like the financial crisis of 2008. Around the 2010s, globalist policies were rejected in America.

The liberal order began to decay: "Although Russia has avoided any direct military challenge to NATO, it has nonetheless shown a growing willingness to disrupt the status quo: through its use of force in Georgia in 2008 and Ukraine since 2014, its often indiscriminate military intervention in Syria, and its aggressive use of cyber-warfare to attempt to affect political outcomes in the United States and Europe. All of these represent a rejection of the principal constraints associated with the old order…The liberal order is exhibiting its own signs of deterioration. Authoritarianism is on the rise not just in the obvious places, such as China and Russia, but also in the Philippines, Turkey, and Eastern Europe. Global trade has grown, but recent rounds of trade talks have ended without agreement, and the World Trade Organization (WTO) has proved unable to deal with today's most pressing challenges, including nontariff barriers and the theft of intellectual property."[149] The EU is struggling with Brexit and disputes over migration and sovereignty. More countries are resisting U.S. supremacy. The violation of the Nuclear Nonproliferation Treaty has threatened world peace.

Why is all this happening? Gideon Rose views that "It is instructive to look back to the gradual demise of the Concert of Europe. Today's world order has struggled to cope with power shifts: China's rise, the appearance of several medium powers (Iran and North Korea, in particular) that reject important aspects of the order, and the emergence of nonstate actors (from drug cartels to terrorist networks) that can pose a serious threat to order within and between states. The technological and political context has changed in important ways, too. Globalization has had destabilizing effects, ranging from climate change to the spread of technology into far more hands than ever before, including a range of groups and people intent on disrupting the order. Nationalism and populism have surged—the result of greater inequality within countries, the dislocation associated with the financial crisis, job losses caused by trade and technology, increased flows of migrants and refugees, and the power of social media to spread hate."[150]

China's Global Ambition: *U.S. Vice President Mike Pence* delivered a searing speech at a Washington think tank in early October 2018, enumerating a long list of reproaches against China. "From territorial disputes in the South China Sea to alleged Chinese meddling in U.S. elections, Pence accused Beijing of breaking international norms and acting against American interests." Yan Xuetong, a China's professor criticized on it that "Such historical analogies are as popular as they are misleading, but the comparison contains a kernel of truth: the post–Cold War interregnum of U.S. hegemony is over, and bipolarity is set to return, with China playing the role of the junior superpower. The transition will be a tumultuous, perhaps even violent, affair, as China's rise sets the country on a collision course with the United States over a number of clashing interests. But… Beijing has no clear plan for filling this leadership vacuum and shaping new international norms from the ground up."[151]

Chinese President Xi Jinping is calling for his nation to lead the reform of the global governance system moving with *its three grand strategies*. (i) "Beijing intends to weaken liberal democratic principles and augment or replace them with authoritarian governance principles." (ii) "Beijing aims to reduce U.S. dominance and give developing nations a stronger voice," because it views that the United States designed the prevailing system for themselves. (iii) Beijing wants the global system to effectively address global challenges. Since China is dependent on the global system, "it is in China's national interest to work collaboratively with other nations to address challenges that threaten global safety and prosperity."[152] Its ultimate goal is "to push the United States out of the Indo-Pacific and rival it on the global stage." History has shown that "a country was able to sustain its rise, the rising power ended up overtaking the dominant power…To remain dominant, Washington will have to change course."[153]

The Belt and Road Initiative is a massive regional infrastructure project that China launched in 2013. "China has spent $400 billion on the initiative, and it has convinced 86 countries and international organizations to sign some 100 related cooperation agreements. Chinese aid, which primarily takes the form of loans from banks controlled by the Chinese Communist Party…the Belt and Road Initiative is intended to enable China to better use its growing economic clout to achieve its ultimate political aims without provoking a countervailing response or a military conflict." Beijing tried to hide its true intentions of the military dimensions, but many observers recognized that it would eventually have a strong military component. "Even if the initiative is not the prelude to an American-style global military presence…China could still use the economic and political influence generated by the project to limit the reach of American power…it could pressure dependent states in Africa, the Middle East, and South Asia to deny the U.S. military the right to enter their airspace or access their ground facilities."[154]

Anti-Access/Area Denial (A2/AD): "China has emerged as an assertive regional power in the Asia-Pacific with forceful A2/AD capabilities, using advanced ballistic and cruise missiles in conjunction with air and maritime defense systems to deter U.S. military operations in the region. China's A2/AD is concentrated around Taiwan and the South China Sea, putting U.S. military forces…and installations in the region within range of precision-guided cruise and ballistic missiles. This regional A2/AD threat also severely mitigates the ability of U.S. forces to conduct operations in the Asia-Pacific."[155] "China has engaged in subtler activities, such as harassing U.S. ships and aircraft with nonmilitary means, which allow it to maintain a degree of deniability and discourage a U.S. response…China has made significant political and territorial gains without crossing the threshold…"[156]

Exploiting Existing Gaps: China has exploited existing gaps without triggering immediate concern. (i) China initially chose to focus on leveraging its economic power "to build influence in Africa, Central Asia, and Southeast Asia" and Iran, North Korea, and Sudan. (ii) China is trying to shape the rules governing this new technology in favor of its own companies. (iii) China promulgates the Chinese view of Internet regulation by pushing the notion of cyber-sovereignty. (iv) Naval vessels' freedom of navigation is enshrined in international law, but China argues about it.[157] China benefits greatly from the United Nations as a permanent member of UN Security Council allowing it to help set the international agenda and block resolutions it disagrees with. "The World Bank has lent China tens of billions of dollars for domestic infrastructure projects. The World Trade Organization (WTO), which China joined in 2001, dramatically opened up the country's access to foreign markets, leading to a surge in exports that drove a decade plus of impressive economic growth. China wants to alter parts of global order.

Made in China 2025 is a strategic plan of China issued by the Chinese cabinet in 2015 as a blueprint to upgrade the manufacturing capabilities of Chinese industries including Information Technology, Robotics, Green energy & green vehicles, Aerospace equipment, Ocean engineering and high-tech ships, Railway equipment, Power equipment, New materials, Medicine and medical devices, and Agriculture machinery. The goals of Made in China 2025 include increasing the Chinese-domestic content of core materials to 40 percent by 2020 and 70 percent by 2025. It is an initiative to comprehensively upgrade Chinese industry, to be directly competitive with the United States, by investing $300 billion US dollars to achieve this plan. "U.S. President Donald Trump and his administration has a strong concern over the potential threat of Made in China 2025 on U.S. economy and national security, therefore he urged China to stop the whole plan, and put import tariffs on products which are listed. As a result, Chinese government downplayed the plan and seek to revise the list in 2018, hoping to loosen the trade tension between U.S. and China."[158]

"China is unabashedly undermining *the U.S. alliance system* in Asia. It has encouraged the Philippines to distance itself from the United States, it has supported South Korea's efforts to take a softer line toward North Korea, and it has backed Japan's stance against American protectionism. It is building offensive military systems capable of controlling the sea and air-space within the so-called first island chain and of projecting power past the second. It is blatantly militarizing the South China Sea, no longer relying on fishing vessels or domestic law enforcement agencies to exercise its conception of sovereignty. It has even started engaging in military activities outside Asia, including establishing its first overseas base, in Djibouti. All these moves suggest one thing: China...seeks to directly challenge its position in the Indo-Pacific region."[159]

In telecommunication, "China has been violating an agreement with the United States aimed at stopping cyber espionage through the hacking of government and corporate data."[160] U.S. authorities also assert that Huawei "retained control of Skycom, using it to sell telecom equipment to Iran and move money out via the international Banking system."[161] The Chinese government accesses "to massive citizen databases, state control over media, and lack of privacy rights and other individual freedoms, may create new forms of digital authoritarianism...exploit AI for military and political uses." China uses facial recognition technology to develop a hyper-surveillance system able to monitor and target its ethnic minorities, including the Muslim Uighur population."[162] A serious violation of human rights!

U.S.-China Trade Talks: Washington considers Chinese trade practices as establishing an unfair advantage for Chinese producers, which is a reasonable topic for discussion and negotiation. "But such negotiations are also a powerful alternative strategy for dealing with China's potential emergence as a global power. For Beijing, the buildup in the South China Sea is an attempt to break out of the ring of islands surrounding the sea and, therefore, undermine a geographic advantage the U.S. would have if it chose to blockade China...If China broke out of the South China Sea, it could become a Pacific threat." "China is heavily dependent on exports, which account for roughly one-fifth of its gross domestic product – possibly more given doubts over the accuracy of Chinese GDP figures. About 18 percent of Chinese exports are destined for the United States. In contrast, U.S. exports to China account for only about 0.5 percent of U.S. GDP. This is classic asymmetric warfare. China is far more dependent on its exports to the United States than the United States is on exports to China. Certainly, some Americans will be hurt by a trade war, but the U.S. as a whole is much less vulnerable than China is. The U.S. has therefore found a way to threaten vital Chinese interests without threatening war." The new strategy is to intimidate adversary, threaten to carry out military action, and then resort to economic warfare by initiating or extending sanctions or a blockade.[163]

Russia: (a) ***Russia annexed Crimea*** in 2014. "The U.S. had submitted a UN Security Council resolution declaring the referendum illegal; it was vetoed by Russia on March 15 with China abstaining and the other 13 Security Council members voting for the resolution…On March 24, 2014, the U.S. and its allies in the G8 political forum suspended Russia's membership thereof…From March 2014 to 2016, six rounds of sanctions were imposed by the US, as well as by the EU, and some other countries allied to the U.S…The end of 2014 saw the passage by the US of the Ukraine Freedom Support Act of 2014, aimed at depriving certain Russian state firms of Western financing and technology while also providing $350 million in arms and military equipment to Ukraine, and the imposition by the US President's executive order of yet another round of sanctions…relations between Russia and the U.S. that denounced Russia's actions were in 2014 said to be at their worst since the end of the Cold War."[164]

(b) ***Russian military intervention in Syria***: "On September 30, 2015, Russia began the air campaign in Syria on the side of the Syrian government headed by president Bashar al-Assad of Syria…Three weeks into the Russian campaign in Syria, on October 20, 2015, Russian president Vladimir Putin met Bashar Assad in Moscow to discuss their joint military campaign and a future political settlement in Syria, according to the Kremlin report of the event. The meeting provoked a sharp condemnation from the White House… While one of the original aims of the Russian leadership may have been normalization of the relationship with the U.S. and the West at large, the resultant situation in Syria was said in October 2015 to be a proxy war between Russia and the U.S."[165] By the end of 2017, Russia produced significant gains for the Syrian government.

(c) ***Russian Hacking in the U.S. 2016 Elections***: "The Russian government interfered in the 2016 U.S. presidential election with the goal of harming the campaign of Hillary Clinton, boosting the candidacy of Donald Trump, and increasing political or social discord in the United States. Russia's covert activities were first publicly disclosed by members of the United States Congress on September 22, 2016, confirmed by the United States Intelligence Community on October 7, 2016, and further detailed by the Director of National Intelligence office three months later. According to U.S. intelligence agencies, the operation was ordered directly by Russian President Vladimir Putin. Former FBI director Robert Mueller led the Special Counsel investigation into the interference from May 2017 to March 2019…The Special Counsel's report, made public on April 18, 2019, examined numerous contacts between the Trump campaign and Russian officials but concluded that there was insufficient evidence to bring any conspiracy or coordination charges against Trump."[166] The U.S. can do little militarily in eastern Ukraine or Crimea, but has organized painful sanctions against Russia and made clear that additional sanctions are possible.

Iran and North Korea: *Denuclearization of Iran*: "The Iran nuclear deal framework was a preliminary framework agreement reached in 2015 between the Islamic Republic of Iran and a group of world powers: the P5+1 (the permanent members of the United Nations Security Council—the United States, the United Kingdom, Russia, France, and China—plus Germany) and the European Union…On July 14, 2015, the Joint Comprehensive Plan of Action between Iran and the P5+1 and EU, a comprehensive agreement based on the April 2015 framework, was announced. On May 8, 2018, United States President Donald Trump announced the United States was withdrawing from the deal."[167] In May 2019, Washington declared the sanction on Iranian oil exports in order to stop its nuclear development in line with North Korea. As economic containments are used to China, the U.S. has applied a similar approach to Ira.

North Korean Denuclearization: U.S. President Donald Trump met North Korean leader Kim Jung Un two times in June 2018 and February 2019. Trump and Kim's second summit, "held in Victnam, collapses after the leaders disagree over sanctions relief and denuclearization. Trump says Kim agreed to dismantle the nuclear and fissile material production facilities at Yongbyon in exchange for complete sanctions relief, but the U.S. president wanted more substantial steps on denuclearization and verification. North Korean officials dispute Trump's account, saying Kim demanded only partial sanctions relief. Both leaders leave Vietnam early, without signing a planned joint statement, but indicate talks will continue. Trump says they parted on friendly terms, while North Korea's foreign ministry warns it will not change its position."[168]

Trump Administration may consider several alternatives that North Korea to take. (i) The complete, verifiable, inconvertible denuclearization (CVID) that is the best option to be achieved in this negotiation. (ii) Regime change: If North Korea does not give up nuclear arsenals, the change of regime could be an option that could happen by internal uprising. (iii) Military operations: This may be the last option to be taken since it might cause war on the Korean peninsula. (iv) The U.S. allows Kim to maintain part of his nuclear arsenal while perhaps dismantling his ICBM program to reduce the direct threat to U.S. national security, which might be the worst choice. To save his bid for reelection "Trump might resort to radical solutions in nuclear diplomacy — war with Iran and/or an agreement with North Korea well short of complete denuclearization. As a proud disrupter, Trump is exactly the kind of president who just might be tempted by these unorthodox, radical outcomes."[169] If the regime is not changed, the military option might be a possible choice to be taken. The United States, in concert with the United Nations, introduced strict sanctions to limit Pyongyang's nuclear program. It even seized a North Korean cargo ship that allegedly was used to violate sanctions.[170]

The New Containment: Michael Mandelbaum writes that three have launched active efforts to revise security arrangements in *Foreign Affairs* 98(2). "Russia has invaded Crimea and other parts of Ukraine and has tried covertly to destabilize European democracies. China has built artificial island fortresses in inter-national waters, claimed vast swaths of the western Pacific, and moved to organize Eurasia economically in ways favorable to Beijing. And... Iran has expanded its influence over much of Iraq, Lebanon, Syria, and Yemen and is pursuing nuclear weapons."[171]

(a) *Stronger Together*: "(i) In Europe, ground troops are needed to deter Russian aggression. The Putin regime has already sent forces into Georgia and Ukraine. The United States is committed to protecting its NATO allies. These include the Baltic states, tiny countries on Russia's border. By defending them, the United States could encounter some of the same difficulties it did defending West Berlin, including, in the worst case, having to decide whether to bring nuclear weapons into play rather than accept military defeat. (ii) East Asia requires a robust U.S. naval presence to fend off China's campaign to dominate the western Pacific. The United States is committed to protecting allies such as Japan, South Korea, and Taiwan and maintaining open sea-lanes, and it conducts what it calls "freedom-of-navigation operations" in international waters newly claimed by China to make clear that the rest of the world does not accept Chinese claims and Chinese dominance there. (iii) And in the Middle East, American naval and air forces are needed to safeguard shipments of Persian Gulf oil to Europe and Asia and to support a successful rollback of the Iranian nuclear program, should that become necessary." In history, "Working with partners exploits Washington's greatest strength: its ability to attract allies and create powerful coalitions against isolated opponents."

(b) *Making It Official*: The United States joined with the Soviet Union to defeat the Nazis and then aligned with Mao Zedong's China to defeat the Soviet Union. "Post-Soviet Russia would have been a natural partner for the West. But Moscow was needlessly alienated from its logical geopolitical partnership by NATO expansion, which brought foreign armies to its doorstep over its objections. At this point, all three revisionist regimes rely for domestic support on nationalist hostility to the United States specifically and Western democracies more generally and reject being part of a U.S.-led coalition. Fortunately, Russia is much weaker than the Soviet Union, China is restrained by both deterrence and the knowledge that military conflict would damage its economy, and Iran is a regional power. So the United States can afford to pursue the containment of all three simultaneously (so long as it does so as part of robust coalitions)." "Cold War containment was an open-ended policy with a hoped-for eventual outcome. The same will be true for the new version...A well-executed policy of containment could increase the chances of disruption by creating an external context."

(c) ***Beware of Free Riders***: The biggest obstacles to a new policy of containment come, ironically, not from the countries doing the containing. "(i) In Europe, although all countries are wary of Russia, some are more so than others. Those closest to Russia's borders most strongly support an enhanced Western military presence. Years of crisis over Europe's common currency, meanwhile, have taken a political toll, increased intra-European tensions, and made cooperation of all kinds more difficult. The continuing Brexit drama will only compound the problems. (ii) In Asia, the Philippines and South Korea have sometimes taken a more benign view of Chinese power than other countries in the region. And among those agreeing on the need to check Chinese ambitions (including Australia, India, Indonesia, and Japan), developing common policies is difficult because they are an amorphous, heterogeneous group. (iii) In the Middle East, crucial American allies, such as Qatar (which hosts a U.S. air base) and Saudi Arabia, are sharply at odds. The government of Turkey, a member of NATO, identifies with the Muslim Brotherhood, which Egypt and Saudi Arabia regard as a mortal enemy. Ironically, the one unproblematic member of the anti-Iran coalition is Israel, a country that for decades was anathematized as the root of all the problems in the Middle East but that is now recognized as a dependable counterweight to Persian power." All coalitions encounter free-rider problems, and the dominant members usually pay more.

(d) ***Will America Lead***?: "The skepticism has deepened because of the county's recent misadventures abroad. The interventions in Afghanistan, Iraq, and Libya turned out poorly, and the public has little taste for more. This view has much to recommend it. But it need not threaten the prospects of a new containment, because that course is quite different from the failed crusades of recent decades. Those involved efforts to transform the internal politics and economies of weak states. Containment involves the opposite, checking the external conduct of strong states. If national leaders can appreciate and explain the difference, they may be able to bring the public along. The resurgence of populism, finally, makes any such project more difficult. The essence of populism is hostility to elites, and the design and conduct of foreign policy are elite activities. The foreign policy establishment favors a robust American role in the world." "Washington might forgo leading coalitions to contain the three revisionist powers, in which case their strength will increase. Emboldened by the American abdication, they may grow aggressive and try to coerce their neighbors. Those neighbors currently rely on the American nuclear arsenal to protect them; if they come to doubt the credibility of American security guarantees, they may follow Israel and opt to develop or acquire their own arsenals in order to protect themselves. An American retreat would thus make the world more dangerous and nuclear proliferation more likely." Americans have been able to pay less attention to its foreign policy than other nationals.

Michael Mandelbaum also published *The Rise and Fall of Peace on Earth* in 2019 consisting of four chapters. (i) Europe - The Loss of Peace: "What brought Russia and China together was not a common ideology but a parallel interest. Central Asia aside, neither played a significant role in the other's home region: Russia was a minor presence in Asia; China was economically but not strategically significant in Europe. In Asia, however, China, like Russia in Europe, was mounting a challenge to the political and military arrangements in place at the end of the Cold War...As Russia had done in Europe, China put an end to the post-Cold War peace in Asia."[172]

(ii) East Asia: The Commercial Peace: "The claim of the American military deployments in the Asia-Pacific region on the public purse had to compete not only with programs providing direct benefits to American taxpayers and voters but also with similar military and diplomatic efforts in other parts of the world. The coalition that opposed Russia's revisionist aspirations in Europe depended on American military power, as did the one opposed to China's ambitions in Asia. Placing even greater strain on foreign policy was a comparable role in yet a third region of the world. There, as in the other two, a revisionist power sought military and political supremacy at the expense of countries aligned with, and that depended on, the United States. That the third region was the Middle East."[173]

(iii) The Middle East: The Hegemonic Truce: "The Middle East after the post-Cold War peace differed from Europe and East Asia in yet another way: the extent to which countries outside the region became involved in its affairs. The United States was active in all three; but despite the budding Sino-Russian friendship China had little impact on the international relations of Europe, and Russia had virtually none on East Asia, although, like the other countries of the region, it bordered on the Pacific Ocean. By intervening in the Syrian civil war, Russia inserted itself into the Middle East, and China had major economic interests there, even without a military presence, because of the region's oil and because Beijing hoped to include Iran in its One Belt One Road project."[174]

(iv) Peace Regained?: "The post-Cold War peace ended because three countries brought security competition back to their regions by adopting foreign policies of aggressive nationalism. Yet nationalism by itself does not explain the end of peace...Their abandonment of peaceful policies, leading to the destruction of the post-Cold War peace, coincided with the rise of a serious domestic problem for their governments: the loss, both actual and prospective, of public support for the ruling regime." "The rest of the world has a great deal at stake in whether the three revisionist powers that ended the peace in their respective regions acquire political systems that would lead to its restoration; but beyond working to make their own democratic political systems attractive models, other countries can do very little to assist the force of democracy in Russia, China, and Iran."[175]

The Resurgence of Realism with Nationalism: Stephen M. Walt, who writes on "The End of Hubris and the New Age of American Restraint" *Foreign Affairs* 98(3), analyzes the current status of U.S. Foreign policy and suggests a new strategy to maximize national interests.[176] According to Walt, "Today's world presents a seemingly endless array of challenges: a more powerful and assertive China, novel threats from cyberspace, a rising tide of refugees, resurgent xenophobia, persistent strands of violent extremism, climate change, and many more. But the more complex the global environment, the more Washington needs clear thinking about its vital interests and foreign policy priorities. Above all, a successful U.S. grand strategy must identify where the United States should be prepared to wage war, and for what purposes...A quarter century ago, after the Cold War ended, foreign policy elites abandoned realism in favor of an unrealistic grand strategy - liberal hegemony - that has weakened the country and caused considerable harm at home and abroad. To get back on track, Washington should return to the realism and restraint that served it so well in the past."

(a) *If It Ain't Broke*: As the Soviet Union collapsed, "U.S. leaders rejected the realism that had worked well for decades and tried to remake global politics in accordance with American values. A new strategy—liberal hegemony—sought to spread democracy and open markets across the globe. That goal is the common thread linking President Bill Clinton's policy of 'engagement and enlargement,' President George W. Bush's 'freedom agenda,' and President Barack Obama's embrace of the Arab revolts of 2010–11 and his declaration that 'there is no right more fundamental than the ability to choose your leaders and determine your destiny.' Such thinking won broad support from both political parties, the federal bureaucracies that deal with international affairs, and most of the think tanks, lobbies, and media figures that constitute the foreign policy establishment. At bottom, liberal hegemony is a highly revisionist strategy." Nonetheless, "The results were dismal: failed wars, financial crises, staggering inequality, frayed alliances, and emboldened adversaries."

(b) *Hegemonic Hubris*: "The United States was not solely responsible for all these adverse developments, but it played a major role in most of them. And the taproot of many of these failures was Washington's embrace of liberal hegemony. For starters, that strategy expanded U.S. security obligations without providing new resources with which to meet them. The policy of dual containment, aimed at Iran and Iraq, forced the United States to keep thousands of troops on the Arabian Peninsula, an additional burden that also helped convince Osama bin Laden to strike at the U.S. homeland. NATO expansion committed Washington to defend weak and vulnerable new members, even as France, Germany, and the United Kingdom let their military forces atrophy. Equally important, U.S. efforts to promote democracy, the open-ended expansion of NATO, and the extension of the alliance's mission far beyond its original parameters poisoned relations with Russia. And fear of U.S.-led regime change encouraged several states to pursue a nuclear deterrent—in the case of North Korea, successfully. When the United States did manage to topple a foreign foe, as it did in Afghanistan, Iraq, and Libya, the results were not thriving new democracies but costly occupations, failed states, and hundreds of thousands of dead civilians. It was delusional for U.S. leaders to expect otherwise: creating a functional democracy is a difficult process under the best of circumstances but trying to do it in fractured societies one barely under-stands is a fool's errand. Finally, globalization did not deliver as promised. Opening up markets to trade and investment brought great benefits to lower and middle classes in China, India, and other parts of the developing world. It also further magnified the already staggering wealth of the world's richest one percent. But lower- and middle-class incomes in the United States and Europe remained flat, jobs in some sectors there fled abroad, and the global financial system became much more fragile."

(c) ***Realism in Practice***: "Today, there is no potential regional hegemon in Europe, whose states should gradually take full responsibility for their own defense. The countries of the European Union are home to more than 500 million people and boast a combined annual GDP exceeding $17 trillion, whereas Russia—the main external threat to EU states—has a population of just 144 million and an annual GDP of only $1.6 trillion." The United States is no more the first line of EU defender. "As an offshore balancer, the United States would establish normal relations with all countries in the region, instead of having special relationships with a few states and profoundly hostile relations with others. No country in the Middle East is so virtuous or vital that it deserves unconditional U.S. support, and no country there is so heinous that it must be treated as a pariah. The United States should act as China, India, Japan, Russia, and the EU do, maintaining normal working relationships with all states in the region—including Iran. Among other things, this policy would encourage rival regional powers to compete for U.S. support, instead of taking it for granted."

With its relationships with Europe and the Middle East right-sized and rationalized, an offshore-balancing United States could focus primarily on China. "If China's power continues to grow, it is likely to press its neighbors to distance themselves from Washington and accept China as the dominant power in the Asia-Pacific. Were China to become a regional hegemon in Asia, it would be better positioned to project power around the world and extend its influence into the Western Hemisphere. To counter this possibility, the United States should maintain and deepen its current security ties with Australia, Japan, the Philippines, and South Korea and continue to nurture its strategic partnerships with India, Singapore, and Vietnam. Once the United States is no longer subsidizing its wealthy European allies or squandering trillions of dollars on costly quagmires in the greater Middle East, it can more readily afford the military capabilities…to balance China."

(d) *Offshore Venture*: "As an offshore balancer, the United States would be deeply engaged diplomatically, economically, and, in some areas, militarily. It would still possess the world's mightiest armed forces, even if it spent somewhat less money on them. The United States would continue to work with other countries to address major global issues such as climate change, terrorism, and cyber-threats. But Washington would no longer assume primary responsibility for defending wealthy allies that can defend themselves, no longer subsidize client states whose actions undermine U.S. interests, and no longer try to spread democracy via regime change, covert action, or economic pressure. Instead, Washington would use its strength primarily to uphold the balance of power in Asia—where a substantial U.S. presence is still needed—and would devote more time, attention, and resources to restoring the foundations of U.S. power at home. By setting an example that others would once again admire and seek to emulate, an offshore-balancing United States would also do a better job of promoting the political values that Americans espouse."

(e) *Out with the Old*: "Consider the officials responsible for the bungled Middle East peace process, the misguided expansion of NATO, the botched wars in Afghanistan and Iraq, the CIA's torture of detainees in the war on terrorism, the National Security Agency's warrantless surveillance of Americans, the disastrous NATO intervention in Libya, and the American machinations in Ukraine that gave Russia a pretext to seize Crimea. None of those officials or commentators has suffered significant professional penalties for his or her mistakes or malfeasance…Despite the stagnation within the foreign policy establishment, the prospects for a more realist, more restrained U.S. foreign policy are better today than they have been in many years. For all his flaws, Trump has made it easier to propose alternatives to liberal hegemony by expressing such disdain for the elite consensus. Younger Americans are more skeptical of their country's imperial pretensions than are their elders…"

"Furthermore, powerful structural forces are working against liberal hegemony and in favor of offshore balancing. China's rise and the partial revival of Russian power are forcing the United States to pay closer attention to balance-of-power politics, especially in Asia. The intractable problems of the Middle East will make future presidents reluctant to squander more blood and treasure there—especially in chasing the siren song of democracy promotion. Pressure on the defense budget is unlikely to diminish, especially once the costs of climate change begin to bite, and because trillions of dollars' worth of domestic needs cry out for attention. For these reasons, the foreign policy elite will eventually rediscover the grand strategy that helped build and sustain American power over most of the nation's history."

The New Nationalism: *Foreign Affairs* (March/April 2019) covers the new nationalism with several essays from which four essays are selected to review its various aspects. The magazine's editor Gideon Rose writes that "The nation-state is so dominant today that it seems natural. But no political arrangements are natural, and any concept with a hyphen has a fault line running through it by definition. States are sovereign political structures. Nations are unified social groups. What does each owe the other?"[177]

(a) **REIVEW** *Why Nationalism Works?* (Andreas Wimmer)[178] (i) Civic versus Ethnic: Civic nationalism considers all citizens, regardless of their cultural background, count as members of the nation; while ethnic nationalism is that ancestry and language determine national identity. "Yet efforts to draw a hard line between good, civic patriotism and bad, ethnic nationalism overlook the common roots of both. Patriotism is a form of nationalism. They are ideological brothers, not distant cousins. At their core, all forms of nationalism share the same two tenets: first, that members of the nation, understood as a group of equal citizens with a shared history and future political destiny, should rule the state…second, that they should do so in the interests of the nation. Nationalism is thus opposed to foreign rule."

(ii) The Nation Is Born: "The doctrine of nationalism—rule in the name of a nationally defined people—spread gradually across the globe. Over the next two centuries, empire after empire dissolved into a series of nation-states." "Europe's competitive and war-prone multistate system drove rulers to extract ever more taxes from their populations and to expand the role of commoners in the military. This, in turn, gave commoners leverage to demand from their rulers increased political participation, equality before the law, and better provision of public goods. In the end, a new compact emerged: that rulers should govern in the population's interests, and that as long as they did so, the ruled owed them political loyalty, soldiers, and taxes. Nationalism at once reflected and justified this new compact. It held that the rulers and the ruled both belonged to the same nation and thus shared a common historical origin and future political destiny. Political elites would look after the interests of the common people rather than those of their dynasty." "As the nation-states of Western Europe and the United States came to dominate the international system, ambitious elites around the world sought to match the West's economic and military power by emulating its nationalist political model." Nationalism was also attractive for the common people, because the nation-state offered a better exchange relationship with the government than any previous model of statehood had.

(iii) The Benefits of Nationalism: Democracy flourished where national identity was able to supersede other identities, such as those centered on religious, ethnic, or tribal communities. "Nationalism provided the answer to the classic boundary question of democracy…By limiting the franchise to members of the nation and excluding foreigners from voting, democracy and nationalism entered an enduring marriage." "Nationalism also helped establish modern welfare states. A sense of mutual obligation and shared political destiny popularized the idea that members of the nation…should support one another in times of hardship. The first modern welfare state was created in Germany during the late nineteenth century at the behest of the conservative chancellor Otto von Bismarck."

(iv) Bloody Banners: "Globally, the rise of nationalism has increased the frequency of war: over the last two centuries, the foundation of the first nationalist organization in a country has been associated with an increase in the yearly probability of that country experiencing a full-scale war, from an average of 1.1 percent to an average of 2.5 percent." "Ethnic cleansing is perhaps the most egregious form of nationalist violence, but it is relatively rare. More frequent are civil wars, fought either by nationalist minorities who wish to break away from an existing state or between ethnic groups competing to dominate a newly independent state."

(v) Inclusive and Exclusive: "Whether the configuration of power in a specific country developed in a more inclusive or exclusive direction is a matter of history, stretching back before the rise of the modern nation-state. Inclusive ruling coalitions—and a correspondingly encompassing national-ism—have tended to arise in countries with a long history of centralized, bureaucratic statehood. Today, such states are better able to provide their citizens with public goods. This makes them more attractive as alliance partners for ordinary citizens, who shift their political loyalty away from ethnic, religious, and tribal leaders and toward the state, allowing for the emergence of more diverse political alliances. A long history of centralized statehood also fosters the adoption of a common language, which again makes it easier to build political alliances across ethnic divides. Finally, in countries where civil society developed early, multiethnic alliances for promoting shared interests have been more likely to emerge, leading to multiethnic ruling elites and more encompassing national identities."

(vi) Building a Better Nationalism: "Western governments should develop public goods projects that benefit people of all colors, regions, and class backgrounds, thereby avoiding the toxic perception of ethnic or political favoritism. Reassuring working-class, economically marginalized populations…might go a long way toward reducing the appeal of resentment -driven, anti-immigrant populism." It is unclear if transnational institutions such as the European Union will ever be able to assume the core functions of national governments. "The challenge for both old and new nation-states is to renew the national contract between the rulers and the ruled by building inclusive coalitions that tie the two together. Benign forms of popular nationalism follow from political inclusion. They cannot be imposed by ideological policing from above, nor by attempting to educate citizens about what they should regard as their true interests."

(b) **REVIEW** *False Flags: The Myth of the Nationalist Resurgence* (Jan-Werner Muller):[179] (i) The People and the Nation: In the past few years, what have seen is not the rise of nationalism but the rise of one variant of it: nationalist populism. Nationalism and populism are often conflated, but they differ. Nationalism is the idea that cultural communities should possess their own states and loyalty to fellow nationals ought to trump other obligations. Populists criticize sitting governments and other parties.

(ii) Populism is not a doctrine; "From the late 1990s until his death in 2013, the Venezuelan populist leader Hugo Chávez created a disastrous socialism for the twenty-first century in his country, wrecking its economy and demonizing all of his opponents in the process. Today's right-wing populists mostly draw on nationalist ideas, such as distrust of international institutions, economic protectionism, and hostility to the idea of providing development aid to other countries."

(iii) Don't Believe the Hype: The potent combination of nationalism and populism has spread in recent years. It appears that nationalist populists have profited from a bitter backlash against globalization and increasing cultural diversity. "This has become the conventional wisdom not only among populists themselves but also among academics and liberal opponents of populism." Although critics often charge populists with peddling reductive messages, "it is these same critics who now grasp at simple explanations for populism's rise. In doing so, many liberal observers play right into their opponents' hands by taking at face value and even amplifying the dubious stories that nationalist populists tell about their own success."

(iv) Not every fight is cultural: "Once in power, most nationalist populists don't actually work to take back control on the people's behalf, as they promised to do. Instead, they perform a sort of nationalist pantomime of largely symbolic gestures: for example, promising to build walls (which achieve nothing concrete other than inciting hatred against minorities) or occasionally having the state seize a multinational company. Behind the scenes, such leaders are generally quite accommodating of international institutions and multinational corporations. They are concerned less with reasserting their countries' autonomy than with appearing to do so."

(v) Beat them, don't join them: "This argument may sound like liberal wishful thinking: People are not nearly as nationalist as populists claim! Conflicts are really all about material interests and not about culture! But the point is not that fights over culture and identity are illusory or illegitimate just because populists always happen to promote them. Rather, the point is that establishment institutions are too quickly turning to culture and identity to explain politics. In this way, they are playing into populists' hands." Populists attack globalists but nationalist populists cynically exploit them in order to weaken democratic institutions and lump together advocates of globalization, transnational tax evaders, and like.

(c) **REVIEW** *Building a Better Nationalism* (Yael Tamir):[180] "For most political thinkers and elites in the developed West, nationalism is a dangerous, divisive, illiberal impulse that should be treated with skepticism or even outright disdain. Yes, nationalism helped give rise to the modern state system, served as a liberating force in anticolonial independence struggles, and fueled anti-Soviet sentiment during the Cold War." In *The Virtue of Nationalism* (2018), Yoram Hazony presents "a spirited defense of nationalism and the nation-state. Although he does not ignore nationalism's flaws, he rightly contends that Western intellectuals have been too quick to dismiss it and that the topic deserves a more balanced and nuanced analysis than what the academy has offered in recent years."

(i) Liberal or Imperial?: "A nation…is constituted of a number of tribes with a common language or religion, and a past history of acting as a body. A nation offers the best, most legitimate basis for a state, he argues, because it allows for the realization of the human aspiration to achieve self-rule and collective freedom in the fullest and most satisfactory way. Nation-states represent durable political unions that confer meaning on their individual members, celebrating and giving voice to what Hazony calls the particular. Giving such nations the ability to govern themselves promotes a healthy competition that inspires them to excel, opening up new opportunities for fellow nationals while allowing the international community…to prosper."

"Imperialism, he notes, produced the greatest destroyers the earth has known, with moderns such as Napoleon, Hitler and Stalin not least among them. Hazony is right that many empires have been driven by universal ideologies that turned oppressive. Yet he ignores the vast and often brutal imperial and colonial enterprises launched by nation-states, such as Belgium, England, Portugal, and Spain. This leaves the reader with the odd idea that, by their very nature, nation-states are bound to live happily within their borders, never looking to expand or conquer. If that were true, the reputation of nationalism would be much easier to defend."

Hazony confuses the liberal belief in internationalism with a desire to erect political empires. "In reality, the nation-state has no serious institutional competitors. International organizations are weak and ineffective; international corporations are powerful and effective but have no desire to spend their energy on governing. The struggle that Hazony describes between noble nationalists and hate-filled imperialists is largely a fantasy. What does exist is a tension between nationalism and neoliberal globalism. Nationalism, in this context, is a theory not just about self-rule but also about the right of states to intervene in the market in order to defend their citizens and control the malignant effects of hyperglobalism: bringing jobs back home, supporting domestic production, limiting immigration, and raising tariffs. Such policies collide with liberal beliefs in the primacy of free trade and the free movement of people. The real debate between nationalists and globalists is less about identity than about economics." Until recently, this debate seemed to have been settled in favor of globalism. "But recently, national preferences have exploded into full view. The anger over the economic and social outcomes of neoliberal globalism has stirred a populist backlash, some of which has taken on a nationalist bent. Consequently, politicians on both sides of the Atlantic are competing for popular support by claiming to represent the people and by blaming elites for adopting self-serving policies. Critics accuse these newly minted nationalists of racism and nativism and of grounding their appeals in fears of the other." Moreover, "The nationalist resurgence is not solely a right-wing phenomenon. Progressive and left-wing leaders and voters are becoming more openly comfortable with policies that have a distinctly nationalist flavor."

(ii) A Kinder, Gentler Nationalism: "The kind of semantic acrobatics Macron performed would be unnecessary if he and other liberals were willing to openly embrace some forms of nationalism. After all, it is only natural for political leaders to look at global issues from a national perspective and to put their own countries' interests first. Macron and German Chancellor Angela Merkel endorse a pro-EU position as they identify their countries' national interests with membership in the union and with a measured degree of regional and global collaboration. The government of British Prime Minister Theresa May holds the opposite view and therefore supports Brexit. Slogans aside, Trump makes similar calculations, operating from a belief that the United States benefits less than it should from those global agreements he wants to renegotiate. And on the other side of the globe, Chinese President Xi Jinping has developed the One Belt, One Road initiative, which seeks to tie together vast swaths of the Eastern Hemisphere in a Chinese-dominated network of infrastructure and supply chains: a nationalist project with a globalist twist."

The main struggle in international politics is "not between nationalists and imperialists but between different approaches to balancing national interests with the demands of a globalized economy. When liberals indiscriminately attack all forms of nationalism, they fuel an unnecessary ideological struggle…If liberalism is to regain power, it needs to develop its own form of nationalism, one that reassures citizens that their leaders work for them and put their well-being first." In conclusion, "For too long, the least well-off citizens of powerful states have paid the price of globalism. Their demand that leaders protect their interests is just and timely. One need not embrace Trump's crude, zero-sum worldview to believe that the wealth of nations should be produced and distributed as part of a relatively narrow social contract among particular individuals. Liberals should not promote national egoism but support policies that will help make their fellow citizens feel connected and committed to a worthy and meaningful community. Liberalism and nationalism are not mutually exclusive."

(d) **REVIEW** *Blood for Soil* (Fars-Erik Cederman):[181] "In 2016, British voters chose to leave the EU out of a belief that the post-national vision… undermined British sovereignty and threatened to overwhelm the United Kingdom with immigrants from Africa, the Middle East, and the less developed parts of Europe." Moreover, Donald Trump tapped into fears that the United States was being invaded by Mexicans and Muslims.

(i) It's Back: "At the end of the Cold War, there were warning signs that ethnic conflict might return. But at the time, any fear of that actually happening seemed unwarranted…despite the violence in the former Yugoslavia and in Rwanda, the frequency of ethnic conflict had actually decreased since the mid-1990s. Pointing to inclusive policies and pragmatic compromises that had prevented and resolved ethnic conflicts…the trend toward peace would continue…Globalization was transforming the world." And ethnic conflict is far less common than it was three decades ago.

(ii) The Road to Violence: "Rising ethnic nationalism leads to conflict in several different ways. The key variable…is access to power. When ethnic groups lack it, they are especially likely to seek it through violence. Oftentimes in multiethnic states, elites of a particular group come to dominate the government and exclude other, weaker groups, even if the leaders' own group represents a minority of the country's population.

(iii) The Path to Peace: It may be tempting to see "ethnic nationalism as part of the solution rather than the problem. Instead of trying to resist such urges, the thinking goes, one should encourage them, since they are likely to bring political borders in line with national borders, thus eliminating the grievances at the root of the problem. Some scholars, such as Edward Luttwak, have even recommended that ethnic groups simply be allowed to fight it out, arguing that the short-term pain of war is worth the long-term benefit of the stability that comes when ethnic dominance replaces ethnic diversity. Yet as the case of Syria has shown, such harsh strategies tend to perpetuate resentment, not consolidate peace."

(iv) Containing Nationalism: Nationalism should therefore be contained, not abolished. And to truly contain ethnic nationalism, governments will have to address its deeper causes, not just its immediate effects. Both supply and demand—that is, the willingness of governments to implement ethno-nationalist policies and the appetite for such policies among populations—will have to be decreased. Within international organizations, governments must defend core liberal values more strenuously. Ethnic nationalism tends to attract the most support from those who have been disadvantaged by globalization and *laissez-faire* capitalism." Populists may exploit growing socioeconomic inequalities between centers and peripheries. However, the answer to ethnic nationalism goes beyond narrow economic fixes; political elites must argue "for ethnic tolerance and supranational cooperation, portraying them as matters of basic human decency and security."

5. Which Power Will Run the World?

Since the collapse of the Soviet Union in 1991, the United States has been the unipolar power controlling international affairs economically and strategically. However, the rising China has challenged the U.S. supremacy; Russia annexed Crimea in 2014 and intervened in Syria in 2015; Iran and North Korea have developed nuclear weapons threatening world peace; and Great Britain voted for the withdrawal from the European Union in 2016, which raised a question: what would happen when Europe comes apart. The countries challenging the current world order must be primarily China, and secondarily Russia, Iran, and North Korea. We face two arising questions. First, whether China or other challengers are able to win the war against the United States. Second, whether the United States is able to maintain its unipolar supremacy, and for which what kind of strategies the United States should take. This section consists of four parts: (i) three book reviews on world order; (ii) An evaluation on China, Russia, Iran and North Korea; (iii) the change of world powers in the 21st century; and (iv) concluding remarks.

BOOK REVIEWS ON WORLD ORDER

BOOK REVIEW 1: World Order (Henry Kissinger, 2014): (a) *Europe: The Pluralistic International Order*: *Westphalian System* of 1648 first attempted to institutionalize an international order on the basis of agreed rule and limits and to base it on a multiplicity of powers. The balance of power was thought an improvement over the exactions of religious wars. Thomas Hobbes published his *Leviathan* in 1651 in which the social contract does not apply beyond borders of states. *The French Revolution and its Aftermath*: Imperial Russia and its power raised fundamental issues for the balance of power in Europe, and its aspirations threatened to make impossible a return to the prerevolutionary equilibrium.

(b) *The European Balance-of-Power System and its End*: In 1815 *The Congress of Vienna* was three tiers of institutions buttressed the Vienna system: the Quadruple Alliance to defeat challenges to the territorial order; the Holy Alliance to overcome threats to domestic institutions; and a concert of powers institutionalized through periodic diplomatic conferences of the heads of government of the alliance to define their common purposes or to deal with emerging crisis. The balance was the signal achievement of the Congress of Vienna. *The premises of international order*: The Congress of Vienna system began to fray under the impact of three events: the rise of nationalism, the revolution of 1848, and the Crimean War (1853-56). *Metternich and Bismarck*: Metternich considered the search for truth the most important task of the statesman and viewed that the interest of Austria was a metaphor for the overall interest of Europe; while Bismarck challenged the established wisdom of his period and pursued the German unity by combining nationalism with liberalism. *The Dilemmas of the Balance of Power*: A war arose from a series of miscalculations made by serious leaders who did not understand the consequences of their planning. The military planning ran away with diplomacy. *Legitimacy and power between the World Wars*: In the end the Versailles order achieved neither legitimacy nor equilibrium. *The postwar European order*: The traditional European balance of power had been based on the equality of its members. The Cold War international order reflected two sets of balances, which for the first time in history were largely independent of each other: the nuclear balance between the Soviet Union and the United States, and the internal balance within the Atlantic Alliance. The collapse of the Soviet Union changed the emphasis of diplomacy. *The Future of Europe*: In foreign policy, EU embraces universal ideals without the means to enforce them, and cosmopolitan identity in contention with national loyalties   with European unity accompanied by cast-west and north-south divides and an ecumenical attitude toward autonomy movements challenging the integrity of states.

   (c) ***Islamism and the Middle East: A World in Disorder***: Islam's rapid advance across three continents provided proof to the faithful of its divine mission. "Pan-Arabists accepted the premise of a state-based system. But the state they sought was a unified Arab nation, a single ethnic, linguistic, and cultural entity. By contrast, political Islam insisted on reliance on the common religion as the best vehicle for a modern Arab identity. The Islamists were often drawn from highly educated members of the new middle class. Islamism as a way to join the postwar era without having to abandon their values, to be modern without having to become Western." The conflict now is religious and geopolitical. "A Sunni bloc consisting of Saudi Arabia, the Gulf States, and to some extent Egypt and Turkey confront a block led by Shia Iran, which backs Bashar al-Assad's portion of Syria, Nuri al-Maliki's central and southern Iraq, and the militias of Hezbollah in Lebanon and Hamas in Gaza. The Sunni bloc supports uprising in Syria against Assad and in Iraq against Maliki; Iran aims for regional dominance by employing non-state actors ties to Tehran ideologically on order to undermine the domestic legitimacy of its regional rival."

   (d) ***The United States and Iran: Approaches to Order***: The peace in the Middle East has focused on the highly technical subject of nuclear weapon in Iran. "These goals reached because three conditions were met: an active American policy, the thwarting of designs seeking to establish a regional order by imposing universalist principles through violence, and the emergence of leaders with a vision of peace." Violent intimidation does challenge the hopes for world order, but when they are thwarted, there may come a moment similar to what led to the breakthroughs recounted here.

(e) *The Multiplicity of Asia*: Asia and Europe have Different concepts of balance of power. "In Asia's historic diplomatic systems, whether based on Chinese or Hindu models, monarch was considered an expression of divinity or, at the very least, a kind of paternal authority; tangible expressions of tribute were thought to be owed to superior countries by their inferiors. This theoretically left no room for ambiguity as to the nature of regional power relationship, leading to a series of rigid alignments."

The contemporary Asian order includes "outside powers as an integral feature: the United States, whose role as an Asia-Pacific power was explicitly affirmed in joint statements by U.S. President Barack Obama and Chinese President Hu Jintao in January 2011, and Chinese President Xi Jinping in June 2014. Russia, geographically an Asian power and participant in Asian groupings such as the Shanghai Cooperation Organization, even if over three-quarters of its population lives in the European portion of Russia territory." In forming the regional order, under contemporary conditions, essentially two balance of power are emerging: one in South Asia, the other in East Asia. "The United States has refrained from treating the contemporary internal South Asian balance primarily as a military problem. But it will have to be active in the diplomacy over establishing a regional order lest a vacuum is created, which would inevitably draw all surrounding countries into a regional confrontation."

(f) *Toward an Asian Order: Confrontation or Partnerships*? As a longer perspective on world order with China, "On the Chinese side, many American actions are interpreted as a design to thwart China's rise, and the American promotion of human rights is seen as a project to undermine China's domestic political structure," designed to keep China permanently in a secondary position. "On the American side, the fear is that a growing China will systematically undermine American preeminence and thus American security…Both sides are reinforced in their suspicions by the military maneuvers and defense programs of the other." Two other issues are contributing to tension in Sino-American relations. "China rejects the proposition that international order is fostered by the spread of liberal democracy and that the international community has an obligation to bring this about, and especially to achieve its perception of human rights by international action. The United States may be able to adjust the application of its views on human rights in relation to strategic priority. But…America can never abandon these principles of altogether." Deng Xiaoping said: "Their talk about human rights, freedom and democracy is designed only to safeguard the interests of the strong, rich countries, which take advantage of their strength to bully weak countries, and which pursue hegemony and practice power politics." In Asia, order must combine "a balance of power with a concept of partnership. A purely military definition of the balance will shade into confrontation." A pure partnership raises fears of hegemony.

(g) ***The United States and its Concept of Order***: Woodrow Wilson (1913-1921) pursued peace through the League of Nations, although his collective security could not prevent another world war. Franklin Roosevelt (1933-1945) "hoped for a peace based on legitimacy, that is, trust between individuals, respect for international law, humanitarian objectives, and goodwill. But confronted with the Soviet Union's insistently power-based approach, he would likely have reverted to the Machiavellian side that had brought him to leadership and made him the dominant figure of his period."

(h) ***The United States: Ambivalent Superpower***: When the Soviet Union challenged the world order, the nature of international order was at issue. Former Secretary of State George Shultz has articulated the American ambivalence wisely: "Americans, being a moral people, want their foreign policy to reflect the values we espouse as a nation. But Americans, being a practical people, also want their foreign policy to be effective."

(i) ***Technology, Equilibrium, and Human Consciousness***: The United State has been challenged with nuclear proliferation, cyber and space warfare, human factors in technology, and foreign policy in the digital era. The spread of networked digital devices will become a positive engine of history: The great human achievements of technology must be fused with enhanced powers of humane, transcendent, and geopolitical judgment.

(j) ***World Order in Our Time?*** The structure of the 21st century lacks in world order in four dimensions. (1) The nature of state itself has been subjected to a multitude of pressures: attacked and dismantled by design, in some regions corroded from neglect, often submerged by the sheer rush of events. Failed states. (2) The international economic system has become global, while the political structure of the world has remained based on the nation-state. The issues of globalization thus merged with the issues of the conduct of democratic foreign policy. (3) Economic globalization causes a conflict with political and strategic interests between nations. A contemporary structure of international rules and norms cannot merely be affirmed by point declarations; it must be fostered as a matter of common conviction. (4) American leadership has sought a balance between stability and advocacy of universal principles not always reconcilable with principles of sovereign non-interference or other nation's historical experience. The quest for that balance, between the uniqueness of the American experience and the idealistic confidence in its universality, between the poles of overconfidence and introspection, is inherently unending. What it does not permit is withdrawal. *Where Do We Go from Here?*

The reconstruction of world order is an ultimate challenge to statesmanship in our time. "For the United States, the quest for world order functions on two levels: the celebration of universal principles needs to be praised with a recognition of the reality of other regions' histories and cultures…Is it possible to translate divergent cultures into a common system?"

BOOK REVIEW 2: The Accidental Superpower (Peter Zeihan, 2014): [182] "Peter Zeihan, founder of Zeihan on Geopolitics, adds that America hit the jackpot, geopolitically speaking, inheriting '…the best lands in the world for a very low price in terms of blood, treasure, and time.' He downplays the claim that American power is declining, pointing out that in 1945, we produced one quarter of the world's gross domestic product and spent as much on the military and controlled as much naval tonnage at the rest of the world combined. The change in 2014: zero. But some things are changing. Resources are diminishing, energy prices are rising, and demographics are inverting. Baby boomers are now retiring to collect benefits paid for by a shrinking number of younger, working taxpayers. The majority of industrialized nations face financial disaster, except America, which faces only inconvenience. Thanks to fracking, oil and gas production are skyrocketing, and America could be energy independent in five years. Thanks to immigration and vast numbers of child-friendly single-family houses, Americans remain younger than nearly every major culture. Within 30 years, Zeihan predicts, some nations (Greece, Libya, Yemen) will collapse, others (Brazil, India, Canada) will shrink, some (Britain, France, Sweden) will muddle through, and a few (Russia, Germany, Japan, Turkey) will become aggressive. Self-sufficient in food and energy, America will turn inward, reverting to the role it played before World War II: a global power without global interests."[183]

"More by luck than by design, America will prosper in the coming decades while the world goes to hell, according to this eye-opening, contrarian survey of geopolitics. Geopolitical analyst Zeihan bases his predictions on accidental factors of the U.S.'s terrain (navigable rivers and rich farmland), resources (abundant shale gas and oil), demography (a relatively young, vigorous population), location (oceans that guard against invasion), and economics (vast consumer markets and cheap capital). The rest of the globe, he argues, will suffer from aging populations, dwindling resources, and the lack of a stable modern-day equivalent to the post-WWII Bretton Woods regime, which fostered free trade, protected sea lanes, and served the world's export market; the collapse of the international order will include the collapse of China, the breakup of Canada, and war in Europe. Zeihan's freewheeling, very readable analyses draw on historical examples, from ancient Egypt to modern Denmark, and a wealth of statistics, packaged with interesting maps and graphs. His generalizations can seem over-simplified, and his prognostications eccentric, such as the prediction that a 'wave of young Uzbeks will wash asunder all foolish enough to stand in their way.' Still, Zeihan's provocative take on how land, climate, energy, and population determine wealth and power makes for a stimulating challenge to conventional wisdom."[184] Zeihan writes on **the China Wars** in Chapter 14 in the same book to be summarized as follows.

Regarding the China Wars, (i) It was the American who removed Japan as a threat. Japan and China had been locked in a bilateral war for nearly five years before the American joined World War II. Japan's subsequent folding into the growing Bretton Woods network in 1955 ended Japan's imperial interest in China. (ii) World War II's conclusion radically changed the region's naval balance of power. By war's end, the Americans had wiped the Pacific clean of Japanese forces, but that was only one piece of the puzzle. While Japan was certainly the country guiltiest of suppressing the Chinese, they were far from the only one. (iii) "Bretton Woods turned out to not just be for America's Western European allies and the defeated Axis. As a part of American Cold War strategic maneuvering, the Chinese themselves were eased into the system starting in the early 1970s...China could access the global market. Instead of being raided for raw materials, China was guaranteed access to global supplies. The endless supplies of cheap labor that the Europeans and Japanese ruthlessly tapped now allowed China to generate its own goods for export, this time with the revenues flowing to the Chinese instead of overseas interests."

(a) ***Problem 1: The Financial System***: (i) The Chinese financial system subsidizes prices for finished outputs. This drives down the price of Chinese finished goods and allows their exports to displace most global competition. (ii) The Chinese financial system subsidizes the consumption for inputs. In effect, the Chinese system doesn't care whether oil costs $8 a barrel or $180 a barrel. (iii) When you don't care about prices or output or debt or quality or safety or reputation, your economic growth is truly impressive. (iv) China has expanded so much that in some sectors demand has swallowed up all that remained of several industrial commodities in the world at large, forcing its state-owned firms to venture out and invest in projects that otherwise shouldn't have happened. (v) As cheap and plentiful as Chinese capital is, it isn't available for everyone. Because the Chinese system is ultimately managed by the Communist Party and because the leaders of localities hold so much power versus the center, there is extreme collusion between bank management and the local Communist Party leaderships. (vi) "The various means of capital profusion had become so many and so lax that the government actually lost control of its own financial network." Shadow lending was exceeding all other forms of credit combined by the first quarter of 2013.

(b) ***Problem 2: Demography***: "During the period from 1979 to 2003 when one-child policy was strictly enforces, the birth rate dropped by half. That slashed everything from health care to education to food costs, but it gutted the most recent generation. After three decades of the policy, there has been a European style hollowing out of the younger segments of the population. This presents China with three unavoidable – system-killing - problems." (i) China is aging far more quickly than it is getting rich. The Chinese will pass the Americans in average age in 2019 and by 2040 will be

42.9 years old versus 39.6 for the Americans. Chinese call it the 4:2:1 problem: four parents to two parents to one child. (ii) China will never be able to move away from its current export-driven model. China appears to be succeeding somewhat in its current efforts to switch from an export-led to a consumption-led economy. But their successors are ever smaller population cohorts, so that consumption growth has never beat out investment/loan-driven activity and is now nearly played out. (iii) So too is the Chinese development model. "China has run out of surplus labor; its presence on the low-cost side of global manufacturing has run its course. This is already reflected in Chinese labor costs, which have sextupled since 2002." China faces a far darker demographic future than Japan.

(c) *Problem 3: Dependency on America*: (i) Roughly 10 percent of China's GDP depends upon direct exports to the United States. Another 5 percent of GDP is locked up in supply chains whose ultimate destination is the American market. "Should American trade access be revoked, it would be as if China suffered from an equivalent of three American Great Recessions all at once." (ii) China is now the world's largest importer of nearly everything. The most strategic of China's world's-largest is of course oil. China's oil supply lines run past a lot of rivals. Oil shipped in from the Middle East of Africa must pass by India, Myanmar, Thailand, Singapore, Vietnam, the Philippines, and Taiwan. The sea lanes are guaranteed by the U.S. navy. (iii) "Ultimately, the Americans will not be worried about China because it is a non-naval power and really not a significant threat to American power in a post-free trade world. The Japanese will face many similar constraints to the Chinese: They will need to guarantee access to their own oil supplies, raw materials, and foreign markets. But they will be different from China in two critical ways. First, on average Japan's dependency on the outside world is less than half that of the Chinese in absolute terms. Second, unlike the Chinese, the Japanese actually have a blue-water navy – the world's second most powerful. They are able to sail up and down the Chinese coast." (iv) "Even if China did have a blue-water navy, it could not use it freely. Bisecting the Chinese coastline is of course Taiwan. The biggest challenge Taiwan presents to the mainland is not its ability to make a mockery of the concept of a united China simply by its existence, but rather the fact that it is far cheaper to use a land-based military to threaten sea lanes than a sea-based military. Taiwanese cruise missiles and aircraft can deny Chinese shipping and even military vessels access to a wide swath of territory. And Taiwan isn't alone." Japan-Taiwan-Indonesia-Singapore forms a line.

(d) *The New/Old China*: The Chinese will face three crushing challenges. "First, Japan is likely to start acting less like an NGO and more like the Japan of ages past. Second, China's geography is nearly as riven as Europe's, with the great myth of Chinese history that unity is normal soon to give way to a more complex and messier reality. Third, everything that made the Chinese economy a success, everything that has put cars on the road, roads on the map, money in the citizens' pockets, and food in their mouths, is completely dependent upon an international economic and strategic environment wholly maintained by country that doesn't like China all that much." "A slow-motion American retreat could leave the Chinese starving for raw materials, which would trigger not just poverty in the coastal regions of Shanghai and to its south but also a contest with Japan and Taiwan that the American might or might not participate in. A break in the Chinese financial system would cause a national collapse in development and mass uprisings in the interior." "China's ability to employ its population will end. China's ability to source the materials to modernize will end. The impacts will vary by region. As poor as the interior is already, it is the region that will…see the sharpest contractions in standard of living."

(e) *Scared New World* (Reverberation of a Fallen Giant): China's explosive rise has impacted nearly every corner of the world, but four outcomes are worthy of particular mention. (i) "China vacuumed up much of the global market share for mid and especially low-skilled industries… Chinese success has meant failure for countries ranging from Mexico to Morocco to India that had previous success in such industries. As china unwinds, much of this productive capacity will fall into disuse for any mix of financial, security, or trade access reasons. The biggest winners will likely be Mexico and the countries of Southeast Asia" with partial relocation back to the United States." (ii) "China's growth resulted in unprecedented demand for every industrial commodity under the sun. Producers dependent upon the mix of Chinese-driven high prices and American-guaranteed shipping security will be those most impacted, with most output from places such as Brazil and Africa being put in extreme danger. The producers who survive will be those with lower production costs and better relations with and access to the United States: Canada, Australia, and Mexico and Southeast Asia." (iii) "China's rise also led to an improvement in diet for most of its 1.35 billion citizens. As with industrial commodities, much of China's food is sourced abroad. However, there will not be a wholesale collapse in international demand in basic foodstuffs. Most of China's food imports serviced China's coastal populations, which will be able to somewhat access international supplies. The demise of the financial system will hurt Chinese food production and may well necessitate greater food import rather than the opposite." (iv) Throughout this entire process, U.S.-dollar denominated assets and especially U.S. government bonds, will become ever more popular. There is not any competition to the U.S. dollar. If any currencies decided to partially fund their bailouts, either Euro or Japanese Yen, their candidacy for status as a global currency will end. Except for U.S. Treasuries, what can you hold?

BOOK REVIEW 3: The Next 100 Years (George Friedman, 2009)·
George Friedman in *The 100 Years: A Forecast for the 21st Century* predicts
"that the United States will remain the dominant global superpower throughout the 21st century, and that the history of the 21st century will consist
mainly of attempts by other world powers to challenge American dominance.
Although mainly about the geopolitics and wars of the century, the book
also makes some economic, social, and technological predictions for the
21st century."[185]

(a) *Second Cold War*: "In the 2010s, the conflict between the US and
Islamic fundamentalists will die down, and a second Cold War, less
extensive and shorter than the first, will take place between the United States
and Russia. It will be characterized by Russian attempts to expand its sphere
of influence into Central and Eastern Europe, coupled with a buildup of
Russian military capabilities. During this period, Russia's military will pose
a regional challenge to the United States. The United States will become a
close ally to some Central and Eastern European countries, all of whom will
be dedicated to resisting Russian geopolitical threats during this period.
Friedman speculates in the book that the United States will probably become
a close ally of some Eastern European countries: Poland, the Czech Republic,
Slovakia, Hungary, and Romania. Around 2015, a Polish-led military
alliance of countries in Eastern Europe will begin to form, which is referred
to in the book as the Polish Bloc."

(b) *Russian and Chinese fragmentation*: "In the early 2020s, the New
Cold War will end when the economic strain and political pressure on Russia,
coupled with Russia's declining population, and poor infrastructure, cause
the federal government of Russia to completely collapse, much like the
dissolution of the Soviet Union. Other former Soviet countries will fragment
as well. Around this time, China (PRC) will politically and culturally
fragment as well. The book asserts that the rapid economic development of
China since 1980 will cause internal pressures and inequalities in Chinese
society. Regional tension in the PRC will grow between the prosperous
coastal regions and the impoverished interior regions. Friedman gives two
possible scenarios: that the Chinese central government will expel outside
interests and rule with an iron fist to keep the country together, or that China
will fragment, with the central government gradually losing much of its real
power and the provinces becoming increasingly autonomous. He works on
the assumption that fragmentation is the most likely scenario. In the 2020s,
the collapse of the Russian government and the fragmentation of mainland
China will leave Eurasia in general chaos. Other powers will then move into
annex or establish spheres of influence in the area, and in many cases,
regional leaders will secede. In Russia, Chechnya and other Muslim regions,
as well as the Pacific Far East will become independent, Finland will annex
Karelia, Romania will annex Moldova, Tibet will gain independence with

help from India, Taiwan (ROC) will extend its influence into mainland China, while the United States, European powers, and Japan will re-create regional spheres of influence in mainland China."

(c) **New powers arise**: "In the 2020s and 2030s, three main powers will emerge in Eurasia: Turkey, Poland, and Japan. (i) Initially supported by the United States, Turkey will expand its sphere of influence and become a regional power, much as it was during the time of the Ottoman Empire. The Turkish sphere of influence will extend into the Arab world, which will have increasingly fragmented by then, and north into Russia and other former Soviet countries. Israel will continue to be a powerful nation and will be the only country in the immediate region to remain outside the Turkish sphere of influence. However, Israel will be forced to come to an accommodation with Turkey due to Turkey's military and political power." (ii) "Japan will expand its economic influence on regions of coastal China, the Russian Far East, and many Pacific Islands. Friedman predicts that Japan will change its foreign policy…becoming more geopolitically aggressive, beginning a major military buildup…that Japan will build military strength capable of regionally projecting power across East Asia during this time." (iii) "Finally, Poland will continue to lead its military alliance, the Polish Bloc. Poland and its allies will be a major power, much like the time of the Polish-Lithuanian Commonwealth. Now possessing substantial military strength, Poland will expand its economic influence into what was formerly European Russia and will begin to compete with Turkey for influence in the important economic region of the Volga River Valley. Around this time, space programs for military use will begin to emerge, and Japan and Turkey will increasingly begin to develop military capabilities in space."

(d) *Tensions build*: "At the beginning of this period, the United States will be allied with all three powers. By 2020, the United States will have been allied with Turkey and Japan for over 75 years. However, in the years after the end of the Second Cold War and collapse of Russia, the United States will gradually become uneasy as Turkey and Japan expand their military power and economic influence. Establishing regional spheres of influence, Turkey and Japan will begin to threaten American interests. The growth of Turkish and Japanese naval power, and their military activities in space will be particularly disturbing to the United States. The book asserts that Japan and Turkey, having similar interests, probably will form an alliance near the end of this period, in an effort to counter the overwhelming global power of the United States. The book also speculates that Germany and Mexico may possibly join this anti-United States coalition, although it is generally unlikely. In this coming confrontation, the United States will be allied with the Polish Bloc, probably with Britain, a re-stabilized China, India, and a reunified Korea. By the 2040s, there will be global tension and competition between these two alliances."

(e) ***Demographic change***: "The book also predicts that decades of low birthrates in developed countries, especially in Europe, will result in dramatic cultural, social, and political shifts through the first half of the 21st century. These countries will experience economic and social strain, caused by a diminishing working age demographic and a rapidly aging population. As a result, in the 2020s and 2030s, Western nations will begin to compete for immigrants. In particular, the United States will greatly ease immigration controls, and will begin trying to entice foreigners - especially Mexicans - to immigrate to the United States. However, later in the century, as robots begin to make human work obsolete, mass unemployment will result, and the United States…will move to limit immigration again."

(f) ***World War III***: "In the mid-21st century, around the year 2050, a Third World War will take place, between the United States, the Polish Bloc, Britain, India, and China on one side, and Turkey and Japan on the other, with Germany and France entering the war in its late stages on the side of Turkey and Japan. According to the book, the war will probably be started by a coordinated Turkish-Japanese sneak attack against the United States and its allies. In the book, Friedman predicts that the attack will take place at a time in which the Americans will be taken completely off guard and hypothesizes 5:00 p.m. on November 24, 2050 as a potential time."

"The Turkish-Japanese alliance's initial strike will cripple the military capabilities of the United States and its allies. The Turkish-Japanese alliance will then attempt to enter negotiations, demanding the United States accept the Turkish-Japanese's alliance's status as a fellow superpower. However, the United States will reject the terms and go to war, refusing to accept Turkish and Japanese hegemony over Eurasia. The Turkish-Japanese alliance will initially possess a military advantage after crippling the United States' military during its first strike. However, as the war progresses, the balance of power will begin to shift as the United States rebuilds and increases its military capabilities and pioneers the use of new military technologies. The war will ultimately end with a victory by the United States and its allies." "According to Friedman, the war will be a limited war, and very different precision-guided munition will minimize collateral damage."

(g) ***Post-World War III***: "Following the war, the United States will enjoy a new post-war boom. This boom will begin in the 2050s after the war and last throughout the 2060s. The economic boom will come as a result of increased defense expenditures that lead to the development of new technologies, which will foster dramatic economic growth and increase American influence worldwide." "The United States will continue to be militarily and politically dominant over the world and will also cement its hegemony over space. In particular, it will work to keep other powers from developing military capabilities in space. Meanwhile, Turkey will retain the bulk of its sphere of influence, although its de facto empire will become increasingly restive as a result of defeat, while Japan will lose its own sphere of influence. Under the US-dictated treaty that will end World War III, military restrictions will be imposed on both Japan and Turkey, although in practice they will be unenforceable and merely a gratuitous humiliation victor's enjoy imposing on the vanquished."

"Poland's power will grow due to the expanded size of the Polish Bloc as a result of the war. Although its infrastructure and economy will have been shattered, and despite having suffered particularly heavy casualties, Poland will exploit the Polish Bloc's increased sphere of influence to rebuild its economy. The United States will begin to look at the Polish Bloc's growing strength as a potential future threat. To prevent Polish hegemony in Europe, the United States will ally with its former enemies Japan and Turkey, as well as Britain, to prevent Poland from dominating Eurasia, and will prevent Poland from making use of space for military purposes."

(h) *U.S.-Mexican Conflict*: "According to the book, North America will remain the center of gravity for the global economic and political system for at least a few more centuries following the 21st century. However, this does not guarantee that the United States will always dominate North America. In the decades following the war, starting in the 2070s, tensions between Mexico and the United States will rise." "During this period, many ethnic Mexicans living in the Southwestern United States, especially those living in the Mexican Cession, will increasingly shun assimilation into American culture, due to the fact that they will live in a predominantly Mexican region, as well as the close proximity of Mexico. These demographic changes will be irreversible. Most Mexicans in the US Southwest will identify as Mexicans rather than Americans, and their national loyalty will be to Mexico and not the United States...An extended crisis between the United States and Mexico will ensue, one that the United States will be unable to resolve through the use of military force."

(i) *Technological Predictions*: "Among the technological predictions made in the book are the development of hypersonic aircraft and missiles, new space-based technology that will foster the development of military bases on the Moon and manned military orbiting platforms (referred to in the book as Battle Stars), and armored robotic battle suits for infantrymen that run on solar power. In addition, the Earth will come to be powered by solar energy collected from satellites beaming the energy down in the form of radiation to receiving stations on Earth, which will end dependence on hydrocarbons, and dramatic advances in robotics and genetic science will lead to a great increase in labor productivity, unemployment as robots make human work obsolete, and significant increases in human longevity. It also hints at more widespread nuclear proliferation, claiming that Japan, Turkey, and Poland will have nuclear weapons by mid-century, as the technology will be a century old by that time."[186]

THE CHANGE OF WORLD ORDER: AN EVALUATION
China, Russia, and the United States

CHINA: With the *Belt and Road Initiative* of 2013, China developed infrastructure in 152 countries in Asia, Europe, Africa, the Middle East, and the Americas; through which China wants to develop new markets for its advanced technology. The *Made in China 2025* is Beijing's industrial policy intending to position China as a high-tech global superpower. "China is spending billions of dollars on science and technology, developing research in genomics, quantum computing, robotics, and advanced materials."[187]

U.S. policy makers worry about market distortions in the future due to China's subsidies and intellectual property theft - its technology companies are merely extensions of its government. "US intelligence warned that Chinese recruitment of foreign scientists and its targeted acquisition of US firms constituted an unprecedented threat to America's industrial base." Regardless of the U.S. worrisome, "China is becoming the main power in Africa and Latin America, providing desperately needed infrastructure and connectivity. China's Asian Infrastructure Investment Bank (AIIB) now rivals the World Bank and its BRI ensures China's long-term leadership across emerging economies." Although Trump administration launched a bid to curb China's rise, "China's deep pools of capital and professional skill underwrites the integration of Asia, the Middle East, Africa and Europe."[188]

Nevertheless, many obstacles are observed against China. First, the United States has built a great leadership with trust for the world to follow democratic values towards peace and prosperity. Second, China is ruled by the Communist Party pursuing dictatorial socialism, which system was never proved to be successful in history. Third, the United States has many powerful leverages to overcome or control violations of China in various aspects. For example, ZTE faces a supply ban that was sparked by its violation - illegally shipping U.S. goods to Iran.[189] Moreover, Huawei has been charged in "two sets of indictments with nearly two dozen counts of stealing trade secrets, violating economic sanctions and concealing its Iran business dealings via an unofficial subsidiary."[190]

The Chinese economy is declining because of several reasons as follows. China may face a financial crisis with a long recession because of low growth coming from the impending trade war with as well as strategic containments by the United States to maintain her unipolar supremacy.

(a) The allocation of resources matters. China's economic policies are decided by the Communist Party, so that major decisions are based on political considerations; which creates bottlenecks and idle capacities in the economy. We can assume that the direction of the *Belt and Road Initiative* is ambitious and great, but the amount of investment in projects should be based on economic efficiency. Each investment project should be profitable

to be able to pay off. China built express railroads with many stations, for example, where numerous apartment towns were built, but the occupancy rates are so low due to lack of jobs there that both railways and apartments are continuously losing money being paid off by taxes. Projects such as construction of foreign ports are also losing money. "In 2018, Malaysian Prime Minister Mahathir Mohamad cancelled China-funded projects and warns there is a new version of Colonialism happening."[191]

(b) The management of corporation matters: The corporations owned by the government also cause problems. In order to maintain the political engine of the Communist Party, the China's government provides jobs for party members in state-owned enterprises (SOEs). Their business decisions are oriented by political considerations. It is not their concern whether the company can make profits or not, because the loss of money is paid by taxes. Recently, "Beijing has sought to strengthen its state-owned enterprises with moves to consolidate industries, reduce output capacity, and shrink the debt amount in the economy. But in doing so, it has strengthened government control over many private businesses and created additional uncertainty and anxiety in both the private sector and society at large."[192] Now SOEs are concentrated in vital or high-profit industries such as finance, power, energy, telecommunications and defense manufacturing.

(c) Debt Finance: Debt levels in the economy have skyrocketed, since the central government injected massive sums of money into the economy as part of a stimulus plan to fight the Great Recession. "Total debt of China exceeds that of the US and was estimated to be twice as high as the average of emerging market economies…Fueled by real estate and shadow banking, total debt has more than quadrupled since 2007, rising to 317% of Chinese GDP. Throughout history and across countries, a rapid growth in debt has been shown to prelude financial crisis. The challenge China faces today is…to find a way to deleverage that will not harm economic growth…A number of reforms of the credit system were introduced from 2016 onwards, including macroprudential measures for the banking sector and regulatory guidelines targeting shadow banking activities…resulted in a significant slowdown in debt growth."[193] An essay of *Financial Times* views that "In the short term, a financial crisis would be followed by weaker investment. Given the decline in the trend rate of growth, the economically justified rate can hardly be higher than it was in 2000, when it was 34 per cent of GDP. That is 10 percentage points below the actual rate in 2017. If this adjustment were to come quickly, in the aftermath of a crisis, such a decline would generate an outright recession."[194] Lixin Sun of Shandong University predicts that "China's public debt from the central government and external debt are sustainable, whereas the highly indebted local governments, non-financial corporations and the shadow banks could lead to potential risk for China's financial stability."[195]

(d) Income inequality in China is problematic. In addition to income gap between urban and rural areas, the imbalance between regions has not been improved particularly between the east and the west. "If measured by the per capita disposable income of urban residents, the most developed areas in the eastern part of the country in 2015 exceeded the most poverty-stricken areas in the west by more than 29,000 yuan, twice as much as the poorest areas in the west." The income inequality was largely created "as a result of government policy favoring urban centers begets further rural-urban income inequality, which creates a vicious cycle and further reinforces regional and rural-urban inequalities." It may cause social instability.

(e) Population decline: Among 56 distinct ethnic groups, "the largest of which are Han, who constitute 91.51% of the total population in 2010. Ethnic minorities constitute 8.49% or 113.8 million of China's population in 2010. During the past decades ethnic minorities have experienced higher growth rates than the majority Han population, because they are not under the one-child policy." China's population has begun to decline and is rapidly aging so that its economic vitality will keep waning. According to China's Bureau of Statistics, "the number of people theoretically able to enter the Chinese labor force (aged 15 to 59), shrank slightly to 937.27 million people in 2012, a decrease of 3.45 million from 2011. This trend…is anticipated to continue for at least the next 20 years, to 2030."[196]

(f) Foreign exchange: China's central bank uses a modified version of a traditional fixed exchange rate, being different from the floating exchange rate the United States and many other countries use. To achieve fairer and more balanced trade, China's currency practices should be monitored and reviewed. "China's leaders must slow economic growth to avoid inflation and a future collapse. They've pumped too much liquidity into state-run companies and banks. In turn, they've invested those funds into ventures that aren't profitable. That's why China's economy must reform or collapse. But China must be careful as it slows growth. China's leaders could create a panic as some of these unprofitable businesses shut down…They could all default if interest rates rise too fast or if growth is too slow. China's central bank must walk a fine line to avoid a financial crisis."[197]

(g) Corruption prevailed: The CCP has retained "control over major sectors of the economy and still plays a leading role in the allocation of capital, land, and labor. But beginning in the 1990s, the party began to decentralize its administrative hierarchy. Today, each level of government controls appointments in the level immediately below it; the party thus retain a high degree of loyalty and influence, but individual bureaucrats, especially local party chiefs, also enjoy a decent amount of autonomy. This combin-ation of state control and decentralized authority has created…unlimited opportunities for corruption, as officials exploit state assets and resources for their own private gain." [198] Hence, efficiency has been falling.

RUSSIA: "Russia is a revanchist power, but its economic stagnation renders it more a spoiler than a genuine challenger. With an acute dependency on oil and a projected economic growth rate hovering around two percent, Russia is likely to see its international power decline over the next decade. Yet Russia is far more economically and politically stable today than it was in the 1990s, allowing it to project power far beyond its borders. And Russian President Vladimir Putin has played a bad hand well: he has integrated Russia's significant hybrid warfare, cyberwar, and nuclear capabilities into an asymmetric defense strategy that lets the country punch well above its weight. Moscow will never truly challenge U.S. dominance, but it will disrupt the democratic processes of EU and NATO members and threaten former Soviet states for the foreseeable future."[199]

According to Michael McFaul, the current relations between the United States and Russia is not a new Cold War but "a new qualitative arms race in nuclear delivery vehicles, missile defenses, and digital weapons. The two countries are no longer engulfed in proxy wars, but over the last decade, Russia has demonstrated less and less restraint in its use of military power. The worldwide ideological struggle between capitalism and communism is history, but Russian President Vladimir Putin has anointed himself the leader of a renewed nationalist, conservative movement fighting a decadent West...the Russian government has made huge investments in television and radio stations, social media networks, and Internet troll farms, and it has spent lavishly in support of like-minded politicians abroad. The best description of the current hostilities is not cold war but hot peace."[200]

In confronting the Kremlin, McFaul believes that real political change in Russia will likely begin only after Putin steps down. He favors the containment strategy to be maintained: (i) Limiting Putin's ability to influence U.S. election should be priority one. The Trump administration should mandate enhanced cybersecurity resilience. Congress should also pass laws to provide greater transparency about Russian media activities inside the United States. (ii) Europe and NATO members must pay greater attention to combating Russian disinformation and devote more time and resources to promoting their own values with more defense spending to reaffirm their commitment to collective security. (iii) Building a secure, wealthy, democratic Ukraine is the best way to restrain Russian ideological and military aggression in Europe. The U.S. must increase its support for Ukraine. (iv) In the Middle East, more aggressive strategy is necessary to contain Russia's most important ally, Iran, and to support Syrian militias fighting Iranian soldiers and their allies in Syria. (v) Western countries must contain economic activities led by the Russian government, while private sector companies inside Russia should be encouraged with Western markets. (vi) Western foundations and philanthropists must provide more support for independent journalism both inside and outside Russia.[201]

THE UNITED STATES: The world can be divided into two groups of countries, free and non-free or democratic and non-democratic countries. The non-free or non-democratic countries are run by authoritarian rulers such as in China, Russia, North Korea, and so on. China is ruled by the Communist Party and Xi Jinping who extended his dictatorial rule for life. Vladimir Putin, a former KGB man, took power as acting president in 1999, and has been holding his power until now. Authoritarian rulers do not respect democratic values - freedom, equality, and humanity. A nation state exists in order to make its people happy and prosperous, without hurting peoples living in other countries; that is the prevailing values of democratic countries. Nevertheless, the opposite norms and rules are affluent in non-democratic countries, invading foreign countries and suppressing peoples.

Threatening Ukraine, Russia annexed the Crimean Peninsula to Russian Federation in February-March 2014, and since then it has been administered as two Russian federal subjects - the Republic of Crimea and the federal city of Sevastopol. Putin's motives seem to be a response to the threat of NATO's further expansion, part of Russian project to recapture the former territories of the Soviet Union, and a response to the unforeseen fall of Ukrainian President Viktor Yanukovych.[202] Chinese buildup in South China Sea is like preparing for World War III. "Beijing's ongoing expansion into the Spratly archipelago agitates neighboring nations and continues to challenge international law, an assertiveness the U.S. Navy attempts to check through routine freedom of navigation operations, or FONOPs."[203] The Chinese authorities have detained…"millions of Uyghurs, Kazakhs, Kyrgyz, Hui (Muslims) and other ethnic Turkic Muslims, Christians, and also some foreign citizens such as Kazakhstanis to be kept in these secretive internment camps throughout the region. The United Nations and many international media reports have stated that more than 1 million people have been held in such re-education camps in recent years." "Chinese authorities are using a mobile app to carry out illegal mass surveillance and arbitrary detention of Muslims in China's western Xinjiang region."

There are two issues: one is external invasion and the other is internal rule without humanity. First in international relations, such rulers of non-democratic countries as China and Russia invade foreign countries with the expansionist strategy: they plunder resources in other countries for their own benefits, which is not acceptable in the twenty-first century. They are the evil states taking happiness away from others for their own state or people. Second in domestic politics, such rulers as Putin and Xi ignore democratic values like human rights and suppress any individuals or groups who are politically against the ruling party. Their people pay taxes for their peace and prosperity, so that they have to be equally treated with others. If a ruler violates common virtues in society, the social contract existing between them is null and void, so that there is no reason why for them to obey.

Another cruel and painful example can be seen in North Korea. Last three decades, the Kim's regime has closed its door to avoid freedom waves coming from communications with foreign countries and developed nuclear weapons by putting all resources into its programs. Pyongyang wants to use nuclear weapons in two ways: one is to threaten national defense of South Korea, and the other is to sell nuclear weapons to such countries as Iran and Syria. However, the UN sanctions are blocking its desire, either selling or threatening. North Korea is extremely an evil regime because of two reasons as discussed above. First, selling and spreading nuclear weapons threaten world peace tremendously. Second, Kim's regime made people die of hunger and sickness because of the use of their resources to develop nuclear weapons. "Conditions inside North Korean prison camps are unsanitary and life-threatening. Prisoners are subject to torture and inhumane treatment. Public and secret executions of prisoners, even children, especially in cases of attempted escape, are commonplace. Infanticides also often occur. The mortality rate is very high, because many prisoners die of starvation, illnesses, work accidents, or torture." This regime should be punished.[204]

Then, who can win the war to lead the world? Non-democratic countries like Russia and China are not qualified to lead the world. Then, among democratic countries, the United States is the mostly powerful and qualified candidate to run the world. Of course, democratic values are not the only factor to be included in nation's power, but it is fortunate that America is the most powerful democratic country that can lead human civilization in the future in terms of leadership with acceptable norms and rules of the world. Hence, Washington should take reasonable and responsible strategies and policies to achieve the mission to construct the world order.

First, the United States should take the containment strategy based on realism by escaping from the order of liberal hegemony that was taken for 25 years in international relations since the Cold War ended. It resulted in the wars in Afghanistan, Iraq, Libya, and Syria, along with the 2008 financial crisis and the rise of populism; being considered as "an unmitigated disaster."[205] Since 1991 "foreign policy elites abandoned realism in favor of an unrealistic grand strategy – liberal hegemony – that has weakened the country and caused considerable harm at home and abroad. To get back on track, Washington should return to the realism and restraint that serve it so well in the past." The foreign policy community must become more responsive to the public. "The foreign policy establishment needs to work harder to engage the public and open its ranks to more itinerant participation. The government should actively involve civic groups and nongovernmental organizations in foreign policy, trusting that activity outside the govern- ment's direct control can still be in its interest. And Congress needs to claw back some of the powers it has ceded over the years to the executive branch by exercising its authority over the use of military force."[206]

Second, military superiority should be accompanied with diplomacy. The diplomacy without military power is unable to contain bad behaviors of bad countries. The militaries that embrace and adapt to advanced technologies will dominate those that do not. "Cyberattacks, communication jamming, electronic warfare, and other attacks on a system's software will become as important as those that target a system's hardware, if not more so. The rate of fire, or how fast weapons can shoot, will accelerate rapidly thanks to new technologies such as lasers, high-powered microwaves, and other directed-energy weapons. But what will really increase the rate of fire are intelligent systems that will radically reduce the time between when targets can be identified and when they can be attacked." Hypersonic munitions and space-based weapons can strike targets anywhere in the world nearly instantly. Technology in military communications based on 5G technology will carry data with faster speeds.

Third, economic growth should not be disturbed by defense spending. It is essential to balance business investment with defense expenditures in order to maintain sustainable nation's power. Democratic politics and market economy cam maximize economic efficiency. However, sometimes overextension of armed forces may require an unexpected expansion of defense budget. The balance of bread and gun must be always considered by avoiding greed for expansionism. Moreover, we have to pay attention to development of science and technology, which are the source of productivity and the engine of economic growth.

Fourth, harmony of society is essential for a healthy nation. "The world can be divided in many ways - rich and poor, democratic and authoritarian - but one of the most striking is the divide between the societies with an individualist mentality and...a collectivist mentality...The individualistic countries tend to put rights and privacy first. People in these societies tend to overvalue their own skills and overestimate their own importance to any group effort. People in collective societies tend to value harmony and duty. They tend to underestimate their own skills and are more self-effacing when describing their contributions to group efforts...The ideal of a harmonious collective may...be as attractive as the ideal of the American Dream."[207]

Finally, the United Nations has been the center of conflict resolution among nation states based on liberal democratic values. It was established by the spirit of President Franklin D. Roosevelt. Major activities are, among others, peace keeping and security, promoting and encouraging respect for human rights, economic development and humanitarian assistance, and other activities have been important for world peace. It is essential for the United States to make the United Nations...function actively to resolve problems between countries. U.S. contribution to the UN fund is 22% of total budget (China is 12%) for 2019. The UN is an excellent vehicle to support America to lead the world towards peace and prosperity.[208]

A HYPOTHETICAL CHANGE OF WORLD POWERS
In the Twenty-Frist Century

The Western Roman Empire collapsed in 476 because its political-military institutions could not be supported by its economy and socio-cultural means. Europe had passed more than one thousand years of transition to establish a new world order. Owing to the progress of shipbuilding, navigation devices, mounted cannons, and mapping skills, Spain funded Christopher Columbus to sail to reach the new world of America by crossing the Atlantic Ocean in 1492. A Portuguese expedition led by Vasco da Gama reached India by sailing around Africa in 1498, opening up direct trade with Asia. Soon, the Portuguese sailed further eastward, to the valuable Spice Islands in 1512, landing in China one year later. Despite conflict with the Turks and others, commercial activities were followed by the Dutch, English, and France who sold manufactured goods for raw materials, spices, or luxury goods to Africa, America, or Asia. Pursuing commercial interests and industrialization, the European states dominated the world for five hundred years but exhausted themselves in endless wars with each other as experienced in World Wars.

The United States emerged from World I as a global power. U.S. President Woodrow Wilson led the Treaty of Versailles creating the League of Nations, though it failed to achieve peace. After World War II, U.S. President Harry S. Truman founded the United Nations, launched the Marshall Plan, organized NATO to defend Europe, and firmly established peace in Japan. The United States emerged as a superpower controlling the North Atlantic and ruling all the world oceans. Thus, the Europeans lost their empire that enjoyed imperialistic profits throughout the world and sat behind the driver. The U.S.-Soviet confrontation created the painful Cold War, but the fall of the Soviet Union elevated the U.S. to the unipolar superpower as the center of gravity of the international system. While U.S. aircraft carriers are able to access to and stay at every corner of the world, Washington can maintain cooperative relations with Atlantic nations in the west and develop favorable relations with Indo-Pacific nations in the east. Fortunately, the shale energy made the United States to start the new American age.

After the collapse of USSR, the Yugoslavian wars and the September 11 attacks happened. The former was a series of separate but related ethnic conflicts, which were the wars of independence and insurgencies fought in the former Yugoslavia during 1991-2001, breaking up the Yugoslav state, which was painful but mostly a response to the collapse of the Soviet Union. The latter "ended the interregnum between the end of the Cold War and the beginning of the next era: the U.S.-Jihadist war." Since divisions in the Islamic world were too powerful to overcome, as long as Muslims are fighting each other, the United States has won its war. Then, which power would run the world in the coming century?

China and Russia in around 2020. *China*: Japan has been in friendly relations with the United States containing China's expansion. China has violated fair trade agreements as a member of the WTO in some serious cases - government subsidies, technology theft, currency manipulation and incompliance with UN sanctions. China's economic growth strengthens its military capabilities threatening U.S. national security, so that Washington contains China's trade and investment. In the worst case, the United States can contain it by controlling of sea lanes transporting energy and of foreign exchanges. In the past three decades, the Chinese economy has been rapidly expanded with over-investment by debt financing without returning profits, causing slow growth and failure of debt-repayments, resulting in default of numerous firms. The situations would be worse because of trade conflicts with the United States. Poverty and unemployment with the added pressure of slow growth may cause political and social instability. Beijing may try to limit disintegration by appealing to nationalism such as blaming foreigners to cause problems and confronting foreign governments diplomatically as well as militarily if possible. China has two options: to recentralize its rule that restricts the regional capabilities to maneuver, and to fragment itself into regional powers along traditional regional lines, while the central government becomes weakened and less powerful. The latter is more plausible, but the result is dependent upon the degree of interactions.

Russia: Russia clashed with the rest of the world in the Napoleonic Wars, the Crimean War, World Wars, and the Cold War, but survived until now although USSR fragmented in 1991. The Russian borders are broad and uncontrollable, and its population has been declined to 144.5 million in 2017. Russia shifted its strategy in around 2000 from industrial development to exporters of natural resources - energy, minerals, agricultural products, lumber, and precious metals. Moscow tries to recover effective control over the former USSR with recreating the buffer states; to create the second-tier buffers beyond the boundary of the former Soviet Union; and to prevent anti-Russian coalitions from forming. For Russia, Ukraine and Belarus are most important, and three Baltic countries are secondary. The United States will increase the power of Poland and three Baltic countries, and Georgia is a secondary flash point. Russia will try to break up NATO and isolate eastern Europe. "If Russia's resurgence is to be a minimal crisis, the Russians will dominate Central Asia and the Caucasus and possibly absorb Moldova, but they will not be able to absorb the Baltic states or dominate any nations west of the Carpathians."[209] In the U.S.-Russian confrontation, in the end, Russian military power will be severely strained by the fraction of American military power. The Russian military will collapse, considering the difference of GDP in 2017 - the Russian GDP was US$ 1.58 trillion, while the U.S. GDP US$ 19.39 trillion, that is more than 12 times of Russia's (over 10 times of defense spending).[210]

A New World during 2020-50: In the next thirty years, we can predict that non-democratic countries will be weakened and divided and partially merged into rising powers. More specifically, Russia and China decline continuously and fragment into the line of traditional regions. In Asia, *Japan* strengthens its economic-military power with the U.S.-Japanese Security Alliance and increases its economic influence in China and the eastern shore of Russia including Vladivostok. The unified Korea, with the population of over 80 million approaching to G5 in economy, feels trapped in the middle, so that the Koreans counteract to balance Japanese power. They demand the United States to support them against a rising Japan. If the United States can balance the role of Japan and Korea to contain China from the beginning, both countries can fairly share contributions and benefits coming from the collapse of Russia and China. When the Japanese economic and military powers are dominant in the East Asia, Japan becomes more assertive. Then, the United States evaluates whether the Japanese assertiveness threatens the U.S. strategic interests, which challenges the U.S. Navy in the Pacific. If the strategic interests between Washington and Tokyo are seriously different, Washington would seek an alliance with China plus Korea to weaken and isolate Japan from the regional coalition as well as U.S. military power. The unified Korea would be a more reliable ally with the U.S. than Japan.

The collapse of Russia creates two fronts of the rising powers in Europe: Islamic states in the south and European states in the west. Among Islamic states, *Turkey* rises because it is not only an economically viable country but also a strategically crucial one. "Turkey enjoys one of the strongest geographic locations of any Eurasian country. Turkey has easy access to the Arab world, Iran, Europe, the former Soviet Union, and the Mediterranean. The Turkish economy grows in part because Turkey is a center of regional trade as well as a productive economic power in its own right."[211] Since Turkey is critical in the U.S.-Russia confrontation, Washington encourages Turkey to press north in the Caucasus and to influence Muslim areas of the Balkans, as well as in the Arab states to the south.[212] In the absence of the Russian threat, NATO cease to exist; France and Germany decline. *Poland* rises with continuous U.S. supports. "Poland is a developed market and a regional power in Central Europe, with the largest Stock Exchange in the East-Central European zone. It has the sixth largest economy by GDP (PPP) in the European Union and one of the most dynamic economies in the world, simultaneously achieving a very high rank on the Human Development Index. Poland is a developed country, which maintains a high-income economy along with very high standards of living, life quality, safety, education, and economic freedom."[213] The Polish try to create a buffer zone in Belarus and Ukraine against Russian influence. As the U.S.-Russian conflict ends, the immediate American interest in the region declines, but will emerge again in the U.S. crisis with Japan and Turkey.[214]

The World Order after 2050: After Russian retreat and Chinese instability, the new world order is established by major actors - Japan in Asia, Poland in Europe, and Turkey in the Middle East under the unipolar power of the United States during the three decades until 2050 as discussed. In the second half of the twenty-first century, major actors maintain favorable relations with the U.S. leadership, and lead regional as well as international politics based on the balance of power. Since the regional environments differ each other, possible noises are expected.

In the Pacific basin, Japan aggressively advances toward China and Siberia with rapidly growing maritime power of the sea-based and space-based missile systems, increasingly uses its power to secure the sea-route importing oil from the Persian Gulf and patrols the Indian Ocean to protect its maritime interests. The Japanese will share waters with the American Seventh Fleet, and space with the U.S. Space Command. But American policy must be complex because Washington should keep a stable China to check the rising Japan if necessary. So Korea may take a positive role.

In the Middle East, Turkey try to achieve its strategic goal - to control of Mediterranean and Black Seas. The Turkish influence will spread northward, beyond the Caucasus into Russia and Ukraine. They create deep relationships into Russia, dominate Iraq and Syria, and influence Saudi Arabia as well as the Balkans. While Israel remains stable, Turkey gets into Egypt and controls the Suez Canal; which consolidates Turkish control over the Arabian Peninsula. Turkey will go beyond the Red Sea and enter the Indian Ocean, where Japan and Turkey will meet. Moving deep into Russia and Balkans, Turkey collides with Poland and the rest of Eastern Europe.

In Europe, after the collapse of Russia, Poland will have an opportunity to create the regional power since Germany will have neither appetite nor the power to challenge the Polish bloc. The Polish bloc will collide with the Turks in the Balkans and Russia itself. The Poles need the Americans to help them resist the Turks in the Mediterranean. Americans will help the Poles in order to balance regional powers. Unlike the Turks, the Poles won't be an immediate threat to any American interests. The Americans will arm the Polish bloc and encourage its confrontation with the Turks.[215]

In the conflict between Turkey and Japan, Americans demand that both states withdraw all forces from the border. But both countries have an interest in limiting American power by forming a natural coalition. George Friedman views that the United States decides to go war against them. The key to warfare in the twenty-first century will be speed, range, and accuracy with unmanned hypersonic aircraft. Americans win wars and then suffer through the aftermath. Global war becomes space War. "Most of the world's communications systems rely heavily on the presence of satellites in orbit around Earth. Protecting these assets might motivate nations dependent upon them to consider deploying more space-based weaponry."[216]

CONCLUDING REMARKS

Realism was a dominant theory explaining international relations until the oil crisis of 1980, when the world recognized that economic interdependence is more influential than the power of military forces, so that liberals became more influential as the Cold War ended in 1991. With the relaxed and less controlled borders, liberal hegemony prevailed with globalization for a couple of decades, but decayed due to challenges of the rising China, returning of Russia, and the development of nuclear weapons of Iran and North Korea; resulting in the resurgence of realism with the new nationalism. The theoretical disagreements between realism and liberalism are obvious. Realists, like John Mearsheimer, believe that a powerful state can pursue liberal hegemony only in a unipolar system without threat from other great powers. When the world is bipolar or multipolar, great powers have little choice but to act according to the balance of power. On the other hand, liberals, like Robert Keohane and Joseph Nye, view that complex inter-dependence demands to use multiple channels of action between societies, in the absence of a hierarchic agenda, with the decline of military force as a policy tool. Realists criticize that since the international system is anarchic, liberalism cannot work without the balance of power. A nation-state where liberalism co-exists with nationalism undercuts a liberal foreign policy.

Since 1991 the United States has provided a liberal trading system and the world became prosperous despite regional disorder and the financial crisis. But the liberal order began to decay. Russia attacked Georgia in 2008, and invaded and merged Crimea in 2014. China launched the Belt and Road Initiative with a massive regional infrastructure project, which intends to use growing economic power ultimately to achieve its political goals, challenging the U.S. dominance. Moreover, China issued a plan of Made in 2025 to upgrade its manufacturing capabilities to catch up advanced U.S. technology with government subsidies and technology theft if possible. China also has violated U.N. sanctions prohibiting products selling to Iran and North Korea. In October 2018, Vice President Mike Pence accused Beijing of breaking international norms and acting against American interests. The U.S. grand strategies against law breakers appear as sanctions or trade restrictions.

Both Russia and China will weaken mainly because of the decline of their economies. China faces various problems: bad resource allocation, inefficiency of corporate management, over extended investment financed by debt without profit-making, high degree of income inequality between regions as well as classes, the decline of labor forces with aging population, foreign exchange manipulation, and prevailed corruption. The trade war with the United States exacerbates its slow growth. Within a couple of decades, Russia will retreat, and China will be destabilized. After the collapse of both, under the U.S. supremacy, Japan will rise in Asia, and

Turkey in the Middle East, and Poland in Europe while France and Germany decline. The world order after 2050 would be the power game of four powers - the United States, Japan, Turkey, and Poland with the deployment of space-based weapons equipped with speed, range, and accuracy.

In concluding the Part I, we have to consider some important issues in future studies of international relation. First, fundamental goals of states lie in national security and economic prosperity of the people, that is to enforce social contract. If any state, either democratic or non-democratic, cannot achieve those goals, there is no reason why that state to exist. In this regard, the collapse of non-democratic Russia and China is the natural course of history. Second, as the Soviet Union collapsed, China could survive by opening four economic special zones in order to take capitalistic benefits, while maintaining one party politics under the Communist Party. Likewise, North Korea wants to survive without giving up Kim's dictatorial system, making the people hungry and diseased. It became obvious that a non-democratic state can be rich for a while, but that is not sustainable if its political system does not respect democratic values without guaranteeing the free market system. In the American age, the United States is responsible to enhance world order supporting democratic values. Third, the United States has discovered and developed the Shale oil and gas, which strengthens her economic and strategic powers. Defense budget is saved from not standing forward deployment, and the U.S. can control the production of energy and its supplies, which can be a leverage for powerful diplomacy. This windfall should be used for peace and prosperity of the world.

Endnotes

[1] Pierre Riche, *The Carolingians: A Family who Forged Europe*, Translated from French by Michael Idomir Allen (Philadelphia, PN: Univ. of Pennsylvania Press, 1993), 168-9.
[2] Hungarian invasions of Europe, accessed 3 June 2019, https://en.wikipedia.org/wiki/Hungarian_invasions_of_Europe.
[3] J. M. Roberts, *The New History of the World* (New York: Oxford University Press, 2003), 331. The Arabs were recruited from hungry fighters who left the Arab dessert, pushed by the over-population demanding more, taught by the prophet that death on the battlefield against the infidel guided them to paradise, and equipped with a religious ideal that they were doing God's will and creating a new brotherhood.
[4] Abbasid Caliphate, accessed 3 November 2019, https://en.wikipedia.org/wiki/Abbasid_Caliphate. "The Abbasid line of rulers, and Muslim culture in general, re-centred themselves in the Mamluk capital of Cairo in 1261. Though lacking in political power, the dynasty continued to claim religious authority until after the Ottoman conquest of Egypt in 1517."
[5] Caliphate, accessed 3 June 2019, https://en.wikipedia.org/wiki/Caliphate.
[6] Hugh Kennedy, *The Prophet and the Age of the Caliphates: The Islamic Near East from the Sixth to the Eleventh Century* (New York: Longman Group, 1986), 144-6.
[7] South Slavs, accessed 2 April 2019, https://en.wikipedia.org/wiki/South_Slavs.

[8] Massilius of Padua, *The Defender of the Peace*, Trans. Annabel Brett (New York: Cambridge University Press, 2005), xxix. The pope is not a judge - the civic judge is the prince, and the divine judge is Christ - so that the papacy has no jurisdictional primacy over the faithful.

[9] Golden Bull of 1356, accessed 2 April 2019, https://en.wikipedia.org/wiki/Golden_Bull_of_1356#Prince-electors.

[10] Seven Years' War, accessed 1 November 2019, https://en.wikipedia.org/wiki/Seven_Years%27_War.

[11] Richard J. Evans, *The Pursuit of Power: Europe 1815-1914* (New York: Viking Press, 2016), 3.

[12] Concert of Europe, accessed 17 March 2017, https://en.wikipedia.org/wiki/Concert_of_Europe.

[13] Revolution of 1830 in Belgium, accessed 18 March 2017, https://en.wikipedia.org/wiki/Revolutions_of_1830#In_Belgium.

[14] November Uprising, accessed 18 March 2017, https://en.wikipedia.org/wiki/November_Uprising.

[15] Revolution of 1830 in Italy, accessed 18 March 2017, https://en.wikipedia.org/wiki/Revolutions_of_1830#In_Italy.

[16] Latin American wars of independence, accessed 18 March 2017, https://en.wikipedia.org/wiki/Latin_American_wars_of_independence.

[17] Greek War of Independence, accessed 18 March 2017, https://en.wikipedia.org/wiki/Greek_War_of_Independence.

[18] Revolution of 1848. Origins, accessed 26 August 2016, https://en.wikipedia.org/wiki/Revolutions_of_1848#Origins.

[19] Revolution of 1848: Legacy, accessed 10 September 2016, https://en.wikipedia.org/wiki/Revolutions_of_1848#Legacy.

[20] Austro-Hungarian Compromise of 1867, accessed 19 March 2017, https://en.wikipedia.org/wiki/Austro-Hungarian_Compromise_of_1867.

[21] Alexander II of Russia, accessed 19 March 2017, https://en.wikipedia.org/wiki/Alexander_II_of_Russia.

[22] American Civil War, accessed 19 March 2017, https://en.wikipedia.org/wiki/American_Civil_War.

[23] Meiji Restoration, accessed 19 March 2017, https://en.wikipedia.org/wiki/Meiji_Restoration.

[24] Europe 1871-1914 Summary, accessed 19 March 2017, http://www.sparknotes.com/history/european/1871-1914/summary.html.

[25] Russo-Turkish War (1877-1878), accessed 19 March 2017, https://en.wikipedia.org/wiki/Russo-Turkish_War_(1877%E2%80%931878).

[26] Berlin Conference, accessed 23 April 2019, https://en.wikipedia.org/wiki/Berlin_Conference.

[27] Europe 1871-1914 Summary, accessed 19 March 2017, http://www.sparknotes.com/history/european/1871-1914/terms.html.

[28] Islamic modernism and Islamic revival, accessed 8 September 2019, http://www.oxfordislamicstudies.com/article/opr/t253/e9.

[29] World War I: Russian Revolution, accessed 24 September 2017, https://en.wikipedia.org/wiki/World_War_I#Russian_Revolution.

[30] https://en.wikipedia.org/wiki/Paris_Peace_Conference,_1919#Overview_and_direct_results, Paris Peace Conference 1919, accessed 24 September 2017.

[31] Interwar period, accessed 24 September 2017, https://en.wikipedia.org/wiki/Interwar_period.

[32] World War II, accessed 25 September 2017,
https://en.wikipedia.org/wiki/World_War_II.
[33] *Ibid.*, accessed the same.
[34] *Ibid.*, accessed the same.
[35] Cold War, accessed 25 September 2017, https://en.wikipedia.org/wiki/Cold_War.
[36] *Ibid.*, accessed the same.
[37] *Ibid.*, accessed the same.
[38] Post-Cold War era: Background, accessed 25 September 2017,
https://en.wikipedia.org/wiki/Post%E2%80%93Cold_War_era#Background.
[39] https://en.wikipedia.org/wiki/Post%E2%80%93Cold_War_era#Consequences_of_the
_Fall_of_Communism, Post-Cold War era: Consequences of the Fall of Communism,
accessed 25 September 2017.
[40] Post-Cold War era, accessed 25 September 2017,
https://en.wikipedia.org/wiki/Post%E2%80%93Cold_War_era.
[41] War on Terror, accessed 4 November 2019,
https://en.wikipedia.org/wiki/War_on_Terror.
[42] Neo-nationalism, accessed 6 November 2019, https://en.wikipedia.org/wiki/Neo-
nationalism.
[43] Paul R. Viotti and Mark V. Kauppi, *International Relations Theory: Realism,
Pluralism, Globalism, and Beyond*, 3rd ed. (Needham Heights, MA: A Viacom
Company, 1999), 1-2.
[44] Realism (international relations), accessed 28 April 2019,
https://en.wikipedia.org/wiki/Realism_(international_relations).
[45] Hans J. Morgenthau, *Politics among Nations: The Struggle for Power and Peace*,
brief ed. (New York: McGraw-Hill, Inc., 1993), 13-5.
[46] Edward Hallett Carr, *The Twenty Years' Crisis, 1919-1939* (New York: Harper
Collins, 1939), 11-21, Chapter 2 Utopia and Reality.
[47] *Ibid.*, 102, Chapter 8 Power in the International Politics.
[48] Paul R. Viotti and Mark V. Kauppi, *International Relations Theory*, 64-5.
[49] Power (international relations), accessed 29 April 2019,
https://en.wikipedia.org/wiki/Power_(international_relations).
[50] *Ibid.*, accessed the same. For further for Hard Power, see John J. Mearsheimer, *The
Great Delusion: Liberal Dreams and International Realities* (New Haven, CT: Yale
University Press, 2018); and fore Soft Power, see Joseph S. Nye, Jr., *Soft Power: The
Means to Success in World Politics* (New York: Public Affairs, 2004).
[51] Paul R. Viotti and Mark V. Kauppi, *International Relations Theory*, 71-4.
[52] *Ibid.*, 74-5.
[53] *Ibid.*, 76-9.
[54] *Ibid.*, 79-82.
[55] Conclusion: The Cautionary and Changing Character of Realism, accessed 29 April
2019, https://plato.stanford.edu/entries/realism-intl-relations/#ConcCautChanCharReal.
[56] Liberalism (international relations), accessed 29 April 2019,
https://en.wikipedia.org/wiki/Liberalism_(international_relations).
[57] Paul R. Viotti and Mark V. Kauppi, *International Relations Theory*, 199-200.
[58] *Ibid.*, 201-2.
[59] *Ibid.*, 202.
[60] Liberalism (international relations), accessed 6 February 2019,
https://en.wikipedia.org/wiki/Liberalism_(international_relations).
[61] Liberalism (international relations): Neoliberalism, accessed 20 April 2019,
https://en.wikipedia.org/wiki/Liberalism_(international_relations)#Neoliberalism.

[62] Paul R. Viotti and Mark V. Kauppi, *International Relations Theory*, 206.

[63] *Ibid.*, 219-20.

[64] Earnest B. Hass, *When Knowledge Is Power: Three Models of Change in International Organizations* (Berkeley, CA: University of California Press, 1990).

[65] James N. Rosenau, *Turbulence in World Politics: A Theory of Change and Continuity* (Princeton, NJ: Princeton University Press, 1990).

[66]https://en.wikipedia.org/wiki/Neoliberalism_(international_relations)#Keohane_and_Nye, Neoliberalism (international relations): Keohane and Nye, accessed 1 May 2019.

[67] Nationalism, accessed 1 May 2019, https://en.wikipedia.org/wiki/Nationalism.

[68] Nationalism: English Puritanism and nationalism, accessed 1 May 2019, https://www.britannica.com/topic/nationalism.

[69] Andrew Heywood, *Political Ideologies: An Introduction*, 3rd ed. (New York: Palgrave, 2003), 155-6.

[70] German nationalism, accessed 1 May 2019, https://en.wikipedia.org/wiki/German_nationalism.

[71] Nationalism: History, accessed 5 January 2017, http://www.infoplease.com/encyclopedia/history/nationalism-history.html.

[72] Andrew Heywood, *Political Ideologies: An Introduction*, 160-2

[73] *Ibid.*, 163.

[74] *Ibid.*, 165-6.

[75] *Ibid.*, 167-8.

[76] *Ibid.*, 169-80.

[77] *Ibid.*, 181-5.

[78] Guillaume Serina, A*n Impossible Dream: Reagan, Gorbachev, and a World Without the Bomb* (New York: Pegasus Books, 2019).

[79] 1973 oil crisis, accessed 3 May 2019, https://en.wikipedia.org/wiki/1973_oil_crisis, and 1979 oil crisis, accessed the same date, https://en.wikipedia.org/wiki/1979_oil_crisis.

[80] Robert O. Keohane and Joseph S. Nye, *Power and Interdependence*, 2nd ed. (New York: Longman, 1989), 10.

[81] *Ibid.*, 11.

[82] *Ibid.*, 20.

[83] *Ibid.*, 24-9.

[84] *Ibid.*, 37.

[85] Complex Interdependence, accessed 4 May 2019, https://en.wikipedia.org/wiki/Complex_interdependence.

[86] John J. Mearsheimer, *The Great Delusion: Liberal Dreams and International Realities* (New Haven, CT: Yale University Press, 2018), 1-13.

[87] *Ibid.*, 14-33

[88] *Ibid.*, 33-8.

[89] *Ibid.*, 47-54.

[90] *Ibid.*, 83-102.

[91] *Ibid.*, 102-8.

[92] *Ibid.*, 120-30.

[93] *Ibid.*, 152-3.

[94] *Ibid.*, 154.

[95] *Ibid.*, 156-87.

[96] Democratic peace theory, accessed 4 November 2019, https://en.wikipedia.org/wiki/Democratic_peace_theory.

[97] John J. Mearsheimer, *The Great Delusion*, 203.

[98] *Ibid.*, 6 and 188-216.

[99] *Ibid.*, 217-8.

[100] Richard Haass, "How a World Order Ends and What Comes in Its Wake," *Foreign Affairs* 98(1) (January/February 2019), 22.

[101] https://www.rand.org/content/dam/rand/pubs/perspectives/PE200/PE226/RAND_PE 226.pdf, RAND Corporation, "The Concert of Europe and Great-Power Governance Today: What Can the Order of 19th Century Europe Teach Policymakers about International order in the 21st Century?" accessed 18 May 2019.

[102] Richard Haass, "How a World Order Ends and What Comes in Its Wake," 24.

[103] Gideon Rose, "The Fourth Founding: The United States and the Liberal Order," *Foreign Affairs* 98 (1) (January/February 2019), 13.

[104] *Ibid.*, 14.

[105] Hegemonic stability theory, accessed 6 May 2019, https://en.wikipedia.org/wiki/Hegemonic_stability_theory.

[106] Hegemon stability theory: Hegemon rise, accessed 6 May 2019, https://en.wikipedia.org/wiki/Hegemonic_stability_theory#Hegemonic_rise.

[107] Robert O. Keohane, *After Hegemony: Cooperation and Discord in the World Political Economy* (Princeton, NJ: Princeton University Press, 1984), 46.

[108] Hegemonic stability theory: Long cycle theory, accessed 6 May 2019, https://en.wikipedia.org/wiki/Hegemonic_stability_theory#Long_cycle_theory.

[109] https://en.wikipedia.org/wiki/Hegemonic_stability_theory#The_neorealist_interpreta tion, Hegemonic stability theory: The neorealist interpretation, accessed 6 May 2019.

[110] https://en.wikipedia.org/wiki/Hegemonic_stability_theory#The_neoliberal_interpreta tion, Hegemonic stability theory: The neoliberal interpretation, accessed 6 May 2019.

[111] Robert O. Keohane, *After Hegemony*, 178.

[112] Robert Gilpin, *War and Change in World Politics* (New York: Cambridge University Press, 1981), 20-10.

[113] Helen V. Milner, "The Enduring Legacy of Robert Gilpin: How He Predicted Today's Great Power Rivalry," *Foreign Affairs* 97(4)), accessed 8 May 2019, https://www.foreignaffairs.com/articles/2018-08-15/enduring-legacy-robert-gilpin.

[114] *Ibid.*, accessed the same.

[115] The Reagan Years: The End of the Cold War, accessed 8 May 2019, http://www.ushistory.org/us/59e.asp.

[116] *Ibid.*, accessed the same.

[117] The Rise and Fall of the Great Powers, accessed 21 February 2019, https://en.wikipedia.org/wiki/The_Rise_and_Fall_of_the_Great_Powers.

[118] The End of History and the Last Man, accessed 21 February 2019, https://en.wikipedia.org/wiki/The_End_of_History_and_the_Last_Man.

[119] *Ibid.*, accessed the same.

[120] The End of History and the Last Man: Criticisms, accessed 8 May 2019, https://en.wikipedia.org/wiki/The_End_of_History_and_the_Last_Man#Criticisms.

[121] *Clash of Civilizations*, accessed 21 February 2019, https://en.wikipedia.org/wiki/Clash_of_Civilizations.

[122] https://en.wikipedia.org/wiki/Clash_of_Civilizations#Huntington's_thesis_of_civiliz ational_clash, Huntington's thesis of civilizational clash, accessed 8 May 2019.

[123] *Ibid.*, accessed the same.

[124] *Ibid.*, accessed the same.

[125] Clash of Civilizations: The West versus the Rest, accessed 8 May 2019, https://en.wikipedia.org/wiki/Clash_of_Civilizations#The_West_versus_the_Rest.

126 Clash of Civilizations: Criticism, accessed 8 May 2019, https://en.wikipedia.org/wiki/Clash_of_Civilizations#Criticism.
127 Book Review, Culture Matters, accessed 8 May 2019, http://www.futurecasts.com/book%20review%209-2.htm.
128 Lawrence E. Harrison and Samuel P. Huntington, ed., *Culture Matters: How Values Shape Human Progress* (New York: Basic Books, 2000), xxiv-xxxiv.
129 Globalization, accessed 8 May 2019, https://en.wikipedia.org/wiki/Globalization.
130 Globalization: Economic, Cultural, Political globalization, accessed 10 September 2019, https://en.wikipedia.org/wiki/Globalization.
131 Globalization: Other dimensions – Movement of people, accessed 8 May 2019, https://en.wikipedia.org/wiki/Globalization#Movement_of_people.
132 Globalization: Other dimensions – Movement of information, accessed 8 May 2019, https://en.wikipedia.org/wiki/Globalization#Movement_of_information.
133 The World Is Flat: Ten flatteners, accessed 9 May 2019, https://en.wikipedia.org/wiki/The_World_Is_Flat#Ten_flatteners.
134 The Earth Is Flat: Proposed remedies, accessed 9 May 2019, https://en.wikipedia.org/wiki/The_World_Is_Flat#Proposed_remedies.
135 The Earth Is Flat: Conflict Prevention, accessed 9 May 2019, https://en.wikipedia.org/wiki/The_World_Is_Flat#Proposed_remedies.
136 G. John Ikenberry, Book Review on The Paradox of American Power, accessed 26 May 2019, https://www.foreignaffairs.com/reviews/capsule-review/2002-03-01/paradox-american-power-why-worlds-only-superpower-cant-go-it-alone.
137 The Paradox of American Power by Joseph S. Nye, accessed 26 May 20-19, https://www.ukessays.com/essays/politics/the-paradox-of-american-power.php.
138 Why Globalization Works: The Global Opposition, accessed 8 May 2019, https://www.economist.com/media/globalexecutive/why_globalization_wks_e_02.pdf.
139 *Ibid.*, accessed the same.
140 Why Globalization Works: A Brighter Tomorrow? Accessed the same.
141 Globalization and Its Contents, accessed 1 March 2019, https://en.wikipedia.org/wiki/Globalization_and_Its_Discontents.
142 *Ibid.*, accessed the same.
143 *Ibid.*, accessed the same.
144 War on Terror, accessed 8 May 2019, https://en.wikipedia.org/wiki/War_on_Terror.
145 *Ibid.*, accessed the same.
146 War on Terror: Criticism, accessed 8 May 2019, https://en.wikipedia.org/wiki/War_on_Terror#Criticism.
147 War on Terror: Other Wars on Terror, accessed 8 May 2019, https://en.wikipedia.org/wiki/War_on_Terror#Other_Wars_on_Terror.
148 Gideon Rose, "The Fourth Founding," 14-7.
149 Richard Haass, "How a World Order Ends and What Comes in Its Wake," 27-8.
150 *Ibid.*, 28.
151 Yan Xuetong, "The Age of Uneasy Peace: Chinese Power in a Divided World," *Foreign Affairs* 98(1) (January/February), 40.
152 Mapping China's Global Governance Ambitions, accessed 13 May 2019, https://www.americanprogress.org/issues/security/reports/2019/02/28/466768/mapping-chinas-global-governance-ambitions/.
153 Oriana Skylar Mastro, "The Stealth Superpower: How China Hid Its Global Ambitions," *Foreign Affairs* 98(1) (January/February 2019), 32.
154 *Ibid.*, 32-3.

[155] China's Anti-Access Area Denial, accessed 14 May 2019, http://missiledefenseadvocacy.org/missile-threat-and-proliferation/todays-missile-threat/china-anti-access-area-denial-coming-soon/.

[156] Oriana Skylar Mastro, "The Stealth Superpower," Foreign Affairs 98(1), 33-4.

[157] *Ibid.*, 34-6.

[158] Made in China 2015, accessed 12 May 2019, https://en.wikipedia.org/wiki/Made_in_China_2025.

[159] Oriana Skylar Mastro, "The Stealth Superpower," 36-7.

[160] U.S. accuses China of violating bilateral anti-hacking deal, accessed 23 May 2019, https://www.reuters.com/article/us-usa-china-cyber/u-s-accuses-china-of-violating-bilateral-anti-hacking-deal-idUSKCN1NE02E.

[161] New documents link Huawei to suspected front companies in Iran, Syria, accessed 23 May 2019. https://www.cnbc.com/2019/01/08/new-documents-link-huawei-to-suspected-front-companies-in-iran-syria.html.

[162] China: facial recognition and state control, accessed 23 May 2019, https://www.youtube.com/watch?v=lH2gMNrUuEY.

[163] US-China Trade Talks and American Strategy, accessed 24 May 2019, https://geopoliticalfutures.com/us-china-trade-talks-and-american-strategy/.

[164] Russia-United States relations: Ukraine crisis, accessed 13 May 2019, https://en.wikipedia.org/wiki/Russia%E2%80%93United_States_relations#Ukraine_crisis,_sanctions_(2014%E2%80%93present).

[165] Russian military intervention in the Syrian civil war, accessed 13 May 2019, https://en.wikipedia.org/wiki/Russia%E2%80%93United_States_relations#Russian_military_intervention_in_the_Syrian_Civil_War_(from_September_30,_2015).

[166]https://en.wikipedia.org/wiki/Russian_interference_in_the_2016_United_States_elections, Russian interference in the 2016 United States elections, accessed 13 May 2019.

[167] Iran Nuclear Deal Framework, accessed 14, May 2019, https://en.wikipedia.org/wiki/Iran_nuclear_deal_framework.

[168] North Korean Nuclear Negotiations, accessed 14 May 2019, https://www.cfr.org/timeline/north-korean-nuclear-negotiations.

[169] Trump's denuclearization strategies for Iran and North Korea are totally opposite. Why? Accessed 14 May 2019, https://www.washingtonpost.com/opinions/2019/03/01/trumps-denuclearization-strategies-iran-north-korea-are-totally-opposite-why/?utm_term=.0e076e7a79de.

[170] US-China Trade Talks and American Strategy, accessed 16 May 2019, https://geopoliticalfutures.com/us-china-trade-talks-and-american-strategy/.

[171] Michael Mandelbaum, "The New Containment: Handling Russia, China, and Iran," *Foreign Affairs* 98(2) (March/April 2019), 123-31.

[172] Michael Mandelbaum, *The Rise and Fall of Peace on Earth* (New York: Oxford University Press, 2019), 43-4.

[173] *Ibid.*, 95.

[174] *Ibid.*, 132.

[175] *Ibid.*, 155-6.

[176] Stephen M. Walt, "The End of Hubris and the New Age of American Restraint," *Foreign Affairs* 98(3) (May/June 2019), 29-35.

[177] What's Inside, accessed 10 September 2019, https://www.foreignaffairs.com/articles/2019-02-12/new-nationalism.

[178] Andreas Wimmer, "Why Nationalism Works and Why It isn't Going Away," *Foreign Affairs* 98(2) (March/April 2019), 27-34.

[179] Jan-Werner Muller, "False Flags: The Myth of the Nationalist Resurgence," *Foreign Affairs* 98(2) (March/April 2019), 35-41.

[180] Yael Tamir, "Building a Better Nationalism: The Nation's Place in a Globalized World," *Foreign Affairs* 98(2) (March/April 2019), 48-53.

[181] Lars-Erik Cederman, "Blood for Soil: The Fatal Temptations of Ethnic Politics," *Foreign Affairs* 98(2) (March/April 2019), 61-8.

[182] Peter Zeihan, The Accidental Superpower: The Next Generation of American Preeminence and the Coming Global Disorder (New York: Twelve, 2014).

[183] Kirk US Review, accessed 23 February 2019, https://www.kirkusreviews.com/book-reviews/peter-zeihan/the-accidental-superpower/.

[184] The Accidental Superpower, accessed 23 February 2019, https://www.publishersweekly.com/978-1-4555-8366-9.

[185]https://en.wikipedia.org/wiki/The_Next_100_Years:_A_Forecast_for_the_21st_Cent ury, *The Next 100 Years*, accessed 22 February 2019.

[186] *Ibid.*, the same. The summary of this book here is all quoted from Wikipeida.org.

[187] https://www.forbes.com/sites/danielaraya/2019/01/14/chinas-grand-strategy/#3c0e07111f18, China's Grand Strategy, accessed 20 May 2019.

[188] *Ibid.*, accessed the same.

[189] https://www.cnbc.com/2018/04/17/chinas-zte-may-lose-android-license-as-us-problems-build.html, "China's ZTE may lose Android license," accessed 21 May 2019,

[190] https://www.scmp.com/news/china/politics/article/3004756/chinese-telecom-giant-huawei-was-under-secret-us-surveillance, "Chinese telecoms giant Huawei was under secret US surveillance, US fraud hearing told," accessed 21 May 2019.

[191]https://en.wikipedia.org/wiki/Belt_and_Road_Initiative#Accusations_of_neocolonial ism, Belt and Road Initiative: Accusations of neocolonialism, accessed 20 May 2019.

[192] State-Owned Enterprises Are a Hard Habit China Doesn't Want to Break, accessed 20 May 2019, https://worldview.stratfor.com/article/state-owned-enterprises-are-hard-habit-china-doesnt-want-break.

[193] Alice Jetin Duceux, An Overview of Chinese Debt, accessed 20 May 2019, http://www.cadtm.org/An-Overview-of-Chinese-Debt.

[194] China's debt threat: time to rein in the lending boom, accessed 20 May 2019, https://www.ft.com/content/0c7ecae2-8cfb-11e8-bb8f-a6a2f7bca546.

[195] Lixin Sun, "The structure and sustainability of China's debt," *Cambridge Journal of Economics* 43(3) (May 2019), 695-715.

[196] Demographics of China: Labor force, accessed 20 May 2019, https://en.wikipedia.org/wiki/Demographics_of_China#Labor_force.

[197] China's Influence on the U.S. Dollar, accessed 20 May 2019, https://www.thebalance.com/how-does-china-influence-the-u-s-dollar-3970466.

[198] Dali Yang, "Dirty Deeds: Will Corruption Doom China?," Foreign Affairs 96(4) (July/August 2017), accessed 13 September 2019, https://www.foreignaffairs.com/reviews/review-essay/2017-06-13/dirty-deeds.

[199] Mira Rapp-Hooper and Rebecca Friedman Lissner, "The Open World: What America Can Achieve after Trump," *Foreign Affairs* 98(3) (May/June 2019), 19-20.

[200] Michael McFaul, "Russia as It Is: A Grand Strategy Confronting Putin" *Foreign Affairs* 97(4) (July/August 2018), accessed 25 May 2019, https://www.foreignaffairs.com/articles/russia-fsu/2018-06-14/russia-it.

[201] *Ibid.*, accessed the same.

[202] https://www.foreignaffairs.com/articles/ukraine/2016-04-18/why-russian-president-putin-took-crimea-from-ukraine, Daniel Treisman, "Why Putin Took Crimea," *Foreign Affairs* 95(3) (May/June 2016), accessed 25 May 2019.

203 https://www.navytimes.com/news/your-navy/2019/01/29/senator-chinese-buildup-in-south-china-sea-like-preparing-for-world-war-iii/, Senator: Chinese buildup in South China Sea like 'preparing for World War III', accessed 25 May 2019.
204 Prisons in North Korea, accessed 26 May 2019, https://en.wikipedia.org/wiki/Prisons_in_North_Korea.
205 Daniel W. Drezner, "This Time Is Different: Why U.S. Foreign Policy Will Never Recover," Foreign Affairs 98(3) (May/June 2019), accessed 26 May 2019, https://www.foreignaffairs.com/articles/2019-04-16/time-different?fa_package=1124201.
206 Kori Schake, "Back to Basic: How to Make Right What Trump Gets Wrong," *Foreign Affairs* 98(3) (May/June 2019), accessed 26 May 2019, the same.
207 David Brooks, "Harmony and the Dream," *New York Times*, August 11, 2008, accessed 26 May 2019, https://www.nytimes.com/2008/08/12/opinion/12brooks.html.
208 U.S. Funding to the United States System, accessed 13 September 2019, https://fas.org/sgp/crs/row/R45206.pdf.
209 George Friedman, *The Next 100 Years: A Forecast for the 21st Century* (New York: Anchor Books, 2009), 110-11.
210 List of countries by military expenditures, accessed 29 May 2019, https://en.wikipedia.org/wiki/List_of_countries_by_military_expenditures.
211 George Friedman, *The Next 100 Years*, 145.
212 *Ibid.*, 147.
213 Poland, accessed 30 May 2019, https://en.wikipedia.org/wiki/Poland.
214 George Friedman, *The Next 100 Years*, 148-151.
215 *Ibid.*, 164.
216 Space Warfare: Possible warfare in the space, accessed 30 May 2019, https://en.wikipedia.org/wiki/Space_warfare#Possible_warfare_over_space.

Photo I-End-1. Trade tensions reflects US-China battle
for 21st century world order,
https://thehill.com/opinion/finance/380625-trade-tensions-reflect-us-china-battle-for-21st-century-world-order, accessed 11 November 2019

REFERENCES
Part I. World Order in the Twenty-First Century

Acharya, Amitav. *Constructing Global Order: Agency and Change in World Politics*. New York: Cambridge University Press, 2018.

Adamsky, Dmitry. *Russian Nuclear Orthodoxy: Religion, Politics, and Strategy.*Stanford, CA: Stanford University Press, 2019.

Ahmed, Akbar. *Journey Into Europe: Islam, Immigration, and Identity*. Washington, DC: Brookings Institution Press, 2018.

Albright, David and Andrea Stricker. *Taiwan's Former Nuclear Weapons Program: Nuclear Weapons On-Demand*. Washington, DC: Institute for Science and International Security, 2018.

Aleksashenko, Sergey. *Putin's Counterrevolution*. Washington, DC: Brookings Institution Press, 2018.

Allcock, Thomas Tunstall. *Thomas C. Mann: President Johnson, the Cold War, and the Restructuring of Latin American Foreign Policy*. Lexington, KY: University Press of Kentucky, 2018.

Allison, Graham T. "Conceptual Models and the Cuban Missile Crisis." *American Political Science Review* 63 (September 1969), 689-718.

Andersson, Jenny. *The Future of the World: Futurology, Futurists, and the Struggle for the Post-Cold War Imagination*. Oxford, UK: Oxford University Press, 2018.

Asserate, Asfa-Wossen. *African Exodus: Migration and the Future of Europe*. London, UK: Haus Publishing, 2014.

Baldwin, Rocjard. *The Globotics Upheaval: Globalization, Robotics, and the Future of Work*. New York: Oxford University Press, 2019.

Baldwin, Tom. *Ctrl Alt Delete: How Politics and the Media Crashed Our Democracy*. London, UK: C. Hurst & Co., Ltd., 2018.

Barton, Frederick D. P*eace Works: America's Unifying Role in a Turbulent World*. Lanham, MD: Rowman & Littlefield, 2018.

Beckley, Michael. *Unrivaled: Why America Will Remain the World's Sole Superpower*. Ithaca, NY: Cornell University Press, 2018.

Bernanke, Ben S., Timothy F. Geithner, and Henry M. Paulson, Jr. *Fire Fighting: The Financial Crisis and Its Lessons*. New York: Penguin, 2019.

Black, Jeremy. *English Nationalism: A Short History*. London: Hurst, 2018.

Blanchard, Olivier and Lawrence H. Summers. *Evolution or Revolution: Rethinking Macroeconomic Policy After the Great Recession*. Cambridge, MA: MIT Press, 2019.

Bleck, Jaimie and Nicolas van de Walle. *Electoral Politics in Africa Since 1990: Continuity in Change*. New York: Cambridge Univ. Press, 2018.

Boix, Carles. *Democratic Capitalism at the Crossroads: Technological Change and the Future Politics*. Princeton, NJ: Princeton Univ. Press, 2019.

Brand, Hal and Charles Edel. *The Lessons of Tragedy: Statecraft and World Order*. New Haven, CT: Yale University Press, 2019.

Brigden, Noelle Kateri. *The Migrant Passage· Clandestine Journeys From Central America*. Ithaca, NY: Cornell University Press, 2018.

Brockman, John, ed. *Possible Minds: Twenty-Five Ways of Looking at AI*. New York: Penguin Press, 2019.

Brookhiser, Richard. *John Marshall: The Man Who Made the Supreme Court*. New York: Basic Books, 2018.

Brooks, Max, John Amble, ML Cavanaugh, and Jaym Gates, eds. *Strategy Strikes Back: How "Star Wars" Explains Modern Military Conflict*. Lincoln, NB: Potomac Books, 2018.

Bull, Hedley. *The Anarchical Society*. New York: Columbia Univ. Press, 1977.

Burns, William J. *The Back Channel: A Memoir of American Diplomacy and the Case for Its Renewal*. New York: Random House, 2019.

Calder, Kent E. *Super Continent: The Logic of Eurasian Integration*. Stanford, CA: Stanford University Press, 2019.

Caldwell, Beth C. *Deported Americans: Life After Deportation to Mexico*. Durham, NC: Duke University Press, 2019.

Campbell, John I. and Ove K. Pedersen. "The Rise of Neoliberalism and Structural Analysis." In *The Rise of Neoliberalism and Structural Analysis*. Eds. John I. Campbell and Ove K. Pedersen. Princeton, NJ: Princeton University Press, 2001.

Campbell, Susanna P. *Global Governance and Local Peace: Accountability and Performance in International Peacebuilding*. New York: Cambridge University Press, 2018.

Carr, Edward Hallett. *The Twenty Years' Crisis, 1919-1939*. New York: Harper Perennial, 1964.

Carson, Austin. *Secret Wars: Convert Conflict in International Politics*. Princeton, NJ: Princeton University Press, 2018.

Cheru, Fantu, Christopher Cramer, and Arkebe Oqubay. *The Oxford Handbook of the Ethiopian Economy*. New York: Oxford University Press, 2019.

Chowdhury, Arjun. *The Myth of International Order: Why Weak States Persist and Alternatives to the State Fade Away*. New York: Oxford University Press, 2018.

Clarke, Colin P. *After the Caliphate: The Islamic State and the Future Terrorist Diaspora*. Cambridge, UK: Polity Press, 2019.

Clausing, Kimbely. *Open: The Progressive Case for Free Trade, Immigration, and Global Capital*. Cambridge, MA: Harvard University Press, 2019.

Collier, Paul. *The Future of Capitalism: Facing the New Anxieties*. New York: HarperCollins Publishers, 2019.

Cormac, Rory. *Disrupt and Deny: Spies, Special Forces, and the Secret Pursuit of British Foreign Policy*. New York: Oxford University Press, 2018.

Crawford, Susan. *Fiber: The Coming Tech Revolution – and Why America Might Miss It*. New Haven, CT: Yale University Press, 2019.

Crouch, Colin. *The Globalization Backlash*. Cambridge, UK: Polity, 2018.

Daalder, Ivo H. and James M. Lindsay. *The Empty Throne: America's Abdication of Global Leadership*. New York: Public Affairs, 2018.

Dam, Nikolaos Van. *Destroying a Nation: The Civil War in Syria.* London, UK: I.B. Tauris, 2017.

D'Aveni, Richard. *The Pan-Industrial Revolution: How New Manufacturing Titans Will Transform the World.* Boston, MA: Houghton Mifflin, 2018.

De, Rohit. *A People's Constitution: The Everyday Life of Law in the Indian Republic.* Princeton, NJ: Princeton University Press, 2018.

Diamond, Jared. *Guns, Germs, and Steel: The Fates of Human Societies.* New York: W. W. Norton & Company, 1997.

Doyle, Michael W. "Liberalism and World Politics." *American Political Science Review* 80:4 (December 1986), 1151-69.

Durrani, Asad. *Pakistan Adrift: Navigating Troubled Waters.* London, UK: C. Hurst & Co., Ltd., 2018.

Economy, Elizabeth C. *The Third Revolution: Xi Jinping and the New Chinese State.* New York: Oxford University Press, 2018.

Eisenman, Joshua. *Red China's Green Revolution: Technical Innovation, Institutional Change, and Economic Development Under the Commune.* New York: Columbia University Press, 2018.

Elgindy, Khaled. *Blind Spot: America and the Palestinians, From Balfour to Trump.* Washington, DC: Brookings Institution Press, 2019.

Ellis, R. Evan. *Transnational Organized Crime in Latin America and the Caribbean: From Evolving Threats and Responses to Integrated, Adaptive Solutions.* New York: Lexington Books, 2018.

_____. *The Future of Latin America and the Caribbean in the Context of the Rise of China.* Washington, DC: CSIS, 2018.

Erisman, H. Michael and John M. Kirk, ed. *Cuban Foreign Policy: Transformation Under Raul Castro.* Lanham, MD: Rowman, 2018.

Farrell, Henry and Abraham Newman. *Of Privacy and Power: The Transatlantic Struggle Over Freedom and Security.* Princeton, NJ: Princeton University Press, 2019.

Fifield, Anna. *The Great Successor: The Divinely Perfect Destiny of Brilliant Comrade Kim Jong Un.* Public New York: Affairs, 2019.

Fincher, Leta Hong. *Betraying Big Brother: The Feminist Awakening in China.* London, UK: Verso Books, 2018.

Foster, Elizabeth A. *African Catholic: Decolonization and the Transformation of the Church.* Cambridge, MA: Harvard University Press, 2019.

Frantz, Erica. *Authoritarianism: What Everyone Needs to Know.* New York: Oxford University Press, 2018.

Fravel, M. Taylor. *Active Defense: China's Military Strategy Since 1949.* Princeton, NJ: Princeton University Press, 2019.

Freedman, Lawrence. *Ukraine and the Art of Strategy.* New York: Oxford University Press, 2019.

Fridman, Ofer. *Russian "Hybrid Warfare": Resurgence and Politicization.* New York: Oxford University Press, 2018.

Frey, John Carlos. *Sand and Blood: America's Stealth War on the Mexico Border.* New York: Bold Type Books, 2019.

Friedman, George. *The Next 100 Years: A Forecast for the 21st Century.* New York: Anchor Books, 2009.

Friedman, Thomas L. *The World Is Flat: A Brief History of the Twentieth-first Century.* New York: Farrar, Straus and Giroux, 2005.

Fukuyama, Francis. *The End of History and the Last Man.* New York: Avon Books, 1992.

_____. *State-Building: Governance and World Order in the 21st Century.* Ithaca, NY: Cornell University Press ,2004.

_____. *Identity: The Demand for Dignity and the Politics of Resentment.* New York: Farrar, Straus and Giroux, 2018.

Gallagher, Kelly Sims and Xiaowei Xuan. *Taitans of the Climate: Explaining Policy Process in the United States and China.* Cambridge, MA: MIT Press, 2019.

Gertel, Jorg and Ralf Hexel. *Coping With Uncertainty: Youth in the Middle East and North Africa.* London, UK: Saqi Books, 2018.

Gills, Barry and Ronen P. Palan. "The Neo-structuralist Agenda in International Relations." In *Transcending the State-Global Divide: A Neo-structuralist Agenda in International Relations.* Eds. Ronen P. Palan and Barry Gills. Boulder, CO: Lynne Rienner, 1994.

Gilpin, Robert, *War and Change in World Politics.* New York: Cambridge University Press, 1981.

Glosserman, Brad. *Peak Japan: The End of Great Ambition.* Washington, DC: Georgetown University Press, 2019.

Goldstein, Judith and Robert O. Keohane, "Ideas and Foreign Policy: An Analytical Framework." In *Ideas and Foreign Policy: Beliefs, Institutions, andPolitical Change.* Eds. Judith Goldstein and Robert O. Keohane. Ithaca, NY: Cornell University Press, 1993.

Gonzalez, Anabel. *Latin America-China Trade and Investment Amid Global Tensions: A Need to Upgrade and Diversify.* Washington, DC: Atlantic Council, 2018.

Gopnik, Adam. *A Thousand Small Sanities: The Moral Adventure of Liberalism.* New York: Basic Books, 2019.

Greenfeld, Liah. *Nationalism: A Short History.* Washington, DC: The Brookings Institution, 2019.

Gregg, Heather Selma. *Building the Nation: Missed Opportunities in Iraq and Afghanistan.* Lincoln, NB: Potomac Books, 2018.

Griffiths, James. *The Great Firewall of China: How to Build and Control an Alternative Version of the Internet.* London, UK: Zed Books, 2019.

Grotius, Hugo. *On the Law of War and Peace.* New York: Cambridge University Press, 2012.

Haas, Ernest B. *When Knowledge Is Power: Three Models of Change in International Organizations.* Berkeley, CA: U.C. Press, 1990.

Hanson, Victor Davis. *The Case for Trump.* New York: Basic Books, 2019.

Harberkorn, Tyrell. *In Plain Sight: Impunity and Human Rights in Thailand.* Madison, WI: University of Wisconsin Press, 2018.

Harrison, Lawrence E. "Why Culture Matters." In *Culture Matters: How Values Shape Human Progress*. Eds. Harrison and Huntington. New York: Basic Books, 2000.

Hastings, Max. *Vietnam: An Epic Tragedy, 1845-1975*. New York: Harper Collins Publishers, 2018.

Hennette, Stephanie, Thomas Piketty, Guillaume Sacriste, and Anthony Vauchez. *How to Democratize Europe*. Cambridge, MA: Harvard University Press, 2019.

Hill, William H. *No Place for Russia: European Security Institutions Since 1989*. New York: Columbia University Press, 2018.

Hiro, Dilip. *Cold War in the Islamic World: Saudi Arabia, Iran, and the Struggle for Supremacy*. London, UK: C. Hurst & Co., Ltd., 2019

Ho, Ming-Sho. *Challenging Beijing's Mandate of Heaven: Taiwan's Sunflower Movement and Hong Kong's Umbrella Movement*. Philadelphia, PA: Temple University Press, 2019.

Hobbes, Thomas. *Leviathan*. New York: Cambridge University Press, 2005.

Hobson, John A. *Imperialism: A Study*. First published in 1902. London, UK: Macat International Ltd., 2017.

Holsti, Ole R. "Crisis Decision Making." In *Diplomacy: New Approaches in History, Theory and Policy*. New York: Free Press, 1979.

Huntington, Samuel P. *The Clash of Civilizations: Remaking of World Order*. New York: A Touchstone Book, Simon & Schuster, 1997.

Hyslop, Stephen G. *Atlas of World War II: History's Greatest Conflict Revealed Through Rare Wartime Maps and New Cartography*. Washington, DC: National Geographic, 2018.

Ikenberry, G. John, ed. *American Foreign Policy: Theoretical Essays*. New York: Harper Collins Publishers, 1989.

Joshi, Yogesh and Frank O'Donnell. *India and Nuclear Asia: Forces, Doctrine, and Dangers*. Washington, DC: Georgetown University Press, 2018.

Karnad, Bharat. *Staggering Forward: Narendra Modi and India's Global Ambition*. New York: Penguin Viking, 2018.

Kenny, Michael. *The Islamic State in Britain: Radicalization and Resilience in an Activist Network*. New York: Cambridge University Press, 2018.

Klinger-Vidra, Robyn. *The Venture Capital State: The Silicon Valley Model in East Asia*. Ithaca, NY: Cornell University Press, 2018.

Jervis, Robert. *Perception and Misperception in International Politics*. Princeton, NJ: Princeton University Press, 1976.

Jervis, Robert, ed. *Chaos in the Liberal Order: The Trump Presidency and International Politics in the Twenty-First Century*. New York: Columbia University Press, 2018.

Kant, Immanuel. *Perpetual Peace: A Philosophical Essay*. Amazon Digital Service, 2011.

Kaplan, Robert David. "The Coming Anarchy." *The Atlantic* (February 1994).

Ohmae, Kenich. *The End of the Nation State: The Rise of Regional Economies*. New York: The Free Press, 1995.

_____. *Monsoon: The Indian Ocean.* New York: Random House, 2010.

Kaushal, Neeraj. *Blaming Immigrants: Nationalism and the Economics of Global Movement.* New York: Columbia University Press, 2019.

Kennan, George F. *American Diplomacy.* Chicago, IL: University of Chicago Press, 1951.

Kennedy, Paul. *The Rise and Fall of the Great Powers: Economic Change and Military Conflict from 1500 to 2000.* New York: Vintage Books, 1989.

Keohane, Robert O. and Joseph S. Nye, Jr. *Power and Interdependence: World Politics in Transition.* Boston, MA: Brown University Press, 1977.

Keohane, Robert O. "The Theory of World Politics: Structural Realism and Beyond." In *Political Science: The State of the Discipline.* Ed. Ada W Finifter. Washington, DC: APSA, 1983

Kissinger, Henry. *World Order.* New York: Penguin Book, 2014.

_____. *Does America Need a Foreign Policy? Toward a Diplomacy for the 21st Century.* New York: Simon & Schuster, 2001.

Koss, Daniel. *Where the Party Rules: The Rank and File of China's Communist State.* New York: Cambridge University Press, 2018.

Krasner, Stephen. "The Accomplishments of International Political Economy." In *International Theory: Positivism and Beyond*, ed. Steve Smith. New York: Cambridge University Press, 1966.

Lackner, Helen. *Yemen in Crisis: Autocracy, Neoliberalism and the Disintegration of a State.* London, UK: Saqi Books, 2017.

Lacroix, Stephane and Jean-Pierre Filiu. *Revisiting the Arab Uprising: The Politics of a Revolutionary Moment.* London, UK: C. Hurst & Co., 2019.

Lepore, Jill. "A New Americanism: Why a Nation Needs a National Story." *Foreign Affairs* 98(2) (March/April 2019), 10-19.

Linter, Bertil. *The Costliest Pearl: China's Struggle for India's Ocean.* London, UK: Hurst Publishers, 2019.

Lundestad, Geir. *The World's Most Prestigious Prize: The Inside Story of the Nobel Prize.* New York: Oxford University Press, 2019.

Lutes, Jason. *Berlin.* Montreal, Canada: Drawn & Quarterly, 2018.

Macekura, Stephen J. and Erez Manela. *The Development Century: A Global History.* New York: Cambridge University Press, 2018.

Machiavelli, Niccolo. *The Prince.* Norwalk, CT: The Easton Press, 1980.

Mandelbaum, Michael. *The Rise and Fall of Peace on Earth.* New York: Oxford University Press, 2019.

_____. *Mission Failure: America and the World in the Post-Cold War Era.* New York: Oxford University Press, 2016.

Marriott, David and Karl Lacroix. *Fault Lines on the Face of China: 50 Reasons Why China May Never Be Great.* Tokyo, Japan: Random House Kodansha, 2010.

Mason, Paul. *Postcapitalism: A Guide to Our Future.* New York: Farrar, Straus and Giroux, 2015.

McFate, Sean. *The New Rules of War: Victory in the Age of Durable Disorder.* New York: William Morrow, 2019.

McMahon, Dinny. *China's Great Wall of Debt*. New York: Houghton Mifflin Harcourt, 2018.

Mearsheimer, John J. *The Tragedy of Great Power Politics*. New York: W. W. Norton & Company, 2001.

_____. John J. *The Great Delusion: Liberal Dreams and International Realities*. New Haven, CT: Yale University Press, 2018.

Meek, James. *Dreams of Leaving and Remaining*. New York: Verso, 2019.

Middelaar, Luuk van. *Alarums and Excursions: Improving Politics on the European Stage*. New York: Agenda Publishing, 2019.

Miller, James. *Can Democracy Work? A Short History of a Radical Idea, From Ancient Athens to Our World*. New York: Farrar, Straus and Giroux, 2018.

Moravcsik, Andrew. "Taking Preferences Seriously: A Positive Liberal Theory" *International Organization*, 51:4 (Autumn 1997), 513-33.

Morgan, Michael Cotey. *The Final Act: The Helsinki Accords and the Transformation of the Cold War*. Princeton, NJ: Princeton University Press, 2018.

Morgenthau, Hans. *Politics among Nations*. New York: McGraw-Hill, 1948.

Morris, Benny and Dror Ze'evi. *The Thirty-Year Genocide: Turkey's Destruction of Its Christian Minorities, 1894-1924*. Cambridge, MA: Harvard University Press, 2019.

Morse, Yonatan L. *How Autocrats Compete: Parties, Patrons, and Unfair Elections in Africa*. New York: Cambridge University Press, 2018.

Murphy, Craig N. *International Organization and Industrial Change: Global Governance Since 1850 (Europe and International Order)*. New York: Oxford University Press, 1994.

Nagorski, Andrew. *1941: The Year Germany Lost the War*. New York: Simon & Schuster, 2019.

Natalegawa, Marty. *Does ASEAN Matter? A View From Within*. Singapore: ISEAS-Yusof Ishak Institute, 2018.

Nesser, Petter. *Islamist Terrorism in Europe*. New York: Oxford University Press, 2018.

Niebuhr, Reinhold. *The Irony of American History*. Chicago, IL: University of Chicago Press, 1952.

Nisley, Thomas J. *The Peace Corps and Latin America: In the Last Mile of U.S. Foreign Policy*. Lanham, MD: Lexington Books, 2018.

Nyabola, Nanjala. *Digital Democracy, Analogue Politics: How the Internet Era Is Transforming Politics in Kenya*. London, UK: Zed Books, 2018.

Nye, Jr., Joseph S. *The Paradox of American Power: Why the World's Only Superpower Can't Go It Alone*. New York: Oxford Univ. Press, 2002.

Panagariya, Arvind. *Free Trade and Prosperity*. New York: Oxford University Press, 2019.

Pike, William. *Combatants: A Memoir of the Bush War and the Press in Uganda*. London, UK: Self-Published, 2019.

Polanyi, Karl. *The Great Transformation: The Political and Economic Origins of Our Time*. New York: Amereon House, 1944.

Pollack, Kenneth M. *Armies of Sand: The Past, Present, and Future of Arab Military Effectiveness*. New York: Oxford University Press, 2019.

Ratner-Rosenhagen, Jennifer. *The Ideas That Made America: A Brief History*. New York: Oxford University Press, 2019.

Rayburn, Joel D. and Frank K. Sobchak. *The U.S. Army in the Iraq War. Vol. 1: Invasion, Insurgency, Civil War, 2003-2006*. Carlisle, PA: Strategic Studies Institute and the U.S. Army War College Press, 2019.

Reinert, Sophus A. *The Academy of Fisticuffs: Political Economy and Commercial Society in Enlightenment Italy*. Cambridge, MA: Harvard University Press, 2018.

Reus-Smit, Christian. *On Cultural Diversity: International Theory in a World of Difference*. New York: Cambridge University Press, 2019.

Rosenau, James N. *The Scientific Study of Foreign Policy*. London, UK: Frances Printer, 1980.

Rosenau, James N. *Turbulence in World Politics: A Theory of Change and Continuity*. Princeton, NJ: Princeton University Press, 1851.

Rosenblatt, Helena. *The Lost History of Liberalism: From Ancient Rome to the Twenty-first Century*. Princeton, NJ: Princeton University Press, 2018.

Rousseau, Jean Jacques. *The Social Contract and Discourses*. Norwalk, CT: Easton Press, 1991.

Rudd, Kevin. *The PM Years*. Sydney, Australia: Pan Macmillan, 2018.

Saikal, Amin. *Iran Rising: The Survival and Future of the Islamic Republic*. Princeton, NJ: Princeton University Press, 2019.

Sand, Shlomo. *The End of the French Intellectual*. London, UK: Verso, 2018.

Schneider, Christina. *The Responsive Union: National Elections and European Governance*. New York: Cambridge University Press, 2018.

Schomerus, Mareike, Pierre Englebert, and Lotje de Vries, ed. *Secessionism in African Politics*. London, UK: Palgrave Macmillan, 2018.

Sen, Amartya. *Development as Freedom*. New York: Anchor Books, Random House, 1999.

Shadikhodjaev, Sherzod. *Industrial Policy and the World Trade organization*. New York: Cambridge University Press, 2018.

Sharma, Shalendra D. *A Political Economy of the United States, China, and India: Prosperity With Inequality*. New York: Cambridge U. Press, 2018.

Sharman, J. D. *Empires of the Weak: The Real Story of European Expansion and the Creation of the New World Order*. Princeton, NJ: Princeton University Press, 2019.

Sharp, Alan. *Versailles 1919: A Centennial Perspective*. London, UK: Haus Publishing, 2018.

Shelley, Louise I. *Dark Commerce: How a New Illicit Economy Is Threatening Our Future*. Princeton, NJ: Princeton University Press, 2018.

Shifrinson, Joshua R. Itzkowitz. *Rising Titans, Falling Giants: How Great Powers Exploit Power Shifts*. Ithaca, NY: Cornell University Press, 2018.

Skidelsky, Robert. *Money and Government: The Past and Future of Economics*. New Haven, CT: Yale University Press, 2018.

Sky, Emma. *In a Time of Monsters: Travels Through a Middle East in Revolt.* London, UK: Atlantic Books, 2019.

Smith, Daniel M. *Dynasties and Democracy: The Inherited Incumbency Advantage in Japan.* Stanford, CA: Stanford University Press, 2018.

Smith, Sheila A. *Japan Rearmed: The Politics of Military Power.* Cambridge, MA: Harvard University Press, 2019.

Smith, Steve, Ken Booth, and Marysia Zalewski, eds. *International Theory: Positivism and Beyond.* New York: Cambridge University Press, 1996.

Sokolski, Henry D. *Underestimated Second Edition: Our Not So Peaceful Nuclear Future.* Carlisle, PA: Strategic Studies Institute, 2018.

Srnicek, Nick and Alex Williams. *Inventing the Future: Postcapitalism and a World Without Work.* Brooklyn, NY: Verso, 2015.

Stapleton, Timothy. *Africa: War and Conflict in Twentieth Century.* New York: Routledge Publishing, 2018.

Stein, Arthur A. *Why Nations Cooperate: Circumstance and Choice in International Relations.* Ithaca, NY: Cornell University Press, 1990.

Stent, Angela. *Putin's World: Russia Against the West and With the Rest.* New York: Twelve Hachette Book Group, 2019.

Stiglitz, Joseph E. *Globalization and Its Discontents.* New York: W. W. Norton & Co., 2002.

Stoker, Donald. *Why America Loses Wars: Limited War and US Strategy From the Korean War to the Present.* New York: Cambridge Univ. Press, 2019.

Straumann, Tobias. *1931: Debt, Crisis, and the Rise of Hitler.* New York: Oxford University Press, 2019.

Streeck, Wolfgang. "How Will Capitalism End?" *New Left Review* 87 (May/June 2014), 35-64.

Sy, Amadou. *Africa Through an Economic Lenz.* Washington, DC: Brookings Institution, 2018.

Tamir, Yael. *Why Nationalism.* Princeton, NJ: Princeton University Press, 2019.

Thucydides. *History of the Peloponnesian War.* New York: Penguin, 1954.

Toffler, Alvin. *The Third Wave.* New York: Bantam Books, 1980.

Trenin, Dmitri. *What Is Russia Up To in the Middle East?* Cambridge, UK: Polity, 2017.

Volker, Paul A. and Christine Harper. *Keeping At It: The Quest for Sound Money and Good Government.* New York: Public Affairs, 2018.

Vuuren, Hennie van. *Apartheid Guns and Money: A Tale of Profit.* London, UK: C. Hurst & Co., Ltd., 2019.

Walker, William O. *The Rise and Decline of the American Century.* Ithaca, NY: Cornell University Press, 2018.

Wallerstein, Immanuel. "Patterns and Perspectives of the Capitalist World Economy." *Contemporary Marxism*, No. 9. San Francisco: Synthesis Publications, 1984.

_____. *World Systems Analysis: An Introduction.* Durham, NC: Duke University Press, 2004.

_____. *The Modern World-System I: Capitalist Agriculture and the Origins of the European World-Economy in the Sixteenth Century*. Berkeley, CA: University of California Press, 1974.

_____. *The Modern World-System II: Mercantilism and the Consolidation of the European World-Economy, 1600-1750*. Berkeley, CA: University of California Press, 2011.

_____. *The Modern World-System III: The Second Era of Great Expansion of the Capitalist World-Economy, 1730s-1840s*. Berkeley, CA: University of California Press, 2011.

_____. *The Modern World System: Centrist Liberalism Triumphant, 1789 1914*. Berkeley, CA: University of California Press, 2011.

Waltz, Kenneth N. *Man, the State and War*. New York: Colombia University Press, 1959.

_____. *Theory of International Politics*. New York: Random House, 1979.

Wang, Ke. *The East Turkestan Independence Movement, 1930s to 1940s*. Hong Kong, China: Chinese University Press, 2019.

Warlouzet, Laurent. *Governing Europe in a Globalizing World: Neoliberalism and Its Alternatives Following the 1973 Oil Crisis*. New York: Routledge Publishing, 2017.

Weisman, Steven R. *The Chosen Wars: How Judaism Became an American Religion*. New York: Simon & Schuster, 2018.

Wendt, Alexander. "Anarchy Is What State Make of It: The Social Construction of Power Politics." In *International Organization* 46: 2 (Spring 1992), 391-425.

Weyland, Kurt and Raul L. Madrid. *When Democracy Trumps Populism: European and Latin American Lessons for the United States*. New York: Cambridge University Press, 2019.

Wolf, Martin. *Why Globalization Works*. New Haven, CT: Yale University Press, 2004.

Wood, Tony. *Russia Without Putin: Money, Power, and the Myths of the New Cold War*. New York: Verso Books, 2018.

Woodward, Bob. *Fear: Trump in the White House*. New York: Simon & Schuster, 2018.

Xuetong, Yan. *Leadership and the Rise of Great Powers*. Princeton, NJ: Princeton University Press, 2019.

Yeo, Andrew and Danielle Chubb. *North Korean Human Rights: Activists and Networks*. New York: Cambridge University Press, 2018.

Zakaria, Fareed. *The Post-American World*. New York: W.W. Norton & Company, 2008.

Zeihan, Peter. *The Accidental Superpower: The Next Generation of American Preeminence and The Coming Global Disorder*. New York: Twelve Hachette Book Group, 2014.

Part II. The Future of Capitalism:
Efficiency in Growth vs. Equality in Distribution

The economic system has transformed from the ancient agrarian economy to present time continuously. During the Middle Ages, external invasions caused the shortage of currency, which made workers unable to get money wages, so that they became vassal of the lord by receiving protection and taking a piece of land with returning of promised services. This was the beginning of feudalism held between landowners and free workers. Around 1450, the European economy began to revive from famine, disease, and wars. The rising population increased demand for food with other necessities, which caused the progress of agriculture, industry, commerce, and finance. With the geographical discovery and after the first industrial revolution in England, industrial capitalism was spread throughout the world in the following century. Moreover, advanced European states created colonies and pursued industrialization with imperialism by selling manufactured goods to their colonies for raw materials in the nineteenth century. Modern capitalism was harnessed by transportation and communications with highly advanced technology pulling the economy globalized.

Part II consists of five sections as listed above: history of economic transformation; theoretical background of capitalism; a historical overview of socialism, capitalism and democracy – efficiency versus equality; and the future of capitalism. On the one hand, capitalism tries to maximize the objective function or profits subject to constraints or available resources. So capitalist economy pursues efficiency that is to gain more profits per unit cost; which is the source of economic growth. On the other hand, socialism tries to minimize the gap between the rich and the poor in distribution. So socialist economy pursues equality that is to collect more taxes from the rich and to distribute wealth to the poor as equally as possible. But they are in trade-off relations, so that government policies for more growth lose some of equality, while government policies for better distribution lose some of efficiency. If a state chooses its political system or its economic policies towards extreme equality, the loss of efficiency will destroy its economy. Eventually, the falling economy is unable to support its political system, so that the state cannot maintain law and order just like former Soviet Union. In this regard, this section evaluates issues on efficiency versus equality.

1. History of Economic Transformation

As we did in Part I, history here is divided by three periods before the death of Louis XIV in 1715, and another three periods after the same. The Greek civilization was built by city states but was destroyed by the war between Athens and Sparta. The Romans united the Italian Peninsula and established the Roman Empire, but problems were risen by Christianity internally and the Germans externally migrating with Romanization, militarization, and barbarization. The Christians were the internal creative minority and the Germans were the external 'creative minority', both which helped destroy the 'dominant minority' of the Roman Empire. After the collapse of Western Empire, a thousand years elapsed to establish a new civilization in Europe.

The Renaissance was a rediscovery of humanism, which begun in Italy and spread to Europe. The Reformation brought religious freedom, although the conflict between Catholics and Protestants remained unresolved. The conflict between state and church was still continuous. The geographical discovery by Portugal and Spain opened a new world, at first for spice trade or precious metals, followed by the Dutch, English, and French; who were eager to gain commercial profits. Moreover, the scientific development in mathematics, physics, chemistry, astronomy, geography, biology, medicine, and others made scientists begin to displace religious authority, such as the Copernicans changed the concept of geocentric medieval astronomy.

The liberal ideas of Enlightenment encouraged the French Revolution, and the capitalistic ideas expedited the Industrial Revolution in the eighteenth century. The Napoleonic Wars spread liberal ideas and abolished the feudal tradition throughout Europe. After the fall of Napoleon, the Concert of Europe reestablished the conservative order by crushing any movements against legitimate rulers. However, liberalism stimulated the independence of European colonies; Socialism and Marxism encouraged revolutionary movements; and Nationalism helped both Italy and Germany unified; while Imperialism of European powers challenged the world peace.

The unified Germany became the main cause of two World Wars. In 1948 the United States launched the Marshal Plan to reconstruct European economies, since economic revival provides political stability. Owing to the NATO alliance, the Soviet Union collapsed in 1991, since inefficiency of the planned economy caused the continuous decline of its national income. Then, why is China to rise unlikely? Until 2015 China was largely benefited from trade and investment with undisturbed violations of norms and rules of the World Trade Organization. It has challenged American interests with the unfair trade surplus that is not sustainable. The current trade war between the United States and China may not be resolved until China stops their existing violations. If China challenges the U.S. strategic supremacy in this way, the United States may encounter the challenges by all means.

The Ancient Agrarian Economy (- 750 A.D.): *Ancient Near East*: The economy was largely dominated by agriculture, but industry and trade grew as the farm surplus demanded exchanges for other needs. In ancient Mesopotamia, the Sumerians utilized a land of fertile soil overflowed from the rivers and developed an irrigation system. They produced abundant crops, woolen textiles, pottery, and the metal work mixed with copper and tin to produce bronze. They traded with the eastern Mediterranean by using wheels and with India by water. Goods were traded by barter, but gold and silver were used as standards of value. They developed a feudal system: the king gave lands to his chieftains after victories of wars; and his generals run the estates and provided soldiers, supplies, and finance for the king in return. Meanwhile, ancient Egypt was surrounded by natural barriers and relatively isolated from Mesopotamia, so that their land was naturally protected from foreign invasions. The agriculture owed to fertile soil overflowed from the Nile. The land was owned by the Pharaoh, the feudal barons, or wealthy men. The ruling class managed king's lands, and the farmers worked on the land mostly owned by the upper class or partially by them-selves. The government monopolized mining for industry and military purposes: copper was mined in small quantity, iron was imported from Arabia, and gold mines were founded along the eastern coast of Nubia, while they used bronze weapons and wheels. The Egyptian engineers were superior to the Greeks or Romans or even to any Europeans before the industrial revolution: they constructed canals from the Nile to the Red Sea, built ships, and provided transport by water, but roads were few and bad except the military highway through Gaza to Euphrates. The ancient Persians depended on agriculture that was considered as the noblest occupation. The peasant proprietors engaged in farming on lands jointly with several families; and the feudal barons cultivated their lands in part by tenants in return for shares of crops, and in part by foreign slaves. They used the irrigation system guiding water from the mountainous high lands to low fields, produced barley and wheat, and ate meat and drank wine. Major crops included barley, dates, wheat, lentils, peas, beans, olives, pomegranates, grapes, vegetables, and pistachios.

The ancient Greeks learned science and technology from the Egyptians of geometry and skills in pottery, textile, metalworking, and ivory; from the Phoenicians of the alphabet and shipbuilding technique; from the Babylonians of the system of weight-measure, water clock and sundial, monetary units, astronomical principles, instruments, records, and calculations. Lydia traded with the Ionian Greeks which promoted banking by issuing a state-guaranteed coinage, which spread to Greece. The Greek economy was agricultural, but the Athenians imported grain mostly from Egypt and Sicily: the rising population was a problem in Greek cities so that politicians favored emigration to overseas to resolve the problem. Attica was rich in marble, iron, zinc, silver, and lead; and the mines of Laurium were the source of Athenian treasury. The Athenians made clothes and blankets at home and bought necessities directly from craftsmen. The public project of the Delian League revived the Athenian economy. The growth of industry and trade made manufacturers and merchants rich, which created a new social class. The landed aristocracy having political power united rich merchants and manufacturers having economic power; which created the political-economic complex through marriages and other ways. This produced an upper class of oligarchs and divided Greek society into two cities: the rich and the poor. Since the poor captured the Assembly and imposed heavy taxes on property and income, the middle-class distrusted democracy. This was the beginning of the collapse of Athens and the rise of Macedonia. The Hellenistic economy in Greece and Macedonia, Syria, Pergamum, and Egypt were basically not different from the Greek period. Trade was expanded with reduced barriers, and improved conditions of roads and harbors which facilitated transportations from India to the Persian Gulf or Red Sea, from Seleucia to Antioch and Ephesus, and from Coptos on Nile to Alexandria and the Mediterranean. Money transactions replaced barter, and bankers provided credit for trade. However, the Hellenic society had no integrated system to form an empire.

The Roman conquest made the Hellenistic territories the property of the Roman state, and capital was concentrated in the hands of Roman citizens and of residents in the Italian cities. The influx of goods, slaves, and money from the Roman provinces into Italy stimulated its economy. The abundant slaves lowered wages and replaced rural peasants, many of whom sold their lands and either settled in cities or migrated to the east. Similarly, slaves replaced urban workers, which raised the number of urban proletariats. The decrease in small-land holders and the increase in urban proletariats changed the traditional aristocratic regime to an oligarchy of rich noble families, which threatened the republic and caused the civil war. Augustus ended internal and external wars, which revived the economy: he pursued no interference in the market and made Italy the economic center in the west. In the first and second centuries, the ownership of land was concentrated to city bourgeoisie, the imperial aristocracy, and the state; and small land-owners became tenant farmers. Hence, agriculture gradually decayed by low productivity without incentives. The growth of commerce within as well as between provinces decentralized markets and challenged Italian merchants. The provinces specialized their manufacturing, which expedited industrial decentralization. While the major cities in provinces were urbanized with the rising population, the economic gravity of the empire gradually shifted from Italy to the provinces. In the third and fourth centuries, the imperial finance was desperate due to civil war followed by external wars; causing to raise taxes. The constitutional monarchy was assisted by experts based on the city bourgeoisie, but the military monarchy was assisted by non-experts based on country peasants. Hence, the empire suffered from corruption and inefficiency of the bureaucracy, causing itself impoverished. The taxpayers were robbed by the state, and the bourgeoisie was ruined by repeated confiscations, so their number constantly decreased and finally disappeared. Diocletian (286-305) pursued structural reforms but faced continuous inflation and empty of the treasury. As a result, higher civilization of Greece and Rome was absorbed by barbarism in the end.

The Germans penetrated into Roman society through the Romanization, militarization, and barbarization. The Roman army legions stationed in the frontier provinces and became a powerful engine of economic transformation. They used slaves and barbarians to fight other barbarians, and the latter were rapidly assimilated; and the wealthy elite monopolized the economy and became powerful landlords holding their dependents bounded to the land, which was the preliminary stage of the feudalism. After the fall of the Roman Empire, the ownership of lands could not be stable, but was passed to new conquerors: the Ostrogoths, Lombards, Visigoths, Burgundians, and Franks. Royal property was scattered and often lay side by side with church property. The Franks produced primarily wheat and barley and grew vine and made wine; though their majority still lived in the countryside, the cities played a vital role as commercial and industrial centers. Despite barbarian pillages and Gallo-Roman internal wars, Roman roads and commercial waterways functioned continuously, which helped circulate goods in the sixth and seventh centuries. The Byzantine kept a centralized administration at Constantinople. Until Justinian, foreign trade flourished owing to well-maintained Roman roads, and building of maritime fleets with many ports in the east and the west. All Syria throve in trade because of its location linking Constantinople with Persia and Egypt. After the collapse of the Justinian order, the expansion of Persia and the rise of Islam seriously reduced holdings of lands and people. The Persians developed industry and commerce. Silk weaving was introduced from China; Chinese merchants came to Persia to sell raw silk and buy rugs, jewels, rouge; and Armenians, Syrians, and Jews connected Persia, Byzantium, and Rome. The Arabs were nomad Beduins, herdsmen moving with their flocks; but after the Muslim conquest, their economy covered the wider range. Moslem merchants dominated the Mediterranean until the Crusades controlled the Red Sea from Ethiopia and reached over the Caspian into Mongolia up to Volga.

Agrarian Capitalism and Feudalism (750-1400): *(a) Feudalism*: The external invasions caused the shortage of currency, and workers hired in farms or elsewhere could not receive money for wages, so that they could not purchase their necessities. For survival, a free man voluntarily became a vassal of the lord by receiving protection and taking a piece of land with returning of promised services. This was the beginning tie of feudalism between landowners and free workers· the free peasantiy shifted to serfdom to be the subject of the lords. Feudalism was based on the manorial system, where a manor was an agricultural unit owned by a noble or a knight, managed by a vassal or sub-vassal, and worked by peasants. The kings needed armed services for protection of the people against foreign invasions, so that the lord-vassal relation was voluntarily established between kings and knights, becoming a lower level of lords. The hierarchy of feudalism starts from the king on the top to the lords in the middle and to the vassals at the bottom. The feudal system ascended by war and anarchy with the rise of cavalry, but declined by peace and order, the fall of cavalry, and the general use of money in exchanges. Feudalism strengthened the local power of dukes and weakened the central power of the monarchy and created a nobility class of knights; and the military function of feudalism remained until the rise of the standing army.

In the High Middle Ages, the agricultural production rapidly increased in Europe owing to the change of climate, population, arable lands, and technology. The rising population demanded more food and more cultivated lands producing more grain; and the heavy wheeled plow with the iron ploughshare was pulled by 6-8 horses wearing the iron shoes and a new horse collar. The watermills were widely used, dams were constructed to increase waterpower, and the windmills were developed to harness the wind power. The farmers applied the three-field system and used the fertilizer of dung, urine, human excrement, ashes, and decayed vegetable matter. The government improved and extended the irrigation system and provided incentive programs to overcome the man-power shortage in the new settlements. Agriculture was hampered in some regions by grazing of sheep in the pastures. The rising demand for produce in towns and cities raised food prices, which made the farming profitable. As agricultural markets began to grow and money is generally circulated, landlords favored a new tenant system by leasing lands to tenants for fixed rents. The lords became manorial operators to collect rents or to pay wages to laborers; while unfree serfs became independent free peasants. The political and legal powers previously exercised by feudal lords were reclaimed by the rising monarchical power in the High Middle Ages.

(b) The Commercial Revolution: During 750-1000, foreign trade was limited to a few goods via some secured routes. As the agricultural sector made surplus in the High Middle Ages, the agrarian community demanded non-farm products, and the rising population in towns and cities demanded more. A few landed rich demanded luxurious goods, while many poor wanted necessities: the former played a more role than the latter in the medieval economy. The regional fairs provided foreign markets throughout years, which were supported by better transportation and security. Europe formed two commercial regions - northern Italy and Flanders - and

Champagne of France became a commercial center by linking two regions at the fairs. Merchants of Venice moved into the east to Byzantine, Muslim states, and Russia via the Black Sea; while those of the Flanders moved into Scandinavia and Russia to Constantinople and Baghdad in addition to trade with the neighboring states. The major commercial centers in Europe included Constantinople, Venice and Genoa, Florence and Millan, the fairs of Champagne, and the towns of the Hanseatic League that protected the bourgeoisie against the barons and promoted the liberation of cities from feudal control. As more money was needed with the growth of trade in those commercial centers in Europe, a new credit system was provided for easy transactions. The joint-stock companies were born; the banking system was developed; and merchant guilds provided insurance for their members.

Industrial needs for a medieval estate were mostly provided in manorial workshops; while military provisions were made by craftsmen in royal manors. Except textiles and mining, most industries in the High Middle Ages remained at the handicraft stage serving a local market by working at homes. The woolen industry was prosperous in Flanders in the north and Italy in the south; and the northern textiles flew into the south and invaded Italian markets in the late twelfth century. To improve competitiveness in the market, Italian producers imported wools of high quality from Spain, Africa, France, England, and Scotland with four times the prices of native wools. As the south produced the finer wools, the north abandoned the wool production. When the relations of Flanders with England and France became worse, the trade of woolen products became favorable for Italy, which lifted the southern industry into the front. Mining industry was demanded for a reliable gold coinage, the passion for jewelry, weapons for knights, church bells, ploughshares, and other tools. Rich veins of gold and silver were chiefly in Central Europe, and German immigrants took the leading role in mining technology. In construction with the stone, feudal lords built strongholds (walls and towers of castle) for defense; churches and monasteries recovered destroyed buildings or needed new ones; and the rising populations demanded private housing as well as public buildings. Meanwhile, the authority of medieval towns and cities pursued complete monopoly of trade and investment by controlling trade routes, dominating commodity sources, and keeping the right of access to markets throughout all regions. But the authority also defended interests of consumers or community for their public welfare by securing consistent supply of necessities at reasonable prices. The guilds were most effective vehicles of monopoly, while town councils tried to reduce monopolies and to minimize conflicts between merchants and artisans, between different guilds, or capitalists and laborers. Though the feudal authority had power issuing and executing economic policies at the local level, the measures of policies and their effectiveness were significantly different by region or state.

(c) Economic growth and Democratization: As feudal lordship became stronger and oppressive during the tenth and eleventh centuries, the conflict of lords with peasants stimulated a new spirit of association for solidarity among villagers. From the economic growth, there were two aspects of democratization in the High Middle Ages. First, the newly cultivated area needed more people to work so that the lords offered attractive programs by providing more rights with less responsibility. As the lords became more profitable with efficient management, villagers were allowed to create self-government of the community by electing their own officials. Second, the commercial revolution urbanized towns and created a new middle class led by the burghers - rich merchants and artisans - the mercantile bourgeoisie challenged the landed nobility and clergy. Around 1200, European towns or cities established communes, and town councils were the ultimate source of authority of the local government. After the Black Death, sudden changes of capital and labor prices disturbed the economy and society. In economy, rising wages and falling rents changed factor intensity in the production. The land-intensive production became attractive, so that wheat fields were converted into pasture; and labor-saving devices were invented: printing machine, maritime transport, and firearms. From economic causes, three developments in politics were seen. First, peasants and other workers gained from the cost of the nobility and clergy, so that the two upper classes tried to reverse the trend by legislation against interest of the third order, which caused revolts. Second, as the lords lost economic power in various regions, political power shifted from lords to kings. This was in the process shifting from the feudal system to the absolute monarchy with the rise of mercantilism. Third, the problems between church lands and state revenues became serious. As the church owned large part of the land and collected huge revenues, the state tried to impose taxes on church revenues and to judge clerical crimes at the royal court. However, the lands owned by church were untouched in France until Napoleon confiscated them.

Mercantilism (1400-1715): *The population* in Europe declined from 73 million in 1300 to 45 million in 1400 due to famines, diseases, and wars; but reviving from 1450 recovered to 81 million in 1500 and 105 million in 1600; and the rising pace of growth was disturbed down to 115 million in 1700 because of the recurrences of the same. In agriculture, the old feudal system rapidly declined in the sixteenth century due to the impoverishment of the landed aristocracy and the massive loss of inhabitants. Liberating the serfs by 1500, most countries in the west of the Elbe like Germany and France developed a tenant farmer system; and rural society in countries like England was transformed into a three-tier structure: landlords, the tenant farmers, and the agricultural laborers. However, countries in the east like Poland, Russia, or Romania restored the feudal system benefiting from the recurrence of wars by forcing serfs not to leave the land. During 1350-1450, the falling population reduced the demand for food stuffs, which caused their prices to fall, and resulted in low rents and high wages in production. The landowners adjusted the use of land by switching from labor-intensive farming to land-intensive pasturing or planting of cash crops. During 1450-1600, the rising population caused the opposite, so that high rents and low wages caused overpopulation problems which are resolved by two ways: either increasing production or reducing population.

The ways increasing *agricultural output* are in the more cultivated area, the more frequency of cropping, shifting to higher yielding crops, technical advance in farming, the division of labor and regional specialization, and domestic industry and seasonal migration. The ways of demographic adjustments include fertility control, migration, and mortality. The agrarian production was affected by weather conditions, available land and soil fertility, a wide range of corps and rotation, plant or animal diseases, advanced tools and equipment, proper knowledge and management skill. Colonial crops were introduced into Europe like maize and potato; and European crops and livestock were transferred to America such as sugarcane, vine, and cattle. Asian spices and beverages were also introduced and spread into Europe and America through the East India companies.

The industries were affected and expanded by the rising population, the discovery of new lands, the longer period and the larger scale of wars, and more by technical achievements with the use of water and wind powers. In mining, a reversible water wheel was built with ten meters in diameter that was able to lift 100 cubic meters in 8 hours. The production of precious metals was greatly increased after the German experts transferred mining skills to America. In the iron industry, there were three key innovations: the substitution of coal for charcoal, the use of water- or wind-powered bellows and hammers, and an improvement of the blast furnace. Abraham Darby's new furnace replacing coal for charcoal revolutionized iron industry. In the textile sector, the spinning wheel was improved with a flyer, and the weaving process by increasing the number of threads; and the cotton industry followed the same processes used in the woolen and linen industries. The Dutch introduced a lighter and cheaper fabric, which skill was transferred to England or Germany by Dutch immigrants. In building, fortifications for war influenced on the construction of walls, towers and gateways encircling towns; the dyke-building used windmills to pump water; dwelling houses and shipbuilding demanded sawmills driven by waterpower; and making glass and pottery spread widely in the sixteenth century. In shipbuilding, the Portuguese developed carrack for capacity of 400 to 600 tons with 3 to 4 masts and guns during 1450-1500; and invented a galleon in 1535 as a superior fighting ship. The Dutch and the English modified the Portuguese models for their own ships, and the former became to lead shipbuilding in the seventeenth century by producing large mercantile fleet with cheaper raw materials. The emergence of naval artillery with advanced ship-building contributed to the technical progress of naval warfare, while navigation skills were improved. The innovation of the printing process expanded the demand for paper, which induced the growing number of paper mills. The mass consumption of food and beverage, particularly, more appeared in armies and navies.

Commerce: During the twelfth and thirteenth centuries, the Champagne fairs connected the industrial cities of Italy to the Hanseatic towns in the Low Countries by land. The progress of shipbuilding and navigation skills linked them directly by sea in the fourteenth century, which caused Italian ports of Venice and Genoa to rise, while the towns of Champagne fairs declined due to bypassing of fair towns in France. Hence, Venice-Bruges-London running from south to north became the main axis of European trade. The Portuguese invented the carrack in the second half of the fifteenth century, which made them possible to explore African coasts and to discover the sea route to the East Indies via the Cape. While the Portuguese secured the sea route to the East Indies and monopolized the spice trade, the Spanish discovered America and had imported huge amounts of precious metals for over a century. They used Antwerp as the trading center, while the Mediterranean trade declined, and Venice began further to fall because of the rise of the Ottoman Turks. In 1576, Philip II intervened in the Spanish Netherlands, and the southern population moved to the United Provinces, so that Amsterdam became a new trading center substituting Antwerp. In 1596, the Dutch designed a new commercial vessel Fluyt to maximize carrying capacity and to minimize constructing and operating costs. Portugal and Spain were dominant sea powers in the sixteenth century but was challenged by the Dutch who replaced them in the world trade in the seventeenth century. The Dutch, by naval blockade and capture, took control over the Portuguese bases in the East Indies, and stepped in America as carriers for Spain and Portugal. The Dutch was regularly engaged in the Baltic and North Sea trades with 735 ships in 1670. Meanwhile, the English entered the trade competition with Asia and America. Most importantly, the English Navigation Act of 1651 ignited the three Anglo-Dutch Wars during 1652-74, which constrained the expansion of commercial power of the Dutch. As a result, the Dutch declined, and the English naval and commercial power began to rise in the eighteenth century. In the meantime, the French entered the competition in Asia and America with mercantilist strategies.

In finance, local small land holders borrowed money from businessmen in town who were entitled to seize the property in pledge if repayments were defaulted. In the fifteenth century, Italian cities established the "mount of piety" that offered loans from the charitable donations at a low interest to the poor; the Netherlands introduced municipal pawnshops in Amsterdam in 1614; and Sweden established a private bank in Stockholm in 1664 accepting deposits and providing loans. Many private banks appeared in Florence and Bruges in the fourteenth century, but the number was much reduced because of financial mismanagement, defaults of government loans, and the stigma of usury. Charles V legalized commercial loans at 12 percent of interest by 1541, which trend was prevailed in the major European countrics. The bill of exchange linked sellers and buyers through the banks of each side, and the promissory notes (that was transferable bonds) were circulated from hand to hand. The fairs of exchange were an international clearing system in which all merchants from different areas to settle all transactions by credit first to minimize cash payments. Nevertheless, the progress of commodity wholesale trading throughout the year required a regulated banking system where merchants could safely deposit and withdraw their assets. Venice authorized a public bank in 1584, Amsterdam opened the Exchange Bank in 1609, and there appeared 25 public banks in Europe by 1697. In company finance, marine partnership appeared by sharing the cost of ship and its cargo in two ways: a basic capital (corpo: share) and an additional capital (sopracorpo: bond). As the partnership became transferable by trading the shares, joint-stock companies were founded such as the English or Dutch East India Company that also issued bonds. In public finance, the state governments had always faced budget deficit financed by borrowing due to high inflation as well as larger and longer wars. The repayments of public debts were often restructured into annuity: for example, Philip II converted all the floating state debts into redeemable annuities with 5 percent interest in 1557.

Industrial Capitalism (1715-1815): *(a) Population growth*: Europe had about 80 million inhabitants in 1500, and three centuries later it rose to 190 million by 1800. During 1650-1750, the European economy suffered from a serious recession; but since then, their population exploded from 140 million in 1750 to 266 million (rising by 1.9 times) by 1850. The factors changing the population are in (i) that the crisis such as famine, disease, war, and unemployment that increased mortality, postponed marriages, reduced marital fertility through birth control or abortion, and the inverse conditions may result in the opposite; (ii) that the social structure that affected the population growth - higher fertility in industrial villages than in agricultural areas was observed from 1730 onwards; and (iii) that group characteristics like religious minorities affecting the population change - Jews were forced to reside in an unhealthy urban environment, but their medical skill, hygienic regulations, and family structure were favorable for demographic growth. The impact of population growth as follows. First in production, over-population reduces labor prices and falling wages make producers use more labor and less capital, resulting in labor-intensive production; and underpopulation results in capital-intensive production by labor-saving technology. Secondly in consumption, population growth demands particularly more supply of food, which raises food prices, making agriculture profitable; but inversely, the falling population reduces food prices, making the agrarian sector decline. Thirdly, overpopulation induces migration from rural to towns, and urbanization forces political power to shift to the bourgeoisie. As the surplus population migrated to the colonies, the major powers in Europe exploited commercial gains and fought each other for more colonies, which caused imperial wars. To avoid social unrest, European rulers sent the surplus population to their colonies. Fourthly, overpopulation stimulated social changes: a different composition of the people required new rules and created new customs of faiths, particularly after the religious reformation and migration to foreign countries.

(b) The agricultural revolution began in England when the growing population rapidly reached unprecedented levels from 5.7 million in 1750 to 16.6 million by 1850, and surprisingly demanded more food, that raised prices of farm produce, particularly in London and its suburbs, which stimulated the agricultural production in the countryside. Both landlords and tenants made profits by increasing the farm production owing to the removal of common property rights to land through enclosure movement; the selective breeding of livestock; and new systems of production with new science and technology - new methods of cultivating, sowing, harvesting, threshing, and transport; including triple crop yields, crop rotation involving turnips and clover. The English experienced remarkable expansion and improvement in agriculture in the eighteenth century as the growing population and increasing demand for farm produce raised its prices and made agriculture profitable, so that landlords and tenants tried to maximize output by reducing costs. There were three classes in farming of England: first, the great landlords and gentry were an educated class of rulers and administrators who drew their income from the rents of land and such estate profits as arose from sales of timber and mining royalties; secondly, the owner-occupiers or yeomen were farming their own land in a small scale and sometimes renting additional land from a landlord; thirdly, the cottagers were landless rural people who had cottages and rights to use common land, and laborers were hired year by year and lived in with the farmer and his family as farm servants. The farmers in England and Wales numbered about 330,000 at the end of the seventeenth century, among which 150,000 were the great landlords and gentry, and the remaining 180,000 were owner-occupiers. In the continent, the rising population stimulated agricultural development; and the grassland was converted to the ploughland for arable farming. During the French Revolution, the property of clergy and emigres was confiscated. Some of the revolutionaries wanted these estates to benefit the small peasants and landless proletariat with redistribution.

(c) The first industrial revolution was led by Britain during 1760-1830 due to following reasons. First, in the demand side, the population of England Wales tripled during 1751-1851, which generated a tremendous demand for their necessities. The agricultural revolution created the surplus of farm produce, and rising profits allowed them to purchase more manufacturing goods. The emergence of the middle class, who lived above the level of subsistence, generated demand. The consumer revolution preceded the industrial revolution. Overseas markets in America, Africa, and Asia were crucial for them to export manufactured goods for raw materials.

Second, in the supply side, industrial output was expanded by utilizing more input and by improving productivity with technological advances. The rapid growth of population in the second half of the century provided a pool of unskilled labor for new factories; and a relatively large number of skilled mechanics and technicians was available. Business investments were financed by an effective central bank and well-developed and flexible credit facilities as well as security markets buying and selling stocks and bonds. The rich mineral resources, like coal and iron ore, were largely available for the manufacturing process. The adoption of new technology through invention and innovation was essential for industrialization: the rapid mechanization of the cotton industry, the new process of smelting iron ore with coke, and the invention of steam engines with continuous improvement; which made a breakthrough towards industrialization.

Third, in the market side, the British government protected private property and provided a favorable market environment through an effective intervention with fewer restrictions, lower trade barriers, lower interest rates, or lower taxation to encourage business activities. The British abandoned mercantilist protectionism and embraced free trade policies, which stimulated her trade volume doubled during 1700-70. But colonial markets were significant for some industries over the course of the eighteenth century, so that protection measures were applied for her imperial interests.

Fourth, in transportation and communications, Britain improved roads and new turnpike with better designed and lighter carriers. They utilized rivers and constructed canals, and renovated harbors and constructed the dock system for coastal and cross-channel shipping, though the ocean shipping sector was relatively late. Farm transport was upgraded by replacing two-wheel carts with four-wheel wagons carrying much heavier loads. Better transport saved time and labor, which made farm products flow rapidly into London and other cities in Britain with lower costs. The appearance of the railway reduced the cost of transportation.

In continental Europe, the industrial revolution was substantially slower than in Britain because of unfavorable internal and external conditions, although there were at least 2,000 skilled British mechanics on the Continent, and British equipment was being sold abroad by 1825. There were some differences between Britain and continental states. First, the British had 'a premium on empiricism, pragmatism, and individual utilitarianism' for technical advances by applying useful knowledge, which was different from the Cartesian or rational approach in continental countries. Even after importing the machinery, the French could not compete with the British in the market due to lack of the immense details. Secondly, in the Continent, the state absorbed a large share of engineering talent; but in Britain, skilled artisans were hired mostly by the private sector, which generated more efficient output. Unlike in France, 'the state was not the enemy' of the people in Britain. Thirdly, the French Revolution and the Napoleonic wars destroyed production capacities and distorted the allocation of resources in continental economies; and the Continental System of Napoleon disturbed the British trade with continental countries. But the British environment was safer and more peaceful than the Continent to develop agriculture and to promote industry during the century. The costs of raw materials, financial services, and transportation were more expensive in France than Britain. The French were so poor that they were far from generating mass consumption of industrial goods, while the British was much richer than the French.

(d) The mercantilists policies were taken by the European rulers to protect home industries or to increase tax revenues. The mercantilist position had been the prevailing reality of political economy in Europe until the mid-eighteenth century, although the degree of intervention was different by time and place. In addition to the Navigation Acts, England passed other Trade Acts that continued to control colonial trade. "The colonists became increasingly angry as each new Act was passed and began to find ways around these restrictions. Smuggling and piracy became a big business. During the French and Indian War, England needed the cooperation of the colonies so that they did not work hard to stop the law breakers. After the war, England cracked down on the colonies and passed new and more restrictive Acts. Another way the colonies get around trade restrictions was through the triangular trade routes. To trade with European merchants, the colonial merchants shipped their products to European ports. There they were traded for goods that were not available in England, such as fruits and wines. Next, the fruits and wine were traded in England for manufactured goods. Finally, the manufactured goods from England were sold in the colonies. Another triangle trade route brought African slaves to America. First, colonists traded their products for sugar and molasses in the West Indies. Ships carried sugar and molasses back to the colonies where they were made into rum. In the next step, ships carried rum and guns to Africa. In Africa these were exchanged for slaves. Then slaves were shipped to the West Indies or to the colonies. As this form of trade grew, great fortunes were made by merchants, slave traders, ship captains, and England." In France, Napoleon issued the Berlin Decree in 1806 in response to the naval blockade of the French coast, which brought a large-scale embargo against British trade. As Napoleon realized that extensive trade was going through Spain and Russia, he invaded both countries, though he lost the war.

(e) Finance and banking: As a nation state claimed the right to collect taxes in case of fiscal needs for war, his subjects demanded the right to be consulted: the ruler allowed his subjects to send their representatives to participate in the decision making process of the state, which created institutions of political representation such as the House of Commons in Britain or the Third Estate of France. Thus, property rights of the people made it possible for them to participate in decision-making over taxes, while lack of consent resulted in tax evasion or the fiscal uprising. The legitimacy of taxation required representation with proper negotiations and agreements between sovereign and subjects in the political institutions. The fiscal institutions collected taxes, and the monetary institutions managed the rising public debts. Debasement was the practice of lowering the value of currency by reducing the quantity of gold, silver, copper or nickel in coins; and monarchies had engaged in the debasement of the coinage to reduce the debt. To avoid state default, financial institutions introduced annuity as a long-term investment instrument to the financial markets such as in the Netherlands, Britain, and France. The European colonies in Americas adopted the fiscal and monetary institutions to their own resources and environments. On the other hand, the French Revolution destroyed the old regime, and restructured the society, so that no privileged classes were accepted by society; thus, economic transformation also changes society. First, with the growth of population, the rapid urbanization intensified problems of housing, sanitary conditions, and adulteration of food for the working class. Second, the rise of capitalism created the industrial middle class (bourgeoisie) and the working class (proletariat): the inequality of income and of wealth became wider, while working conditions remained problematic. Third, the Industrial Revolution transformed morality of the protestant ethics, while capitalistic efficiency with profit motive is emphasized, which was different from the agricultural regime. Fourth, the first Industrial Revolution spread the capitalism as much as the socialism. Capitalism preached the doctrine of economic liberalism – *laissez faire* in trade and investment, while socialism propagated the idea of political and economic equality for the low class.

Imperialism (1815-1914): "Until the year 1000, everyone was equally poor, but we learn that as early as the year 1500 Western Europe had achieved some very limited economic prosperity; until the early 19th century the region could slowly increase the economic wealth. But the wealth enjoyed at the time is still incomparably low with the level that Europe enjoys now at the beginning of the 21st century." In addition to rising income, the Industrial Revolution fundamentally altered societies around the world. "Products were no longer made in cottage industries but as manufacturing took place on a vast scale in city factories. Transportation dramatically changed. Steam-powered trains moved people and products across Britain in a fraction of the time taken by road or by canal. By the end of the 18th century, Britain was the most advanced country in Europe. The 19th century saw the spread of the Industrial Revolution. Other European countries acquired the tools and skills needed to revolutionize their economies. The United States also underwent an industrial revolution in the 19th century." In the pattern of economic activity, as a community develops economically, the number of its workers engaged in agriculture tends to decline, at first relatively to those engaged in manufacturing or the provision of services, and later absolutely as more and more of its resources are devoted to the production of industrial goods. It is a common trend for a country to shift from agriculture to non-agricultural sector in the process of economic development. In Great Britain, for example, by 1800 around 40 percent of the labor force were engaged in the primary sector, but by 1901 about 8.5 percent of the labor force was in the same. The share of the primary sector in the gross national product was 40-45 percent in around 1750, about a fifth in 1851 and about a tenth in 1881; which pattern has been prevailed in other industrialized countries.

(a) *Population*: The population of Europe was 150 million in 1800 and increased to 291 million in 1900, almost doubled in a century. In 1800 there were 23 towns of more than 100,000 inhabitants in Europe, with a total of 5.5 million inhabitants; but in 1900 there were 135 cities, with a total of 46 million. One of the most profound effects of the Industrial Revolution was to stimulate the growth of cities, leading to rapid urbanization. Throughout Europe, only 17% of the population lived in cities in 1801, which increased to 35% by 1851, and 54% by 1891. This is parallel to the decline of the labor force in agriculture. The mortality rate in England and Wales declined from 22.2 to 15.4 souls annual per 1000 souls in average from 1851-60 to 1901-10; in France from 24.0 to 19.4 souls; in Germany 26.4 to 18.7 souls for the same period. The number of survivors in average annual out of 10,000 born in France was also increased from 7,930 in 1801-07 to 8,410 for male in 1900-2, and from 8,240 to 8,680 for female in the same period. The life expectancy was also improved, for example, in England, from 39.9 in 1838-53 to 48.5 in 1901-10 for male and 41.8 to 52.3 for female during the same period. The birth rate is in conjunction with the marriage rate, since the majority of birth in Europe are engendered by married couples. Since most married couples did not traditionally practice voluntary birth control, "the fertility rate for married couples was very high in the first half of the eighteenth century, at any rate above the present average of Western Europe. Married women of under 39 had an average of two children every five years, and women under 30 gave birth to three almost as often as to two children in the same period." Annual average births per 1,000 population during 1908-12 was 24.9 in England, 19.5 in France; 29.5 in Germany. In the eighteenth, there are two types of global migration: spontaneous or governmental sponsored. Emigration from Europe to the rest of the world was counted more than 30,000-40,000 people each year until 1840, who were chiefly farm laborers or domestic staffs. Organized migration ceased in the first half of the nineteenth century, as most emigrants left their homes for personal motives, and made their own arrangements for the unknown journey.

(b) Agriculture: "The main problem in sustaining agriculture in one place for a long time was the depletion of nutrients, most importantly nitrogen levels, in the soil. To allow the soil to regenerate, productive land was often let fallow and in some places crop rotation was used. The Dutch four-field rotation system was popularized...The system (wheat, turnips, barley and clover), opened up a fodder crop and grazing crop allowing livestock to be bred year-round...The mechanization and rationalization of agriculture was another important factor. Robert Bakewell and Thomas Coke introduced selective breeding and initiated a process of inbreeding to maximize desirable traits from the mid-18th century...Machines were invented to improve the efficiency of various agricultural operation, such as Jethro Tull's seed drill of 1701 that mechanized seeding at the correct depth and spacing and Andrew Meikle's threshing machine of 1784. Ploughs were steadily improved, from... iron plough in 1730 to...improved Scots Plough metal in 1763...Powered farm machinery began with Richard Trevithick's stationary steam engine, used to drive a threshing machine, in 1812. Mechanization spread to another farm uses through the 19th century. The first petrol-driven tractor was built in America by John Froclich in 1892. The scientific investigation of fertilization began at the Rothamsted Experimental Station in 1843 by John Bennet Lawes. He investigated the impact of inorganic and organic fertilizers on crop yield and founded one of the first artificial fertilizer manufacturing factories in 1842. Fertilizer, in the shape of sodium nitrate deposits in Chile, was imported to Britain by John Thomas North as well as guano. The first commercial process for fertilizer production was the obtaining of phosphate from the dissolution of coprolites in sulfuric acid." Dan Albone (1860-1906) constructed the first gasoline-powered general-purpose tractor in 1901, and its improved models largely replaced animal power by 1923. Since then, agriculture in the developed nations, and to a lesser extent in the developing world, has seen large rises in productivity as human labor has been replaced by mechanization, and assisted by synthetic fertilizers, pesticides, and selective breeding.[1]

(c) Industrial Revolution: The first Industrial Revolution was led by Great Britain during 1760-1830. In the demand side, the rising population generated huge demand for eating, closing, housing and other necessities. The agricultural revolution created the surplus of farm production, and the

rising profits allowed them to purchase more manufactured goods. Moreover, overseas markets in Asia, Africa, and the Americas were crucial to export their manufactured goods for raw materials. In the supply side, industrial output was expanded by more factor inputs, and by the improvement of productivity with new technologies and management. Business investments were financed by effective central banks and credit facilities as well as security markets; and the rich mineral resources were available in the process of industrialization. Particularly, the rapid mechanization of the cotton industry, the new process of smelting iron ore with coke, and the invention and improvements of steam engines made a breakthrough toward industrialization. In the market side, the British government protected private property and provided favorable market conditions with less restrictions, lower trade barriers, lower interest rates, and lower taxation to encourage business activities. The system of transportation was improved through the utilization of rivers, constructed canals, renovated harbors and the new dock system for coastal and cross-channel shipping. The railway system, though appeared later, largely reduced transportation costs. By 1850, Britain had become the first industrialized country in the world. Europe and America shared a common cultural heritage with Britain that was geographically close to the rest of Europe. Moreover, "constant contact with Britain meant that its knowledge could not be kept secret. Designs for steam engines and locomotives were bound to leak out, and they did with incredible impact. The first step most countries took to industrialize was to build railroads to link coal to iron deposits and factories to markets. Once a transportation system was in place, factory building, and production could proceed." Both petroleum and steel industries were established within a decade.

(d) Commerce: In North America, major attractive items to export to Europe were furs, timber, tobacco, and cotton. The Hudson's Bay Company sent the two or three trading ships into the bay every year to buy and sell furs. New England and Canada exported timber to Europe, and the American industrial revolution also caused the national demand for timber to spike. Tobacco was cultivated by the Virginia settlers for years, which was successfully exported to Europe. Raw cotton had been one of the chief exports from the United States to England. The discovery of gold nuggets in the Sacramento Valley in early 1848 sparked the Gold Rush, which stimulated the economy, but after 1850 the surface gold in California largely disappeared, so that the adjustment of labor forces to agriculture was unavoidable. In Australia, the first gold rush began in 1851, and gold rushes caused a huge influx of people from overseas. "The famous pastoralists, John and Elizabeth Macarthur, established a colonial wool industry in Australia in the early decades of the 1800s with rare Spanish sheep. Compared to growing crops, sheep could be grazed with little labor. Rail transport made wool production competitive while the visual success of this

industry was reflected in the enormous wool stores erected all over cities. In New Zealand, British settlers were engaged in whaling and sealing in the Southern Ocean. In Canada, the economy was primarily based on export of a series of staples including fish, fur, timber, and wheat differently from Quebec, Rupert's Land and British Columbia. The Portuguese settlers in Brazil earned its independence in 1822 (38% white, 34% pardos, 20% black in 1872). Their exports include sugar, cotton, coffee, and others: the share of major Brazilian exports of the total during 1841-50 was 26.7%, 7.5%, 41.4%, and 24.4% respectively. Argentina possesses comparative advantages in agriculture, as the country is endowed with a vast amount of highly fertile land, so their major exports were grain, meat, seafood, and dairy products. Between 1860 and 1930, exploitation of the rich land of the pampas strongly pushed economic growth. During the first three decades of the 20th century, Argentina outgrew Canada and Australia in population, total income, and per capita income. By 1913, Argentina was the world's 10th wealthiest nation per capita.

(e) Transportation: "In the mid-19th century transport was revolutionized by railways. They made travel much faster. The Stockton and Darlington railway opened in 1825. However, the first major railway was from Liverpool to Manchester. It opened in 1830. In the 1840s there was a huge boom in building railways and most towns in Britain were connected. In the late 19th century many branch lines were built connecting many villages. The first underground railway in Britain was built in London in 1863. Steam locomotives pulled the carriages. The first electric underground trains began running in London in 1890. The Central Line opened in 1900. The Bakerloo Line and the Piccadilly Line both opened in 1906. Meanwhile the Paris Metro opened in 1900. From 1829 horse drawn omnibuses began running in London. They soon followed in other towns. In the 1860s and 1870s horse drawn trams began running in many towns. Meanwhile the first traffic lights were installed in London in 1868. They were worked by gas and unfortunately they soon blew up. Karl Benz and Gottlieb Daimler made the first cars in 1885 and 1886. The motorbike was patented in 1885. Cars developed quickly. The electric car heater was invented by Canadian Thomas Ahearn in 1890. Also, in the 1880s the safety bicycle was invented and cycling soon became a popular hobby. Meanwhile at sea 19th century transportation was revolutionized by the steam ship. By 1815 steamships were crossing the English Channel. The Savannah became the first steamship to cross the Atlantic in 1819. Furthermore, it used to take several weeks to cross the Atlantic. Then in 1838 a steam ship called the Sirius made the journey in 19 days. However, steam did not completely replace sail until the end of the 19th century when the steam turbine was used on ships. At the end of the 18th century several men designed lifeboats. By the mid-19th century lifeboats were commonly used on ships."

(g) Finance and Banking: Banking for industrialization in Europe can be considered by supply of and demand for money in the capital market. "The English banking system does not appear to have been fully equipped to cope with the needs of modernized industrial units. The merchant bankers were much more interested in large-scale international trade and its concomitant financial transactions; as well as the state's requirements. The interest that they could take in industrial investment and credit facilities for industry was limited by the size of their available capital, and it was rather low in relation to the sudden high demand. When they backed industry, they did so first and foremost to support their own business activities. The English provincial banks, in their turn, were very small affairs with limited funds put up by small groups of partners. They received deposits and made payments; discounting bills was the only activity open to them in the absence of any long-term commitments. At the end of the eighteenth century, the use of shares was more widespread in England than in any other country. This meant that English industry could draw on the vast wealth of the gentry and nobility, many of whom were willing to invest: the industrialist had relatively large amount of capital to work with, and the capitalists held securities that were more or less negotiable." On the continent Europe, in corresponding to technical improvements, the first large industrial ventures were very largely supported by the governments.

(g) Mass society: The industrial revolution had far reaching social conse-quences, which varied across class and regions. "Between the late 18th and early 20th centuries, (i) new family and class structures emerged to adjust to the new wage economy and production shifted out of the house to large scale production in factories. (ii) Industrialization also caused population migration from rural areas to urban areas, as factory emerged around towns. Marvin Perry says in 1800, about 10% of the Europeans lived in cities. But by 1850 this increased to -52% of Englishmen living in cities, 25% Frenchmen and 36% Germans. As rural production couldn't compete with cheaper factory production, rural workers moved to work in factories." Industrialization and capitalism changed the class structure: it destroyed the old division of society into clergy, nobility, and commoners, and created the new class…Hence, it is concerned with "the rise to power of the bourgeoisie via the economic, social, and political revolution that it brought about with an increasing awareness of its role and its strength; and a parallel formation of the working mass, which, created by the industrial activity of the bourgeoisie, gradually acquired the forms and values of a social class by attaining self-consciousness in its turn." Though they were partners of the economy, both classes crashed over the radical opposition in their material interests as well as other aspirations.

(h) States and the Industrial Revolution: Continental nations had three advantages: "(i) Continental European nations had a rich tradition of skilled

urban artisans, putting out enterprises and merchant capitalism. This made it easy for their economies to adapt and survive in changing market conditions. (ii) Continental capitalists did not have to undergo the trial and error method which had slowed development in Britain. They simply had to borrow ideas from their British counterparts. (iii) France and Russia had strong independent governments which could - and did - use the power of the state to promote economic growth and eventually catch up with Britain". Banks were more involved in industrial development on the continent in Europe. "British banks had been secretive partnerships in which all partners were liable for the debts of the firm, meaning that should the bank fail, each partner stood to lose all his personal assets, not just his investment in the company...As a result, the banks were able to attract numerous shareholders and were able to lend money for industrial development. Similar corporate banks developed in France and Germany in the mid nineteenth century, which helped in the financing of railroad construction and heavy industrial development. The most famous French bank was the Crédit Mobilier of Paris, founded by two Jewish journalists, Isaac and Emile Pereire. The company advertised extensively, used the savings of thousands of small investors and built railroads all over Europe."

Modern Capitalism (1914-2015): In the late nineteenth century, industrialization was encouraged by technical changes as well as by policy changes: the introduction of electricity and its applications, with communications (through the telephone and telegraph), transport (by railroads and steamships), and much more. "The introduction of the railroad led to a steep decline in the costs of moving freight, and there were further dramatic drops in the costs of ocean shipping following the introduction of steamships...a drop in costs of transport between the U.S. and Europe from about 80 per cent of the price of the commodity to less than 20 percent during that period. The sharp decline in transport costs came at a time when most European countries had lower tariff levels than earlier in the 19th century. The U.K. had zero tariffs on agriculture and manufacturing until 1914, and Dutch and Scandinavian tariffs were also low. The impact of rapidly falling transport costs, combined with the reduced levels of protection, undoubtedly led to a major net reduction in barriers - both natural and artificial - to trade. As a consequence, world trade grew rapidly - at an annual rate of 3.4 percent between 1870 and 1914, with growth not only in industrial goods but also in raw materials." The European countries exported manufactured goods to their colonies for raw materials. Simultaneously, integration of world capital markets proceeded rapidly. "By the early 20th century, it is estimated that foreign-owned assets were about equal in value to about 20 percent of world GDP. The United Kingdom was, as is well known, the world's banker and at its peak, owned 80 percent of foreign assets globally. Its capital outflows were as much as 10 percent of GDP in some years and averaged 4.5 percent of GDP per year between 1870 and 1914."[2]

The growth of real incomes, the growth of world trade, and the integration of the world economy were causally linked. "But while real wages and living standards rose throughout the world, the rate of increase was much faster in the industrial countries. Until the early 1700s, it is estimated that living standards were not significantly different between different geographic regions of the world. But by the end of the nineteenth century, economic growth had been sufficiently rapid in the industrial countries that the world had bifurcated in terms of living standards and rates of economic growth. "The First World War, however, led to an abrupt reversal in the degree of globalization. As transport routes were disrupted and countries experienced different degrees of inflation in response to the differential strains of their wartime expenditures, the earlier integration of the international economy was largely reversed. Despite efforts to restore the status quo ante after the war, disequilibria associated with the over-valuation of the pound sterling following the British return to the Gold Standard in 1925, German reparations, and other imbalances led to slow progress in the 1920s. At the end of that decade, markets were not as integrated as they had been prewar. But the Great Depression reversed even that progress." Real incomes dropped dramatically, unemployment rates rose sharply, and prices of goods and services fell abruptly.

"The policy response intensified the difficulties: the 1930s were characterized by rising trade barriers and competitive devaluations, often referred to as beggar they neighbor policies, and by rapidly falling volumes of trade and prices of traded goods. As each country attempted to reverse its own downward spiral by imposing ever-higher tariffs, devaluing its currency, and other measures, they in effect exported part of their own deflationary pressures, only to be hit by deflationary pressures resulting from similar actions in other countries. Britain was forced off the gold standard in 1931, while the United States followed suit in 1933 and simultaneously experienced a banking holiday as banks were hard hit by nonperforming loans in their portfolios. Worse still, the American Congress had enacted the Hawley-Smoot tariff in the early 1930s, giving an average tariff level of 59 percent in 1932 in the United States: the highest level since the 19th century. As it became evident with hindsight that the Hawley-Smoot Tariff Act had greatly intensified the Great Depression."[3] The Act raised U.S. tariffs on over 20,000 imported goods: the tariffs under the act were the second highest in the United States in 100 years, exceeded by a small margin by the Tariffs of 1828. "The Act and following retaliatory tariffs by America's trading partners were major factors of the reduction of American exports and imports by more than half during the Depression." The Reciprocal Trade Agreement Act of 1934 allowed tariff reduction.[4]

(a) The Situation at the End of the War 1945-46: The postwar planners proposed a framework for international economic cooperation.

(i) International Monetary Fund (IMF): "The IMF was originally laid out as a part of the Bretton Woods system exchange agreement in 1944. During the Great Depression, countries sharply raised barriers to trade in an attempt to improve their failing economies. This led to the devaluation of national currencies and a decline in world trade. This breakdown in international monetary cooperation created a need for oversight. The representatives of 45 governments met at the Bretton Woods Conference in the Mount Washington Hotel in Bretton Woods, New Hampshire in the United States, to discuss a framework for postwar international economic cooperation and how to rebuild Europe." "The IMF formally came into existence on 27 December 1945, when the first 29 countries ratified its Articles of Agreement. By the end of 1946 the IMF had grown to 39 members."[5]

(ii) International Bank for Reconstruction and Development (IBRD): The IBRD was established by delegates at the Bretton Woods Conference in 1944 and became operational in 1946. "The IBRD was established with the original mission of financing the reconstruction efforts of war-torn European nations following World War II, with goals shared by the later Marshall Plan. The Bank issued its inaugural loan of $250 million ($2.6 billion in 2012 dollars) to France in 1947 to finance infrastructure projects. The institution also established its first field offices in Paris, France, Copenhagen, Denmark, and Prague in the former Czechoslovakia. Throughout the remainder of the 1940s and 1950s, the Bank financed projects seeking to dam rivers, generate electricity, and improve access to water and sanitation...Following the reconstruction of Europe...In 1960, the International Development Association (IDA) was established to serve as the Bank's concessional lending arm and provide low and no-cost finance and grants to the poorest of the developing countries."[6]

(iii) General Agreement on Tariffs and Trade (GATT) was a legal agreement between many countries, "whose overall purpose was to promote international trade by reducing or eliminating trade barriers such as tariffs or quotas...its purpose was the substantial reduction of tariffs and other trade barriers and the elimination of preferences, on a reciprocal and mutually advantageous basis. It was first discussed during the United Nations Conference on Trade and Employment and was the outcome of the failure of negotiating governments to create the International Trade Organization (ITO). GATT was signed by 23 nations in Geneva on October 30, 1947 and took effect on January 1, 1948. It remained in effect until the signature by 123 nations in Marrakesh on April 14, 1994 of the Uruguay Round Agreements, which established the World Trade Organization (WTO) on January 1, 1995. The WTO is in some ways a successor to GATT, and the original GATT text is still in effect under the WTO framework."[7]

(iv) European and Japanese economic recovery was successful after the first two difficult postwar years. "Prewar output levels were generally attained by the early 1950s and were only the start of a period of sustained rapid growth. From a situation in the late 1940s when most European economies traded through bilateral payments arrangements with each other (or used Marshall Plan aid), they moved to multilateral clearing arrangements. Simultaneously, tariff reductions were taking place and quantitative restrictions were being removed. With the groundwork laid by the Marshall Plan, increas-ingly free exchange regimes and tariff reductions (spurred both by the GATT multilateral tariff reductions and intra-European liberalization undertaken in the context of the Marshall Plan), the world economy embarked upon a quarter century of sustained and unprecedentedly rapid economic growth." While developing countries grew, they did so without integrating the world economy.[8]

(b) The Changing Postwar World: "While the rest of the industrialized world grew rapidly, and at rates well above those achieved in the first half of the twentieth century, it was the phenomenal growth of Europe and Japan which led to the biggest changes in the world economy. In 1950, it could fairly be said that the United States dominated; by the early 1970s, Europe and Japan were also major players in the world economy. During the golden quarter century, tariff reductions continued. The rate of growth of world trade averaged almost 8 percent per year from 1950 to 1973. Quite clearly, trade was an engine of growth, just as it had been in the late 19th century, growing at about twice the rate of growth of world output. But whereas in the late 19th century, it was primarily reductions in transport costs that facilitated that growth, it was reductions in tariff and nontariff barriers to trade were the major stimulus to the growth of trade in the postwar years."

The very rapid economic growth of that era took place in a relatively non-inflationary environment, but individual countries experienced balance of payments crises, and rates of growth fluctuated through recession and boom periods. "Nonetheless, the world economy as a whole was relatively stable. Through the provision of financial assistance to countries in balance of payments crises, the IMF played an important role in enabling adjustment to take place without the disruption to the international system that had characterized the inter-war period. Many of the industrial countries - and many developing countries - took advantage of the IMF's lending facilities... Part of that stability derived from the relative size and dominance of the American economy. From 1950, when 79 percent of foreign exchange reserves of the industrial countries were held in gold...By 1973, more than 90 percent of the foreign exchange reserves holdings of those industrial countries that reported such data were held in U.S. dollars. International prices, and settlements of accounts even between other countries, were predominantly denominated in U.S. dollars."[9]

(c) The World from the Early 1970s to the 1990s: The 1970s were the worst decade of industrial performance since the Great Depression. The oil shocks of 1973 and 1979 added to the existing ailment and conjured high inflation throughout the world for the rest of the decade. As a result, U.S. manufacturing industries began to decline, running its last trade surplus in 1975. In contrast, Japan and West Germany experienced economic booms, overtaking the U.S. as the world's leading manufacturers. In 1970, Japan became the world's second-largest economy until 1994 when the EU came into effect. "In the US, the average annual inflation rate from 1900 to 1970 was approximately 2.5%. From 1970–1979, however, the average rate was 7.06%, and topped out at 13.29% in December 1979. This period is also known for stagflation, a phenomenon in which inflation and unemployment steadily increased. It led to double-digit interest rates that rose to unprecedented levels (above 12% per year). The prime rate hit 21.5 in December 1980, the highest in history. By the time of 1980, when U.S. President Jimmy Carter was running for re-election against Ronald Reagan, the misery index (the sum of the unemployment rate and the inflation rate) had reached an all-time high of 21.98%. The economic problems of the 1970s would result in a sluggish cynicism replacing the optimistic attitudes of the 1950s and 1960s and a distrust of government and technology. Faith in government was at an all-time low in the aftermath of Vietnam and Watergate, as exemplified by the low voter turnout in the 1976...presidential election."[10]

"Great Britain also experienced considerable economic turmoil during the decade as outdated industries proved unable to compete with Japanese and German wares. Labor strikes happened with such frequency as to almost paralyze the country's infrastructure. Breadlines and trash piling up in the street became common sights, and in 1979, Margaret Thatcher was elected prime minister with the promise of cleaning up the economic mess. In Eastern Europe, Soviet-style command economies began showing signs of stagnation, in which successes were persistently dogged by setbacks. The oil shock increased East European, particularly Soviet, exports, but a growing inability to increase agricultural output caused growing concern to the governments of the COMECON block, and a growing dependence on food imported from democratic nations. On the other hand, export-driven economic development in Asia, especially by the Four Asian Tigers, resulted in rapid economic transformation and industrialization. Their abundance of cheap labor, combined with educational and other policy reforms, set the foundation for development in the region during the 1970s and beyond."[11]

"By the late 1980s, inflation was contained in most industrial countries, and debt was being restructured (the Brady Plan) in the heavily indebted developing countries. The oil price had peaked in real terms in 1979 and fell sharply in 1986. The stimulus from lower real oil prices and stable price levels resulted in a period of sustained growth of the industrial countries.

Trade barriers...continued to drop, as quantitative restrictions had been... eliminated and tariffs were being further reduced under the influence of successive rounds of trade negotiations under the GATT." However, the lost decade of the 1980s led a number of countries to begin reducing their trade barriers and other impediments to growth. After the collapse of the Soviet Union, transition economies were adjusting to the free market system; while China opened the four coastal specific economic zones in 1979, which was expanded continuously. In 1994, the North American Free Trade Agreement (NAFTA) was signed by the United States, Canada, and Mexico...Unlike European Union, the free trade agreement allows the flow of goods and services without tariffs, but mobility of labor (employment) between nations is not allowed. In the 1990s, a number of financial crises appeared. In late 1994 in Mexico, investors became reluctant to finance the current account deficits that had been 7.6 percent of GDP. Mexican officials took swift action – adjusting monetary and fiscal policy - with a large loan from the IMF. In 1997 South Korea had a shortage of foreign reserve holding to pay back foreign loans: stock prices fell by 4% on 7 November 1997, by 7% next day, and fell further on fears that the IMF would demand tough reforms. The IMF provided US$58.4 billion package, subject to taking restructuring measures of the ROK government.[12]

At the turn of the century, American economy experienced rapid growth, with more rapid rates of productivity increase than had earlier occurred. "Europe had begun a process of increasing integration with the opening of trade and financial flows under the Marshall Plan. The Treaty of Rome [forming EU in 1957] had started the process of movement toward an integrated internal market, undertaken within the context of lowered trade barriers from the multilateral trading rounds under the GATT. As additional countries joined the European enterprise, and policy harmonization deepened, the European Union emerged as a major force in the global economy with 38 percent of world trade and 26 percent of world GDP as of 2000. By contrast, after four decades of growth and rapidly rising living standards, the Japanese economy had entered a period of stagnation by around 1990, and Japanese growth remained sluggish a decade later, primarily as a consequence of the asset bubble of the late 1980s and the policy challenges posed both by the need for reform of the financial sector. Despite the difficulties of countries such as South Korea, growth in developing countries accelerated during the 1990s as a result of their policy changes and the supportive global environment. By 2000, developing countries as a group accounted for about 47 per cent of world GDP and a third of world trade. And, of course, the East Asian economies, in addition to Japan, were by 2000 large enough to be significant...South Korea, the ASEAN countries, and China, were also gaining share. India had embarked upon reforms." Rising trade and investment enhanced economic growth.

(d) The Global Economy around 2000: As the world became more open place, our economy and society has been changed. Anne O. Krueger, a U.S. economist, considers three changes of the global economy: the structure of international economy, the economic power, and integration of global financial markets.[13]

(i) First of all, the structure of international economy was dramatically changed. The technology transformed tools and ways of transportation and communication, which significantly reduced their costs: "in constant 1998 prices the cost of a three-minute phone call from New York to London had been $293 in 1931 and had (by 2001) fallen to around $1 for a much better-quality connection. In 2006 that same call costs just a few cents. Other technical changes, and above all the reduction in tariff and other barriers to trade, had played a role in opening up the global economy...For manufactured goods...average tariff rates among industrial countries are now less than 5 percent; within areas such as the European Union, they are zero. With airfreight, the internet, and other changes, goods can be ordered from one part of the world and received elsewhere in a matter of hours, contrasted with the months the same transaction would have taken two hundred years ago...Consequently, the relative importance of inter-national trade in the world economy had greatly increased: from 5.5 percent in 1950 to 17.2 percent in 2000...Much more trade was in intermediate goods, as producers were able to locate each stage of the production process in the country or countries where costs of production were lower. And, whereas in 1950, 45 percent of merchandise exports were agricultural, and 37 percent were manufactures, the composition of trade was radically altered, and trade in services grew in importance. By 1980, services trade constituted 15 percent of all goods and services trade, agriculture accounted for 12 percent and manufactures for 45 percent. The comparable numbers for 2004 show agriculture down to 7 percent, services up to almost 20 percent, and manufactures to 59 percent...other international transactions had increased in importance: tourism, other services items, and capital flows."

(ii) The second major change is in the economic power with increased macroeconomic stability based on reasonable domestic economic policies. Whereas "in 1950 the United States was the economic power; and by the mid-1970s Europe and Japan were clearly established as major global players; by 2000, emerging Asia - especially China and India, but also a number of other countries - had become a significant economic force in the international economy. Much of Europe...is now in the European Union and has achieved an even higher degree of internal integration than that realized externally. And the emerging Asian economies are already so large as to have global significance and impact. Assuming that their relatively high rates of economic growth persist, they will become increasingly important in the years to come." Their life expectancy has risen greatly.

(iii) The third is the rapid increase in integration of global financial markets. In 1952, only seven countries had "free exchange rate regimes for current account transactions. Now, 164 countries have accepted its obligations, while capital account transactions are much freer than they were.

(iv) Sustainable economic growth is basically dependent upon two ways: mobilization of more input factors, and productivity growth with new technology). If both are equal to others, the third factor could be government policies, including either monetary or fiscal policies. The government intervention needs to be limited to encouraging competitiveness and removing monopoly from the market to allocate resources efficiently without bottlenecks and idle capacities. It is important to maintain full employment with moderate levels of inflation in the long run. Anne O Krueger also writes three challenges: First, the Doha Round has encountered serious resistance in multi-lateral trade negotiations with 149 WTO members. Second, the international financial system needs to give Asia appropriate weight in its system, including IMF itself. Third, domestic policies and measures are important to bring more opportunities for growth in the short-run, and more education is necessary in the medium and longer terms.

Economic globalization has caused conflict with political and strategic interests between nations. The non-free or non-democratic countries such as in China, Russia, North Korea, do not respect democratic values - freedom, equality, and humanity. U.S. policy makers worry about market distortion due to China's subsidies and intellectual property theft. China's technology companies are merely extensions of its government. In this regard, the trade war between the United States and China seems to be much longer.

Photo II-1-1. The digitization of manufacturing will transform the way goods are made and change the politics of jobs too (The Economist, April 21st, 2012)
http://cdn.static-economist.com/sites/default/files/imagecache/full-width/images/printedition/20120421_LDP001_0.jpg, Accessed 9 July 2017

2. Theoretical Background of Capitalism

The difference between capitalism and socialism mainly comes from the extent of government intervention in the economy. A capitalist economy is based on private ownership of assets and business and relies on free markets to determine price, income, wealth, and distribution of goods and services. A socialist economy is characterized by greater intervention of the state to re-allocate resources in a more egalitarian way. Their major differences are as follows. First, private businesses are owned by private individuals or companies in capitalism, while in socialism the state owns and controls the means of production. In some models of socialism, worker cooperatives own businesses, instead of the government. Second, prices are determined by supply and demand in markets in capitalism, while in socialism they are controlled by the government. Third, income is determined by market forces in capitalism, while in socialism it is determined by redistribution through the government. Fourth, limited taxes are imposed for government spending in capitalism; while in socialism high progressive taxes are imposed to meet higher spending on public services. Fifth, healthcare left to free market in capitalism; while it is provided by the government free at point of use in the socialism. Sixth, in capitalism, the unemployment rates fluctuate according to the business cycle, while in socialism, the state provide full employment even without proper working loads.

The issue arising from capitalism and socialism lies in the problems of efficiency and equality. The capitalist economy is efficient but unequal: the goals of business firm are to maximize the shareholders wealth (or profits) subject to constraints - limited resources such as capital, labor, technology, and materials. If firms fail to keep up, they will go out of business. But this business failure allows resources to flow into new more efficient areas of the economy, that is known as the creative destruction. Market incentives encourage firms to cut costs with technological advances and managerial improvement, which makes the capitalist economy efficient. Capitalism inevitably leads to monopolies and oligarchies, and the system's use of resources is unsustainable. The successful business and individuals have more income, but the failed business and individuals lose income, which widens the gap between the rich and the poor, creating inequality in society. The socialist economy is equal but inefficient. Since socialism favors the community over the individuals, the loss of freedoms and rights is deemed "undemocratic at best and totalitarian at worst." Regarding incentives, "The right to private property is the fundamental right, for if one cannot own the fruits of one's labors, then the person is always subject to the state." Without proper compensation for one's efforts, the incentive to do well is taken away. Moreover, the market in the socialist system is basically non-reactive to prices, that would lead to irrational economic decisions and policies.[14]

"Analysis in economic history is undertaken using a combination of historical methods, statistical methods and the application of economic theory to historical situations and institutions...In Germany in the late 19th century, scholars in a number of universities, led by Gustav von Schmoller, developed the historical school of economics. It ignored quantitative and mathematical approaches. Historical approach dominated German and French scholarship for most of the 20th century. The approach was spread to Great Britain by William Ashley, 1860–1927, and dominated British economic history for much of the 20th century. In France, economic history was heavily influenced by the Annales School[15] from the early 20th century to the present. It exerts a worldwide influence through its Journal Annales, *Histoire, Sciences Sociales.*"[16]

"Academics at the London School of Economics (LSE) and the University of Cambridge had numerous disputes over the separation of economics and economic history in the interwar era. Cambridge economists believed that pure economics involved a component of economic history and that the two were inseparably entangled. Those at the LSE believed that economic history warranted its own courses, research agenda and academic chair separated from mainstream economics. In the initial period of the subject's development, the LSE position of separating economic history from economics won out... Indeed, the Economic History Society had its inauguration at LSE in 1926 and the University of Cambridge eventually established its own economic history programme. However, the past twenty years have witnessed the widespread closure of these separate programmes in the UK and the integration of the discipline into either history or economics departments. Only the LSE retains a separate economic history department...Meanwhile, in the US, the field of economic history has in recent decades been largely subsumed into other fields of economics... As a consequence, there are no specialist economic history graduate programs at any universities anywhere in the country."[17]

"In the history of economic thought, a school of economic thought is a group of economic thinkers who share or shared a common perspective on the way economies work. While economists do not always fit into particular schools, particularly in modern times, classifying economists into schools of thought is common. Economic thought may be roughly divided into three phases: premodern (Greco-Roman, Indian, Persian, Islamic, and Imperial Chinese), early modern (mercantilist, physiocrats) and modern (beginning with Adam Smith and classical economics in the late 18th century). Systematic economic theory has been developed mainly since the beginning of what is termed the modern era. Currently, the great majority of economists follow an approach referred to as mainstream economics (sometimes called 'orthodox economics'). Within the mainstream in the United States, distinctions can be made between the Saltwater school (associated with Berkeley, Harvard, MIT, Pennsylvania, Princeton, and Yale), and the more laissez-faire ideas of the Freshwater school (represented by the Chicago school of economics, Carnegie Mellon University, the University of Rochester and the University of Minne-sota). Both of these schools of thought are associated with the neoclassical synthesis. Some influential approaches of the past, such as the historical school of economics and institutional economics, have become defunct or have declined in influence, and are now considered heterodox approaches," which include Austrian economics and Marxian economics."[18]

Neoclassical economics developed in the 1870s. There were three main independent schools. (i) The Cambridge School was founded with the 1871 publication of Jevons' *Theory of Political Economy*, developing theories of partial equilibrium and focusing on market failures. Its main representatives were Stanley Jevons, Alfred Marshall, and Arthur Pigou. "Alfred Marshall (1842–1924) is also credited with an attempt to put economics on a more mathematical footing. The first professor of economics at the University of Cambridge, his 1890 work *Principles of Economics* abandoned the term political economy for his favorite economics." (ii) The Austrian School of Economics was made up of Austrian economists Carl Menger, Eugen von Böhm-Bawerk, and Friedrich von Wieser, who developed the theory of capital and tried to explain economic crises. Carl Menger (1840-1921) published *Principles of Economics* (1871), restating the basic principles of marginal utility: "Consumers act rationally by seeking to maximize satisfaction of all their preferences; people allocate their spending so that the last unit of a commodity bought creates no more satisfaction than a last unit bought of something else." (iii) The Lausanne School, led by Léon Walras and Vilfredo Pareto, developed the theories of general equilibrium and Pareto efficiency. Leon Walras (1834-1910) published *Elements of Pure Economics* (1874): Walras constructed his basic theory of general equilibrium by beginning with simple equations and then increasing the complexity in the next equations. Pareto introduced the notion of Pareto optimality, enjoying maximum economic satisfaction.

(iv) Institutional economics was led by Torstein Veblen, Wesley Clair Mitchell, John R. Commons, and John H. Hobson. John R. Commons (1862–1945) published *Institutional Economics* (1934), based on the concept that the economy is a web of relationships between people with diverging interests, including monopolies, large corporations, labor disputes, and fluctuating business cycles. (v) In debate concerning economic systems – capitalism versus socialism – Ludwig von Mises, Friedrich A. Hayek, Oscar R. Lange, and Joseph A. Schumpeter were highly influential, particularly in the cold war period. (vi) Socio-cultural evolutionism became popular with Herbert Spencer, August Comte, Lewis H. Morgan, and Max Weber (1864-1920), who wrote *The Protestant Ethic and the Spirit of*

Capitalism (1904) and *Economy and Society* (1921-22). (vii) Keynesianism was led by John Maynard Keynes (1988-1946), who wrote *The Economic Consequences of the Peace* (1919) and *The General Theory of Employment, Interest and Money* (1936). He dealt with the Great Depression, based on the theories written in the latter.

Neoclassical economics transformed itself so rapidly in the 1940s and 1950s that someone ought to invent an entirely new label for post-war orthodox economics. "Economics is a social science concerned chiefly with description and analysis of production, consumption, and distribution of goods and services. Economics focuses on the behavior and interactions of economic agents and how economies work. Microeconomics analyzes basic elements in the economy, including individual agents and markets, their interactions, and the outcomes of interactions. Individual agents may include...households, firms, buyers, and sellers. Macroeconomics analyzes the entire economy (meaning aggregated production, consumption, savings, and investment) and issues affecting it, including unemployment of resources (labor, capital, and land), inflation, economic growth, and the public policies that address these issues (monetary, fiscal, and other policies). Other broad distinctions within economics include those between positive economics, describing *what is*, and normative economics, advocating *what ought to be*; between economic theory and applied economics; between rational and behavioral economics; and between mainstream economics and heterodox economics."[19] In methodology, econometrics and other empirical methods were developed. Modern heterodox economic thought developed such radicals, institutionalists, post-Keynesians, and so on. Let's review economic theories of microeconomics, macroeconomics, methodology, and heterodox economics.

MODERN MICROECONOMICS

"Neoclassical economics was not a single entity: it was a multidimensional school of thought that evolved over time. It focused on marginalism, assumptions of rationality, and a strong policy presumption that markets worked, although that was subject to a number of provisos. The neoclassical school was quite fluid: as soon as neoclassical economists became the orthodoxy, and possibly even before, it started to change. Bit by bit economics moved away from its neoclassical footing. Marginalist calculus was replaced by set theory; rationality assumptions were modified by insights from psychology; the set of issues to which economic analysis was applied expanded; evolutionary game theory raised the possibility that individuals exhibit class-consciousness; and sociological explanations were used to supplement analyses of the labor market. As these and similar changes occurred, what had .been seen as necessary components of neoclassical thought ceased to be components of modern thought. Our belief is that sufficient components have changed to warrant a new term to describe modern economics. Many elements of neoclassical economics still exist within modern microeconomics, but what distinguishes modern microeconomics is not these elements; it is a modeling approach to problems. The assumptions and conclusions of the model are less important than whether the model empirically fits reality. In this chapter we discuss the evolution of microeconomics from neoclassical to modern. We trace that path from the 1930s through a highly formalistic stage in which there was an attempt to tie microeconomics together within a single theory with little regard for that theory's empirical relevance to its modern state, in which microeconomics consists of a set of models focused almost entirely on empirical relevance. We start our story in the 1930s with the fall of Marshallian economics."[20]

Table II-2-1. Major Writers on Modern Microeconomic Theory

A. Cournot, *Researches into the Mathematical Principles of the Theory of Wealth* (1838)
Leon Walras, *Elements of Pure Economics* (1874)
F. Y. Edgeworth, *Mathematical Psychics* (1881)
Irving Fisher, *Mathematical Investigations in the Theory of Value and Prices* (1892)
Vilfredo Pareto, *Manual of Political Economy* (1906)
Gustav Cassel, *Theory of Social Economy* (1918)
John R. Hicks, *Value and Capital* (1939)
John von Neumann and Oskar Morgenstern, *Theory of Games and Economic Behavior* (1944)
P. A. Samuelson, *Foundations of Economic Analysis* (1947)
Kenneth Arrow, *Social Choice and Individual Values* (1951)
Herbert Simon, *Models of Man* (1957)
Gerald Debreu, *Theory of Value, an Axiomatic Analysis of Economic Equilibrium* (1959)

Source: Harry Landreth and David C. Colander, *History of Economic Thought* (Boston, MA: Houghton Mifflin, 2002), 388.

Away from Marshallian Economics: "Marshall's engine of analysis, combining supply and demand curves with common sense, could answer certain questions, but others exceeded its scope. Supply-and-demand analysis was partial equilibrium analysis applied to problems of relative prices. But many of the questions economists were trying to answer, such as what determines the distribution of income or what effect certain laws and taxes would have either introduced problems beyond the applicability of partial equilibrium analysis or violated its assumptions. Nonetheless, economists continued to apply partial equilibrium arguments to such issues, assuming that the aggregate market must constitute some as yet unknown combination of all the partial equilibrium markets. Most economists were content with this state of affairs for quite a while. After all, Marshallian economics did provide a workable, if not formally tight, theory that was able to answer many real-world questions…In the United States, a group called the institutionalists wanted simply to eliminate the theory, arguing that history and institutions should be emphasized, and the inadequate theory dropped. Other critics, whom we will call formalists, went in the opposite direction: they believed that economics should be a science, not an engineering field, and that if economics were to conclude that the market worked well, we needed a theory to show how and why it did so. These formalists agreed with the institutionalists that Marshallian economic theory was inadequate, but their answer was not to eliminate the theory: they wanted to provide a better, more rigorous general equilibrium foundation that could adequately answer…complicated questions."[21]

The Formalist Revolution in Microeconomics: "In the late 1930s the formalist research program won, and the Marshallian approach started to wane. By the 1950s the formalists had reformulated microeconomics into a mathematical structure dependent on Walras, not Marshall. Applications became less important than logical consistency. The formalist revolution reached its apex in 1959 with the publication of the Arrow-Debreu model. With the completion of that general equilibrium work, economists turned once again to applied work. But they did not return to Marshall's engine of analysis approach, which down-played the use of mathematics and stressed judgment. Instead, they integrated policy prescriptions into the mathematical models. As that happened, the neoclassical era evolved into the modern modeling era. In the modeling approach, mathematics is used to develop simple models that ideally capture the essence of the problem. Then econometric techniques are used to test those models. This development and empirical testing of models have become the modern economic method."[22]

(a) ***The Battle over Formalist Approaches***: The mathematical approach is rooted in the thought of several prominent economists. Antoine Augustine Cournot attempted Researches on the *Mathematical Principles of the Theory of Wealth* (1838) in describing a spring water duopoly that now bears his name. Later, "William Stanley Jevons's *Theory of Political Economy* (1871), Carl Manger's *Principles of Economics* (1871), and Léon Walras's *Elements of Pure Economics*: Or the theory of social wealth (1874–77) gave way to what was called the Marginal Revolution. Some common ideas behind those works were models or arguments characterized by rational economic agents maximizing utility under a budget constrain. This arose as a necessity of arguing against the labor theory of value associated with classical economists such as Adam Smith, David Ricardo and Karl Marx. Walras also went as far as developing the concept of general equilibrium of an economy."[23]

Irving Fisher also advocated the use of mathematics in the development of his economic theory, particularly in his quantity theory of money (MV=PT) in *The Theory of Interest* (1930).

"In the early 1930s this situation began to change. Expositions of the many geometric tools that now provide the basis for undergraduate microeconomics began to fill the journals. The marginal revenue curve, the short-run marginal cost curve, and models of imperfect competition and income-substitution effects were discovered and explored during this period. Though rooted in Marshall, these new tools formalized his analysis, and as they did so they moved farther and farther from the actual institutions they represented. The Marshallian approach to interrelating theory and institutions had been like a teeter-totter: it had worked as long as the two sides balanced. But once the theory side gained a bit, the balance was broken, and economics fell hard to the theoretical side, leaving history and institutions suspended in air. History and institutions were abandoned because the new mathematical tools required stating precisely what was being assumed and what was changing and stating it in such a way that the techniques could handle the entire analysis. History and particular institutions no longer fit in. One could no longer argue, as in the earlier Marshallian economics, that a reasonable businessman would act in a certain way, appealing to the reader's sensibility to know what reasonable meant. Instead, reasonableness was transformed into a precise concept – rational – that was defined as making choices in conformance with certain established axioms. Similarly, the competitive economy was defined as one in which all individuals are price takers. Developing one's models mathematically required non-contextual argumentation, abstracted from any actual setting..."[24]

"Though the use of geometry as a tool in Marshallian analysis was a relatively small step, it was the beginning of the end for Marshallian economics. When geometry disclosed numerous logical problems with Marshallian economics, the new Marshallians responded with further formalization. Thus, by 1935 economics was ripe for change...The first step in the mathematization of microeconomic theory was to extend the marginal analysis of the household, firm, and markets and to make it more internally consistent. As economists shifted to higher-level mathematical techniques, they were able to go beyond partial equilibrium to general equilibrium, because the mathematics provided a method by which to keep track more precisely of items they had formerly kept somewhat loosely in the back of their heads. The second step was to reformulate the questions in a manner consistent with the tools and techniques available for dealing with them. The third step was to add new techniques to clarify unanswered questions. This process is continuing today. These steps did not follow a single path. One path had strong European roots; it included generalizing and formalizing general equilibrium theory. An early pioneer on this path was Gustav Cassel

(1866-1945), who simplified the presentation of Walras's general equilibrium theory in his *Theory of Social Economy* (1918; English versions 1924, 1932), making it more accessible."[25]

"In the 1930s two mathematicians, Abraham Wald (1902-1950) and John von Neumann (1903-1957), turned their attention to the study of equilibrium conditions in both static and dynamic models. They quickly raised the technical sophistication of economic analysis, exposing the inadequacy of much of previous economists' policy and theoretical analysis. Their work was noted by economists such as Kenneth Arrow (1921-2017) and Gerard Debreu (1921-2004), who extended it and applied it to Walras's theory to produce a more precise formulation of his general equilibrium theory. Following Wald's lead, Arrow and Debreu then rediscovered the earlier writings of Edgeworth. So impressed were they by these writers that they declared Edgeworth, not Marshall, to be the rightful forefather of modern microeconomics. The work of these theorists, in turn, has continued a highly formalistic tradition of general equilibrium theorists. Some of the questions that general equilibrium analysis has addressed are Adam Smith's questions: Will the unfettered use of markets lead to the common good, and if so, in what sense? Will the invisible hand of the market promote the social good? What types of markets are necessary for that to be the case? Because they involve the entire system, these are essentially general equilibrium questions, not questions of partial equilibrium. They could not, therefore, be answered within the Marshallian framework...General equilibrium theorists have found the answer to the question 'Does the invisible hand work?' to be yes, as long as certain conditions hold true. Their proof, for which Arrow and Debreu received Nobel prizes, was a milestone in economics because it answered the conjecture Adam Smith had made to begin the classical tradition in economics. Much subsequent work has been done in general equilibrium theory to articulate the invisible-hand theorem more elegantly and to modify its assumptions, but by first proving it, Arrow and Debreu earned a place in the history..."[26]

An Edgeworth box, named after Francis Ysidro Edgeworth, is "a way of representing various distributions of resources. Edgeworth made his presentation in his book *Mathematical Psychics: An Essay on the Application of Mathematics to the Moral Sciences*, 1881. Edgeworth's original two-axis depiction was developed into the now familiar box diagram by Pareto in his 1906 book *Manual of Political Economy* and was popularized in a later exposition by Bowley. The modern version of the diagram is commonly referred to as the Edgeworth–Bowley box. The Edgeworth box is used frequently in general equilibrium theory. It can aid in representing the competitive equilibrium of a simple system or a range of such outcomes that satisfy economic efficiency...the difficulty of moving to an efficient outcome in the presence of bilateral monopoly."[27]

(b) ***Imperfect Competition***: "In 1929 Harold Hotelling published *Stability in Competition* addressing the problem of instability in the classic Cournout model: Bertrand emphasized it for lacking equilibrium for prices as independent variables and Edgeworth constructed a dual monopoly model with correlated demand with also lacked stability. Hotteling proposed that demand typically varied continuously for relative prices, not discontinuously as suggested by the later authors. Following Sraffa he argued for the existence with reference to each seller of groups who will deal with him instead of his competitors in spite of difference in price, he also noticed that traditional models that presumed the uniqueness of price in the market only made sense if the commodity was standardized and the market was a point: akin to a temperature model in physics, discontinuity in heat transfer (price changes) inside a body (market) would lead to instability. To show the point he built a model of market located over a line with two sellers in each extreme of the line, in this case maximizing profit for both sellers leads to a stable equilibrium. From this model also follows that if a seller is to choose the location of his store so as to maximize his profit, he will place his store the closest to his competitor: the sharper competition with his rival is offset by the greater number of buyers he has an advantage."[28]

"A new impetus was given to the field when 1933 Joan Robinson and Edward II. Chamberlin published respectively, *The Economics of Imperfect Competition* (1933) and *The Theory of Monopolistic Competition* (1933), introducing models of imperfect competition. Although the monopoly case was already exposed in Marshall's Principles of Economics and Cournot had already constructed models of duopoly and monopoly in 1838, a whole new set of models grew out of this new literature. In particular the monopolistic competition model results in a non-efficient equilibrium. Chamberlin defined monopolistic competition as, '...challenge to traditional viewpoint of economics that competition and monopoly are alternatives and that individual prices are to be explained in terms of one or the other.' He continues, 'By contrast it is held that most economic situations are composite of both competition and monopoly, and that, wherever this is the case, a false view is given by neglecting either one of the two forces or regarding the situation as made up entirely of the other'."[29]

"Later, some market models were built using game theory, particularly regarding oligopolies. A good example of how microeconomics started to incorporate game theory, is the Stackelberg competition model published in 1934, which can be characterized as a dynamic game with a leader and a follower, and then be solved to find a Nash Equilibrium. William Baumol provided in his 1977 paper the current formal definition of a natural monopoly where an industry in which multiform production is more costly than production by a monopoly: mathematically this equivalent to sub-additivity of the cost function. He then sets out to prove 12 propositions related to strict economies of scale, ray average costs, ray concavity and transray convexity: in particular strictly declining ray average cost implies strict declining ray subadditivity, global economies of scale are sufficient but not necessary for strict ray subadditivity. In 1982 paper Baumol defined a contestable market as a market where entry is absolutely free and exit absolutely costless, freedom of entry in Stigler sense: the incumbent has no cost discrimination against entrants. He states that a contestable market will never have an economic profit greater than zero when in equilibrium and the equilibrium will also be efficient. According to Baumol this equilibrium emerges endogenously due to the nature of contestable markets, that is the only industry structure that survives in the long run is the one which minimizes total costs."[30]

(c) *Paul Samuelson* (1915-2009) "entered the University of Chicago at age 16, during the depths of the Great Depression, and received his PhD in economics from Harvard. After graduating, he became an assistant professor of economics at Massachusetts Institute of Technology (MIT) when he was 25 years of age and a full professor at age 32. In 1966, he was named Institute Professor, MIT's highest faculty honor. He spent his career at MIT where he was instrumental in turning its Department of Economics into a world-renowned institution by attracting other noted economists to join the faculty, including Robert M. Solow, Franco Modigliani, Robert C. Merton, Joseph E. Stiglitz, and Paul Krugman, all of whom went on to win Nobel Prizes. He served as an advisor to Presidents John F. Kennedy and Lyndon B. Johnson, and was a consultant to the United States Treasury, the Bureau of the Budget and the President's Council of Economic Advisers. Samuelson wrote a weekly column for Newsweek magazine along with Chicago School economist Milton Friedman, where they represented opposing sides: Samuelson, as a self-described Cafeteria Keynesian, took the Keynesian perspective but adapted it accepting what he felt was good. By contrast, Friedman represented the monetarist perspective. Samuelson died on December 13, 2009, at the age of 94."[31] Samuelson was the first American to win the Nobel Memorial Prize in Economic Sciences.

Foundations of Economic Analysis (1946) is derived from his doctoral dissertation and was inspired by the classical thermodynamic methods. "The book proposes to: (i) examine underlying analogies between central features in theoretical and applied economics; and (ii) study how operationally meaningful theorems can be derived with a small number of analogous methods, in order to derive a general theory of economic theories. The book showed how these goals could be parsimoniously and fruitfully achieved, using the language of the mathematics applied to diverse subfields of economics. The book proposes two general hypotheses as sufficient for its purposes: (i) maximizing behavior of agents (including consumers as to utility and business firms as to profit); and (ii) economic systems (including a market and an economy) in stable equilibrium. In the first tenet, his views presented the idea that all actors, whether firms or consumers, are striving to maximize something. They could be attempting to maximize profits, utility, or wealth, but it did not matter because their efforts to improve their well-being would provide a basic model for all actors in an economic system. His second tenet was focused on providing insight on the workings of equilibrium in an economy. Generally, in a market, supply would equal demand. However, he urged that this might not be the case and that the important thing to look at was a systems natural resting point. Foundations presents the question of how an equilibrium would react when it is moved from its optimal point. Samuelson was also influential in providing explanations on how the changes in certain factors can affect an economic system. For example, he could explain the economic effect of changes in taxes or new technologies. In the course of analysis, comparative statics, (the analysis of changes in equilibrium of the system that result from a parameter change of the system) is formalized and clearly stated. The chapter on welfare economics attempt(s) to give a brief but fairly complete survey of the whole field of welfare economics. It also...develops what became commonly called the Bergson–Samuelson social welfare function. It shows how to represent (in the maximization calculus) all real-valued economic measures of any belief system that is required to rank consistently different feasible social configurations in an ethical sense as better than, worse than, or indifferent to each other."[32]

Economics (1948): "Samuelson is also author (and since 1985 co-author) of an influential principles textbook, Economics, first published in 1948, now in its 19th edition. The book has been translated into forty-one languages and sold over four million copies; it is considered the best-selling economics textbook in history...Written in the shadow of the Great Depression and the Second World War, it helped to popularize the insights of John Maynard Keynes. A main focus was how to avoid, or at least mitigate, the recurring slumps in economic activity. Samuelson wrote: 'It is not too much to say that the widespread creation of dictatorships and the resulting World War II stemmed in no small measure from the world's failure to meet this basic economic problem adequately.' This reflected the concern of Keynes himself with the economic causes of war and the importance of economic policy in promoting peace. Samuelson's influential textbook has been criticized for including comparative growth rates between the United States and the Soviet Union that were inconsistent with historical GNP differences. The 1967 edition extrapolates the possibility of Soviet/US real GNP parity between 1977 and 1995. Each subsequent edition extrapolated a date range further in the future until those graphs were dropped from the 1985 edition. Samuelson commented on the economics of the Soviet Union and Marxism in 1989" with many skeptics.[33]

(d) ***Equilibrium and Stability***: "Equilibrium is a state of a system which does not change. If the dynamics of a system is described by a differential equation (or a system of differential equations), then equilibria can be estimated by setting a derivative (all derivatives) to zero. For example, in a logistic model, to find equilibria we have to solve the equation: $dN/dt = 0$: This equation has two roots: $N=0$ and $N=K$. An equilibrium may be stable or unstable... An equilibrium is considered stable (for simplicity we will consider asymptotic stability only) if the system always returns to it after small disturbances. If the system moves away from the equilibrium after small disturbances, then the equilibrium is unstable. The notion of stability can be applied to other types of attractors (limit cycle, chaos), however, the general definition is more complex than for equilibria. Stability is probably the most important notion in science because it refers to what we call 'reality'. Everything should be stable to be observable. For example, in quantum mechanics, energy levels are those that are stable because unstable levels cannot be observed."[34]

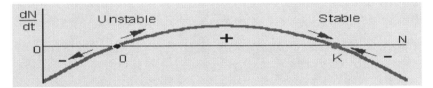

Figure II-2-1. Equilibrium: 1 Stable and 1 Unstable Points
Accessed 27 August 2017, https://www.ma.utexas.edu/users/davis/375/popecol/lec9/equilib.html

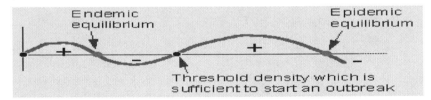

Figure II-2-2. Equilibrium: 2 Stable and 2 Unstable Points
Accessed 27 August 2017, https://www.ma.utexas.edu/users/davis/375/popecol/lec9/equilib.html

Figure II-2-1 examines stability of 2 equilibria points in the logistic model. "In this figure, population growth rate, dN/dt, is plotted versus population density, N. This is often called a phase-plot of population dynamics. If $0 < N < K$, then $dN/dt > 0$ and thus, population grows (the point in the graph moves to the right). If $N < 0$ or $N > K$ (of course, $N < 0$ has no biological sense), then population declines (the point in the graph moves to the left). The arrows show that the equilibrium $N=0$ is unstable, whereas the equilibrium $N=K$ is stable. From the biological point of view, this means that after small deviation of population numbers from $N=0$ (e.g., immigration of a small number of organisms), the population never returns back to this equilibrium. Instead, population numbers increase until they reach the stable equilibrium N=K. After any deviation from N=K the population returns back to this stable equilibrium. The difference between stable and unstable equilibria is in the slope of the line on the phase plot near the equilibrium point. Stable equilibria are characterized by a negative slope (negative feedback) whereas unstable equilibria are characterized by a positive slope (positive feedback)." "The second example is the bark beetle model with two stable and two unstable equilibria. Stable equilibria correspond to endemic and epidemic populations. Endemic populations are regulated by the number of susceptible trees in the forest. Epidemic populations are limited by the total number of trees because mass attack of beetle females may overcome the resistance of any tree."[35]

(e) Formalists, Mathematics, Pedagogy: "In foundations of mathematics, philosophy of mathematics, and philosophy of logic, formalism is a theory that holds that statements of mathematics and logic can be considered to be statements about the consequences of certain string manipulation rules. For example, Euclidean geometry can be considered a game whose play consists in moving around certain strings of symbols called axioms according to a set of rules called rules of inference to generate new strings. In playing this game one can prove that the Pythagorean theorem is valid because the string representing the Pythagorean theorem can be constructed using only the stated rules. According to formalism, the truths expressed in logic and mathematics are not about numbers, sets, or triangles or any other contented subject matter – in fact, they aren't about anything at all. They are syntactic forms whose shapes and locations have no meaning unless they are given an interpretation."[36]

"Formalism is associated with rigorous method. In common use, a formalism means the outturn of the effort towards formalization of a given limited area. In other words, matters can be formally discussed once captured in a formal system...Complete formalization is in the domain of computer science. Formalism stresses axiomatic proofs using theorems, specifically associated with David Hilbert. A formalist is an individual who belongs to the school of formalism, which is a certain mathematical-philosophical doctrine descending from Hilbert. Formalists are relatively tolerant and inviting to new approaches to logic, non-standard number systems, new set theories, etc. The more games they study, the better. However, in all three of these examples, motivation is drawn from existing mathematical or philosophical concerns. The games are usually not arbitrary. Recently, some formalist mathematicians have proposed that all formal mathematical knowledge should be systematically encoded in computer-readable formats, in order to facilitate automated proof checking of mathematical proofs and the use of interactive theorem proving in the development of mathematical theories and computer software."[37]

"But the introduction of formalism presented a pedagogical problem: the Walasian general equilibrium approach is very difficult. In order to master it, one must learn a new language (mathematics) and be able to grasp highly abstract, non-contextual argumentation. But most economics undergraduates have no intention of becoming economists and hence have little incentive to acquire the considerable mathematical skill necessary to comprehend the complexities of general equilibrium interactions. This pedagogical problem has occasioned the current bifurcation of micro-economics, because the preferred graduate economics theory is too difficult for the typical undergraduate. Paul Samuelson responded to the special needs of undergraduate education by writing an elementary economics textbook that has sold several million copies and gone through many editions. Samuelson's text dominated the field for some thirty years from its first edition in 1947, and most other introductory texts have copied his format. This elementary text shaped modern undergraduate economics, just as his Foundations did graduate economics."

"In his undergraduate text Samuelson graphically presented micro-economics as a logical extension of the interactions of rational individuals within a competitive market structure. Retaining the Marshallian tools but eliminating most of the platitudes and homey analogies of earlier economic texts, Samuelson constructed a largely non-contextual theory that is more consistent with general equilibrium analysis. It was in this manner that the current division of graduate and undergraduate economics developed. Undergraduate introductory texts kept the Marshallian approach, emphasizing two-dimensional graphical techniques rather than multivariate calculus, and graduate microeconomics moved on to the full mathematical approach that is far more consistent with Walras and Cournot than with Marshall."[38]

Milton Friedman and the Chicago Approach: "Milton Friedman (1912-2006) was an American economist who received the 1976 Nobel Memorial Prize in Economic Sciences for his research on consumption analysis, monetary history and theory, and the complexity of stabilization policy. With George Stigler and others, Friedman was among the intellectual leaders of the second generation of Chicago price theory, a methodological movement at the University of Chicago's Department of Economics, Law School, and Graduate School of Business from the 1940s onward. Several students and young professors that were recruited or mentored by Friedman at Chicago went on to become leading economists; they include Gary Becker, Robert Fogel, Thomas Sowell, and Robert Lucas, Jr. Friedman's challenges to what he later called naive Keynesian theory began with his 1950s reinterpretation of the consumption function. In the 1960s, he became the main advocate opposing Keynesian government policies, and described his approach (along with mainstream economics) as using Keynesian language and apparatus yet rejecting its initial conclusions. He theorized that there existed a natural rate of unemployment and argued that employment above this rate would cause inflation to accelerate. He argued that the Phillips curve was, in the long run, vertical at the natural rate and predicted what would come to be known as stagflation. Friedman promoted an alternative macroeconomic viewpoint known as monetarism, and argued that a steady, small expansion of the money supply was the preferred policy. His ideas concerning monetary policy, taxation, privatization and deregulation influenced government policies, especially during the 1980s. His monetary theory influenced the Fed...to the global financial crisis of 2007–08."[39]

"Friedman was an advisor to Republican U.S. President Ronald Reagan and Conservative British Prime Minister Margaret Thatcher. His political philosophy extolled the virtues of a free market economic system with minimal intervention. He once stated that his role in eliminating U.S. conscription was his proudest accomplishment. In his 1962 book *Capitalism and Freedom*, Friedman advocated policies such as a volunteer military, freely floating exchange rates, abolition of medical licenses, a negative income tax, and school vouchers. His support for school choice led him to found the Friedman Foundation for Educational Choice...Friedman's works include monographs, books, scholarly articles, papers, magazine columns, television programs, and lectures, and cover a broad range of economic topics and public policy issues. His books and essays have had global influence, including in former communist states. A survey of economists ranked Friedman as the second-most popular economist of the twentieth century after John Maynard Keynes, and The Economist described him as the most influential economist of the second half of the 20th century."[40]

The Chicago approach has stimulated many new ideas. "Among those new ideas that have been stimulated has been Armen Alchian's (1914-2013) and Harold Demsetz's (1930-) work on property rights as underlying markets. Since the Chicago view is that it is best to assume that markets depend upon property rights; thus, the study of property rights is of paramount importance to economics." The most important follower of Friedman was Gary Becker (1920-2014), who had used microeconomic models to study decisions about crime, courtship, marriage, and childbearing. Becker had shown that the simple-maximization microeconomic model based on the assumption of rational individuals had potentially infinite applications. "Market incentives make a difference in people's behavior, and noneconomic specialists have often not included a sufficient consideration of these incentives in their analyses. But analyses can go astray when only economic incentives are considered, and insufficient attention is paid to institutional and social incentives." After Milton Friedman, George Stigler, and Gary Becker, Chicago economics changed, becoming more mathematical and less intuitive.[41]

Classical-Neoclassical-Modern Microeconomics: "Classical econo-mics was founded by economists including Adam Smith, David Ricardo, and John Stuart Mill. Neoclassical economics was developed by authors and scholars such as William Stanley Jevons, Carl Menger, and Leon Walras. The two schools of thought are quite different to each other in that classical economics was developed historically, and neo classical economics encom-passes the kinds of economic principles and concepts followed and accepted today. (a) *Classical economic theory* is the belief that a self-regulating economy is the most efficient and effective because as needs arise people will adjust to serving each other's requirements. According to classical economic theory there is no government intervention and the people of the economy will allocate scare resources in the most efficient manner to meet the needs to individuals and businesses. Prices in a classical economy are decided based on the raw materials used to produce, wages, electricity and other expenses that have gone into deriving a finished product. In classical economics, government spending is minimum, whereas spending on goods and services by the general public and business investments are considered as the most important to stimulate economic activity."[42]

(b) Neoclassical economics are the economic theories and concepts that are practiced in the modern world. "One of the major underlying principles of neoclassical economics is that prices are determined by the forces of demand and supply. There are three fundamentals assumptions that govern neoclassical economics. Neoclassical economics assumes that individuals are rational in that they act in a manner that brings forth the best personal advantage; individuals have limited income and, therefore, strive to maximize utility and organizations have constraints with regard to cost and, therefore, use the available resources to maximize profits. Finally, neoclassical economics assumes that individuals act independently of one another and have full access to the information required for decision making. Despite its acceptability in the modern world, neo-classical economics has invited some criticism. Some critiques question whether neo-classical economics is a true representation of reality."[43]

(c) Modern Microeconomics: (i) During the 1990s, "growth was a key topic; and the new growth theory is decidedly mainstream and non-neoclassical. In fact, it is generally contrasted with neoclassical growth theory." (ii) "Few modern economists accept utilitarianism…In his Nobel Prize speech, Amartya Sen recounted the problems of utilitarianism. While it is true that…students are still taught versions of utilitarianism, these are presented for pedagogical reasons only, not because utilitarianism is the reigning approach of modern economists." (iii) "In modern graduate microeconomics, game theory has almost completely replaced calculus as the central modeling apparatus." (iv) "In modern economics, bounded rationality, norm-based rationality, and empirically determined rationality

are fully acceptable approaches to problems." (v) "While individualism still reigns, it is under attack by certain branches of modern economics. Complexity theorists challenge the entire individualistic approach, at least when that approach is used to understand the aggregate economy. Evolutionary game theorists are attempting to show how such norms develop and constrain behavior. New institutionalists consistently operate within a framework that is at odds with methodological individualism." (vi) "In modern economics, theoretical economists are quite willing to consider multiple equilibria…modern work in policy generally avoids any discussion of multiple equilibria, and that is one of the contradictions."[44]

MODERN MACROECONOMICS

Macroeconomics deals with the economy as a whole like national, regional, and global economics. "In contrast to macroeconomics, microeconomics is the branch of economics that studies the behavior of individuals and firms in making decisions and the interactions among these individuals and firms in narrowly defined markets. Macroeconomists study aggregated indicators such as GDP, unemployment rates, national income, price indices, and the interrelations among the different sectors of the economy to better understand how the whole economy functions. Macroeconomists develop models that explain the relationship between such factors as national income, output, consumption, unemployment, inflation, savings, investment, international trade and international finance. While macroeconomics is a broad field of study, there are two areas of research that are emblematic of the discipline: the attempt to understand the causes and consequences of short-run fluctuations in national income, and the attempt to understand the determinants of long-run economic growth."[45] Macroeconomic models and their forecasts are used by governments to assist in application of economic policy.

"Macroeconomic theory has its origins in the study of business cycles and monetary theory. In general, early theorists believed monetary factors could not affect real factors such as real output. John Maynard Keynes attacked some of these classical theories and produced a general theory that described the whole economy in terms of aggregates rather than individual, microeconomic parts. Attempting to explain unemployment and recessions, he noticed the tendency for people and businesses to hoard cash and avoid investment during a recession. He argued that this invalidated the assumptions of classical economists who thought that markets always clear, leaving no surplus of goods and no willing labor left idle. The generation of economists that followed Keynes synthesized his theory with neoclassical microeconomics to form the neoclassical synthesis. Although Keynesian theory originally omitted an explanation of price levels and inflation, later

Keynesians adopted the Phillips curve to model price-level changes. Some Keynesians opposed the synthesis method of combining Keynes's theory with an equilibrium system and advocated disequilibrium models instead. Monetarists, led by Milton Friedman, adopted some Keynesian ideas, such as the importance of the demand for money, but argued that Keynesians ignored the role of money supply in inflation. Robert Lucas and other neoclassical macroeconomists criticized Keynesian models that did not work under rational expectations. Lucas argued that Keynesian empirical models would not be as stable…based on microeconomic foundations."[46]

The new classical school culminated in real business cycle theory (RBC). "RBC models assumed that markets clear and that business cycles are driven by changes in technology and supply, not demand. New Keynesians tried to address many of the criticisms leveled by Lucas and other… economists…New Keynesians adopted rational expectations and built models with micro-foundations of sticky prices that suggested recessions could still be explained by demand factors because rigidities stop prices from falling to a market-clearing level, leaving a surplus of goods and labor. The new neoclassical synthesis combined elements of both new classical and new Keynesian macroeconomics into a consensus. Other economists avoided the new classical and new Keynesian debate on short-term dynamics and developed the new growth theories of long-run economic growth. The Great Recession led to a retrospective on the state of the field and some popular attention turned toward heterodox economics."[47]

Table II-2-2. Major Writers on Modern Macroeconomic Thought

Knut Wicksell, *Interest and Prices* (1898)
Irving Fisher, *Purchasing Power of Money* (1911)
Joseph Schumpeter, *Theory of Economic Development* (1911)
Wesley Clair Mitchell, *Business Cycles* (1913)
Friedrich Hayek, *Prices and Production* (1931)
Michal Kalecki, *Studies in the Theory of Business Cycles* (1933-39)
Dennis Robertson, "Saving and Hoarding" (1933)
John Maynard Keynes, *The General Theory* (1936)
John R. Hicks, "Mr. Keynes and the Classics" (1937)
Gunnar Myrdal, *Monetary Equilibrium* (1939)
Paul A. Samuelson, "Interaction between the Multiplier Analysis and
the Principle of Acceleration" (1939)
Alvin Hansen, *Fiscal Policy and Business Cycles* (1941)
Abba P. Lerner, *The Economics of Control* (1944)
Milton Friedman, *Studies in the Quantity Theory of Money* (1956)
Robert Solow, *A Contribution to the Theory of Growth* (1956)
John Muth, "Rational Expectations and the Theory of Price Movements" (1961)
Robert E. Lucas, Jr., *Studies in Business-Cycle Theory* (1981)

Source: Harry Landreth and David C. Colander, *History of Economic Thought*
(Boston, MA: Houghton Mifflin, 2002), 408.

Forerunners of Modern Macroeconomics: *(a) Joseph Schumpeter's Economic Growth*: Joseph Schumpeter (1883-1950) was born in Triesch, Habsburg Moravia to Catholic German-speaking parents. "His father owned a factory, but he died when Joseph was only four years old. In 1893, Joseph and his mother moved to Vienna. After attending school at the Theresianum, Schumpeter began his career studying law at the University of Vienna under the Austrian capital theorist Eugen von Böhm-Bawerk, taking his Ph.D. in 1906. In 1909, after some study trips, he became a professor of economics and government at the University of Czernowitz. In 1911, he joined the University of Graz, where he remained until World War I. In 1918, Schumpeter was a member of the Socialization Commission established by the Council of the People's Deputies in Germany. In March 1919, he was invited to take office as Minister of Finance in the Republic of German-Austria. He proposed a capital levy as a way to tackle the war debt and opposed the socialization of the Alpine Mountain plant. In 1921, he became president of the private Biedermann Bank…His resignation was a condition of the takeover of the Biedermann Bank in September 1924."[48]

"From 1925 to 1932, Schumpeter held a chair at the University of Bonn, Germany. He lectured at Harvard in 1927–1928 and 1930. In 1931, he was a visiting professor at The Tokyo College of Commerce. In 1932, Schumpeter moved to the United States, and soon began what would become extensive efforts to help central European economist colleagues displaced by Nazism. Schumpeter also became known for his opposition to Marxism and socialism that he thought would lead to dictatorship, and even criticized President Franklin Roosevelt's New Deal. In 1939, Schumpeter became a US citizen. In the beginning of World War II, the FBI investigated him and his wife (a prominent scholar) for pro-Nazi leanings but found no evidence of Nazi sympathies. At Harvard, Schumpeter was considered a memorable character, erudite and even showy in the classroom. He became known for his heavy teaching load and his personal and painstaking interest in his students. He served as the faculty advisor of the Graduate Economics Club and organized private seminars and discussion groups."[49]

The Theory of Economic Development (1911) introduces four main features. (i) Circular Flow means a continuous activity and no destruction. "It is the characteristic of an economy in stationary state. The circular flow is similar to circulation in blood in an animal organism. Circular flow is based upon a state of perfect competitive equilibrium in which costs are equal to receipts and prices to average costs. 'The circular flow is a stream that is fed from the continually flowing springs of labor power and land and flow in every economic period into the reservoir which we call income, in order to be transformed into satisfaction of wants'. The main features of circular flow are as under a) All economic activities are essentially repetitive and follow a familiar routine course. b) All the producers know the aggregate demand for goods and adjust the supply of output accordingly. This means demand and supply are in equilibrium at each point of time. c) The economic system has the optimum level of output and its maximum use and there is no possibility of wastage of resources. d) The firms working in a system are in a state of competitive equilibrium; e) Under the stationary equilibrium, the prices are equal to the average cost. The above stated features imply that circular flow is used in a static setting. To make it dynamic and consistent with development, changes must take place in flow system. These changes can be brought through innovations. Innovation may be defined as a change in existing production system to be introduced by the entrepreneur with a view to make profits and reduce costs...Any innovation may consist of a) The introduction of a new product. b) The introduction of a new method of production. c) The opening up of a new market. d) The conquest of a new source of supply of raw materials or semi manufactured goods. e) The carrying out of the new organization of any industry like the creation of a monopoly. The new combinations of these factors are essential for the development process to start."[50]

(ii) Role of the Entrepreneur: "As in economic system, there is high degree of risk, thus entrepreneur is motivated: a) The desire to find a private commercial kingdom. b) The will to conquer and prove his superiority. c) The joy of creating, getting things done or simply of exercising one's energy and ingenuity." For the entrepreneurial performance, "a) Technical know-how should be available to the entrepreneur for introducing new products and new combinations of production factors. b) Capital resource can enable the entrepreneurs to have command over factors of production. For this, he needs purchasing power in the form of credit and capital which he can borrow from banks and other financial institutions. Thus, credit and bank play a vital role in economic development. Credit enables the entrepreneur to buy producer's goods which he needs for conducting new experiments and innovations. The invention in one field of the economic activity will induce inventions in the related fields. Thus, credit creation becomes an important part of the development model." c) Role of Profits: An entrepreneur innovates to earns profits. "Profits arise due to dynamic changes resulting from an innovation. d) Breaking the Circular Flow: They continue to exist till the innovation becomes general...Schumpeter regards economic development as a dynamic and discontinuous process. The society progresses through trade cycles. In order to break the circular flow, the innovating entrepreneurs are financed by bank credit expansion. Since investment in innovation is risky, they must be paid bank interest on it. Once the innovations become successful and profitable, other entrepreneurs follow it in 'swarm like clusters'. Innovations in one field may induce other innovations in related fields." The emergence of auto industry stimulated the construction of highways, rubber tires and petroleum products etc.[51]

(iii) Business Cycle: "According to Schumpeter, the creation of bank credit is assumed to accelerate money incomes and prices in the economy. It creates a cumulative expansion throughout the economy. With the increase in the purchasing power of the consumers, the demand for the products increases in relation to supply. The rising prices and the high rates of profits stimulate producers to raise investments by borrowing from the banks...During the boom period, the new products start appearing in the market with the entrance of new entrepreneurs. These products displace the old ones and thus decrease their demand in the market. Consequently, the prices of old products fall. With a view to liquidating their stocks, the old firms start selling their goods at a low price and hence most of the firms incur losses and some firms are even forced to run into loss...The business cycle continues to fall below the level of equilibrium with the beginning of the recession and ultimately reaches the point of depression. In the end, the retake of economic activities leads to revival of the economy."[52]

(iv) The Decay of Capitalism: The continuous technical progress results in an unbounded increase in total and per capita output. "As long as technological progress takes place, the rate of profit is positive. Hence, there can be no drying up of sources of investible funds nor any vanishing of investment opportunities. There is, therefore, no prior ceiling to the level of per capita income in a capitalist society. Nevertheless, the economic success of capitalism will eventually lead to its decay" because of following reasons: The Obsolescence of Entrepreneurial Function, Destruction of Industrial Framework, and Destruction of Protecting Political Strata.[53]

Capitalism, Socialism, and Democracy (1942): "While he agrees with Karl Marx that capitalism will collapse and be replaced by socialism, Schumpeter predicts a different way this will come about. While Marx predicted that capitalism would be overthrown by a violent proletarian revolution, which actually occurred in the least capitalist countries, Schumpeter believed that capitalism would gradually weaken by itself and eventually collapse. Specifically, the success of capitalism would lead to corporatism and to values hostile to capitalism, especially among intellectuals. Intellectuals are a social class in a position to critique societal matters for which they are not directly responsible and to stand up for the interests of other classes. Intellectuals tend to have a negative outlook of capitalism, even while relying on it for prestige, because their professions rely on antagonism toward it. The growing number of people with higher education is a great advantage of capitalism, according to Schumpeter. Yet, unemployment and a lack of fulfilling work will cause intellectual critique, discontent and protests. Parliaments will increasingly elect social democratic parties, and democratic majorities will vote for restrictions on entrepreneurship. Increasing workers' self-management, industrial democracy and regulatory institutions would evolve non-politically into liberal capitalism. Thus, the intellectual and social climate needed for thriving entrepreneurship will be replaced by some form of laborism. This will exacerbate creative destruction (an endogenous replacement of old ways of doing things by new ways), which will ultimately undermine and destroy the capitalist structure."[54]

History of Economic Analysis (1954): "Schumpeter thought that the greatest 18th century economist was Turgot, not Adam Smith, as many consider, and he considered Léon Walras to be the greatest of all economists, beside whom other economists' theories were like inadequate attempts to catch some particular aspects of Walrasian truth. Schumpeter criticized John Maynard Keynes and David Ricardo for the Ricardian vice. According to Schumpeter, Ricardo and Keynes reasoned in terms of abstract models, where they would freeze all but a few variables. Then they could argue that one caused the other in a simple monotonic fashion. This led to the belief that one could easily deduce policy conclusions directly from a highly abstract theoretical model. In this book, Joseph Schumpeter recognized the implication of a gold monetary standard compared to a fiat monetary standard...An 'automatic' gold currency is part and parcel of a *laissez-faire* and free-trade economy. It links every nation's money rates and price levels with the money-rates and price levels of all the other nations that are 'on gold.' However, gold is extremely sensitive to government expenditure and even to attitudes or policies that do not involve expenditure directly, for example, to foreign policy, to certain policies of taxation, and, in general, to precisely all those policies that violate the principles of [classical] liberalism. This is the reason why gold is so unpopular now and also why it was so popular in a bourgeois era."[55] (The floating exchange rate since 1973)

(b) Quantity Theory of Money: "Classical and neoclassical theorists maintained an interest in at least one macroeconomic question: what determines the generalized level of prices? They addressed this economic question by utilizing the supply-and-demand approach developed in micro-economic theory. The supply of money was assumed to be determined by the monetary authorities, so some orthodox economists contended that the basic issues to be analyzed were on the side of demand. The household and firm are assumed to be rational and to have a demand for money...Walras, Menger, and others developed a supply-and-demand analysis to explain the value of money, but the most famous...is probably the one developed by Marshall, which has become known as the Cambridge cash-balance version of the quantity theory of money."[56]

Cambridge Approach: [Alfred Marshall, A.C. Pigou, and John Maynard Keynes associated with Cambridge University, took a slightly different approach to the quantity theory, focusing on money demand instead of money supply] "The first clear statement of the quantity theory of money was made by David Hume in 1752. This theory, as it came down through the literature, held that the general level of prices depended upon the quantity of money in circulation. Marshall's version of the quantity theory was an attempt to give microeconomic underpinnings to the macroeconomic theory that prices, and the quantity of money varied directly. He did this by elaborating a theory of household and firm behavior to explain the demand for money. Marshall reasoned that households and firms would desire to hold in cash balances a fraction of their money income. If M is money (currency plus demand deposits), PY is money income, and k is the proportion of their income that households and firms desire to hold in the form of money, the fundamental cash-balance equation is $M = k\ PY$. Because Marshall accepted Say's Law, full employment is assumed. An increase in the quantity of money, assuming k remains constant, will lead to an increase in money income, PY. Because full employment is assumed, an increase in the quantity of money will result in higher prices and a consequent increase in money income; real income, however, will not change. Decreases in the quantity of money will result in a fall in money income as prices fall; real income again will remain constant. We shall not examine the many different aspects of Marshall's formulation; the important point is that Marshall's version of the quantity theory made an attempt to integrate the microeconomic behavior of maximizing firms and households with ... the general level of prices."[57]

Irving Fisher (1869-1947): A group of economists, led by Irving Fisher developed another form of the quantity theory known as the transactions version. "However, they showed little interest in finding a microeconomic foundation for the macroeconomic analysis of the general level of prices. In this version, MV = PT where M is the quantity of money, V is the velocity of money, P is a measure of the price level, and T is the volume of transactions. Although have important differences, they have one element in common: they were both designed to explain the force that determine the general price level. They were not used to explain the level of real income, which was assumed to be at full employment and fixed by non-monetary forces in the economy. [Thus far the theory is not particularly controversial, as the equation of exchange is an identity. A theory requires that assumptions be made about the causal relationships among the four variables in this one equation. There are debates about the extent to which each of these variables is dependent upon the others. Without further restrictions, the equation does not require that a change in the money supply would change the value of any or all of P, Q, or PQ.] Not all economists were satisfied with this analysis. For example, Knut Wicksell argued that the quantity theory of money failed to explain why the monetary or pecuniary demand for goods exceeds or falls short of the supply of goods in given conditions. Wicksell tried to develop a so-called income approach to explain the general level of prices...to develop a theory of money that explains fluctuations in income as well as fluctuations in price levels."[58]

(c) Business Cycle Theory: For almost 200 years, we have recognized the cycle of expansion-boom-contraction-depression in the economy, so-called the business cycle, the downward and upward movement of gross domestic product (GDP) around its long-term growth trend. There are four different theories explaining the business cycles – Austrian Theory, Keynesian Theory, Mone-tarist Theory, and Real Business Cycle Theory.

(i) *Austrian Business Cycle Theory*: This theory was originated in the work of Austrian School economists Ludwig von Mises and Friedrich Hayek. "Hayek won the Nobel Prize in economics in 1974 (shared with Gunnar Myrdal) in part for his work on this theory. Proponents believe that a sustained period of low interest rates and excessive credit creation result in a volatile and unstable imbalance between saving and investment. According to the theory, the business cycle unfolds in the following way: low interest rates tend to stimulate borrowing from the banking system. This leads to an increase in capital spending funded by newly issued bank credit. Proponents hold that a credit-sourced boom results in widespread mal-investment. A correction or credit crunch – commonly called a recession or bust – occurs when the credit creation has run its course. Then the money supply contracts causing a curative recession and eventually allowing resources to be reallocated back towards their former uses. The Austrian explanation of the business cycle differs significantly from the mainstream understanding of business cycles and is generally rejected by mainstream economists."[59] Theoretically, "Some economists argue that the Austrian business cycle theory requires bankers and investors to exhibit a kind of irrationality, because their theory requires bankers to be regularly fooled into making unprofitable investments by temporarily low interest rates."[60] Empirically, Jeffery Hummel argues "that the Austrian explanation of the business cycle fails on empirical grounds...that investment spending remained positive in all recessions where there are data, except for the Great Depression...In 1969, economist Milton Friedman, after examining the history of business cycles in the U.S., concluded that The Hayek–Mises explanation of the business cycle is contradicted by the evidence."[61]

(ii) *Keynesian Business Cycle Theory*: According to Keynes, business cycle is caused by variations in the rate of investment caused by fluctuations in the Marginal Efficiency of Capital, which means the expected profits from new investments. "Business cycles are periodic fluctuations of employment, income and output. According to Keynes, income and output depend upon the volume of employment. The volume of employment is determined by three variables: the marginal efficiency of capital, the rate of interest and the propensity to consume. In the short period the rate of interest and the propensity to consume are more or less stable...fluctuations in the volume of employment are caused by fluctuations in the marginal efficiency of capital. Towards the end of the period, the high marginal efficiency of capital receives a setback from two directions: (i) The cost of production of new capital assets increases as shortages and bottlenecks of materials and of labor arise, and (ii) Owing to the abundance of output, profits are lowered below expectation. Soon business optimism gives way to skepticism and then to pessimism. The marginal efficiency of capital collapses with catastrophic suddenness. When businessmen find the investment expected to yield 10% yield only 3%, reducing incomes still further. The downward movement proceeds cumulatively, because every decrement of investment causes a multiple decrement in income. The economy proceeds towards a crisis and depression. Recovery begins when confidence revives, that is, when the marginal efficiency of capital again increases. This will happen after the period of time necessary for (i) the wearing out and obsolescence of part of the durable capital and (ii) the exhaustion of excess stock of consumer goods accumulated during the depression. Gradually the growing scarcity of capital goods and consumer goods increases profits... The marginal efficiency of capital revives, and expansion commences."[62]

(iii) ***Monetarist Business Cycle Theory***: Milton Friedman, as opposed to Keynes, "lays stress on the exogenous changes in money stock that causes fluctuations in aggregate demand and hence in economic activity while Keynes emphasized autonomous changes in investment that bring about changes in aggregate demand and hence in economic activity. Besides, Friedman and other monetarists put forward the concept of money multiplier which relates the statis-tical relationship between changes in money stock with changes in real income (i.e. $\Delta Y/\Delta M$ is money multiplier where ΔY stands for change in national income and ΔM stands for change in money stock in a given period) as against investment multiplier of Keynes, which states the relationship between change m autonomous investment (ΔT) and resulting change in income (ΔY), that is, $\Delta Y/\Delta I$ measures the size of multiplier. According to Friedman and other monetarists, money multiplier shows greater stability than the Keynesian investment multiplier which varies depending on the various leakages such as the extent of imports and the degree of taxation of income. They assert that apparently greater stability of money multiplier shows prima facie evidence in favor of the monetarist's explanation of cyclical fluctuations."[63]

"Finally, there is issue of transmission mechanism through which changes in money supply affect the level of national output and employment. Friedman explains it through portfolio adjustment consequent to changes in money stock where portfolios are considered to be comprising a spectrum of assets ranging from money (liquid-funds) through financial assets (bonds and equities to physical assets, durable producer and consumer goods. When there is increase in money stock by the Central Bank of the country, individuals and firms would have temporarily more money balances (i.e., cash or liquid funds) in their portfolio of assets than desired by them, they readjust their portfolio by spending some of the extra money balances on consumer goods and services; some part of extra money balances goes to purchasing new bonds and equity shares, some part to durable consumer goods such as houses. The new expenditure on bonds and shares raise their prices and lead to the fall in the rate of interest. The fall in interest and increase in wealth of the people will induce more investment and consumption demand. More investment will cause rise in demand for capital goods. Thus, increase in money stock causes increase in aggregate demand for goods and services either directly through portfolio adjustment or indirectly through increase in wealth and fall in rate of interest caused in this adjustment process. The transmission process is quite complex as it involves not only readjustment of portfolio of the individuals but also of firms, banks and other financial institutions."[64]

(iv) *Real Business Cycle Theory* (RBC): "RBC theory sees business cycle fluctuations as the efficient response to exogenous changes in the real economic environment. That is, the level of national output necessarily maximizes expected utility, and governments should therefore concentrate on long-run structural policy changes and not intervene through discretionary fiscal or monetary policy designed to actively smooth out economic short-term fluctuations. According to RBC theory, business cycles are therefore real in that they do not represent a failure of markets to clear but rather reflect the most efficient possible operation of the economy, given the structure of the economy. Real business cycle theory categorically rejects Keynesian economics and the real effectiveness of monetary policy as promoted by monetarism and New Keynesian economics, which are the pillars of mainstream macroeconomic policy. RBC theory differs in this way from other theories of the business cycle such as Keynesian economics and monetarism." RBC theory is associated with the Chicago School.[65]

The real business cycle theory relies on three assumptions which are unrealistic: "1) The model is driven by large and sudden changes in available production technology. Summers noted that Prescott is unable to suggest any specific technological shock for an actual downturn apart from the oil price shock in the 1970s. Furthermore, there is no microeconomic evidence for the large real shocks that need to drive these models. Real business cycle models as a rule are not subjected to tests against competing alternatives which are easy to support. 2) Unemployment reflects changes in the amount people want to work. Paul Krugman noted that this assumption would mean that 25% unemployment at the height of the Great Depression (1933) would be the result of a mass decision to take a long vacation. 3) Monetary policy is irrelevant for economic fluctuations. Nowadays it is widely agreed that wages and prices do not adjust as quickly as needed to restore equilibrium. Therefore, most economists, even among the new classicals, do not accept the policy-ineffectiveness proposition."[66]

Keynesian Macroeconomics: John Maynard Keynes (1883-1946) was a British economist whose ideas changed the theory and practice of macroeconomics and the economic policies of governments. "In the 1930s, Keynes spearheaded a revolution in economic thinking, challenging the ideas of neoclassical economics that held that free markets would, in the short to medium term, automatically provide full employment, as long as workers were flexible in their wage demands. He instead argued that aggregate demand determined the overall level of economic activity and that inadequate aggregate demand could lead to prolonged periods of high unemployment. Keynes advocated the use of fiscal and monetary policies to mitigate the adverse effects of economic recessions and depressions. Following the outbreak of World War II, the leading Western economies adopted Keynes's policy recommendations, and in the two decades following Keynes's death in 1946, almost all capitalist governments had done so. Keynes's influence waned in the 1970s, partly as a result of the stagflation that plagued the Anglo-American economies during that decade, and partly because of criticism of Keynesian policies by Milton Friedman and other monetarists. He and other economists had disputed the ability of government to regulate the business cycle favorably with fiscal policy. However, the advent of the global financial crisis of 2007–08 caused a resurgence in Keynesian thought."[67]

(a) Economic Theories: Keynes attended the Paris Peace Conference of 1919 as a delegate of the British Treasury. He published *The Economic Consequences of the Peace* (1919), arguing for a much more generous peace, not out of a desire for justice or fairness. "The book was a best-seller throughout the world and was critical in establishing a general opinion that the treaties were a Carthaginian peace designed to crush the defeated Central Powers, especially Germany. It helped to consolidate American public opinion against the treaties and against joining the League of Nations." "In 1925 he opposed Britain's return to the gold standard at the prewar dollar-pound ratio of $4.86; and, long before the Great Depression, Keynes expressed concern over the persistent unemployment of British coal miners, shipyard workers, and textile laborers. Reconciled by this time with Lloyd George, he supported the Liberal Party's program of public works to take the unemployed off welfare by placing them in useful jobs. But respectable economists still expected the automatic adjustments of the free market to solve these problems, and the Treasury was convinced that public works were useless because any increase in the government deficit would likely cause an equal decline in private investment."[68]

Keynes published *The General Theory of Employment, Interest and Money* (1936) which argues that "demand, not supply, is the key variable governing the overall level of economic activity. Aggregate demand, which equals total un-hoarded income in a society, is defined by the sum of consumption and investment. In a state of unemployment and unused production capacity, one can only enhance employment and total income by first increasing expenditures for either consumption or investment. Without government intervention to increase expenditure, an economy can remain trapped in a low employment equilibrium – the demonstration of this possibility has been described as the revolutionary formal achievement of the work. The book advocated activist economic policy by government to stimulate demand in times of high unemployment, for example by spending on public works. 'Let us be up and doing, using our idle resources to increase our wealth,' he wrote in 1928. 'With men and plants unemployed, it is ridiculous to say that we cannot afford these new developments. It is precise with these plants and these men that we shall afford them'."[69]

(b) Later Works and Assessment: "Keynes's long-run influence has not been as significant as his short-run impact. The Keynesian model was a core part of economics textbooks from the late 1940s until the late 1980s. But as economists have become more concerned about economic growth, and more informed about inflation and unemployment, the Keynesian model has lost prominence. *The General Theory* was Keynes's last major written work. In 1937 he suffered a severe heart attack. Two years later, though not completely recovered, he returned to teaching at Cambridge, wrote three influential articles on war finance entitled *How to Pay for the War* (1940), and served once more in the Treasury as an all-purpose adviser. He also played a prominent role at the Bretton Woods Conference in 1944…His last major public service was his negotiation in the autumn and early winter of 1945 of a multibillion-dollar loan granted by the United States to Britain."[70]

(c) Keynesian Ascendancy (1939-79):): "From the end of the Great Depression to the mid-1970s, Keynes provided the main inspiration for economic policy makers in Europe, America and much of the rest of the world. While economists and policy makers had become increasingly won over to Keynes's way of thinking in the mid and late 1930s, it was only after the outbreak of World War II that governments started to borrow money for spending on a scale sufficient to eliminate unemployment. According to the economist John Kenneth Galbraith, in the rebound of the economy from wartime spending, one could not have had a better demonstration of the Keynesian ideas. The Keynesian Revolution was associated with the rise of modern liberalism in the West during the post-war period. Keynesian ideas became so popular that some scholars point to Keynes as representing the ideals of modern liberalism, as Adam Smith represented the ideals of classical liberalism. After the war, Winston Churchill attempted to check the rise of Keynesian policymaking in the United Kingdom and used rhetoric critical of the mixed economy in his 1945 election campaign." Despite his popularity as a war hero, Churchill was defeated by Clement Attlee whose economic policy continued to be influenced by Keynes's ideas.[71]

Modern Macroeconomics After Keynes: *(a) Neo-Classical Synthesis or Neo-Keynesian Synthesis*: It refers to "the post-war macroeconomic development which combined elements of Keynesian macroeconomics with more classical microeconomic theory. Up until the 1930s, economics had been dominated by classical economists who argued that markets were self-regulating, markets would clear, and markets were the most efficient method of distributing resources. Keynesian theory, however, suggested that markets weren't self-regulating, and could be below full employment for a considerable time. The neo-classical synthesis suggests that Keynes was right in the short term, and classical economists were correct in the long-term. Markets may be subject to short term shocks which puts them out of equilibrium. But, in the long-term, free markets were best for distributing resources. The neo-classical synthesis suggests government intervention should primarily be concentrated on the short-term, stimulating demand in a recession, and dealing with rigidities in labor markets - monopolies, minimum wages and monopsonies."[72]

Key People in the Neo-Classical Synthesis: (i) John Hicks. Hicks developed the IS/LM model in 1937, which is based on Keynesian macroeconomic insights. (ii) Paul Samuelson: "In the post-war period, Samuelson was one of the first economists to popularize Keynesian theory with his amendments. His *Economics: An Introductory Analysis* (1948) was instrumental in sharing Keynesian macroeconomic principles, alongside more classical microeconomic theory." On the other hand, in Politics of the Neo-Classical Synthesis, "There was a belief that Keynesian economics was partly inspired by Communist ideas. This was in the 'McCarthyite era' with great suspicion of any left-wing ideas. Samuelson's synthesis helped to dilute Keynesian economics to give it more market-based approach and this became the more widespread version."[73]

Key Elements of the Neoclassical Synthesis: "(i) Full Employment is possible: Government intervention could help the economy be maintained close to full employment. For example, in an economic downturn, the government could pursue expansionary fiscal policy to boost demand. In the 1950s and 1960s, these ideas received widespread support as most major economies experienced two decades of economic expansion and close to full employment. Richard Nixon, said in early 1970s 'we're all Keynesians now'. (ii) Monetary and Fiscal Policy: Keynes had concentrated on the role of fiscal policy in managing the economy. However, the neo-Keynesians became more accepting that monetary policy could also be used to manage demand and the rate of economic growth. By the late 1990s, the neo-classical synthesis had embraced the role of monetary policy in achieving inflation targets. (iii) *Phillips Curve*: In the post-war, the Phillips curve had significant importance. It appeared there was a trade-off between inflation and unemployment and the government could decide which to prioritize."[74]

(b) Monetarism: "Throughout the 1950s and 1960s, the primary foil to the Keynesians was the monetarists. Under the leadership of Milton Friedman, they provided an effective opposition to Keynesian policy and theory. The consumption function model used by Keynesians in the 1950s had no role for money, nor did it consider prices or the price level. The initial lack of concern about money supply and prices manifested itself in policy based on Keynesian analysis. In an agreement with the Treasury that developed during World War II, the Federal Reserve Bank agreed to buy whatever bonds were necessary to maintain the interest rate at a fixed level. In so doing, the Fed relinquished all control of the money supply. Monetarist argued that the money supply played an important role in the economy and should not be limited to a role of holding the interest rate constant... Keynesians soon willing to concur with the monetarists that money mattered ...The debate was resolved by means of the IS-LM Keynesian-neoclassical synthesis, in which the monetarists assumed a highly inelastic LM curve and Keynesians assumed a highly elastic IS curve. Thus at least in terms of the textbook presentation, monetarist and Keynesian analysis came together in the general neo-Keynesian IS-LM model, about which they differed slightly on some parameters."[75] "The model was developed by John Hicks in 1937, and later extended by Alvin Hansen, as a mathematical representation of Keynesian macroeconomic theory. Between the 1940s and mid-1970s, it was the leading framework of macroeconomic analysis."[76]

(c) The IS/LM Model: The IS-LM model represents two intersecting curves. "The investment/saving (IS) curve is a variation of the income-expenditure model incorporating market interest rates (demand), while the liquidity preference/money supply equilibrium (LM) curve represents the amount of money available for investing (supply). The model explains the decisions made by investors when it comes to investments with the amount of money available and the interest they will receive. Equilibrium is achieved when the amount invested equals the amount available to invest. Despite many shortcomings, the IS-LM model has been one of the main tools for macroeconomic teaching and policy analysis. The IS-LM model describes the aggregate demand of the economy using the relationship between output and interest rates. In a closed economy, in the goods market, a rise in interest rate reduces aggregate demand, usually investment demand and/or demand for consumer durables. This lowers the level of output and results in equating the quantity demanded with the quantity produced. This condition is equal to the condition that planned investment equals saving. The negative relationship between interest rate and output is known as the IS curve. The second relationship deals with the money market, where the quantity of money demanded increases with aggregate income and decreases with the interest rate."[77] Thus, they are interactions of the market for goods and services with market for money at equilibrium.

(d) Keynesian Economics Unfavored: "Keynesian economics were officially discarded by the British Government in 1979, but forces had begun to gather against Keynes's ideas over 30 years earlier. Friedrich Hayek had formed the Mont Pelerin Society in 1947, with the explicit intention of nurturing intellectual currents to one day displace Keynesianism and other similar influences. Its members included the Austrian School economist Ludwig von Mises along with the then young Milton Friedman. Initially the society had little impact on the wider world — according to Hayek it was as if Keynes had been raised to sainthood after his death and that people refused to allow his work to be questioned. Friedman however began to emerge as a formidable critic of Keynesian economics from the mid-1950s, and especially after his 1963 publication of *A Monetary History of the United States*...Criticisms of Keynes's ideas had begun to gain significant acceptance by the early 1970s, as they were then able to make a credible case that Keynesian models no longer reflected economic reality." "A key cause of economic problems afflicting America in the 1970s was the refusal to raise taxes to finance the Vietnam War, which was against Keynesian advice." "However, many officials on both sides of the Atlantic retained a preference for Keynes, and in 1984 the Federal Reserve officially discarded monetarism, after which Keynesian principles made a partial comeback as an influence on policy making."[78]

(e) Keynesian Resurgence (2008-09): "The global financial crisis of 2007–08 led to public skepticism about the free market consensus." In March 2008, an essay of the *Financial Times* announced the death of the dream of global free-market capitalism. By the end of December 2008, the same journal reported "that the sudden resurgence of Keynesian policy is a stunning reversal of the orthodoxy of the past several decades. In December 2008, Paul Krugman released his book *The Return of Depression Economics and the Crisis of 2008*, arguing that economic conditions similar to what existed during the earlier part of the 20th century had returned, making Keynesian policy prescriptions more relevant than ever...While the need for stimulus measures was broadly accepted among policy makers, there had been much debate over how to fund the spending. Some leaders and institutions...expressed concern over the potential impact on inflation, national debt and the risk that a too large stimulus will create an unsustainable recovery...Although many economists...supported Keynesian stimulus, others did not believe higher government spending would help the United States economy recover from the Great Recession. Some economists, such as Robert Lucas, questioned the theoretical basis for stimulus packages. Others say that empirical evidence for beneficial effects from Keynesian stimulus does not exist. However, there is a growing academic literature that shows that fiscal expansion helps an economy grow in the near term, and that certain types of fiscal stimulus are particularly effective."[79]

(f) Rational Expectations Theory: "Rational expectations ensure internal consistency in models involving uncertainty. To obtain consistency within a model, the predictions of future values of economically relevant variables from the model are assumed to be the same as that of the decision-makers in the model, given their information set, the nature of the random processes involved, and model structure. The rational expectations assumption is used especially in many contemporary macroeconomic models. Since most macroeconomic models today study decisions under uncertainty and over many periods, the expectations of individuals, firms, and government institutions about future economic conditions are an essential part of the model. To assume rational expectations is to assume that agents' expectations may be wrong but are correct on average over time. In other words, although the future is not fully predictable, agents' expectations are assumed not to be systematically biased and collectively use all relevant information in forming expectations of economic variables. This way of modeling expectations was originally proposed by John F. Muth (1961) and later became influential when it was used by Robert Lucas, Jr. in macroeconomics."[80] He received the Nobel Prize in Economics in 1995. "Lucas (1972) incorporates the idea of rational expectations into a dynamic general equilibrium model...based on the available information, they form expectations about future prices and quantities, and based on these expectations they act to maximize their expected lifetime utility."[81]

(g) The Solow Growth Model: The growth model of Robert Solow is a standard neoclassical model of economic growth, which has three basic sources for GDP: labor (L), capital (K) and knowledge (A). Knowledge is a sort of catch-all category used to augment labor (AL), called effective labor. "The model assumes the growth rates of knowledge and labor are constant. The portion of production saved for investment, S, is also assumed to be constant (and exogenous), as well as the rate of depreciation. It should be noted that S and Y (output) directly affect the growth of k in the economy. The Solow model is so straightforward, it's worth pointing out what it does not include. Government, multiple goods, changes in employment, natural resources, geography and social institutions are main features the model ignores. It is, however, this simplification that allows us to better understand the role of capital, labor and knowledge in our study of economic growth. The Solow model predicts conditional convergence. This means that countries with similar characteristics converge to the same steady state (situation in which k stays the same). Similar characteristics means in this model that the savings rate of both countries is same."[82] He was awarded the Nobel Memorial Prize in Economic Sciences in 1987, and "the Presidential Medal of Freedom in 2014. Four of his PhD students, George Akerlof, Joseph Stiglitz, Peter Diamond and William Nordhaus later received Nobel Memorial Prizes in Economic Sciences in their own right."[83]

ECONOMETRICS AND EMPIRICAL METHODS

"The debate about empirical methods in economics has had both a micro-economic and a macroeconomic front. The microeconomic front has, for the most part, been concerned with empirically estimating production functions and supply-and-demand curves; the macroeconomic front has generally been concerned with the empirical estimation of macroeconomic relationship and their connections to individual behavior. The macroeconomic estimation problems include all the microeconomic problems plus many more, so it is not surprising that empirical work in macroeconomics is far more in debate than empirical work in microeconomics."[84]

We can consider four different approaches to relating theories to the real world: common-sense empiricism, statistical analysis, classical econometric analysis, and Bayesian econometric analysis. *Common-sense empiricism* is an approach that relates theory to reality through direct observation of real-world events with a minimum of statistical aids. The *statistical analysis* approach also requires one to look at reality but emphasizes aspects of events that can be quantified and thereby be subject to statistical measure and analysis. The *classical econometric* approach is a method of empirical analysis that directly relates theory and data; and this approach makes use of classical statistical methods to formally test the validity of a theory. The *Bayesian approach* directly relates theory and data, but in the interpretation of any statistical test, it takes the position that the test is not definitive. It is based on the Bayesian approach to statistics that seeks probability laws not as objective laws but as subjective degree of belief, so researchers must simply use the statistical tests to modify their subjective opinions."

With computer technology, statistical tests were possible by computer programs. "Recently a group of empirical economists have been focusing more on agent-based modeling. These are simulations in which local individual optimization goals of heterogeneous agents are specified and modeled. But instead of being deductively determined, the results are simulated to determine the surviving strategies."[85] Another change that we have seen is the development and use of a technique called calibration in macroeconomic models. Models are not tested but calibrated to see if the empirical evidence is consistent with what the model could have predicted. "The final change has been the development of a natural experiment approach to empirical work. This approach uses intuitive economic theory rather than structural models and uses natural experiments as the data points." There are important *quantitative methods* in empirical economics such as mathematics, statistics, and econometrics with various ways of application. Particularly, quantitative research deals in numbers, logic, and an objective stance, focusing on numeric and unchanging data and detailed, convergent reasoning rather than divergent.[86]

Table II-2-3. Major Writers on Econometrics and
Empirical Methods in Economics

William Petty, *Political Arithmetic* (1690)
Charles Davenant, *An Essay upon the Probable Methods of Making a People Gainer in the Balance of Trade* (1699)
Clement Juglar, *Des crises commerciales et de leur retour periodique en France, en Angleterre et aux Etats-Unis* (1862)
W. S. Jevons, "The Solar Period and the Price of Corn" (1875)
Henry L. Moore, *Laws of Wages* (1911)
W. C. Mitchell, *Business Cycles* (1913)
Irving Fisher, *The Making of Index Numbers* (1922)
E. J. Working, "What Do Statistical Demand Curves Show?" (1927)
Henry Schultz, *Statistical Laws of Demand and Supply* (1928)
Ragnar Frisch, *Statistical Confluence Analyses by Means of Complete Regression Systems* (1934)
Jan Tinbergen, *Statistical Testing of Business Cycle Theories* (1939)
Wassily Leontief, *The Structure of the American Economy, 1919-1929* (1941)
Trygve Haavelmo, "The Probability Approach to Econometrics" (1944)
Vernon Smith, "An Experimental Study of Competitive Market Behavior" (1962)
Robert W. Fogel, *Railroads and American Economic Growth: Essays in Econometric History* (1964)

Source: Harry Landreth and David C. Colander, *History of Economic Thought*
(Boston, MA: Houghton Mifflin, 2002), 436-7.

Mathematical Economics: (a) ***Differential Calculus***: "Vilfredo Pareto analyzed micro-economics by treating decisions by economic actors as attempts to change a given allotment of goods to another, more preferred allotment. Sets of allocations could then be treated as Pareto efficient (Pareto optimal is an equivalent term) when no exchanges could occur between actors that could make at least one individual better off without making any other individual worse off. Pareto's proof is commonly conflated with Walrasian equilibrium or informally ascribed to Adam Smith's Invisible hand hypothesis. Rather, Pareto's statement was the first formal assertion of what would be known as the first fundamental theorem of welfare economics. These models lacked the inequalities of the next generation of mathematical economics. In the landmark treatise *Foundations of Economic Analysis* (1947), Paul Samuelson identified a common paradigm and mathematical structure across multiple fields in the subject, building on previous work by Alfred Marshall. Foundations took mathematical concepts from physics and applied them to economic problems. This broad view drives the fundamental premise of mathematical economics: systems of economic actors may be modeled, and their behavior described much like any other system. This extension followed on the work of the marginalists in the previous century and extended it significantly. Samuelson approached the problems of applying individual utility maximization over aggregate groups with comparative statics, which compares two different equilibrium states after an exogenous change in a variable." These methods provided the foundation for mathematical economics in the 20th century.[87]

(b) *Linear Models*: "Restricted models of general equilibrium were formulated by John von Neumann in 1937. Unlike earlier versions, the models of von Neumann had inequality constraints. For his model of an expanding economy, von Neumann proved the existence and uniqueness of an equilibrium using his generalization of Brouwer's fixed point theorem. Von Neumann's model of an expanding economy considered the matrix pencil $A - \lambda B$ with nonnegative matrices A and B; von Neumann sought probability vectors p and q and a positive number λ that would solve the complementarity equation $pT (A - \lambda B) q = 0$, along with two inequality systems expressing economic efficiency. In this model, the (transposed) probability vector p represents the prices of the goods while the probability vector q represents the intensity at which the production process would run. The unique solution λ represents the rate of growth of the economy, which equals the interest rate. Proving the existence of a positive growth rate and proving that the growth rate equals the interest rate were remarkable achievements, even for von Neumann. Von Neumann's results have been viewed as a special case of linear programming, where von Neumann's model uses only nonnegative matrices. The study of von Neumann's model of an expanding economy continues to interest mathematical economists with interests in computational economics."[88]

Input-Output Model developed by Wassily Leontief produces outputs using constant proportions of inputs, regardless of the price of inputs, reducing the value of Leontief models for understanding economies but allowing their parameters to be estimated relatively easily. The U.S. Department of Commerce have used the Input-Output Account for current industrial analysis with regular industrial survey every five years.[89]

(c) *Mathematical Optimization*: Mathematical optimization refers to the selection of a best element from some set of available alternatives through application of mathematic methods such as linear programming, non-linear programming, variational calculus and optimal control, and functional analysis. Generally speaking, optimization means to maximize the objective function subject to constraints or given necessary conditions. For example in microeconomics, consumers try to maximize utility subject to their budget constraint or to minimize the expenditure for a given level of utility; while producers try to maximize their output subject to input costs like capital or labor costs. Moreover, in exchange, either partial or general equilibrium, optimization of the use of resources comes from no waste, which means that consumption budget equals to production cost. This can be induced by solving the Lagrangian Function as follows.

In Consumption: To Maximize Utility

Maximize Utility: $U(x, y)$

Subject to Budget Constraint: $B = x\, Px + y\, Py$

In order to maximize $U(x, y)$ subject to $B = x\, P_x + y\, P_y$ where $U(x, y)$ is a Utility Function, and $B = x\, P_x + y\, P_y$ is a budget constraint in which x and y are Good x and Good y, and P_x and P_y are Prices of Good x and Good y; we can formulate a Lagrangian Function as follows;

$$Z = U(x, y) + \lambda\,(B - x\,P_x - y\,P_y)$$

In Production: To Maximize Output

Maximize Output: $Q = f(K, L)$

Subject to Cost: $C = r\,K + w\,L$

In 2-Input production model, Output Q is a function of Capital (K) and Labor (L). C is cost, r is unit capital cost, and w is unit labor cost. We can formulate a Lagrangian function as follows:

$$Z = f(K, L) + \mu\,(1 - r\,K - w\,L)$$

In Exchange: Simultaneous General Equilibrium of Production and Consumption

$$MRTS_{XY}^{A} \equiv MRS_{XY}^{A} \equiv MRS_{XY}^{B} \equiv MRTS_{XY}^{B}$$

$$x\,Px + y\,Py = B = C = r\,K + w\,L \quad \text{where Budget = Cost}$$

Therefore, consumption and production are satisfied in the Robinson Crusoe Economy; which is efficient as a Pareto Optimal. If this condition is violated, continuous adjustment is necessary for economic efficiency. Hence, the production with factor inputs (L and K appeared on Contract Curve) is expressed by combination of 2 Goods (X and Y) on the production possibility frontier of the graph below. Consumer Indifference Curve (CIC) meets PPF at point F, where Consumption Budget $\equiv$ Production Cost.

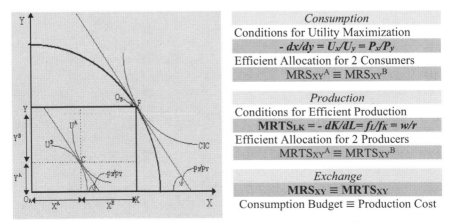

Consumption

Conditions for Utility Maximization

$- dx/dy = U_x/U_y = P_x/P_y$

Efficient Allocation for 2 Consumers

$MRS_{XY}^{A} \equiv MRS_{XY}^{B}$

Production

Conditions for Efficient Production

$MRTS_{LK} = - dK/dL = f_L/f_K = w/r$

Efficient Allocation for 2 Producers

$MRTS_{XY}^{A} \equiv MRTS_{XY}^{B}$

Exchange

$MRS_{XY} \equiv MRTS_{XY}$

Consumption Budget $\equiv$ Production Cost

Figure II-2-3. The Paretian System – General Equilibrium
Accessed 5 March 2017, http://cruel.org/econthought/essays/paretian/image/pareto7.gif

(d) *Differential decline and rise*: "John von Neumann's work on functional analysis and topology broke new ground in mathematics and economic theory. It also left advanced mathematical economics with fewer applications of differential calculus. In particular, general equilibrium theorists used general topology, convex geometry, and optimization theory more than differential calculus, because the approach of differential calculus had failed to establish the existence of an equilibrium. However, the decline of differential calculus should not be exaggerated, because differential calculus has always been used in graduate training and in applications. Moreover, differential calculus has returned to the highest levels of mathematical economics, general equilibrium theory (GET), as practiced by the GET-set. In the 1960s and 1970s, however, Gérard Debreu and Stephen Smale led a revival of the use of differential calculus in mathematical economics. In particular, they were able to prove the existence of a general equilibrium, where earlier writers had failed."[90]

(e) *Game Theory*: John von Neumann working with Oskar Morgenstern on the theory of games "broke new mathematical ground in 1944 by extending functional analytic methods related to convex sets and topological fixed-point theory to economic analysis. Their work thereby avoided the traditional differential calculus, for which the maximum operator did not apply to non-differentiable functions. Continuing von Neumann's work in cooperative game theory, game theorists...influenced economic research in politics and economics... For example, cooperative game theory was used in designing the water distribution system of Southern Sweden and for setting rates for dedicated telephone lines in the USA. Earlier neoclassical theory had bounded only the range of bargaining outcomes and in special cases, for example bilateral monopoly or along the contract curve of the Edgeworth box. Von Neumann and Morgenstern's results were similarly weak. Following von Neumann's program, however, John Nash used fixed–point theory to prove conditions under which the bargaining problem and non-cooperative games can generate a unique equilibrium solution."[91]

(f) *Agent-based computational economics* (ACE) as a named field is relatively recent, dating from about the 1990s as to published work. It studies economic processes, including whole economies, as dynamic systems of interacting agents over time. As such, it falls in the paradigm of complex adaptive systems...The rules are formulated to predict behavior and social interactions based on incentives and information. The theoretical assumption of mathematical optimization by agents markets is replaced by the less restrictive postulate of agents with bounded rationality adapting to market forces. ACE models apply numerical methods of analysis to computer-based simulations of complex dynamic problems for which more conventional methods, such as theorem formulation, may not find ready use." It requires continuing improvements in modeling techniques.[92]

Statistics in Empirical Economics: *Mathematical economics* refers only to the application of mathematical techniques to the formulation of hypotheses. "It is formal, abstract analysis used to develop hypotheses and clarify their implications. The term *statistics* refers to a collection of numerical observations, and statistical analysis refers to the use of statistical tests derived from probability theory to gain insight into those numerical observation. *Econometrics* combines mathematical economics, which is used to formulate hypotheses, and statistical analysis, which is used to formally test hypotheses. The combination is not symmetrical; one can do mathematical economics without doing econometrics, but one cannot do econometrics without first doing mathematical economics."[93]

What economists hoped to gain from mathematical economics was a precision of hypothesis testing that would make it possible to reduce the ambiguity of tests. For example, instead of relying on common sense and a general heuristic understanding that demand curves slope downward, they wanted to be able to prove empirically that demand curves slope downward, they wanted to be mathematical formalization of economic theory, economists employed words to state economic theories and hypotheses. Testing of general hypotheses was done in relation to current circumstances or in relation to historical events, but in either case the use of statistics was minimal. This essentially heuristic approach did not permit hypotheses to be tested in a manner acceptable to formal economists. The 1960s and 1970s saw enormous advances in formal statistical testing and in an understanding of econometric methods. Advance in computer technology made it possible to conduct extremely complicated empirical work. Statistical tests that earlier would have taken days now could be done in seconds. During that period the hopes for econometrics were high."[94]

"Economic statistics is a topic in applied statistics that concerns the collection, processing, compilation, dissemination, and analysis of economic data. It is also common to call the data themselves 'economic statistics', but for this usage see economic data. The data of concern to economic statistics may include those of an economy of region, country, or group of countries. Economic statistics may also refer to a subtopic of official statistics for data produced by official organizations (e.g. national statistical services, inter-governmental organizations such as United Nations...). Analyses within economic statistics both make use of and provide the empirical data needed in economic research, whether descriptive or econometric. They are a key input for decision making as to economic policy. The subject includes statistical analysis of topics and problems in microeconomics, macroeconomics, business, finance, forecasting, data quality, and policy evaluation. It also includes such considerations as what data to collect in order to quantify some particular aspect of an economy and of how best to collect in any given instance."[95]

The Rise of Econometrics: Econometrics applies "statistical methods to economic data and is described as the branch of economics that aims to give empirical content to economic relations. More precisely, it is the quantitative analysis of actual economic phenomena based on the concurrent development of theory and observation, related by appropriate methods of inference. An introductory economics textbook describes econometrics as allowing economists to sift through mountains of data to extract simple relationships. The first known use of the term econometrics was by Polish economist Paweł Ciompa in 1910. Jan Tinbergen is considered by many to be one of the founding fathers of econometrics. Ragnar Frisch is credited with coining the term in the sense in which it is used today. The basic tool for econometrics is the multiple linear regression model. Econometric theory uses statistical theory and mathematical statistics to evaluate and develop econometric methods. Econometricians try to find estimators that have desirable statistical properties including unbiasedness, efficiency, and consistency. Applied econometrics uses theoretical econometrics and real-world data for assessing economic theories, developing econometric models, analyzing economic history, and forecasting."[96]

(a) Basic Model - Linear Regression: "The basic tool for econometrics is the multiple linear regression model. Estimating a linear regression on two variables can be visualized as fitting a line through data points representing paired values of the independent and dependent variables. For example, consider Okun's law, which relates GDP growth to the unemployment rate. This relationship is represented in a linear regression where the change in unemployment rate (Δ Unemployment) is a function of an intercept (β_0), a given value of GDP growth multiplied by a slope coefficient β_1 and an error term, ε: Δ Unemployment $= \beta_0 + \beta_1$ Growth $+ \varepsilon$. The unknown parameters β_0 and β_1 can be estimated...The model could then be tested for statistical significance as to whether an increase in growth is associated with a decrease in the unemployment, as hypothesized. If the estimate of β_1 were not significantly different from 0, the test would fail to find evidence that changes in the growth rate and unemployment rate were related. The variance in a prediction of the dependent variable as a function of the independent variable is given in polynomial least squares."[97]

(b) Econometric Theory: "Econometric theory uses statistical theory and mathematical statistics to evaluate and develop econometric methods. Econometricians try to find estimators that have desirable statistical properties including unbiasedness, efficiency, and consistency. An estimator is unbiased if its expected value is the true value of the parameter; it is consistent if it converges to the true value as sample size gets larger, and it is efficient if the estimator has lower standard error than other unbiased estimators for a given sample size. Ordinary least squares (OLS) is often used for estimation since it provides the BLUE or best linear unbiased

estimator given the Gauss-Markov assumptions. When these assumptions are violated, or other statistical properties are desired, other estimation techniques such as maximum likelihood estimation, generalized method of moments, or generalized least squares are used. Estimators that incorporate prior beliefs are advocated by those who favor Bayesian statistics over traditional, classical or frequentist approaches."[98]

(c) Methods: "Applied econometrics uses theoretical econometrics and real-world data for assessing economic theories, developing econometric models, analyzing economic history, and forecasting. Econometrics may use standard statistical models to study economic questions, but most often they are with observational data, rather than in controlled experiments. In this, the design of observational studies in econometrics is similar to the design of studies in other observational disciplines, such as astronomy, epidemiology, sociology and political science. Analysis of data from an observational study is guided by the study protocol, although exploratory data analysis may be useful for generating new hypotheses. Economics often analyzes systems of equations and inequalities, such as supply and demand hypothesized to be in equilibrium. Consequently, the field of econometrics has developed methods for identification and estimation of simultaneous-equation models. These methods are analogous to methods used in other areas of science, such as the field of system identification in systems analysis and control theory. Such methods may allow researchers to estimate models and investigate their empirical consequences, without directly manipulating the system. One of the fundamental statistical methods used by econometricians is regression analysis."

(d) Examples: Let's take a simple example of econometrics, [$\ln(\text{wage}) = \beta_0 + \beta_1 (\text{years of education}) + \varepsilon$]. This assumes that "the natural logarithm of a person's wage is a linear function of the number of years of education that person has acquired. The parameter β_1 measures the increase in the natural log of the wage attributable to one more year of education. The term β_0 and β_1 under specific assumptions about the random variable ε. For example, if ε is uncorrelated with years of education, then the equation can be estimated with ordinary least squares. If the researcher could randomly assign people to different levels of education, the data set thus generated would allow estimation of the effect of changes in years of education on wages. In reality, those experiments cannot be conducted…Given this kind of data, the estimated coefficient on Years of Education in the equation above reflects both the effect of education on wages and the effect of other variables on wages, if those other variables were correlated with education. For example, people born in certain places may have higher wages and higher levels of education. Unless the econometrician controls for place of birth in the above equation, the effect of birthplace on wages may be falsely attributed to the effect of education on wages."[99]

Bayesian Econometrics is based on a degree-of-belief interpretation of probability, as opposed to a relative-frequency interpretation. "The Bayesian principle relies on Bayes' theorem which states that the probability of B conditional on A is the ratio of joint probability of A and B divided by probability of B. Bayesian econometricians assume that coefficients in the model have prior distributions."[100] "In Bayesian analysis the interpretation of an estimator is quite different. Instead of producing a point estimate of data, Bayesian analysis produces a density function of data, which is called a posterior density function. The density function is not a sampling distribution. It can be interpreted only in reference to a prior conviction about what one believed. It is normally discussed as the odds a researcher would give when taking bets on the true value of data. It is a subjective notion of probability rather than an objective or frequentist notion of probability, as is the classical approach. Thus, in the Bayesian approach one must specify one's initial degree of belief and use empirical evidence as a means of changing that degree of belief. One has both a prior density function and a posterior density function. In the Bayesian analysis one is simply sing empirical data to modify one's prior beliefs, whereas in the classical approach one is continually attempting to establish the true nature of the model…most part, economists have not used Bayesian methods."[101]

"The ideas underlying Bayesian statistics were developed by Rev. Thomas Bayes during the 18th century and later expanded by Pierre-Simon Laplace. As early as 1950, the potential of the Bayesian inference in econometrics was recognized by Jacob Marschak. The Bayesian approach was first applied to econometrics in the early 1960s…The central motivation behind these early endeavors in Bayesian econometrics was the combination of the parameter estimators with available uncertain information on the model parameters that was not included in a given model formulation. From the mid-1960s to the mid-1970s, the reformulation of econometric techniques along Bayesian principles under the traditional structural approach dominated the research agenda, with Zellner's *An Introduction to Bayesian Inference in Econometrics* in 1971 as one of its highlights, and thus closely followed the work of frequentist econometrics. Therein, the main technical issues were the difficulty of specifying prior densities without losing either economic interpretation or mathematical tractability and the difficulty of integral calculation in the context of density functions. The result of the Bayesian reformulation program was to highlight the fragility of structural models to uncertain specification…Bayesian econometrics also became attractive to Christopher Sims' attempt to move from structural modeling to VAR modeling due to its explicit probability specification of parameter restrictions. Driven by the rapid growth of computing capacities from the mid-1980s on, the application of Markov chain Monte Carlo simulation to statistical and econometric models…1990s, enabled Bayesian analysis."[102]

Experimental Economics and Simulation: In economic simulation, "Experimentalists argue that laboratory tests provide information about naturally occurring economic behavior, because economic behavior is governed by basic principles which apply both inside and outside the lab. These axioms of rationality are the basis of economic theory, which makes no distinction between, for instance, maximizing utility inside and outside the laboratory. The cash incentives ensure that better decisions inside the laboratory result in more utility outside the laboratory (money earned in the experiment can be spent outside the laboratory). The external validity of any particular result depends on how well the experimental design captures the incentives present in the naturally occurring situation being modeled... Laboratory analysis can complement traditional field data modeling by testing economic theories in several ways. First, laboratory experimentation offers a degree of control which allows economists to generate tests of alternative policies at low cost, or to give theories their best chance by testing them in environments which exactly satisfy their assumptions. Second, laboratory analysis facilitates replication; it is often difficult to find an independent field sample with which to accomplish this critical step in the scientific method. Finally, experimentation allows economists to have information they could not know in the field. For instance, many economic theories suggest that people respond to their beliefs in particular ways. Beliefs are difficult or impossible to measure in the field, but they can be naturally integrated into an experimental design."[103]

There are many ways to categorize experiments, but one of the more useful is by which models they are attempting to test. Most experiments can be characterized by one or more of these objectives: (1) Testing theoretical predictions: "Economic theories make predictions which can be tested in the laboratory. For instance, general equilibrium theory predicts market prices at the intersection of supply and demand. Experiments have shown this prediction is accurate with a wide variety of trading institutions." (2) Testing robustness of theories: "Economic theories often include strong assumptions, and experiments can test the sensitivity of their predictions to weakening of those assumptions." (3) Testing assumptions: "Rather than testing the predictions of a theory, models are sometimes examined by testing their assumptions. This technique is frequently used by behavioral economists who seek to replace standard rationality assumptions with more descriptively accurate, yet mathematically tractable, models." (4) Identifying stylized facts: "Because replication is straightforward in the laboratory, experiments are often used to identify patterns in behavior which may or may not be consistent with theory." (5) Comparing institutional designs: "Theory does not always provide guidance when deciding among institutions. The alternative institutions, or policies, can be implemented in laboratory and the outcomes compared on the basis of efficiency."[104]

MODERN HETERODOX ECONOMIC THOUGHT

Table II-2-4. Major Writers on Modern Heterodox Economic Thought

Joseph Schumpeter, *The Theory of Economic Development* (1912)
Gunnar Myrdal, *The Political Element in the Development of Economic Theory* (1930)
Michal Kalecki, "Essays on Business Cycle Theory" (1933)
F. A. Hayek, "Economics and Knowledge" (1937)
Maurice Dobb, *Political Economy and Capitalism* (1937)
Ludwig von Mises, *Human Action* (1940)
Joan Robinson, *An Essay on Marxian Economics* (1942)
Paul Sweezy, *The Theory of Capitalist Development* (1942)
Clarence Ayres, *The Theory of Economic Progress* (1944)
John Kenneth Galbraith, *American Capitalism* (1952)
Piero Sraffa, *Production of Commodities by Means of Commodities* (1960)
James Buchanan and Gordon Tullock, *The Calculus of Consent* (1962)
Paul Sweezy, *Monopoly Capital* (1966)
Paul Davidson, *Money and the Real World* (1972)
Herbert Gintis, *Schooling in Capitalist America* (1976)
I. M. Kirzner, *Competition and Entrepreneurship* (1973)

Source: Harry Landreth and David C. Colander, *History of Economic Thought* (Boston, MA: Houghton Mifflin, 2002), 448.

"Heterodoxy is a term that may be used in contrast with orthodoxy in schools of economic thought or methodologies, that may be beyond neoclassical economics. Heterodoxy is an umbrella term that can cover various schools of thought or theories. These might for example include institutional, evolutionary, Georgist, Austrian, feminist, social, post-Keynesian, ecological, Marxian, socialist and anarchist economics, among others. Economics may be called orthodox or conventional economics by its critics. Alternatively, mainstream economics deals with the rationality–individualism–equilibrium nexus and heterodox economics is more radical in dealing with the institutions–history–social structure nexus. Many economists dismiss heterodox economics as fringe and irrelevant, with little or no influence on the vast majority of academic mainstream economists in the English-speaking world. A recent review documented several prominent groups of heterodox economists since at least the 1990s as working together with a resulting increase in coherence across different constituents…In defining a common ground in the critical commentary, one writer described fellow heterodox economists as trying to do three things: (1) identify shared ideas that generate a pattern of heterodox critique across topics and chapters of introductory macro texts; (2) give special attention to ideas that link methodological differences to policy differences; and (3) characterize the common ground in ways that permit distinct paradigms to develop common differences with textbook economics in different ways."[105]

3. A Historical Overview of Socialism

Socialism is a range of economic and social systems "characterized by social ownership of the means of production and workers' self-management, as well as the political theories and movements associated with them. Social ownership can be public, collective or cooperative ownership, or citizen ownership of equity…Socialist systems are divided into non-market and market forms. Non-market socialism involves replacing factor markets and money with engineering and technical criteria based on calculation performed in-kind, thereby producing an economic mechanism that functions according to different economic laws from those of capitalism. Non-market socialism aims to circumvent the inefficiencies and crises traditionally associated with capital accumulation and the profit system. By contrast, market socialism retains the use of monetary prices, factor markets and in some cases the profit motive, with respect to the operation of socially owned enterprises and the allocation of capital goods between them. Profits generated by these firms would be controlled directly by the workforce of each firm or accrue to society at large in the form of a social dividend. The socialist calculation debate concerns the feasibility and methods of resource allocation for a socialist system."[106]

"The socialist political movement includes a set of political philosophies that originated in the revolutionary movements of the mid-to-late 18th century and out of concern for the social problems that were associated with capitalism. By the late 19th century, after the work of Karl Marx and his collaborator Friedrich Engels, socialism had come to signify opposition to capitalism and advocacy for a post-capitalist system based on some form of social ownership of the means of production. By the 1920s, social democracy and communism had become the two dominant political tendencies within the international socialist movement…It is a political ideology, a wide and divided political movement' and while the emergence of the Soviet Union as the world's first nominally socialist state led to socialism's widespread association with the Soviet economic model, some economists and intellectuals argued that in practice the model functioned as a form of state capitalism or a non-planned administrative or command economy. Socialist parties and ideas remain a political force with varying degrees of power and influence on all continents, heading national governments in many countries around the world. Today, some socialists have also adopted the causes of other social movements, such as environmentalism, feminism and progressivism."[107] This section deals with (i) the meaning of socialism; (ii) utopian socialism before Marx; (iii) revolutionary versus evolutionary socialism; (iv) Marxism; (v) socialist theory after Marx – orthodox Marxism, Marxism-Leninism, social democracy or revisionism, and communism in China or Maoism.

The Meaning of Socialism: Socialism is not only an economic system but a social, political, and moral philosophy. A particular kind of socialism was envisioned by Marx, but Marxism is one variant of that ideology. All Marxists are socialists, but not all socialists are Marxists. The meaning of socialism can be divided into three features: ownership of production, the welfare states, and the socialist intent pursuing economic equality.

(a) Ownership of Production: "The concept of public ownership and control of the major means of production, distribution, and finance is a fundamental principle of socialism. The traditional way to socialize an economy is by nationalization. Nationalization exists when government owns and operates an industry. In Western societies nationalized industries are usually managed by boards or commissions appointed by government officials but insulated in some way from political pressure; that is, the commissions are usually appointed to office for specific term and may be removed only by parliamentary or congressional vote. Some good examples of this kind of arrangement are the British Broadcasting Corporation, the Tennessee Valley Authority in the United States...In the few remaining communist countries, a government-owned industry is more likely to be closely connected to the society's political leaders than is true in non-communist countries...Non-communists usually try to differentiate between the political and economic functions of society. In a Marxist state, however, ideology teaches that politics result from economic conditions and that both are inseparable parts of the same historical development."[108]

In the Western states, following the Scandinavian model, socialists have increasingly turned to cooperatives as a means of socializing the economy. "A cooperative enterprise is made up of individuals who collectively own the enterprise. They share in both the work and the profits. Usually they elect a board of directors to manage the enterprise. Such cooperatives can become quite extensive...Cooperatives were developed because serious problems with nationalization became apparent as various enterprises were expropriated by the state...The cooperative is an attempt to combine the virtues of private motivation with the benefits of collective ownership."

"When a large part of society's production, exchange, distribution, and employment is controlled by the government, the latter's involvement in the lives of individuals is greatly increased. Totalitarian states are born of such enormous power. Any free society must be very cautious of centralized power." Therefore, socialist countries not only differ on the method of socializing the economy but also vary greatly in the degree to which their economies are socialized. "Socialist planning does not presuppose public ownership of all the means of production. It is compatible with the existence of private ownership in important fields" like agriculture, retail trade, small and middle-sized industries. In all socialist countries except like North Korea, large portion of the economy remain under private ownership.[109]

(b) The Welfare State: In general, the welfare state is "a concept of government in which the state plays a key role in the protection and promotion of the social and economic well-being of its citizens. It is based on the principles of equality of opportunity, equitable distribution of wealth, and public responsibility for those unable to avail themselves of the minimal provisions for a good life. The general term may cover a variety of forms of economic and social organization." [110] "To the socialist, the importance lies in the distribution of goods and services produced in society, but to the capitalist, private property is the reward for individual effort and economic achievement...The Great Depression of the 1930s caused a quarter of the workforce to lose jobs, which ruined their lives. Losing confidence in the *laissez-faire* myth, the public viewed society in a more realistic way and capitalism was modified, becoming more humane. In the 1930s, President Franklin D. Roosevelt introduced the New Deal, a massive reform program that injected enough socialism into the system to give capitalism a human face. "Since the 1930s, the welfare state in this country has been expanded to include public health plans for the elderly, job training, federal aid to education, public funding for small business...and so on." [111]

"The communist countries tried to invoke total socialism; but their efforts have failed in large measure. More successful are the Western European countries, which have nationalized their banks, utilities, transportation, and some manufacturing, while also developing extensive social welfare policies...generous housing subsidies, parental leave plans, grants to the poor, public health protections, educational aid, unemployment benefits...Regardless of the specific programs used, socialism is not always completely egalitarian. It tends to narrow the gap between the haves and the have-nots. Yet, only the most fanatic socialist wants to eliminate all differences in material status. Most socialists recognize that people are different: Some are more talented or hard working than others and should be regarded for their extra contributions. Still, they believe that all people have a right to a reasonably comfortable life, given the economy's ability to produce enough for all...Consequently, they want to eliminate poverty." "While Western Europe has successfully reduced poverty and its accompanying social anxiety, these gains have not been achieved without great costs. The tax rates in these societies are extremely high. Indeed, the United States enjoy the lowest tax rate as a percentage of the gross national product of all industrial countries. Also, many European states are experiencing serious economic difficulties in maintaining these generous social welfare benefits and are beginning to trim them. General economic decline of the 1990s, joined by a growing materialism among Europeans and an overall disenchantment with socialism following the collapse of the Soviet Union, has led several European states to question the extent of their social welfare programs...the welfare state is currently in retreat across the board." [112]

(c) The Socialist Intent: Economic Equality: "In previous eras, scarcity made it necessary for people to compete with one another. In this competition for goods, they treated each other inhumanely in order to survive. Forced into conflict with each other in order to make a living, people became trapped in a pattern of conduct that not only was harmful to them but also prevented them from developing their nobler aspects. Now...technology has created a situation in which people can produce enough to satisfy all their basic needs. If the Industrial Revolution had indeed brought the ultimate freedom...People will emerge into a reformed society with new values and new modes of conduct. Competition, formerly the necessary yet destructive mode of human conduct, will become increasingly less effective than cooperation. The replacement of competition with cooperation will lead to a new era of greater productivity, thus improving the lifestyles of individuals even more." As the general material conditions of the society improve, social relationships within a particular state greatly improves. "Socialism is an economic equivalent of democracy, if democracy can be equated with individual political equality."[113]

Socialism is characterized by its belief in social equality and socialists have argued at least three points in favor of equality. (i) Social equality upholds justice or fairness. "Socialists are reluctant to explain the inequality of wealth in terms of innate differences of ability amongst individuals. Socialist believe that just as capitalism has fostered competitive and selfish behavior, human inequality very largely reflects the unequal structure of society...Nevertheless, socialists believe that the most significant forms of human inequality are a result of unequal treatment by society, rather than unequal endowment by nature." (ii) Social equality underpins community and cooperation. "If people live in equal social circumstances, they will be more likely to identify with one another and work together for common benefit. Equal outcomes therefore strengthen social solidarity. Social inequality...leads to conflict and instability. This is most clearly reflected in socialist theories about class conflict, or even class war." (iii) Socialists support social equality "because they hold that need-satisfaction in the basis for human fulfilment and self-realization. A need is necessary: it demands satisfaction; it is not simply a frivolous wish or a passing fancy. Basic needs ...are fundamental to the human condition, which means that, for socialists, their satisfaction is the very stuff of freedom. Since all people have broadly similar needs, distributing wealth on the basis of need-satisfaction has clearly egalitarian implications. Unlike liberals, socialists therefore believe that freedom and equality are compatible principles." (iv) "Marxist and communists believe in absolute social equality, brought about by the abolition of private property and collectivization of productive wealth." Social democrats believe in relative social equality, through the redistribution of wealth in the welfare state with progressive taxation. [114]

Utopian Socialism before Marx: Socialist ideas espousing common or public ownership have existed since antiquity. After the French Revolution, "activists and theorists like François-Noël Babeuf, Étienne-Gabriel Morelly, Philippe Buonarroti and Auguste Blanqui influenced the early French labor and socialist movements. In Britain, Thomas Paine proposed a detailed plan to tax property owners to pay for the needs of the poor in Agrarian Justice while Charles Hall wrote The Effects of Civilization on the People in European States, denouncing capitalism's effects on the poor of his time which influenced the utopian schemes of Thomas Spence."[115]

"The first self-conscious socialist movements developed in the 1820s and 1830s. The Owenites, Saint-Simonians and Fourierists provided a series of coherent analyses and interpretations of society. They also, especially in the case of the Owenites, overlapped with a number of other working-class movements like the Chartists in the United Kingdom. The Chartists gathered significant numbers around the People's Charter of 1838, which sought a number of democratic reforms focused on the extension of suffrage to all male adults. Leaders in the movement also called for a more equitable distribution of income and better living conditions for the working classes. The very first trade unions and consumers' cooperative societies also emerged in the hinterland of the Chartist movement...A later important socialist thinker in France was Pierre-Joseph Proudhon, who proposed his philosophy of mutualism in which 'everyone had an equal claim, either alone or as part of a small cooperative, to possess and use land.'"[116]

West European social critics were the first modern socialists who criticized the excessive poverty and inequality of the Industrial Revolution. "They advocated reform, with some such as Robert Owen advocating the transformation of society to small communities without private property... Charles Fourier advocated phalansteres which were communities that respected individual desires, affinities and creativity and saw that work has to be made enjoyable for people. The ideas of Owen and Fourier were tried in practice in numerous intentional communities around Europe and the American continent in the mid-19th century."[117] As we will review below, "Utopian socialism is often described as the presentation of visions and outlines for imaginary or futuristic ideal societies, with positive ideals being the main reason for moving society in such a direction."[118]

Table II-3-1. Timeline of the Socialists Movement (Dates are approximate)

Humanitarian Socialism	Utopian		Fabians	Social Democracy	
			Revisionism		
Scientific Socialism		Marxism	Orthodox		
				M-Leninism	Maoism
Active Years	1810	1850	1890	1930	1950

Source: Leon P. Baradat, Political Ideologies (Upper Saddle, NJ: Prentice Hall, 2000), 194.

Francois-Noel Babeuf (1760-97) was a political journalist and agitator in Revolutionary France whose strategies provided a model for left-wing movements of the 19th century. "The son of a tax farmer, Babeuf worked in the 1780s as a feudal law expert, maintaining records of dues owed and paid by the peasants to the local seigneuries. His increasing distaste for the injustices of this system led him to begin an active career as a political journalist (1788–92). In 1789 he wrote a pamphlet advocating tax reform and went to Paris in hopes of becoming a journalist. He returned to his native Picardy, where he was arrested and briefly imprisoned in 1790. Following his release, he founded a journal, *Le Correspondant picard.* He advocated a program of radical agrarian reforms, including the abolition of feudal dues and the redistribution of land...he served as an administrator in the Mont-didier district of the Somme, but in February 1793 he returned to Paris, where, during the Reign of Terror, Maximilien Robespierre's radical-democratic regime, he was again arrested and imprisoned. After his release following Robespierre's fall in July 1794, he founded a new journal, *Le Journal de la liberté de la presse*, in which he at first defended the Thermidorians and attacked the Jacobins. When he began to attack the Thermidorians, he was arrested (1795) and imprisoned at Arras."[119]

"During this brief imprisonment, Babeuf continued to formulate his egalitarian doctrines, advocating an equal distribution of land and income, and after his release he began a career as a professional revolutionary. He quickly rose to a position of leadership in the Society of the Pantheon, which sought political and economic equality in defiance of the new French Constitution of 1795. After the society was dissolved in 1796, he founded a "secret directory of public safety" to plan an insurrection. On May 8, 1796, a general meeting of Babouvist, Jacobin, and military insurrectionary committees took place in order to plan the raising of a force of 17,000 men to overthrow the Directory and to institute a return to the Constitution of 1793, which the committee members considered the document most legitimately sanctioned by popular deliberation." "Babeuf published the paper 'Scout of the People, or Defender of Twenty-Five Million Oppressed', which was passed from group to group secretly in the streets of Paris. At the same time, Issue 40 of Babeuf's *Tribune* caused immense sensation as it praised the authors of the September Massacres as 'deserving well of their country' and declared that a more complete '2 September' was needed to destroy the government, which consisted of 'starvers, bloodsuckers, tyrants, hangmen, rogues and mountebanks'...On May 10, however, the conspirators were arrested after an informant revealed their plans to the government. The trial took place...All conspirators were acquitted except Babeuf and his companion, Augustin Darthé, both of whom were guillotined. Babeuf was revered as a hero by 19th- and 20th-century revolutionaries because of his advocacy of communism and his conviction..."[120]

(a) Henri de Saint-Simon (1760-1825) was born of an impoverished aristocratic family. After an irregular education, he entered military service at 17. "He was in the regiments sent by France to aid the American colonies in their war of independence against England and served as a captain of artillery at Yorktown in 1781." During the French Revolution, he was in France and was imprisoned during the Reign of Terror. In *Letters of an Inhabitant of Geneva to His Contemporaries* (1803), he proposed that scientists take the place of priests in the social order. "He argued that the property owners who held political power could hope to maintain themselves against the property-less only by subsidizing the advance of knowledge. By 1808 Saint-Simon was impoverished, and the last 17 years of his life were lived mainly on the generosity of friends." Among his many later publications were *On the Reorganization of European Society* (1814) and *Industry* (1816–18, with Auguste Comte)." In 1823, Saint-Simon attempted to kill himself with a pistol but succeeded only in putting out one eye.[121]

"Throughout his life Saint-Simon devoted himself to a long series of projects and publications through which he sought to win support for his social ideas. As a thinker, Saint-Simon was deficient in system, clearness, and coherence, but his influence on modern thought, especially in the social sciences, is undeniable. Apart from the details of his socialist teachings, his main ideas are simple and represented a reaction against the bloodletting of the French Revolution and the militarism of Napoleon. Saint-Simon correctly foresaw the industrialization of the world, and he believed that science and technology would solve most of humanity's problems. Accordingly, in opposition to feudalism and militarism, he advocated an arrangement whereby businessmen and other industrial leaders would control society. The spiritual direction of society would be in the hands of scientists and engineers, who would thus take the place occupied by the Roman Catholic church in the European Middle Ages. What Saint-Simon desired...was an industrialized state directed by modern science, and one in which society would be organized for productive labor by the most capable men. The aim of society would be to produce things useful to life." He proposed that the states of Europe form an association to suppress war, which ideas had influenced on the philosopher Auguste Comte.[122]

"Although the contrast between the laboring and the propertied classes in society is not emphasized by Saint-Simon," the cause of the poor is discussed in his work, *The New Christianity* (1825), "it takes the form of a religion. It was this development of Saint-Simon's teaching that occasioned his final rupture with Comte. Before the publication...Saint-Simon had not concerned himself with theology, but in this work, beginning with a belief in God, he tries to resolve Christianity into its essential elements, and he finally propounds this precept: that religion should guide the community toward the great aim of improving...the conditions of the poorest class."[123]

(b) Robert Owen (1771–1858), born to a family of postmaster, attended local schools until the age of 10, when he became an apprentice to a clothier. "His employer had a good library, and Owen spent much of his time reading. His reading of books on religious controversies led him to conclude at an early age that there were fundamental flaws in all religions. Excelling in business, by the time he was 19 he had become superintendent of a large cotton mill in Manchester, and he soon developed it into one of the foremost establishments of its kind in Great Britain. Owen made use of … cotton ever imported into Britain and made improvements in the quality of the cotton spun…Owen induced his partners to purchase the New Lanark mills."[124]

"There were 2,000 inhabitants of New Lanark, 500 of whom were young children from the poorhouses and charities…The children, especially, had been well treated by the former proprietor, but their living conditions were harsh: crime and vice were bred by demoralizing conditions; education and sanitation were neglected; and housing conditions were intolerable. Owen improved the houses and…encouraged the people in habits of order, cleanliness, and thrift. He opened a store that sold sound-quality goods at little more than cost and strictly supervised the sale of alcoholic beverages. His greatest success was in the education of the young, to which he devoted special attention. In 1816 he opened the first infant school in Great Britain at the New Lanark mills and gave it his close personal supervision. The schools, which eschewed corporal punishment and other traditional methods, emphasized character development and included dancing and music in the curriculum. Although Owen initially was regarded with suspicion as an outsider, he quickly won the confidence of the people."[125]

"In 1813 Owen published two of the four essays in *A New View of Society*; or, Essays on the Principle of the Formation of the Human Character, in which he expounded the principles on which his system of educational philanthropy was based. Having lost all belief in the prevailing forms of religion, he developed his own creed that he took to be an entirely new and original discovery. The chief point in Owen's philosophy was that man's character was formed by circumstances over which he had no control. For this reason, man was not a proper subject of either praise or blame. These convictions led him to the conclusion that the great secret in the right formation of man's character was to place him under the proper influences from his earliest years. The non-responsibility of man and the effect of early influences were the hallmark of Owen's entire system of education and social amelioration."[126] "In 1824, Owen travelled to America, where he invested the bulk of his fortune in an experimental socialistic community at New Harmony, Indiana, the preliminary model for Owen's utopian society. The experiment was short-lived, lasting about two years. Other Owenite utopian communities met a similar fate. In 1828, Owen returned to the United Kingdom and settled in London."[127]

(c) Charles Fourier (1772–1837) was a son of a small businessman. When his father died in 1781, "Fourier received two fifths of his father's estate, valued at more than 200,000 francs. This inheritance enabled Fourier to travel throughout Europe at his leisure. In 1791 he moved from Besancon to Lyon, where he was employed by the merchant M. Bousquet. Fourier's travels also brought him to Paris, where he worked as the head of the Office of Statistics for a few months. Not satisfied with making journeys on behalf of others for their commercial benefit, and desiring to seek knowledge in everything he could, Fourier would often change business firms and residences in order to explore and experience new things. From 1791 to 1816 Fourier was employed in Paris, Rouen, Lyon, Marseille, and Bordeaux. As a traveling salesman and correspondence clerk, his research and thought were time-limited: he complained of serving the knavery of merchants...He took up writing, and his first book was published in 1808."[128]

"Fourier declared that concern and cooperation were the secrets of social success. He believed that a society that cooperated would see an immense improvement in their productivity levels. Workers would be recompensed for their labors according to their contribution. Fourier saw such cooperation occurring in communities he called phalanxes, based around structures called Phalanstères...These buildings were four-level apartment complexes where the richest had the uppermost apartments and the poorest enjoyed a ground-floor residence. Wealth was determined by one's job; jobs were assigned based on the interests and desires of the individual. There were incentives: jobs people might not enjoy doing would receive higher pay. Fourier considered trade, which he associated with Jews, ...be forced to perform farm work in the phalansteries."[129]

"Fourier characterized poverty (not inequality) as the principal cause of disorder in society, and he proposed to eradicate it by sufficiently high wages and by a decent minimum for those who were not able to work." In *Work and Liberated Passions*, "The idea of libidinal work relations in a developed industrial society finds little support in the tradition of thought, and where such support is forthcoming it seems of a dangerous nature. The transformation of labor into pleasure is the central idea in Fourier's giant socialist utopia." In *Women's Rights*, "Fourier was also a supporter of women's rights in a time period when influences like Jean-Jacques Rousseau were prevalent. Fourier believed that all important jobs should be open to women." In *Children and Education*, "Fourier felt that civilized parents and teachers saw children as little idlers. Fourier felt that this way of thinking was wrong. He felt that children as early as age two and three were very industrious. He listed the dominant tastes in all children to include, but not limited to: Rummaging or inclination to handle everything, examine everything, look through everything; to constantly change occupations...; and Progressive attraction of the weak toward the strong."[130]

(d) Étienne Cabet (1788–1856) was born in Dijon, Côte-d'Or, educated as a lawyer. He was appointed attorney-general in Corsica and represented the government of Louis Philippe, after having headed an insurrectionary committee and participated actively during the July Revolution of 1830. He was dismissed from this position for his attack upon the conservatism of the government in his *Histoire de la révolution de* (1830). "Nonetheless, in 1831, Cabet was elected to the Chamber of Deputies in France as the representative of Côte d'Or...Accused of treason in 1834 because of his bitter attacks on the government...Cabet was convicted and sentenced to five years' exile. He fled to England and sought political asylum. Influenced by Robert Owen, Thomas More and Charles Fourier, Cabet wrote *Travel and Adventures of Lord William Carisdall in Icaria* (1840), which depicted a utopia in which a democratically elected governing body controlled all economic activity and closely supervised social life." (Icaria is the name of ideal society)[131]

"In 1839, Cabet returned to France to advocate a communitarian social movement, for which he invented the term communisme. Cabet's notion of a communal society influenced other socialist writers and philosophers, notably Karl Marx and Friedrich Engels. Some of these other writers ignored Cabet's Christian influences, as described in his book *The real Christianity according to Jesus Christ* (1846). This book described Christ's mission to be to establish social equality and contrasted primitive Christianity with the ecclesiasticism of Cabet's time to the disparagement of the latter...contained a popular history of the French Revolutions from 1789 to 1830."[132]

"In 1847, after realizing the economic hardship caused by the depression of 1846, Cabet gave up on the notion of reforming French society. Instead, after conversations with Robert Owen and Owen's attempts to found a commune in Texas, Cabet gathered a group of followers from across France and traveled to the United States to organize an Icarian community. They entered into a social contract, making Cabet the director-in-chief for the first ten years, and embarked from Le Havre, February 3, 1848, for New Orleans, Louisiana. They expected to settle in the Red River valley in Texas...by disease, about one-third of the colonists returned to France."[133]

"The remainder moved to Nauvoo, Illinois, to a site recently vacated by the Mormons, in 1849. Because of the improved location, it developed into a successful agricultural community. By 1855, the Nauvoo Icarian community had expanded to about 500 members with a solid agricultural base, shops, schools, and a newspaper. Amidst this success, however, Cabet was forced to return to France in May 1851 to settle charges of fraud brought up by his previous followers in Europe. When he returned in July 1852, the community was suffering economically, and a split developed regarding the work division and food distribution. In attempts to save the community upon his return, Cabet issued a series of edicts...After disputes...Cabet went to St. Louis, Missouri, in 1855, where he died the following years."[134]

Revolutionary versus Evolutionary Socialism: Two major issues had divided competing traditions and tendencies within socialism: the goals or ends for which socialist should strive; and the means they should use to achieve ends or the roads to socialism. This concern with means follows from the fact the socialism has always had an oppositional character: either revolutionary or evolutionary, with interconnected means and ends.

(a) ***Revolutionary Socialism***: Social revolution is necessary to change the structure of society. It is the view that "revolution is a necessary precondition for a transition from capitalism to socialism. Revolution is not necessarily defined as a violent insurrection; it is defined as seizure of political power by mass movements of the working class so that the state is directly controlled by the working class as opposed to the capitalist class and its interests. Revolutionary socialists believe such a state of affairs is a precondition for establishing socialism." In fact, revolutionary socialism "is opposed to social movements that seek to gradually ameliorate the economic and social problems of capitalism through political reform."[135]

During the nineteenth century, revolutionary tactics were "attractive to socialists for two reasons. First, the early stages of industrialization produce stark injustice as the working masses were afflicted by grinding poverty and widespread unemployment. Capitalism was viewed as a system of naked oppression and exploitation, and the working class was thought to be on the brink of revolution. When Marx and Engels wrote in 1848 that 'A specter is haunting Europe – the specter of Communism', they were writing against a background of revolt and revolution in many parts of the continent. Second, the working classes had few alternative means of political influence, indeed, almost everywhere they were excluded from political life." As universal male suffrage was introduced like in France in 1848, the country was in predominantly agricultural and still deeply religious, so that the majority of the electorate were politically conservative. Therefore, political revolution was the only realistic way to introduce socialism to the working masses.[136]

Meanwhile, "revolutionary socialists view the state as an agent of class oppression, acting in the interest of capital and against those of labor. Marxists, for example, believe that political power reflects class interests, and that the state is a bourgeois state, inevitably biased in favor of capital. Political reform and gradual change are clearly pointless. Universal suffrage and regular and competitive elections are at best a façade, their purpose being to conceal the reality of unequal class and to misdirect the political energies of the working class. A class-conscious proletariat thus has no alternative: in order to build socialism, it has first to overthrow the bourgeois state through political revolution. Marx believed that this revolution would be followed by a temporary period called the dictatorship of the proletariat, during which the revolution would need to be protected against the danger of counter-revolution carried out by the disposed bourgeoisie."[137]

"In the second half of the twentieth century, faith in revolution was most evident amongst socialists in the developing world. In the post-1945 period, many national liberation movements embraced the armed struggle in the belief that colonial rule could neither be negotiated nor voted out of existence. In Asia, the Chinese Revolution of 1949, led by Mao Zedong, was the culmination of a long military campaign against both Japan and the Chinese Nationalists, the Kuomintang. Vietnamese national unity was achieved in 1975 after a prolonged war fought first against France and subsequently against the United States. Until his death in 1967, Che Guevara, the Argentine revolutionary, led guerrilla forces in various parts of South America and commanded troops during the Cuban revolution of 1959, which overthrew the US-backed Batista regime and brought Fidel Castro to power. Similar revolutionary struggles took place in Africa; for example, the bitter war through which Algeria eventually gained independence from France in 1962. In the light of the Algerian experience, the French revolutionary theorists Frantz Fanon (1925-61) argued in *The Wretched of the Earth* (1961) that violent insurrection was not merely a political necessity but was also a psychological desirable feature of the anticolonial struggle. Fanon believed that years of colonial rule had engendered a paralyzing sense of inferiority and impotence amongst the black people of Africa, which could only be purged by the experience of revolt."[138]

"The choice of revolutionary or insurrectionary political means had profound consequences for socialism. For example, the use of revolution usually led to the pursuit of fundamentalist ends. Revolution had the advantage that it allowed the remnants of the old order to be overthrown and an entirely new social system to be constructed...Capitalism could be abolished, and a qualitatively different socialist society established in its place. Socialism in this context, usually took the form of state collectivization, modelled upon the Soviet Union during the Stalinist period. The revolution road was also associated with a drift towards dictatorship and the use of political repression. This occurred for a number of reasons. Frist, the use of force accustomed the new rulers to regard violence as a legitimate instrument of policy, as Mao put it, power resides in the barrel of a gun. Second, revolutionary parties typically adopted military-style structures, based upon strong leadership and strict discipline; that were merely consolidated once power was achieved. Third, in rooting out the vestiges of the old order, all oppositional forces were also removed, effectively preparing the way for the construction of totalitarian dictatorships. The revolutionary socialist tradition, nevertheless, was fatally undermined by the collapse of communism in what were, effectively, the counterrevolutions of 1989-91. This finally ended the divide that had opened up in socialist politics in 1917 and completed the conversion of socialism to constitutional and democratic politics." It survives such as in Peru and Nepal.[139]

(b) ***Evolutionary Socialism***: "Capitalism itself had matured and by the late nineteenth century the urban working class had lost its revolutionary character and been integrated into society. Wages and living standards had started to rise, partly as a result of colonial expansion into Africa and Asia after 1875. The working class had also begun to develop a range of institutions – working men's clubs, trade unions, political parties and so on – which both protected their interests and nurtured a sense of security and belonging within industrial society. Furthermore, the gradual advance of political democracy led to the extension of franchise (the right to vote) to the working classes. By the end of the First World War, a large majority of western state had introduced universal manhood suffrage, with a growing number extending voting rights also to women. The combined effect of these factors was to shift the attention of socialists away from violent insurrection and to persuade them that there was an alternative evolutionary, democratic or parliamentary road to socialism. It is notable, for example, that towards the end of his life Marx was prepared to speculate about the possibility of a Western Europe, and Engels openly approved of the electoral tactics increasingly employed by the German Social Democratic Party (SPD). Where revolutionary doctrines continued to dominate it was usually in economically and politically backward countries such as Russia."[140]

The Fabian Society is a British socialist organization advocating "to advance the principles of democratic socialism via gradualist and reformist effort in democracies, rather than by revolutionary overthrow." "This would occur through a combination of political action and education. Political action required the formation of a socialist party, which would compete for power against established parliamentary parties rather than prepare for violent revolution. They therefore accepted the liberal theory of the state as a neutral arbiter, rather than the Marxist belief that it was an agent of class oppression…The Fabians also believed that elite groups, such as politicians of all parties, civil servants, scientists and academics, could be converted to socialism through education. These elite groups would be permeated by socialist ideas as they recognized that socialism is morally superior to capitalism…A socialist economy…could avoid the waste involved in class conflict and debilitating poverty."[141] In British politics, "As one of the founding organizations of the Labor Representation Committee in 1900, and as an important influence upon the Labor Party which grew from it, the Fabian Society has had a powerful influence on British politics. Other members of the Fabian Society have included political leaders from countries formerly part of the British Empire, such as Jawaharlal Nehru, who adopted Fabian principles as part of their own political ideologies. The Fabian Society founded the London School of Economics and Political Science in 1895. Today, the society functions primarily as a think tank and is one of 21 socialist societies affiliated with the Labor Party."[142]

(c) ***The Inevitability of Gradualism?*** The advent of democracy in the late nineteenth and early twentieth centuries caused "a wave of optimism to spread throughout the socialist movement" as shown in the Fabian Society of the inevitability of gradualism. "Marx had predicted the inevitable over-throw of capitalist society in a proletarian revolution. However, whereas Marx believed that history was driven by the irresistible forces of class conflict, evolutionary socialists highlighted the logic of the democratic process itself. Their optimism was founded on a number of assumptions. First, the progressive extension of the franchise would eventually lead to the establish-ment of universal adult suffrage and therefore of political equality. Second, political equality would, in practice, work in the interests of the majority, that is, those who decide the outcome of elections. Socialists thus believed that political democracy would invest power in the hands of the working class, easily the most numerous class in any industrial society. Third, socialism was thought to be the natural home of the working class. As capitalism was seen as a system of class exploitation, oppressed workers would naturally be drawn to socialist parties, which offered them the prospect of social justice and emancipation. The electoral success of socialist parties would therefore be guaranteed by the numerical strength of the working class. Fourth, once in power, socialist parties would be able to carry out a fundamental transformation of society through a process of social reform. In this way, political democracy not only open up the possibility of achieving socialism peacefully, it made this process inevitable."[143]

Such optimistic expectations have, however, not been borne out in reality. Some have even argued that democratic socialism is founded upon a contradiction: in order to respond successfully to electoral pressures, socialist have been forced to revise or water down their ideological beliefs. Socialist parties have enjoyed periods of power in virtually all liberal democracies, with the exception of North America. However, they have certainly not been guaranteed power. The Swedish Social Democratic Labor Party (SAP) has been the most successful in this respect, having been in power alone or as a senior partner in a coalition for most of the period since 1951. Nevertheless, even the SAP has only once achieved 50 percent of the popular vote (in 1968). The UK labor Party gained its greatest support (49 percent) in 1951, equaled by the Spanish Socialist Workers' Party in 1982. The SPD in Germany got 46 percent of the vote in 1972 and the combined socialist and communist vote in Italy in 1976 amounted to 44 percent. Moreover, although these parties have undoubtedly introduced significant social reforms when in power, usually involving the expansion of welfare provision and economic management, they have certainly not presided over any fundamental social transformation. At best, capitalism has been reformed, not abolished." Moreover, socialist parties have been forced to acknowledge the ability of capitalism to deliver the goods.[144]

Marxism: Karl Marx (1818-83): Born in Trier, Germany, Marx studied law and philosophy at university. "He married Jenny von Westphalen in 1843. Due to his political publications, Marx became stateless and lived in exile with his wife and children in London for decades, where he continued to develop his thought in collaboration with German thinker Friedrich Engels and publish his writings, researching in the reading room of the British Museum. His best-known titles are the 1848 pamphlet, *The Communist Manifesto*, and the three-volume *Das Kapital*. His political and philosophical thought had enormous influence on subsequent intellectual, economic and political history, and his name has been used as an adjective, a noun and a school of social theory. Marx's critical theories about society, economics and politics – collectively understood as Marxism – hold that human societies develop through class struggle. In capitalism, this manifests itself in the conflict between the ruling classes (known as the bourgeoisie) that control the means of production and the working classes (known as the proletariat) that enable these means by selling their labor power in return for wages. Employing a critical approach known as historical materialism, Marx predicted that, like previous socio-economic systems, capitalism produced internal tensions which would lead to its self-destruction and replacement by a new system known as socialism."[145]

"For Marx, class antagonisms under capitalism, owing in part to its instability and crisis-prone nature, would eventuate the working class' development of class consciousness, leading to their conquest of political power and eventually the establishment of a classless, communist society constituted by a free association of producers. Marx actively pressed for its implementation, arguing that the working class should carry out organized revolutionary action to topple capitalism and bring about socio-economic emancipation. Marx has been described as one of the most influential figures in human history, and his work has been both lauded and criticized. His work in economics laid the basis for much of the current understanding of labor and its relation to capital, and subsequent economic thought. Many intellectuals, labor unions, artists and political parties worldwide have been influenced by Marx's work, with many modifying or adapting his ideas. Marx is cited as one of the principal architects of modern social science."[146]

"The legacy of Marx's thought has become contested between numerous tendencies, each of which sees itself as Marx's most accurate interpreter. In the political realm, these tendencies include Leninism, Marxism–Leninism, Trotskyism, Maoism, Luxemburgism and libertarian Marxism. Various currents have also developed in academic Marxism, often under influence of other views, resulting in structuralist Marxism, historical Marxism, phenomenological Marxism, analytical Marxism and Hegelian Marxism. From an academic perspective, Marx's work contributed to the birth of modern sociology…three masters of the school of suspicion…"[147]

(a) Philosophy: Rejecting the idealism of Hegel, "Marx held material circumstances to be fundamental to all forms of social and historical development. This reflected the belief that the production of the means of subsistence is the most crucial of all human activities. Since humans cannot survive without foot, water, shelter and so on, the way in which these are produced conditions all other aspects of life." In *A Contribution to the Critique of Political Economy* (1859), Marx gave a theory suggesting "that social consciousness and the legal and political super-structure arise from the economic base, the real foundation of society. This base consists essentially of the mode of production or economic system – feudalism, capitalism, socialism and so on ...it undoubtedly led Marx to conclude that political, legal, cultural, religious, artistic and other aspects of life could primarily be explained by reference to economic factors."[148]

"Although in other respects a critic of Hegel, Marx nevertheless embrace his belief that the driving force of historical change was the dialectic, a process of interaction between competing forces that leads to a higher stage of development. In effect, progress is the consequence of internal conflict. For Hegel, this explained the movement of the world spirit towards self-realization through conflict between the thesis and its opposing force, an antithesis, producing a higher level, a synthesis, which in turn constitutes a new thesis. Marx, as Engels put it, turned Hegel on his head by investing this Hegelian dialectic with a materialistic interpretation. Marx thus explained historical change by reference to internal contradictions within each mode of production arising from the existence of private property ... Conflict between capitalism and the proletariat will therefore lead to a higher stage of development in the establishment of a socialist, and eventually a communist, society."[149]

"Marx's theory of history is therefore teleological, in the sense that it invests history with meaning...reflected in its goal: classless communism. This goal would nevertheless only be achieved once history had developed through a series of stages or epochs, each characterized by its own economic structure and class system. In *The German Ideology* (1846), Marx identified four such stages: (1) primitive communism or tribal society, in which material scarcity provided the principal source of conflict; (2) slavery, covering classical or ancient societies and characterized by conflict between master and slave; (3) feudalism, marked by antagonism between land owners and serfs; and (4) capitalism, dominated by the struggle between the bourgeoisie and the prole-tariat. Human history had therefore been a long struggle between the oppressed and the oppressor, the exploited and the exploiter...Marx envisaged an end of history, which would occur when a society was constructed that embodied no internal contradictions or antagonisms. This, for Marx, meant communism, a classless society based on the common ownership of productive wealth."[150]

(b) Economics: "Marx studies capitalism and the ideas of Locke, Smith, Ricardo, Malthus, and others very carefully, analyzing them perceptively in *Das Kapital*. In this work he concludes that capitalism has within it the seeds of its own destruction. In short, Marx believed that the fall of capitalism was inevitable and that it would lead to socialism."

(i) The Theory of Work: Marx believed that work is the process through which people develop their humanity and fulfill themselves. The essence of human beings, therefore, becomes closely related to their work.

(ii) The Theory of Self-Alienation suggests that capitalism has separated people from their genuine or essential natures, that is, from their capacity as workers to develop skills, talents and understanding through the experience of free productive labor. "Since capitalism is a system of production for exchange, it alienates humans from the product of their labor: they work to produce not what they need or what is useful, but commodities to be sold for profit. They are also alienated from the process of labor, because most are forced to work under the supervision of foremen or managers… individuals are encouraged to be self-interested and are therefore alienated from fellow human beings. Finally, workers are alienated from themselves. Labor itself is reduced to a mere commodity, and work becomes a depersonalized activity instead of a creative and fulfilling one."[151]

(iii) The Labor Theory of Value: Marx assumed that the intrinsic value of any object is determined by the amount of labor needed to produce it. "The price of the object, the amount of money it will fetch on the market at any given time, is determined by supply and demand. However, the value of the object is determined by the labor time needed for its production."

(iii) The Theory of Surplus Value: Ricardo suggested that capitalists, driven by the need to make profits and capital, will pay their workers only subsistence wages because that much is necessary to bring them back to work the next day. Marx views that workers are not only slaves, but also the meager wage earners paid by their masters, regardless of how much value they may produce. "Thus, the capitalists force workers to produce in excess, or *surplus value*, and they keep that sum for themselves as a profit. According to this theory, the workers' intrinsic value is the money needed to feed themselves and their families. Anything they produce above the subsistence level is surplus value…the capitalists pay only a subsistence wage, they keep the surplus value produced by the workers as their profit…Accordingly, any profit the capitalists make from the labor of their employees is ill-gotten and exploitative. The capitalist is, therefore, a villain, a parasite who lives by sucking the economic lifeblood of the proletariat and must be erased from society when the proletariat takes over. Needless to say, Ricardo, the capitalist economist, would not have agreed with conclusion. Ricardo believed that the capitalists' control of property distinguished them from other people and justified their exploitation…"[152]

(c) Politics: "Marx predicted the demise of capitalism. Competition, he argues, would force the capitalists to buy more machinery. Yet, only human labor can produce a surplus value; thus, the capitalists' profits would decline as they employed fewer people. At the same time, unemployment would increase among the proletariat as competition forced increasing numbers of former capitalists into the proletarian ranks. On the other hand, the size of the proletariat and the depth of its misery would increase; on the other, the wealth in the society would be controlled by fewer people. Marx predicted that every capitalist society would be subject to increasingly frequent and ever more serious economic convulsions. Eventually, the misery of the proletariat would increase to a point that could no longer be endured and a revolution would erupt...Marx envisioned a spontaneous uprising of the workers. Conditions for the common people in pre-revolutionary France had degenerated to miserable levels. Yet little was done in the way of advanced planning for a popular revolt prior to its eruption in Paris in 1789...after centuries of aristocratic abuse, the people of France had quietly reached the breaking point...some ordinarily trivial event sparked a public fury that culminated in a frightful period of social and political chaos."[153]

"Marx's most important prediction was that capitalism was destined to be overthrown by a proletarian revolution. This would be not merely a political revolution that would...overthrow the state machine, but a social revolution that would establish a new mode of production and culminate with the achievement of full communism. In Marx's view, the epoch of social revolution would begin when the class system, the relations of production, became a fetter upon the further development of productive techniques and innovation, the so-called forces of production. Such a revolution, he anticipated, would occur in the most mature capitalist countries...where the forces of production had expanded to their limit within the constraints of the capitalist system...revolution would not simply be determined by the development of objective conditions. The subjective element would be supplied by a class-conscious proletariat would recognize the fact of its own exploitation and become a revolutionary force: a class-for-itself...The initial target of this revolution was to be the bourgeois state."[154] Marx sees "that the proletarian revolution would triumph, since human social evolution is driven by technological development, and since the proletarian revolution would be integrally tied to the more technically advanced system of automated industry. Thus, socialism would be established on a foundation of advanced and automated industry; ownership of the factories would be collective; private property would be abolished; class distinctions would be eliminated; governments, which exit only to promote the interests of the dominant classes, would not be necessary; and human emancipation from oppressive forms of work and from domination of one social group by another would be established."[155]

(d) Communist Manifesto (1848) is divided into a preamble and four sections, the last of these a short conclusion. The introduction proclaims that "A spectre is haunting Europe—the spectre of communism."[156]

(i) Bourgeois and Proletarians elucidates the materialist conception of history, "that the history of all hitherto existing society is the history of class struggles. Societies have always taken the form of an oppressed majority exploited under the yoke of an oppressive minority. In capitalism, the industrial working class, or proletariat, engage in class struggle against the owners of the means of production, the bourgeoisie. As before, this struggle will end in a revolution that restructures society, or the common ruin of the contending classes. The bourgeoisie, through the constant revolutionizing of production and uninterrupted disturbance of all social conditions have emerged as the supreme class in society, displacing all the old powers of feudalism. The bourgeoisie constantly exploits the proletariat for its labor power, creating profit for themselves and accumulating capital. However, in doing so the bourgeoisie serves as its own gravediggers; the proletariat inevitably will become conscious of their own potential and rise to power through revolution, overthrowing the bourgeoisie."

(ii) Proletarians and Communists are the relationship of conscious communists to the rest of the working class. "The communists' party will not oppose other working-class parties, but unlike them, it will express the general will and defend the common interests of the world's proletariat as a whole, independent of all nationalities. This section goes on to defend communism from various objections, including claims that it advocates free love or dis-incentivizes people from working. At the end, it outlines a set of short-term demands - among them a progressive income tax; abolition of inheritances and private property; free public education; nationalization of the means of transport and communication; centralization of credit via a national bank; expansion of publicly owned etc. - the implementation of which would result in the precursor to a stateless and classless society.

(iii) Socialist and Communist Literature "distinguishes the socialist doctrines prevalent at the time - these being broadly categorized as Reactionary Socialism...While the degree of reproach toward rival perspectives varies, all are dismissed for advocating reformism and failing to recognize the pre-eminent revolutionary role...Position of the Communists in Relation to the Various Opposition Parties, the concluding section of the Manifesto, briefly discusses the communist position on struggles in specific countries in the mid-nineteenth century such as France, Switzerland, Poland, and Germany, this last being on the eve of a bourgeois revolution, and predicts that a world revolution will soon follow. It ends by declaring an alliance with the social democrats, boldly supporting other communist revolutions, and calling for united international proletarian action - Working Men of All Countries, Unite!."[157]

(e) Das Kapital (3 volumes, 1867, 1885, 1894) is one of his major works. Volume I (1867): *The Critic of the Political Economy of Capitalism* deals with that wage-labor is the basic cell-form of a capitalist society. The economic formation of society is a process of natural history. The structural contradictions of a capitalist economy describe the contradictory movement originating from the class-struggle between labor and capital. The economic crises are the conditions that propitiate proletarian revolution. "In a capitalist economy, technological improvement and its consequent increased production augment the amount of material wealth in society, while simultaneously diminishing the economic value of the same wealth, thereby diminishing the rate of profit - a paradox characteristic of economic crisis in a capitalist economy; poverty in the midst of plenty consequent to over-production and under-consumption."[158]

Volume II (1885): *The Process of Circulation of Capital*: The social intertwining of the different capitals, of the component parts of capital and of revenue, conceived "as a movement of commodities and of money, enabled Marx to work out at least the essential elements, if not the definitive form of a coherent theory of the trade cycle, based upon the inevitability of periodic disequilibrium between supply and demand under the capitalist mode of production. Volume II of Capital has indeed been not only a sealed book, but also a forgotten one. To a large extent, it remains so to this very day. Part 3 is the point of departure for a topic given its Marxist treatment later in detail by, among others, Rosa Luxemburg."[159]

Volume III (1894): *The Process of Capitalist Production as a Whole*: "It is in seven parts: (1) The conversion of Surplus Value into Profit and the rate of Surplus Value into the rate of Profit; (2) Conversion of Profit into Average Profit; (3) The Law of the Tendency of the Rate of Profit to Fall; (4) Conversion of Commodity Capital and Money Capital into Commercial Capital and Money-Dealing Capital (Merchant's Capital); (5) Division of Profit Into Interest and Profit of Enterprise, Interest Bearing Capital; (6) Transformation of Surplus-Profit into Ground Rent; and (7) Revenues and Their Sources. The work...says that as the organic fixed capital requirements of production rise as a result of advancements in production generally, the rate of profit tends to fall. This result, which orthodox Marxists believe is a principal contradictory characteristic leading to an inevitable collapse of the capitalist order, was held by Marx and Engels to, as a result of various contradictions in the capitalist mode of production, result in crises whose resolution necessitates the emergence of an entirely new mode of production as the culmination of the same historical dialectic that led to the emergence of capitalism from prior forms...The first three parts are concerned with the division of surplus value amongst individual capitals, where it takes the form of profit. The following parts are concerned with merchants' capital, interest-bearing capital and landed capital." [160]

(f) The Marxist Political System: Marx expected that the proletarian state would create a dictatorship. "The purpose of the dictatorship of the proletariat would be to eliminate all but a single proletarian class. "Since Marx insisted on a democratic format in all other things and since he never attempted to form a communist party as Lenin later did, it is highly unlikely that he meant to imply the model Lenin employed...[In the first Marxist state] Marx expected that the over-whelming number of people in society would be among the proletariat when the revolution occurred. Hence, if he meant that the dictatorship was to be by the proletariat, the situation would indeed be different. The huge majority of people – the proletariat – would impose its egalitarian policies on the tiny corps of remaining capitalists... such a system would be more democratic than that which Lenin used."[161]

"In any event, as the dictatorship succeeded in redirecting the society toward the socialist utopia, more and more people would adopt the socialist ethic, meaning willingness to work to one's capacity and to share the fruits of labor with the rest of society. This concept is clearly the most revolution-ary aspect of Marx's thought. Like all Leftists, he believed people could change, redirecting their lives and actions toward more desirable goals. To this end Marx expected the dictatorship to encourage people to abandon their selfish, atomistic ways, adopting collective, or organic, values which accrue to the good of society as a whole. The new society would operate on the principle from each according to his ability, to each according to his needs."

"If people could be encouraged to enjoy their labor, they would become more productive than was possible in a capitalist system. If the productivity was shared equally by all, social anxieties and frustrations would most probably abate, creating a happy, contented populace. Thus, crime, war, and human turmoil would disappear. As strife and anxiety declined, a gradual change of society's foundations would lead to the second Marxist state. The need for the dictatorship would disappear. Eventually, when the last non-proletariat was gone, the state would have withered away: The police state would have ceased to exist. Then, all the individuals in society would be free to govern themselves responsibly for the good of all, and the system would have evolved into a democratic utopia similar to that desired by many anarchists. Only a skeletal shell of the former state would be left, and it would simply administer the economy...'In the final state of communism, the government of men will change to the administration of things."[162]

Marx expected that socialism would be adopted in every country in the world sooner or later by a law of historical development. He argued that nation-states were organized by the capitalists to keep people who really had a great deal in common separated from one another. National boundaries were only artificial separations designed to reinforce the capitalist system. Since workingmen have no country, all national boundaries would have withered away, and the entire world would be a single socialist utopia.

SOCIALIST THEORY AFTER MARXISM

"The International Workingmen's Association (IWA), known as *The First International*, was founded in London in 1864. "Victor Le Lubez, a French radical republican living in London, invited Karl Marx to come to London as a representative of German workers. The IWA held a preliminary conference in 1865 and had its first congress at Geneva in 1866... Russian revolutionary Mikhail Bakunin and his collectivist anarchist associates joined the First International. They allied with the federalist socialist sections of the International, who advocated the revolutionary overthrow of the state and the collectivization of property."[163] An uprising in Paris established *The Paris Commune* in 1871, that was a government that briefly rule Paris. The Commune was the result of an uprising in Paris after France was defeated in the Franco-Prussian War. Anarchists participated actively in the establishment of the Paris Commune." The socialist movement was then decapitated and deeply affected for years.[164]

In 1889, "*The Second International* was founded, with 384 delegates from 20 countries representing about 300 labor and socialist organizations. Anarchists were ejected and not allowed in mainly because of the pressure from Marxists. Just before his death in 1895, Engels argued that there was now a single generally recognized, crystal clear theory of Marx and a single great international army of socialists."[165] *Anarchism* was associated with the working-class movements of the 19th century and the Spanish Civil War-era struggles against fascism. "In 1907, the International Anarchist Congress of Amsterdam gathered delegates from 14 different countries...in particular concerning the organization of the anarchist movement, popular education issues, the general strike or antimilitarism."[166]

By the time of Marx's death in 1883, "His influence was particularly strong within *the Social Democratic Party of Germany* (SPD), which was formed in 1875 by the merger of a Marxist party and a party created by Marx's German rival, Ferdinand Lassalle. "In 1896, Eduard Bernstein argued that once full democracy had been achieved, a transition to socialism by gradual means was both possible and more desirable than revolutionary change. Bernstein and his supporters came to be identified as revisionists, because they sought to revise the classic tenets of Marxism."[167] In the chaotic circumstances of postwar Europe, the revolutionary socialism prevailed in Russia. "Communist parties were formed, often from minority or majority factions in most of the world's socialist parties, which broke away in support of the Leninist model."[168] *The Third International*, *Comintern* (1919-43) was founded under Lenin and was dissolved by Joseph Stalin in 1943. Finally, when Marx died, the socialist movement lost the dominant guidance, but eventually three socialist doctrines emerged: Orthodox Marxism, Marxism-Leninism, and Social Democracy.

Orthodox Marxism: The Orthodox Marxists were led by ***Karl Kautsky*** (1854-2938) after Engel's death in 1895. As a Czech-Austrian philosopher, journalist, and Marxist theoretician, Kautsky was recognized as among the most authoritative promulgators of Orthodox Marxism…until the outbreak of World War I in 1914. Following the war, Kautsky was an outspoken critic of the Bolshevik Revolution, engaging in polemics with Vladimir Lenin and Leon Trotsky on the nature of the Soviet state." "Karl Kautsky, born in Prague of a middle-class artistic family…moved with his family to Vienna at the age of seven. He studied history, philosophy and economics at the University of Vienna from 1874 and became a member of the Social Democratic Party of Austria in 1875. In 1880 he joined a group of German socialists in Zürich who were supported financially by Karl Höchberg, and who smuggled socialist material into the Reich at the time of the Anti-Socialist Laws (1878–1890). Influenced by Eduard Bernstein, Karl Höchberg's secretary, he became a Marxist."[169]

"In 1883, Kautsky founded the monthly *Die Neue Zeit* (The New Times) in Stuttgart, which became a weekly in 1890. He edited the magazine until September 1917: this gave him a steady income and allowed him to propagate Marxism. From 1885 to 1890 he spent time in London, where he became a close friend of Friedrich Engels. His position as a prominent Marxist theorist was assured in 1888, when Engels put him to the task of editing Marx's three-volume work Theories of Surplus Value. In 1891 he co-authored the Erfurt Program of the Social Democratic Party of Germany together with August Bebel and Eduard Bernstein. Following the death of Engels in 1895, Kautsky became one of the most important and influential theoreticians of Marxism…and outlining a Marxist theory of imperialism. When Bernstein attacked the traditional Marxist position of the necessity for revolution in the late 1890s, Kautsky denounced him."[170]

"In 1914, when the German Social-Democrat deputies in the Reichstag voted for war credits, Kautsky suggested abstaining. Kautsky claimed that Germany was waging a defensive war against the threat of Czarist Russia. However, in June 1915…In 1917 he left the SPD for the Independent Social Democratic Party of Germany (USPD), which united Socialists…After the November Revolution in Germany, Kautsky served as under-secretary of State in the Foreign Office in the short-lived SPD-USPD revol-utionary government and worked at finding documents which proved the war guilt of Imperial Germany. After 1919 Kautsky's prominence steadily diminished. He visited Georgia in 1920 and wrote a book in 1921 on this Social Democratic country still independent of Bolshevist Russia. In 1920, when the USPD split, he went with a minority of that party back into the SPD. In 1924, at the age of 70, he moved back to Vienna…and remained there until 1938. At the time of Hitler's Anschluss he fled to Czechoslovakia and thence by plane to Amsterdam, where he died in the same year."[171]

Marxism-Leninism: *Vladimir I. Lenin* (1870-1924) from a middle-class family in Simbirsk "embraced revolutionary socialist politics following his brother's 1887 execution. Expelled from Kazan Imperial University for participating in protests against the Tsarist government, he devoted the following years to a law degree. "He moved to Saint Petersburg in 1893 and became a senior Marxist activist. In 1897, he was arrested for sedition and exiled to Shushenskoye for three years, where he married Nadezhda Krupskaya. After his exile, he moved to Western Europe, where he became a prominent theorist in the Marxist Russian Social Democratic Labor Party (RSDLP). In 1903, he took a key role in a RSDLP ideological split, leading the Bolshevik faction against Julius Martov's Mensheviks. Encouraging insurrection during Russia's failed Revolution of 1905, he later campaigned for the First World War to be transformed into a Europe-wide proletarian revolution, which as a Marxist he believed would cause the overthrow of capitalism and its replacement with socialism. After the 1917 February Revolution ousted the Tsar and established a Provisional Government, he returned to Russia to play a leading role in the October Revolution, in which the Bolsheviks overthrew the new regime."[172]

"Lenin's Bolshevik government initially shared power with the Left Socialist Revolutionaries, elected soviets, and a multiparty Constituent Assembly, although by 1918 it had centralized power in the new Communist Party. Lenin's administration redistributed land among the peasantry and nationalized banks and large-scale industry. It withdrew from the First World War by signing a treaty conceding territory to the Central Powers and promoted world revolution through the Communist International. Opponents were suppressed in the Red Terror, a violent campaign administered by the state security services; tens of thousands were killed or interned in concentration camps. His administration defeated right and left-wing anti-Bolshevik armies in the Russian Civil War from 1917 to 1922 and oversaw the Polish–Soviet War of 1919–1921. Responding to wartime devastation, famine, and popular uprisings, in 1921 Lenin encouraged economic growth through the market-oriented New Economic Policy. Several non-Russian nations had secured independence from the Russian Empire after 1917, but three were re-united into the new Soviet Union in 1922. His health failing, Lenin died in Gorki, and Joseph Stalin succeeded him."[173]

(i) *Theory of Revolution and Revolutionary*: Lenin devoted himself to developing a revolutionary doctrine and applying Marxism to a real situation. Lenin drew the same conclusion as Marx: "Violent revolution is the only action that will bring about meaningful change. Unlike Marx, however, Lenin never wavered from this conviction dedicating himself single-mindedly to the cause of overthrowing the tsars by force. Marx also taught that the revolution would take place when the workers had developed a clear awareness (class-consciousness) of the exploitation and hopelessness of their station...Relying on the trade unions and other agitators to teach the workers to be conscious of the oppression they endured, Marx expected that the proletarian revolution would eventually erupt automatically, ending the bourgeois state and bringing the worker to power. Lenin also contradicted Marx on this point. He argued that the proletariat would not develop class consciousness without the intervention of a revolutionary group. Thinking labor unions too easy for capitalists to control, Lenin believed that a different group was needed to ignite the revolution. To justify this concept, he expanded on Marx's rather than unimportant theory of *the vanguard of the proletariat*...Marx believed the vanguard could speed the approach of revolution by helping the proletariat develop class-consciousness, but he gave the vanguard no other major task...Lenin saw the vanguard itself as the principal revolutionary agent that would overthrow the government and establish a socialist state before the proletariat developed self-awareness."[174]

"This disagreement is what lies behind an important difference in expectations between Marx and Lenin. Marx expected that the proletariat would rebel only after it had become an overwhelming majority in the society and was clearly aware of itself as a class. Consequently, he believed that *the dictatorship of the proletariat* would exist for a relatively brief period during which the small number of remaining non-proletarians would be reeducated, creating a classless society. In Lenin's plan, by contrast, the vanguard would trigger a revolution long before the conditions that Marx anticipated actually developed. In this case, socialism would be imposed on the society by a minority instead of being forced upon the governing elite by the majority. Not only would socialism be hard to attain under these conditions, but the dictatorship of the proletariat would last much longer because such a huge percentage of the population would have to be transformed into socialist proletariat before the ideal society could be realized. Lenin was very specific about the structure of his revolutionary vanguard: *a small, disciplined, totally dedicated group*. It must include only the best in the society because its job of carrying out the revolution demanded total commitment. The vanguard of the proletariat in Russia was the Bolshevik Party (renamed the Communist party in 1918)...You will recall that Marx's statements on the dictatorship of the proletariat were vague. One cannot be sure whether he intended the proletariat to assume the role of dictator itself until only one class existed, or if a dictator was to govern all, including the proletariat. Lenin, on the other hand, was quite specific on this subject. The vanguard of the proletariat was to become a collective dictatorship. In other words, the Bolshevik party would carry out the revolution and then impose a dictatorship on the entire society until it was prepared to enter the utopian stage. Thus...the dictatorship of the proletariat was not to be a dictatorship by the proletariat but a dictatorship of Bolsheviks over the proletariat."[175]

"Lenin also created a structure for the vanguard of the proletariat at the international level. In 1919, he created the International Communist Movement, the Comintern. It was supposed to encourage socialist revolutions throughout Europe. Rebellions in Bulgaria, Hungary, and Germany were successful briefly but were eventually suppressed. These failures were a great disappointment to Lenin and his associates, who were convinced that the Bolshevik could not stay in power long in Russia unless they received some help from the more advanced Western European countries. As it turned out, they not only sustained themselves without help from the West, but they actually resisted concerted Western efforts to bring down the Soviet Union. This success, however, was achieved only at the cost of creating a totalitarian dictatorship under Joseph Stalin. As for the Comintern, while Lenin generally allowed it to function as an international revolutionary catalyst, Stalin turned it into a mere appendage of Soviet foreign policy. Thus, socialist internationalism was overwhelmed by Russian nationalism. In the short run, the efficacy of Lenin's activist and elitist tactics seemed borne out by the 1917 event in Russia. However, while Lenin's scheme successfully brought about the revolution, non-Marxist-Leninists argue that the recent collapse of the Soviet Union proved that Marx was in the long run correct. A successful Marxist society cannot be created by an elite group that imposes from the top down such a society on unwilling masses. Rather, it can only be successful when the people are fully prepared to accept it."[176]

(ii) *Imperialism*: The core of the Marx's theory, dialectic materialism, predicted a proletarian revolution that never occurred. The conditions of labor were "improving in the industrial countries, making the revolution appear to be myth. Hard pressed to explain this seeming contradiction, Lenin studied the trends of capitalism in search of a solution to the dilemma. His conclusion was a cleaver analysis that went far beyond a simple rationalization of Marx's error. Since Marx's death a new kind of capitalism had developed. As he predicted, firms became larger though less numerous, their financial needs growing along with their corporate size. But, needing vast amounts of capital to sustain their huge enterprises, the corporations became increasingly dependent on banks for financing, until the bankers themselves gained control of the monopolies. Marx had not foreseen this new financial structure, which Lenin called finance capitalism. *Finance capitalism* marked a new, much more exploitative stage than the previous condition of industrial capitalism. Under these new conditions the owners of the means of production (bankers and financiers) contributed absolutely nothing to the productivity of the plants they controlled...Lenin believed that the ownership class had begun to realize the truth in the Marxist prediction of a revolution by a proletariat whose misery could no longer be borne. This led the owners to find new sources of cheap labor and resources. Thus, they began to export their exploitation through colonialism."[177]

"The new colonialism, which Lenin called imperialist capitalism, also delayed the proletarian revolution. Driven to increase profits yet needing to protect themselves against a rebellion by their domestic proletariat, the capitalist began to exploit the labor of the colonial people…the capitalists shared some of their new profits with their domestic workers…Allowing themselves to be bought off by profits stolen from the colonial proletariat, the domestic workers became partners in the capitalist exploitation of the unfortunate colonial people. This economic prostitution disgusted Lenin, who saw it as yet another evil policy of the capitalist enemy. Capitalist imperialism, however, was ultimately self-destructive. Eventually, all the colonial resources would be consumed by the various capitalist states. With no more colonies to subdue, the profit-hungry imperialist nations would begin to feed off each other, causing strive and conflict that would end in a general confrontation among the capitalist imperialist powers. Imperialism, Lenin declared in 1916, is *the final stage of capitalism*. It will ultimately lead to a conflict in which the capitalists will destroy each other. Thus, Lenin concluded that World War I was a giant struggle in which the imperialist nations hoped to finally settle their colonial conflicts, and that socialists should take advantage of this conflict by seizing control of Western governments after the capitalists had exhausted…in futile fraternal warfare.[178]

Lenin defined imperialism embracing following five essential points: "(1) The concentration of production and capital developed to such a high stage that it created monopolies which play a decisive role in economic life. (2) The merging of bank capital with industrial capital, and the creation, on the basis of this finance capital, of a financial oligarchy. (3) The export of capital, which has become extremely important, as distinguished from the export of commodities. (4) The formation of international capitalist monopolies which share the world among themselves. (5) The territorial division of the whole world among the greatest capitalist power is completed. Imperialism is capitalism in that stage of development in which the dominance of monopolies and finance capital has established itself…the division of all territories…has been completed."[179] Developing his theory of the weakest link, Lenin argued that colonialism gave the advanced industrial countries a tremendous competitive advantage over the less developed, non-colonialist capitalist states. "If the latter were to compete against the cheap labor and raw materials available to their imperialist opponents, they would have to exploit their own labor force even more. The increased exploitation suffered by the workers in the less advanced countries would naturally push them toward revolution at the very moment when the proletariat of the advance capitalist countries was being bought off with a share of the colonial spoils. Russia, Lenin concluded, was the weakest link in the capitalist chain, making the first Marxist revolution there quite logical. Lenin's multipurpose theory served yet another, unanticipated function."[180]

(iii) ***Achieving the Utopia***: "Lenin outlined the economic and political development of the future workers' paradise. The economic system to be used by the Bolshevik dictatorship of the proletariat was what Lenin called *state socialism*. According to this theory, the state was to control elements of the economy. The workers, employees of the state, would produce a profit and the profit, or surplus value, would then be returned to the society byway of investments to increase productivity, social and governmental programs to aid and protect the citizens, and consumer goods to benefit the society. The formula for the distribution of goods to the citizens is one that colonial Virginia's John Smith would have been proud of : *From each according to his ability, to each according to his work*. This formula is even more practical than it appears at first glance. Marx had seen the dictatorship creating a single proletarian class imbued with the socialist ethic by one of two methods: educating the masses to convince them of the wisdom of socialism, or simply removing them from the society. Here Lenin introduced a third technique for achieving the single-class utopia. Because socialists are supposed to enjoy the process of labor, Lenin expected that they would be more productive than those who did not accept socialism. Paying workers according to the labor they performed would reward the socialists, while the slackers would be penalized for lack of productivity."[181]

"When the nonconformists had been starved into the socialist mold, all the people would be convinced of the value of labor and the utopian stage would be at hand. As more people became proletariat and socialist, class differences would diminish and strife among the people would be reduced. As human strife disappeared, the need for the state would wither away, just as Marx had predicted. Eventually there would emerge a utopian existence in which people might live and work in peace. Sharing their labor, they would also share the fruits of their production. In the utopia the economic system would have evolved from socialism to communism, which Lenin, echoing Marx, describes as an economy in which the people give according to their abilities and take back according to their needs. More practical than Marx, Lenin contradicted the German master several times. More an activist than an ideologue, he has always concerned with the workability of a process, often leaving theoretical inconsistencies to sort themselves out. He ignored the democratic spirit of Marx's theory in favor of an elitist revolution, claiming that its utopian ends justified its extreme means. He violated the dialectic by demanding an early revolution, which he followed with an elitist dictatorship that Marx almost surely never intended. He used his theory of imperialism to describe a stage of capitalism not foreseen by Marx; he then used it to explain why the revolution happened first in Russia and failed to take place in the highly industrialized countries. Finally, along with state socialism, Lenin proposed a new kind of labor exploitation about which Marx would have had serious qualms."[182]

Lenin's Publications: *The Development of Capitalism in Russia* (1896-99) argues that Russia is indeed on the capitalist path and cannot escape the Marxian destiny of a proletarian revolution. *What Is to Be Done?* (1902) argues that Marxists should form a political party. *Imperialism: The Highest Stage of Capitalism* (1917) explains how the mature capitalist government has been able to stave off the inevitable revolution. *The State and Revolution* (1917) describes the role of the state and society, the necessity of proletarian revolution, and the theoretic inadequacies of social democracy in achieving revolution to establish the dictatorship of the proletariat. *The Day After the Revolution* (1917) consists of writings from after the Soviet victory of understanding the philosophical potential of Lenin's revolutionary ideology and its significance to leftism.

Leon Trotsky (1879-1940) was a Soviet revolutionary, Marxist theorist, and politician "whose particular strain of Marxist thought is known as Trotskyism. "Initially supporting the Menshevik-Internationalists faction within the Russian Social Democratic Labor Party, he joined the Bolsheviks just before the 1917 October Revolution, immediately becoming a leader within the Communist Party. He would go on to become one of the seven members of the first Politburo, founded in 1917 to manage the Bolshevik Revolution. During the early days of the Russian Soviet Federative Socialist Republic (RSFSR) and the Soviet Union, he served first as People's Commissar for Foreign Affairs and later as the founder and commander of the Red Army, with the title of People's Commissar of Military and Naval Affairs. He became a major figure in the Bolshevik victory in the Russian Civil War (1918–1922). After leading a failed struggle of the Left Opposition against the policies and rise of Joseph Stalin in the 1920s and against the increasing role of bureaucracy in the Soviet Union, Trotsky was removed as Commissar for Military and Naval Affairs (1925)…expelled from the Communist Party (1927)…and exiled from the Soviet Union (1929). As the head of the Fourth International (1938), Trotsky continued to oppose the Stalinist bureaucracy in the Soviet Union while in exile. Trotsky was assassinated in Mexico City (1940)."[183]

According to a leading Russian historian, "Trotsky bears a great deal of responsibility both for the victory of the Red Army in the civil war, and for the establishment of a one-party authoritarian state with its apparatus for ruthlessly suppressing dissent... He was an ideologist and practitioner of the Red Terror. He despised 'bourgeois democracy'; he believed that spineless-ness and soft-heartedness would destroy the revolution, and that the suppression of the propertied classes and political opponents would clear the historical arena for socialism. He was the initiator of concentration camps, compulsory 'labor camps,' and the militarization of labor, and the state takeover of trade unions. Trotsky was implicated in many practices which would become standard in the Stalin era, including summary executions."[184]

Joseph Stalin (1878-1953): In 1912, Lenin, then in exile in Switzerland, appointed Joseph Stalin to serve on the first Central Committee of the Bolshevik Party. "Three years later, in November 1917, the Bolsheviks seized power in Russia. The Soviet Union was founded in 1922, with Lenin as its first leader. During these years, Stalin had continued to move up the party ladder, and in 1922 he became secretary general of the Central Committee of the Communist Party, a role that enabled him to appoint his allies to government jobs and grow a base of political support. After Lenin died in 1924, Stalin eventually outmaneuvered his rivals and won the power struggle for control of the Communist Party. By the late 1920s, he had become dictator of the Soviet Union."[185]

"Starting in the late 1920s, Joseph Stalin launched a series of five-year plans intended to transform the Soviet Union from a peasant society into an industrial superpower. His development plan was centered on government control of the economy and included the forced collectivization of Soviet agriculture, in which the government took control of farms. Millions of farmers refused to cooperate with Stalin's orders and were shot or exiled as punishment. The forced collectivization also led to widespread famine across the Soviet Union that killed millions. Stalin ruled by terror and with a totalitarian grip in order to eliminate anyone who might oppose him. He expanded the powers of the secret police, encouraged citizens to spy on one another and had millions of people killed or sent to the Gulag system of forced labor camps. During the second half of the 1930s, Stalin instituted the Great Purge, a series of campaigns designed to rid the Communist Party, the military and other parts of Soviet society from those he considered a threat. Additionally, Stalin built a cult of personality around himself in the Soviet Union...In 1939, on the eve of World War II, Joseph Stalin and German dictator Adolf Hitler signed a nonaggression pact. Stalin then proceeded to annex parts of Poland and Romania, as well as the Baltic states of Estonia, Latvia and Lithuania. He also launched an invasion of Finland. Then, in June 1941, Germany...invaded the USSR."[186]

"While some historians view Stalinism as a reflection of the ideologies of Leninism and Marxism, some argue that it stands separate from the socialist ideals it stemmed from. After a political struggle that culminated in the defeat of the Bukharinists, Stalinism was free to shape policy without opposition, ushering forth an era of harsh authoritarianism that soldiered toward rapid industrialization regardless of the cost. From 1917 to 1924, Vladimir Lenin, Leon Trotsky and Stalin often appeared united, but they had discernible ideological differences. In his dispute with Trotsky, Stalin de-emphasized the role of workers in advanced capitalist countries. Stalin also polemicized against Trotsky on the role of peasants as in China whereas Trotsky's position was in favor of urban insurrection over peasant-based guerrilla warfare. Whilst all other October Revolution 1917 Bolshevik leaders regarded their revolution more or less just as the beginning, they saw Russia as the leap-board on the road towards the Worldwide Revolution, Stalin eventually introduced the idea of Socialism in One Country by the autumn of 1924. This did not just stand in sharp contrast to Trotsky's Permanent Revolution, but in contrast also to all earlier Socialistic theses. But by time and through circumstances, the revolution did not spread outside Russia, as Lenin had assumed it soon would. Not even within the other former territories of the Russian Empire such as Poland, Finland, Lithuania, Latvia and Estonia had the revolution been a success. On the contrary, all these countries had returned to capitalist bourgeois rule...by the autumn of 1924, Stalin's idea of socialism in Soviet Russia alone, initially was next to blasphemy in the ears of the other Politburo members."[187]

The Soviet Union was more profoundly affected by Stalin's second revolution in the 1930s than it had been by the October Revolution. Stalin's most import ideological shift was to embrace the doctrine of Socialism in One Country, initially developed by Bukharin. Announced in 1924, this proclaimed that the Soviet Union could succeed in building socialism without the need for international revolution. This clearly distinguished him from his rival for power, Leon Trotsky, who maintained an unswerving commitment to internationalism...However, Stalin oversaw a dramatic economic and political upheaval, commencing with the announcement of the first Five Year Plan in 1928. Under Lenin's New Economic Policy, introduced in 1921, the Soviet Union had developed a mixed economy in which agriculture and small-scale industry remained in private hands, while the state controlled only what Lenin called the commanding heights of the economy. Stalin's Five-Year Plans, however, brought about rapid industrialization...From 1929 agriculture was collectivized, and Soviet peasants were forced at the cost of literally millions of lives to give up their land and join state of collective farms. Economic Stalinism...took the form of state collectivization or state socialism."[188]

Major political changes accompanied this second revolution. "Party officials were appointed from above by a system known as the *nomenklatura*, rather than being elected from below. Democratic centralism became less democratic and more centralized, leading to a circular flow of power in which the party leader acquired unrivalled authority by virtue of his control over patronage and promotion. During the 1930s Stalin used this power to brutal effect, removing anyone suspected of disloyalty or criticism in an increasingly violent series of purges carried out by the secret policy...The membership of the Communist Party was almost halved, over a million people lost their lives...many millions were imprisoned in labor camps, or *gulags*. Political Stalinism was therefore a form of totalitarian dictatorship, operating through a monolithic ruling party, in which all forms of debate or criticism were eradicated by terror."[189]

Maoism - Communism in China: "Maoism is the Chinese communist variety of Marxism–Leninism that Mao Zedong developed for realising a socialist revolution in the agricultural, pre-industrial society of the People's Republic of China. The philosophic difference between Maoism and Marxism–Leninism is that the peasantry is the revolutionary vanguard in pre-industrial societies, rather than the proletariat. From the 1950s until the Chinese economic reforms of Deng Xiaoping in the late 1970s, Maoism was the political and military ideology of the Communist Party of China and of Maoist revolutionary movements throughout the world."[190]

(a) The Initial Stage of the Revolution: "In 1911 the Manchu Dynasty ended with the child emperor, Pu Yi, abdicating in response to over-whelming pressure. The leader of the victorious republican forces was an unimposing, idealistic man, *Dr. Sun Yat-sen* (1866-1925). His ideology was a somewhat confused mixture of Western political theories, mild socialist economic ideas, and Eastern traditions…In the meantime, the Communist Party of China (CPC) was founded in 1921. Attending the first party congress was a radical young school-teacher *Mao Tse-tung* (1893-1976). Coming from a well-to-do peasant family, Mao pursued an education and graduated from a teacher's college in 1918. Although he began at a low rank, his devotion to the cause and his keen insight into the problems of the revolution soon caught the attention of his superiors. The Soviet Union was becoming increasingly interested in China. Lenin sent agents to coordinate the Comintern efforts in China. He favored an alliance between the CPC and the Kuomintang (Sun's political party) against the reactionary elements in China. More important, Stalin also supported such an alliance, actively encouraging it after Lenin became ill in 1923. Repeatedly rebuffed in his appeals for aid from the United States and Western Europe because he was a socialist, Sun Yat-sen turned to the Soviet Union for support, agreeing to the first Communist-Kuomintang alliance (1924-1927). The purpose of the first alliance was to break the power of the reactionary warlords who controlled China's far-flung provinces. The alliance's initial success was darkened in 1925 when Sun Yat-sen died. He was succeeded by his lieutenant *Chang Kai-shek* (1887-1975), a much more conservative leader. As world events made right-wing extremism increasingly acceptable, Chiang's Communist allies became a troublesome embarrassment. Sudden-ly, in 1927 he ordered his armies to attack the communists. The CPC was nearly exterminated by this treachery as Chiang slaughtered all who fell into his hands. In desperation, the communists saved themselves by fleeing the cities to seek safety in the provinces."[191]

The Ruralization of Chinese Communism: "The two years before the Kuo-mintang attacked the communists, Mao had become unhappy with the progress of the revolution. Thus, he had returned to his native Hunan province in southern China and studies the peasantry as a revolutionary force.

In Hunan, Mao produced his first significant work, Report on the *Hunan Peasant Movement*, which called upon communists to abandon the cities for the countryside, because the peasants, not the proletariat were China's true revolutionaries. With this document he laid the foundation of Maoist thought, and it, together with Chiang's betrayal and the communist failure to rouse the proletariat in the cities, ended the domination of the Soviet Union over the CPC. Though always an important factor, Stalin's influence was clearly secondary in China after 1927 as a distinctly Chinese brand of communism began to develop."[192]

The Long March: "Finally gaining an almost decisive military advantage over the communists in 1934, the Kuomintang army surrounded them and threatened their destruction. To avoid annihilation, the communists broke out of the encirclement – leaving their southern base behind – and fled to safety in northern China. This epic retreat, called the Long March, was the low point of the CPC's history and lasted a full year. About 100,000 people set out on a journey that took them 6,000 miles. Since it was more a running battle than a march, scarcely 35,000 survived. As if the hardships of the trek and attacks by the forces of Chiang and the warlords were not enough, the Long March precipitated a leadership struggle within the CPC, and Mao gained the top position in the party...it made him dominant in the movement...The march finally ended in Shensi province in north-central China, where a new base was established in 1936. Hostilities between the communists and the Kuomintang would have continued if the Japanese had not become an overriding threat in the same year. Ever the nationalistic pragmatist, Stalin encouraged the Chinese communists to form a new alliance with the Koumintang because he wanted to preoccupy Japan with a war in China, thus preventing it from invading the Soviet Union. This alliance actually only a truce, however, permitting two enemies to deal with a third force threatening both. Nevertheless, the war efforts of each partner were restrained, since each saved its energy for the inevitable struggle that would take place when the Japanese were defeated."[193]

When the Japanese were finally vanquished in 1945, the China question emerged once again. The United States, which clearly favored the Koumintang, tried to negotiate a coalition government between Mao and Chiang. Ironically, Stalin, who believed that the communists could not yet defeat Chiang, also pressured Mao to join in a coalition government. Mao and Chiang were both convinced that they could win the struggle, however, so they each refused to compromise. The upshot was the last phase of the belligerent period of the Chinese Revolution (1946-1949), as the two sides locked in mortal combat. Because he had not been able to control the warlords and because his government was cruel. Corrupt, and foolish, Chiang had lost popular support. His military superiority, so obvious on paper, melted away. Mao, on the other hand, enjoyed great popular support in the north and considerable appeal in the south. A series of stunning defeats saw Chiang giving ground until finally, in 1949, all was lost, and he fled to the island province of Taiwan."[194]

(b) The Political Stage of the Revolution: "The communist regime in China has been marked by a series of important, sometimes traumatic, events. Mao Tse-tung remained a radical force in Chinese politics, often plunging China into tumultuous programs aimed at achieving great goals for his people. When they failed, the reform periods were followed by period of consolidation that evolved into the staging grounds for the next set of Mao's radical reforms. This behavior pattern was repeated again and again."

The First Five Year Plan: "Moving quickly but cautiously, Mao struck at the absentee landlords who dominated China's vast countryside. Knowing the peasants would have to be led gradually to collectivized farming, he encouraged them to join the authorities in taking the land from its absent and exploitative owners. In only two years this popular policy saw most of the large estates reduced to peasant ownership. At the same time, Mao launched drives to increase social justice. Perhaps the most important of these campaigns was to improve the status of women. Declaring that 'women hold up half the sky,' Mao demanded that women be freed from traditional male bondage."[195] "The next task was to socialize the economy. The first Five-Year Plan, based on the Soviet model, was designed to achieve economic centralization. Its goals were to increase heavy industrial production, socialize light industry and retail enterprises, and collectivize the farms. Though heavy industrial production improved considerably, resistance to the socialization program grew in intensity until forceful measures were used. Although the merchants and artisans were displeased by the takeover of their business, the greatest problems faced by the collectivization program arose on the farms. Mindful of the disastrous Soviet experience, however, the Chinese collectivized the firms more gradually. Eventually, private ownership of the land was abandoned altogether, and the peasant found themselves on giant communes. By 1957 the goals of the first Five-Year Plan had been largely achieved...Yet, political conditions within the party remained unsettled. Khrushchev's de-Stalinization campaign encouraged for a brief moment attempts at liberalizing reforms within the Soviet bloc. Meanwhile, the moderate in the CPC, the army, and the government believed that Mao had outlived his usefulness and began to maneuver for the old radical's retirement. For his part, Mao felt exposed. The adulation accorded him by the masses suddenly became uncomfortably similar to Stalin's personality cult. Wishing to disassociate himself with his former personality cult policy and hoping to outflank his moderate detractors, Mao surprised his adversaries with a sudden liberalization of his own."[196]

Great Leap Forward: "In 1958, after China's first Five-Year Plan, Mao called for 'grassroots socialism' in order to accelerate his plans for turning

China into a modern industrialized state. In this spirit, Mao launched the Great Leap Forward, established People's Communes in the countryside, and began the mass mobilization of the people into collectives. Many communities were assigned production of a single commodity—steel. Mao vowed to increase agricultural production to twice 1957 levels."[197]

"The Great Leap was an economic failure. Many uneducated farmers were pulled from farming and harvesting and instead instructed to produce steel on a massive scale, partially relying on backyard furnaces to achieve the production targets set by local cadres. The steel produced was low quality and largely useless. The Great Leap reduced harvest sizes and led to a decline in the production of most goods except substandard pig iron and steel. Furthermore, local authorities frequently exaggerated production numbers, hiding and intensifying the problem for several years. In the meantime, chaos in the collectives, bad weather, and exports of food necessary to secure hard currency resulted in the Great Chinese Famine... The famine caused the deaths of 30+ million people."[198]

"The Great Leap's failure reduced Mao's prestige within the Party. Forced to take major responsibility, in 1959, Mao resigned as the President of the People's Republic of China...and was succeeded by Liu Shaoqi. In July, senior Party leaders convened at the scenic Mount Lu to discuss policy. At the conference, Marshal Peng Dehuai, the Minister of Defense, criticized Great Leap policies in a private letter to Mao, writing that it was plagued by mismanagement and cautioning against elevating political dogma over the laws of economics. Despite the moderate tone of Peng's letter, Mao took it as a personal attack against his leadership. Following the Conference, Mao had Peng removed from his posts, and accused him of being a right-opportunist. Peng was replaced by Lin Biao, another revolutionary army general who became a stauncher Mao supporter later in his career. While the Lushan Conference served as a death knell for Peng, Mao's most vocal critic, it led to a shift of power to moderates led by Liu Shaoqi and Deng Xiaoping, who took effective control of the economy following 1959."[199]

The Cultural Revolution was a sociopolitical movement in the People's Republic of China from 1966 until 1976. "Launched by Mao Zedong, then Chairman of the Communist Party of China, its stated goal was to preserve Chinese Communism by purging remnants of capitalist and traditional elements from Chinese society, and to re-impose Mao Zedong Thought (Maoism) as the dominant ideology in the Communist Party of China. The Revolution marked Mao's return to a position of power after a period of less radical leadership to recover from the failures of the Great Leap Forward, whose leftist policies led to a famine and approximately 30 million deaths only 5 years earlier. The Cultural Revolution paralyzed China politically, damaged its economy and society, and killed an estimated 500,000 to 2,000,000 people. Mao launched the movement in May 1966, soon calling on young people to bombard the headquarters and proclaiming that "to rebel is justified". Mao charged that bourgeois elements had infiltrated the government and society and that they aimed to restore capitalism. Lin Biao, head of the People's Liberation Army (PLA), was written into the constitution as Mao's successor; Lin had compiled the Little Red Book, a selection of Mao's sayings, that became a sacred text for Mao's personality cult. To eliminate his rivals within the Communist Party of China (CPC) and in schools, factories, and government institutions, Mao insisted that revisionists be removed through violent class struggle." [200]

China's youth responded by forming Red Guard groups around the country, which split into rival factions and sometimes open battle. Schools and universities were closed. Urban workers likewise split into factions, and the PLA had to be sent to restore order. Senior officials, most notably Liu Shaoqi and Deng Xiaoping, were purged or exiled. Millions of people were accused of being Rightists, and persecuted or suffered public humiliation, imprisonment, torture, hard labor, seizure of property, and sometimes execution or harassment into suicide. Many urban intellectual youths were sent to the countryside in the Down to the Countryside Movement. Red Guards destroyed historical relics and artifacts or ransacked cultural and religious sites. Mao officially ended the Cultural Revolution in 1969, but its active phase lasted until at least 1971, when Lin Biao fled and died in a plane crash, accused of plotting to overthrow Mao. After Mao's death and the arrest of the Gang of Four in 1976, Deng Xiaoping gradually dismantled the Maoist policies associated with the Cultural Revolu-tion. In 1981, the Party declared that the Cultural Revolution was responsible for the most severe setback and the heaviest losses suffered by the Party, the country, and the people since the founding of the People's Republic." [201]

On June 27, 1981, the Central Committee adopted the *Resolution on Certain Questions in the History of Our Party…* officially affirming that the Cultural Revolution brought serious disaster and turmoil to the Communist Party and the Chinese people, in terms of Communist Party opinions.

(c) The Principles of Maoism: "The two differences between Maoism and Marxism are how the proletariat are defined and what political and economic conditions would start a communist revolution: (1) For Karl Marx, the proletariat were the urban working class, which was determined in the revolution by which the bourgeoisie overthrew feudalism. For Mao Zedong, the proletariat were the millions of peasants, to whom he referred as the popular masses. Mao based his revolution upon the peasants, because they possessed two qualities: (i) they were poor, and (ii) they were a political blank slate; in Mao's words, 'A clean sheet of paper has no blotches, and so the newest and most beautiful words can be written on it'. (2) For Marx, proletarian revolution was internally fueled, by the capitalist mode of production; that, as capitalism developed, a tension arises between the

productive forces and the mode of production. The political tension between the productive forces (the workers) and the owners of the means of production (the capitalists) would be an inevitable incentive to proletarian revolution, which would result in a Communist society as the main economic structure. Mao did not subscribe to Marx's proposal of inevitable cyclicality in the economic system. His goal was to unify the Chinese nation and so realize progressive change for China in the form of Communism, hence, revolution was needed as soon as possible. In The Great Union of the Popular Masses (1919), Mao said: The decadence of the state, the sufferings of humanity, and the darkness of society have all reached an extreme."[202]

(i) *New Democracy*: "The theory of the New Democracy was known to the Chinese revolutionaries from the late 1940s. This thesis held that for the majority of the people of the planet, the long road to socialism could only be opened by a national, popular, democratic, anti-feudal and anti-imperialist revolution, run by the communists."[203]

(ii) *People's war*: "Maoism emphasizes the revolutionary struggle of the vast majority of people against the exploiting classes and their state structures, which Mao termed a people's war. Mobilizing large parts of rural populations to revolt against established institutions by engaging in guerrilla warfare…focuses on surrounding the cities from the countryside."[204]

(iii) *Mass line*: "Contrary to the Leninist vanguard model employed by the Bolsheviks, the theory of the mass line holds that party must not be separate from the popular masses, either in policy or in revolutionary struggle. To conduct a successful revolution the needs and demands of the masses must be told to the party so that the party can interpret them."[205]

(iv) *Cultural Revolution*: "The theory of the Cultural Revolution states that the proletarian revolution and the dictatorship of the proletariat does not wipe out bourgeois ideology—the class-struggle continues and even intensifies during socialism, therefore, a constant struggle against these ideologies and their social roots must be conducted…is directed also against traditionalism." The road to socialism must be a permanent revolution.[206]

(v) *Contradiction*: Matter always develops through a dialectical contradiction: "The interdependence of the contradictory aspects present in all things and the struggle between these aspects determine the life of things and push their development forward. There is nothing that does not contain contradiction; without contradiction nothing would exist…Revolution is necessary to fully resolve antagonistic contradictions."[207]

(vi) *Three Worlds Theory*: "Three Worlds Theory states that during the Cold War two imperialist states formed the first world—the United States and the Soviet Union. The second world consisted of the other imperialist states in their spheres of influence. The third world consisted of the non-imperialist countries. Both the first and the second world exploit the third world, but the first world is the most aggressive party. The workers in the first and second world are bought up by imperialism, preventing socialist revolution. On the other hand, the people of the third world have not even a short-sighted interest in the prevailing circumstances, hence revolution is most likely to appear in third world countries."[208]

(vii) *Agrarian socialism*: Maoism departs from European-inspired Marxism in that its focus is on the agrarian countryside, rather than the industrial urban forces—this is known as agrarian socialism. Maoist parties in Peru, Nepal, and the Philippines have adopted equal stresses on urban and rural areas, depending on the country's focus of economic activity. Maoism broke with the state capitalist framework of the Soviet Union under Nikita Khrushchev, dismissing it as revisionist, a pejorative term among communists referring to those who fight for capitalism in the name of socialism and who depart from historical and dialectical materialism."[209]

(viii) *Guerrilla warfare*: "Perhaps the Maoist idea most widely applied is the theory of guerrilla warfare. Both Marx and Lenin believed that power could be seized at a single stroke and that the violent portion of a Marxist revolution would be very short. The two differed only on tactics, Marx believing that the revolution would happen by itself, Lenin supporting a conspiratorial approach. Mao, by contrast, argued that revolutions in the less developed world would have to extend over a long period. Lacking a doctrine to justify such a revolution, Mao developed one himself, setting down its principles in his famous work *Yu Chi Chan* (Guerrilla Warfare). In this book, Mao divides guerrilla warfare into two basic parts: military and political. Mao saw the military part of a guerrilla war as having three distinct phases. During the first phase the soldiers concentrate on building secure bases, or safe zones, in which to rest, refit, and training their troops. The second phase involves numerous small groups attacking the enemy by means of ambush and other guerrilla activities. The final phase begins only after victory is certain and consists of large troop maneuvers and battles similar to those of a conventional war.'"[210]

"The military goal of a guerrilla war is very clear. The first law of war, Mao wrote, is to preserve ourselves and destroy the enemy. Mao clearly warns against seeing territorial gains as a major goal. The only real objective must be to destroy the fighting capacity of the opponents. With this in mind Mao also warned that a guerrilla force should carefully choose when it fights, avoiding any battel it is unsure of winning. The only territory essential to the guerrilla is the safe zones…In a guerrilla war, there may be no defensive battles. If any area is given up to a superior force, with patience and cunning it will be regained later. This strategy is most clearly expressed in Mao's famous dictum, 'When guerrillas engage a stronger enemy, they withdraw when he advances; harass him when he stops; strike when he is weary, pursue him when he withdraws'." "More important to Mao than military operations were the political activities of the guerrilla force."[211]

Democratic Socialism is a political philosophy that advocates political democracy alongside a socially owned economy, "with an emphasis on workers' self-management and democratic control of economic institutions within a market or some form of a decentralized planned socialist economy. Democratic socialists argue that capitalism is inherently incompatible with the values of freedom, equality and solidarity and that these ideals can be achieved only through the realization of a socialist society. Although most democratic socialists are seeking a gradual transition to socialism, democritic socialism can support either revolutionary or reformist politics as a means to establish socialism. Democratic socialism is distinguished from Marxist–Leninist-inspired socialism which to many is viewed as being undemocratic or authoritarian in practice. Democratic socialists oppose the Stalinist political system and the Soviet-type economic system, rejecting the perceived authoritarian form of governance and highly centralized command economy that took form in the Soviet Union and other Marxist–Leninist states in the early 20th century."[212]

"Democratic socialism is also distinguished from reformist social democracy on the basis that democratic socialists are committed to systemic transformation of the economy from capitalism to socialism whereas social democrats are opposed to ultimately ending capitalism and are instead supportive of progressive reforms to capitalism. In contrast to modern social democrats, democratic socialists believe that policy reforms and state interventions aimed at addressing social inequalities and suppressing the economic contradictions of capitalism will ultimately exacerbate the contradictions, seeing them emerge elsewhere in the economy under a different guise. Democratic socialists believe the fundamental issues with capitalism are systemic in nature and can only be resolved by replacing the capitalist economic system with socialism, i.e. by replacing private owner-ship with collective ownership of the means of production and extending democracy to the economic sphere. The origins of democratic socialism can be traced to 19th-century utopian socialist thinkers and the British Chartist movement that differed in detail, yet all shared the essence of democratic decision making and public ownership of the means of production as positive characteristics of the society they advocated. In the late 19th century and early 20th century, democratic socialism was also influenced by social democracy. For instance, the gradualist, reformist socialism promoted by the British Fabian Society and Eduard Bernstein's evolutionary socialism in Germany influenced…democratic socialism."[213]

In his *Contemporary Political Ideologies*: *A Comparative Analysis* (2008), Lyman Tower Sargent writes that "The Principles of Democratic Socialism can be characterized as follows: (i) Much property held by the public through a democratically elected government, including most major industries, utilities, and transportation systems; (ii) A limit on the accumulation of private property; (iii) Governmental regulation of the economy; (iv) Extensive publicly financed assistance and pension programs; (v) Social costs and the provision of services added to purely financial considerations as the measure of efficiency. Publicly held property is limited to productive property and significant infrastructure; it does not extend to personal property, homes, and small businesses. And in practice in many democratic socialist countries, it has not extended to many large corporations."[214]

Some tendencies of democratic socialism advocate for revolution in order to transition to socialism, distinguishing it from some form of social democracy. "Democratic socialists have promoted a variety of different models of socialism ranging from market socialism where socially-owned enterprises operate in competitive markets and are self-managed by their workforce to non-market participatory socialism based on decentralized economic planning. Historically, democratic socialism has been committed to a decentralised form of economic planning where productive units are integrated into a single organization and organized on the basis of self-management as opposed to Soviet-style economies in Marxist–Leninist states...Democratic socialists, especially contemporary proponents of market socialism, have argued that...the major reason for the economic shortcomings of Soviet-type economies was their failure to create rules and operational criteria for the efficient operation of state enterprises in their administrative, command allocation of resources and commodities and the lack of democracy in the political systems that the Soviet-type economies were combined with. As a result, their form of socialism explicitly rejects authoritarian allocation in favor of democracy."[215]

After the Cold War, many democratic socialist parties have adopted neoliberal market policies - privatization, deregulation and financialization. "They abandoned their pursuit of moderate socialism in favor of market liberalism...In the late-1990s, the Labor Party under the leadership of Tony Blair enacted policies based on the liberal market economy to deliver public services via the private finance initiative. Influential in these policies was the idea of a Third Way which called for a re-evaluation of welfare state policies. In 1995, the Labor Party re-defined its position on socialism by re-wording Clause IV of their Constitution, effectively rejecting socialism by removing all references to public, direct worker or municipal ownership of the means of production." Now the Constitution stated: "The Labor Party is a democratic socialist party. It believes that, by the strength of our common endeavor we achieve more than we achieve alone, so as to create, for each of us, the means to realize our true potential, and, for all of us, a community in which power, wealth, and opportunity are in the hands of the many, not the few'." Democratic socialism became a synonym in American politics more recently for social democracy due to social democratic policies being adopted by progressives and reform liberals."[216]

(a) ***Ethical Socialism***: As discussed, "Marx's scientific method was based upon historical materialism, the belief that human thought and behavior are conditioned by the economic circumstances of life." Socialism is portrayed as morally superior to capitalism because human beings are ethical creatures, bound to one another by the ties of love, sympathy and compassion. Such ideas have often given socialism a markedly utopian character. The moral vision that underlies ethical socialism has been based upon both humanistic and religious principles." Socialism in France, the UK and other Commonwealth countries has been more strongly influenced by the utopian ideas than by the scientific creed of Karl Marx. "The Christian ethic that has inspired British socialism is that of universal brotherhood, the respect that should be accorded all individuals as creations of God, a principle embodied in the commandment 'Though shalt love thy neighbor as thyself'. In his *The Acquisitive Society* (1921), R. H. Tawney (1880-1962) condemned unregulated capitalism because it is driven by the sin of avarice rather than faith in a common humanity. In *Equality* (1931) Tawney condemned the British class system as particularly detestable to Christians and called for a substantial reduction of social inequality."[217]

"Such religious inspiration has also been evident in the ideas of liberation theology, which has influenced many Catholic developing world states, especially in Latin America. After years of providing support for repressive regimes in Latin America, Roman Catholic bishops meeting at Medellin, Colombia, in 1968 declared a preferential option for the poor. The religious responsibilities of the clergy were seen to extend beyond the narrowly spiritual and to embrace the social and political struggle of ordinary people. Despite the condemnation of Pope John Paul II and the Vatican, radical priests in many parts of Latin America campaigned against poverty and political oppression and at times even backed socialist revolutionary movements. Similarly, socialist movements in the predominantly Muslim countries of North Africa, the Middle East and Asia have been inspired by religion. Islam is linked to socialism in that it exhorts the principles of social justice, charity and cooperation, and...prohibits usury of profiteering. In abandoning scientific analysis in favor of moral or religious principles, however, social democracy weakened the theoretical basis of socialism. Social democracy has been primarily concerned with the notion of a just or fair distribution of wealth in society. This is embodied in the overriding principle of social democracy: social justice, implying a commitment to greater equality and reflected in values such as caring and compassion. Social democracy consequently came to stand for a broad range of views, extending from a left-wing commitment to extending equality and expanding the collective ownership of wealth, to more right-wing acceptance of the need for market efficiency and individual self-reliance...indistinguishable from...liberalism or conservatism."[218]

(b) ***Revisionist Socialism***: Eduard Bernstein (1850-1932) had held close association to Karl Marx and Friedrich Engels, "but he saw flaws in Marxist thinking and began to criticize views held by Marxism when he investigated and challenged the Marxist materialist theory of history. He rejected significant parts of Marxist theory…based upon Hegelian metaphysics and rejected the Hegelian dialectical perspective."[219] In *Evolutionary Socialism* (1898), Bernstein. saw little evidence that the specter of Communism was still haunting Europe. "Rather than class conflict intensifying, dividing capitalist society into two great classes, the bourgeoisie and the proletariat, Bernstein suggested that capitalism was becoming increasingly complex and differentiated…the ownership of wealth had widened as a result of the introduction of joint stock companies, owned by a number of shareholders, instead of a single powerful industrialist. The ranks of the middle classes had also swollen, the throwing number of salaried employees, technicians, government officials and professional workers being neither capitalists nor proletarians. In Bern-stein's view, capitalism was no longer a system of naked class oppression. Capitalism could…be reformed by the nationalization of major industries and the extension of legal protection and welfare benefits to the working class, a process which Bernstein was confident could be achieve peacefully and democratically."[220]

"An attempt to give theoretical substance to these developments, and in effect update Bernstein, was made by the UK politician and social theorist Anthony Crosland (1908-77) in the *Future of Socialism* (1956). Crosland argued that modern capitalism bore little resemblance to the nineteenth century model that Marx had had in mind. Crosland was influenced by the ideas of James Burnham (1905-87), who *in The Managerial Revolution* (1941) suggested that a new class of managers, experts and technocrats had sur-planted the old capitalist class and come to dominate all advanced industrial societies, both capitalist and communist. Crosland believed that the ownership of wealth had become divorced from its control. Whereas shareholders are principally concerned with profit, salaried managers, who make day-to-day business decisions, have a broader range of goals, including the maintenance of industrial harmony as well as the public image of their company. Marxism had therefore become irrelevant; if capitalism could no longer be viewed as a system of class exploitation, the fundamentalist goals of nationalization and planning were simply outdated. However,…Crosland remained faithful to the goal of social justice, which he understood to mean a more equal distribution of wealth. Wealth need not be owned in common, it could be redistributed through a welfare state, financed by progressive taxation. The welfare state would raise the living standards of the poor and the more vulnerable sections in society, while progressive taxation would ensure that the prosperous and strong bore the burden of expanded welfare support."[221]

(c) Compatibility of Socialism and Democracy: Among scholars who argued that socialism and democracy are compatible, Joseph Schumpeter was hostile to socialism. "In his book *Capitalism, Socialism and Democracy* (1942), Schumpeter emphasizes that political democracy was thoroughly compatible with socialism in its fullest sense, noting that he did not believe that democracy was a good political system, but rather advocated republican values." In 1963, Indian Prime Minister Jawaharlal Nehru stated that "Political Democracy has no meaning if it does not embrace economic democracy. And economic democracy is nothing but socialism." Political historian Theodore Draper wrote that "I know of no political group which has resisted totalitarianism in all its guises more steadfastly than democratic socialists." Historian and economist Robert Heilbroner argued that "there is, of course, no conflict between such a socialism and freedom as we have described it; indeed, this conception of socialism is the very epitome of these freedoms, referring to open association of individuals in political and social life; the democratization and humanization of work; and the cultivation of personal talents and creativities." Bayard Rustin, long-time member of the Socialist Party of America and National Chairman of the Social Democrats, USA, wrote: "For me, socialism has meaning only if it is democratic. Of the many claimants to socialism only one has a valid title—that socialism which views democracy as valuable per se, which stands for democracy unequivocally, and which continually modifies socialist ideas and programs in the light of democratic experience. This is the socialism of the labor, social-democratic, and socialist parties of Western Europe."[222]

Table II-3-2. Tensions within Socialism: Social Democracy vs. Communism

Social Democracy (Eduard Bernstein)	*Communism* (Lenin, Stalin, Mao)
Ethical socialism	Scientific Socialism
Revisionism	Fundamentalism
Reformism	Utopianism
Evolution/Gradualism	Revolution
Humanize capitalism	Abolish Capitalism
Ameliorate Class Conflict	Classless Society
Relative Equality	Absolute Equality
Mixed Economy	State Collectivization
Economic Management	Central Planning
Parliamentary Party	Vanguard Party
Political Pluralism	Dictatorship of Proletariat
Liberal-Democratic State	Proletarian/People's State

Source: Andrew Heywood, Political Ideologies: An Introduction, 3rd ed. (New York: Palgrave Macmillan, 2003), 145.

4. Capitalism and Economic Development

As discussed previously, Joseph Schumpeter views that capitalism is being killed by its achievements, and a socialism form of society will inevitably emerge from an equally inevitable decomposition of capitalist society. But the collapse of communism evidenced that democratic politics cannot be successful without free market economy.

The capitalist economy pursues economic growth by maximizing the objective function (profits) subject to constraints (available resources). The growth of national income or GDP is generated by two ways: one is to use more inputs including labor, capital, and other resources with corresponding demand such as increased population or new territory; the other is the productivity growth with advanced technology and improved management, introducing new goods and services to the markets.[223]

Economic efficiency can be achieved, in the general equilibrium, by maximizing utility subject to budget constraint for consumption; maximizing output subject to unit cost in production; and equalizing the marginal rate of substitution (MRS) in consumption with the marginal rate of technical substitution in production for exchange. In order to optimize social welfare, we may face conflicts of economic efficiency with income equality, from which the government chooses either growth policy or distribution policy; that is the main issue of contemporary political economy.

When trade takes place between two or more nations, various factors such as politics and law, economy, science and technology, society and culture affect trade. Considering comparative advantages of two nations, nation A and nation B can enjoy higher utility at point E where the combined indifference curve of (A+B) hits the line connecting two transaction points on the production possibility frontiers of each nation. Tariffs and trade barriers are used to protect domestic consumers or producers as well as national security. However, "tariffs have a negative effect on economic growth and economic welfare while free trade and the reduction of trade barriers has a positive effect on economic growth."[224]

Finally, the capitalist states try to maximize profits, more GDP, or efficiency that is output divided by input; increasing the income gap between the rich and the poor. In order to reduce income inequality, the government collects more taxes from the rich and uses them to build more and better infrastructure, improve education and health care, and provide social services for the less advantaged peoples. However, the available resources are so limited that the government cannot fully meet the demand of the poor. If the government collect high taxes above the acceptable limit, taxpayers refuse to obey, and the state cannot maintain law and order, just like in the former USSR. Hence, capitalist efficiency in economy and democratic equality in politics should compromise each other.

ALLOCATION OF RECOURCES
AVAILABLE RESOURCES AND POPULATION

Allocation of Resources: "In the traditional static economic theory, allocation of resources is regarded as optimal or efficient when any transfer of resources between different sectors will not raise real national income any further. The principle to obtain such a point of optimality is to equate marginal productivities of different inputs in alternative activities. However, the peculiar characteristics of the LDCs generally account for a separate discussion of *the investment criteria*. For example, the different markets in the LDCs are so imperfect that the market prices of resources, i.e. wages and interest, do not reflect their true social opportunity costs. Thus, market prices may give wrong signals for allocating resources and, given the divergences between the marginal private net benefits (net costs) and marginal social net benefits (net of costs), the use of marginal principles will result in misallocation of resources. Second, the LDCs may not be interested in the static principles of resource allocation. Given these principles, the LDCs may wish to maximize immediate rather than future output and consumption. But this may not lead to the attainment of a future optimal level. Third, it is normal in the application of the static principles that the existing distribution of income is assumed to be optimal and remains unaltered by the choice of development strategy. This is questionable if the choice of a strategy leads to maximum output but a more uneven distribution of income. That this can occur in practice has been shown in the process of Green Revolution in many LDCs. Fourth, the question of externalities in many sectors could well lead to divergencies between social and private costs."[225]

In addition to this, "Problems of investment criteria in LDCs are also related to macro and micro level decision-making processes. However, these processes could be, and sometimes are, interrelated. Thus, the planners may have to decide on the sectoral allocation of investments. Next, within the different sectors, given the resources, decisions regarding the choice of projects should be made; finally, the project managers must also decide the techniques of production, given the relative prices of different inputs. The choice of techniques could easily be influenced by the sectoral allocation of resources. Likewise, project allocation could be influenced by sectoral allocation. Again the choice of techniques may influence project allocation. The debate among the different schools advocating different investment criteria has generally centered round the question of allocating scarce inputs in the LDCs (usually capital and sometimes foreign exchange) in the most efficient way to attain the best combination between present and future consumption, subject to the economic and social constraints. Since the arguments are different, and each has some merits and limits, we will proceed to discuss them in turn."

(a) The Capital Turnover Criterion: "The problems of investment strategies in most LDCs center round the choice of values of the different variables of the Harrod-Domar growth model to maximize growth rates. Assuming that S is the saving-income ratio and C is the capital-output ratio, the Harrod-Domar model states that g=S/C where g is the rate of growth of output. It is obvious from this equation that to raise the growth rate we are required either to raise S or to lower the value of C." Given the scarcity of capital in LDCs, C should be minimized in this model. This is known as the capital turnover criteria. Given some capital scarcity in LDCs, a high capital turnover criterion would lead to an efficient allocation of resources. However, the theory is criticized on many grounds. (i) The use of this criterion ignores the externalities arising out of investments. Given the complementarities of different projects, a project which involves a higher capital-output ratio need not be assigned always a lower priority. (ii) The time element plays a crucial role because quick-yielding projects with a lower capital-output ratio in the short run do not necessarily have a lower ratio in the long run. (iii) In some projects, particularly within the agricultural sector in LDCs, fixed capital may form a small proportion of total inputs of working capital. The fixed capital-output ratio may fluctuate substantially because of factors other than capital investment. (iv) The use of the capital turnover criterion may go against the objective of maximizing the rate of economic growth if resources such as skill and management are scarce."[226]

(b) The Social Marginal Productivity Criterion: It has been contended that in allocating investment, it is necessary to consider the total net contribution of the marginal unit of investment to national output (i.e. the social marginal productivity, SMP) and not merely portion of contribution (or of its costs) which may accrue to the private investor. "Efficient allocation consists of maximizing the value of national product and the principle to obtain this objective is to equate the SMP of capital in different uses. Where the social opportunity cost of labor is zero there is no difference between the capital turnover criterion and the SMP criterion." "The SMP principle also suffers from the following major criticisms. (i) The SMP principles ignores the multiplier effects on future income levels. (ii) The SMP criterion does not make due allowance for the changes in the nature and quality of factors of production such as population and labor that may take place as a result of present investment. (iii) In the labor-surplus economies where the opportunity cost of labor may be zero, the SMP criterion is open to the same criticisms as can be levelled against the capital turnover criterion."[227]

(c) The Rate of Creation of Investible Surplus: The main objective is to maximize per capita real income at the future point of time, by emphasizing the role of capital accumulation to achieve a higher rate of growth. The main argument rests on following premises. "First, national income can be divided into two parts: wages and profits. Second, wage

earners savings are zero but profit earners, which makes output per unit of labor a function of capital per unit of labor, prevails in the whole economy. Third, one production function, which makes output per unite of labor a function of capital per unit of labor, prevails in the whole economy. Given these assumptions, maximization of per capital real income at some future point of time would require an increase of capital per unit of labor at present. This implies the maximization of investment at each preceding period which in turn requires that profit share in national income should maximize (or wage share be minimized). The implication is to choose those projects which involve higher capital intensity, i.e. where the capital-labor ratio is highest. Allocation efficiency is achieved by distributing the available capital in different uses in such a way that the marginal per capita reinvestment quotient of capital is equal in different projects."[228]

In evaluation, "Per capita real income maximization at some future point of time has not been considered as a very realistic goal." "There is not enough evidence to assume that the propensity of the workers to save will be zero and that of the profit earners will be equal to one." "Maximum use of capital in some projects may well reduce the rate of profit particularly where we do not assume that production is the same function of capital for all sectors." In labor-surplus economies, large unemployment may well be a social and political objective, which may call for the use of the capital turnover rather than the rate of creation of investible surplus.[229]

(d) The Re-investible Surplus Criterion: In this model, the economy is divided into two sectors: one is modern, the other is backward. The modern sector is again subdivided into two parts: sector A is producing machinery with only labor, and sector B is producing corn by using machinery and labor. In the backward sector corn (i.e. a consumer good) is produced by labor alone. Labor productivity in the modern sector A is given by the capital intensity of the technology applied there where the capital intensity is given by the total number of man-years necessary in sector A to turn out enough machinery for one unit of labor in sector B. The model distinguishes between the following aims: "(i) maximization of current output (i.e. corn); (ii) maximization of the rate of growth of output; (iii) maximization of the undiscounted flow of output over a finite period of time. The choice of capital intensity will differ according to the nature of the objective. Sen (1968) describes how a conflict can arise between the current output maximization principle and the criterion to maximize the rate of growth of output." [230] The choice between maximization of output and that of employment is more complex than the previous analysis would suggest. "Output is a heterogenous concept; so is employment. Since both output and employment change over time and since present output and employment may affect future levels, both intra- and inter-temporal weighting is very important. It is possible to state that generation of more output (with given

capital and technology) will require more labor and to that extent the conflict between the objectives to maximize employment and output is more apparent than real. However, the conflict between the two objectives would be more real if it is assumed that a new technology is chosen."[231]

(e) Balanced and Unbalanced Growth: (i) *The balanced growth theory* is pioneered by Ragnar Nurkse (1907–1959). "The theory hypothesizes that the government of any underdeveloped country needs to make large investments in a number of industries simultaneously. This will enlarge the market size, increase productivity, and provide an incentive for the private sector to invest. Nurkse was in favor of attaining balanced growth in both the industrial and agricultural sectors of the economy. He recognized that the expansion and inter-sectoral balance between agriculture and manufacturing is necessary so that each of these sectors provides a market for the products of the other and in turn, supplies the necessary raw materials for the development and growth of the other. Nurkse and Paul Rosenstein-Rodan were the pioneers of balanced growth theory and much of how it is understood today dates back to their work. Nurkse's theory discusses how the poor size of the market in underdeveloped countries perpetuates its underdeveloped state. Nurkse has also clarified the various determinants of the market size and puts primary focus on productivity. According to him, if the productivity levels rise in a less developed country, its market size will expand and…become a developed economy."[232]

(ii) *Unbalanced Growth Theory*: According to Albert O. Hirschman, "Underdeveloped countries display common characteristics: low levels of GNI per capita and slow GNI per capita growth, large income inequalities and widespread poverty, low levels of productivity, great dependence on agriculture, a backward industrial structure, a high proportion of consumption and low savings, high rates of population growth and dependency burdens, high unemployment and underemployment, technological backwardness and dualism (existence of both traditional and modern sectors). In a less-developed country, these characteristics lead to scarce resources or inadequate infrastructure to exploit these resources. With a lack of investors and entrepreneurs, cash flows cannot be directed into various sectors that influence balanced economic growth."[233]

Unbalancing the Economy: "Development, according to Hirschman, can take place only by unbalancing the economy. This is possible by investing either in social overhead capital (SOC) or indirectly productive activities (DPA). Social overhead capital creates external economies whereas directly productive activities appropriate them. (i) Excess of investment in Social Overhead Capital: Social over-head capital are concerned with those series without which primary, secondary and tertiary services cannot function. In SOC we include investment on education, public health, irrigation, water drainage, electricity etc. Investment in SOC favorably affect private investment in directly productive activities (DPA). Investment in SOC is called autonomous investment which is made with the motive of private profit...Similarly irrigation facilities lead to development of agriculture. As imbalance is created in SOC, it will lead to investment in DPA. (ii) Excess of Investment in Directly Productive Activities: Directly productive activities include those investments which lead to direct increase in the supply of goods and services. Investment in DPA means investment in private sector which is done with a view to maximize profit. In those projects, investment is made first where high profits are expected. In this way, DPA are always induced by profits."[234]

"Priorities: Excess SOC or Excess DPA: (i) Unbalancing the economy with SOC: Imbalance can be created both by SOC and DPA. But the question before us is that in which direction the investment should be made first so as to achieve continuous and sustained economic growth. The answer is quite simple. The government should invest more in order to reap these economies, the private investors would make investment in order to enjoy profits. This would raise the production of goods and services. Thus investment in SOC would bring automatically investment in DPA. (ii) Unbalancing the economy with DPA: In case investment is made first in DPA, the private investors would be facing a lot of problems in the absence of SOC. If a particular industry is setup in a particular region, that industry will not expand if SOC facilities are not available. In order to have SOC facilities, the industry has to put political pressure. That is really a tough job. Thus, excess DPA path is full of strains or pressure- creating whereas excess SOC path is very smooth or pressure relieving."[235]

Domestic Resources for Growth: Domestic resource mobilization (DRM) is "the process through which countries raise and spend their own funds to provide for their people – is the long-term path to sustainable development finance. DRM not only provides governments with the funds needed to alleviate poverty and deliver public services but is also a critical step on the path out of aid dependence. DRM does not necessarily mean new taxes or higher tax rates. Governments often see their revenues rise though improved audits or simplified filing processes. Successful DRM programs are cost-effective; they return many times what is invested in them."[236]

(a) Money and Economic Growth: Monetary expansion aids economic growth of LDCs. For the LDCs, evidence suggests a positive and significant relationship between the ratio of investment to income and the growth of per capital income. "First, money replaces barter transactions which are frequently wasteful and time-consuming to strike the right balance between demand and supply. Notice that the relative cost of printing money is small. Second, money as a medium of exchange induces specialization and increases productivity. Specialization in the production of specific crops in

a peasant economy would increase the interdependence and exchange among the various sectors and increasing monetization (i.e. increase in the ratio of monetary transaction (M) to total transactions (T) and increase in M/T could only facilitate this process of increasing productivity. Third, in a developing country, to match increasing output and the demand for money, it is necessary to increase money supply. (Fourth, if barter transactions are replaced by monetary transactions, then real resources will be released to promote growth. In fact, increasing monetization would require the promotion of banking and credit institutions which could help considerably the promotion of saving, investment and growth. Fifth, money can also act as a store of value, and the government by incurring public debt can provide alternative channels to mobilize enough saving to achieve equality between the natural rate and the warranted growth rate of capital."[237]

(b) Inflation and Economic Growth: "It is tempting for the LDCs to resort to inflation as a major tax to finance their public expenditure to promote economic development, particularly when the tax revenue as a proportion of GNP is low and tax elasticity with respect to income is not always greater than unity. Given certain demand for money assumptions, inflation can raise revenues. Second, by increasing profitability of industries, inflation can provide incentives to investment. Third, the government will be less obliged to depend upon foreign resources if it can raise more revenue at home. Fourth, it has been argued that inflationary financing could promote the growth of banks and other financial institutions. These agencies may include the public to hold financial rather than physical assets and thus release real resources for economic growth."

"On the debit side, inflation could easily distort the efficient allocation of resources and reduce real growth. Second, a high level of inflation will reduce a country's competitive power in the export market, and it may eventually price itself out. The LDCs which suffer from a chronic balance of payments deficit, therefore, should exercise greater caution in the use of inflationary policies. Third, inflation may make the distribution of income more equal. Many LDCs experience significant inequalities in the distribution of income and, as such, inflationary financing, which often tends to redistribute income in favor of profits rather than wages, may arouse public hostility. However…even if inflation promotes more inequality, it tends to raise profit share and thereby the saving ratio in national income and this could have a beneficial effect on growth in the LDCs. Fourth, a high level of inflation could easily shake people's confidence in the currency, and this could induce greater holding of physical rather than financial assets with detrimental effects on growth. Finally, hyper-inflation could only have disastrous consequences on the currency and financial system without conferring much significant benefit on the real growth of a country." The weight seems to be in favor of mild inflation for promoting growth.[238]

Because the rising prices reflect a growing economy that leads to pay hikes; inflation is better than deflation that cuts consumer spending and hampers growth indefinitely; and rising prices could help end the housing bust.[239] Are the rising stock prices good news too? In general, maximization of intrinsic stock value benefits society because the rising wealth provide quality of life; the wealth allows consum-ers to purchase more; and employees gain more benefits when the company becomes rich.

"A realistic policy of financial reform is called for to promote real saving and growth and employment in the LDCs. Rates of interest should be raised to reflect more correctly the relative scarcity of capital and this would have beneficial effect upon the choice of technology, employment and income distribution. Although the attraction of an inflation tax is obvious in situations where the relative values of revenues from other taxes are falling with rising prices and when inflation is a taxation without representation, which even the weakest government could enforce upon its people, it could be used only in moderate amounts to mobilize resources and great caution is needed to handle it before it gets out of hand."[240]

(c) Fiscal Policy and Growth: Objectives of Fiscal Policy in LDCs are as follows: (i) to raise revenues for the government; (ii) to stabilize prices by changing aggregate demand; (iii) to promote economic growth by mobil-izing surplus; (iv) to promote foreign investment should it be considered desirable; (v) to change the pattern of income distribution according to some social objective, e.g. more equal distribution of income; and to minimize the adverse effects to resource allocation. Most governments in LDCs try to achieve a combination of some of these major objectives.[241] "In order to utilize capital stock fully, the necessary growth of demand must be equal to the required investment growth which in itself is functionally related to changes both in taxes and in public expenditure. Should actual growth be less than desired growth, actual growth could be raised by inducements to invest or to lower the desired growth by altering fiscal policies. Thus changes in taxes or public expenditure should considerably influence the equality between desired and actual growth rate. For LLDCs it is of prime importance to utilize fully both capital and labor. In this sense, the HD model loses some of its appeal for devising fiscal policies for the LDCs, though the advocates of prior-saving theory may find it useful."[242]

(d) Deficit Financing and LDCs: "Deficit financing (DF) has played an important role in many LDCs. Given the inability of their governments to mobilize enough resources to achieve a desired rate of growth, unreliability of foreign investment and lack of tax elasticity, the temptation to adopt DF is understandable. The impact of money supply on prices, saving and growth has already been discussed. It remains to be pointed out that for DF to be effective in the LDCs the supply of output must be elastic with respect to demand. Otherwise, inflation is inevitable. To count the net

benefit of DF, it is necessary to examine the costs of inflation against the possible gains in resource mobilization. Among these, the most important are (i) distortions of real rates of return; (ii) inefficiency in allocation; (iii) inequalities in income distribution; and (iv) an increase in imports and unemployment. Among the possible benefits are the stimulus to profitability and investment, greater utilization of capacity because of increased demand and consequent lowering of the costs of production should there be excess capacity, and a larger investment provided that private investment was not forthcoming in any case. The other points which have been mentioned in its favor are, first, if an increase in money supply can stimulate growth, its presence can be tolerated. Here it is important to find the optimal level of money supply. Second, if income distribution becomes more unequal because of DF, then a rise in profit share will stimulate investment. If, however, profits are not reinvested, then growth is likely to suffer. Also, if private saving is not forthcoming spontaneously, government may resort to DF for generating more savings."

(e) The Tax Structure in LDCs: "The tax structures of most LDCs are narrow based, inelastic with respect to changes in income and greatly dependent upon indirect rather than direct taxes. Thus, if fiscal policy is to play a more vigorous role to promote revenue, growth and stability, it is imperative that the tax base should be broadened, that the tax revenue should be more elastic with respect to income and that there should be a relative expansion of the role of direct taxes in comparison with indirect taxes."

(i) Direct taxes in LDCs: "The major direct taxes in LDCs consist of income tax, corporation tax, wealth tax and property tax. Usually in LDCs, the proportion of direct taxes in total tax is much lower than that of indirect taxes, and direct taxes on agricultural income are generally very low... Second, with the growth of agriculture from the late 1960s in many Asian countries and the emergence of a Kulak or relatively well-off class of peasants who have been the main beneficiaries of the Green Revolution, it is argued that agricultural income taxation should be made progressive ...The high marginal tax rates plus... corruption have resulted in large-scale tax evasion and revenue losses."[243]

(ii) Indirect taxes in LDCs: "Indirect taxes in LDCs usually consist of sales taxes, excise taxes (like on fuel, tabaco, alcohol) and custom duties. Sometimes, marketing boards offer less than international prices to the domestic producers, the differential being the tax. Tariffs on imports are also recognized as an important type of indirect tax. Value-added tax and payroll taxes are now increasingly regarded as important types of indirect taxation for LDCs. The indirect taxes are generally borne by the consumers and as such they are sometimes regarded as consumption-based taxes...Countries earning less than $100 per capita collect 68 percent of total tax revenue in indirect taxes, whereas DCs...32 percent of their total tax revenues."[244]

(f) Taxation and Domestic Resource Mobilization in LDCs: "The demand for generating greater tax revenue in LDCs emanates from the necessity to finance public investment projects. The desire to raise more revenue, however, could be in conflict with equity objectives as taxes affect income distribution, provision of public goods and services, and general programmes of stabilization. Given variety of objectives, tax systems vary significantly across LDCs...the main differences between the DCs and LDCs are (i) the greater share of tax revenue from income and profit taxes and social insurance payments in the former group and (ii) the greater importance of various trade taxes in the latter group. Further, LDCs generally implement a more complex set of consumption and excise taxes than DCs and frequently offer subsidies on basic wage goods. Some African countries use marketing boards to tax exports of mainly agricultural goods. Other LDCs are now using sales and VAT. Despite the importance of price signals in LDCs, the effects of taxes on prices are too marginal to have a major impact on incentives for growth. Even a more progressive tax system has minor effects on income distribution. Most LDCs depend very heavily on import duties (tariffs) as a revenue source. Such high duties provide strong incentives for smuggling or evading tariffs. Taxes, however, influence incentives to save and invest. In most LDCs, expenditure-based taxes are regarded as more inductive for growth in private savings than are income-based taxes. Changes in taxes are also regarded as instruments for macroeconomic taxes."[245]

(g) Tax Reforms in LDCs: "The problem of tax reform in LDCs is to observe tax alterations which will raise social welfare but reave tax revenue constant or vise versa. When current taxes are suboptimal, then there must be one 9if not many) welfare-raising tax reforms...The aim of taxation should be similar in both DCs and LDCs; the main differences in the types of tax structure lie in the constraint facing government: the weakness of administration, limited experience with taxation, poor accounting, the low level of monetization in the economy, the high share of agriculture and the fact that tax handles are generally few in number relative to developed countries will have a different structure and emphasis. In view of growing public debt in LDCs, it is acknowledged that such expenditure should be checked to tackle the insolvency problem of many LDC governments. However, some cuts in government expenditure, sometimes advocated by some international lending agencies, could have a disastrous effect on the rate of economic growth of many poor countries. In particular, it is necessary to focus on the composition of public expenditure before deciding on cuts. In addition, given the narrow bond market and the limited ability of LDCs governments to finance deficits by selling bonds, and the inflationary effects of money finance, there are not very many real substitutes for taxation to increase revenue for the governments to avoid the insolvency problem."[246]

Foreign Resources for Growth: The flow of foreign resources (FR) are many types. "Frist, there are institutions which provide grants to many countries to alleviate the after-effects of a natural disaster such as famine, flood or earthquakes. Such grants need not be repaid by the recipient countries, nor do they carry any interest charges. Indeed, grants are genuine aids, but they usually form a tiny fraction of the total inflow of FR. Second, some loans are given, chiefly by the international lending agencies at interest rates which are lower than those in the market. Here the foreign resources are provided on soft terms which reflect a desire to aid the receiving countries. Where the loans are granted to the LDCs at a concessary rate for very long periods, the inflow of FR takes the character of genuine foreign aid as the net present value of FR provided at a concessionary rate and to be repaid fifty years hence would be almost the same as the value of grants. However, foreign private investments in the LDCs are not exactly foreign aid as they are made on commercial terms. Foreign private investment usually carries commercial interest rates…Foreign private investment usually forms a significant proportion of the total inflow of FR. Government lending could be carried out on a bilateral or multilateral basis. Sometimes, several governments could set up a consortium to provide FR to a country or countries. Such lending could carry commercial terms; but frequently these loans are provided at concessionary rates and they have to be repaid after a long period. Sometimes, grace periods are offered to relieve the burden of debt repayments. It seems clear that all FR are not aid or charities, some parts of them being international lending on a commercial basis."[247]

(a) Criteria for Distribution of Foreign Resources: Several criteria for allocating FR are highlighted here. First, FR are usually given for political reasons. It is generally the case that FR will not be given to one's enemies. A large part of American aid to the LDCs is allocated on the grounds of keeping intact America's political interest as far as possible. Second, FR are supposed to replenish the dearth of domestic saving in the LDCs. Generally, the difference between planned investment and planned saving is taken as the FR. Third, absorptive capacity means a country's ability to absorb capital and to sue it in a productive way. Such productive use of capital is measured by positive reasonable rates of return on total investment. Obviously, it would depend upon the level of income and its growth rate, the supply of skill and the level of average and marginal rates of savings. Other criteria may include historical factors, maintenance and promotion of the private sector of the economy, the principle of achieving maximum efficiency, and the principle of stability chiefly in prices and in trade balance. "Above discussion suggests that the difficulties which are inherent in finding out an appropriate value-free index to measure the performance of FR on growth and development of the LDCs not only at a point in time, but also over time. Any decision regarding the most desirable…is likely to be subjective."[248]

(b) Types of Foreign Resources: Allocation of FR can assume different forms. They can be tied to the imports from donor countries (i.e. tying by sources); alternatively, their use could be linked to a specific project (i.e. tying by end use). The reasons for tying are: "First, tying helps to increase the exports of the donor countries and protects their income and employment. However, such an argument is inconsistent with humanitarian motives for transferring resources. Second, tying of resources by some deficit donor countries may increase pressure in surplus donor countries to similar tying because tying by the deficit countries is supposed to enhance their relative share in the competitive market for exports. Such a phenomenon is regarded as competitive aid-tying. Their, tying is supposed to result in efficient utilization of resources. Fourth, project tying is supposed to be effective as the projects could be identified easily. Also, such tying is expected to enhance the reputation of the donor countries. Fifth, when resources are tied both by sources and by uses, then it increases a monopolistic situation in favor of the donor country which it can easily exploit."[249]

Tying of resources has created so much resentment. First, tying does not help the recipient countries to obtain resources at the cheapest prices. In many instances, prices paid by the LDCs are much above their world prices. Second, tying will not necessarily improve the balance of payments of the donor country fi the cause of such deficit is an excess demand for resources. Third, the objective of tying resources will be defeated if a recipient country decides to spend on goods and services of the donor country, for its total reserves of foreign earning, a fraction which is greater than or equal to the value of tied resources. Fourth, resources may be tied to the construction of a specific project which does not satisfy the objective of the national plan. Fifth, in the event of a double-tying, the monopo-listic position of the lender may result in a situation which could be less than optimal from the point of view of the recipient country. Sixth, costs of tying of resources have been regarded as considerable for some LDCs. Seventh, the informal agreement about servicing over the life of the capital projects as well as some indirect costs of tying may well reduce the true value of the tied FR."[250]

(c) Foreign Resources for Projects or Plans: "Sometimes FR are given to a particular project or projects in LDCs. The point has been made that such FR may fail to promote the basic objective of the national plan and hence it is necessary to work at the problem of financing the plan rather than the projects. It is clear that such a problem could only arise if the aim in the national plans is different from the one in the project. But to the extent that projects included in the plan are so selected as to achieve some national objectives, the problem of financing the plan or the project disappears, and the possibility of switching arises. Donor countries may reveal their preference for financing the projects rather than the plans if the national plans are likely to be revised suddenly with frequent changes."[251]

(d) Private Foreign Investment and Transfer of Technology: Options open to the LDCs for the transfer of technology and alternatives may include "(i) import the final product; (ii) import the technology for producing the final product suing imported raw materials, indigenous raw materials, or adopt some combination of imported and indigenous raw materials; (iii) import an intermediate product, suing indigenous plant for the final mixing of the product; (iv) develop indigenous technology similar to the imported technology; and develop indigenous alternative technology." Most LDCs try to meet the gap between domestic demand and supply through imports of products of technology, or some combination of the two. Here the policies of the different governments are generally reflected regarding the import of the final product or technology. An LDC strongly in favor of import substitution would prefer to import technology rather than the final product. The difference in public policies could also reflect the differences in market size, expected economies of scale and the level of skill." There are benefits and costs of transfer of technology to the multinational corporations.[252]

(e) Special Drawing Rights and Link: Special drawing rights (SDR) are supplementary foreign exchange reserve assets defined and maintained by the IMF. "SDRs are units of account for the IMF, and not a currency per se. They instead represent a claim to currency held by IMF member countries for which they may be exchanged. SDRs were created in 1969 to supplement a shortfall of preferred foreign exchange reserve assets, namely gold and U.S. dollars. SDRs are allocated by the IMF to countries and cannot be held or used by private parties. The number of SDRs in existence was around XDR 21.4 billion in August 2009. During the global financial crisis of 2009, an additional XDR 182.6 billion was allocated to provide liquidity to the global economic system and supplement member countries' official reserves. By October 2014, the number of SDRs in existence was XDR 204 billion. The value of a SDR is based on a basket of key international currencies reviewed by IMF every five years. The weights assigned to each currency in the XDR basket are adjusted to consider their current prominence in terms of inter-national trade and national foreign exchange reserves." The Renminbi (Chinese yuan) was added on 1 October 2016. The XDR basket now consists of the five currencies: U.S. dollar 41.73%, euro 30.93%, renminbi 10.92%, Japanese yen 8.33%, British pound 8.09%.[253]

"An IMF member country that requires actual *foreign currency* may sell its SDRs to another member country in exchange for the currency. To sell a part or all its SDRs, the country must find a willing party to buy them. The IMF acts as an intermediary in this voluntary exchange. The IMF also has the authority under the designation mechanism to ask member countries with strong foreign exchange reserves to purchase XDRs from those with weak reserves. The maximum obligation any country has under this mechanism is currency equal to twice the amount of its SDR allocation."[254]

(f) Foreign Aid and Economic Growth: Types of foreign aid may include bilateral aid, multilateral aid, project aid, technical assistance, humanitarian aid, soft loans, tied aid, and debt relief. But now exports from DCs are more than 40 times the level of official aid flows.

"Does overseas aid help or hinder economic growth and development? Aid has a range of economic, social, environmental and political objectives Economic development can take place without aid - China and Vietnam have both experienced sustained and rapid growth over nearly two decades without receiving much in the way of international aid payments measured as a share of their GDP. Well directed and targeted aid can enhance a country's growth potential, but the effects may not be seen for many years e.g. Aid might help finance the building of a power station contributes directly to aggregate demand and increases supply potential. Or aid that is designed to put more children through school or humanitarian aid to vaccinate kids and prevent them dying will have an impact over a longer time horizon Different kinds of aid projects can affect growth at different times and to different degrees." On the other hand, aid provides a financial inflow for low income countries, which helps to overcome the saving gap. Infrastructure projects increase the capital stock lifting a country's growth potential, and long-term aid for health and education projects builds human capital and raises productivity. Well targeted aid might add around 0.5% to growth rate of poorest countries.[255]

Counterarguments or disadvantages of overseas aid. "(i) Corruption: In poorly governed countries much of the aid flow to politicians and relatively little may directly benefit the poorest communities in greatest need. (ii) Ruling Elites: Aid can act as a barrier to true democracy - politicians pay more attention to aid donors than to their citizens. Aid-dependent governments are accountable to donors, not to their population. (iii) Aid dependency: A dependency culture on aid might be generated - the aid paradox is that aid tends to be most effective where it is needed least. (iv) Market distortions: Aid for example in the form of food aid in emergencies may lead to a distortion of market forces and a loss of economic efficiency. In the 'The Bottom Billion' Professor Paul Collier suggests that, ceteris paribus, overseas aid may have added around 1% per year to the growth rate of the poorest countries of the world during the past 30 years. There are few economists who argue that aid has led to a reduction in economic growth of donor countries. Most of those who are critical of overseas aid focus instead on dependency and corruption. It is possible for countries to grow quickly without aid – but equally there are countries who were initially heavy aid recipients who have grown and developed and are now aid donors themselves…Many external factors may reduce or enhance the impact of aid on economic growth, for example the quality of government, the efficiency of financial systems and also the absence of conflict.[256]

Population and Income Distribution: *(a) Population and Economic Development*: The growth of population could have some beneficial effects on economic growth due to demand generation and supply of labor. "First, a growing population enlarges the size of the market by raising aggregate demand. Second, a rising population supplies more labor for employment. Third, if the labor supply is a constraint on growth, then an expansion of the labor force will raise output and growth. The major harmful effects of rapid population growth can be summarized as follows."

"(i) If the rise in per capita income or output growth is regarded as a rough indicator of the improvement of the average standard of living in the society, then it is obvious that in an economy with stagnant total income and rising population, the average standard of living could only worsen. Similarly, if the population growth rate is faster than the growth rate of real income, again the average standard of living will fall. (ii) The positive effects of population growth on output growth could only be obtained if labor could be productively employed with the available resources. In LDCs given the paucity of capital, the availability of more labor does not add much to output growth. (iii) The rise in population lowers the man-land or the man-resources rations. This implies that a static, backward economy without any technical progress could only experience greater poverty with growing population pressure on available resources. (iv) The lack of enough physical and social capital along with structural and technical rigidities in the LDCs render the curve for supply of output rather inelastic and a rise in population coupled with an increased supply of labor leads to greater under-employment and open unemployment, particularly in the agricultural sector.

(v) A high level of population or its rapid growth creates additional demands on social capital like education, housing and health services. Since the supply of such facilities is usually inadequate in LDCs, a growth in population tends to overstrain the existing limited supply. (vi) If supply of food is inelastic in LDCs, then a rising population with an increase in demand could lead to inflation. In order to cope with the problem, many LDCs import food grains from abroad and this causes an important drain on valuable foreign exchange which could have been used for better purposes. (vii) The rapid growth of population leads to a high dependency ratio, i.e. the proportion of non-working to working population. (viii) High population growth rates and/or a high level of population could lead to pollution and many environmental problems like the growth of shanty towns or *bustees*, juvenile delinquency. Squalor, congestion etc. (ix) A rising population in a fairly static and poor economy could aggravate the problems of inequalities in income distribution. Since, poor families tend to be larger than rich families, as long as there is only one bread winner in both these income classes, per capita, real income and real consumption will clearly be lower in poor income groups in comparison with richer ones."[257]

(b) Population Explosion in LDCs: "According to the theory of demographic transition, in the pre-industrial, backward society a high birth rate (BR) is generally accompanied by a high death rate (DR) with the result that the net growth rate of population remains low. Evidence from most countries seems to back up this argument. In the passage of economic growth, it is argued that BR remains high while DR falls resulting in a very rapid rise in population growth or population explosion. In a more mature phase of economic development, BR tends to decline and DR falls to its lowest level and remains fairly stationary. Eventually, BR falls to a low level and the net growth population becomes low and stable. Although the theory of demographic transition is supposed to be a theory, it is not really a theory. Rather, it is a description of facts."[258]

(c) Low-level Equilibrium Trap: This theory suggests that, "as long as per capita income remains below a critical level, a population growth rate that exceeds the income growth rate will always bring the economy back to a low-level equilibrium trap. To avoid this trap, it is necessary to introduce technical progress so that the production function which accounts for the output or real income growth rate will lie above the population growth rate, and as long as that happens the trap will cease to operate."[259]

(d) Fertility and Population Growth in LDCs: (i) Factors affecting fertility; (ii) Fertility and mortality; (iii) Fertility and education: Higher education is generally expected to reduce fertility; (iv) Fertility and income: "It is sometimes argued that fertility and per capital real income are inversely correlated so that a rise in per capita real income would tend to reduce fertility." (v) Fertility and urbanization: "The hypothesis is often put forward that fertility should be inversely correlated with urbanization. To the extent that higher per capital real income, better education, greater employment opportunities, particularly for women, are all associated with greater urbanization in LDCs, the hypothesis seems to be valid, at least theoretically." (vi) Fertility, compulsory sterilization and incentive payments: "One of the direct methods to reduce fertility could be compulsory sterilization. But the efficiency of such a method could be very much doubted, particularly in a democratic society."[260]

(e) Poverty and Income Distribution: Persistence of absolute poverty and the increase in relative inequality in LDCs are serious.

(i) Income Inequality: "The socialist countries have the highest degree of overall equality with the average income of the lowest 40 percent amounting to about 25 percent of total incomes." "Developed countries are next in income equality ranging equally between low and moderate inequality with the income share of the lowest 40 percent averaging about 16 percent of total incomes." "Most underdeveloped countries have more inequality than developed countries with about half falling into the high inequality arrange" - the lowest 40% shares 12.5% of total incomes.[261]

(ii) Absolute Poverty: "Most of those living in absolute poverty are to be found in countries with low average level of per capita income rather than in countries with very unequal income distribution patters." (i) Growth, inequality, and poverty: "In most countries the poorest would be found among four identifiable economic groups. The rural landless, small farmers, the urban under-employed and the urban unemployed...the poor are disproportionately located in the rural areas. It is estimated that at least 70 percent of the poor are to be found in this sector, mostly landless farm workers and self-employed small farmers, but also including small traders and artisans located in the rural areas. The dimensions of this group have obvious implications for policies aimed at reducing poverty."[262]

(iii) Distribution with Growth: *Redistribution of Growth* (Chenery et al. 1974) describes a set of four basic approaches to increase the income of low-income groups. These approaches are: "(i) maximizing GNP growth through raising saving and allocating resources more efficiently, with benefits to all groups in society; (ii) redirecting investment to poverty groups in the form of education, access to credit, public facilities and so on; (iii) redistributing income (or consumption) to poverty groups through the fiscal system or through direct allocation of consumer goods; (iv) a transfer of existing assets to poverty groups, as in land reform."[263]

(f) The Employment Problem: "Classical economics, neo-classical economics, and the Austrian School of economics argued that market mechanisms are reliable means of resolving unemployment. These theories argue against inter-ventions imposed on the labor market from the outside, such as unionization, bureaucratic work rules, minimum wage laws, taxes, and other regulations that they claim discourage the hiring of workers. Keynesian economics emphasizes the cyclical nature of unemployment and recommends government interventions in the economy that it claims will reduce unemploy-ment during recessions. This theory focuses on recurrent shocks that suddenly reduce aggregate demand for goods and services and thus reduce demand for workers. Keynesian models recommend government interventions designed to increase demand for workers; these can include financial stimuli, publicly funded job creation, and expansionist monetary policies. Its namesake economist, John Maynard Keynes, believed that the root cause of unemploy-ment is the desire of investors to receive more money rather than produce more products, which is not possible without public bodies producing new money. A third group of theories emphasize the need for a stable supply of capital and investment to maintain full employment. They argue accordingly that government should guarantee full employment through fiscal policy, monetary policy and trade policy as stated, for example, in the US Employment Act of 1946, by counteracting private sector or trade investment volatility, and reducing inequality."[264]

(g) Migration Theory and Evidence: "International migration occurs when people cross state boundaries and stay in the host state for some minimum length of time. Migration occurs for many reasons. Many people leave their home countries in order to look for economic opportunities in another country. Others migrate to be with family members who have migrated or because of political conditions in their countries. Education is another reason for inter-national migration, as students pursue their studies abroad. While there are several different potential systems for categorizing international migrants, one system organizes them into nine groups: temporary labor migrants; irregular, illegal, or undocumented migrants; highly skilled and business migrants; refugees; asylum seekers; forced migration; family members; return migrants; and long-term, low-skilled migrants. These migrants can also be divided into two large groups, permanent and temporary. Permanent migrants intend to establish their permanent residence in a new country and possibly obtain that country's citizenship. Temporary migrants intend only to stay for a limited period of time; perhaps until the end of a particular program of study or for the duration of their work contract or a certain work season."[265] Both types of migrants have a significant effect on the economies and societies of both sides.

"Similarly, the countries which receive these migrants are often grouped into four categories: traditional settlement countries, European countries which encouraged labor migration after World War II, European countries which receive a significant portion of their immigrant populations from their former colonies, and countries which formerly were points of emigration but have recently emerged as immigrant destinations."[266]

(h) Migration and Employment Policy: (i) Rural development with all that is involved in improving rural incomes and job opportunities is seen to be the most important way of reducing the push from the countryside. (ii) Positive policies should be introduced to increase productivity and incomes in the informal urban sector. (iii) An income policy to reduce or at least prevent a widening of the gap between earnings in the modern sector and in the rest of the economy is widely stressed in the literature.[267] On the other hand, migrant workers we have to consider productive policies. "A migrant worker is a person who either migrates within their home country or outside it to pursue work. Migrant workers usually do not have an intention to stay permanently in the country or region in which they work. Migrant workers who work outside their home country are also called foreign workers. They may also be called expatriates or guest workers, especially when they have been sent for or invited to work in the host country before leaving the home country. The International Labor Organization estimated in 2014 there were 232 million international migrants worldwide who were outside their home country for at least 12 months and approximately half of them were estimated to be economically active."[268]

INDUSTRIZATION, TRADE, DEVELOPMENT PLANNING, AND STRUCTURAL TRANSFORMATION

Agriculture and Green Revolution: *(a) The Role of Agriculture* in economic development: (i) Agriculture provides labor to the non-agricultural sector. (ii) Food and raw materials are supplied by agriculture. (iii) Exports of agricultural products can help a country to earn valuable foreign exchange. (iv) The rate of capital formation in LDCs can be considerably improved by the agricultural sector. (v) Agriculture in LDCs may play a crucial role in expanding the size of the home market.[269]

(b) The Concept of Marketed Surplus: (i) Marketed surplus and capital formation: "Defining marketed surplus as the difference between total food production and total food consumption, it may be argued that, if per capita consumption remains fixed, surplus could be mobilized for real capital formation." (ii) Marketed surplus and terms of trade: "The method of turning the terms of trade against agriculture is supposed to be similar to that of a country's use of its favorable terms of trade with other countries for its capital formation." (iii) Empirical estimates of the relationship between terms of trade and marketed surplus do not yield any conclusive answer.[270] Given the role of agriculture in the economic development of the LDCs, it is imperative "to invest considerable resources for their agricultural develop -ment. Unfortunately…agriculture is synonymous with backward-ness, and planners too often equate development with urban industrialization."[271]

(c) The Green Revolution "is set of research technology transfer initiatives occurring between 1950 and the late 1960s, that increased agricultural production worldwide, particularly in the developing world, beginning most markedly in the late 1960s. The initiatives resulted in the adoption of new technologies, including high-yielding varieties (HYVs) of cereals, especially dwarf wheats and rices, in association with chemical fertilizers and agro-chemicals,and with controlled water-supply (usually involving irrigation) and new methods of cultivation, including mechanization. All of these together were seen as a 'package of practices' to supersede 'traditional' technology and to be adopted as a whole. Both the Ford Foundation and the Rockefeller Foundation were heavily involved. One key leader was Norman Borlaug, the "Father of the Green Revolution", who received the Nobel Peace Prize in 1970. He is credited with saving over a billion people from starvation. The basic approach was the development of high-yielding varieties of cereal grains, expansion of irrigation infrastructure, modernization of management techniques, distribution of hybridized seeds, synthetic fertilizers, and pesticides to farmers. The term *Green Revolution* was first used in a speech on 8 March 1968 by the administrator of the U.S. Agency for International Development (USAID), William S. Gaud, who noted the spread of the new technologies."[272]

Industrialization and Trade Policies: *(a) Reasons for Industrialization in LDCs*: "Industrialization has been regarded as a major strategy for achieving a faster rate of economic growth and a higher standard of living in many LDCs. Several reasons are advanced to justify such a strategy. First, it is contended that economically advanced countries are usually more industrialized than the economically poor countries. The strength of this argument is derived from the lessons of economic history developed countries. Second, industrialization is sometimes regarded as the major way to solve the problem of unemployment and under-employment in LDCs, many of which suffer from problems of a highly adverse man-land ratio. Third, the nature of trade of many LDCs prompts them to choose industrialization as an avenue to solve the problem of instabilities in the earning from exports which chiefly consists of primary products. The demand for primary products in the international market is usually price and income inelastic. The LDCs also suffer from a chronic balance of payments deficit. Fourth, it is argued that industrialization alone can alter the present economic and social structure of many LDCs which is not conductive to achieving a higher level of economic development since dynamic externalities concomitant which industrialization are necessary conditions for attaining a high level of growth. Some of the advocates of the big-push theory have actually emphasized the need for industrialization on the strength of dynamic externalities. Fifth…industrialization is supposed to improve productivity by increasing efficiency. Sixth, the desire to attain self-sufficiency has promised many LDCs to choose the path of industrialization. Finally, industrialization is regarded as an important policy to affect fundamental economic and social changes in LDCs which are considered as necessary conditions to raise their growth potentials."[273]

(b) The Role of Tariffs in Economic Development: "Classical economists like Smith, Ricardo and Mill advocated the doctrine of free trade based on the theory of comparative advantage. Such a doctrine is an offshoot of the principles of laissez-faire, although it was soon realized that the principles of laissez-faire may not be the best for a country to follow, as some of the basic assumptions such as perfect competition and optimal income distribution may not hold. Several qualifications of the doctrine of free trade were made, and indeed Mill has suggested the use of tariffs to protect the infant industries. Some others have shown the case for tariffs to improve upon a country's terms of trade through trade restriction. This has now been regarded as the optimum tariff argument."[274] In fact, "A tariff is a tax on imports or exports between sovereign states. It is a form of regulation of foreign trade and a policy that taxes foreign products to encourage or safeguard domestic industry. Traditionally, states have used them as a source of income. Now, they are among the most widely used instruments of protectionism, along with import and export quotas."[275]

Tariffs and trade barriers are used as follows: (i) Protecting domestic employment: The possibility of increased competition from imported goods can threaten domestic industries, that may fire workers or shift production abroad to cut costs, which means higher unemployment. (ii) Protecting consumers: "A government may levy a tariff on products that it feels could endanger its population. For example, South Korea may place a tariff on imported beef from the United States if it thinks that the goods could be tainted with a disease." (iii) Infant industries: "The use of tariffs to protect infant industries can be seen by the Import Substitution Industrialization (ISI) strategy employed by many developing nations. (iv) National security: "Barriers are also employed by developed countries to protect certain industries that are deemed strategically important, such as those supporting national security." (v) Retaliation: tariffs are imposed "as a retaliation technique if they think that a trading partner has not played by the rules. There are several types of tariffs and barriers that a government can employ. Specific tariffs are a fixed fee levied on one unit of an imported good. Ad Valorem tariffs is levied on a good based on a percentage of that good's value. Non-tariff barriers to trade includes licenses, import quotas, voluntary export restraints, and local content requirements. Tariffs increase government revenue, and reduce competition of domestic companies, but domestic consumers have to pay more." [276]

"Imposing an import tariff has the following effects, shown in Figure II-4-1. Economic Effects of Tariffs: *Price rises from world price Pw to higher tariff price Pt. *Quantity demanded by domestic consumers falls from C1 to C2, a movement along the demand curve due to higher price. *Domestic suppliers are willing to supply Q2 rather than Q1, a movement along the supply curve due to the higher price, so the quantity imported falls from C1-Q1 to C2-Q2. *Consumer surplus (the area under the demand curve but above price) shrinks by areas A+B+C+D, as domestic consumers face higher prices and consume lower quantities. *Producer surplus (the area above the supply curve but below price) increases by area A, as domestic producers shielded from international competition can sell more of their product at a higher price. *Government tax revenue is the import quantity (C2-Q2) times the tariff price (Pw - Pt), shown as area C. *Areas B and D are deadweight losses, surplus formerly captured by consumers that now is lost to all parties. *The overall change in welfare = Change in Consumer Surplus + Change in Producer Surplus + Change in Government Revenue = (-A-B-C-D) + A + C = -B-D. The final state after imposition of the tariff is indicated in the second diagram, with overall welfare reduced by the areas labeled "societal losses", which correspond to areas B and D in the first diagram. The losses to domestic consumers are greater than the combined benefits to domestic producers and government. That tariffs overall reduce welfare is not a controversial topic among economists."[277]

Figure II-4-1 Economic Effects of Tariffs
Accessed 24 September 2019,
https://en.wikipedia.org/wiki/Tariff#/media/File:EffectOfTariff.svg

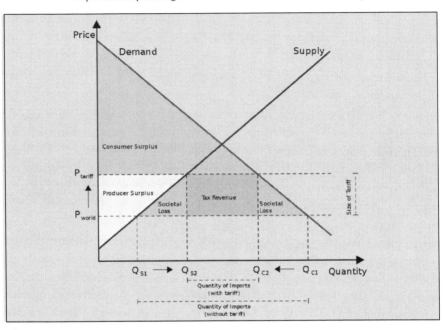

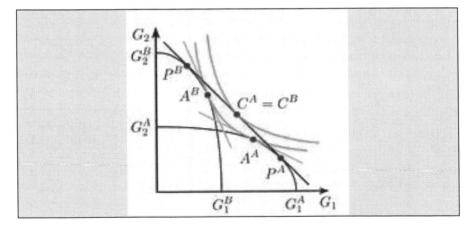

Figure II-4-2. Two-Country Equilibrium in International Trade
Accessed 24 September 2019,
https://tse3.mm.bing.net/th?id=OIP.tzs0fLdz28Ctv1ZsaKg-6gHaGy&pid=Api&P=0&w=175&h=162

(c) Optimal Tariff: "For economic efficiency, free trade is often the best policy, however levying a tariff is sometimes second best. A tariff is called an optimal tariff if it is set to maximize the welfare of the country imposing the tariff. It is a tariff derived by the intersection between the trade indifference curve of that country and the offer curve of another country. In this case, the welfare of the other country grows worse simultaneously, thus the policy is a kind of beggar thy neighbor policy. If the offer curve of the other country is a line through the origin point, the original country is in the condition of a small country, so any tariff worsens the welfare of the original country. It is possible to levy a tariff as a political policy choice, and to consider a theoretical optimum tariff rate. However, imposing an optimal tariff will often lead to the foreign country increasing their tariffs as well, leading to a loss of welfare in both countries. When countries impose tariffs on each other, they will reach a position off the contract curve, meaning that both countries' welfare could be increased by reducing tariffs."[278]

(d) The Infant Industry: "An infant industry is a new industry, which in its early stages experiences relative difficulty or is absolutely incapable in competing with established competitors abroad. Governments are sometimes urged to support the development of infant industries, protecting home industries in their early stages, usually through subsidies or tariffs. Subsidies may be indirect, as in when import duties are imposed or some prohibition against the import of a raw or finished material is imposed... Economists argue that state support for infant industries is justified only if there are external benefits. That is underscored by the fact that the original bastions of the infant industry argument argued that external benefits aside, it is undeniable that both the US and Britain rose to become relative superpowers in economic terms by following their approach for an extended period of time...After about 100 years of protectionism of this wool industry, the country finally decided that duties on exports would be lifted."[279]

(e) Distortion in the Factor Markets: "In many LDCs, distortions exist in the factor markets. For instance, in the presence of large-scale unemployed labor, particularly in agriculture, low wages in agriculture and high wages in industry, a tariff on importable industry is sometimes advocated as an offset against high const of labor. The differences in wages between agriculture and industry overestimate the private cost of labor in industry since industrial wages exceed the social opportunity cost of labor. Such a situation shows inefficiency in resource allocation and under-estimation of the benefits of industrial transformation. The aim is to increase real income over and above the level of suboptimal free trade by raising the relative price of industrial output via tariffs on industries, and a better allocation of resource (here, labor) is attempted by transferring labor from agriculture to industry."[280] In the LDCs, a tariff can never be the optimal policy and a subsidy is better than the policy of importing tariffs.

(f) The Balance of Payments: "Tariffs have been regarded as an effective weapon to reduce the balance of payments deficit. Both DCs and LDCs have taken resort to tariffs to reduce their trade deficits from time to time." However, it brings equilibrium through a contraction of foreign trade; inhibits the advantages of a large and expanding world trade and prosperity and adjusts the equilibrium without mitigating the root cause of disequilibrium. Sometimes, the imposition of a new or higher tariff may aggravate a disequilibrium in case of a country already experiencing a surplus in its balance of payments.[281]

(g) Income and Employment Effect: Imposition of tariff would lead to expansion of employment and incomes. "By reducing imports, tariffs stimulate employment and output in the import-competing industries. A new flow of income will be generated with its 'multiplier effect.' In an expanding economy, more capital goods investment will also be made which produces 'acceleration effect.' Thus, under conditions of less than full employment, the interaction of multiplier-accelerator will lead to a cumulative expansion of investment, employment, output and income in the country. Another possible impact of tariffs is that the imposition of tariff duties may attract foreign capital in the country concerned, when they find that they may lose market for their products in the country due to contraction of import demand and expansion of home industries under the protective effects of tariffs."[282]

(h) Economic Growth and Trade: "The Ricardian and the Hecksher-Ohlin models are modified in the current theories of trade to take into account the effects of growth...The effects of the growth of factor supplies can first be mentioned in the light of the Rybczynski theorem. Let us assume a rise in the supply of labor. If the terms of trade are given, then the Rybczynski theorem says that with an increase in the supply of labor relative to capital, the production of a labor-intensive good will fall. This may be labelled the pro-trade bias at given terms of trade (TT). On the other hand, capital accumulation will imply an increase in the production of capital-intensive goods and a fall in the production of labor-intensive goods at given TT, and this impact on production has been labelled anti-trade bias. The impact on consumption can be measured by noting that at given TT and within fixed factor properties and marginal products, an increase in labor with fixed stock of capital will transfer income to labor. If the marginal propensity to consume by the laborers is high for the labor-intensive good, then a larger proportion of society's income will be spent on the labor-intensive good in comparison with the capital-intensive commodity. This is anti-trade bias because of consumption."[283]

(i) Terms of Trade between DCs and LDCs: "The TT is generally defined as the ratio of export price to import price paid by the LDCs in their trade with DCs. If the TT moves against the LDCs for some time, it would imply that the LDCs are losing out in their trade with the DCs. During the

1960s it was suggested that such an index of TT had actually moved against the LDCs vis-à-vis the DCs for a long time, and hence existing trade theory is inadequate to help the LDCs and a new economic order is called for both internationally and nationally, chiefly via protection and industrialization." "An improvement of a nation's terms of trade benefits that country in the sense that it can buy more imports for any given level of exports. The terms of trade may be influenced by the exchange rate because a rise in the value of a country's currency lowers the domestic prices of its imports but may not directly affect the prices of the commodities it exports."[284]

(j) Non-Tariff Barriers: "With the exception of export subsidies and quotas, NTBs are most similar to the tariffs. Tariffs for goods production were reduced during the eight rounds of negotiations in the WTO and the General Agreement on Tariffs and Trade (GATT). After lowering of tariffs, the principle of protectionism demanded the introduction of new NTBs such as technical barriers to trade (TBT). According to statements made at United Nations Conference on Trade and Development (UNCTAD, 2005), the use of NTBs, based on the amount and control of price levels has decreased significantly from 45% in 1994 to 15% in 2004, while use of other NTBs increased from 55% in 1994 to 85% in 2004. Increasing consumer demand for safe and environment friendly products also have had their impact on increasing popularity of TBT." The types of non-tariff barriers are: (i) Protectionist policies: import quotas, local content requirements, public procurement practices, and anti-dumping laws; (ii) Assistance policy: domestic subsidies and industry bailouts; and (iii) Non-protectionist policies: licensing, packaging, and labelling requirements; sanitary and phytosanitary rules; food, plant and animal inspections; import bans based on objectionable harvesting or fishing methods."[285]

(k) Trade Liberalization: "Free trade is a trade policy that does not restrict imports or exports; it can also be understood as the free market idea applied to international trade. In government, free trade is predominantly advocated by political parties that hold liberal economic positions while economically left-wing and nationalist political parties generally support protectionism. the opposite of free trade...There is a broad consensus among economists that protectionism has a negative effect on economic growth and economic welfare while free trade and the reduction of trade barriers has a positive effect on economic growth and economic stability. However, liberalization of trade can cause significant and unequally distributed losses, and the economic dislocation of workers in import-competing sectors."[286]

"Trade policies in the LDCs, despite making some gains in industrialization and import substitution, have also caused some of their welfare loss in terms of negative value added at world prices in some of their industries. The ERP has remained quite high in many cases and the policy has promoted monopoly rather than competition and inefficiency in many sectors."[287]

Development Planning: "Economic planning is a mechanism for the allocation of resources between and within organizations which is held in contrast to the market mechanism. As an allocation mechanism for socialism, economic planning replaces factor markets with a direct allocation of resources within a single or interconnected group of socially owned organizations. There are various forms of economic planning. The level of centralization in the decision-making depends on the specific type of planning mechanism employed. As such, one can distinguish between centralized planning and decentralized planning. An economy primarily based on planning is referred to as a planned economy. In a centrally planned economy, the allocation of resources is determined by a comprehensive plan of production which specifies output requirements. Planning may also take the form of directive planning or indicative planning. A distinction can be made between physical planning and financial planning . Physical planning involves economic planning and coordination conducted in terms of disaggregated physical units whereas financial planning involves plans formulated in terms of financial units. "[288]

(a) In Socialism: Different forms of economic planning have been featured in various models of socialism. These range from decentralized-planning systems which are based on collective decision-making and disaggregated information to centralized systems of planning conducted by technical experts who use aggregated information to formulate plans of production. In a fully developed socialist economy, engineers and technical specialists, overseen or appointed in a democratic manner, would coordinate the economy in terms of physical units without any need or use for financial-based calculation. The economy of the Soviet Union never reached this stage of development, so planned its economy in financial terms throughout the duration of its existence. Nonetheless, a number of alternative metrics were developed for assessing the performance of non-financial economies in terms of physical output. (i.e. net material product vs. GDP)"[289]

(i) Concept of socialist planning: "The classical conception of socialist economic planning held by Marxists involved an economic system where goods and services were valued, demanded and produced directly for their use-value as opposed to being produced as a by-product of the pursuit of profit by business enterprises. This idea of production for use is a fundamental aspect of a socialist economy. This involves social control over the allocation of the surplus product and in its most extensive theoretical form calculation-in-kind in place of financial calculation. For Marxists in particular, planning entails control of the surplus product (profit) by the associated producers in a democratic manner. This differs from planning within the framework of capitalism which is based on the planned accumulation of capital in order to either stabilize the business cycle (when undertaken by governments) or to maximize profits (when undertaken by firms) as opposed to the socialist concept of planned production for use...the state would become a coordinating economic entity rather than a mechanism of political and class-based control."[290]

(ii) Planning versus command: "The concept of a command economy is differentiated from the concepts of a planned economy and economic planning, especially by socialists and Marxists who liken command economies to that of a single capitalist firm, organized in a top-down administrative fashion based on bureaucratic organization akin to that of a capitalist corporation. Economic analysts have argued that the economy of the former Soviet Union actually represented an administrative or command economy as opposed to a planned economy because planning did not play an operational role in the allocation of resources among productive units in the economy since in actuality the main allocation mechanism was a system of command-and-control. As a result, the phrase administrative command economy gained currency as a more accurate descriptor..."[291]

(b) In Capitalism: (i) Intra-firm and intra-industry planning: "Large corporations use planning to allocate resources internally among their divisions and subsidiaries. Many modern firms also use regression analysis to measure market demand to adjust prices and to decide upon the optimal quantities of output to be supplied. Planned obsolescence is often cited as a form of economic planning that is used by large firms to increase demand for future products by deliberately limiting the operational lifespan of its products...Many socialists viewed these tendencies, specifically the increasing trend toward economic planning in capitalist firms, as evidence of the increasing obsolescence of capitalism..."[292]

(ii) State development planning: "State development planning or national planning entails macroeconomic policies and financial planning conducted by governments to stabilize the market or promote economic growth in market-based economies. This involves the use of monetary policy, industrial policy and fiscal policy to steer the market toward targeted outcomes. Industrial policy includes government taking measures aimed at improving the competitiveness and capabilities of domestic firms and promoting structural transformation. In contrast to socialist planning, state development planning does not replace the market mechanism and does not eliminate the use of money in production. It only applies to privately owned and publicly owned firms in the strategic sectors of the economy and seeks to coordinate their activities (such as tax breaks or subsidies)."[293]

(c) Criticism on Economic Planning: "The most notable critique of economic planning came from Austrian economists Friedrich Hayek and Ludwig von Mises. Hayek argued that central planners could not possibly accrue the necessary information to formulate an effective plan for production because they are not exposed to the rapid changes that take place in an economy in any particular time and place and so they are unfamiliar

with those circumstances. The process of transmitting all the necessary information to planners is thus inefficient. Mises also had a similar opinion. Proponents of decentralized economic planning have also criticized central economic planning. For example, Leon Trotsky believed that central planners, regardless of their intellectual capacity, operated without the input and participation of the millions of people who participate in the economy and so they would be unable to respond to local conditions quickly enough to effectively coordinate."[294]

(d) Methodology: (i) Macro-econometric Models in Development Planning: "The Development Planning Centre (DPC) specializes in macro-econometric analysis with special expertise in building macro-models, which are used for the analysis of macroeconomic behavior and policy and for providing forecasts. This research programme was greatly stimulated after India began to implement the structural adjustment program in 1991. Since then, the research on macroeconomics has widened its scope from domestic closed economy models to open economy macro models. The models and analysis also began to focus more and more on the market-determined behavior of the exchange rate, interest rate, private investment and foreign trade. The techniques of analysis have also been constantly updated. The simple regression analysis has been extended to structural macro modeling, time series analysis, co-integration, vector auto-regression (VAR) and Bayesian forecasting. The econometric analysis now uses not only annual time series data but also higher frequency data, including quarterly and monthly data."[295]

(II) The Input-Output Model: Wassily Leontief (1906-99) developed the input-output model that was the first to use a matrix representation of a national economy. "The model depicts inter-industry relationships within an economy, showing how output from one industrial sector may become an input to another industrial sector. In the inter-industry matrix, column entries typically represent inputs to an industrial sector, while row entries represent outputs from a given sector. This format therefore shows how dependent each sector is on every other sector, both as a customer of outputs from other sectors and as a supplier of inputs. Each column of the input–output matrix shows the monetary value of inputs to each sector and each row represents the value of each sector's outputs. Say that we have an economy with n sectors. Each sector produces x_i units of a single homogeneous good. Assume that the *jth* sector, in order to produce 1 unit, must use a_{ij} units from sector i. Furthermore, assume that each sector cells some of its output to other sectors (intermediate output) and some of its output to consumers (final output, or final demand). Call final demand in the *ith* sector d_i. Then we might write $[x_i = a_{i1}x_1 + a_{i2}x_2 + \ldots + a_{in}x_n + d_i]$ or total output equals intermediate output plus final output. If we let A be the matrix of coefficients a_{ij}, x be the vector of total output, and d be the vector of final demand, then

our expression for the economy becomes $[x = Ax + d]$ which after re-writing becomes $[(I − A)x = d]$. If the matrix $I − A$ is invertible then this is a linear system of equations with a unique solution, and so given some final demand vector, the required output vector x is non-negative."[296] "The mathematics of input–output economics is straightforward, but the data requirements are enormous because the expenditures and revenues of each branch of economic activity have to be represented." The U.S. Government has used the Input-output model for the national economic survey every five years.

(iii) The Linear Programing Model: "Linear programming (LP) is really a mathematical tool which is now being increasingly used in economic analysis. Its use in the field of development planning is of much interest chiefly because it helps the planner to allocate resources optimally among alternative uses within the specific constraints. At the micro level, the technique could be used to find out optimal and efficient (least expensive) methods of production. Actually, LP can be regarded as a powerful and complementary tool which can be sued to analyze the IO table in order to solve the problems of choice of techniques on the supply side as well as the problem of choice of final demand. It is important to emphasize that the LP technique helps to tackle the major problems of investment planning: (i) consistency between sectors; (ii) feasibility of plans; and (iii) optimality in resource allocation. However, it should be pointed out that eth important assumption that is made in LP analysis is that variables are interrelated in a linear way. This assumption may not be very realistic in all cases. But if it is, then LP is indeed very useful planning. On the other hand, if the relationship among the variables are non-linear, then on-linear programming can be used to solve the problems.

For example, Maximize output $[Y = f(K, L, T)]$ is the function of capital, labor, and technology inputs. The constraints could be available resources in terms of capital, labor, and technology. Hence we can write $[K < \$ 100$ million, $L < 100$ thousand men, $T =$ current level of technology]. Therefore, we can use mathematical methodology – linear programming or non-linear programming method to get maximization conditions. For this, the general equilibrium model is attached in the Appendix at the end of Part II.

(iv) Cost-Benefit Analysis "is a systematic approach to estimating the strengths and weaknesses of alternatives used to determine options which provide the best approach to achieving benefits while preserving savings. A CBA may be used to compare completed or potential courses of actions, or to estimate the value against the cost of a decision, project, or policy. It is commonly used in commercial transactions, business or policy decisions, and project investments. CBA has two main applications: To determine if an investment is sound, ascertaining if its benefits outweigh its costs. To provide a basis for comparing investments, comparing the total expected cost of each option with its total expected benefits."[297]

Growth and Structural Transformation: Income growth changes the composition of "domestic demand and production, and, conversely, rising investment rates and the reallocation of labor tend to increase aggregate growth. The transformation is by no means uniform across countries, however, for it is affected by resource endowments and the initial structure of the economy as well as by the choice of development policies. In extreme case, large structural changes may be associated with little or no growth...It presents a simple multisectoral model designed to stimulate the effects of changing demand and trade on the structure of production.."[298] "In common features of industrialization, the model of industrialization traces the rise of industry to shifts in domestic demand, the growing intermediate use of industrial products, and the transformation of comparative advantage as factor proportions change. Although these phenomena can be observed in virtually all developing countries, their relative importance varies according to each initial structure, resource endowment, and development policies."[299]

Shift in Domestic Demand: "In almost all cases, the largest single change in demand is the fall in the share of food consumption. The reduction is even steeper for Israel, Japan, Korea, and Turkey in relation to their levels of income." "Two major shifts occur in virtually all cases: first, a substantial fall in the share of food demand with the rise in per capita income; and second, increases in producer goods, machinery, and social overhead, produced by rises in both investment and consumer demand."

Rise in Intermediate Use: "As with final demand, this phenomenon can be broken down into two parts: a shift in output mix toward manufacturing and other sectors that use more intermediate inputs; and second, technological changes within a sector that lead to a greater use of intermediate inputs. The second aspect is illustrated by the increased use of manufactured inputs in agriculture and transportation" with increasing mechanization.

Changes in Comparative Advantage: "Through import substitution and the expansion of manufactured exports, developing countries shift away from the specialization in primary products that is characteristic of early stages of development. Underlying this shift are changes in supply conditions – accumulation of skills and physical capital plus the greater availability of intermediate inputs – as well as economies of scale based on a growing domestic market for manufactured goods."

Reallocation of Capital and Labor: "The shift in the composition of output with rising income is reflected in varying degree in the reallocation of labor and capital from primary production to manufacturing and services." "The rise of employment in industry is much smaller than the decline in agriculture, and consequently most of the shift takes place from agriculture to services." "The pattern of capital use shows a much higher proportion in social overhead," which is larger than primary and secondary combined.[300]

ECONOMIC POLICIES FOR GROWTH AND STABILITY
In the Capitalist Economy

The governments of capitalist countries have intervened in markets in order to promote competition and to reduce monopoly by laws and regulations. Moreover, the world economic system moves toward strict reciprocity in trade and investment for international justice and fairness.

Economic Growth vs. Income Distribution: In capitalism, individuals or corporates own the means of production, and prices are determined by market forces, and each individual works hard to maximize profits and to accumulate his own wealth with continuous innovation and managerial improvement. There is a large gap between rich class and poor class because of unequal distribution of wealth as opposed to the socialism where there is no such gap because of equal distribution by the state. With the progressive tax policies, more taxes are collected from the rich in order to transfer the tax money for the benefits to the low-income class through investment in the public sector for the infrastructure, healthcare, and education. However, problems appear in the limited funds from tax revenues, while wide regional disparities in economic activity, growth, wellbeing, and insufficient diversification; which cannot overcome the income inequality.

(a) Trade-off Relations: Growth and Distribution: "In his influential 1975 book *Equality and Efficiency: The Big Tradeoff*, Arthur Okun argued that pursuing equality can reduce efficiency (the total output produced with given resources). The late Yale University and Brookings Institution economist said that not only can more equal distribution of incomes reduce incentives to work and invest, but the efforts to redistribute-through such mechanisms as the tax code and minimum wages- can themselves be costly. Okun likened these mechanisms to a 'leaky bucket.' Some of the resources transferred from rich to poor "will simply disappear in transit, so the poor will not receive all the money that is taken from the rich"-the result of administrative costs and disincentives to work for both those who pay taxes and those who receive transfers."[301]

"In recent work, we discovered that when growth is looked at over the long term, the trade-off between efficiency and equality may not exist. In fact equality appears to be an important ingredient in promoting and sustaining growth. The difference between countries that can sustain rapid growth for many years or even decades and the many others that see growth spurts fade quickly may be the level of inequality. Countries may find that improving equality may also improve efficiency, understood as more sustainable long-run growth."[302] But if government spends more not for new jobs but simply hiring temporary jobs by increasing more positions in the government or publicly owned corporations, the growth would be opposite.

(b) The Measurement of Inequality: Among the most common metrics used to measure inequality are the Gini index (known as Gini coefficient).

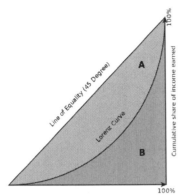

Figure II-4-3. Graphical Representation of the Gini Coefficient

The graph shows that the Gini coefficient is equal to the area marked A divided by the sum of the areas marked A and B, that is, Gini = A/(A + B). It is also equal to 2A and to $1 - 2B$ due to the fact that A + B = 0.5 (since the axes scale from 0 to 1).

The range of the Gini index is between 0 and 1 (0% and 100%), where 0 indicates perfect equality (area A is zero) and 1 (100%) indicates maximum inequality.

"The Gini index is the most frequently used inequality index. The reason for its popularity is that it is easy to understand how to compute the Gini index as a ratio of two areas in Lorenz curve diagrams. As a disadvantage, the Gini index only maps a number to the properties of a diagram, but the diagram itself is not based on any model of a distribution process. The "meaning" of the Gini index only can be understood empirically. Additionally the Gini does not capture where in the distribution the inequality occurs. As a result, two very different distributions of income can have the same Gini index."[303]

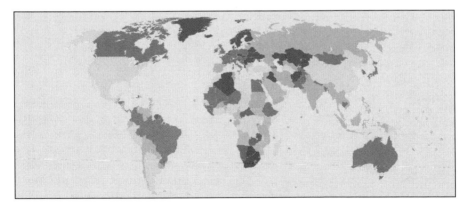

Map II-4-1. Countries by their most recent Gini coefficient score, according to the World Bank. ▮ ≤ 30 ▮ 30-34.9 ▮ 35-39.9 ▮ 40-44.9 ▮ 45-49.9 ▮ 50-54.9 ▮ 55-59.9 ▮ 60-64.9
▮ Data unavailable, accessed 5 September 2019,
https://upload.wikimedia.org/wikipedia/commons/d/d1/World_Bank_Gini_Map.svg.

(c) How Monopoly Impact Income Inequality: Joseph Stiglitz writes: "For 200 years, there have been two schools of thought about what determines the distribution of income – and how the economy functions. One, emanating from Adam Smith and nineteenth-century liberal economists, focuses on competitive markets. The other, cognizant of how Smith's brand of liberalism leads to rapid concentration of wealth and income, takes as its starting point unfettered markets' tendency toward monopoly. For the nineteenth-century liberals individuals' returns are related to their social contributions. Capitalists are rewarded for saving rather than consuming. Differences in income were then related to their ownership of assets – human and financial capital. Scholars of inequality thus focused on the determinants of the distribution of assets, including how they are passed on across generations. The second school of thought takes as its starting point power, including the ability to exercise monopoly control or, in labor markets, to assert authority over workers. Scholars in this area have focused on what gives rise to power, how it is maintained and strengthened, and other features that may prevent markets from being competitive. Work on exploitation arising from asymmetries of information is an important example. In the West...the liberal school of thought has dominated. Yet, as inequality has widened and concerns about it have grown, the competitive school, viewing individual returns in terms of marginal product, has become increasingly unable to explain how the economy works."[304]

"So, today, the second school of thought is ascendant. After all, the large bonuses paid to banks' CEOs as they led their firms to ruin and the economy to the brink of collapse are hard to reconcile with the belief that individuals' pay has anything to do with their social contributions...The top ten banks' share of the deposit market, for example, increased from about 20% to 50% in just 30 years, from 1980 to 2010. Some of the increase in market power is the result of changes in technology and economic structure: consider network economies and the growth of locally provided service-sector industries. Some is because firms have learned better how to erect and maintain entry barriers, often assisted by conservative political forces that justify lax anti-trust enforcement and the failure to limit market power on the grounds that markets are naturally competitive. Large banks, for example, lobbied the US Congress to amend or repeal legislation separating commercial banking from other areas of finance. The consequences are evident in the data, with inequality rising at every level, not only across individuals, but also across firms. Joseph Schumpeter...argued that monopolies would only be temporary. There would be fierce competition for the market, and this would replace competition in the market and ensure that prices Today's markets are characterized by the persistence of high monopoly profits. The implications of this are profound. If markets are based on exploitation, the rationale for *laissez-faire* disappears."[305]

(d) Social Cost of Monopoly: "An important difference between monopoly and perfect competition is that whereas under perfect competition allocation of resources is optimum and therefore social welfare is maximum, under monopoly resources are misallocated causing loss of social welfare. When a product is produced and sold under conditions of monopoly, the monopolist gains at the expense of consumers, for they have to pay a price higher than marginal cost of production. This results in loss of consumers' welfare. Which is greater? Monopolist's gain or consumers' loss."[306]

"Consumer's surplus, is the surplus of price which consumers are prepared to pay for a commodity over and above what they actually pay for it. The dead-weight loss in consumer's welfare due to monopoly can be shown through Figure II-4-3 where TD is the demand curve for the monopolist product MR is the corresponding marginal revenue curve. It is assumed that the industry is a constant cost industry so that average cost (AC) remains the same as output is increased and marginal cost is equal to it. Under perfect competition firms equate price with marginal cost and industry's output is determined by demand for and supply of the product. Since we are considering a constant cost industry, a horizontal line (AC=MC) is the supply curve of the industry…Firms will be equating price OPc with their marginal cost. The consumer surplus enjoyed by the consumers is equal to the area TKPc. It may be noted that consumer surplus reflects social welfare as it is excess of what consumers are willing to pay."[307]

"Now, the monopolist would not produce OPc output as he equates marginal revenue (MR) with marginal cost (MC) to maximize his profits. It will be seen…that marginal revenue and marginal cost are equal at output level OM. Therefore the monopolist will produce OM output and charge ML or OPm price…monopolist has restricted output to OM and raised price to OPm. As a result monopolist makes profits equal to the area PmLEPc. On the other hand, as a result of rise in price to Pm, the consumers' surplus has been reduced to the area TLPm and they suffer a loss of consumer surplus equal to the area PcKLPm. Thus there is a redistribution of income from consumers to the monopolist, but it is important to note that loss of consumer surplus PcKLPm which is greater than the profits made by the monopolist by the area of triangle LKE." This is the social cost of monopoly."[308]

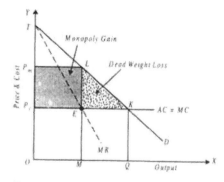

Fig. 26.12. *Dead-weight Loss or Social Cost of Monopoly*

Figure II-4-4. Social Cost of Monopoly, accessed 15 September 2019,
https://tse1.mm.bing.net/th?id=OIP.T-4i8ej-Rt7a0nonoJ6F5QHaHa&pid=Api&P=0&w=300&h=300

Policies for Stability: *(a) Fiscal and Monetary Policies*: "Fiscal policy depicts the picture of how the government spends money and collects revenue and the whole thing about fiscal policy are to ensure that the spending and revenue collections happen appropriately…Monetary policy talks about the movement and supply of money. It is handled by the central bank of the country by changing factors like interest rates, cash reserve ratio etc." Then, how they are different? "The fiscal policy ensures that the economy develops and grows through the government's revenue collections and government's appropriate expenditure….monetary policy ensures that there is liquidity in the economy and the economy remains stable throughout. Fiscal policy is controlled by the ministry of finance of the country. Monetary policy, on the other hand, is controlled by the central bank of the country. The fiscal policy ensures the overall well-being of the economy. Monetary policy is the subset of fiscal policy. Fiscal policy is formed every year after reviewing the results of the previous year. Monetary policy is formed as per the economic conditions of the country. Both fiscal policy and monetary policy can be used as expansionary and contractionary policies in different conditions."[309]

The expansionary fiscal policy requires the government minimizes taxes and increases public spending; while the contractionary fiscal policy requires the government increases taxes and reduce public expenditure. The expansionary monetary policy requires that Federal Reserve increases the money supply through the purchase securities on the open market; lower the Federal Discount Rate; and lower Reserve Requirements. "Expansionary monetary policy causes an increase in bond prices and a reduction in interest rates. Lower interest rates lead to higher levels of capital investment. The lower interest rates make domestic bonds less attractive, so the demand for domestic bonds falls and the demand for foreign bonds rises. The demand for domestic currency falls and the demand for foreign currency rises, causing a decrease in the exchange rate. A lower exchange rate causes exports to increase, imports to decrease and the balance of trade to rise."[310]

The contractionary monetary policy requires FOMC to sell securities on the open market, known as Open Market Operations; to raise the Federal Discount Rate, to raise Reserve Requirements. "Contractionary monetary policy causes a decrease in bond prices and an increase in interest rates. Higher interest rates lead to lower levels of capital investment. The higher interest rates make domestic bonds more attractive, so the demand for domestic bonds rises and the demand for foreign bonds falls. The demand for domestic currency rises and the demand for foreign currency falls, causing an increase in the exchange rate. A higher exchange rate causes exports to decrease, imports to increase and the balance of trade to decrease." Finally, monetary and fiscal policies should be used as complementary cooperation to stabilize the economy.[311]

(b) Foreign Exchange Rates and Trade Deficit: The exchange rate is the price of a foreign currency. "A high exchange rate – a week dollar – reduces imports and increases exports, stimulating aggregate demand. Under fixed exchange rates, central banks buy and sell foreign currency to peg the exchange rate. Under floating exchange rates, the market determines the value of one currency in terms of another. If a country wishes to maintain a fixed exchange rate in the presence of a balance of payments deficit, the central bank must buy back domestic currency, using its reserves of foreign currency and gold or borrowing reserves from abroad. If the balance of payments deficit persists long enough for the country to run out of reserves, it must allow the value of its currency to fall. In the very long run, exchange rates adjust so as to equalize the real cost of goods across countries." In perfect capital mobility, fiscal policy is powerful with fixed exchange rates, and monetary policy is powerful with floating exchange rates.[312]

"Purchasing power parity (PPP) is a way of determining the value of a product after adjusting for price differences and the exchange rate...The real exchange rate is the purchasing power of a currency relative to another at current exchange rates and prices." "The balance of payments model holds that foreign exchange rates are at an equilibrium level if they produce a stable current account balance. A nation with a trade deficit will experience a reduction in its foreign exchange reserves, which ultimately lowers, or depreciates, the value of its currency. If a currency is undervalued, its nation's exports become more affordable in the global market while making imports more expensive. After an intermediate period, imports will be forced down and exports will rise, thus stabilizing the trade balance and bringing the currency towards equilibrium."[313]

"The primary objective of foreign exchange market intervention is to manage the volatility and/or influence the level of the exchange rate. Governments prefer to stabilize the exchange rate because excessive short-term volatility erodes market confidence and affects both the financial market and the real goods market." "Direct currency intervention is generally defined as foreign exchange transactions that are conducted by the monetary authority and aimed at influencing the exchange rate. Depending on whether it changes the monetary base or not, currency intervention can be distinguished between non-sterilized intervention and sterilized intervention, respectively."[314] "Currency manipulation occurs when a country that runs a large trade surplus intervenes in the foreign exchange market with the aim of artificially depressing the value of its currency and making its exports cheaper on the global market. Although... policies, such as cutting interest rates or buying domestic financial assets, can affect exchange rates, manipulation...is conceptually different. Whereas the aim of the former policies is to ease domestic financial conditions, the purpose ...is simply to weaken a currency or to keep it from rising when it should."[315]

(c) Government-Owned Company: (i) "Characteristics of a Government Company: *1. A government company is formed and registered under the Companies Act, 1956 as a public company or a private company. *2. It has a separate legal entity, perpetual succession and a common seal. *3. It can sue and be sued, enter into contracts and acquire property in its own name. *4. A government company may be owned wholly by the government or partly by the government and partly by the private investors. When these companies are owned by both the government and private investors, not less than 51 per cent of the paid-up share capital of government company is held by the Government. *5. The government company is managed by Board of Directors. The directors are appointed by the government and other shareholders. *6. The auditor of a government company is appointed by the Central Government on the advice of the Comptroller and Auditor-General of India. *7. The annual report of the working of the government company is required to be presented every year to the Parliament."[316]

(ii) Advantages of a Government Company: "A government company enjoys the following advantages or benefits: *1. A government company is formed easily as no statute is required to be enacted. *2. It has a separate legal entity and so can manage its affairs on its own. *3. These companies are run on sound business lines. They earn surpluses to finance their own expansion plans. *4. This form of management has greater flexibility than the department management. The 'Memorandum of Association' and 'Articles of Association' of government company can be altered according to the provisions of the Indian Companies Act, 1956 as and when required. *5. It is the only form of management by which the government can make use of managerial skill and technical know-how of the private sector. *6. Tie directors of a government company are free to take decisions. They can take prompt decisions. They will not let an opportunity slip away."[317]

(iii) Limitations of a Government Company: *1. The relatively independent character of the Government company has proved to be farce. Government being the sole or the bulk shareholder dictates its terms and the management is conducted by the Board of Directors...*2. Ministerial interference in the working of the Government company is found to be frequent and far-reaching. *3. The powers of the Board of Directors are subject to the approval of the concerned Ministry. *4. The control exercised by the Government over these companies is so vast or all-pervading that they are reduced to mere adjuncts to the ministries. *5. The autonomy of the Govern-ment companies is vitiated by the executive orders of the Government issued without reference to the Parliament. *6. The Boards of Management are dominated by officials from the ministerial departments in their ex-officio capacity. *7. The departmental officers appointed to top posts in the executive control of these companies. *8. It evades the constitutional responsibility to the Government and the Parliament.[318]

(d) The Global Financial Crisis 2007-2008: "It began in 2007 with a crisis in the subprime mortgage market in the United States and developed into a full-blown international banking crisis with the collapse of the investment bank Lehman Brothers on September 15, 2008. Excessive risk-taking by banks such as Lehman Brothers helped to magnify the financial impact globally. Massive bailouts of financial institutions and other palliative monetary and fiscal policies were employed to prevent a possible collapse of the world financial system. The crisis was nonetheless followed by a global economic downturn, the Great Recession. The Asian markets immediately impacted and volatilized after the U.S. sub-prime crisis. The European debt crisis, a crisis in the banking system of the European countries using the euro, followed later."[319]

(i) Subprime mortgage bubble: "The precipitating factor for the Financial Crisis of 2007–2008 was a high default rate in the United States subprime home mortgage sector, i.e. the bursting of the subprime bubble. This happened when many housing mortgage debtors failed to make their regular payments, leading to a high rate of foreclosures." *Low interest rates encouraged mortgage lending. *Many mortgages were bundled together and formed into new financial instruments called mortgage-backed securities, in a process known as securitization. *Lax regulation allowed predatory lending in the private sector. The Community Reinvestment Act, a 1977 US federal law designed to help low- and moderate-income Americans get mortgage loans encouraged banks to grant mortgages to higher risk families. *Reckless lending by, for example, Bank of America's Countrywide Financial unit, caused Fannie Mae and Freddie Mac to lose market share and to respond by lowering their own standards. * Mortgage guarantees. Many of the subprime (high risk) loans were bundled and sold, finally accruing to the quasi-government agencies Fannie Mae and Freddie Mac.[320]

(ii) Banking crisis: "High mortgage approval rates led to a large pool of homebuyers, which drove up housing prices. This appreciation in value led large numbers of homeowners (subprime or not) to borrow against their homes as an apparent windfall. This "bubble" would be burst by a rising single-family residential mortgages delinquency rate beginning in August 2006 and peaking in the first quarter, 2010. The high delinquency rates led to a rapid devaluation of financial instruments."[321]

(iii) Consequence: "While the collapse of large financial institutions was prevented by the bailout of banks by national governments, stock markets still dropped worldwide. In many areas, the housing market also suffered, resulting in evictions, foreclosures, and prolonged unemployment." The crisis caused the failure of key businesses, "declines in wealth estimated in trillions of US dollars, and a downturn in economic activity leading to the Great Recession of 2008–2012 and contributing to the European sovereign-debt crisis."[322] Congress passed the Reinvestment Act of 2009.

Environment and Development: The implication of government failure could be damaging to the economy as those of market failure. "Such failures comprise: 1 intervention in markets and present wrong price signals which distort allocation; 2 market controls; 3 land use controls; 4 inappropriate fiscal policies (e.g. taxes and subsidies); 5 the general failure of bureaucracies to formulate and implement rational national resource policies in LDCs. Some of these failures will have a clear impact on natural resource degradation in LDCs. It is now increasingly acknowledged that relative prices matter; otherwise there will be a natural desire to exhaust the lowest priced resource first regardless of its true scarcity and benefits."[323]

"In the absence of general economic policies to prevent the over-use of physical and economic resources, it is very likely that resource use will be inefficient. Such inefficiencies are quite common in LDCs with common property resources or open access resources and the effect on the environment could be very damaging. The final result would be tragic when a common property, say in parts of Africa or Asia, is overgrazed." Why are scarce resources so underpriced in LDCs? The main reasons could be as follow: (i) For common property/open access resources, since everyone's property belongs to no one, on owner is interested in preventing air/water pollution to keep the private cost of cleaning the environment down to the minimum...(ii) The cost of monitoring the use of common property resources is high; so are the costs of collection tariffs. Hence, governments sometimes decide to stay away from the duty of protecting the environment." Thus, policy failures and market failures contribute to this.[324]

"ESCAP (as UN Education and Social Commission for Asia Pacific) pursues a development agenda that focuses on integrating environmental sustainability into development policy making, in particular by turning resource constraints and the climate crisis into an economic opportunity that generates a double dividend of higher economic growth necessary to reduce poverty with lower environmental impact by improving the efficiency of resource use and increasing investments in human and natural capital. Economic growth cannot be an end in itself. Gains from current growth have not been evenly distributed and environmental and social externalities are growing worse. However, poverty reduction and decent job creation are not possible without economic growth. This is why we need an economic growth with different economic, social and ecological qualities, such as high economic dynamism, social inclusion and ecological sustainability. The green growth approach, promoted in the ESCAP region since 2005, focuses on improving the ecological quality of economic growth as an important tool for sustainable development..." ESCAP is now directing policies to integrate environment and development making toward green growth and green economy, quality growth, urban development, water resource management, energy security, and so on to recover previous damages.[325]

(a) Externalities, Natural Resource Degradation and Economic Policies: (i) The pollution tax: polluters pay principle: "In economic theory, the simple way to solve the problem of pollution from an industry would be to equate the marginal abatement cost MAC [i.e. the cost of abating or controlling pollution, also known as marginal control cost which rises with increasing pollution and lowers marginal private net benefits (MPNB)] to the marginal benefit from abating pollution. When the latter benefits are regarded as the cost of the damage avoided, they can also be regarded as marginal damage or external cost (MDC)" rising with increasing pollution. The socially optimum level of pollution occurs at...MAC = MDC."[326]

(ii) The fixed standard, bargaining and the Coase theorem: "Other principles to achieve a socially desirable level of pollution involve the least cost method of a fixed standard of environmental quality, the principle of bargaining (under which victims of pollution negotiate directly with the polluters and a deal is struck where the victims marginal damage is equal to the firm's marginal benefit) and regulations to achieve a certain standard. It has been persuasively argued that a competitive market economy can reach an optimum level of pollution through bargaining among the affected parties when the property rights are well defined."[327]

(b) Fuelwoods in Household Energy Consumption: "This is mainly because of their low cost, ready availability and the extremely modest cooking facilities needed to convert them into useful energy. Estimates of worldwide consumption of fuelwoods indicate that in 1978, 2 billion people relied on fuelwoods and biomass as their...household energy."[328]

(c) An Alternative Farming System: "West African agricultural productivity has been sustained through shifting cultivation methods. However, owing to an increase in population pressure on arable land, fallow periods have been shortened with adverse consequences on the natural restoration of the physical, chemical and biological properties of soils. The long forest and bush fallow have been replaced by short grass fallow. The result has been a decline in crop productivity and the availability of food pea capital over the last decade or so. A set of new technologies developed elsewhere is most often inappropriate to the unstable soils found in much of sub-Saharan Africa. Of the various technologies developed by scientists, alley cropping has shown the most promise. Alley cropping mimics the natural land management system by introducing leguminous trees/shrubs in hedgerows with crop grown between the alleys. The leguminous trees contribute by fixing nitrogen, recovering nutrients leached in subsoil, recycling soil erosion. The long-term use reduces demand for idling of land and thus enables an increased proportion of the land to remain in cultivation. The replacement of bush fallow cultivation methods by a semi-permanent cultivation system is a desirable strategy to meet the growing food needs of tropical sub-Saharan Africa."[329]

Climate Change Problems: "Climate change, periodic modification of Earth's climate brought about as a result of changes in the atmosphere as well as interactions between the atmosphere and various other geologic, chemical, biological, and geographic factors within the Earth system."

Causes: "(i) Fossil-fuel combustion, deforestation, rice cultivation, livestock ranching, industrial production, and other human activities have increased since the development of agriculture and especially since the start of the Industrial Revolution. (ii) Greenhouse gases (GHGs) in the atmosphere, such as carbon dioxide, methane, and water vapor, absorb infrared radiation emitted from Earth's surface and reradiate it back, thus contributing to the greenhouse effect. (iii) Ice sheets, sea ice, terrestrial vegetation, ocean temperatures, weathering rates, ocean circulation, and GHG concentrations are influenced either directly or indirectly by the atmosphere. (iv) Periodic changes in Earth's orbit and axial tilt with respect to the Sun affect how solar radiation is distributed on Earth's surface. (v) Tectonic movements, which change the shape, size, position, and elevation of the continental masses and the bathymetry of the oceans, have had strong effects on the circulation of both the atmosphere and the oceans. (vi) The brightness of the Sun continues to increase as the star ages and it passes on an increasing amount of this energy to Earth's atmosphere."[330]

Outcomes: "(i) The most familiar and predictable phenomena are the seasonal cycles, to which people adjust their clothing, outdoor activities, thermostats, and agricultural practices. (ii) Human societies have changed adaptively in response to climate variations, although evidence abounds that certain societies and civilizations have collapsed in the face of rapid and severe climatic changes. (iii) The complex feedbacks between climate components can produce "tipping points" in the climate system, where small, gradual changes in one component of the system can lead to abrupt climate changes. (iv) The history of life has been strongly influenced by changes in climate, some of which radically altered the course of evolution."[331]

How Cities Can Respond: "Climate change impacts are now a permanent feature of our world...There are several steps that cities and states in particular, standing as they do at the frontlines of these climate impacts, can take as they shift climate policies from triage to chronic care. First, cities and states clearly must acknowledge not only the need to reduce greenhouse gas emissions but also the need to manage the physical impacts of chronic climate change. Cities in particular should commission climate risk analysis using available climate science modeling that factors in both acute and chronic climate conditions over several decades. Once this analysis is in hand, cities need to incorporate climate risk considerations into local planning decisions every time they consider an investment in infra-structure, real estate, or other long-term, place-based assets. They should consider adding staff with relevant expertise and requiring contractors..."[332]

China-United States Trade War is an ongoing economic conflict between the world's two largest national economies, China and the United States. "The conflict, initiated by President of the United States Donald Trump, has been characterized by increasing tariffs and other trade barriers with the goal of forcing China to make changes to what the U.S. says are unfair trade practices. Among the trade practices and their effects which the U.S. claims are unfair are the growing trade deficit, the theft of intellectual property, and the forced transfer of American technology to China."[333]

"Since the 1980s, Trump advocated tariffs to reduce the U.S. trade deficit and promote domestic manufacturing, saying the country was being ripped off by its trading partners; imposing tariffs became a major plank of his presidential campaign. Although some economists and politicians argue that the United States' persistent trade deficit is problematic, many economists argue that it is not a problem, and very few advocate tariffs as a solution, citing historical evidence that escalating tariff conflicts result in no winners. In the United States, the trade war has brought struggles for farmers and manufacturers and higher prices for consumers. In other countries it has also caused economic damage, though some countries have benefited from increased manufacturing to fill the gaps. It has also led to stock market instability. The governments of several countries...have taken steps to address some of the damage. The trade war has been criticized internationally; in the U.S., businesses and agricultural organizations have also been critical, though most farmers continued to support Trump. Among U.S. politicians the response has been mixed. The trade war has caused a significant deterioration in China–United States relations."[334]

Chinese domestic reactions: "Communist Party newspaper People's Daily has stated that China will be able to withstand the trade war, and that Trump's policies are affecting American consumers. In September 2019, Lu Xiang, an analyst at the Chinese Academy of Social Sciences, expressed pessimism about the outcome of upcoming talks, called Trump 'unpredictable', and said, 'We can only try to find sensible clues in his nonsense.' Domestic reporting on the trade war is censored." United States domestic reactions: "Senate Democratic leader Chuck Schumer praised President Trump's higher tariffs against China's alleged taking advantage of the U.S. and said Democrats, Republicans, Americans of every political ideology, every region in the country should support these actions" International reactions: "U.S. allies have warned Trump about escalating tariffs....UK Prime Minister Boris Johnson said, 'We don't like tariffs on the whole.' European Council President Donald Tusk said the trade war risked causing a global recession. On June 1, 2018...the European Union launched WTO legal complaints against China's alleged forced ownership-granting and usage of technology that is claimed to discriminate against foreign firms and undermine the intellectual property rights of EU companies."[335]

5. Capitalism and Democracy
Economic Efficiency versus Political Equality

"Most modern societies are made up of three sectors: the state, the market, and civil society. Most political philosophies contain an implicit bias toward one of these three sectors. *Socialists* tilt toward the state. They believe that government bears primary responsibility for improving the lives of its citizens. To this end, state ownership of the means of production is favored. A softer version of this model, which I will call democratic socialism, sees some role for markets given the past failure of planned economies, but a bigger role for government than currently exists in many European countries and especially in the U.S. The Nordic countries come closest to embodying this philosophy and left-leaning politicians in other countries point to their example as one that is worth copying. *Capitalists* believe that free markets are the best way to organize a society. Markets, they argue, are not only the most efficient way to allocate resources but also preserve individual freedom in the process. Markets produce good outcomes precisely because, when unfettered, they optimize growth, efficiency, and a distribution of income that is acceptable because it is assumed to reflect each person's contributions to the economy. A softer version of capitalism, that we might call liberal democracy or the mixed-economy model, accepts the importance of markets but recognizes the need for government to correct market failures and address distributional questions. This type of a mixed economy prevailed in the three decades following World War II in the U.S. and was championed in a weaker way by Third Way leaders such as Tony Blair and Bill Clinton in the 1990s and Obama in the 2000's. *Social capitalists* believe that the good society is built on a foundation of respect for tradition and authority, and for the civic virtues or morals that enable us to fulfill various responsibilities to one another. That society is based on private property but also on the little platoons of family, church, and voluntary associations. It celebrates virtuous social norms and habits that shape how people behave. I call this social capitalism, not because of its emphasis on private property (although that institution is celebrated) but because of its emphasis on the little platoons that in the aggregate create social capital."[336]

In most societies, all three of these sectors – the state, the market, and civil society – play a role. "The question is not whether there is a role for each. The question is what's the right balance or mix. If we got the mix right we might have a Goldilocks economy and a well-woven society – one in which all three sectors play a prominent role but in which they complement each other and provide a kind of checks and balances against the weaknesses of each. Right now, the predominant paradigm in the U.S. is market fundamentalism. But it is being challenged on both the left and the right, by both left-leaning Democrats and some conservative intellectuals."[337]

Social Democracy is a political, social and economic philosophy that supports economic and social interventions to promote social justice within the framework of liberal democracy and capitalist economy. "The protocols and norms used to accomplish this involve a commitment to representative and participatory democracy, measures for income redistribution, regulation of the economy in the general interest and social welfare provisions. Due to longstanding governance by social democratic parties during the post-war consensus and their influence on socioeconomic policy in the Nordic countries, social democracy became associated with the Nordic model and Keynesianism within political circles in the late 20th century. Social democracy aims to create the conditions for capitalism to lead to greater democratic, egalitarian and solidaristic outcomes. It is characterized by a commitment to policies aimed at curbing inequality, eliminating oppression of underprivileged groups, and eradicating poverty, including support for universally accessible public services like care for the elderly, childcare, education, health care and workers' compensation. The social democratic movement often has strong connections with the labor movement and trade unions which are supportive of collective bargaining rights for workers as well as measures to extend decision-making beyond politics into the economic sphere in the form of co-determination for employees and other economic stakeholders."[338]

"Social democracy originated as an ideology within the socialist and labor movement, whose goal at different times has been a social revolution to move away from capitalism to a post-capitalist economy such as socialism, a peaceful revolution as in evolutionary socialism, or the establishment and support of a welfare state. Social democracy's origins lie in the 1860s German Empire as a form of revolutionary socialism associated with orthodox Marxism. Starting in the 1890s, there was a dispute between committed revolutionary social democrats such as Rosa Luxemburg and reformist evolutionary social democrats such as revisionist Eduard Bernstein who supported a more gradual approach grounded in liberal democracy, with Karl Kautsky representing a centrist position. By the 1910s, social democracy had spread worldwide and transitioned towards advocating an evolutionary and peaceful change from capitalism to socialism using established political processes. In the late 1910s, socialist parties that were committed to revolutionary socialism renamed themselves as communist parties, causing a split in the socialist movement between these supporting the October Revolution and those opposing it. Social democrats who were opposed to the Bolsheviks later named themselves democratic socialists in order to highlight their differences from communists and later in the 1920s from Marxist–Leninists, disagreeing with them on topics such as their opposition to bourgeois democracy, although sharing some common ideological roots."[339]

"In the early post-war era in Western Europe, social democratic parties rejected the Stalinist political and economic model then current in the Soviet Union, committing themselves either to an alternative path to socialism or to a compromise between capitalism and socialism. During the post-war period, social democrats embraced a mixed-market economy based on the predominance of private property, with only a minority of essential utilities and public services being under public ownership. As a result, social democracy became associated with Keynesian economics, state interventionism and the welfare state while abandoning the prior goal of replacing the capitalist system (as manifested in factor markets, private property and wage labor) with a qualitatively different socialist economic system."[340]

(a) Response to Neoliberalism: As a matter of fact, "The economic crisis in the Western world during the mid to late 1970s resulted in the rise of neoliberalism and politicians elected on neoliberal platforms such as British prime minister Margaret Thatcher and United States president Ronald Reagan. The rise in support for neoliberalism raised questions over the political viability of social democracy, with sociologist Ralf Dahrendorf predicting the end of the social democratic century...The collapse of Marxist–Leninist states in Eastern Europe after the end of the Cold War and the creation of multi-party democracy in many of those countries resulted in the creation of multiple social democratic parties. Alhough many of these parties did not achieve initial electoral success, they became a significant part of the political landscape of Eastern Europe. In Western Europe, the prominent Italian Communist Party transformed itself into the post-communist Democratic Party of the Left in 1991."[341]

(b) Third Way and Great Recession (1991-2007): "In the 1990s, the ideology of the Third Way developed, and many social democrats became adherents of it. The social democratic variant of the Third Way has been advocated by its proponents as an alternative to both capitalism and what it regards as the traditional forms of socialism (Marxian socialism and state socialism) which Third Way social democrats reject. It officially advocates ethical socialism, reformism and gradualism which includes advocating a humanized version of capitalism, a mixed economy, political pluralism and liberal democracy. The Third Way has been strongly criticized within the social democratic movement for being neoliberal in nature. Left-wing opponents of the Third Way claim that it is not a form of socialism and that it represents social democrats who responded to the New Right by accepting capitalism. Supporters of Third Way ideals argue that they merely represent a necessary or pragmatic adaptation of social democracy to the realities of the modern world, noting that traditional social democracy thrived during the prevailing international climate of the post-war Bretton Woods consensus which collapsed in the 1970s."[342] Andrew Heywood identified the beliefs of the third way as follows.

(i) Socialism, at least in the form of top-down state intervention, is dead: there is no alternative to what clause 4 of the UK Labor Party's constitution, re-written in 1995, refers to as a dynamic market economy. (ii) The third way emphasizes upon community and moral responsibility. Community has a long socialist heritage associated with a critique of liberal individualism. (iii) The supporters of the third way tend to adopt a consensus view of society, in contrast to socialism's conflict view of society. (iv) The third way has substituted a concern with social inclusion for the traditional socialist commitment to equality. (v) "Where neoliberals argue that the state should be confined to its minimal or night-watchman role, and social democrats wish to use the state to counter-balance the injustices of capitalism, the third way embraces the idea of a competition or market state."[343]

(c) Decline and rejection of the Third Way (2007-present): "With the global economic crisis in the late 2000s and early 2010s, the social democratic parties that had dominated some of the post-World War II political landscape in Western Europe were under pressure in some countries to the extent that a commentator in Foreign Affairs called it an implosion of the centre-left. The first country that saw this development was Greece in the aftermath of the Great Recession and the ongoing Greek government-debt crisis. Support for the Greek social democratic party PASOK declined from 43.9% in the 2009 legislative election to 4.68% in the January 2015 legislative election. The decline subsequently proved to not be isolated to Greece as it spread to a number of countries in Western Europe, a phenomenon many observers described as Pasokification."

Table II-5-1. Tensions between The Third Way and Social Democracy

The Third Way	Social Democracy
Pragmatic	Ideological
Globalization	Nation-State
Information Society	Industrial Society
Community	Class Politics
Market Economy	Mixed Economy
Full Employment	Full Employment
Equality of Opportunity	Equality of Outcome
Meritocracy	Concern for Underdog
Opportunity for All	Social Justice
Promote Inclusion	Eradicate Poverty
Rights and Responsibilities	Social Rights
Welfare-to-Work	Cradle-to-Grave Welfare
Competition/Market State	Social-Reformist State

Source: Andrew Heywood, *Political Ideologies: An Introduction*, 3rd ed.
(New York: Palgrave Macmillan, 2003), 152.

Post-Capitalism Societies: "Post-capitalism includes a number of proposals for a new economic system to replace capitalism, or otherwise speculate on the fate of the current form of the socio-economic order. According to some classical Marxist and some social evolutionary theories, post-capitalist societies may come about as a result of spontaneous evolution as capitalism becomes obsolete. Others propose models to intentionally replace capitalism. The most notable among them are socialism and anarchism."[344] Nevertheless, I don't think both would happen.

Peter Drucker outlined a possible evolution of capitalistic society in his book *Post-Capitalist Society* (1993). "The book stated that knowledge, rather than capital, land, or labor, is the new basis of wealth. The classes of a fully post-capitalist society are expected to be divided into knowledge workers or service workers, in contrast to the capitalists and proletarians of a capitalist society. In the book, Drucker estimated the transformation to post-capitalism would be completed in 2010–2020. Drucker also argued for rethinking the concept of intellectual property by creating a universal licensing system. Consumers would subscribe for a cost and producers would assume that everything is reproduced and freely distributed."[345]

Paul Mason published *Post Capitalism: A Guide to our Future* (2105). He views that "Much of the speculation surrounding the proposed fate of the capitalist system stems from predictions about the future integration of technology into economics. The evolution and increasing sophistication of both automation and information technology is said to threaten jobs and highlight internal contradictions in Capitalism which will allegedly ultimately lead to its collapse." He argues that centralized planning of socialism…is unachievable."[346]

Robin Hahnel published *Of the People, By the People: The Case of a Participatory Economy* (2012). "The participatory economy focuses on the participation of all citizens through the creation of worker councils and consumer councils. Hahnel emphasizes the direct participation of worker and consumers rather than appointing representatives. The councils are concerned with large-scale issues of production and consumption and are broken into various bodies tasked with researching future development projects. In a participatory economy, economic rewards would be offered according to need, the amount of which would be determined democratically by the workers council. Hahnel also calls for economic justice by rewarding people for their effort and diligence rather than accomplishments or prior ownership. A worker's effort is to be determined by their co-workers. Consumption rights are then rewarded according to the effort ratings. The worker has the choice to decide what they consume using…" "It is utopian to expect more from a system than it can possibly deliver. To expect equality and justice from capitalism is utopian. To expect social solidarity from markets, or self-management from central planning, is equally utopian."[347]

"Crony capitalism is an economy in which businesses thrive not as a result of risk, but rather as a return on money amassed through a nexus between a business class and the political class. This is often achieved by using state power rather than competition in managing permits, government grants, tax breaks, or other forms of state intervention over resources where the state exercises monopolist control over public goods, for example, mining concessions for primary commodities or contracts for public works. Money is then made not merely by making a profit in the market, but through profiteering by rent seeking using this monopoly or oligopoly. Entrepreneurship and innovative practices which seek to reward risk are stifled since the value-added is little by crony businesses, as hardly anything of significant value is created by them, with transactions taking the form of trading. Crony capitalism spills over into the government, the politics, and the media, when this nexus distorts the economy and affects society to an extent it corrupts public-serving economic, political, and social ideals."[348]

"While the problem is generally accepted across the political spectrum, ideology shades the view of the problem's causes and therefore its solutions. Political views mostly fall into two camps which might be called the socialist and capitalist critique. The socialist position is that crony capitalism is the inevitable result of any strictly capitalist system and thus broadly democratic government must regulate economic, or wealthy, interests in order to restrict monopoly. The capitalist position is that natural monopolies are rare, therefore governmental regulations generally abet established wealthy interests by restricting competition."[349]

Capitalism in economy provides efficiency in fair market competition without monopoly, while democracy in politics pursues equal opportunity in society. Any future system is not sustainable if it cannot support both demands. In this regard, the answer to question about the future system we pursue is definitely democracy with market economy. Capitalism pursues efficiency that brings more profits or personal income. If businesses become prosperous, it is very possible to create the political-economic complex in the absence of appropriate checks and balances in the system. There are many reasons for income inequality in society, including the labor, innate ability, education, race, gender, culture, wealth condensation, development patterns and personal preference for work, leisure and risk." Mitigating factors in government sponsored approach may include public education, progressive taxation, minimum wage regulation, nationalization of essential goods and services. "In a market-driven economy, too much economic disparity could generate pressure for its own removal. In an extreme example, if one person owned everything, that person would immediately (in a market economy) have to hire people to maintain his property, and that person's wealth would immediately begin to dissipate."[350]

Efficiency in Growth vs. Equality in Distribution: Capitalism tries to maximize business profits subject to constraints, pursuing efficiency, which increases the income gap between the rich and the rich. Democracy is based freedom and on equality (such as a vote a person). In order to reduce income inequality, the government collect more taxes from the rich, and uses funds to build more and better infrastructure, improve better education and health care, and provide other social services for the less advantaged peoples. However, available resources are so limited in a limited period of time that the nation state is unable to provide their demand fully. If the state collects taxes above the acceptable limited, taxpayers refuse to obey, and if enforced, the state cannot maintain law and order. Hence, capitalist efficiency in economy should be compromised with democratic equality in politics.

In a microeconomic level, the fundamental cause of income inequality comes from *different initial conditions* between individuals. A person who is born to the rich will get better education and receive some inheritance, which generate labor income with additional rent income, while a person born to the poor generate labor income only. A person, who inherited better gene with wiser brain, warmer heart, and better physical abilities, can achieve better output that a person who inherited not better gene. Hence, this person will perform better in works and get paid more in working place. Therefore, the initial condition makes individual person achieve differently. As mentioned above, there are mitigating factors to reduce individual differences by the government or private organizations, but resources are limited in a state during a limited period of time. Unfortunately, there is no way to change this kind of initial conditions. The only way to overcome differences lies in personal motivation to overcome his or her fate.

The state government usually choose fiscal and monetary policies to adjust to the business cycle of its economy. The economic policies could be either for growth (efficiency) or for distribution (equality). Theoretically, it is wise to take the growth strategy first and the distribution strategy later, because a bigger pie can hold more ingredient to divide equally in distribution. However, politicians are often eager to follow the populism for more votes so that they choose the distribution strategy first for popular votes by getting even smaller pie to divide into pieces. Generally speaking in U.S. politics, the President from the Republican Party often pursues the growth strategy rather than the distribution strategy, however, the President from the Democratic Party often takes the opposite strategy, which trend causes voters to switch the political party of the President.

Therefore, the world should maintain not only capitalist economy for efficiency in growth by promoting competition and minimizing monopoly, but also democratic politics for equality in distribution by enforcing such policies as progressive taxation, public education, minimum wages, nationalization of essential goods and services, and so on.

TWO ESSAYS ON EFFICIENCY AND EQUALITY

Idolization of Human Equality
This is my first essay on this issue published in a newspaper in 2018
titled Idolization of Human Equality.[351]

We live ideologically with the idol of "human beings are equal," but we realize that there is a hierarchy in terms of political, economic, and social aspects in our daily lives. Ordinary people who do not have a parent's legacy would be fortunate to be able to work hard, get paid, pay their bank bills, pay basic living expenses, pay for their children's education, and save a little while. The average person should be at least 50 years old, except for those who are lucky enough to be able to accumulate capital on their own and buy stocks or bitcoins. If young people at age 20 to 30 had good luck gambling with bitcoin investments, that seed money probably wouldn't be their own.

The source of personal income is capital and labor; in addition to income from their own labor, they add income from inherited capital, rent or interest; but those born into poor families are all income from their own labor; and children from wealthy families receive the highest level of education under better conditions, and the difference in personal income increases as they receive a higher level of income in the profession. Even if the intellectual, emotional, and physical conditions are equal, the gap in personal income naturally occurs between wealthy and poor families, except in special cases. Although humans are equal, it is difficult to move between layers or classes because of different starting conditions of individuals.

The Greek society around 400 B.C. was engaged in the class war between the rich and the poor, so that many intellectuals such as Aristophanes intended that "there shall only be one and the same condition of life for all....I shall begin by making land, money, everything that is private property, common to all." Like other intellectuals of his time, Plato's communism is not a nationalization of the land by the state, but an equal sharing of wealth by the citizens, that can be achieved by proper policy measures. Plato's communism was far different from the Marxism experienced and failed in the former Soviet Union and its satellites. Meanwhile, China is transitioning to a capitalist economic system under the control of the Chinese Communist Party, which has created many problems of inefficiency. Then, how can we make human society equal?

Many European countries have adopted socialist policies to pursue equality but failed and returned to the capitalist system. The country like Greece chose socialist policies with huge welfare benefits to the people, which brought a state bankruptcy, begging money to the ECB. The fundamental issue here is that if the state chooses a growth strategy, the gap between rich and poor is widened, and that if the government choose a distribution strategy, the productivity is declines and so does the growth. The answer is in that firstly choose the growth policy and accumulate the nation's wealth, and secondly choose the distribution policy with increased national wealth. However, the people are not patient, and politicians tend to use popular tactics such as free meals or a half of tuition and fees. In the United States, the Republican Party has pursued a growth-oriented policy, and the Democratic party has done a distribution-oriented policy, which changes the ruling party switching the policy-orientation.

There is no answer to the question: what form of politics will allow human start-up conditions to be equal except that each individual must overcome these through his or her own efforts. The state only can collect more taxes from the rich and invest the fund for the benefits of the poor such as to the construction of infrastructure, healthcare, education, and so on. Nevertheless, the supply of resources is limited but the demand for free ride is endless. Therefore, the state policies to reduce the income inequality in the capitalist economy must be minimal in their effectiveness. Moreover, there are differences in abilities that each individual has inherently, so that each's willingness to overcome individual differences is even more important. Considering the North Korean political system, it would be an extravagant idea for South Korean young people to blame the government for the happiness of ordinary people. It would be wiser to depend on oneself rather than the state for their future.

In other words, the national government provides national security against foreign threat and public safety against domestic violations for the payments of your taxes. The socialist government tries to distribute available resources for the well-being of all. It should be especially important to keep in mind that socialist policies can lead to a crisis of state wealth as we have seen in Cuba and Venezuela. Human equality is a humanitarian idol. Without individual efforts to overcome human inequality, what a nation can do is very limited.

How to overcome the unfavorable initial conditions of individuals. The answer to this question is simple: Maximize your objective function subject to constraints such as available resources including capital, labor, and technology. You may use more input factors with improved productivity as appeared below: "Economics of Happiness: You Can Have a Happy Life."

(End of essay)

Economics of Happiness- You can have a happy life
This is my second essay published in 2016, which suggests how to overcome an unfavorable initial condition of man, that has not been resolved until now.

Everyone wants to live happily, so the human effort to pursue happiness continues until the end of its life. What is happiness and how can we obtain it? How many happiness figures are you currently in? Gradually, the average life expectancy of modern people will be extended so that they can live healthily until the age of 90, and a person who has been pushed out of work at age 60 will have another 30 years of activity, so a lecture on economics of happiness is needed.

● *Definition of happiness*: Being happy can be seen as a degree of satisfaction in one's life. If you are happy with your daily life, you will be happy, and you will not be happy if you are dissatisfied. Therefore, the question of what happiness is and how to achieve it can be seen as what the value of the individual seeks and how to achieve it. This is the theory of utility in economics, and it can be said that the pursuit of maximum satisfaction of the individual with limited resources and time. The economics of happiness can be divided into two parts: objective function and constraints. Objective functions are difficult to simplify and describe because each person has different values and different levels of desire. Maslow's motivation theory suggests that humans develop from basic needs to social and self-realization needs. Since each position of desire is different between individuals, the degree of satisfaction with the same achievement is different between them.

● *Reconciliation of goals*: The first secret of happiness can be found in the individual's objective function. If your situation is not able to change the constraints, you need to set goals that are appropriate for your abilities. If your greed is so high that it is beyond the limits of your abilities, you will always be dissatisfied. By reducing the lust, you become satisfied when your accomplish-ments exceed expectations. The economics of happiness lies in the old saying that you should whip yourself by looking at the top and comfort the body by looking down the other who is less competitive to you. If there is less return from daily affairs with greed, it becomes painful with a sense of dissatisfaction. The time given to humans is finite, so if you set a goal that suits your abilities, you become happy with fruitful days. When you have a lot of work to do, it's wise to prioritize and do it and forget about the rest. You can't do everything if you try to finish them all, so the result would be the same.

● *Easing of constraints*: The second secret to happiness is to achieve the goals setting above your abilities by easing constraints. This is an aggressive measure to fill the shortfall in the current income by adding additional available resources such as more capital and or more labor. If you work 40 hours per week, you would get additional returns by adding more working hours, or by adding more capital to expand production facilities. In the 1980s, Professor Paul Krugman argued that economic growth in East Asian countries had increased investment and that rural idle labor was employed in manufacturing, that is, by increasing input factors in production, and that growth without productivity had reached its limits. However, *The Economist* saw differently that East Asian countries are continuing to grow as a result of technological innovation, research and development, educational investment, and transformation of the industrial structure to drive productivity growth.

● *Increased productivity*: This is an economic development theory, but it can be applied to the economics of happiness. In other words, the third secret to happiness is to increase individual productivity. By introducing new technologies and management methods in the industry, you can develop your own skills as if you were increasing productivity. You worked in the past 50 hours a week but now you work 40 hours a week to produce the same. This may seem like a physical or mechanical phenomenon, but it can be applied equally to metaphysical events. Setting goals for happiness will vary by age, but efforts to improve productivity should continue for all ages. Improving productivity through the development of individual skills will develop the national economy on a macro scale and increased disposable income will improve the happiness index that you can enjoy. Adjusting the goal is a passive approach and easing constraints to increase input will soon reach its limits, but increased productivity is a challenge to infinite possibilities.

Conclusion: Increased productivity of individuals and corporations is a wise way for mankind to leap toward a new civilization, in which the happiness of individuals and humanity lies. Thus, productivity is the main course of happiness.

(End of essay)

Endnotes

[1] Modern agriculture/British agricultural revolution, accessed 17 November 2019, https://en.wikipedia.org/wiki/History_of_agriculture#Modern_agriculture.

[2] The Facts of Economic Growth, accessed 25 September 2017, https://web.stanford.edu/~chadj/facts.pdf.

[3] *Ibid.*, accessed the same.

[4] The World Economy at the Start of the 21st Century, Remarks by Anne O. Krueger, First Deputy Managing Director, IMF, accessed 17 November 2019, https://www.imf.org/en/News/Articles/2015/09/28/04/53/sp040606.

[5] International Monetary Fund: History, accessed 25 September 2017, https://en.wikipedia.org/wiki/International_Monetary_Fund#History.

[6] https://en.wikipedia.org/wiki/International_Bank_for_Reconstruction_and_Development, IBRD, accessed 25 September 2017,

[7] General Agreement on Tariffs and Trade, accessed 25 September 2017, https://en.wikipedia.org/wiki/General_Agreement_on_Tariffs_and_Trade.

[8] "The World Economy at the Strat of the 21st Century," accessed the same.

[9] *Ibid.*, accessed the same.

[10] 1970s: Economy, accessed 25 September 2017, https://en.wikipedia.org/wiki/1970s#Economy.

[11] *Ibid.*, accessed the same.

[12] "The World Economy at the Strat of the 21st Century," accessed the same.

[13] *Ibid.*, accessed the same.

[14] Capitalism vs. Socialism, accessed 3 September 2019, https://www.diffen.com/difference/Capitalism_vs_Socialism.

[15] Annales School, accessed 27 August 2017, https://en.wikipedia.org/wiki/Annales_School.

[16] Economic history, accessed 26 August 2017, https://en.wikipedia.org/wiki/Economic_history.

[17] Economic history: Development as a separate field, accessed 26 August 2017, https://en.wikipedia.org/wiki/Economic_history#Development_as_a_separate_field.

[18] School of economic thought, accessed 26 August 2017, https://en.wikipedia.org/wiki/Schools_of_economic_thought.

[19] Economics, accessed 26 August 2017, https://en.wikipedia.org/wiki/Economics.

[20] Modern microeconomics theory analysis, accessed 27 August 2017, http://www.economictheories.org/2008/07/modern-microeconomics-theory-analysis.html.

[21] Movement Away from Marshallian Economics, accessed 27 August 2017, http://www.economictheories.org/2008/07/marshallian-economics-marshallian.html.

[22] Harry Landreth and David C. Colander, *History of Economic Thought*, 4th ed. (Boston, MA: Houghton Mifflin Company, 2002), 390.

[23] Evolution of microeconomics: Traditional marginalism, accessed 27 August 2017, https://en.wikipedia.org/wiki/Evolution_of_microeconomics#Traditional_marginalism.

[24] Harry Landreth and David C. Colander, *History of Economic Thought*, 392

[25] *Ibid.*, 392-3.

[26] *Ibid.*, 393.

[27] Edgeworth box, accessed 27 August 2017, https://en.wikipedia.org/wiki/Edgeworth_box.

[28] Evolution of microeconomics: Imperfect competition and game theory, accessed 27 August 2017,

https://en.wikipedia.org/wiki/Evolution_of_microeconomics#Imperfect_competition_and_game_theory.

[29] *Ibid.*, accessed the same.

[30] *Ibid.*, accessed the same.

[31] Paul A. Samuelson, Nobel Laureate, accessed 20 September 2019, http://economics.mit.edu/faculty/samuelson/biography.

[32] Paul Samuelson: Foundations of Economic Analysis, accessed 27 August 2017, https://en.wikipedia.org/wiki/Paul_Samuelson#Foundations_of_Economic_Analysis.

[33] Paul Samuelson: Economics, accessed 27 August 2017, https://en.wikipedia.org/wiki/Paul_Samuelson#Economics.

[34] Equilibrium: Stable or Unstable? Accessed 27 August 2017, https://www.ma.utexas.edu/users/davis/375/popecol/lec9/equilib.html.

[35] *Ibid.*, accessed the same.

[36] Formalism (philosophy of mathematics), accessed 27 August 2017, https://en.wikipedia.org/wiki/Formalism_(philosophy_of_mathematics).

[37] *Ibid.*, accessed the same.

[38] *Ibid.*, accessed the same.

[39] Milton Friedman, accessed 27 August 2017, https://en.wikipedia.org/wiki/Milton_Friedman.

[40] *Ibid.*, accessed the same.

[41] Harry Landreth and David C. Colander, *History of Economic Thought*, 401-2.

[42] Difference between classical economics and vs. neoclassical economics, accessed 5 September 2017, http://www.differencebetween.com/difference-between-classical-economics-and-vs-neoclassical-economics/.

[43] *Ibid.*, accessed the same.

[44] Comparison of Neoclassical and Modern Microeconomics, accessed 6 September 2017, http://www.economictheories.org/2008/07/comparison-of-neoclassical-and-modern.html.

[45] Microeconomics, accessed 27 August 2017, https://en.wikipedia.org/wiki/Macroeconomics.

[46] History of macroeconomic thought, accessed 27 August 2017, https://en.wikipedia.org/wiki/History_of_macroeconomic_thought.

[47] *Ibid.*, accessed the same.

[48] Joseph Schumpeter: Life, accessed 29 August 2017, https://en.wikipedia.org/wiki/Joseph_Schumpeter#Life.

[49] *Ibid.*, accessed the same.

[50] 4 Main Features of Schumpeter's Theory of Economic Development, accessed 21 September 2019, http://www.economicsdiscussion.net/schumpeters-theory/4-main-features-of-schumpeters-theory-of-economic-development/13001.

[51] *Ibid.*, accessed the same.

[52] *Ibid.*, accessed the same.

[53] *Ibid.*, accessed the same.

[54] Joseph Schumpeter: Demise of Capitalism, accessed 21 September 2019, https://en.wikipedia.org/wiki/Joseph_Schumpeter#Demise_of_capitalism.

[55] Joseph Schumpeter: History of Economic Analysis, accessed 21 September 21, 2019, https://en.wikipedia.org/wiki/Joseph_Schumpeter#History_of_Economic_Analysis.

[56] Harry Landreth and David C. Colander, *History of Economic Thought*, 416.

[57] *Ibid.*, 416.

[58] *Ibid.*, 416-7.

[59] Austrian business cycle theory, accessed 20 August 2017,
https://en.wikipedia.org/wiki/Austrian_business_cycle_theory.

[60] Austrian business cycle theory: Theoretical objections, accessed 30 August 2017,
https://en.wikipedia.org/wiki/Austrian_business_cycle_theory#Theoretical_objections.

[61] Austrian business cycle theory: Empirical objections, accessed 30 August 2017,
https://en.wikipedia.org/wiki/Austrian_business_cycle_theory#Empirical_objections.

[62] http://www.economicsdiscussion.net/keynesian-economics/keynes-theory/keyness-theory-of-business-cycle-economics/26055, Keynes's Theory of Business Cycle Economics, accessed 30 August 2017.

[63] http://www.yourarticlelibrary.com/macro-economics/theories-macro-economics/the-friedmans-monetarist-theory-of-business-cycles-explained-with-diagram/38073/, The Friedman's Monetarist Theory of Business Cycles (Explained with Diagram), accessed on August 31, 2017.

[64] *Ibid.*, accessed the same.

[65] Real business cycle theory, accessed 31 August 2017,
https://en.wikipedia.org/wiki/Real_business-cycle_theory.

[66] Real business cycle theory: Criticisms, accessed 31 August 2017,
https://en.wikipedia.org/wiki/Real_business-cycle_theory#Criticisms.

[67] John Maynard Keynes, accessed 31 August 2017,
https://en.wikipedia.org/wiki/John_Maynard_Keynes.

[68] *Ibid.*, accessed the same.

[69] *Ibid.*, accessed the same.

[70] *Ibid.*, accessed the same.

[71] John Maynard Keynes: Keynesian ascendancy, accessed 31 August 2017,
https://en.wikipedia.org/wiki/John_Maynard_Keynes#Keynesian_ascendancy_1939.E2.80.9379.

[72] Neo-Classical Synthesis, accessed 4 September 2017,
http://www.economicshelp.org/blog/6930/economics/neo-classical-synthesis/.

[73] *Ibid.*, accessed the same.

[74] *Ibid.*, accessed the same.

[75] Harry Landreth and David C. Colander, *History of Economic Thought*, 425.

[76] IS-LM-BP model, accessed 5 September 2017, http://policonomics.com/is-lm-bp/.

[77] IS-LM model, accessed 5 September 2017,
http://macroeconomicanalysis.com/macroeconomics-wikipedia/is-lm-model/.

[78] https://en.wikipedia.org/wiki/John_Maynard_Keynes#Keynesian_economics_out_of_favour_1979.E2.80.932007, John Maynard Keynesian economics out of favor, accessed 31 August 2017.

[79] John Maynard Keynes: Keynesian resurgence 2008, accessed 31 August 2017,
https://en.wikipedia.org/wiki/John_Maynard_Keynes#Keynesian_resurgence_2008.E2.80.9309.

[80] Rational expectations, accessed 20 November 2019,
https://en.wikipedia.org/wiki/Rational_expectations.

[81] Robert Lucas, Jr.: Rational expectations, accessed 5 September 2017,
https://en.wikipedia.org/wiki/Robert_Lucas_Jr.#Rational_expectations.

[82] Solow Growth Model, accessed 5 September 2017,
http://economics.wikia.com/wiki/Solow_Growth_Model.

[83] Robert Solow, accessed 5 September 2017,
https://en.wikipedia.org/wiki/Robert_Solow.

[84] Harry Landreth and David C. Colander, *History of Economic Thought*, 437.

[85] *Ibid.*, 439-40.

[86] Organizing Your Social Sciences Research Paper: Quantitative Methods, accessed 6 September 2017,
http://libguides.usc.edu/writingguide/quantitative.

[87] Mathematic economics: Differential calculus, accessed 27 August 2017,
https://en.wikipedia.org/wiki/Mathematical_economics#Differential_calculus.

[88] Mathematical economics: Linear models, accessed 27 August 2017,
https://en.wikipedia.org/wiki/Mathematical_economics#Linear_models.

[89] Wassily Leontief, Pioneer of Input-Output Analysis by Eugene Garfield on *Current Comments* Number 37 (1986), accessed 27 August 2017,
https://www.bea.gov/papers/pdf/IOmanual_092906.pdf.

[90] Mathematic economics: Differential decline and rise, accessed 27 August 2017,
https://en.wikipedia.org/wiki/Mathematical_economics#Differential_decline_and_rise.

[91] Mathematic economics: Game theory, accessed 27 August 2017,
https://en.wikipedia.org/wiki/Mathematical_economics#Game_theory.

[92] https://en.wikipedia.org/wiki/Mathematical_economics#Agent-based_computational_economics, Mathematic economics: Agent-based computational economics, accessed 27 August 2017.

[93] Harry Landreth and David C. Colander, *History of Economic Thought*, 440-1.

[94] *Ibid.*, 441-2.

[95] Economic statistics, accessed 6 September 2017,
https://en.wikipedia.org/wiki/Economic_statistics.

[96] Econometrics, accessed 7 September 2017,
https://en.wikipedia.org/wiki/Econometrics.

[97] Econometrics: Basic models: Linear regression, accessed 7 September 2017,
https://en.wikipedia.org/wiki/Econometrics#Basic_models:_linear_regression.

[98] Econometrics: Theory, accessed 7 September 2017,
https://en.wikipedia.org/wiki/Econometrics#Theory.

[99] Econometrics: Example, accessed 7 September 2017,
https://en.wikipedia.org/wiki/Econometrics#Example.

[100] Bayesian econometrics, accessed 7 September 2017,
https://en.wikipedia.org/wiki/Bayesian_econometrics.

[101] Harry Landreth and David C. Colander, *History of Economic Thought*, 462-3.

[102] Bayesian econometrics: History, accessed 7 September 2017,
https://en.wikipedia.org/wiki/Bayesian_econometrics#History.

[103] Experimental economics, accessed 7 September 2017,
http://web.uri.edu/simlab/experimental-economics/.

[104] *Ibid.*, accessed the same.

[105] Heterodox economics, accessed 22 November 2019,
https://en.wikipedia.org/wiki/Heterodox_economics.

[106] Socialism, accessed 16 September 2019, https://en.wikipedia.org/wiki/Socialism.

[107] *Ibid.*, accessed the same.

[108] Leon P. Baradat, Political Ideologies: Their Origins and Impact, 7th ed. (Upper Saddle River, NJ: Prentice Hall, 1999), 185-6.

[109] *Ibid.*, 187.

[110] Welfare state, accessed 27 December 2016,
https://en.wikipedia.org/wiki/Welfare_state.

[111] Leon P. Baradat, *Political Ideologies: Their Origins and Impact*, 189.

[112] *Ibid.*, 189-90.

[113] *Ibid.*, 191.

[114] Andrew Heywood, *Political Ideologies: An Introduction*, 3rd ed. (New York: Palgrave Macmillan, 2003), 111-2.
[115] Socialism: History, accessed 16 September 2019, https://en.wikipedia.org/wiki/Socialism#History.
[116] *Ibid.*, accessed the same.
[117] *Ibid.*, accessed the same.
[118] Utopian socialism: Development, accessed 27 December 2016, https://en.wikipedia.org/wiki/Utopian_socialism#Development.
[119] Francois Noel Babeuf, accessed 27 December 2016, https://www.britannica.com/biography/Francois-Noel-Babeuf.
[120] *Ibid.*, accessed the same.
[121] Henry de Saint-Simon, accessed 16 September 2019, https://www.britannica.com/biography/Henri-de-Saint-Simon.
[122] *Ibid.*, accessed the same.
[123] *Ibid.*, accessed the same.
[124] Robert Owen, accessed 27 December 2016, https://www.britannica.com/biography/Robert-Owen.
[125] *Ibid.*, accessed the same.
[126] *Ibid.*, accessed the same.
[127] Robert Owen, accessed 16 September 2019, https://en.wikipedia.org/wiki/Robert_Owen.
[128] Charles Fourier: Life, accessed 27 December 2016, https://en.wikipedia.org/wiki/Charles_Fourier#Life.
[129] Charles Fourier: Ideas, accessed 27 December 2016, https://en.wikipedia.org/wiki/Charles_Fourier#Ideas.
[130] Charles Fourier: Children and education, accessed 27 December 2016, https://en.wikipedia.org/wiki/Charles_Fourier#Children_and_education.
[131] Étienne Cabet, accessed 27 December 2016, https://en.wikipedia.org/wiki/%C3%89tienne_Cabet.
[132] *Ibid.*, accessed the same.
[133] *Ibid.*, accessed the same.
[134] *Ibid.*, accessed the same.
[135] Revolutionary socialism, accessed 27 December 2016, https://en.wikipedia.org/wiki/Revolutionary_socialism.
[136] Andrew Heywood, *Political Ideologies: An Introduction*, 118.
[137] *Ibid.*, 118-9.
[138] *Ibid.*, 119.
[139] *Ibid.*, 120.
[140] *Ibid.*, 120.
[141] *Ibid.*, 121.
[142] Fabian Society, accessed 22 November 2019, https://en.wikipedia.org/wiki/Fabian_Society.
[143] *Ibid.*, 122.
[144] Ibid., 122-3.
[145] Karl Marx, accessed 23 November 2019, https://en.wikipedia.org/wiki/Karl_Marx.
[146] *Ibid.*, accessed the same.
[147] Karl Marx/Legacy, accessed 23 November 2019, https://en.wikipedia.org/wiki/Karl_Marx#Legacy.
[148] Andrew Heywood, *Political Ideologies: An Introduction*, 125-6.
[149] *Ibid.*, 126-7.

[150] *Ibid.*, 127.

[151] Leon P. Baradat, *Political Ideologies: Their Origins and Impact*, 176-7.

[152] *Ibid.*, 178.

[153] *Ibid.*, 179-80.

[154] Andrew Heywood, *Political Ideologies: An Introduction*, 130.

[155] http://www.globallearning-cuba.com/blog-umlthe-view-from-the-southuml/marx-on-the-revolutionary-proletariat, Marx on the revolutionary proletariat, accessed 16 September 2019.

[156] The Communist Manifesto: Synopsis, accessed 30 December 2016, https://en.wikipedia.org/wiki/The_Communist_Manifesto#Synopsis.

[157] *Ibid.*, accessed the same.

[158] Das Kapital: Themes, accessed 30 December 2016, https://en.wikipedia.org/wiki/Capital:_Critique_of_Political_Economy#Themes.

[159] Das Capital: Synopsis Volume II, accessed 30 December 2016, https://en.wikipedia.org/wiki/Capital:_Critique_of_Political_Economy#Capital.2C_Volume_II.

[160] Das Kapital: Synopsis Volume III, accessed 30 December 2016, https://en.wikipedia.org/wiki/Capital,_Volume_III.

[161] Leon P. Baradat, *Political Ideologies: Their Origins and Impact*, 181.

[162] *Ibid.*, 182.

[163] https://en.wikipedia.org/wiki/History_of_socialism#International_Workingmen.27s_Association_.28First_International.29, History of socialism: International Workingmen's Association (First International), accessed 30 December 2016.

[164] History of socialism: Paris Commune, accessed 20 December 2016, https://en.wikipedia.org/wiki/History_of_socialism#Paris_Commune.

[165] History of socialism: The Second International, accessed 30 December 2016, https://en.wikipedia.org/wiki/History_of_socialism#The_Second_International.

[166] History of socialism: Anarchism, accessed 30 December 2016, https://en.wikipedia.org/wiki/History_of_socialism#Anarchism.

[167] History of socialism: Social democracy to 1917, accessed 30 December 2016, https://en.wikipedia.org/wiki/History_of_socialism#Social_democracy_to_1917.

[168] https://en.wikipedia.org/wiki/History_of_socialism#Revolutionary_socialism_and_the_Soviet_Union_.281917-39.29, History of socialism: Revolutionary socialism and the Soviet Union, accessed 30 Dec. 2016.

[169] Karl Kaustky: Life and career, accessed 31 December 2016, https://en.wikipedia.org/wiki/Karl_Kautsky#Life_and_career.

[170] Karl Kaustky: Political career, accessed 31 December 2016, https://en.wikipedia.org/wiki/Karl_Kautsky#Political_career.

[171] Karl Kaustky: Polemics with the Bolshevics, accessed 31 December 2016, https://en.wikipedia.org/wiki/Karl_Kautsky#Polemics_with_the_Bolsheviks.

[172] Vladimir Lenin, accessed 17 September 2019, https://en.wikipedia.org/wiki/Vladimir_Lenin.

[173] *Ibid.*, accessed the same.

[174] Leon P. Baradat, *Political Ideologies: Their Origins and Impact*, 202.

[175] *Ibid.*, 203.

[176] *Ibid.*, 203-4.

[177] *Ibid.*, 205.

[178] *Ibid.*, 206.

[179] V. I. Lenin, *Imperialism: The Highest Stage of Capitalism: A Popular Outline* (New York: International Publishers, 1939), reprinted in 1997, 89.

[180] Leon P. Baradat, *Political Ideologies: Their Origins and Impact*, 205-6.

[181] *Ibid.*, 206.

[182] *Ibid.*, 206-7.

[183] Leon Trotsky, accessed 23 November 2019,
https://en.wikipedia.org/wiki/Leon_Trotsky.

[184]https://en.wikipedia.org/wiki/Leon_Trotsky#Trotsky's_contribution_to_the_Russian
_Revolution, Leon Trotsky's contribution, accessed 23 November 2019.

[185] Joseph Stalin, accessed 31 December 2016, http://www.history.com/topics/joseph-stalin.

[186] *Ibid.*, accessed the same.

[187] Stalinism: Stalinist Policies, accessed 17 September 2019,
https://en.wikipedia.org/wiki/Stalinism#Stalinist_policies.

[188] Andrew Heywood, *Political Ideologies: An Introduction*, 133-4.

[189] *Ibid.*, 134.

[190] Maoism, accessed 24 November 2019, https://en.wikipedia.org/wiki/Maoism.

[191] Leon P. Baradat, *Political Ideologies: Their Origins and Impact*, 217-8.

[192] *Ibid.*, 218.

[193] *Ibid.*, 218-9.

[194] *Ibid.*, 219.

[195] *Ibid.*, 220.

[196] *Ibid.*, 220-1.

[197] Cultural Revolution: Background, Great Leap Forward, accessed 18 September
2019, https://en.wikipedia.org/wiki/Cultural_Revolution#Great_Leap_Forward.

[198] *Ibid.*, accessed the same.

[199] *Ibid.*, accessed the same.

[200] Cultural Revolution, accessed 18 September 20109,
https://en.wikipedia.org/wiki/Cultural_Revolution.

[201] *Ibid.*, accessed the same.

[202] Maoism//Differences between Maoism and Marxism, accessed 24 November 2019,
https://en.wikipedia.org/wiki/Maoism#Differences_between_Maoism_and_Marxism.

[203] Maoism: New Democracy, accessed 18 September 2019,
https://en.wikipedia.org/wiki/Maoism#New_Democracy.

[204] Maoism: People's war, accessed 18 September,
https://en.wikipedia.org/wiki/Maoism#People's_war.

[205] Maoism: Mass line, accessed 18 September,
https://en.wikipedia.org/wiki/Maoism#Mass_line.

[206] Maoism: Cultural Revolution, accessed 18 September 18, 2019,
https://en.wikipedia.org/wiki/Maoism#Cultural_Revolution.

[207] Maoism: Contradiction, accessed 18 September 2019,
https://en.wikipedia.org/wiki/Maoism#Contradiction.

[208] Maoism: Three Worlds Theory, accessed 18 September 18, 2019,
https://en.wikipedia.org/wiki/Maoism#Three_Worlds_Theory.

[209] Agrarian socialism, accessed 18 September 2019,
https://en.wikipedia.org/wiki/Maoism#Agrarian_socialism.

[210] Leon P. Baradat, *Political Ideologies: Their Origins and Impact*, 227.

[211] *Ibid.*, 228.

[212] Democratic socialism, accessed 25 November 2019,
https://en.wikipedia.org/wiki/Democratic_socialism.

[213] *Ibid.*, accessed the same.

[214] *Ibid.*, accessed the same.

[215] Democratic socialism/Economics, accessed 25 November 2019, https://en.wikipedia.org/wiki/Democratic_socialism#Economics.

[216] Democratic socialism/21st century, accessed 25 November 2019, https://en.wikipedia.org/wiki/Democratic_socialism#21st_century.

[217] Andrew Heywood, *Political Ideologies: An Introduction*, 141.

[218] *Ibid.*, 142.

[219] Eduard Bernstein, accessed 25 November 2019, https://en.wikipedia.org/wiki/Eduard_Bernstein.

[220] *Ibid.*, 143-4.

[221] *Ibid.*, 145.

[222] https://en.wikipedia.org/wiki/Democratic_socialism#Views_on_compatibility_of_so cialism_and_democracy, Democratic socialism/Views on compatibility of socialism and democracy, accessed 26 November 2019.

[223] Economic growth, accessed 25 September 2019, https://en.wikipedia.org/wiki/Economic_growth.

[224] Tariff, accessed 26 November 2019, https://en.wikipedia.org/wiki/Tariff.

[225] Subrata Ghatak, *Introduction to Development Economics*, 3rd ed. (New York: Routledge, 1995, 101.

[226] *Ibid.*, 103.

[227] *Ibid.*, 103-4.

[228] *Ibid.*, 104.

[229] *Ibid.*, 105.

[230] *Ibid.*, 106.

[231] *Ibid.*, 109.

[232] Ragnar Nurkse's balanced growth theory, accessed 22 September 2019, https://en.wikipedia.org/wiki/Ragnar_Nurkse%27s_balanced_growth_theory.

[233] Strategy of unbalanced growth, accessed 22 September 2019, https://en.wikipedia.org/wiki/Strategy_of_unbalanced_growth.

[234] Unbalanced Growth Theory: Explanation, Process and Priorities, accessed 22 September 2019, http://www.economicsdiscussion.net/economic-development/unbalanced-growth-theory-explanation-process-and-priorities/4630.

[235] *Ibid.*, accessed the same.

[236] https://www.usaid.gov/what-we-do/economic-growth-and-trade/domestic-resource-mobilization, Domestic Resource Mobilization, accessed 23 September 2019.

[237] Subrata Ghatak, *Introduction to Development Economics*, 120-1.

[238] *Ibid.*, 122-3.

[239] https://money.usnews.com/money/blogs/flowchart/2011/03/23/4-reasons-rising-prices-are-good-news, 4 Reasons Rising Prices Are Good News, accessed 23 September 23, 2019.

[240] Subrata Ghatak, *Introduction to Development Economics*, 128.

[241] *Ibid.*, 128.

[242] *Ibid.*, 132.

[243] *Ibid.*, 135.

[244] *Ibid.*, 138.

[245] *Ibid.*, 143.

[246] *Ibid.*, 144.

[247] *Ibid.*, 145-6.

[248] *Ibid.*, 150.

[249] *Ibid.*, 150.

[250] *Ibid.*, 151.

[251] *Ibid.*, 151-2.

[252] *Ibid.*, 164-172.

[253] Special drawing rights, accessed 23 September 2019, https://en.wikipedia.org/wiki/Special_drawing_rights.

[254] *Ibid.*, accessed the same.

[255] Overseas Aid and Economic Development, accessed 23 September 2019, https://www.tutor2u.net/economics/reference/overseas-aid-and-development.

[256] *Ibid.*, accessed the same.

[257] Subrata Ghatak, *Introduction to Development Economics*, 231-3.

[258] *Ibid.*, 233-4.

[259] *Ibid.*, 234-5.

[260] *Ibid.*, 236-42.

[261] *Ibid.*, 243-6.

[262] *Ibid.*, 249.

[263] *Ibid.*, 250-1.

[264] Unemployment, accessed 23 September 2019, https://en.wikipedia.org/wiki/Unemployment.

[265] International migration, accessed 23 September 2019, https://en.wikipedia.org/wiki/International_migration.

[266] *Ibid.*, accessed the same.

[267] Subrata Ghatak, *Introduction to Development Economics*, 263-4.

[268] Migrant worker, accessed 23 September 23, 2019, https://en.wikipedia.org/wiki/Migrant_worker.

[269] Subrata Ghatak, *Introduction to Development Economics*, 272.

[270] *Ibid.*, 273-81.

[271] *Ibid.*, 289-90.

[272] Green Revolution, accessed 24 September 2019, https://en.wikipedia.org/wiki/Green_Revolution.

[273] Subrata Ghatak, Introduction to Development Economics, 320.

[274] *Ibid.*, 321.

[275] Tariff, accessed 24 September 2019, https://en.wikipedia.org/wiki/Tariff.

[276] The Basics of Tariffs and Trade Barriers, accessed 15 September 2019, https://www.investopedia.com/articles/economics/08/tariff-trade-barrier-basics.asp.

[277] Tariff: Economic Analysis, accessed 24 September 2019, https://en.wikipedia.org/wiki/Tariff#Economic_analysis.

[278] Tariff: Optimal tariff, accessed 24 September 24, 2019, https://en.wikipedia.org/wiki/Tariff#Optimal_tariff.

[279] Infant industry, accessed 24 September 2019, https://en.wikipedia.org/wiki/Infant_industry.

[280] Subrata Ghatak, Introduction to Development Economics, 327.

[281] How Tariffs Affect the Trade? Accessed 24 September 24, 2019, http://www.preservearticles.com/economics/how-tariffs-affects-the-trade/19638.

[282] *Ibid.*, accessed the same.

[283] *Ibid.*, accessed the same.

[284] Terms of Trade, accessed 24 September 2019, https://en.wikipedia.org/wiki/Terms_of_trade.

[285] https://en.wikipedia.org/wiki/Non-tariff_barriers_to_trade#Non-tariff_barriers_today, Non-tariffs barriers to trade, accessed 24 September 2019.

[286] Free Trade, accessed 24 September 24, 2019, https://en.wikipedia.org/wiki/Free_trade.

[287] Subrata Ghatak, Introduction to Development Economics, 357.

[288] Economic planning, accessed 24 September 24, 2019, https://en.wikipedia.org/wiki/Economic_planning.

[289] Economic planning: In socialism, accessed 24 September 24, 2019, https://en.wikipedia.org/wiki/Economic_planning#In_socialism.

[290] *Ibid.*, accessed the same.

[291] *Ibid.*, accessed the same.

[292] Economic planning: Intra-firm and intra-industry planning, accessed 24 September 24, 2019, https://en.wikipedia.org/wiki/Economic_planning#Intra-firm_and_intra-industry_planning.

[293] Economic planning: State development planning, accessed 24 September 24, 2019, https://en.wikipedia.org/wiki/Economic_planning#State_development_planning.

[294] Economic planning: Criticism, accessed 24 September 24, 2019, https://en.wikipedia.org/wiki/Economic_planning#Criticism.

[295] Macroeconomics Analysis and Policy, accessed 24 September 24, 2019, http://iegindia.org/dpc/Macroeconomics-Analysis-and-Policy.

[296] Input-output model: basic derivation, accessed 24 September 2019, https://en.wikipedia.org/wiki/Input%E2%80%93output_model#Basic_derivation.

[297] Cost-benefit analysis, accessed 24 September 24, 2019, https://en.wikipedia.org/wiki/Cost%E2%80%93benefit_analysis.

[298] Hollis Chenery and Moshe Syrquin, "3. Typical Patterns of Transformation," in *Industrialization and Growth: A Comparative Study*, Hollis Chenery, Sherman Robinson, and Moshe Syrquin (New York: Oxford University Press, 1986), 37.

[299] *Ibid.*, 38.

[300] *Ibid.*, 64-66.

[301] "Equality and Efficiency: Is there a trade-off between the two?" accessed 5 September 2019, http://regardssurlaterre.com/en/equality-and-efficiency-there-trade-between-two. For further, see Arthur M. Okun, *Equality and Efficiency: The Big Tradeoff* (Washington, DC: Brookings Institution, 1975).

[302] Equality and Efficiency, *Finance & Development* 48(3) (September 2011), accessed 27 November 2019, https://www.imf.org/external/pubs/ft/fandd/2011/09/Berg.htm.

[303] Income inequality matrix: Gini Index, accessed 5 September 2019, https://en.wikipedia.org/wiki/Income_inequality_metrics#Gini_index.

[304] Susan Davis, How Monopolies Impact Incomes, accessed 2 September 2019, https://www.w-t-w.org/en/33653-2/.

[305] *Ibid.*, accessed the same.

[306] Social Cost of Monopoly: Monopoly and Inefficiency, accessed 15 September 2019, http://www.yourarticlelibrary.com/economics/monopoly/social-cost-of-monopoly-monopoly-and-inefficiency/37215.

[307] *Ibid.*, accessed the same.

[308] *Ibid.*, accessed the same.

[309] Fiscal Policy vs. Monetary Policy: Differences, accessed 5 September 2019, https://www.wallstreetmojo.com/fiscal-policy-vs-monetary-policy/.

[310] Expansionary vs. contractionary monetary policy, accessed 5 September 2019, https://www.thoughtco.com/expansionary-vs-contractionary-monetary-policy-1146303.

[311] *Ibid.*, accessed the same.

[312] Rudiger Dornbusch, Stanley Fisher, and Richard Startz, *Macroeconomics*, 10th ed. (New York: McGraw-Hill /Irwin, 2008), 279.

[313] Exchange Rates, accessed 15 September 2019, https://courses.lumenlearning.com/boundless-economics/chapter/exchange-rates/.

[314] Currency intervention, accessed 15 September 2019, https://en.wikipedia.org/wiki/Currency_intervention.
[315] "How Not to Fight a Currency War: Branding China a 'Currency Manipulator' Will Only Hut the United States, accessed 15 September 2019, Foreign Affairs 98(5) (September/October 2019), accessed 15 September 2019, https://www.foreignaffairs.com/articles/china/2019-08-28/how-not-fight-currency-war.
[316] https://www.businessmanagementideas.com/management/government-company-characteristics-advantages-and-limitations/9028, Government Company: Characteristics, Advantages, and Limitation, accessed 24 September 24, 2019.
[317] *Ibid.*, accessed the same.
[318] *Ibid.*, accessed the same.
[319] Financial crisis of 2007-2008, accessed 24 September 24, 2019, https://en.wikipedia.org/wiki/Financial_crisis_of_2007-2008.
[320] Financial crisis of 2007-2008: Subprime mortgage bubble, accessed 24 September 24, 2019, https://en.wikipedia.org/wiki/Financial_crisis_of_2007-2008#Subprime_mortgage_bubble.
[321] Financial crisis of 1007-2008: Banking crisis, accessed 24 September 2019, https://en.wikipedia.org/wiki/Financial_crisis_of_2007-2008#Banking_crisis.
[322] Financial crisis of 1007-2008: Consequence, accessed 24 September 24, 2019, https://en.wikipedia.org/wiki/Financial_crisis_of_2007-2008#Consequences.
[323] Subrata Ghatak, Introduction to Development Economics, 450.
[324] *Ibid.*, 453-4.
[325] Environment and Development, accessed 24 September 24, 2019, https://www.unescap.org/our-work/environment-development.
[326] Subrata Ghatak, Introduction to Development Economics, 455-6.
[327] *Ibid.*, 457-8.
[328] *Ibid.*, 459.
[329] *Ibid.*, 465-6.
[330] Stephen T. Jackson, Climate Change (Last updated 22 August 2019), accessed 24 September 2019, https://www.britannica.com/science/climate-change.
[331] *Ibid.*, accessed the same.
[332] https://www.foreignaffairs.com/articles/united-states/2018-09-18/climate-change-chronic-condition, Kate Gordon and Julio Friedmann, "Climate Change Is a Chronic Condition," *Foreign Affairs* (September 18, 2018), accessed 24 September 24, 2019.
[333] China-United States trade war, accessed 24 September 24, 2019, https://en.wikipedia.org/wiki/China%E2%80%93United_States_trade_war.
[334] *Ibid.*, accessed the same.
[335] https://en.wikipedia.org/wiki/China%E2%80%93United_States_trade_war#Reactions, China-United States trade war: Reaction, accessed 24 September 2019.
[336] file:///G:/5A%20Political%20Economy/Pub%2021st%20Century/Sawhill_Capitalism-and-the-Future-of-Democracy-.pdf, Isabel V. Sawhill, "Capitalism and the Future of Democracy," accessed 28 November 2019.
[337] *Ibid.*, accessed the same.
[338] Social democracy/Development, accessed 27 November 2019, https://en.wikipedia.org/wiki/Social_democracy.
[339] *Ibid.*, accessed the same.
[340] *Ibid.*, accessed the same.
[341] Social democracy/Response to neoliberalism, accessed 28 November 2019, https://en.wikipedia.org/wiki/Social_democracy#Response_to_neoliberalism_(1973%E2%80%931991).

[342] Social democracy/Third Way and Great Recession, accessed 28 November 2019, https://en.wikipedia.org/wiki/Social_democracy#Third_Way_and_Great_Recession_(1 991%E2%80%932007).

[343] Andrew Heywood, *Political Ideologies: An Introduction*, 151.

[344] Post-capitalism, accessed 25 September 2019, https://en.wikipedia.org/wiki/Post-capitalism.

[345] *Ibid.*, accessed the same.

[346] *Ibid.*, accessed the same.

[347] *Ibid.*, accessed the same.

[348] Crony capitalism, accessed 25 September 2019, https://en.wikipedia.org/wiki/Crony_capitalism.

[349] *Ibid.*, accessed the same.

[350] Income inequality: Mitigating factors, accessed 25 September 2019, http://www.thefullwiki.org/Income_inequality#Mitigating_factors.

[351] "Idolization of Human Equality," Pen and Mike 25 February 2018, accessed 5 September 2019, http://www.pennmike.com/news/articleView.html?idxno=2655.

Photo II-End-1. Productivity: The main source of happiness
Accessed 25 September 2019
https://smartface.io/wp-content/uploads/2015/01/productivity.jpg

REFERENCES
PART II. The Future of Capitalism
Efficiency in Growth vs. Equality in Distribution

1. The Development of Modern Microeconomics

Balasko, Yves. *General Equilibrium Theory of Value*. *Princeton*, NJ: Princeton University Press, 2011.

Cassel, Gustav. *The Theory of Social Economy*. San Diego, CA: Harcourt, 1932.

Chamberlin, E. *The Theory of Monopolistic Competition*. Cambridge, MA: Harvard Univ. Press, 1939.

Colander, David C. *Microeconomics*, 10th ed. New York: McGraw-Hill, 2016.

Debreu, Gerard. *Theory of Value: Analysis of Economic Equilibrium*. New Haven, CT: Yale University Press, 1972.

Emmett, Ross B., ed. *The Chicago Tradition in Economics*. New York: Routledge, 2001.

Frank, Robert H. *Microeconomics and Behavior*, 8th ed. New York: McGraw Hill/Irwin, 2009

Friedman, Milton. *Price Theory*. New York: Routledge, 2007.

_____. *Capitalism and Freedom*. Chicago, IL: Univ. of Chicago Press, 2002.

Hicks John. *Value and Capital*, 2nd ed. New York: Oxford Univ. Press, 1975.

Jehle, Geoffrey A. and Philip J. Reny. *Advanced Microeconomic Theory*. London, UK: Pearson, 2011.

Jevons, William Stanley. *The Theory of Political Economy*. New York: Palgrave Macmillan, 2013.

Krugman, Paul and Robin Wells. *Microeconomics*, 4th ed. New York: Wroth Publishers, 2014.

Mankiw, N. Gregory. *Principles of Microeconomics*, 8th ed. Boston, MA: Cengage Learning, 2017.

Marshall, Alfred. *Principles of Economics*. New York: Palgrave, 2013.

Newmann, John von and Oskar Morgenstern. *Theory of Games and Economic Behavior*. Princeton,, NJ: Princeton University Press, 2007.

Menger, Carl. *Principles of Economics*. CreateSpace Independent Pub., 2006.

Nicholson, Walter. *Microeconomic Theory*. Boston, MA: Cengage, 2017.

Pareto, Vilfred. *Manual of Political Economy*. New York: Oxford U P, 2014.

Parkin, Michael. *Microeconomics*, 12th ed. London, UK: Pearson, 2015.

Pigou, Arthur Cecil. *The Economics of Welfare*. New York: Routledge, 2001.

Samuelson, Paul A. *Foundations of Economic Analysis*. New York: Atheneum Books, 1965.

Samuelson, Paul A., *Economics*, 19th ed. New York: McGraw-Hill, 2009.

Starr, Toss M. *General Equilibrium Theory: An Introduction*. New York: Cambridge University Press, 2011.

Walras, Leon. *Elements of Pure Economics*. New York: Routledge, 2010.

Yang, Xiaokai. *Economics: New Classical versus Neoclassical Frameworks*. Malden, MA: Blackwell, 2001.

2. The Development of Modern Macroeconomics

Backhouse, Roger E. *The Puzzle of Modern Economics: Science or Ideology?*
New York: Cambridge University Press, 2010.

Baumol, William J. and Charles A. Wilson. *Welfare Economics*, 3 Vol.
Cheltenham, UK: Edward, 2001.

Blanchard, Oliver and David R. Johnson. *Macroeconomics*. 6th ed. London,
UK: Pearson, 2012.

Chugh, Sanjay K. *Modern Macroeconomics.* Cambridge, MA: MIT Press, 2015.

Cowen, Tyler and Alex Tabarrok. *Modern Principles: Macroeconomics*.
Duffield, UK: Worth Pub, 2014.

Fisher, Irving and Harry Gunnison Brown. *The Purchasing Power of Money*.
Andesite Press, 2015.

Friedman, Milton. *Quantity Theory of Money*. Chicago, IL: University of
Chicago Press, 1956.

Goodspeed, Tyler Beek. *Rethinking the Keynesian Revolution: Keynes, Hayek,
and the Wicksell Connection*. New York: Oxford University Press, 2012.

Hayek, Frederick A. *Prices and Production*. CreateSpace Pub., 2008.

Keynes, John M. *The General Theory of Employment, Interest, and Money*.
New York: Harcourt, 1964.

Klein, Lawrence R. *The Keynesian Revolution*. New York: Palgrave, 1980.

Krugman, Paul. *Macroeconomics*. Duffield, UK: Worth Publishers, 2015.

Laidler, David E. W. *The Demand for Money: Theories, Evidence, and
Problems*. London: Pearson, 1997.

Lucas Jr., Robert E. *Studies in Business-Cycle Theory*. Cambridge, MA: MIT
Press, 1983

Lucas Jr., Robert E and Thomas J. Sargent, eds. *Rational Expectations and
Econometric Practice*. Minneapolis, MN: Univ. of Minnesota Press, 1981.

Mankiw, N. Gregory. *New Keynesian Economics,* Cambridge, MA: MIT
Press, 1991.

Mitchell, Wesley Clair. *Business Cycles*. Whitefish, MO: Kessinger, 2010.

Morgan, Mary S. *The History of Econometric Ideas*. New York: Cambridge
University Press, 1990.

Myrdal, Gunnar. *Monetary Equilibrium*. Glasgow, UK: William Hodge &
Company, 1939.

Romer, David. *Advanced Macroeconomics*. New York: McGraw-Hill, 2005.

Schumpeter, Joseph A. *Theory of Economic Development*. New York:
Routledge, 2017.

Sheffrin, Steven M. *Rational Expectations*. New York: Cambridge U P, 1996.

Sidgwick, Henry. *The Principles of Political Economy*. New York: Cambridge
University Press, 2011.

Solow, Robert M. *Growth Theory: An Exposition:* New York: Oxford
University Press, 2000.

Solow, Robert M. and James B. Taylor. *Inflation, Unemployment, and
Monetary Policy*. Cambridge, MA: MIT Press, 1999.

3. A Historical Overview of Socialism

Archer, Robin. *Economic Democracy: The Politics of Feasible Socialism*. New York: Oxford U P, 1995.

Baradat, Leon P. and John A. Phillips. *Political Ideologies: Their Origins*. New York: Routledge, 2016.

Beaud, Michel. *Socialism in the Crucible of History*. Atlantic Highlands, NJ: Humanities Press Intl., 1993

Berki, R. N. *Insight and Vision: The Problem of Communism in Marx's Thought*. London: J. M. Dent, 1984.

Bernstein, Eduard. *The Preconditions of Socialism*, ed. Henry Tudor. New York: Cambridge U P, 1993.

Carver, Terrell, ed. *The Cambridge Companion to Marx*. New York: Cambridge University Press, 1991.

Carver, Terrell and James Farr, eds. *The Cambridge Companion to the Communist Manifesto*. New York: Cambridge University Press, 2015.

Cohen, Carl. *Communism, Fascism, and Democracy*. New York: McGraw Hill Humanities, 1996.

Collins, Peter. *Ideology after the Fall of Communism*. London, UK: Marion Boyars, 1993.

Crosland, Anthony. *The Future of Socialism*. London, UK: Constable, 2006.

Derber, Charles. *What's Left: Radical Politics in the Post-communist Era*. Amherst, MA: UMA Press, 1995.

Diamond, Patrick. *The Crosland Legacy: The Future of British Social Democracy*. Bristol, UK: Policy, 2016.

Fabra, Paul. *Capitalism versus Anti-Capitalism: The Triumph of Recardian over Marxist Political Economy*. Piscataway, NJ: Transaction Publisher, 1993.

Forman, James D. *Capitalism, Economic Individualism*. New Brunswick, NJ: New Viewpoints, 1973.

_____. *Communism: From Marx's Manifesto to 20th Century*. London, UK: Franklin Watts, 1979.

Giddens, Anthony. *The Third Way and its Critics*. Malden, MA: Blackwell, 2000.

Harrington, Michael. *Socialism: Past and Future*. Chandler, AZ: Academic Publishing, 2011.

Hegel, G. W. F. *Hegel: Reason in History*. Upper Saddle R., NJ: Pearson, 1995.

Heilbroner, Robert L. *Marxism: For and Against*. New York: Norton, 1981.

Heywood, Andrew. *Political Ideologies*. New York: Palgrave, 2012.

Holz, Hans Heinz. *The Downfall and Future of Socialism*. Edina, NY: M. E. Pinkham, 1992.

Hook, Sidney. *From Hegel to Marx: Studies in the Intellectual Development of Karl Marx*. New York, CT: Columbia University Press, 1994.

Horvat, Branko. *Political Economy of Socialism*. New York: Routledge, 1983.

Hunt, R. N. Carew. *The Theory and Practice of Communism*. London: Pelican Books, 1964.

Kautsky, Karl. *The Road to Power*. Berkeley, CA: Socialist History, 2007.
_____. *Ethics and the Materialist Conception of History*. London, UK: Forgotten Books, 2012.
Lane, David Stuart. *The Rise and Fall of State Socialism: Industrial Society and the Socialist State*. Cambridge, MA: Polity Publishers, 1996.
Lenin, Vladimia Ilyich. *Essential Works of Lenin: What Is to Be Done? And Other Writings*. New York: Dover Publications, 1987.
_____. *The State and Revolution*. Norwalk, CT: The Easton Press, 1992.
_____. *Imperialism the Highest Stage of Capitalism*. Eastford, CT: Martino Fine Books, 2011.
Martell, Luke, and Others, eds. *Social Democracy: Global Perspectives*. New York: Palgrave, 2001.
Marx, Karl. *Das Kapital, Volume I, A Critique of Political Economy*. New York: Penguin Books, 1976.
_____. *The Condition of the Working Class in England*. New York: Oxford University Press, 2009.
_____. *The Class Struggles in France: 1848-1850*. Amazon.com, 2015.
Marx, Karl and Friedrich Engels. *The Communist Manifesto*. New York: Barnes & Noble Classics, 2005.
McLellan, David. *Karl Marx* (Modern Masters). New York: Penguin, 1976.
_____. *Marxism after Marx*. London, UK: Palgrave Macmillan, 1983.
Mongar, Thomas M. *The Death of Communism and the Rebirth of Original Marxism*. New York: Edwin Mellen Press, 1994.
Moschonas, Gerassimos. *In the Name of Social Democracy*. New York: Verso Books, 2002.
Nove, Alec. *The Economics of Feasible Socialism Revisited*. London, UK: Routledge, 1992.
Pilling, Geoff. *Marxist Political Economy: Essays in Retrieval*. New York: Routledge, 2016.
Russell, Bertrand. *The Practice and Theory of Bolshevism*. Teddington, UK: Echo Library, 2008.
Sargent, Lyman Tower. Contemporary Political Ideologies. Belmore, CA: Wadsworth Publishing, 2008.
Sassoon, Donald. *One Hundred Years of Socialism: The West European Left in the Twentieth Century*. New York: I. B. Tauris, 2014.
Schweickart, David. *Against Capitalism*. New York: Cambridge U P, 1993.
Shortall, Felton. *The Incomplete Marx*. Brookfield, VT: Ashgate, 1994.
Sik, Ota. *Socialism Today?: The Changing Meaning of Socialism*. New York: Palgrave Macmillan, 2014.
Steenson, Gary P. *Karl Kautsky, 1845-1938: Marxism in the Classical Years*. Pittsburgh, PA: University of Pittsburgh Press, 1991.
Steger, Mansfield B. *The Quest for Evolutionary Socialism: Edward Bernstein and Social Democracy*. New York: Cambridge U P. 1997.
Wright, Anthony. *Socialisms: Theories and Practices*. New York: Oxford University Press, 1987.

4. Critiques of Neoclassical Economics: Socialism versus Capitalism

Carayannis, Elias G. and C. Ziemiowicz. *Rediscovering Schumpeter: Creative Destruction Evolving into Mode 3*. New York: Palgrave Macmillan, 2007.

Boudreaux, Donald J. *The Essential Hayek*. Vancouver, Canada: Fraser, 2015.

Bücher, Karl. *Industrial Evolution*. London, UK: Forgotten Books, 1927.

Dalton, Thomas. *Keynes and Hayek: The Meaning of Knowing*. Amazon Digital Services, 2013.

Friedman, Milton. *Capitalism and Freedom: Fortieth Anniversary Edition*. Chicago, IL: Chicago U P, 2002.

_____. *Why Government Is the Problem*. Stanford, CA: Hoover Press, 1993.

Hayek, Friedrich A. *The Road to Serfdom*. Chicago, IL: University of Chicago Press, 2007.

Heertje, Arnold. *Schumpeter on the Economics of Innovation and the Development of Capitalism*. London, UK: Edward Elgar Pub, 2006.

Hobson, John A. *Imperialism: A Study*. TheClassics.us, 2013.

_____. *The Eastern Origins of Western Civilization*. New York: Cambridge University Press, 2004.

Keynes, John Maynard. *The General Theory of Employment, Interest, and Money*. San Diego, CA: Harcourt, Brace & World, 1965.

Lange, Oscar. *On the Economic Theory of Socialism*. Fairfield, NJ: Augustus M. Kelley Pubs, 1970.

Medearis, John. *Joseph A. Schumpeter*. New York: Bloomsbury, 2013.

_____. *Joseph Schumpeter's Two Theories of Democracy*. Cambridge, MA: Harvard University Press, 2001.

Mises, Ludwig von. *Human Action: The Scholar's Edition*. Auburn, AL: Ludwig von Mises Institute, 2010.

_____. *Socialism: An Economic and Sociological Analysis*. Libertyville, IL: Liberty Classics, 1981.

_____. *The Anti-Capitalistic Mentality*. Auburn, AL: Ludwig von Mises Institute, 2016.

Schumpeter, Joseph A. *Capitalism, Socialism, and Democracy*. New York: Harper & Row, 1942.

_____. *The Theory of Economic Development*. London: Transaction, 1982.

_____. *Can Capitalism Survive?: Creative Destruction and the Future of the Global Economy*. New York: Harper Perennial, 2009.

_____. *History of Economic Analysis*. New York: Oxford Univ. Press, 1996.

_____. *The Economics and Sociology of Capitalism*. Princeton, NJ: Princeton University Press, 1991.

Swedberg, Richard. *Schumpeter: A Biography*. Princeton, NJ: Princeton University Press, 1992.

Wapshott, Nicholas. *Keynes Hayek: The Clash that Defined Modern Economics*. New York: Norton, 2012.

Weber, Max. *The Protestant Ethic and the Spirit of Capitalism*. New York: Penguin Books, 2002.

5. Capitalism and Democracy: Efficiency versus Equality

Anthony, James. *The Constitution Needs a Good Party: Good Government Comes from Good Boundaries.* St. Peters, MO: Newwochner Press, 2018.

Boltanski, Luc and Eve Chiapello. *The New Spirit of Capitalism.* New York: Verso Books, 2018.

Boix, Carles. *Democratic Capitalism at the Crossroads: Technological Change and the Future of Politics.* Princeton, NJ: Princeton University Press, 2019.

Borders, Max. *The Social Singularity: How Decentralization Wil Allow Us to Transcend Politics, Create Global Prosperity, and Avoid the Robot Apocalypse.* Austin, TX: Social Revolution, 2018.

Bowles, Samuel and Herbert Gintis. *Democracy and Capitalism: Property, Community, and the Contradictions of Modern Social Thought.* New York: Basic Books, 1987.

Brands, H. W. *The Money Men: Capitalism, Democracy, and the Hundred Year's War Over the American Dollar.* New York: W.W. Norton, 2006.

Carter, Zachary D. *The Price of Peace: Money, Democracy, and the Life of John Maynard Keynes.* New York: Random House, 2020.

Chandler, David. *Digital Objects, Digital Subjects.* London, UK: University of Westminster Press, 2019.

Chen, Fu T. *First Aid for Democracy and Capitalism: A Plan for World Peace.* Amazon Digital Services, 2017.

Collier, Paul. *The Future of Capitalism: Facing the New Anxieties.* New York: Harper Collins Publishers, 2018.

Connolly, William. *Capitalism and Christianity, American Style.* Durham, NC: Duke University Press, 2008.

Crosland, Anthony. *The Future of Socialism.* London, UK: Constable, 2006.

Dahl, Robert A. *On Democracy.* New Haven, CT: Yale University Press, 1998.

Dardot, Pierre and Christian Laval. *Never Ending Nightmare: The Neoliberal Assault on Democracy.* New York: Verso Books, 2019.

Devine, Pat. *Democracy and Economic Planning.* New York: Polity, 2010.

Diamond, Patrick. *The Crisis of Globalization: Democracy, Capitalism and Inequality in the Twenty-First Century.* New York: I. B. Tauris, 2019.

Dobson, William J. *The Dictator's Learning Curve: Inside the Global Battle for Democracy.* New York: Anchor Books, 2013.

Dolgon, Corey. *Kill It to Save It: An Autopsy of Capitalism's Triumph over Democracy.* Chicago, IL: Policy Press, 2018.

Dorrien, Gary. *Social Democracy in the Making: Political and Religious Roots of European Socialism.* New Haven, CT: Yale University Press, 2019.

Friedman, Milton. *Capitalism and Freedom.* Chicago, IL: University of Chicago Press, 2002.

Fung, Archon and Eric Olin Wright, eds. *Deepening Democracy: Institutional Innovations.* New York: Verso Books, 2003.

Gardels, Nathan and Nicolas Berggruen. *Renovating Democracy: Governing in the Age of Globalization.* Oakland, CA: Univ. of California Press, 2009.

Glassman, Ronald M. *The Future of Democracy*. New York: Springer. 2019.

Goldberg, Jonah. *Suicide of the West: How the Rebirth of Tribalism, Populism, Nationalism, and Identity Politics Is Destroying American Democracy*. New York: Crown Forum, 2018.

Hahnel, Robin and Erik Olin Wright. *Alternatives to Capitalism: Proposals for a Democratic Economy*. New York: Verso Books, 2016.

Harvey, David. *Spaces of Global Capitalism: A Theory of Uneven Geographical Development*. New York: Verso Books, 2019.

Hewett, Edward. *Reforming the Soviet Economy: Equality Versus Efficiency*. Washington, DC: Brookings Institution Press, 1990.

Hoppe, Hans-Hermann. *Democracy – The God That Failed: The Economics and Politics of Monarchy*. New York: Routledge, 2017.

Huxley, Aldous. *Brave New World*. New York: Everyman's Library, 2013.

Inversen, Torben and David Soskice. *Democracy and Prosperity*. Princeton, NY: Princeton University Press, 2019.

_____. *Capitalism, Democracy, and Welfare*. New York: Cambridge University Press, 2005.

Kerr, Gavin. *The Property-Owning Democracy; Freedom and Capitalism in the Twenty-First Century*. New York: Routledge, 2019.

Kuttner, Robert. *Can Democracy Survive Global Capitalism?* New York: W. W. Norton and Company, 2019.

Kurlantzick, Joshua. *State Capitalism: How the Return of Statism Is Transforming the World*. New York: oxford University Press, 2016.

Lacalle, Daniel. *Freedom or Equality: The Key to Prosperity Through Social Capitalism*. Nashville, TN: Post Hill Press, 2010.

Liu, Eric and Nick Hanauer. *The Gardens of Democracy: A New American Story of Citizenship, the Economy, and the Role of Government*. Seattle, WA: Sasquatch Books, 2011.

Mannn, James. *The China Fantasy: Why Capitalism Will Not Bring Democracy to China*. New York: Penguin Books, 2008.

Markovits, Daniel. *The Meritocracy Trap: How America's Foundational Myth Feeds Inequality, Dismantles eh Middle Class, and Devours the Elite*. New York: Penguin Press, 2019.

Meede, James E. *Efficiency, Equality and the Ownership of Property*. New York: Routledge, 2013.

Moyo, Eambisa. *Edge of Chaos: Why Democracy Is Failing to Deliver Economic Growth – and How to Fix It*. New York: Basic Books, 2018.

Mueller, John. *Capitalism, Democracy, and Ralph's Pretty Good Grocery*. Princeton, NJ: Princeton University Press, 2001.

Ng, Yew-Kwang. *Efficiency, Equality and Public Policy*. New York: Palgrave Macmillan, 2000.

Novak, Michael. *The Spirit of Democratic Capitalism*. New York: Madison, 1990.

Okun, Arthur M. *Equality and Efficiency: The Big Trade Off*. Washington, DC: Brookings Institution, 1975.

O'Neil, Patrick H., Karl Fields, and Don Share. *Essentials of Comparative Politics with Cases*. New York: W. W. Norton and Company, 2015.

Patel, Raj. *The Value of Nothing: How to Reshape Market Society and Redefine Democracy*. New York: Picador, 2009.

Phillips, Kevin. *Wealth and Democracy: A Political History of the American Rich*. New York: Broadway Books, 2002.

Pomerantsev, Peter. *This Is Not Propaganda: Adventures in the War Against Reality*. New York: Public Affairs, 2019.

Posner, Eric A. *Radical Markets: Uprooting Capitalism and Democracy for a Just Society*. Princeton, NJ: Princeton University Press, 2018.

Przeworski, Adam. *Capitalism and Social Democracy*. New York: Cambridge University Press, 1986.

Rahman, K. Sabeel. *Democracy Against Domination*. New York: Oxford University Press, 2017.

Ranciere, Jacques. *Hatred of Democracy*. New York: Verso Books, 2014.

Reich, Robert B. *Saving Capitalism: For the Many, Not a Few*. New York: Vantage Books, 2016.

_____. *Supercapitalism: The Transformation of Business, Democracy, and Everyday Life*. New York: Vintage Books, 2007.

Schumpeter, Joseph A. *Capitalism, Socialism, and Democracy*, 3rd ed. New York: Harper Perennial Modern Thought, 2008.

_____. *Business Cycle: A Theoretical, Historical, and Statistical Analysis of the Capitalist Process*. Eastford, CT: Martino, 2017.

Schweickart, David. *After Capitalism*. New York: Rowman & Littlefield, 2011.

Servin, Kenneth P. *From Revolution to Power in Brazil*. Notre Dame, IN: University of Notre Dame Press, 2019.

Snyder, Timothy. *The Road to Unfreedom: Russia, Europe, America*. New York: Tim Duggan Books, 2019.

Soros, George. *In Defense of Open Society*. New York: Public Affairs, 2109.

Stiglitz, Joseph E. *People, Power, and Profits: Progressive Capitalism for an Age of Discontent*. New York: W. W. Norton and Company, 2019.

Stockman, David. *The Great Deformation: The Corruption of Capitalism in America*. New York: Public Affairs, 2014.

Streeck, Wolfgang, *How Will Capitalism End?: Essays on a Failing System*. New York: Verso Books, 2017.

Taylor, Astra. *Democracy May Not Exist But We'll Miss it When It's Gond*. New York: Metropolitan Books, 2019.

Tepper, Jonathan and Denise Hearn. *The Myth of Capitalism: Monopolies and the Death of Competition*. Hoboken, NJ: John Wiley & Sons, Inc., 2019.

Wilkinson, T. M. *Freedom, Efficiency and Equality*. New York: Palgrave, 2000.

William, James. *Stand Out of Our Light: Freedom and Resistance in the Attention Economy*. New York: Cambridge University Press, 2018.

Wood, Ellen Meiksins. *Democracy Against Capitalism: Renewing Historical Materialism*. New York: Cambridge University Press, 1995.

Wu, Guoguang. *Globalization against Democracy: A Political Economy of Capitalism after its Global Triumph*. New York: Cambridge U P, 2017.
Yankelovich, Daniel. *Profit with Honor: The New Stage of Market Capitalism*. New Haven, CT: Yale University Press, 2006.

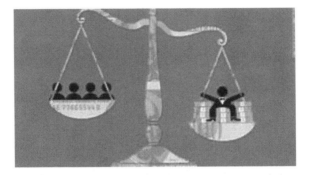

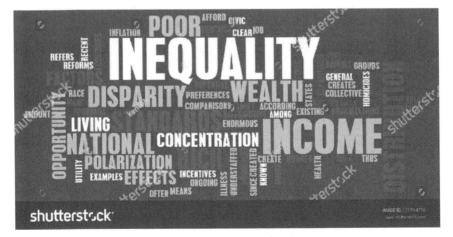

Photos II-End-2. Income Inequality, Accessed 29 November 2019
Upper: https://tse3.mm.bing.net/th?id=OIP.u9fH3YRFULifO-
Pr203edQHaEK&pid=Api&P=0&w=279&h=157
Lower: https://tse2.mm.bing.net/th?id=OIP.ky2TZy0xaHO4HP-
sTGveEQHaDy&pid=Api&P=0&w=367&h=189 (Lower)

Part III. Science, Technology, and National Security

> **1. Digital Transformation and Information Age 322**
> **Cloud Computing, Big Data, AI, Internet of Things**
> **2. Cyberwarfare and National Security 345**
> **3. Space Warfare and National Security 352**
> **4. Weapons of Mass Destruction and National Security 357**
> **5. The Biggest Technology Trends: Prospects 361**
> **Endnotes and References 364-374**

Now we stand on the brink of a technological revolution altering the way we live, work, and relate to one another. "The First Industrial Revolution used water and steam power to mechanize production. The Second used electric power to create mass production. The Third used electronics and information technology to automate production. Now a Fourth Industrial Revolution is building on the Third, the digital revolution that has been occurring since the middle of the last century. It is characterized by a fusion of technologies that is blurring the lines between the physical, digital, and biological spheres." The Fourth is different from the Third Revolution in terms of velocity, scope, and systems impact. "The speed of current breakthroughs has no historical precedent. When compared with previous industrial revolutions, the Fourth is evolving at an exponential rather than a linear pace. Moreover, it is disrupting almost every industry in every country. And the breadth and depth of these changes herald the transformation of entire systems of production, management, and governance."[1]

The progress of science and technology has changed weapons. "The first atomic bombs were tested and used in warfare in 1945. No nuclear weapons have been used in warfare since, due to the added risk of Nuclear holocaust. They remain the most powerful man-made weapons ever built. The first weapons designed to attack targets in space were developed by both the Soviet Union and the United States during the Cold War, particularly with their respective anti-satellite missiles." In the twenty-first century, guided weapons have been increasingly used to reduce the risk of soldiers fatalities and to increase effectiveness. "The first practical laser weapon, called the Laser Weapon System, was built by the United States Navy and installed on the USS Ponce. It is designed to destroy fast and small targets such as incoming missiles, fast attack craft and aircraft."[2] It is important to predict the progress of science and technology for national security. Part III consists of five sections as listed above. The first section deals with digital transformation and information age. Section 2 investigates cyberwarfare; Section 3 space warfare; and Section 4 weapons of mass destruction; which are related to national security. Section 5 investigate the biggest technology trends in the future, particularly in line with national security.

1. Digital Transformation and the Information Age

Generally, a computer system consists of four important components. (i) Input unit consists of input devices such as keyboard, mouse, scanner, and joystick. Input devises are used to send data to the computer. (ii) CPU (Central Processing Unit) is considered as the brain of computer. It is an electronic circuit that carries out the instruction of a computer program. CPU controls operations on all parts of the computer including main memory. (iii) Output unit consists of output devices such as monitor, printer, and speaker; which display the result to the user in an understandable manner. (iv) Memory unit is used for storing digital data for future use. Computer memory stores the information temporarily or permanently.[3]

Figure III-1-1. Important Components of the Computer System
Accessed 20 October 2019
http://www.physics-and-radio-electronics.com/computer-basics/images/computerblockdiagram.png.

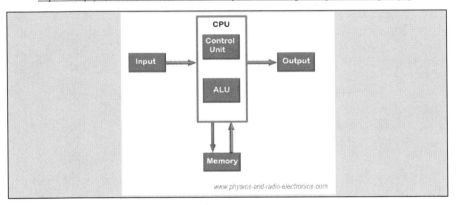

CPU is Central Processing Unit; ALU is Arithmetic Logic Unit.

Five Generations of Computer: "The computer has developed from a large sized simple calculating machine to a small sized most powerful machine. The development of computer up to the current state is defined in terms of generations. Currently, there are five generations of computer."

First generation - Vacuum Tubes (1940-1956): "The first-generation computers used vacuum tubes as the basic components because vacuum tubes are the only electronic components available on those days. Vacuum tubes are used for circuitry and magnetic drums are used for memory. The input to the computer was given through punched cards and paper tapes. The output displayed as printouts. No translator (translates from programming language to machine or computer language) was used to compile the programming language. The instructions to computer was given directly in machine language, i.e. 0's and 1's." They are used for scientific research.[4]

Second generation - Transistors (1956-1963): "The second-generation computers used transistors as the basic components. The first transistor was developed at bell laboratories on 1947 by William Shockley, John Bardeen and Walter Houser Brattain. The size of transistor is small compared to the size of vacuum tubes. Transistors are made from silicon. Transistors that are made from silicon are less sensitive to temperature, so they cannot easily burn up. Second generation computers used magnetic tapes, magnetic disks for secondary memory and magnetic core for primary memory. The input to second generation computers was given through punch cards and the output displayed as printouts," written in assembly language.[5]

Third generation - Integrated Circuits (1964-1971) was invented by Jack Kilby and Robert Noyce. "The electronic circuit formed by constructing electronic components like transistor, resistor and capacitor on a small piece of semiconducting material is called integrated circuit. Integrated circuit is also called as chip or microchip. Large number of transistors is placed on a single chip. In third generation computers input is given through keyboard and output is displayed on monitor. The keyboard and monitor were interfaced through the operating system...allows different appli-cations to run at the same time. The instructions to the computer were written in high level language instead of machine language and assembly language."[6]

Fourth generation - Microprocessor (1971-Present): "Intel 4004 chip was the first microprocessor developed in 1971. The microprocessor is a silicon chip contains millions of transistors that was designed using LSI and VLSI technology. The fourth-generation computers used LSI (Large Scale Integration) and VLSI (Very Large-Scale Integration) technology. Using LSI and VLSI technology thousands of transistors are integrated on a small silicon chip. In fourth generation computers the semiconductor memory is replaced by magnetic core memory resulting in fast random access to memory. Several operating systems like MS-DOS and MS windows developed during this time. The instructions to the computer were written in high level language instead of machine language and assembly language."[7]

Fifth generation (Present and Beyond): "Scientists are working on fifth generation computers. The main aim of fifth generation computing is to develop computers that are respond to surroundings using different types of sensors and capable of learning. Fifth generation computers use super large scale integrated (SLSI) chips that contains millions of components on a single chip. These computers use parallel processing where instructions are executed in parallel manner. Parallel processing is much faster than serial processing. In serial processing each task is performed in serial manner. Whereas in parallel processing multiple tasks are performed simultaneously. Fifth generation computers are based on artificial intelligence. The fifth-generation computers are also called artificial intelligence computers."[8]

Electronic Data Processing (EDP) is the use of automated methods to process commercial data. This uses simple, repetitive activities to process large volumes of similar information. For example: stock updates applied to an inventory, banking transactions applied to account and customer master files, booking and ticketing transactions to an airline reservation.

(a) Data Storage: "IBM introduced the first hard disk drive in 1956, as a component of their 305 RAMAC computer system. Most digital data today is still stored magnetically on hard disks, or optically on media such as CD-ROMs. Until 2002 most information was stored on analog devices, but that year digital storage capacity exceeded analog for the first time. As of 2007 almost 94% of the data stored worldwide was held digitally: 52% on hard disks, 28% on optical devices and 11% on digital magnetic tape. It has been estimated that the worldwide capacity to store information on electronic devices grew from less than 3 exabytes in 1986 to 295 exabytes in 2007, doubling every 3 years."[9]

(b) Data Retrieval: "The relational database model introduced a program-ming-language independent Structured Query Language (SQL), based on relational algebra. The terms data and information are not synonymous. Anything stored is data, but it only becomes information when it is organized and presented meaningfully. Most of the world's digital data is unstructured and stored in a variety of different physical formats even within a single organization. Data warehouses began to be developed in the 1980s to integrate these disparate stores. They contain data extracted from various sources, including external sources such as the Internet, organized in such a way as to facilitate decision support systems (DSS)."[10]

(c) Data Transmission: "Data transmission has three aspects: transmission, propagation, and reception. It can be categorized as broadcasting, in which information is transmitted unidirectionally downstream, or telecommunications, with bidirectional upstream and downstream channels. XML has been increasingly employed as a means of data interchange since the early 2000s, particularly for machine-oriented interactions such as those involved in web-oriented protocols such as SOAP... data-in-transit."[11]

(d) Data Manipulation: Machines' application-specific capacity to compute information per capita "roughly doubled every 14 months between 1986 and 2007; the per capita capacity of the world's general-purpose computers doubled every 18 months during the same two decades; the global telecommunication capacity per capita doubled every 34 months; the world's storage capacity per capita required roughly 40 months to double (every 3 years); and per capita broadcast information has doubled every 12.3 years. Massive amounts of data are stored worldwide every day, but unless it can be analyzed and presented effectively it essentially resides in what have been called data tombs: data archives that are seldom visited. To address that issue, the field of data mining...emerged in the late 1980s."[12]

Digital Transformation: "It arises from the intersection of cloud computing, big data, IoT, and AI, and it is vital to industries across the market today. Some describe it as the power of digital technology applied to every aspect of the organization. Some refer to it using digital technologies [an analog-to-digital conversion] and advanced analytics for economic value, agility, and speed."[13] Digital Transformation must be in line with the Fourth Industrial Revolution that involves "a systemic change across many sectors and aspects of human life: the crosscutting impacts of emerging technologies are even more important than the exciting capabilities they represent. Our ability to edit the building blocks of life has recently been massively expanded by low-cost gene sequencing and techniques such as CRISPR; artificial intelligence is augmenting processes and skill in every industry; neurotechnology is making unprecedented strides in how we can use and influence the brain as the last frontier of human biology; automation is disrupting century-old transport and manufacturing paradigms; and technologies such as blockchain and smart materials are redefining and blurring the boundary between the digital and physical worlds."[14]

"The result of all this is societal transformation at a global scale. By affecting the incentives, rules, and norms of economic life, it transforms how we communicate, learn, entertain ourselves, and relate to one another and how we understand ourselves as human beings. Furthermore, the sense that new technologies are being developed and implemented at an increasingly rapid pace has an impact on human identities, communities, and political structures. As a result, our responsibilities to one another, our opportunities for self-realization, and our ability to positively impact the world are intricately tied to and shaped by how we engage with the technologies of the Fourth Industrial Revolution. This revolution is not just happening to us— we are not its victims—but rather we have the opportunity and even responsibility to give it structure and purpose." "As automation substitutes for labor…the net displacement of workers by machines might exacerbate the gap between returns to capital and returns to labor."[15]

Digital transformation will improve human life: "(i) In medicine, expect very early disease detection and diagnosis, genome-specific preventative care, extremely precise surgeries performed with the help of robots, on-demand and digital health care, AI-assisted diagnoses, and reduced costs of care. (ii) In the automotive industry, expect self-driving cars, reduced crashes and causalities, fewer drunk drivers, lower insurance premiums, and decreased carbon emissions. (iii) In manufacturing, 3D printing and manufacturing-as-a-service will allow for mass, inexpensive customization with low or no distribution costs. (iv) In resource management and sustainability, resources will be matched with need, waste minimized, and constraints alleviated. Digital transformation even has the potential to completely decouple emissions and resource use from economic growth."[16]

The Information Age Accelerates: The four key technologies in the IT world drive and enable digital transformation, which include elastic cloud computing, big data, artificial intelligence, and internet of things.

(a) ***Cloud Computing***: "Cloud computing is a model of accessing shared pools of configurable hardware and software resources – computer networks, servers, data storage, applications, and other services – that can be rapidly provisioned with minimal management effort, typically via the internet." In other words, "cloud computing means storing and accessing data and programs over the Internet instead of your computer's hard drive. The cloud is just a metaphor for the Internet. It goes back to the days of flowcharts and presentations that would represent the gigantic server-farm infrastructure of the Internet as nothing but a puffy, white cumulus cloud, accepting connections and doling out information as it floats."[17]

(b) ***Big Data***: "Big data is a term applied to data sets whose size or type is beyond the ability of traditional relational databases to capture, manage and process the data with low latency. Big data has one or more of the following characteristics: high volume, high velocity or high variety. Artificial intelligence (AI), mobile, social and the Internet of Things (IoT) are driving data complexity through new forms and sources of data. For example, big data comes from sensors, devices, video/audio, networks, log files, transactional applications, web, and social media — much of it generated in real time and at a very large scale."[18]

(c) ***Artificial Intelligence*** (AI) is "the simulation of human intelligence processes by machines, especially computer systems. These processes include learning (the acquisition of information and rules for using the information), reasoning (using rules to reach approximate or definite conclusions) and self-correction. Particular applications of AI include expert systems, speech recognition and machine vision. AI can be categorized as either weak or strong. Weak AI, also known as narrow AI, is an AI system that is designed and trained for a particular task. Virtual personal assistants, such as Apple's Siri, are a form of weak AI. Strong AI, also known as artificial general intelligence, is an AI system with generalized human cognitive abilities. When presented with an unfamiliar task, a strong AI system is able to find a solution without human intervention."[19]

(d) ***Internet of Things***: "The internet of things (IoT) is a computing concept that describes the idea of everyday physical objects being connected to the internet and being able to identify themselves to other devices. The term is closely identified with RFID as the method of communication, although it also may include other sensor technologies, wireless technologies or QR (quick response) codes. The IoT is significant because an object that can represent itself digitally becomes something greater than the object by itself. No longer does the object relate just to its user, but it is now connected to surrounding objects and database data."[20]

(I) CLOUD COMPUTING

"Cloud computing is the on-demand availability of computer system resources, especially data storage and computing power, without direct active management by the user. The term is generally used to describe data centers available to many users over the Internet. Large clouds, predominant today, often have functions distributed over multiple locations from central servers. If the connection to the user is relatively close, it may be designated an edge server. Clouds may be limited to a single organization (enterprise clouds) or be available to many organizations (public cloud). Cloud computing relies on sharing of resources to achieve coherence and economies of scale."[21]

"Advocates of public and hybrid clouds note that cloud computing allows companies to avoid or minimize up-front IT infrastructure costs. Proponents also claim that cloud computing allows enterprises to get their applications up and running faster, with improved manageability and less maintenance, and that it enables IT teams to more rapidly adjust resources to meet fluctuating and unpredictable demand. Cloud providers typically use a pay-as-you-go model, which can lead to unexpected operating expenses if administrators are not familiarized with cloud-pricing models. The availability of high-capacity networks, low-cost computers and storage devices as well as the widespread adoption of hardware virtualization, service-oriented architecture and autonomic and utility computing has led to growth in cloud computing. By 2019, Linux was the most widely used operating system, including in Microsoft's offerings and is thus described as dominant. The Cloud Service Provider (CSP) will screen, keep up and gather data about the firewalls, intrusion identification or/and counteractive action frameworks and information stream inside the network."[22]

During the 1960s, the initial concepts of time-sharing became popularized. "In August 2006, Amazon created subsidiary Amazon Web Services and introduced its Elastic Compute Cloud (EC2). In April 2008, Google released the beta version of Google App Engine." "In February 2010, Microsoft released Microsoft Azure, which was announced in October 2008. In July 2010, Rackspace Hosting and NASA jointly launched an open-source cloud-software initiative known as OpenStack." "On March 1, 2011, IBM announced the IBM SmartCloud framework to support Smarter Planet. Among the various components of the Smarter Computing foundation, cloud computing is a critical part. On June 7, 2012, Oracle announced the Oracle Cloud. This cloud offering is poised to be the first to provide users with access to an integrated set of IT solutions, including the Applications (SaaS), Platform (PaaS), and Infrastructure (IaaS) layers. In May 2012, Google Compute Engine was released in preview, before being rolled out into General Availability in December 2013. In 2019, it was revealed that Linux is most used on Microsoft Azure."[23]

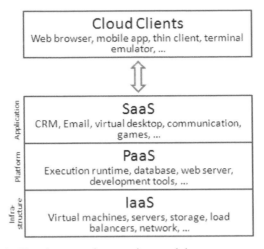

Figure III-1-2. Cloud computing service models, Accessed 30 November 2019,
https://upload.wikimedia.org/wikipedia/commons/3/3c/Cloud_computing_layers.png

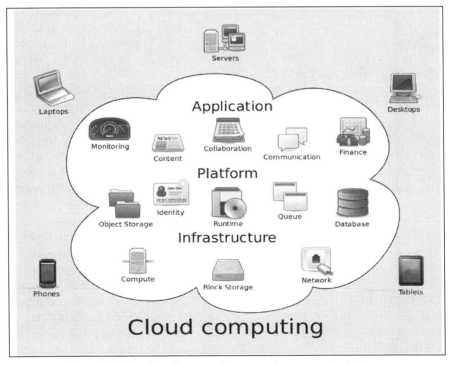

Figure III-1-3. Cloud computing metaphor: networked elements
Lower: https://en.wikipedia.org/wiki/Cloud_computing#/media/File:Cloud_computing.svg
Accessed 30 November 2019.

Similar Concepts: "The goal of cloud computing is to allow users to take benefit from all of these technologies, without the need for deep knowledge about or expertise with each one of them. The cloud aims to cut costs, and helps the users focus on their core business instead of being impeded by IT obstacles. The main enabling technology for cloud computing is virtualization. Virtualization software separates a physical computing device into one or more virtual devices, each of which can be easily used and managed to perform computing tasks. With operating system–level virtualization essentially creating a scalable system of multiple independent computing devices, idle computing resources can be allocated and used more efficiently. Virtualization provides the agility required to speed up IT operations and reduces cost by increasing infrastructure utilization. Autonomic computing automates the process through which the user can provision resources on-demand. By minimizing user involvement, automation speeds up the process, reduces labor costs and reduces the possibility of human errors. Cloud computing uses concepts from utility computing to provide metrics for the services used. Cloud computing attempts to address QoS (quality of service) and reliability problems of other grid computing models."[24]

Characteristics: Cloud computing exhibits such characteristics as agility, cost reduction, device independence, easy maintenance, and so on. "The National Institute of Standards and Technology (NIST)'s definition of cloud computing identifies five essential characteristics: (i) On-demand self-service. A consumer can unilaterally provision computing capabilities, such as server time and network storage, as needed automatically without requiring human interaction with each service provider. (ii) Broad network access. Capabilities are available over the network and accessed through standard mechanisms that promote use by heterogeneous thin or thick client platforms (e.g., mobile phones, tablets, laptops, and workstations). (iii) Resource pooling. The provider's computing resources are pooled to serve multiple consumers using a multi-tenant model, with different physical and virtual resources dynamically assigned and reassigned according to consumer demand. (iv) Rapid elasticity. Capabilities can be elastically provisioned and released, in some cases automatically, to scale rapidly outward and inward commensurate with demand. To the consumer, the capabilities available for provisioning often appear unlimited and can be appropriated in any quantity at any time. (v) Measured service. Cloud systems automatically control and optimize resource use by leveraging a metering capability at some level of abstraction appropriate to the type of service (e.g., storage, processing, bandwidth, and active user accounts). Resource usage can be monitored, controlled, and reported, providing transparency for both the provider and consumer of the utilized service."[25]

Service Models: Cloud-computing providers offer their services according to different models, of which the three standard models per NIST are Infrastructure as a Service (IaaS), Platform as a Service (PaaS), and Software as a Service (SaaS). "These models offer increasing abstraction; they are thus often portrayed as a layers in a stack: infrastructure-, platform- and software-as-a-service, but these need not be related. For example, one can provide SaaS implemented on physical machines (bare metal), without using underlying PaaS or IaaS layers, and conversely one can run a program on IaaS and access it directly, without wrapping it as SaaS."[26]

Infrastructure as a service (IaaS) "refers to online services that provide high-level APIs used to dereference various low-level details of underlying network infrastructure like physical computing resources, location, data partitioning, scaling, security, backup etc." "IaaS-cloud providers supply these resources on-demand from their large pools of equipment installed in data centers. For wide-area connectivity, customers can use either the Internet or carrier clouds (dedicated virtual private networks). To deploy their applications, cloud users install operating-system images and their application software on the cloud infrastructure. In this model, the cloud user patches and maintains the operating systems and the application software. Cloud providers typically bill IaaS services on a utility computing basis: cost reflects the amount of resources allocated and consumed."[27]

Platform as a service (PaaS) provides consumer acquired applications supported by the provider. "The consumer does not manage or control the underlying cloud infrastructure including network, servers, operating systems, or storage, but has control over the deployed applications and possibly configuration settings for the application-hosting environment...In the PaaS models, cloud providers deliver a computing platform, typically including operating system, programming-language execution environment, database, and web server. Application developers develop and run their software on a cloud platform instead of directly buying and managing the underlying hardware and software layers."[28]

Software as a service (SaaS) refers to software applications hosted on cloud infrastructure (either public or private) and accessed by users through the internet via a web browser. "In the software as a service (SaaS) model, users gain access to application software and databases. Cloud providers manage the infrastructure and platforms that run the applications. SaaS is sometimes referred to as on-demand software and is usually priced on a pay-per-use basis or using a subscription fee. In the SaaS model, cloud providers install and operate application software in the cloud and cloud users access the software from cloud clients. Cloud users do not manage the cloud infrastructure and platform where the application runs. This eliminates the need to install and run the application on the cloud user's own computers, which simplifies maintenance and support."[29]

Deployment Models: (a) ***Private Cloud***: is "operated solely for a single organization, whether managed internally or by a third party, and hosted either internally or externally. Undertaking a private cloud project requires significant engagement to virtualize the business environment and requires the organization to reevaluate decisions about existing resources. It can improve business, but every step in the project raises security issues that must be addressed to prevent serious vulnerabilities. Self-run data centers are generally capital intensive. They have a significant physical footprint, requiring allocations of space, hardware, and environmental controls. These assets have to be refreshed periodically, resulting in additional capital expenditures. They have attracted criticism because users still have to buy, build, and manage them and thus do not benefit from less hands-on management, essentially lacking the economic model that makes cloud computing such an intriguing concept."[30]

(b) ***Public Cloud***: The services are rendered over a network that is open for public use. "Public cloud services may be free. Technically there may be little or no difference between public and private cloud architecture, however, security consideration may be substantially different for services (applications, storage, and other resources) that are made available by a service provider for a public audience and when communication is effected over a non-trusted network. Generally, public cloud service providers like Amazon Web Services (AWS), IBM, Oracle, Microsoft, Google, and Alibaba own and operate the infrastructure at their data center and access is generally via the Internet. AWS, Oracle, Microsoft, and Google also offer direct connect services called AWS Direct Connect, Oracle FastConnect, Azure ExpressRoute, and Cloud Interconnect respectively, such connections require customers to purchase or lease a private connection to a peering point offered by the cloud provider."[31]

(c) ***Hybrid Cloud***: It is a composition of a public cloud and a private environment, such as a private cloud or on-premise resources, that remain distinct entities but are bound together, offering the benefits of multiple deployment models. Hybrid cloud can also mean the ability to connect collocation, managed and/or dedicated services with cloud resources. Gartner defines a hybrid cloud service as a cloud computing service that is composed of some combination of private, public and community cloud services, from different service providers. A hybrid cloud service crosses isolation and provider boundaries so that it can't be simply put in one category of private, public, or community cloud service. It allows one to extend either the capacity or the capability of a cloud service, by aggregation, integration or customization with another cloud service... Hybrid cloud adoption depends on a number of factors such as data security and compliance requirements, level of control needed over data, and the applications an organization uses."[32]

Security and Privacy: "Cloud computing poses privacy concerns because the service provider can access the data that is in the cloud at any time. It could accidentally or deliberately alter or delete information. Many cloud providers can share information with third parties if necessary for purposes of law and order without a warrant. That is permitted in their privacy policies, which users must agree to before they start using cloud services. Solutions to privacy include policy and legislation as well as end users' choices for how data is stored. Users can encrypt data that is processed or stored within the cloud to prevent unauthorized access. Identity management systems can also provide practical solutions to privacy concerns in cloud computing. These systems distinguish between authorized and unauthorized users and determine the amount of data that is accessible to each entity. The systems work by creating and describing identities, recording activities, and getting rid of unused identities. According to the Cloud Security Alliance, the top three threats in the cloud are Insecure Interfaces and API's, Data Loss & Leakage, and Hardware Failure—which accounted for 29%, 25% and 10% of all cloud security outages respectively. Together, these forms shared technology vulnerabilities... Fundamentally, private cloud is seen as more secure with higher levels of control for the owner, however public cloud is seen to be more flexible and requires less time and money investment from the user."[33]

Limitations and Disadvantages: "Cloud computing is cheaper because of economics of scale, and—like any outsourced task—you tend to get what you want...the cloud provider might not meet your legal needs and that businesses need to weigh the benefits of cloud computing against the risks. In cloud computing, the control of the backend infrastructure is limited to the cloud vendor only. Cloud providers often decide on the management policies, which moderates what the cloud users are able to do with their deployment. Cloud users are also limited to the control and management of their applications, data and services. This includes data caps, which are placed on cloud users by the cloud vendor allocating certain amount of bandwidth for each customer and are often shared among other cloud users." Privacy and confidentiality are big concerns in some activities. "Cloud computing is beneficial to many enterprises; it lowers costs and allows them to focus on competence instead of on matters of IT and infrastructure. Nevertheless, cloud computing has proven to have some limitations and disadvantages, especially for smaller business operations, particularly regarding security and downtime. Technical outages are inevitable and occur sometimes when cloud service providers (CSPs) become overwhelmed in the process of serving their clients. This may result to temporary business suspension." An individual is unable to access their applications, server or data from the cloud during an outage (of internet).[34]

(II) BIG DATA

Big Data is "a field that treats ways to analyze, systematically extract information from, or otherwise deal with data sets that are too large or complex to be dealt with by traditional data-processing application software. Data with many cases (rows) offer greater statistical power, while data with higher complexity (more attributes or columns) may lead to a higher false discovery rate. Big data challenges include capturing data, data storage, data analysis, search, sharing, transfer, visualization, querying, updating, inform- ation privacy and data source. Big data was originally associated with three key concepts: volume, variety, and velocity. When we handle big data, we may not sample but simply observe and track what happens. Therefore, big data often includes data with sizes that exceed the capacity of traditional usual software to process within an acceptable time and value."[35]

"Current usage of the term big data tends to refer to the use of predictive analytics, user behavior analytics, or certain other advanced data analytics methods that extract value from data, and seldom to a particular size of data set...the quantities of data now available are indeed large, but that's not the most relevant characteristic of this new data ecosystem. Analysis of data sets can find new correlations to spot business trends, prevent diseases, combat crime and so on. Scientists, business executives, practitioners of medicine, advertising and governments alike regularly meet difficulties with large data-sets in areas including Internet searches, fintech, urban informatics, and business informatics. Scientists encounter limitations in e-Science work, including meteorology, genomics, connectomics, complex physics simul- ations, biology and environmental research."[36]

"Data sets grow rapidly, in part because they are increasingly gathered by cheap and numerous information-sensing Internet of things devices such as mobile devices, aerial (remote sensing), software logs, cameras, micro- phones, radio-frequency identification (RFID) readers and wireless sensor networks. The world's technological per-capita capacity to store information has roughly doubled every 40 months since the 1980s; as of 2012, every day 2.5 exabytes (2.5×10^{18}) of data are generated. Based on an IDC report prediction, the global data volume will grow exponentially from 4.4 zettabytes to 44 zettabytes between 2013 and 2020. By 2025, IDC predicts there will be 163 zettabytes of data. One question for large enterprises is determining who should own big-data initiatives that affect the entire organization. Relational database management systems, desktop statistics and software packages used to visualize data often have difficulty handling big data. The work may require massively parallel software running on tens, hundreds, or even thousands of servers. What qualifies as being big data varies depending on the capabilities of the users and their tools and expand- ing capabilities make big data a moving target."[37]

Characteristics: Volume: The quantity of generated and stored data. Variety: The type and nature of the data. Velocity: "The speed at which the data is generated and processed to meet the demands and challenges that lie in the path of growth and development." Veracity: the data quality and data value. Exhaustive: Whether the entire system is captured or recorded or not. Fine-grained and uniquely lexical: " Respectively, the proportion of specific data of each element per element collected and if the element and its characteristics are properly indexed or identified." Relational: "If data collected contains commons fields that would enable a conjoining, or meta-analysis, of different data sets." Extensional: "If new fields in each element of the data collected can be added or changed easily." Scalability: If the size of the data can expand rapidly. Value: "The utility that can be extracted from the data. Variability: "It refers to data whose value or other characteristics are shifting in relation to the context they are being generated."[38]

Architecture: "Big data repositories have existed in many forms, often built by corporations with a special need." Big data analytics for manufacturing applications is marketed as a 5C architecture (connection, conversion, cyber, cognition, and configuration). Factory work and Cyber-physical systems may have an extended 6C system: Connection (sensor and networks), Cloud (computing and data on demand), Cyber (model and memory), Content/context (meaning and correlation), Community (sharing and collaboration), and Customization (personalization and value).[39]

Technologies: "A 2011 McKinsey Global Institute report characterizes the main components and ecosystem of big data as follows: (i) Techniques for analyzing data, such as A/B testing, machine learning and natural language processing; (ii) Big data technologies, like business intelligence, cloud computing and databases; and (iii) Visualization, such as charts, graphs and other displays of the data." "The practitioners of big data analytics processes are generally hostile to slower shared storage, preferring direct-attached storage (DAS) in its various forms from solid state drive (SSD) to high capacity SATA disk buried inside parallel processing nodes. The perception of shared storage architectures—Storage area network (SAN) and Network-attached storage (NAS) —is that they are relatively slow, complex, and expensive. These qualities are not consistent with big data analytics systems that thrive on system performance, commodity infra-structure, and low cost. Real or near-real time information delivery is one of the defining characteristics of big data analytics. Latency is therefore avoided whenever and wherever possible. Data in direct-attached memory or disk is good—data on memory or disk at the other end of a FC SAN connection is not. The cost of a SAN at the scale needed for analytics applications is very much higher than other storage techniques."[40]

Applications: "Big data has increased the demand of information management specialists so much so that Software AG, Oracle Corporation, IBM, Microsoft, SAP, EMC, HP and Dell have spent more than $15 billion on software firms specializing in data management and analytics. In 2010, this industry was worth more than $100 billion and was growing at almost 10 percent a year: about twice as fast as the software business as a whole. Developed economies increasingly use data-intensive technologies... According to one estimate, one-third of the globally stored information is in the form of alphanumeric text and still image data, which is the format most useful for most big data applications. This also shows the potential of yet unused data. While many vendors offer off-the-shelf solutions for big data, experts recommend the development of in-house solutions custom-tailored to solve the company's problem at hand if the company has sufficient technical capabilities."[41]

(i) Government: "The use and adoption of big data within governmental processes allows efficiencies in terms of cost, productivity, and innovation, but does not come without its flaws."

(ii) International development: "Research on the effective usage of information and communication technologies for development suggests that big data technology can make important contributions but also present unique challenges to International development."

(iii) Manufacturing: Improvements in supply planning and product quality provide the greatest benefit of big data for manufacturing. "The generated big data acts as the input into predictive tools and preventive strategies such as Prognostics and Health Management."

(iv) Healthcare: "Big data analytics has helped healthcare improve by providing personalized medicine and prescriptive analytics..."

(v) Education: "A McKinsey Global Institute study found a shortage of 1.5 million highly trained data professionals and managers and a number of universities...have created masters programs to meet this demand."

(vi) Media: Practitioners "in Media and Advertising approach big data as many actionable points of information about millions of individuals."

(vii) Insurance: "Health insurance providers are collecting data on social determinants of health such as food and TV consumption, marital status, clothing size and purchasing habits, from which they make predictions on health costs, in order to spot health issues in their clients."

(viii) Internet of Things (IoT): "Big data and the IoT work in conjuncttion. Data extracted from IoT devices provides a mapping of device interconnectivity. Such mappings have been used by the media industry, companies and governments to more accurately target their audience..."

(ix) Information Technology: Big data has come to "prominence within Business Operations as a tool to help employees work more efficiently and streamline the collection and distribution of Information Technology."

Research activities: "Encrypted search and cluster formation in big data were demonstrated in March 2014 at the American Society of Engineering Education. Gautam Siwach engaged at Tackling the challenges of Big Data by MIT Computer Science and Artificial Intelligence Laboratory and Dr. Amir Esmailpour at UNH Research Group investigated the key features of big data as the formation of clusters and their interconnections. They focused on the security of big data and the orientation of the term towards the presence of different type of data in an encrypted form at cloud interface by providing the raw definitions and real time examples within the technology. Moreover, they proposed an approach for identifying the encoding technique to advance towards an expedited search over encrypted text leading to the security enhancements in big data. In March 2012, The White House announced a national Big Data Initiative that consisted of six Federal departments and agencies committing more than $200 million to big data research projects...Big data sets come with algorithmic challenges that previously did not exist. Hence, there is a need to fundamentally change the processing ways. The Workshops on Algorithms for Modern Massive Data Sets (MMDS) bring together computer scientists, statisticians, mathematicians, and data analysis practitioners to discuss algorithmic challenges of big data. Regarding big data...concepts of magnitude are relative."[42]

Challenges of Big Data in a Modern Enterprise: "Enterprises face a multitude of systems, data sources, data formats, and potential use cases. Generating value requires individuals in the enterprise who are able to understand all these data, comprehend the IT infrastructure used to support these data, and then relate the data sets to business use cases and value drivers. The resulting complexity is substantial."[43] Thomas M. Seibel, in his *Digital Transformation* (2019) views five key challenges that organizations face in today's era of big data: 1. Handling a multiplicity of enterprise source systems "The average Fortune 500 enterprise has, at the very least, a few hundred enterprise IT systems. 2. Incorporating and contextualizing high-frequency data: The challenge gets significantly harder with the censoring of value chains and the resulting inflow of real-time data. 3. Working with data lakes. 4. Ensuring data consistency, referential integrity, and continuous downstream use: "Data arrival rates vary by system; data formats from source systems can change; and data arrive out of order due to networking delays. More nuanced is the choice of which analytics to update and when, in order to support a business workflow." 5. Enabling new tools and skills for new needs: "As the availability and access to data within an enterprise grow, the skills challenge grows commensurately...Enterprise IT and analytics teams need to provide tools that enable employees with different levels of data science proficiency to work with large data sets and perform predictive analytics using a unified data image."[44]

(III) ARTIFICIAL INTELLIGENCE (AI)

Artificial intelligence (AI) is "the study of intelligent agents: any device that perceives its environment and takes actions that maximize its chance of successfully achieving its goals." AI capabilities include "understanding human speech, competing at the highest level in strategic game systems, autonomously operating cars, intelligent routing in content delivery networks, and military simulations."[45] The field of AI was reinvigorated in the 2000s by three major forces: rapid improvement of computational power; access to a large amount of data through internet, and advances of underlying algorithms. "AI has greatly evolved from the use of symbolic logic and expert systems (in the 70s and 80s), to **machine learning** systems in the 2000s, and to **neural networks** and deep learning systems in the 2010s."[46]

"Traditional logic-based algorithms effectively handle a range of different problems and tasks. But they are not effective at addressing many tasks that are often quite easy for humans to do...Many AI algorithms are based on the idea that rather than code a computer program to perform a task, design the program to learn directly from data."[47] "A typical AI analyzes its environment and takes actions that maximize its chance of success. An AI's intended utility function (or goal) can be simple (1 if the AI wins a game of Go, 0 otherwise) or complex (Do mathematically similar actions to the ones succeeded in the past). Goals can be explicitly defined or induced. If the AI is programmed for reinforcement learning, goals can be implicitly induced by rewarding some types of behavior or punishing others. Alternatively, an evolutionary system can induce goals by using a fitness function to mutate and preferentially replicate high-scoring AI systems."[48]

"AI often revolves around the use of algorithms. An algorithm is a set of unambiguous instructions that a mechanical computer can execute. A complex algorithm is often built on top of other, simpler, algorithms...Many AI algorithms are capable of learning from data; they can enhance themselves by learning new heuristics (strategies, or rules of thumb, that have worked well in the past), or can themselves write other algorithms. Some of the learners described below, including Bayesian networks, decision trees, and nearest neighbor, could theoretically, (given infinite data, time, and memory) learn to approximate any function, including which combination of mathematical functions would best describe the world. These learners could, therefore, derive all possible knowledge, by considering every possible hypothesis and matching them against the data. In practice, it is almost never possible to consider every possibility, because of the phenomenon of combinatorial explosion, where the amount of time needed to solve a problem grows exponentially...Compared with humans, existing AI lacks several features of human commonsense reasoning; most notably, humans have powerful mechanisms for reasoning."[49]

Machine Learning: "Machine learning is a subfield of AI based on the idea that computers can learn from data without being explicitly programmed. Machine learning algorithms employ various statistical techniques on the data they are fed in order to make inferences about the data. The algorithms improve as the amount of data they are fed increases and as the inferences they generate are either confirmed or disconfirmed (sometimes by humans, sometimes by machines)."[50] "Machine learning algorithms are used in a wide variety of applications, such as email filtering and computer vision, where it is difficult or infeasible to develop a conventional algorithm for effectively performing the task. Machine learning is closely related to computational statistics, which focuses on making predictions using computers. The study of mathematical optimization delivers methods, theory and application domains to the field of machine learning. Data mining is a field of study within machine learning and focuses on exploratory data analysis through unsupervised learning."[51]

In supervised learning, "techniques require the use of training data in the form of labeled inputs and outputs. A supervised algorithm employs sophisticated statistical techniques to analyze the labeled training data, in order to infer a function that maps inputs to outputs. When sufficiently trained, the algorithm can then be fed new input data it has not seen before, and generate answers about the data (i.e., outputs) by applying the inference function to the new inputs."[52]

In unsupervised learning, "the algorithm builds a mathematical model from a set of data which contains only inputs and no desired output labels. Unsupervised learning algorithms are used to find structure in the data, like grouping or clustering of data points. Unsupervised learning can discover patterns in the data, and can group the inputs into categories, as in feature learning. Dimensionality reduction is the process of reducing the number of features, or inputs, in a set of data."[53]

Semi-supervised learning falls "between unsupervised learning (without any labeled training data) and supervised learning (with completely labeled training data). Many machine-learning researchers have found that unlabeled data, when used in conjunction with a small amount of labeled data, can produce considerable improvement in learning accuracy."[54]

Reinforcement learning is an area of machine learning concerned with how software agents ought to take actions in an environment so as to maximize some notion of cumulative reward. Due to its generality, the field is studied in many other disciplines, such as game theory, control theory, operations research, information theory, simulation-based optimization, multi-agent systems, swarm intelligence, statistics and genetic algorithms. In machine learning, the environment is typically represented as a Markov Decision Process (MDP). Many reinforcement learning algorithms use dynamic programming techniques."[55]

Neural Networks: "The neural network is a set of algorithms patterned after the functioning of the human brain and the human nervous system. A neuron is a mathematical function that takes inputs and then classifies them according to the applied algorithm. It consists of an input layer, multiple hidden layers, and an output layer. It has layers of interconnected nodes. Each node is a perception that feeds the signal into an activation function. Neural networks are trained and taught just like a child's developing brain is trained. They cannot be programmed directly for a particular task. They are trained in such a manner so that they can adapt according to the changing input." There are three methods or learning paradigms: Supervised Learning, Reinforcement Learning, and Unsupervised Learning.[56]

Supervised learning: "As the name suggests, supervised learning means in the presence of a supervisor or a teacher. It means a set of a labeled data set is already present with desired output i.e. the optimum action to be performed by the neural network which is already present for some data sets. The machine is then given new data sets to analyze the training data sets and to produce the correct output."

Reinforcement learning: "In this, learning of input-output mapping is done by continuous interaction with the environment so that the scalar index of performance could be minimized. In this, instead of a teacher, there is a critic that converts the primary reinforcement signal i.e. the scalar input received from the environment into heuristic reinforcement signal (higher quality reinforcement signal) also a scalar input."

Unsupervised learning: As the name suggests, there is no teacher or supervisor available. In this, the data is neither labeled nor classified and no prior guidance is available to the neural network. In this, the machine has to group the provided data sets according to the similarities, differences, and patterns without any training provided beforehand."

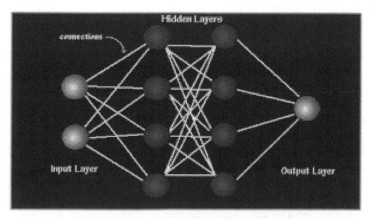

Photo III-1-1. The Neural Network
Accessed 15 December 2019, https://www.educba.com/what-is-neural-networks/

Development and Deployment Workflow in Machine Learning:
Let's look at what's involved in a machine learning development process.

(a) *Data Assembly and Preparation*. "The first step is to identify the required and relevant data sets, and then assemble the data in a unified image that is useful for machine learning."

(b) *Featuring Engineering*: "This involved going through the data and crafting individual signals that the data scientist and domain expert think will be relevant to the problem being solved."

(c) *Labeling the Outcomes*: "This step involves labeling the outcomes the model tries to predict (e.g., engine failure). Often the specific outcomes are not clearly defined in the data since the original source data sets and business processes were not originally defined with AI in mind."

(d) *Setting Up the Training Data*: "Now comes the process of setting up the data set for training the algorithm. There are a number of nuances to this process that may require outside expertise. For classification tasks, data scientists need to ensure that labels are approximately balanced with positive and negative examples to provide the classifier algorithm enough balanced data. Data scientists also need to ensure the classifier is not biased by artificial patterns in the data."

(e) *Choosing and Training the Algorithm*: "The next step is to choose the actual algorithm and then train it with the training data set. Numerous algorithm libraries are available data scientists today, created by companies, universities, research organizations, government agencies, and individual contributors. Many are available as open source software from repositories."

(f) *Deploying the Algorithm into Production*: "The machine learning algorithm then must be deployed to operate in a production environment: It needs to receive new data, generate outputs, and have some action or decision be made based on those outputs. This may mean embedding the algorithm within an enterprise application used by humans to make decisions – for example, a predictive maintenance application that identifies and prioritizes equipment requiring maintenance to provide guidance for maintenance crews. This is where the real value is created – by reducing equipment downtime and servicing costs through more accurate failure prediction that enables proactive maintenance before the equipment actually fails. In order for the machine learning algorithm to operate in production, the underlying compute infrastructure needs to be set up and managed."

(g) *Closed-Loop Continuous Improvement*: "Once in production, the performance of the AI algorithm needs to be tracked and managed. Algorithms typically require frequent retraining by data science teams. As market conditions change, business objectives and processes evolve, and new data sources are identified. Organizations need to maintain technical agility so they can rapidly develop, retrain, and deploy new models as circumstances change." [57]

Business Benefits of AI: "Artificial intelligence can improve customer service with the use of chatbots and recommendation systems, increase revenue by identifying and maximizing sales opportunities, predict product demand, classify customers, predict customer behavior, detect fraudulent credit card transactions, detect malware, review documents, do research, help diagnose patients... The list could go on. The key in looking for the benefits of AI is not in what other people think about it – it's about finding the value it can bring to your organization."[58] One of the newest benefits of cloud computing is that it enables businesses to take advantage of AI. (i) Improving personalized shopping experiences; (ii) Automating customer interactions; (iii) Real-time assistance; (iv) Data mining; (v) Operational automation; (vi) Predicting outcomes; (vii) Improve the recruitment process. Thus, AI systems provide businesses with a wide range of benefits.[59]

Applications: "AI is relevant to any intellectual task. Modern artificial intelligence techniques are pervasive and are too numerous to list here. Frequently, when a technique reaches mainstream use, it is no longer considered artificial intelligence; this phenomenon is described as the AI effect. High-profile examples of AI include autonomous vehicles (such as drones and self-driving cars), medical diagnosis, creating art (such as poetry), proving mathematical theorems, playing games (such as Chess or Go), search engines (such as Google search), online assistants (such as Siri), image recognition in photographs, spam filtering, predicting flight delays, prediction of judicial decisions and targeting online advertisements."[60]

Philosophy and Ethics: *(a) The limits of artificial general intelligence*: "We need not decide if a machine can think; we need only decide if a machine can act as intelligently as a human being. This approach to the philosophical problems associated with artificial intelligence forms the basis of the Turing test." "The brain can be simulated by machines and because brains are intelligent, simulated brains must also be intelligent; thus machines can be intelligent."[61] *(b) Potential harm*: "Widespread use of artificial intelligence could have unintended consequences that are dangerous or undesirable. Scientists from the Future of Life Institute, among others, described some short-term research goals to see how AI influences the economy, the laws and ethics that are involved with AI and how to minimize AI security risks. In the long-term, the scientists have proposed to continue optimizing function while minimizing possible security risks."[62] *(c) Ethical machines*: "Machines with intelligence have the potential to use their intelligence to prevent harm and minimize the risks; they may have the ability to use ethical reasoning to better choose their actions in the world. Research in this area includes machine ethics, artificial moral agents, and friendly AI." Those are significant in the long run.

(IV) THE INTERNET OF THINGS

The Internet of Things (IoT) is "a system of interrelated computing devices, mechanical and digital machines, objects, animals or people that are provided with unique identifiers (UIDs) and the ability to transfer data over a network without requiring human-to-human or human-to-computer interaction. The definition of the Internet of Things has evolved due to the convergence of multiple technologies, real-time analytics, machine learning, commodity sensors, and embedded systems. Traditional fields of embedded systems, wireless sensor networks, control systems, automation (including home and building automation), and others all contribute to enabling the Internet of Things. In the consumer market, IoT technology is most synonymous with products pertaining to the concept of the smart home, covering devices and appliances (such as lighting fixtures, thermostats, home security systems and cameras, and other home appliances) that support one or more common ecosystems, and can be controlled via devices associated with that ecosystem, such as smartphones and smart speakers. There are a number of serious concerns about dangers in the growth of IoT, especially in the areas of privacy and security; and consequently industry and governmental moves to begin to address these."[63]

"The concept of a network of smart devices was discussed as early as 1982, with a modified Coke vending machine at Carnegie Mellon University becoming the first Internet-connected appliance, able to report its inventory and whether newly loaded drinks were cold or not." "***Consumer of IoT*** was further sparked in 2011-12, when several successful products like the Nest remote thermostat and the Philips Hue smart lightbulb were introduced. In 2014, IoT hit the mainstream when Google bought Nest for $3.2 billion, the Consumer Electronics Show showcased IoT, and Apple introduced its first smart watch. Consumer IoT is most visible in the fast-growing adoption of wearables (particularly smart watches) and smart speaker devices like the Amazon Echo, Google Home, and Apple HomePod – a category growing at nearly 48 percent a year in the U.S. Today, we see even more changes in the form factor of computing devices."[64]

The IoT technology solution connects the edge, an IoT platform, and the enterprise. The edge consists of a very broad range of communication-enabled devices, including appliances, sensors, and gateways, that can connect to a network. An IoT platform is the connection between the enterprise and the edge. "IoT platform must be able to aggregate, federate, and normalize large volumes of disparate, real-time operational data." The ability to analyze data on petabyte scale is a critical requirement. The IoT platforms function as application development platforms for enterprises. Rapid development of applications that monitor, control, and optimize products and business units greatly increases productivity.[65]

IoT's Potential and Impact: The Internet of Things will change the way business is done. It begs three questions: why, how, and how much?

(a) *Why*: Why IoT will change the way business is dome? First, "the volume of data that IoT systems can generate is wholly unprecedented. The internet of things is projected to generate 600 zettabytes of data annually by 2020 – that's 600 million petabytes." Second, "the data generated are valuable. As organizations sensor and measure areas of their business, those sensor readings help them make better, more profitable decisions. The data generated by IoT, when analyzed by AI, will enable organizations to better run core business processes." The third reason IoT will transform business is the power of Metcalfe's Law – i.e., the value of a network is proportional to the square of the number of its members. In this case, the network is a company's federated data image, and the members are the data points."[66]

(b) *How*: IoT will change businesses in a major way. The question remains how: how we make decisions, how we execute business processes, and how we differentiate products in the marketplace. First, "decision-making will change, with data-driven decision-making in particular taking on an entirely new meaning. Algorithms will become an integral part of most, if not all, decisions. This is particularly true for the day-to-day decisions that keep a business running." Second, "IoT will change how business processes are executed, resulting in faster, more accurate, and less expensive decision-making. Instead of consulting one's own intuition and experience and doing what feels right, operator will consult an algorithmic recommendation that clearly explains why it suggests a certain course of action. Third, "IoT will change the way products are differentiated in the marketplace. We will see a new level of individualization of product behaviors. Smartphones already adapt to how their owner speaks of types."[67]

(c) *How Much?* "With the total number of connected devices projected to grow from about 20 billion today to 75 billion by 2025, analysts expect IoT will contribute up to $11.1 trillion in annual global economic value by 2025. That is a staggering amount, equivalent to approximately 11 percent of the global economy, based on the World Banks projection of $99.5 trillion in global GDP in 2025. Significant workforce displacement will be a byproduct of IoT adoption and the corresponding automation it enables. I expect the level and timing of job displacement to vary dramatically across industries, but the aggregate statistics are undeniable…However, job displacement doesn't mean people will no longer work. New jobs will emerge even as traditional jobs disappear."[68]

(d) *How IoT Creates Value*: "From a customer's or end user's perspective, IoT's real value comes from services, IoT analytics, and applications, while the rest of the technology stack serves as an enabler with lower value and growth potential. Ultimately, organizations using IoT technologies will capture most of the potential value over time."[69]

Applications: *Consumer applications*: "A growing portion of IoT devices are created for consumer use, including connected vehicles, home automation, wearable technology, connected health, and appliances with remote monitoring capabilities... IoT devices are a part of the larger concept of home automation, which can include lighting, heating and air conditioning, media and security systems. Long-term benefits could include energy savings by automatically ensuring lights and electronics are turned off... One key application of a smart home is to provide assistance for those with disabilities and elderly individuals."

Commercial applications: Medical and healthcare, Transportation, V2X communications, and Building and home automation. "IoT devices can be used to enable remote health monitoring and emergency notification systems. These health monitoring devices can range from blood pressure and heart rate monitors to advanced devices capable of monitoring specialized implants, such as pacemakers, Fitbit electronic wristbands, or advanced hearing aids...The IoT can assist in the integration of communications, control, and information processing across various transportation systems. Application of the IoT extends to all aspects of transportation systems...In vehicular communication systems, vehicle-to-everything communication (V2X), consists of three main components: vehicle to vehicle communication (V2V), vehicle to infrastructure communication (V2I) and vehicle to pedestrian communications (V2P)."

Industrial applications: "Also known as IIoT, industrial IoT devices acquire and analyze data from connected equipment, (OT) operational technology, locations and people. Combined with operational technology (OT) monitoring devices, IIOT helps regulate and monitor industrial systems...The IoT can realize the seamless integration of various manufacturing devices equipped with sensing, identification, processing, communication, actuation, and networking capabilities."

Infrastructure applications: "Monitoring and controlling operations of sustainable urban and rural infrastructures like bridges, railway tracks and on- and offshore wind-farms is a key application of the IoT.[59] The IoT infrastructure can be used for monitoring any events or changes in structural conditions that can compromise safety and increase risk. The IoT can benefit the construction industry by cost saving, time reduction, better quality workday, paperless workflow and increase in productivity."

Military applications: "The Internet of Military Things (IoMT) is the application of IoT technologies in the military domain for the purposes of reconnaissance, surveillance, and other combat-related objectives. It is heavily influenced by the future prospects of warfare in an urban environment and involves the use of sensors, munitions, vehicles, robots, human-wearable biometrics, and other smart technology that is relevant on the battlefield."[70]

2. Cyberwarfare and National Security

Let's define the terms of cyberspace, cyberwarfare, and cyber war. Unlike physical space, "cyberspace is a manmade landscape of inter-connected devices and networks. Organizations must connect, and remain connected, to this internet in order to compete in today's markets. However, consistent governance does not apply across all geographic internet presences…Much of cyberspace is organized and managed by private and cooperative organizations without state or geographical overlap. The internet, which is a central and growing component in this space, is built in a decentralized manner. The ideology of the internet's creators and its leading thinkers is opposed to any type of state management."[71]

"Cyberwarfare is the use of technology to attack a nation, causing comparable harm to actual warfare. 'Cyberwarfare' does not imply scale, protraction or violence which are typically associated with the term 'war'. There is significant debate among experts regarding the definition of cyberwarfare, and even if such a thing exists. The term 'Cyberwarfare' is a misnomer, to date no offensive cyber actions could be described as 'war'. Offensive cyber actions, such as those in Estonia in 2007, Georgia in 2008, Iran in 2010, North Korea have occurred in the context of international relations, only resulting in condemnation and denial by sides. Cyberwarfare may not meet the typical definition of the term war, however, many states including the United States, United Kingdom, Russia, India, China, Israel, Iran, North Korea and Vietnam have active cyber operations for offensive and defensive operations. As states explore the use of cyber operations and combine capabilities the likelihood of physical confrontation and violence playing out as a result of, or part of, a cyber operation is increased. However, meeting the scale and protracted nature of war is unlikely, thus ambiguity remains. The first instance of kinetic military action used in response to a cyber-attack resulting in the loss of human life was observed on May 5, 2019, when the Israel Defense Forces targeted and destroyed a building associated with an on-going cyber-attack."[72]

"Cyberwarfare is used in a board context to denote interstate use of technological force within computer networks in which information is stored, shared or communicated online." It is the act penetrating a state's computer network infrastructure, or that of businesses and organizations within a target nation. "The term 'cyberwarfare' is distinct from the term 'cyber war'. Cyber warfare includes techniques, tactics and procedures which may be involved in a cyber war…the term war inherently refers to a large-scale action, typically over a protracted period of time and may include objectives seeking to utilize violence or the aim to kill. A cyber war could accurately describe a protracted period of back-and-forth cyber-attacks (including in combination with traditional military action) between nations."

Types of Threat: "Cyber warfare can present a multitude of threats towards a nation. At the most basic level, cyber-attacks can be used to support traditional warfare. For example, tampering with the operation of air defenses via cyber means in order to facilitate an air attack. Aside from these hard threats, cyber warfare can also contribute towards soft threats such as espionage and propaganda."[73]

(a) Espionage: "Traditional espionage is not an act of war, nor is cyber-espionage, and both are generally assumed to be ongoing between major powers. Despite this assumption, some incidents can cause serious tensions between nations, and are often described as attacks."[74]

(b) Sabotage: "Computers and satellites that coordinate other activities are vulnerable components of a system and could lead to the disruption of equipment. Compromise of military systems, such as C4ISTAR components that are responsible for orders and communications could lead to their interception or malicious replacement. Power, water, fuel, communications, and transportation infrastructure all may be vulnerable to disruption…the civilian realm is also at risk, noting that the security breaches have already gone beyond stolen credit card numbers, and that potential targets can also include the electric power grid, trains, or the stock market."[75]

(i) Denial-of-service attack: "In computing, a denial-of-service attack or distributed denial-of-service attack is an attempt to make a machine or network resource unavailable to its intended users."

(ii) Electrical power grid: "The federal government of the United States admits that the electric power grid is susceptible to cyberwarfare. The United States Department of Homeland Security works with industries to identify vulnerabilities and to help industries enhance the security of control system networks."

(c) Propaganda: "Cyber propaganda is an effort to control information in whatever form it takes and influence public opinion. It is a form of psycho-logical warfare, except it uses social media, fake news websites and other digital means." Propaganda is "the deliberate, systematic attempt to shape perceptions, manipulate cognitions, and direct behavior to achieve a response that furthers the desired intent of the propagandist. The internet is a phenomenal means of communication. People can get their message across to a huge audience."[76]

(d) Economic disruption: In 2017, "the cyber-attacks, masquerading as ransomware, caused large-scale disruptions in Ukraine as well as to the U.K.'s National Health Service, pharmaceutical giant Merck, Maersk shipping company and other organizations around the world."[77]

(e) Surprise Cyber Attack: "The idea of a cyber Pearl Harbor has been debated by scholars, drawing an analogy to the historical act of war. Others have used 'cyber 9/11' to draw attention to the nontraditional, asymmetric, or irregular aspect of cyber action against a state."[78]

Motivations: "There are a number of reasons nations undertake offensive cyber operations. Sandro Gaycken, a cyber security expert and adviser to NATO, advocates that states take cyber warfare seriously as they are viewed as an attractive activity by many nations, in times of war and peace. Offensive cyber operations offer a large variety of cheap and risk-free options to weaken other countries and strengthen their own positions. Considered from a long-term, geostrategic perspective, cyber offensive operations can cripple whole economies, change political views, agitate conflicts within or among states, reduce their military efficiency and equalize the capacities of high-tech nations to that of low-tech nations, and use access to their critical infrastructures to blackmail them."[79]

(a) Military: Computer network warfare is "evolving so rapidly that there is a mismatch between our technical capabilities to conduct operations and the governing laws and policies. Cyber Command is the newest global combatant and its sole mission is cyberspace, outside the traditional battlefields of land, sea, air and space. It will attempt to find and, when necessary, neutralize cyberattacks and to defend military computer networks." U.S. Cyber Command (USCYBERCOM) unifies the direction of cyberspace operations, which will be discussed separately later.[80]

(b) Civil: "Potential targets in internet sabotage include all aspects of the Internet from the backbones of the web, to the internet service providers, to the varying types of data communication mediums and network equipment. This would include web servers, enterprise information systems, client server systems, communication links, network equipment, and the desktops and laptops in businesses and homes. Electrical grids, financial networks, and telecommunication systems are also deemed vulnerable, especially due to current trends in computerization and automation."[81]

(c) Hacktivism: "Politically motivated hacktivism involves the subversive use of computers and computer networks to promote an agenda, and can potentially extend to attacks, theft and virtual sabotage that could be seen as cyberwarfare – or mistaken for it. Hacktivists use their knowledge and software tools to gain unauthorized access to computer systems they seek to manipulate or damage not for material gain or to cause widespread destruction, but to draw attention to their cause through well-publicized disruptions of select targets. Anonymous and other hacktivist groups are often portrayed in the media as cyber-terrorists, wreaking havoc by hacking websites, posting sensitive information about their victims, and threatening further attacks if their demands are not met…They are politically motivated to change the world, through the use of fundamentalism."[82]

(d) Income generation: "Cyber-attacks, including ransomware, can be used to generate income. States can use these techniques to generate significant sources of income, which can evade sanctions and perhaps while simultaneously harming adversaries (depending on targets)."[83]

Preparedness: "A number of countries conduct exercise to increase preparedness and explore the strategy, tactics and operations involved in conducting and defending against cyber-attacks against nations, this is typically done in the form of war games. The Cooperative Cyber Defense Centre of Excellence (CCDCE), part of the North Atlantic Treaty Organization (NATO), have conducted a yearly war game called Locked Shields since 2010 designed to test readiness and improve skills, strategy tactics and operational decision making of participating national organizations. Locked Shields 2019 saw 1200 participants from 30 nations compete in a red team vs. blue team exercise."[84]

Cyber Activities by Nation: "Approximately 120 countries have been developing ways to use the Internet as a weapon and target financial markets, government computer systems and utilities."

(a) China: "Foreign Policy magazine puts the size of China's "hacker army" at anywhere from 50,000 to 100,000 individuals. Diplomatic cables highlight US concerns that China is using access to Microsoft source code and 'harvesting the talents of its private sector' to boost its offensive and defensive capabilities. The 2018 cyberattack on the Marriott hotel chain that collected personal details of roughly 500 million guests is now known to be a part of a Chinese intelligence-gathering effort that also hacked health insurers and the security clearance files of millions more Americans."[85]

"China has expanded its cyber capabilities and military technology by acquiring foreign military technology...the Chinese government uses new space-based surveillance and intelligence gathering systems, Anti-satellite weapon, anti-radar, infrared decoys, and false target generators to assist in this quest, and that they support their informationization of their military through increased education of soldiers in cyber warfare; improving the information network for military training, and has built more virtual laboratories, digital libraries and digital campuses...they hope to prepare their forces to engage in a different kind of warfare, against technically capable adversaries."[86]

(b) Russia: "When Russia was still a part of the Soviet Union in 1982, a portion of its Trans-Siberia pipeline within its territory exploded[citation needed], allegedly due to computer malware implanted in the pirated Canadian software by the Central Intelligence Agency. The malware caused the SCADA system running the pipeline to malfunction. The Farewell Dossier provided information on this attack and wrote that compromised computer chips would become a part of Soviet military equipment, flawed turbines would be placed in the gas pipeline, and defective plans would disrupt the output of chemical plants and a tractor factor. This caused the most monumental nonnuclear explosion and fire ever seen from space. However, the Soviet Union did not blame the United States for the attack."[87]

"It has been claimed that Russian security services organized a number of denial of service attacks as a part of their cyber-warfare against other countries, most notably the 2007 cyberattacks on Estonia and the 2008 cyberattacks on Russia, South Ossetia, Georgia, and Azerbaijan. One identified young Russian hacker said that he was paid by Russian state security services to lead hacking attacks on NATO computers. He was studying computer sciences at the Department of the Defense of Information. His tuition was paid for by the FSB."[88]

(c) India: "The Department of Information Technology created the Indian Computer Emergency Response Team (CERT-In) in 2004 to thwart cyber-attacks in India. That year, there were 23 reported cyber security breaches. In 2011, there were 13,301. That year, the government created a new subdivision, the National Critical Information Infrastructure Protection Centre (NCIIPC) to thwart attacks against energy, transport, banking, telecom, defense, space and other sensitive areas."[89]

(d) Iran: "Iran has been both victim and predator of several cyberwarfare operations. Iran is considered an emerging military power in the field. In September 2010, Iran was attacked by the Stuxnet worm, thought to specifically target its Natanz nuclear enrichment facility. It was a 500-kilobyte computer worm that infected at least 14 industrial sites in Iran, including the Natanz uranium-enrichment plant. Although the official authors of Stuxnet haven't been officially identified, Stuxnet is believed to be developed and deployed by the United States and Israel. The worm is said to be the most advanced piece of malware ever discovered and significantly increases the profile of cyberwarfare."

(e) North Korea: "Congress and the Trump Administration have elevated North Korea to a top U.S. foreign policy priority…international sanctions imposed by the United Nations Security Council have focused on North Korea's WMD and ballistic missile programs and human rights abuses. According to some experts, another threat is emerging from North Korea: an ambitious and well-resourced cyber program. North Korea's cyber-attacks have the potential not only to disrupt international commerce, but to direct resources to its clandestine weapons and delivery system programs, potentially enhancing its ability to evade international sanctions. As Congress addresses the multitude of threats emanating from North Korea, it may need to consider responses to the cyber aspect of North Korea's repertoire. This would likely involve multiple committees, some of which operate in a classified setting. This report will provide a brief summary of what unclassified open-source reporting has revealed about the secretive program, introduce four case studies in which North Korean operators are suspected of having perpetrated malicious operations, and provide an overview of the international finance messaging service that these hackers may be exploiting."[90]

Cyber-peace: "The rise of cyber as a warfighting domain has led to efforts to determine how cyberspace can be used to foster peace. For example, the German civil rights panel FIfF runs a campaign for cyberpeace – for the control of cyberweapons and surveillance technology and against the militarization of cyberspace and the development and stockpiling of offensive exploits and malware. Measures for cyberpeace include policy-makers developing new rules and norms for warfare, individuals and organizations building new tools and secure infrastructures, promoting open source, the establishment of cyber security centers, auditing of critical infrastructure cybersecurity, obligations to disclose vulnerabilities, disarmament, defensive security strategies, decentralization, education and widely applying relevant tools and infrastructures, encryption..."[91]

Cyber Counterintelligence: "Cyber counter-intelligence are measures to identify, penetrate, or neutralize foreign operations that use cyber means as the primary tradecraft methodology, as well as foreign intelligence service collection efforts that use traditional methods to gauge cyber capabilities and intentions... On 7 April 2009, The Pentagon announced they spent more than $100 million in the last six months responding to and repairing damage from cyber-attacks and other computer network problems... In 2015... released an updated cyber strategy memorandum detailing the present and future tactics deployed in the service of defense against cyberwarfare. In this memorandum, three cyberfictions are laid out. The first cybermission seeks to arm and maintain existing capabilities in the area of cyberspace, the second cybermission focuses on prevention of cyberwarfare, and the third cybermission includes strategies for retaliation and preemption."[92]

Legal Perspective: "Various parties have attempted to come up with international legal frameworks to clarify what is and is not acceptable, but none have yet been widely accepted. The Tallinn Manual, published in 2013, is an academic, non-binding study on how international law, in particular the jus ad bellum and international humanitarian law, apply to cyber conflicts and cyber warfare. It was written at the invitation of the Tallinn-based NATO Cooperative Cyber Defense Centre of Excellence by an international group of approximately twenty experts between 2009 and 2012. The Shanghai Cooperation Organization defines cyberwar to include dissemination of information harmful to the spiritual, moral and cultural spheres of other states. In September 2011, these countries proposed to the UN Secretary General a document called International code of conduct for information security. In contrast, the United States' approach focuses on physical and economic damage and injury, putting political concerns under freedom of speech. This difference of opinion has led to reluctance in the West to pursue global cyber arms control agreements."[93]

United States Cyber Command (USCYBERCOM) is "one of the eleven unified commands of the United States' Department of Defense. It unifies the direction of cyberspace operations, strengthens DoD cyberspace capabilities, and integrates and bolsters DoD's cyber expertise. USCYBERCOM was created in mid-2009 at the National Security Agency (NSA) headquarters in Fort George G. Meade, Maryland. It cooperates with NSA networks and has been concurrently headed by the Director of the National Security Agency since its inception. While originally created with a defensive mission in mind, it has increasingly been viewed as an offensive force. On 18 August 2017, it was announced that USCYBERCOM would be elevated to the status of a full and independent unified combatant command. This elevation occurred on 4 May 2018."[94] "USCYBERCOM plans, coordinates, integrates, synchronizes and conducts activities to: direct the operations and defense of specified Department of Defense information networks and; prepare to…conduct full spectrum military cyberspace operations in order to enable actions in all domains, ensure US/Allied freedom of action in cyberspace and deny the same to our adversaries."[95]

(a) Organization: USCYBERCOM is an armed forces unified command under DoD: Army Cyber Command, Fleet Cyber Command, Air Force Cyber; and Marine Corps Cyberspace Command.

(b) Concerns: "There are concerns that the Pentagon and NSA will overshadow any civilian cyber defense efforts. There are also concerns on whether the command will assist in civilian cyber defense efforts…the command will lead day-to-day defense and protection of all DoD networks. It will be responsible for DoD's networks – the dot-mil world. Responsibility for federal civilian networks – dot-gov – stays with the Department of Homeland Security, and that's exactly how it should be. Alexander notes, however, that if faced with cyber hostilities an executive order could expand Cyber Command's spectrum of operations to include, for instance, assisting the Department of Homeland Security in defense of their networks."[96]

(c) International effects and reactions: "The creation of U.S. Cyber Command appears to have motivated other countries in this arena. In December 2009, South Korea announced the creation of a cyber warfare command. Reportedly, this was in response to North Korea's creation of a cyber warfare unit. In addition, the British GCHQ has begun preparing a cyber force. Furthermore, a shift in military interest in cyber warfare has motivated the creation of the first U.S. Cyber Warfare Intelligence Center. In 2010, China introduced a department dedicated to defensive cyber war and information security in response to the creation of USCYBERCOM."[97]

(d) Operations: "In June 2019, Russia has conceded that it is possible its electrical grid was under cyberattack by the United States. The New York Times reported that hackers from the U.S. Cyber Command planted malware potentially capable of disrupting the Russian electrical grid."[98]

3. Space Warfare and National Security

"Space warfare is combat that takes place in outer space. The scope of space warfare therefore includes ground-to-space warfare, such as attacking satellites from the Earth, as well as space-to-space warfare, such as satellites attacking satellites. As of 2019 no actual warfare has ever taken place in space, though a number of tests and demonstrations have been performed. International treaties are in place that regulate conflicts in space and limit the installation of space weapon systems, especially nuclear weapons."

"From 1985 to 2002 there was a United States Space Command, which in 2002 merged with the United States Strategic Command, leaving Air Force Space Command as the primary American military space force. The Russian Space Force, established on August 10, 1992, which became an independent section of the Russian military on June 1, 2001, was replaced by the Russian Aerospace Defense Forces starting December 1, 2011, but was reestablished as a component of the Russian Aerospace Forces on August 1, 2015. In 2019 India conducted a test of the ASAT missile making it the fourth country with that capability. In April 2019, the government established the Defense Space Agency, or DSA."[99]

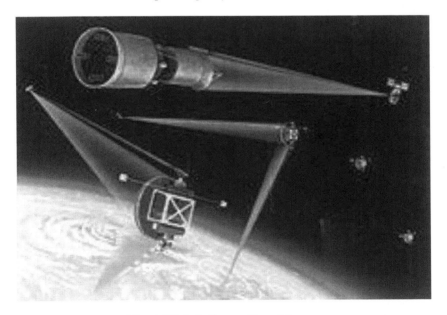

Photo III-3-1. Space-Based Lasers
https://upload.wikimedia.org/wikipedia/commons/thumb/e/e2/Space_lasers.jpg/220px-Space_lasers.jpg, accessed 22 October 2019.

History: *(a) 1960s*: "Early efforts to conduct space warfare were directed at space-to-space warfare, as ground-to-space systems were considered to be too slow and too isolated by Earth's atmosphere and gravity to be effective at the time. The history of active space warfare development goes back to the 1960s when the Soviet Union began the Almaz project, a project designed to give them the ability to do on-orbit inspections of satellites and destroy them if needed...One early test of electronic space warfare took place in 1962, when the United States exploded a ground-launched nuclear weapon in space to test the effects of an electromagnetic pulse. The result was a deactivation of many then-orbiting satellites, both American and Soviet. The deleterious and unfocused effects of the EMP test led to the banning of nuclear weapons in space in the Outer Space Treaty of 1967. In the early 1960s the U.S. military produced a film called Space and National Security which depicted space warfare."[100]

(b) 1970s-1990s: "Through the 1970s, the Soviet Union continued their project and test-fired a cannon to test space station defense. This was considered too dangerous to do with a crew on board, however, so the test was conducted after the crew had returned to Earth. Space warfare strongly influenced the final design of the United States Space Shuttle. The distinctive delta wing shape was needed if the shuttle were to launch a military payload towards the Soviet Union and perform an immediate de-orbit after one rotation to avoid being shot down. Both the Soviets and the United States developed anti-satellite weaponry designed to shoot down satellites. While early efforts paralleled other space-to-space warfare concepts, the United States was able in the 1980s to develop ground-to-space laser anti-satellite weapons...In 1985 a USAF pilot in an F-15 successfully shot down the P78-1, an American research satellite, in a 345-mile (555 km) orbit."[101]

(c) Since 2000: "The People's Republic of China successfully tested (see 2007 Chinese anti-satellite missile test) a ballistic missile-launched anti-satellite weapon on January 11, 2007. This resulted in harsh criticism from the United States of America, Britain, and Japan. The U.S. developed an interceptor missile, the SM-3, testing it by hitting ballistic test targets while they were in space. On February 21, 2008, the U.S. used a SM-3 missile to destroy a spy satellite, USA-193, while it was 247 kilometers above the Pacific Ocean. Japan fields the U.S.-made SM-3 missile, and there have been plans to base the land-based version in Romania and Vietnam...In July 2019 Emmanuel Macron called for a space high command to protect France's satellites. This was followed by a plan released by military officials. French Defense Minister, Florence Parly, announced a space weapons program that would move the country's space surveillance strategy towards active protection of its assets in space, e.g. satellites. The projects outlined include patrolling nano-satellites swarms, ground-based laser systems to blind spying satellites, and machine guns mounted on satellites."[102]

Theoretical Space Weaponry: *(a) Ballistic Warfare*: "When the U.S. gained interest in utilizing space-based lasers for ballistic missile defense, two facts emerged. One being that the ballistic missiles are fragile and two, chemical lasers project missile killing energy. This meant that lasers could be put into space to intercept a Ballistic missile. Systems proposed ranged from measures as simple as ground and space-based anti-missiles to railguns, space-based lasers, orbital mines and similar weaponry. Deployment of these systems was seriously considered in the mid-1980s under the banner of the Strategic Defense Initiative announced by Ronald Reagan in 1983, using the term evil empire to describe the Soviets."[103]

(b) Electronic Warfare: "With the end of the Cold War and continued development of satellite and electronics technology, attention was focused on space as a supporting theatre for conventional warfare. Currently, military operations in space primarily concern either the vast tactical advantages of satellite-based surveillance, communications, and positioning systems or mechanisms used to deprive an opponent of said tactical advantages. Accord-ingly, most space-borne proposals which would traditionally be considered weapons (a communications or reconnaissance satellite may be useful in warfare but isn't generally classified as a weapon) are designed to jam, sabotage, and outright destroy enemy satellites, and conversely to protect friendly satellites against such attacks. To this end, the US (and presumably other countries) is researching groups of small, highly mobile satellites called microsats (about the size of a refrigerator) and picosats (approximately 1 cubic foot in volume) nimble enough to maneuver around and interact with other orbiting objects to repair, sabotage, hijack, or simply collide with them."[104]

(c) Kinetic Bombardment: "Another theorized use involves the extension of conventional weaponry into orbit for deployment against ground targets. Though international treaties ban the deployment of nuclear missiles outside the atmosphere, other categories of weapons are largely unregulated. Traditional ground-based weapons are generally not useful in orbital environments, and few if any would survive re-entry even if they were, but as early as the 1950s, the United States has toyed with kinetic bombardment, i.e. orbiting magazines of non-explosive projectiles to be dropped onto hardened targets from low Earth orbit. Kinetic weapons have always been widespread in conventional warfare—bullets, arrows, swords, clubs, etc.—but the energy a projectile would gain while falling from orbit would make such a weapon rival all but the most powerful explosives. A direct hit would presumably destroy all but the most hardened targets without the need for nuclear weapons. Such a system would involve a 'spotter' satellite, which would identify targets from orbit with high-power sensors, and a nearby 'magazine' satellite to de-orbit a long, needle-like tungsten dart onto it with a small rocket motor or just dropping a very big

rock from orbit (such as an asteroid). This would be more useful against a larger but less hardened target (such as a city). Though a common device in science fiction, there is no publicly available evidence that any such systems have actually been deployed by any nation."[105]

(d) Directed-energy Weapons: "Weapon systems that fall under this category include lasers, linear particle accelerators or particle-beam based weaponry, microwaves and plasma-based weaponry. Particle beams involve the acceleration of charged or neutral particles in a stream towards a target at extremely high velocities, the impact of which creates a reaction causing immense damage. Most of these weapons are theoretical or impractical to implement currently, aside from lasers which are starting to be used in terrestrial warfare. That said, directed-energy weapons are more practical and more effective in a vacuum (i.e. space) than in the Earth's atmosphere, as in the atmosphere the particles of air interfere with and disperse the directed energy. Nazi Germany had a project for such a weapon, considered a wunderwaffe, the sun gun, which would have been an orbital concave mirror able to concentrate the sun's energy on a ground target."[106]

(e) Spaced-Based Lasers: "Light Amplification by the Stimulated Emission of Radiation (acronym LASER) pumps energy into molecules, creating an electronic state that releases energy in the form of photons. The photons pass by other molecules, spreading energy, making more photons. To make an actual laser, a beam has to pass through mass quantities of laser medium by bouncing back and forth between mirrors placed at opposing ends. Then the light beam exits through one of the mirrors which is more transparent than the other. Making a functional laser requires the electrons to not only reach their excited state but is reliant on the time it takes for them to get excited, and also the time for the energy created to reach new electrons. The efficiency of the laser relies on the amount of heat that exits. In terms of lasers, the power of the laser far outweighs the chemical efficiency. Of course the trajectory of the laser matters as well as its ability to hit the target it is aimed at, but when lasers are placed in space, Diffraction can cause interference."[107] (See Photo III-6-1. Space-Based Lasers)

Lethality of Space Lasers: "a beam with an intensity of around 10 million watts per square centimeter would cause the air immediately in front of the target to ionize, which would create a layer of plasma as the beam hits the surface. The plasma would absorb the energy of the laser beam and grow extremely hot. The plasma would distribute this energy in two ways, by emitting ultraviolet radiation and by expanding explosively. These mechanisms could increase the extent of the beam energy attached to the target to approximately 30 percent and reduce the amount of energy the laser would have to produce." Characteristics: "Directed energy weapons might be put on satellites in Earth orbit, but the altitude of the satellite lies would depend on what the laser is supposed to be targeting and where."[108]

Practical Considerations: "Space warfare is likely to be conducted at far greater distances and speeds than terrestrial combat. The vast distances involved pose difficult challenges for targeting and tracking...For example, if attempting to fire upon a target at the distance of the Moon from the Earth, the image one sees reflects the position of the target slightly more than a second earlier. Thus even a laser would need approximately 1.28 seconds, meaning a laser-based weapon system would need to lead a target's apparent position by $1.28 \times 2 = 2.56$ seconds. A projectile from a railgun recently tested by the US Navy would take over eighteen hours to cross that distance, assuming that it would travel in a straight line at a constant velocity of 5.8 km/s along its entire trajectory. Three factors conspire to make engaging targets in space very difficult. First, the vast distances involved mean that an error of even a fraction of a degree in the firing solution could result in a miss by thousands of kilometers. Second, space travel involves tremendous speeds by terrestrial standards—a geostationary satellite moves at a speed of 3.07 km/s whereas objects in low earth orbit can move at up to 8 km/s. Third, though distances are large, targets remain relatively small."[109]

The International Space Station, currently the largest artificial object in Earth orbit, measures slightly over 100m at its largest span. Other satellites can be orders of magnitude smaller, e.g. Quickbird measures a mere 3.04m. External ballistics for stationary terrestrial targets is enormously complicated—some of the earliest analog computers were used to calculate firing solutions for naval artillery, as the problems were already beyond manual solutions in any reasonable time—and the issues in targeting objects in space make a difficult problem even harder. Additionally, though not a problem for orbital kinetic weapons, any directed energy weapon would require large amounts of electricity. So far the most practical batteries are lithium batteries, and the most practical method of generating electricity in space is through photovoltaic modules, which are currently only up to 30% efficient, and fuel cells, which have limited fuel. Current technology might not be practical for powering effective lasers, particle beams, and railguns in space. In the context of the Strategic Defense Initiative, the Lawrence Livermore National Laboratory in the United States worked on a project for expandable space-based x-ray lasers powered by a nuclear explosion, Project Excalibur, a project canceled in 1992 for lack of results."[110]

Possible Warfare over Space: "Most of the world's communications systems rely heavily on the presence of satellites in orbit around Earth. Protecting these assets might seriously motivate nations dependent upon them to consider deploying more space-based weaponry, especially in conflicts involving advanced countries with access to space. Since 2017, the United States Air Force has run an annual military exercise called Space Flag...which involves a red team simulating attacks on U.S. satellites."[111]

4. Weapons of Mass Destruction and National Security

"A weapon of mass destruction (WMD) is a nuclear, radiological, chemical, biological, or any other weapon that can kill and bring significant harm to numerous humans or cause great damage to human-made structures, natural structures, or the biosphere. The scope and usage of the term has evolved and been disputed, often signifying more politically than technically. Originally coined in reference to aerial bombing with chemical explosives during World War II, it has later come to refer to large-scale weaponry of other technologies," such as mentioned above.[112]

Use, Possession and Access: *(a) Nuclear Weapons*: The United States dropped two atomic bombs on the Japanese cities of Hiroshima and Nagasaki during World War II. "There are eight countries that have declared they possess nuclear weapons and are known to have tested a nuclear weapon, only five of which are members of the NPT. The eight are China, France, India, North Korea, Pakistan, Russia, the United Kingdom, and the United States. Israel is considered by most analysts to have nuclear weapons numbering in the low hundreds as well, but maintains an official policy of nuclear ambiguity, neither denying nor confirming its nuclear status. South Africa developed a small nuclear arsenal in the 1980s but disassembled them in the early 1990s, making it the only country to have fully given up an independently developed nuclear weapons arsenal. Belarus, Kazakhstan, and Ukraine inherited stockpiles of nuclear arms following the break-up of the Soviet Union but relinquished them to the Russian Federation. Countries where nuclear weapons are deployed through nuclear sharing agreements include Belgium, Germany, Italy, the Netherlands, and Turkey."[113]

(b) Chemical Weapons: "Chemical weapons have been used around the world by various civilizations since ancient times. In the industrial era, they were used extensively by both sides during World War I, and by the Axis powers during World War II (both in battle and in extermination camp gas chambers) though Allied powers also stockpiled them. Countries in Western Europe renounced the use of such weapons. As of 2018, a handful of countries have known inventories, and many are in the process of being safely destroyed under the Chemical Weapons Convention. Nonetheless, proliferation and use in war zones remains an active concern, most recently the use of chemical weapons in the Syrian Civil War."[114] "Since World War I, several types of chemical agents have been developed into weapons. These include choking agents, blister agents, blood agents, nerve agents, incapacitants, riot-control agents, and herbicides...Chemical weapons can be categorized by their physical characteristics, such as lethality, persistency, mode of action on the human body, and physical state (i.e., gas, liquid, or solid) when being delivered."[115]

(c) Biological Weapons: "Biological weapon, also called germ weapon, any of a number of disease-producing agents—such as bacteria, viruses, rickettsiae, fungi, toxins, or other biological agents—that may be utilized as weapons against humans, animals, or plants. The direct use of infectious agents and poisons against enemy personnel is an ancient practice in warfare. Indeed, in many conflicts, diseases have been responsible for more deaths than all the employed combat arms combined, even when they have not consciously been used as weapons. Biological weapons, like chemical weapons, radiological weapons, and nuclear weapons, are commonly referred to as weapons of mass destruction, although the term is not truly appropriate in the case of biological armaments. Lethal biological weapons may be capable of causing mass deaths, but they are incapable of mass destruction of infrastructure, buildings, or equipment. Nevertheless, because of the indiscriminate nature of these weapons—as well as the potential for starting widespread pandemics, the difficulty of controlling disease effects, and the simple fear that they inspire—most countries have agreed to ban the entire class."[116] "Biological warfare attacks can be made less effective, or ineffective, if the targeted persons have been vaccinated."

Ethics and International Legal Status: "Some commentators classify some or all the uses of nuclear, chemical, or biological weapons during wartime as a war crime (or crime against humanity if widespread) because they kill civilians (who are protected by the laws of war) indiscriminately or are specifically prohibited by international treaties (which have become more comprehensive over time). Proponents of use say that specific uses of such weapons have been necessary for defense or to avoid more deaths in a protracted war. The tactic of terror bombing from aircraft, and generally targeting cities with area bombardment or saturation carpet bombing has also been criticized, defended, and prohibited by treaty in the same way; the destructive effect of conventional saturation bombing is similar to that of a nuclear weapon."[117] **United States Politics**: Due to the indiscriminate effects of WMD, "the fear of a WMD attack has shaped political policies and campaigns, fostered social movements, and has been the central theme of many films. Support for different levels of WMD development and control varies nationally and internationally. Yet understanding of the nature of the threats is not high, in part because of imprecise usage of the term by politicians and the media. Fear of WMD, or of threats diminished by the possession of WMD, has long been used to catalyze public support for various WMD policies. They include mobilization of pro- and anti-WMD campaigners alike, and generation of popular political support. The term WMD may be used as a powerful buzzword or to generate a culture of fear. It is also used ambiguously, particularly by not distinguishing among the different types of WMD."[118]

The 7 Technologies that Transformed Warfare: Here are seven technologies that have transformed warfare.[119]

(a) Drone: "Combat drones, or unmanned aerial vehicles, enable troops to deploy weapons in war while safely remaining thousands of miles away from the front lines of the battlefield...the lives of drone pilots are not in danger, which helps the military limit the number of combat fatalities."

(b) Fly-by-wire technology: "Fly-by-wire technology replaces manual flight controls with an electronic interface that uses signals generated by a computer and transmitted by wires to move control mechanisms. The introduction of fly-by-wire systems in aircraft enabled more precise computer guidance and control. For instance, fly-by-wire systems could automatically help stabilize airplanes, without relying on manual inputs from the pilot."

(c) Submarines: "Submarines revolutionized naval warfare by introducing underwater vessels capable of attacking enemy ships. The first successful submarine attack on a warship occurred during the American Civil War, which lasted from 1861 to 1865. In February...Today, the military uses submarines to carry missiles, conduct reconnaissance, support land attacks, and establish blockades."

(d) Tomahawk Missile: "The Tomahawk is a type of long-range cruise missile designed to fly at extremely low altitudes at subsonic speeds, enabling the weapons to be used to attack various surface targets. These jet engine-powered missiles were first used operationally during Operation Desert Storm in 1991. The missiles travel at speeds of approximately 550 miles per hour (880 km/h) and use GPS receivers to pinpoint their targets more accurately."

(e) Stealth Aircraft: "Stealth aircraft, as their name suggests, help pilots evade detection in the sky. While planes cannot be completely invisible to radar detection, stealth planes use a range of advanced technologies to reduce the aircraft's reflection, radio frequency spectrum, and radar and infrared emissions. Stealth technology increases the odds of a successful attack, since enemies have a harder time finding, tracking and defending against these aircraft."

(f) Space Weapons: "Space weapons include a range of warheads that can attack targets on Earth from space, intercept and disable missiles traveling through space, or destroy space systems or satellites in orbit. During the Cold War, the U.S. and the former Soviet Union both developed space weapons, as political tensions escalated."

(g) Nuclear Weapons: Nuclear bombs are most destructive weapons. "These warheads draw their destructive force from nuclear reactions, which release enormous amounts of explosive energy. The world's first nuclear weapons, or atomic bombs, were developed by physicists working on the Manhattan Project during World War II."

Science, Technology, and the Future of Warfare (Margaret Kosal, 2 October 2016):[120] "We know that emerging innovations within cutting-edge science and technology (S&T) areas carry the potential to revolutionize governmental structures, economies, and life as we know it. Yet, others have argued that such technologies could yield doomsday scenarios and that military applications of such technologies have even greater potential than nuclear weapons to radically change the balance of power. These S&T areas include robotics and autonomous unmanned system; artificial intelligence; biotech-nology, including synthetic and systems biology; the cognitive neurosciences; nanotechnology, including stealth meta-materials; additive manufacturing; and the intersection of each with information and computing technologies, i.e., cyber-everything. These concepts and the underlying strategic importance were articulated at the multi-national level in NATO's May 2010 New Strategic Concept paper: 'Less predictable is the possibility that research breakthroughs will transform the technological battlefield.... The most destructive periods of history tend to be those when the means of aggression have gained the upper hand in the art of waging war'."

"The widespread enthusiasm for emerging technologies is reflected not only in official rhetoric but is also codified in respective national technology strategies and the global upswing of dedicated funding. Military-related programs in potential peer competitors in Asia (China), in states posing regional security challenges in the Middle East (Iran), in the former Soviet Union (Russia), and in rapidly developing areas (including South Asia, Southeast Asia, and Brazil) offer comparisons for advanced, allied states (U.S., western Europe, Japan, ROK) in order to understand the national meanings, organization, and strategic implications surrounding the develop-ment and fielding of emerging technology."

"In the global information age, the most technologically advanced military power no longer guarantees national security. Globalization and the information revolution, including the Internet and other communication leaps – have led to much greater visibility into the availability and potential for science and technology. Science is and will continue to enable new technological develop-ments becoming accessible and affordable to a larger number of nations and within the grasp of non-state actors: advanced technology is no longer the domain of the few. Understanding these changing paradigms and the implications for modern warfare starts with an awareness of the factors driving the capabilities, understanding the underlying science and the challenges of foreign policy, considering the changing nature of technological progress and the changing nature of conflict, and the relationship between science and security domestically and internationally. The importance of bridging the technical and the human domain is increasing; the challenges are organizational, strategic, and enabling the right people to implement and execute it."

5. The 7 Biggest Technology Trends in 2020

By Bernard Marr, 2019

https://www.forbes.com/sites/bernardmarr/2019/09/30/the-7-biggest-technology-trends-in-2020-everyone-must-get-ready-for-now/#2ab79dbc2261

"We are amidst the 4th Industrial Revolution, and technology is evolving faster than ever. Companies and individuals that don't keep up with some of the major tech trends run the risk of being left behind. Understanding the key trends will allow people and businesses to prepare and grasp the opportunities. As a business and technology futurist, it is my job to look ahead and identify the most important trends. In this article, I share with you the seven most imminent trends everyone should get ready for in 2020."[121]

(a) AI-as-a-service: "Artificial Intelligence (AI) is one of the most trans-formative tech evolutions of our times. As I highlighted in my book 'Artificial Intelligence in Practice', most companies have started to explore how they can use AI to improve the customer experience and to streamline their business operations. This will continue in 2020, and while people will increasingly become used to working alongside AIs, designing and deploying our own AI-based systems will remain an expensive proposition for most businesses. For this reason, much of the AI applications will continue to be done through providers of as-a-service platforms, which allow us to simply feed in our own data and pay for the algorithms or compute resources as we use them. Currently, these platforms, provided by the likes of Amazon, Google, and Microsoft, tend to be somewhat broad in scope, with custom engineering required to apply them to the specific tasks an organization may require. During 2020, we will see wider adoption and a growing pool of providers that are likely to start offering more tailored applications and services for specific or specialized tasks. This will mean no company will have any excuses left not to use AI."

(b) 5G data networks: "The 5th generation of mobile internet connectivity is going to give us super-fast download and upload speeds as well as more stable connections. While 5G mobile data networks became available for the first time in 2019, they were mostly still expensive and limited to functioning in confined areas or major cities. 2020 is likely to be the year when 5G really starts to fly, with more affordable data plans as well as greatly improved coverage, meaning that everyone can join in the fun. Super-fast data networks will not only give us the ability to stream movies and music at higher quality when we're on the move. The greatly increased speeds mean that mobile networks will become more usable even than the wired networks running into our homes and businesses. Companies must consider the business implications of having super-fast and stable internet

access anywhere. The increased bandwidth will enable machines, robots, and autonomous vehicles to collect and transfer more data than ever, leading to advances in the area of the Internet of Things (IoT) and smart machinery."

(c) Autonomous Driving: "While we still aren't at the stage where we can expect to routinely travel in, or even see, autonomous vehicles in 2020, they will undoubtedly continue to generate a significant amount of excitement. Tesla chief Elon Musk has said he expects his company to create a truly complete autonomous vehicle by this year, and the number of vehicles capable of operating with a lesser degree of autonomy – such as automated braking and lane-changing – will become an increasingly common sight. In addition to this, other in-car systems not directly connected to driving, such as security and entertainment functions – will become increasingly automated and reliant on data capture and analytics. Google's sister-company Waymo has just completed a trial of autonomous taxis in California, where it transported more than 6200 people in the first month. It won't just be cars, of course – trucking and shipping are becoming more autonomous, and breakthroughs in this space are likely to continue to hit the headlines throughout 2020. With the maturing of autonomous driving technology, we will also increasingly hear about the measures that will be taken by regulators, legislators, and authorities. Changes to laws, existing infrastructure, and social attitudes are all likely to be required before autonomous driving becomes a practical reality for most of us. During 2020, it's likely we will start to see the debate around autonomous driving spread outside of the tech world, as more and more people come around to the idea that the question is not 'if,' but 'when,' it will become a reality."

(d) Personalized and predictive medicine: "Technology is currently transforming healthcare at an unprecedented rate. Our ability to capture data from wearable devices such as smartwatches will give us the ability to increasingly predict and treat health issues in people even before they experience any symptoms. When it comes to treatment, we will see much more personalized approaches. This is also referred to as precision medicine which allows doctors to more precisely prescribe medicines and apply treatments, thanks to a data-driven understanding of how effective they are likely to be for a specific patient. Although not a new idea, thanks to recent breakthroughs in technology, especially in the fields of genomics and AI, it is giving us a greater understanding of how different people's bodies are better or worse equipped to fight off specific diseases, as well as how they are likely to react to different types of medication or treatment. Throughout 2020 we will see new applications of predictive healthcare and the introduction of more personalized and effective treatments to ensure better outcomes for individual patients."

(e) Computer Vision: In computer terms, vision involves systems that are able to identify items, places, objects or people from visual images – those collected by a camera or sensor. It's this technology that allows your smartphone camera to recognize which part of the image it's capturing is a face, and powers technology such as Google Image Search. As we move through 2020, we're going to see computer vision equipped tools and technology rolled out for an ever-increasing number of uses. It's fundamental to the way autonomous cars will see and navigate their way around danger. Production lines will employ computer vision cameras to watch for defective products or equipment failures, and security cameras will be able to alert us to anything out of the ordinary, without requiring 24/7 monitoring. Computer vision is also enabling face recognition, which we will hear a lot about in 2020. We have already seen how useful the technology is in controlling access to our smart phones in the case of Apple's FaceID and how Dubai airport uses it to provide a smoother customer journey. However, as the use cases will grow in 2020, we will also have more debates about limiting the use of this technology because of its potential to erode privacy and enable 'Big Brother'-like state control."

(f) Extended Reality: "Extended Reality (XR) is a catch-all term that covers several new and emerging technologies being used to create more immersive digital experiences. More specifically, it refers to virtual, augmented, and mixed reality. Virtual reality (VR) provides a fully digitally immersive experience where you enter a computer-generated world using headsets that blend out the real world. Augmented reality (AR) overlays digital objects onto the real world via smartphone screens or displays (think Snapchat filters). Mixed reality (MR) is an extension of AR, that means users can interact with digital objects placed in the real world (think playing a holographic piano that you have placed into your room via an AR headset). These technologies have been around for a few years now but have largely been confined to the world of entertainment – with Oculus Rift and Vive headsets providing the current state-of-the-art in videogames, and smartphone features such as camera filters and Pokemon Go-style games providing the most visible examples of AR. From 2020 expect all of that to change, as businesses get to grips with the wealth of exciting possibilities offered by both current forms of XR. Virtual and augmented reality will become increasingly prevalent for training and simulation, as well as offering new ways to interact with customers."

(g) Blockchain Technology: Blockchain is a technology trend that I have covered extensively this year, and yet you're still likely to get blank looks if you mention it in non-tech-savvy company. 2020 could finally be

the year when that changes, though. Blockchain is essentially a digital ledger used to record transactions but secured due to its encrypted and decentralized nature. During 2019 some commentators began to argue that the technology was over-hyped and perhaps not as useful as first thought. However, continued investment by the likes of FedEx, IBM, Walmart and Mastercard during 2019 is likely to start to show real-world results, and if they manage to prove its case, could quickly lead to an increase in adoption by smaller players. And if things are going to plan, 2020 will also see the launch of Facebook's own blockchain-based crypto currently Libra, which is going to create quite a stir."

Endnotes

[1] Klaus Schwab, "The Fourth Industrial Revolution: What It Means and How to Respond," Foreign Affairs (December 12, 2016), accessed 4 December 2019, https://www.foreignaffairs.com/articles/2015-12-12/fourth-industrial-revolution.

[2] History of weapons >>Modern era, accessed 22 October 2019, https://en.wikipedia.org/wiki/History_of_weapons#Modern_Era.

[3] Computer Basics >>Computer system, accessed 20 October 2019, http://www.physics-and-radio-electronics.com/computer-basics/computersystem.html.

[4] Computer basics >>Generations of computer >> First generation, accessed 20 October 2019, http://www.physics-and-radio-electronics.com/computer-basics/generations-of-computer/first-generation.html.

[5] Computer basics >>Generations of computer >> Second generation, accessed 20 October 2019, http://www.physics-and-radio-electronics.com/computer-basics/generations-of-computer/second-generation.html.

[6] Computer basics >>Generations of computer >> Third generation, accessed 20 October 2019, http://www.physics-and-radio-electronics.com/computer-basics/generations-of-computer/third-generation.html.

[7] Computer basics >>Generations of computer >> Fourth generation, accessed 20 October 2019, http://www.physics-and-radio-electronics.com/computer-basics/generations-of-computer/fourth-generation.html.

[8] Computer basics >>Generations of computer >> Fifth generation, accessed 20 October 2019, http://www.physics-and-radio-electronics.com/computer-basics/generations-of-computer/fifth-generation.html.

[9] Information technology >>Data storage, accessed 21 October 2019, https://en.wikipedia.org/wiki/Information_technology#Data_storage.

[10] Information technology >>Data retrieval, accessed 21 October 2019, https://en.wikipedia.org/wiki/Information_technology#Data_retrieval.

[11] Information technology >>Data transmission, accessed 21 October 2019, https://en.wikipedia.org/wiki/Information_technology#Data_transmission.

[12] Information technology >>Data manipulation, accessed 21 October 2019, https://en.wikipedia.org/wiki/Information_technology#Data_manipulation.

[13] Thomas M. Siebel, Digital Transformation: Survive and Thrive in an Era of Mass Extinction (New York: RosettaBooks, 2019), 11.

[14] The Fourth Industrial Revolution, accessed 29 September 2019, https://www.britannica.com/topic/The-Fourth-Industrial-Revolution-2119734.

[15] Ibid., accessed the same.

[16] Thomas M. Siebel, *Digital Transformation*, 27-8.
[17] What Is Cloud Computing? Accessed 30 November 2019, https://www.pcmag.com/article/256563/what-is-cloud-computing.
[18] Big Data, accessed 30 November 2019, https://www.ibm.com/analytics/hadoop/big-data-analytics.
[19] AI, Artificial Intelligence, accessed 30 November 2019, https://searchenterpriseai.techtarget.com/definition/AI-Artificial-Intelligence.
[20] Internet of Things (IoT), accessed 30 November 2019, https://www.techopedia.com/definition/28247/internet-of-things-iot.
[21] Cloud computing, accessed 30 November 2019, https://en.wikipedia.org/wiki/Cloud_computing.
[22] *Ibid.*, accessed the same.
[23] Cloud computing >>2010s, accessed 30 November 2019, https://en.wikipedia.org/wiki/Cloud_computing#2010s.
[24] Cloud computing >> Similar concepts, accessed 30 November 2019, https://en.wikipedia.org/wiki/Cloud_computing#Similar_concepts.
[25] Cloud computing >> Characteristics, accessed 30 November 2019, https://en.wikipedia.org/wiki/Cloud_computing#Characteristics.
[26] Cloud computing >> Service models, accessed 30 November 2019, https://en.wikipedia.org/wiki/Cloud_computing#Service_models.
[27] Cloud computing >> Infrastructure as a service, accexxed 30 November 2019, https://en.wikipedia.org/wiki/Cloud_computing#Infrastructure_as_a_service_(IaaS).
[28] Cloud computing >> Platform as a service, accessed 30 November 2019, https://en.wikipedia.org/wiki/Cloud_computing#Platform_as_a_service_(PaaS).
[29] Cloud computing >> Software as a service, accessed 30 November 2019, https://en.wikipedia.org/wiki/Cloud_computing#Software_as_a_service_(SaaS).
[30] Cloud computing >> Private cloud, accessed 30 November 2019, https://en.wikipedia.org/wiki/Cloud_computing#Private_cloud.
[31] Cloud computing >> Public cloud, accessed 30 November 2019, https://en.wikipedia.org/wiki/Cloud_computing#Public_cloud.
[32] Cloud computing >> Hybrid cloud, accessed 30 November 2019, https://en.wikipedia.org/wiki/Cloud_computing#Hybrid_cloud.
[33] Cloud computing >> Security and privacy, accessed 30 November 2019, https://en.wikipedia.org/wiki/Cloud_computing#Security_and_privacy.
[34] Cloud computing >> Limitations and disadvantages, accessed 30 November 2019, https://en.wikipedia.org/wiki/Cloud_computing#Limitations_and_disadvantages.
[35] Big data, accessed 20 October 2019, https://en.wikipedia.org/wiki/Big_data.
[36] *Ibid.*, accessed the same.
[37] *Ibid.*, accessed the same.
[38] Big data >> Characteristics, accessed 1 December 2019, https://en.wikipedia.org/wiki/Big_data#Characteristics.
[39] Big data >>Architecture, accessed 20 October 2019, https://en.wikipedia.org/wiki/Big_data#Architecture.
[40] Big data >>Technologies, accessed 20 October 2019, https://en.wikipedia.org/wiki/Big_data#Technologies.
[41] Big data >>Applications, accessed 20 October 2019, https://en.wikipedia.org/wiki/Big_data#Applications.
[42] Big data >>Research activities, accessed 20 October 2019, https://en.wikipedia.org/wiki/Big_data#Research_activities.
[43] Thomas M. Siebel, *Digital Transformation*, 76-7.

[44] *Ibid.*, 76-81.

[45] Artificial intelligence, accessed 21 October 2019, https://en.wikipedia.org/wiki/Artificial_intelligence.

[46] Thomas M. Siebel, *Digital Transformation*, 91-2.

[47] Thomas M. Siebel, *Digital Transformation*, 84-5.

[48] Artificial intelligence >>Basics, accessed 21 October 2011, https://en.wikipedia.org/wiki/Artificial_intelligence#Basics.

[49] *Ibid.*, accessed the same.

[50] Thomas M. Siebel, *Digital Transformation*, 93-4.

[51] Machine learning, accessed 15 December 2019, https://en.wikipedia.org/wiki/Machine_learning.

[52] Thomas M. Siebel, *Digital Transformation*, 94.

[53] Machine learning >> Machine learning tasks, accessed 15 December 2019, https://en.wikipedia.org/wiki/Machine_learning#Machine_learning_tasks.

[54] Machine learning >> Approaches >> Semi-supervised Learning, accessed 15 December 2019, https://en.wikipedia.org/wiki/Machine_learning#Approaches.

[55] Machine learning >> Approaches >> Reinforcement learning, accessed 15 December 2019, https://en.wikipedia.org/wiki/Machine_learning#Approaches.

[56] What Is Neural Networks? Accessed 15 December 2019, https://www.educba.com/what-is-neural-networks/.

[57] Thomas M. Siebel, *Digital Transformation*, 98-100.

[58] AI in business: What are the benefits of artificial intelligence? Accessed 15 December 2019, https://neoteric.eu/blog/ai-in-business-what-are-the-benefits-of-artificial-intelligence/.

[59] https://www.eukhost.com/blog/webhosting/7-benefits-of-artificial-intelligence-for-business/, 7 Benefits of AI for business, accessed 15 December 2019.

[60] Artificial intelligence >>Applications, accessed 21 October 2019, https://en.wikipedia.org/wiki/Artificial_intelligence#Applications.

[61] https://en.wikipedia.org/wiki/Artificial_intelligence#The_limits_of_artificial_general_intelligence, Artificial intelligence >>The limits of artificial general intelligence, accessed 21 October 2019.

[62] Artificial intelligence >>Potential harm, accessed 21 October 2019, https://en.wikipedia.org/wiki/Artificial_intelligence#Potential_harm.

[63] The Internet of Things, accessed 15 December 2019, https://en.wikipedia.org/wiki/Internet_of_things.

[64] Thomas M. Siebel, *Digital Transformation*, 113.

[65] *Ibid.*, 113-4.

[66] *Ibid.*, 114-7.

[67] *Ibid.*, 118-9.

[68] *Ibid.*, 119-21.

[69] *Ibid.*, 121-2.

[70] Internet of things >> Applications, accessed 16 December 2019, https://en.wikipedia.org/wiki/Internet_of_things#Applications.

[71] https://www.techrepublic.com/blog/it-security/cyberwarfare-characteristics-and-challenges/, Cyberwarfare, accessed 16 December 2019.

[72] Cyberwarfare, accessed 21 October 2019, https://en.wikipedia.org/wiki/Cyberwarfare.

[73] Cyberwarfare >>Types of threat, accessed 21 October 2019, https://en.wikipedia.org/wiki/Cyberwarfare#Types_of_threat.

[74] Cyberwarfare >>Espionage, accessed 21 October 2019, https://en.wikipedia.org/wiki/Cyberwarfare#Espionage.
[75] Cyberwarfare >>Espionage, accessed 21 October 2019, https://en.wikipedia.org/wiki/Cyberwarfare#Sabotage.
[76] Cyberwarfare >>Propaganda, accessed 21 October 2019, https://en.wikipedia.org/wiki/Cyberwarfare#Propaganda.
[77] Cyberwarfare >>Economic disruption, accessed 21 October 2019, https://en.wikipedia.org/wiki/Cyberwarfare#Economic_disruption.
[78] Cyberwarfare >>Surprise Cyber Attack, accessed 21 October 2019, https://en.wikipedia.org/wiki/Cyberwarfare#Surprise_Cyber_Attack.
[79] Cyberwarfare >>Motivations, accessed 21 October 2019, https://en.wikipedia.org/wiki/Cyberwarfare#Motivations.
[80] Cyberwarfare >>Military, accessed 21 October 2019, https://en.wikipedia.org/wiki/Cyberwarfare#Military.
[81] Cyberwarfare >>Civil, accessed 21 October 2019, https://en.wikipedia.org/wiki/Cyberwarfare#Civil.
[82] Cyberwarfare >>Hacktivism, accessed 21 October 2019, https://en.wikipedia.org/wiki/Cyberwarfare#Hacktivism.
[83] Cyberwarfare >>Income generation, accessed 21 October 2019, https://en.wikipedia.org/wiki/Cyberwarfare#Income_Generation.
[84] Cyberwarfare >>Preparedness, accessed 21 October 2019, https://en.wikipedia.org/wiki/Cyberwarfare#Preparedness.
[85] Cyberwarfare >>Asia, accessed 21 October 2019, https://en.wikipedia.org/wiki/Cyberwarfare#Asia.
[86] *Ibid.*, accessed the same.
[87] *Ibid.*, accessed the same.
[88] *Ibid.*, accessed the same.
[89] *Ibid.*, accessed the same.
[90] North Korean Cyber Capabilities: In Brief by Congressional Research Service, accessed 21 October 2019, https://fas.org/sgp/crs/row/R44912.pdf.
[91] Cyberwarfare >>Cyberpeace, accessed 21 October 2019, https://en.wikipedia.org/wiki/Cyberwarfare#Cyberpeace.
[92] Cyberwarfare >>Cyber counterintelligence, accessed 21 October 2019, https://en.wikipedia.org/wiki/Cyberwarfare#Cyber_counterintelligence.
[93] Cyberwarfare >>Legal perspective, accessed 21 October 2019, https://en.wikipedia.org/wiki/Cyberwarfare#Legal_perspective.
[94] United States Cyber Command, accessed 21 October 2019, https://en.wikipedia.org/wiki/United_States_Cyber_Command.
[95] U.S. Cyber Command >> Mission statement, accessed 21 October 2019, https://en.wikipedia.org/wiki/United_States_Cyber_Command#Mission_statement.
[96] U.S. Cyber Command >>Concerns, accessed 21 November 2019, https://en.wikipedia.org/wiki/United_States_Cyber_Command#Concerns.
[97]https://en.wikipedia.org/wiki/United_States_Cyber_Command#International_effects_ and_reactions, U.S. Cyber Command >>International effects and reactions, accessed 221 October 2019.
[98] U.S. Cyber Command >>Operations, accessed 21 October 2019, https://en.wikipedia.org/wiki/United_States_Cyber_Command#Operations.
[99] Space warfare, accessed 22 October 2019, https://en.wikipedia.org/wiki/Space_warfare.

[100] Space warfare >>1960s, accessed 22 October 2019,
https://en.wikipedia.org/wiki/Space_warfare#1960s.
[101] Space warfare >>170s-1980s, accessed 22 October 2019,
https://en.wikipedia.org/wiki/Space_warfare#1970s%E2%80%931990s.
[102] Space warfare >>Since 2000, accessed 22 October 2019,
https://en.wikipedia.org/wiki/Space_warfare#Since_2000.
[103] Space warfare >>Ballistic warfare, accessed 22 October 2019,
https://en.wikipedia.org/wiki/Space_warfare#Ballistic_warfare.
[104] Space warfare >>Electronic warfare, accessed 22 October 2019,
https://en.wikipedia.org/wiki/Space_warfare#Electronic_warfare.
[105] Space warfare >>Kinetic bombardment, accessed 22 October 2019,
https://en.wikipedia.org/wiki/Space_warfare#Kinetic_bombardment.
[106] Space warfare >>Directed-energy weapons, accessed 22 October 2019,
https://en.wikipedia.org/wiki/Space_warfare#Directed-energy_weapons.
[107] Space warfare >> Space-Based Lasers, accessed 22 October 2019,
https://en.wikipedia.org/wiki/Space_warfare#Space-Based_Lasers.
[108] Space warfare >> Lethality of Space Lasers, accessed 22 October 2019,
https://en.wikipedia.org/wiki/Space_warfare#Lethality_of_Space_Lasers.
[109] Space warfare >> Practical considerations, accessed 22 October 2019,
https://en.wikipedia.org/wiki/Space_warfare#Practical_considerations.
[110] *Ibid.*, accessed the same.
[111] Space warfare >>Possible warfare over space, accessed 22 October 2019,
https://en.wikipedia.org/wiki/Space_warfare#Possible_warfare_over_space.
[112] Weapon of mass destruction (WMD), accessed 22 October 2019,
https://en.wikipedia.org/wiki/Weapon_of_mass_destruction.
[113] https://en.wikipedia.org/wiki/Weapon_of_mass_destruction#Nuclear_weapons,
Weapon of mass destruction >>Nuclear weapons, accessed 22 October 2019.
[114] *Ibid.*, accessed the same.
[115] Chemical weapon, accessed 22 October 2019,
https://www.britannica.com/technology/chemical-weapon.
[116] Biological weapon, accessed 22 October 2019,
https://www.britannica.com/technology/biological-weapon.
[117] https://en.wikipedia.org/wiki/Weapon_of_mass_destruction#Ethics_and_internationa
l_legal_status, Weapon of mass destruction >>Ethics and international legal status,
accessed 22 October 2019.
[118] Weapon of mass destruction >>United States politics, accessed 22 October 2019,
https://en.wikipedia.org/wiki/Weapon_of_mass_destruction#United_States_politics.
[119] 7 Technologies That Transformed Warfare, accessed 22 October 2019,
https://www.livescience.com/41321-military-war-technologies.html.
[120] Science, Technology, and the Future of Warfare, accessed 22 October 2019,
https://mwi.usma.edu/science-technology-future-warfare/.
[121] Bernard Marr, The 7 Biggest Technology Trends In 2020 Everyone Must Get Ready
For Now, accessed 22 October 2019,
https://www.forbes.com/sites/bernardmarr/2019/09/30/the-7-biggest-technology-
trends-in-2020-everyone-must-get-ready-for-now/#2ab79dbc2261.

REFERENCES
PART III. Science, Technology, and National Security

1. Digital Transformation and Information Age

Bahga, Arshdeep and Vijay Madisetti. *Cloud Computing Solutions Architect: A Hands-On Approach*. Arshdeep & Vijay Madisetti, 2019.

Bridgstock, Martin, David Burch, John Forge, John Laurent, and Ian Lowe. *Science, Technology and Society: An Introduction*. New York: Cambridge University Press, 1998.

Campbell-Kelly, Martin, William Aspray, Nathan Ensmenger, and Jeffrey R. Yost. *Computer: A History of Information Machine*, 3rd ed. New York: Routledge, 2019.

Ceruzzi, Paul E. *A History of Modern Computing*, 2nd ed. Cambridge, MA: MIT Press, 2003.

Chou, Timothy. *Precision: Principles, Practices and Solutions for the Internet of Things*. San Jose, CA: Cloudbook, Inc., 2016.

Cobb, Cathy and Harold Goldwhite. *Creation of Fire: Chemistry's Lively History from Alchemy to the Atomic Age*. New York: Basic Books, 1995.

Davenport, Thomas H. *Big Data at Work: Dispelling the Myths, Uncovering the Opportunities*. Cambridge, MA: Harvard Business School P., 2014.

Fara, Patricia. *Science: A Four Thousand Year History*. New York: Oxford University Press, 2009.

Garfinkel, Simon and Rachel H. Grunspan. *The Computer Book: From the Abacus to Artificial Intelligence*. New York: Sterling, 2018.

Greengard, Samuel. *The Internet of Things*. Cambridge, MA: MIT Press, 2015.

Groscurth, Chris. *Future-Ready Leadership: Strategies for the Fourth Industrial Revolution*. Santa Barbara, CA: Praeger, 2018.

Headrick, Daniel R. *Technology: A World History*. New York: Oxford University Press, 2009.

Jackson, Kevin L. and Scott Goessling. *Architecting Cloud Computing Solutions*. Birmingham, UK: Packt Publishing, 2018.

Kane, Gerald C., Anh Nguyen Phillips, Jonathan R. Copulsky, and Garth R. Andrus. *The Technology Fallacy: How People Are the Real Key to Digital Transformation*. Cambridge, MA: MIT Press, 2019.

Karanz, Maciej. *Building the Internet of Things*. New York: John Wiley, 2017.

Kleppmann, Martin. *Designing Data-Intensive Applications: The Big Ideas Behind Reliable, Scalable, and Maintainable Systems*. Sebastopol, CA: O'Reilly Media, 2017.

Krach, Helge. *Quantum Generations: A History of Physics in the Twentieth Century*. Princeton, NJ: Princeton University Press, 1999.

Kurniawan, Agus. *Smart Internet of Things Projects*. Birmingham, UK: Packt Publishing, 2016.

Lee, Kai-Fu. *AI Superpowers: China, Silicon Valley, and the New World Order*. New York: Houghton Mifflin Harcourt Publishing, 2018.

Levitin, Daniel J. *The Organized Mind: Thinking Straight in the Age of Information Overload*. New York: Plume Penguin Random House, 2014.

Marr, Bernard. *Data Strategy: How to Profit from a World of Big Data, Analytics and the Internet of Things*. London, UK: Kogan Page, 2017.

Mayer-Schonberger, Victor and Kenneth Cukier. *Big Data: A Revolution That Will Transform How We Live, Work, and Think*. London, UK: John Murray, 2013.

McClellan III, James E. and Harold Dorn. *Science and Technology in World History: An Introduction*, 2nd ed. Baltimore, MD: Johns Hopkins University, 2006.

Minteer, Andrew. *Analytics for the Internet of Things (IoT): Intelligent analytics for your intelligent devices*. Birmingham, UK: Packt, 2017.

Mitchell, Melanie. *Artificial Intelligence: A Guide for Thinking Humans*. New York: Farrar, Straus and Giroux, 2019.

O'Malley, Martin. *Smarter Government: How to Govern for Results in the Information Age*. Redlands, CA: Eris Press, 2019.

Oreskes, Naomi and John Krige, eds. *Science and Technology in the Global Cold War*. Cambridge, MA: MIT Press, 2014.

Rogers, David. *The Digital Transformation Playbook: Rethink Your Business for the Digital Age*. New York: Columbia University, 2016.

Russell, Stuart. *Human Compatible: Artificial Intelligence and the Problem of Control*. New York: Viking Penguin Random House, 2019.

Saldanha, Tony. *Why Digital Transformation Fail: The Surprising Disciplines of How to Take Off and Stay Ahead*. Oakland, CA: Berrett-Koehler Publishers, Inc., 2019.

Sebastian, D J. *The Selling Revolution: Prospering in the New World of Artificial Intelligence*. Samuelson Publishing, 2019.

Siebel, Thomas M. *Digital Transformation: Survive and Thrive in an Era of Maxx Extinction*. New York: RosettaBooks, 2019.

Schwab, Klaus. *The Fourth Industrial Revolution*. New York: Penguin Random House, 2016.

Sinclair, Bruce. *IoT Inc. : How Your Company Can Use the Internet of Things to Win in the Outcome Economy*. New York: McGraw-Hill Education. 2017.

Stone, James V. *Artificial Intelligence Engines: A Tutorial Introduction to the Mathematics of Deep Learning*. Sebtel Press, 2019.

Taulli, Tom. *Artificial Intelligence Basics: A Non-Technical Introduction*. New York: Apress Media, 2019.

Topol, Eric. *Deep Medicine: How Artificial Intelligence Can Make Healthcare Human Again*. New York: Basic Book, 2019.

Unemyr, Magnus. *The Internet of Things – The Next Industrial Revolution Has Begun*. Amazon Digital Services, 2017.

Vandegrift, David. *The Future of Business: An Introduction to Artificial Intelligence*. Independently Published, 2019.

Veneri, Giacomo and Antonio Capasso. *Hands-On Industrial Internet of Things*. Birmingham, UK: Packt Publishing, 2018.

2. Cyberwarfare and National Security

Akart, Bobby. *Cyber Warfare: Prepping for Tomorrow Series*. Cookeville, TN: Bobby Akart Inc., 2015.

Andress, Jason and Steve Winterfeld. *Cyber Warfare: Techniques, Tactics and Tools for Security Practitioners*, 2nd ed. Cambridge, MA: Syngress, 2013.

Bodmer, Sean, Max Kilger, et al. *Reverse Deception: Organized Cyber Threat Counter-Exploitation*. New York: McGraw-Hill Education, 2012.

Carr, Jeffrey. *Inside Cyber Warfare: Mapping the Cyber Underworld*. Sebastopol, CA: O'Reilly Media, 2011.

Chapple, Mike and David Seidl. *Cyberwarfare: Information Operations in a Connected World*. Burlington, MA: Jones & Bartlett, 2014.

Clark, Robert M. and William L. Mitchell. *Deception: Counterdeception and Counterintelligence*. Washington, DC: CQ Press, 2018.

Cordesman, Anthony H. and Justin G. Cordesman. *Cyber-Threats, Information Warfare, and Critical Infrastructure Protection: Defending the U.S. Homeland*. Westport, CT: Praeger Publishers. 2002.

De Azevedo, Fernando Uilherme Barbosa. *Hackers Exposed: Discover the secret world of cybercrime*. Amazon Digital Service, 2018.

Evans, Lester. *Cybersecurity: An Essential Guide to Computer and Cyber Security for Beginners*. Independently Published, 2018.

Hagestad II, William T. *21st Century Chinese Cyberwarfare*. Cambridgeshire, UK: IT Governance Publishing, 2012.

Kaplan, Fred. *Dark Territory: The Secret History of Cyber War*. New York: Simon & Schuster, 2017,

Rosone, James and Miranda Watson. *Cyber-Warfare and the New World Order: World War III Series, Book 4*. Chicago, IL: Front Line, 2019.

Sanger, David E. *The Perfect Weapons: War, Sabotage, and Fear in the Cyber Age*. New York: Crown Publishing Group., 2018.

Shakarian, Paulo, Jana Shakarian, and Andrew Ruef. *Introduction Cyber Warfare: A Multidisciplinary Approach*. Cambridge, MA: Syngress, 2013.

Singer, P. W. and Allan Friedman. *Cybersecurity and Cyberwar: What Everyone to Know*. New York: Oxford University Press, 2014.

Springer, Paul J., ed. *Encyclopedia of Cyber Warfare*. Santa Barbara, CA: ABC CLIO, 2017.

Thanvi, Irfan Ali. *Cyber Attack in International Warfare: Another Use of Force*. Independently Published, 2018.

Wallace, Pendleton C. *Cyberwarfare: Ted Higuera Series Book 6*. Mooresville, NC: Victory Press, 2018.

Whyte, Christopher and Brian Mazanec. *Understanding Cyber Warfare*. New York: Routledge, 2018.

Winkler, Ira and Araceli Treu Gomes. *Advanced Persistent Security: A Cyberwarfare Approach*. Cambridge, MA: Syngress, 2016.

Zetter, Kim. *Countdown to Zero Day: Stuxnet and the Launch of the World's First Digital Weapon*. New York: Crown Publishing, 2014.

3. Space Warfare and National Security

Altmann, Jurgen. *Military Nanotechnology: Potential Applications and Preventive Arms Control*. New York: Routledge, 2007.

Dawson, Linda. *War in Space: The Science and Technology Behind Our Next Theater of Conflict*. Chichester, UK: Springer, 2018.

Daniel, J. Furman, III and T. K. Rogers. *The First Space War: How the Patterns of History and the Principles of STEM will Shape Its Form*. Lanham, MD: Rowman & Littlefield Publishing, 2019.

Dolman, Everett C. *Pure Strategy: Power and Principle in the Space and Information Age*. New York: Routledge, 2005.

_____. *Astropolitik: Classical Geopolitics in the Space Age*. New York: Routledge, 2001.

Frils, Karstein and Jens Ringsmose, eds. *Conflict in Cyber Space: Theoretical, Strategic and Legal Perspectives*. New York: Routledge, 2016.

Froehlich, Annette and Vincent Seffinga, eds. *The United Nations and Space Security: Conflicting Mandates Between UNCOPUOS and the CD*. Berlin, Germany: Springer Nature, 2019.

Johnson-Freese, Joan. *Space Warfare in the 21st Century*. New York: Routledge, 2016.

Klein, John J. *Understanding Space Strategy: The Art of War in Space*. New York: Routledge, 2019.

Lambakis, Steven. *On the Edge of Earth: The Future of American Space Power*. Lexington, KY: University Press of Kentucky, 2001.

Moltz, James Clay. *The Politics of Space Security: Strategic Restraint and the Pursuit of National Interests*, 3rd ed. Stanford, CA: Stanford U. P., 2019.

National Academy. *National Security Space Defense and Protection: A Report of National Academy of Science, Engineering, Medicine*. Washington, DC: National Academies Press, 2016.

Otto, Lisa. Global *Challenges in Maritime Security: An Introduction*. Berlin, Germany: Springer Nature, 2020.

Pahl, David. *Space Warfare and Strategic Defense*. Seattle, WA: Bookthrift Company., 1988.

Preston, Bob, Dana J Johnson, Sean Edwards, Jennifer Gross, and Michael Miller. *Space Weapons, Earth Wars*. Santa Monica, CA: RAND, 2001.

Rabkin, Jeremy and John Yoo. *Striking Power: How Cyber, Robots, and Space Weapons Change the Rules for War*. New York: Encounter Books, 2017.

Sen, Gautam. *The Purpose of India's Security Strategy: Defense, Deterrence and Global Involvement*. New York: Routledge, 2019.

Temple, L., III. Parker. *Shades of Gray: National Security and the Evolution of Space Reconnaissance*. Reston, VA: American Institute of Aeronautics and Astronautics, 2004.

Wright, John C. Deep *Space Warfare: Military Strategy Beyond Orbit*. Jefferson, NC: McFarland, 2019.

Yuen, Simon. *Treatise on Space Warfare*. Amazon Digital Services, 2019.

4. Weapons of Mass Destruction and National Security

Alibek, Ken. And Stephen Handelman. *Biohazard: The Chilling True Story of the Largest Covert Biological Weapons Program in the World--Told from the Inside by the Man Who Ran It.* New York: Random House, 1999.

Bentley, Michelle. *Weapons of Mass Destruction and US Foreign Policy: The strategic use of a concept.* New York: Routledge, 2014.

_____. *Syria and the Chemical Weapons Taboo.* Manchester, UK: Manchester University Press, 2016.

Cirincione, Joseph, ed. *Repairing the Regime: Preventing the Spread of Weapons of Mass Destruction.* New York: Routledge, 2000.

Croddy, Eric A., Jeffrey A. Larsen, and James J. Wirtz, eds. *Weapons of Mass Destruction.* Santa Barbara, CA: ABC-CLIO, 2018.

Curley, Robert, ed. *Weapons of Mass Destruction.* New York: Rosen Education Service, 2011.

Forest, James and Russell Howard. *Weapons of Mass Destruction and Terrorism.* New York: McGraw-Hill, 2012.

Funderburk, Greg, Dennis McGowan, and Charles Stumph. *Weapons of Mass Destruction.* LawTech Publishing Group, 2017.

Goldstein, Lyle J. *Preventive Attack and Weapons of Mass Destruction: A Comparative Historical Analysis.* Stanford, CA: Stanford U. P., 2005.

Graham, Thomas, Jr. *Common Sense on Weapons of Mass Destruction.* Seattle, WA: University of Washington Press, 2004.

Harris, Robert and Jeremy Paxman. *A Higher Form of Killing: The Secret History of Chemical and Biological Warfare.* New York: Random, 2002.

Hutchinson, Robert. *Weapons of Mass Destruction: The No-Nonsense Guide to Nuclear, Chemical and Biological Weapons Today.* London, UK: Weidenfeld & Nicolson, 2003.

Miller, Martin. *Weapons of Mass Destruction: Specter of the Nuclear Age.* Schiffer Military History, 2017.

Newby, Kris. Bitten: *The Secret History of Lyme Disease and Biological Weapons.* New York: HarperCollins, 2019.

Okawa, Ryuho. *The Just Cause in the Iraq War: Did Saddam Hussein Possess Weapons of Mass Destruction?* New York: IRH Press, 2013.

O'Neil, Cathy. *Weapons of Math Destruction: How Big Data Increases Inequality and Threatens Democracy.* New York: Broadway Books, 2016.

Siracusa, Joseph M. and Aiden Warren. *Weapons of Mass Destruction.* Lanham, MD: Rowman & Littlefield, 2017.

Vanderburg, Margaret. *Weapons of Mass Destruction.* New York: Permanent Press, 2015.

Venter, Al J. Nuclear Terror: *The Bomb and Other Weapons of Mass Destruction in the Wrong Hands.* Barnsley, UK: Pen and Sword, 2018.

United Nations Security Council Resolution 1540. https://en.wikipedia.org/wiki/United_Nations_Security_Council_Resoluton_1540, accessed 17 December 2019.

5. The Biggest Technology Trends

Allocca, Kevin. *Videoccracy: How Youtube Is Changing the World*. New York: Bloomsbury, 2018.

Chavez, Tom, Chris O'Hara, and Vivek Vaidya. *Data Driven: Harnessing Data and AI to Reinvent Customer Engagement*. Audible Studios, 2019.

Juma, Calestous. *Innovation and Its Enemies: Why People Resist New Technologies*. New York: Oxford University Press, 2016.

Kelly, Kevin. *The Inevitable: Understanding the 12 Technological Forces That Will Shape Our Future*. New York: Penguin Books, 2017.

Lok, Johnny Ch. *Information Technology: Economic Influence*. Independent Publisher, 2019.

McGrath, Ryan. *Social Media Marketing: Latest Tips and Trends*. Independently Published, 2018.

Mehta, Neel, Aditya Agashe, and Parth Detroja. *Blockchain Bubble or Revolution: The Present and Future of Blockchain and Cryptocurrencies*. Paravane Ventures, 2019.

Morgan, Jacob. *The Future of Work: Attract New Talent, Build Better Leaders, and Create a Competitive Organization*. New York: John Wiley, 2014.

Pinker, Steven. *Enlightenment Now: The Case for Reason, Science, Humanism, and Progress*. New York: Penguin Audio, 2018.

Reiser, Robert A. and John V. Dempsey. *Trends and Issues in Instructional Design and Technology*, 4th ed. London, UK: Pearson, 2017.

Photo III-Refer-1. U.S. Navy's new stealth destroyer Zumwalt
https://www.stripes.com/polopoly_fs/1.430208.1474471595!/image/image.jpg_gen/derivatives/landscape_900/image.jpg, accessed 22 October 2019

The guided-missile destroyer Pre-Commissioning Unit Zumwalt (DDG 1000) departs from Naval Station Newport, Rhode Island on Sept. 12, 2016 following its maiden voyage from Bath Iron Works Shipyard in Bath, Maine.

Made in the USA
Columbia, SC
12 January 2020